Sir Ernest Satow (1843–1929)

SATOW'S DIPLOMATIC PRACTICE

Seventh Edition

Edited by

SIR IVOR ROBERTS

OXFORD
UNIVERSITY PRESS

OXFORD
UNIVERSITY PRESS

Great Clarendon Street, Oxford, OX2 6DP,
United Kingdom

Oxford University Press is a department of the University of Oxford.
It furthers the University's objective of excellence in research, scholarship,
and education by publishing worldwide. Oxford is a registered trade mark of
Oxford University Press in the UK and in certain other countries

First Edition published in 1917
Seventh Edition published in 2017
First published in paperback 2018

Impression: 1

Published in the United States of America by Oxford University Press
198 Madison Avenue, New York, NY 10016, United States of America

British Library Cataloguing in Publication Data

Data available

Library of Congress Cataloging in Publication Data

Data available

ISBN 978–0–19–873910–4 (Hbk.)
ISBN 978–0–19–882195–3 (Pbk.)

Printed in Great Britain by
Ashford Colour Press Ltd, Gosport, Hampshire

SUMMARY TABLE OF CONTENTS

BOOK I DIPLOMACY IN GENERAL

BOOK II DIPLOMATIC AND CONSULAR RELATIONS

BOOK III PRIVILEGES AND IMMUNITIES

BOOK IV MULTILATERAL DIPLOMACY, HUMAN RIGHTS, AND INTERNATIONAL ORGANIZATIONS

BOOK V INTERNATIONAL DISPUTES AND COURTS

BOOK VI ALTERNATIVE (INCLUDING TRACK 2) DIPLOMACY

TABLE OF CONTENTS

I DIPLOMACY IN GENERAL

3. **Introduction to International Law**
   Elizabeth Wilmshurst

4. **The State: its Concept as a Legal Person in International Law**
   Hazel Fox

II DIPLOMATIC AND CONSULAR RELATIONS

5. Functions of Diplomatic Missions and Consulates
Ivor Roberts

6. Diplomatic Communication
Ivor Roberts

7. **Formal Aspects of Diplomatic Relations: Precedence among Heads of State and States, Selection, *Agrément*, Precedence among Heads of Mission, Chargés d'Affaires, Credentials, Full Powers for Heads of Mission**
   Ivor Roberts

8. **The Appointment and Functions of Consuls**
   Joanne Foakes and Eileen Denza

III PRIVILEGES AND IMMUNITIES

12. Privileges and Immunities of the State, the Head of State, State Officials, and State Agencies

Hazel Fox

15. Special Missions
Hazel Fox and Joanne Foakes

IV MULTILATERAL DIPLOMACY, HUMAN RIGHTS AND INTERNATIONAL ORGANIZATIONS

16. Theory and Practice of Multilateral Diplomacy
Emyr Jones Parry

17. Human Rights
Amal Clooney

18. The United Nations—I The Charter and its Operation

Emyr Jones Parry

23. Other International and Regional Organizations: Commonwealth, NATO, Council of Europe, OAS, AU, ASEAN, CIS, Francophonie, Arab League, Organization of Islamic Cooperation, Gulf Cooperation Council, OSCE

Ivor Roberts

V INTERNATIONAL DISPUTES AND COURTS

24. Prevention and Management of Conflict and Settlement of Disputes
Emyr Jones Parry

VI ALTERNATIVE (INCLUDING TRACK 2) DIPLOMACY

VII TREATIES AND TREATY-MAKING

31. Treaties and Other International Instruments—I General Definition, Treaty Formalities

Frank Berman and David Bentley

32. Treaties and Other International Instruments—II Treaty, Convention, Agreement, Protocol

Frank Berman and David Bentley

VIII ENVOI

36. Advice to Diplomats

Ivor Roberts and Emyr Jones Parry

PREFACE TO THE CENTENARY EDITION

When the sixth edition of *Satow's Diplomatic Practice* came out in 2009, it was the first new edition for 30 years. As this inevitably required a considerable amount of new work and rewriting ('radical surgery' as its Preface explained), we were consequently very gratified by the positive, indeed enthusiastic, reception which the edition enjoyed.

However, in preparing (at the prompting of OUP) a new edition to mark the centenary of Sir Ernest Satow's original work, published in 1917, we felt that we needed to go further. Not just in terms of updating the sixth edition but also even more radically in covering areas which, if not neglected in the last edition, still did not receive an in-depth treatment. Thus we have added an introduction to international law and chapters on the changes in and challenges of modern diplomacy, on human rights, and on public (and digital) diplomacy. For the last two we have been fortunate enough to have secured the services of two contributors, new to the team, whose material has been invaluable. The changes in communication and public diplomacy covered briefly in the last edition have been extensively expanded in a new chapter, and human rights, now so central to the conduct of international affairs, rightly merits a chapter on its own. None of the 'old' chapters from the sixth edition, however, has been left untouched. A great deal of revision to update the last edition has taken place, much new material has been added including on secret intelligence, and certain chapters have undergone a very substantial makeover. The organization of the book follows broadly the plan of its predecessor (and once again we have tried to make the language as gender neutral as possible).

We hope that this edition will prove a fitting milestone to celebrate *Satow's Diplomatic Practice* as it begins its second century.

Ivor Roberts
Trinity College, Oxford
July 2016

PREFACE TO THE 6TH EDITION

Sir Ernest Satow's *Guide to Diplomatic Practice* although first published nearly 100 years ago remains a masterpiece. The book he wrote in 1917 was no dry collection of facts and legal terms. It was suffused with illuminating, interesting, often whimsical, anecdotes, and wise counsel. Nevertheless, when I was invited to edit the first revised edition for 30 years, I quickly realized that nothing less than radical surgery was required. For diplomacy has changed too much in its practice, if not in its essentials. Satow would find much to amaze him in the conduct of diplomacy but not in the underlying purpose. It is still 'the application of intelligence and tact to the conduct of official relations between the governments of independent states, and between governments and international institutions; or, more briefly, the conduct of business between states by peaceful means' (Chapter 1). But it would clearly be a mistake to try to cling to much in earlier editions which has now been entirely superseded. The team of contributors, a note on whom is at xxxiii, has been an enormous source of professional expertise, support, and consistently constructive criticism of my and each other's work. It would be invidious to single anyone out. Their respective contributions are to be found in the Note.

The last edition of this book was written 10 years before the fall of the Berlin Wall. It reads very much like a book of its time, reflecting the immediate post-war disposition and still retaining from the original Satow much of the language of traditional diplomacy. A new edition is needed to illustrate how much the world of diplomacy has changed since the last one. I concluded with regret that it would have by and large to depart from the Satow writing style to make it more contemporary and accessible to the practitioners of the twenty-first century.

We have aimed in this new edition to move the focus away from the UK and Commonwealth (in the last edition, the international organization mentioned first after the United Nations is the Commonwealth) and towards a global audience. We hope that it will be considered an indispensable vademecum in every foreign ministry, as a concise and authoritative guide for their legal advisers and diplomats, and more widely for international lawyers and students of international relations. It aims to be in effect a short primer in diplomacy as well as a guide to diplomatic practice, international organizations, and law. It also comes to terms with the fact that English is the 'new' diplomatic language. (It is striking that so many passages in the 1979 edition are in French.)

At the same time, the book reflects the way modern communications have transformed diplomacy. When the last edition came out, the phrase 'shuttle diplomacy' had just been invented and summit meetings were still a rarity. Videoconferencing was practically unknown and the internet, although conceived of, had yet to acquire a public face. At the time communication technology seemed to stretch only to a hotline to prevent nuclear war. Hand in hand with these changes in communications has come the rise in multilateral organizations and networks which makes diplomacy at the foreign ministerial level far more frequent and accessible. First published a year before the Versailles Peace Conference, the original Satow described a world where the only way for the Great Powers to meet was at a major conference lasting weeks and in some cases months. Berlin and Vienna were perhaps the most famous of these conferences in the preceding century. The changes required to diplomatic practice by monthly meetings and weekly conversations of e.g. EU foreign ministers, thrice-yearly meetings of EU presidents and prime ministers, and regular meetings at ministerial and prime ministerial level in most international organizations need to be documented and the impact on diplomats' lives and work explained. At the time of writing the world is in the grip of a financial and economic crisis that shows little sign of abating. International organizations and institutions are unlikely to emerge unchanged—some may not survive. But diplomacy and diplomats will still be required. The question which the book asks, and I hope answers, is: what, in the twenty-first century, are diplomats for?

Arrangement of the Book

Turning to the detail, Book I 'Diplomacy in General' needed substantial change. The introductory chapter on diplomacy has been expanded to make it a short history of diplomacy which it is hoped will help beginners orientate themselves in the subject. We dropped a good deal of the historical material on precedence and protocol and emphasized how foreign affairs are no longer the exclusive prerogative of the Minister for Foreign Affairs or the president/prime minister. The chapter on language and forms of diplomatic communication while aiming to be comprehensive also reflects how diplomats communicate today increasingly through email and even texting and rather fewer leisurely *Notes Verbales*.

The Books on Diplomatic Agents and Consular Matters have been further broken down into four Books, one on diplomatic relations, a second on diplomatic privileges and immunities, a third on diplomatic missions, and a fourth on consular matters. Most of the material on diplomatic and consular privileges and immunities was rewritten by Eileen Denza for the last edition to reflect the international conferences in Vienna on these subjects which had taken place in the 1960s and the resulting Conventions. No such major but a fair amount of minor revision has now been called for which she has again provided. Previous chapters on attacks on embassies and kidnapping of diplomats have been combined and expanded to reflect the growth in the scourge of terrorism and the often 'soft' target that embassies and diplomats provide. The last edition was written before the most flagrant breach of diplomatic immunity, the seizure of the US embassy in Tehran in 1979 and the detention of its staff for over a year. Since then, of course, many diplomats have been kidnapped, attacked, and even assassinated. The last edition of Satow has no entry in its index under terrorism.

As multilateral diplomacy and international organizations are at the heart of modern diplomacy, the Book devoted to them has been greatly expanded and given a higher priority in the text. The Book (VI) has substantial chapters on the United Nations and its specialized agencies and subsidiary bodies. Those dealing with economic, financial, and trade matters have now been grouped in a separate chapter which also takes in the work of the G8 and G20. The EU requires two chapters, and other international and regional organizations are incorporated in yet another (very substantial) chapter, such has been the exponential growth of these bodies. A new Book VII deals with peaceful settlement of disputes and the development of international tribunals including the International Criminal Court and the war crimes tribunals. Another new Book (VIII) covers non-governmental organizations (NGOs) and others who compete with conventional diplomats in the crowded international market place of conflict resolution. Book IX revises comprehensively, with contemporary examples, earlier material covering congresses, conferences, treaties, and other international instruments. The last chapter, Advice to Diplomats, retains some of the material from earlier editions which is timeless but has been brought into the new century with advice on modern diplomatic practice and a specific section on multilateral diplomacy. It has been important to suggest in my predecessor Lord Gore-Booth's words 'differences in atmosphere and diplomatic technique between bilateral diplomacy in a foreign capital and multilateral diplomacy'.

It is indeed our hope that enough of the original Satow has been retained to give the new reader something of its flavour while satisfying those aficionados of earlier editions. I hope that our extensive use of fresh material will entertain and instruct a new generation of diplomats, academics, students of international relations, and international lawyers and be of practical use to a wider public.

When the last edition of this book was written, Britain had never had a woman prime minister. Since then we have had one, for more than a decade, who saw foreign affairs (but perhaps not diplomacy) as being very much her domain. Meanwhile in the US, so often a pace setter in social affairs, three of the four most recent Secretaries of State have been women. Disappointingly, as my predecessor put it, 'the English language has not yet provided a grammatically elegant way of dealing with this change. We have, therefore, used the compromise of occasionally employing the "he (or she)" formula . . . but its constant repetition would be intolerably tedious.' For this edition, too, to avoid repetition of he/she, the male pronoun has had, very often, to serve both sexes where the plural pronoun 'they' has not been appropriate.

Ivor Roberts
Trinity College, Oxford
April 2009

NOTES ON CONTRIBUTORS

(Sir) Ivor Roberts KCMG: (editor), President of Trinity College, Oxford, former British Ambassador to Yugoslavia, Ireland, and Italy.

David Bentley CB: Former Legal Counsellor, Foreign and Commonwealth Office, Deputy Legal Adviser, Home Office.

(Sir) Frank Berman KCMG, QC: Visiting Professor of International Law in the University of Oxford, Barrister and international arbitrator, former Judge ad hoc of the International Court of Justice, former Legal Adviser to the Foreign and Commonwealth Office.

Paul Berman: Director, Legal Service, Council of the European Union; formerly Director, Cabinet Office European Law Division and Legal Counsellor, Foreign & Commonwealth Office.

Amal Clooney: Barrister, Doughty Street Chambers and Visiting Professor, Columbia Law School.

Eileen Denza CMG: formerly Legal Counsellor, Foreign and Commonwealth Office, Counsel to the EC Committee, House of Lords, and Visiting Professor, University College, London.

Tom Fletcher CMG: Visiting Professor of International Relations, New York University; former British Ambassador to Lebanon and Private Secretary for Foreign Affairs to Prime Ministers Blair, Brown and Cameron.

Joanne Foakes: Associate Fellow, Chatham House and formerly a Legal Counsellor in the Foreign and Commonwealth Office.

(Lady) Hazel Fox CMG, QC: Barrister, formerly Director of the British Institute of International and Comparative Law and General Editor of the International and Comparative Law Quarterly.

(Sir) Emyr Jones Parry GCMG: Chancellor of Aberystwyth University, President of the Learned Society of Wales, former British Permanent Representative to the North Atlantic Council and to the United Nations, New York.

Elizabeth Wilmshurst CMG: Distinguished Fellow, Chatham House, formerly Visiting Professor, University College London, formerly a Deputy Legal Adviser in the Foreign and Commonwealth Office.

BIOGRAPHICAL NOTE ON SATOW

Ernest Mason Satow was born at Clapton, North London, in 1843. He was the son of a merchant from the former Hanseatic seaport of Wismar who had settled in England, and an English lady, Margaret Mason. In his studies at University College, London, he read at an early stage a borrowed copy of Laurence Oliphant's *Narrative of the Earl of Elgin's Mission to China.* This aroused in him a desire to know Asia. In 1861 he came first in an examination for a student interpretership in the Far East. He was assigned to the British Consular Service in Japan.

After a short stay in Peking for Chinese studies, Satow arrived in Japan in 1862, nine years after the 'opening up' of that country by Commodore Perry to foreign presence and commerce. He found himself in the midst of the violent struggle between the partisans of the Shōgun, or chief of government, and the Emperor, which involved constant physical danger to foreign residents in Japan. The victory of the Emperor's party ushered in the great Meiji Restoration period, in which Japan, after three centuries of isolation, assimilated with incredible seriousness and rapidity skills developed during those centuries in the Western world. For over 20 years Satow's linguistic expertise, together with his adventurous travels (including shipwreck off the port of Hakodate) and his personal qualities, gave him a most remarkable position among Japanese of all backgrounds, and contributed greatly to the standing of the British Legation in Tokyo. Satow also started a family with Takeda Kane (1853–1932), his *musumé* (mistress, or common-law wife), with whom he cohabited in Tokyo from the 1870s until his departure from Japan in 1884. They had two sons, the younger of whom came to Britain to study botany some years later.

In 1884 Satow was posted to Siam (Thailand) and subsequently to Uruguay in 1888 ('nothing to do') and Morocco in 1893. But a man with a uniquely expert knowledge of both Chinese and Japanese language and civilization was bound to go back to the Far East, and Satow found himself in Tokyo (1895–1900) and Peking (1900–6), in both places as minister and head of mission. In these last two posts he performed most distinguished service, though, as the years went on, the claims and ambitions of Far Eastern and other powers took the situation out of the control of diplomacy or peaceful foreign policy.

On 25 July 1906, three months before his retirement from the Diplomatic Service, Satow was received in audience by King Edward VII. 'On my going away,' he recorded, 'His Majesty said that my services would receive recognition. Later in the day came a notice that I was to be sworn a member of the Privy Council.' 'I value it,' he wrote to an old friend, 'more than anything else that could have been given me. It was The King's own idea.'

In 1907 Satow represented Britain at the Second Hague Conference on International Peace. For the rest of his life, he lived quietly at his home in Devonshire, devoting his time to study and writing. He died in 1929, having lived a full and fruitful life as a member of that rare calling, the Scholar-Diplomat. As H W V Temperley put it, 'He wrote various studies on international law and history, and delivered his final message in a work full of practical wisdom, legal acumen and antiquarian knowledge, entitled *A Guide to Diplomatic Practice*.'

ACKNOWLEDGEMENTS TO THE CENTENARY EDITION

Many of the acknowledgements in the previous edition still stand. Rather than repeat them, the earlier acknowledgements are to be found below.

I should like personally to thank my present team of collaborators not only for their own contributions but for their assiduity and thoroughness in offering invariably helpful comments and suggestions on the chapters of others. It has eased my editorial burden considerably and resulted, I believe, in a much improved final product. I should like in particular to take the opportunity to thank Eileen Denza whose contribution to both the fifth and sixth editions of this work has been immense. Her influence continues to be felt strongly in this seventh edition as the chapter headings indicate. Her own work on 'Diplomatic Law' is, of course, the gold standard.

As in previous editions, the help and support provided by the Foreign and Commonwealth Office have been invaluable. Jon Davies, the Director of its newly created Diplomatic Academy, has provided constant encouragement. Nick Heath, now of the British Embassy in The Hague, was instrumental in providing a younger perspective on the final chapter, *Advice to Diplomats*. Julian Evans, the Vice-Marshal of the Diplomatic Corps, and his colleagues in Protocol Directorate, Barry Nicholas, Parulpinky Ram, Francesca Flessati, and Rufus Legg have been more than generous with their time and expertise. We also thank Iain Macleod, the FCO Legal Adviser, Rachael Hill, Head of Consular Policy, Dale Harrison and his colleagues in Treaty Section, and Kate Thomson, Team Leader, Human Rights and Democracy Department, for their helpful suggestions. Elsewhere, thanks are due to Sebastian Bates, Keble College, Oxford; Ilan Manor, St Cross College, Oxford; Alexander Kentikelenis, Trinity College, Oxford; Stefan Talmon, University of Bonn; HE Mme Sylvie Bermann, French Ambassador in London; and Fay Miller, Information Resource Center, US Embassy, London. At OUP, we have benefited once again from Merel Alstein and John Louth's encouragement and support as well as that of Emma Endean-Mills.

And, as in the previous edition, for any errors which remain, I take full responsibility.

IAR

ACKNOWLEDGEMENTS TO THE SIXTH EDITION

A collaborative venture is by definition a work of more than one hand. In this case the team of collaborators has acquired debts to many people not least to their predecessors and to the original author, Sir Ernest Satow, in particular. In compiling the present edition the present editor and his colleagues have often made the Foreign and Commonwealth Office their first port of call. We are most grateful, first of all, to Sir Peter Ricketts, Permanent Under-Secretary of State in the FCO, who has given the project full support and to Jane Darby who has channelled many of the enquiries. We should also like to acknowledge the help and counsel of Scott Wightman, Sarah Gillett's team in Protocol Department, and particularly Holly Welch, Paul Barnett and colleagues in Treaty Section, Jane Crellin in the Legal Adviser's Library, Chanaka Wickremasinghe in the UK Mission to the United Nations, and Sir Michael Wood formerly the Legal Adviser to the FCO. Several members of departments also provided indispensable information to help us maintain high standards of accuracy. It has proved impossible to thank them individually but they can rest assured that lack of personal mention does not diminish our indebtedness to them. Although we have made great use of the FCO and other Departments, all former and present public servants and officials in the team are writing in a personal capacity and the views expressed are not intended to represent those of any government or organization.

Elsewhere we should like to thank Vaclav Mikulka and the UN Division for Ocean Affairs and the Law of the Sea, Gleider Hernandez, Eliane Affolter (ICRC), Sir Adrian Beamish, Richard Davy, Professor Sir Adam Roberts, Professor Larry Siedentop, Professor Lorna Lloyd, Professor Richard Sharpe, Thomas Otte, Jeremy Cresswell, Aurel Sari, and Professor John Young. I owe a particular debt to Professor Geoffrey Berridge for commenting extensively on the chapters I wrote.

We benefited from the views of colleagues from other countries and would like to express our thanks to the Ambassador of France in London, HE Monsieur Maurice Gourdault-Montagne and to Anna Girvan of the United States Embassy in London for information on specialized points and to the former Canadian Ambassador Robert Fowler for details of his ordeal in the Sahara. I was particularly grateful to the Italian Ambassador in London, HE Sig. Giancarlo Aragona and his wife Sandra for frequent hospitality during my research.

The rewriting of the section on the Commonwealth was strengthened by the advice of the Commonwealth Secretary-General, Kamalesh Sharma, and the political section of the Commonwealth Secretariat.

Finally, I owe a special debt to the Librarian at Trinity College Oxford, Sharon Cure, for her unfailing help in locating books in other libraries inside and outside Oxford and for her assistance in compiling the bibliography. The Fellows of Trinity deserve thanks for their forbearance and support while I have been carrying through this project and above all for their fellowship. Three of them, Peter Brown, Johannes Zachhuber, and Bryan Ward-Perkins, have provided linguistic advice and my PA, Ulli Parkinson, has provided essential support not least in organizing my time.

At OUP, we have been fortunate indeed with the editorial team led by John Louth and so ably supported by Merel Alstein and her predecessor Gwen Booth, and by Fiona Stables, and at the OED, Associate Editor, Peter Gilliver, provided some fresh insights into the etymology of diplomacy. I am most grateful to my wife, Elizabeth, for assiduously reading and commenting on the chapters for which I am responsible and to my daughter, Hannah, for her valiant work on the bibliography. David Bentley among the team of collaborators has been eternally vigilant in picking up errors and providing helpful advice. For any errors which remain, I take full responsibility.

Sir Ivor Roberts
Oxford

LIST OF ABBREVIATIONS

ACABQ	Advisory Committee on Administrative and Budgetary Questions
AJIL	American Journal of International Law
All ER	All England Law Reports
ASEAN	Association of South-East Asian Nations
AU	African Union
BBC	British Broadcasting Corporation
BFSP	British and Foreign State Papers
BYIL	British Yearbook of International Law
CENTO	Central Treaty Organization
CFSP	Common Foreign and Security Policy (of the European Union)
Cmd, Cmnd, Cm	Command Papers. (UK Parliamentary Papers which derive their name from the fact they are presented to the United Kingdom Parliament nominally by 'Command of Her Majesty'. The current series uses the prefix Cm.)
CMLR	Common Market Law Review
COREPER	Committee of Permanent Representatives (of Member States of the European Union)
CSCE	Conference on Security and Cooperation in Europe
CSDP	Common Foreign and Security Policy (of the European Union)
DGSE	Direction Générale de la Sécurité Extérieure
EC	European Community
ECAFE	Economic Commission for Asia and the Far East
ECHR	European Convention on Human Rights
ECJ	Court of Justice of the European Union
ECLA	Economic Commission for Latin America
ECOSOC	Economic and Social Council of the United Nations. Also used to refer to the Economic and Social Committee of the EU.
ECR	European Court Reports
ECSC	European Coal and Steel Community
ECOWAS	Economic Community of West African States
EDC	European Defence Community
EEA	European Economic Area

EEC	European Economic Community (later the European Community)
EFAR	European Foreign Affairs Review
EFTA	European Free Trade Association
EHRR	European Human Rights Reports
EJIL	European Journal of International Law
ELDO	European Launcher Development Organisation
ELJ	European Law Journal
ELR	European Law Review
EP	European Parliament
ER	English Reports
ESCAP	Economic and Social Commission for Asia and the Pacific
ESRO	European Space Research Organization
EU	European Union
EURATOM	European Atomic Energy Community
EUROCONTROL	Name given to the European Organisation for the Safety of Air Navigation
FAO	Food and Agriculture Organization
FCO	Foreign and Commonwealth Office
FRG	Federal Republic of Germany
FRY	Federal Republic of Yugoslavia
GA	General Assembly of the United Nations
GATT	General Agreement on Tariffs and Trade
GDR	German Democratic Republic
HMSO	Her Majesty's Stationery Office
HR	Académie de Droit International de la Haye Recueil des Cours
IAEA	International Atomic Energy Agency
IBRD	International Bank for Reconstruction and Development
ICAO	International Civil Aviation Organization
ICC	International Criminal Court
ICCPR	International Covenant on Civil and Political Rights
ICLQ	International and Comparative Law Quarterly
ICJ	International Court of Justice
ICJ Rep	International Court of Justice Reports
ICRC	International Committee of the Red Cross
ICTR	International Criminal Tribunal for Rwanda
ICTY	International Criminal Tribunal for the Former Yugoslavia
IDA	International Development Association
IFC	International Finance Corporation

ILC	International Law Commission
ILC Yearbook	Yearbook of the International Commission
ILO	International Labour Organization
ILR	International Law Reports (Older Reports Annual Digest and Reports of International Law Cases (AD))
IMF	International Monetary Fund
IMO	International Maritime Organization
INMARSAT	International Maritime Satellite Organization
INTELSAT	International Telecommunications Satellite Consortium
IRO	International Refugee Organization
ITLOS	Law of the Sea Tribunal
ITU	International Telecommunication Union
LR	Law Reports
MOU	Memorandum of Understanding
NATO	North Atlantic Treaty Organization
NGO	Non-governmental Organization
OAS	Organization of American States
OAU	Organization of African Unity (now AU, *see above*)
OECD	Organisation for Economic Cooperation and Development
OEEC	Organisation for European Economic Cooperation
OIC	Organization of the Islamic Conference
OJ	Official Journal of the European Union
OSCE	Organization for Security and Co-operation in Europe
PAU	Pan-American Union
PCIJ	Permanent Court of International Justice
QC	Queen's Counsel
RGDIP	Revue Générale de Droit International Public
RN	Royal Navy (UK)
SACEUR	Supreme Allied Commander, Europe
SHAPE	Supreme Headquarters Allied Powers, Europe
SOFA	Status of Forces Agreement
SOMA	Status of Mission Agreement
TEU	Treaty on European Union
TLR	Times Law Reports

UKTS	United Kingdom Treaty Series
UNCIO	United Nations Conference on International Organization
UNCTAD	United Nations Conference on Trade and Development
UNEF	United Nations Expeditionary Force
UNESCO	United Nations Educational, Scientific and Cultural Organization
UNFICYP	United Nations (Peacekeeping) Force in Cyprus
UNHCR	United Nations High Commissioner for Refugees
UNICEF	United Nations Children's Fund (1946–53 United Nations International Children's Emergency Fund: in 1953 name changed, original acronym retained)
UPU	Universal Postal Union
UNTS	United Nations Treaty Series
WEU	Western European Union
WHO	World Health Organization
WIPO	World Intellectual Property Organization
WMO	World Meteorological Organization
WTO	World Trade Organization

TABLE OF CASES

NATIONAL COURTS AND TRIBUNALS

INTERNATIONAL COURTS AND TRIBUNALS

European Commission on Human Rights

European Community

European Court of Human Rights

International Court of Justice

Permanent Court of International Justice

TABLE OF INTERNATIONAL TREATIES, CONVENTIONS AND OTHER INTERNATIONAL INSTRUMENTS

li

TABLE OF LEGISLATION

FRANCE

GERMANY

HONG KONG

MALAWI

Book I

DIPLOMACY IN GENERAL

1

DIPLOMACY—A SHORT HISTORY FROM PRE-CLASSICAL ORIGINS TO THE FALL OF THE BERLIN WALL

Ivor Roberts

Definitions

Diplomacy is the application of intelligence and tact to the conduct of official **1.1** relations between the governments of independent States, extending sometimes also to their relations with dependent territories, and between governments within international institutions; or, more briefly, the conduct of business between States by peaceful means. Although the word, diplomacy, has been in the English language for little more than two centuries, it has suffered from misuse and confusion. While diplomacy is properly the conduct or execution of foreign policy, it is sometimes confused with foreign policy itself. But foreign policy is formulated by government, not by diplomats, albeit often on the advice of diplomats.[1] In order to carry out its policy, a government manages its

---

[1] In popular American usage, the United States Secretary of State is sometimes called a 'diplomat'. But the Secretary, though not a member of the Legislature, is essentially a member of the Administration and not of the Diplomatic Service, so that the description 'diplomat' can be misleading. A similar confusion exists elsewhere. The French frequently refer to Foreign Ministers as 'le chef de la diplomatie ruritanienne'.

international relations by applying not only persuasion but also different forms of pressure. How successful these pressures prove will depend to a great extent on the real power, often now referred to as hard power,[2] behind them. The power must be real, but rather than exercise it explicitly, the government may prefer to keep it in reserve with the implication that in certain circumstances it could be used. Nevertheless, in normal circumstances it will conduct its international intercourse by negotiation, a form of soft power. This is diplomacy. Persuasive argument, if applied skilfully and sensitively at the right time, may achieve a better result than persuasion too obviously backed by the threat of force. The latter may provoke resistance and ultimately lead to war. (Smart power, a term coined by Fen Hampson and used by Joseph Nye in 2003, can be defined as the ability to combine hard and soft power resources into effective strategies.)

1.2　The etymology of diplomacy takes us to ancient Greece. The diplomat,[3] says Littré, is so called because diplomas are official documents (*actes*) emanating from princes, and the word 'diploma' comes from the Greek δίπλωμα (δι πλόω, I fold, fold double). A diploma is understood to be a document by which a privilege is conferred: a state paper, official document, a charter. The earliest English instance of the use of this word is in the year 1645[4] though the now disused form *diplome* was borrowed into English as early as 1610, when it appeared in John Donne's book *Pseudo-Martyr* (p. 20: 'If the Pope should write to any of them by

---

[2] 'Everyone is familiar with hard power. We know that military and economic might often get others to change their position. Hard power can rest on inducements ("carrots") or threats ("sticks"). But sometimes you can get the outcomes you want without tangible threats or payoffs. The indirect way to get what you want has sometimes been called "the second face of power." A country may obtain the outcomes it wants in world politics because other countries admire its values, emulate its example, aspire to its level of prosperity and openness. This soft power—getting others to want the outcomes that you want—co-opts people rather than coerces them. Soft power rests on the ability to shape the preferences of others.' J S Nye Jr, 'Soft Power and Leadership' *Compass*, Spring 2004, published by Kennedy School of Government, Harvard University.

[3] Diplomats existed long before the word was employed to denote the class. Machiavelli (1469–1527) is perhaps the most celebrated of men who discharged diplomatic functions in early days. D'Ossat (1536–1604), the Conde de Gondomar (1567–1626), Kaunitz (1710–94), Metternich (1773–1859), Pozzo di Borgo (1764–1842), the first Lord Malmesbury (1764–1820), Talleyrand (1754–1838), and Lord Stratford de Redcliffe (1786–1880) were among the most eminent of the profession in their time. If men who combined fame as statesmen with diplomatic reputation are to be included, the Duc de Richelieu (Cardinal Richelieu, 1585–1642) was in a sense the father of French diplomacy; and Count Cavour (1810–61) and Prince Bismarck (1815–98) enjoyed worldwide celebrity. Outside Europe there were notable 'pioneer' diplomats such as Sir Thomas Roe, British 'lord ambassador' at the court of the Mogul Emperor Jehangir (1615–18) and Townsend Harris, the first American consul-general in Japan (1855–60) with his remarkable gift for comprehending the psychology of a long-isolated people and Dr Henry Kissinger, who served two US Presidents and usually put them in the shade where foreign policy was concerned.

[4] J Howell, *Epistolae Ho-Elianae* (section ii, page 23): 'the King of Spain ... was forcd to publish a Diploma wherein he dispensd with himself (as the Holland Story hath it) from payment.' See also *Oxford English Dictionary* (2nd edn, Oxford: Clarendon Press, 1989), Vol IV, 695.

the name of Sons…it vitiates the whole Diplome, and makes it false'). The meaning here is again 'official document'. The organization of such documents fell to trained archivists who were the first to be called diplomats, i.e. those who dealt with diplomas or archives.[5]

Leibnitz, in 1693, published his *Codex Juris Gentium Diplomaticus;* Dumont, in **1.3** 1726, the *Corps Universel Diplomatique du Droit des Gens.* Both were collections of treaties and other official documents. In these titles *diplomaticus, diplomatique,* are applied to a body or collection of original state papers, but as the subject-matter of these particular collections was what we now call *international* relations, '*corps diplomatique*' appears to have been treated as equivalent to '*corps du droit des gens*', and '*diplomatique*' as 'having to do with international relations'. Hence the application also to the officials connected with such matters. *Diplomatic body*[6] now came to signify the body of ambassadors, envoys, and officials attached to the foreign missions residing at any seat of government, and *diplomatic service* that branch of the public service which supplies the *personnel* of the permanent missions in foreign countries. The earliest example of this use in England appears to be in a satirical work *The Chinese Spy* (a translation, published in 1765, of the French work *L'espion chinois* by Ange Goudar): 'The diplomatic body, as it is called, was at this ball, but without distinguishing itself to any great advantage' (volume VI, p. 198). Burke, in 1796, speaks of the 'diplomatic body', and also uses 'diplomacy' to mean skill or dexterity in the conduct of international intercourse and negotiations. The terms *diplomat, diplomate, diplomatist* (now virtually obsolete) were adopted to designate a member of this body. In the eighteenth century they were scarcely known. Callières, whose book was published in 1716, never uses the word *diplomate*. He always speaks of 'un bon' or 'un habile négociateur'. Disraeli is quoted as using 'diplomatic' in 1826 as 'showing address (adroitness)' in negotiations or intercourse of any kind *(Oxford English Dictionary). La diplomatique* is used in French for the art of deciphering ancient documents, such as charters and so forth.

---

[5] This is still reflected in the title at Oxford University of 'professor of diplomatic'. The current holder, Professor Richard Sharpe, writes 'Oxford has had a teaching post in diplomatic since 1897. The term itself originates with the founding textbook by Dom Jean Mabillon, *De Re Diplomatica* (The Matter of Diplomas), published in 1681, in which he argued that there were criteria to judge the authenticity or otherwise of the early medieval charters in Benedictine archives. In Mabillon's time many subjects were included under the term diplomatic that would not be now, including numismatics. Palaeography is dealt with separately now, but sigillography (sometimes known by its Greek name sphragistics)—the study of seals attached to documents—is still taught as part of diplomatic. The main purpose is to equip postgraduates in medieval history to deal with raw primary evidence, especially charters, deeds, and government records.'

[6] This use of the expression first arose in Vienna around the middle of the eighteenth century. (Ranke, cited by Holtzendorff, Vol 3, 617.)

Early History

1.4 Diplomacy is in fact, as the Duc de Broglie remarked, the best means devised by civilization for preventing international relations from being governed by force alone. The field in which it operates lies somewhere between power politics and civilized usage, and its methods have varied with the political conventions of each age. There is no lack of evidence that the sending of emissaries to open negotiations was a common practice among quite primitive peoples and that in many cases their reception and treatment were regulated, even if only in a rudimentary way, by custom or taboo. The origins may go back at least to the Great Kings of the Ancient Near East in the second and possibly even as early as the late fourth millennium BC, to the cuneiform civilizations of Mesopotamia. The first diplomatic document we possess is a copy of a letter inscribed on a cuneiform tablet sent around 2500 BC from Ibubu, a high official of the Kingdom of Ebla to an envoy of the ruler of the Kingdom of Amazi about 600 miles away concerning the exchange of equids for chariots to cement the alliance between the two monarchs.[7] It was discovered in the palace archives of Ebla (modern Tell Mardikh, Syria) by an Italian archaeological team in 1972.[8] The Mari (also in Syria) archives (seventeenth century BC) provide a fascinating glimpse into 'what gestures and rituals diplomats used to conclude or reject treaties and alliances'.[9] Touching a hem of outer clothing or the throat for instance symbolized the conclusion of an agreement. Thus ambassador plenipotentiary Abum-ekin who had been appointed by Zimri-Lim, the king of Mari, to negotiate a treaty with the Babylonian king, Hammurabi, struck an obstacle over the town of Hît and was forced to report that by the twenty-fifth day Hammurabi 'had not touched his throat'[10] and had explained his reluctance thus: 'Now I have honoured Sin, I will not touch [my throat].' In other words, having consulted the oracle Sin by means of omens, he would not ratify the treaty.

1.5 The Amarna letters discovered in Egypt in 1887 show us a world of quite advanced political interaction among the States of the Near East in the fourteenth century BC. But as Berridge remarks, communications in this period were slow and insecure and the means either messengers or merchant caravans. Diplomatic immunity was nothing more elaborate than the standards of hospitality of the period. By the time of the Greek city states of the fourth and fifth

---

[7] P Michalowski, *Letters from Early Mesopotamia*, ed E Reiner (Atlanta GA: Scholars Press, 1993) 13.

[8] R Cohen in *Innovation in Diplomatic Practice*, ed Jan Melissen (New York: Macmillan, 1999).

[9] K Hamilton and R Langhorne, *The Practice of Diplomacy* (2nd edn, London: Routledge, 2011) 8.

[10] J M Munn-Rankin 'Diplomacy in Western Asia in the Early Second Millenium BC' (Spring 1956) XVII(1) *Iraq* 87.

centuries BC a new more sophisticated diplomacy had developed.[11] The city states frequently despatched and received special embassies with due accreditation, who presented their case, sometimes accompanied by a declaration of war, openly before the rulers or assemblies to whom they were sent and relied on a recognized system of diplomatic immunity. Resident missions with local representation were also introduced whose head was known as *proxenos*.

The principles and methods of Greek diplomacy had in fact been developed by 1.6 the fifth century BC into a recognized system to which much subsequent thinking on the subject owes its origin, and which has provided one of the earliest and clearest illustrations of the difficulty, so familiar to us today, of reconciling efficient negotiation with the processes of democracy. There were epic moments of diplomacy in antiquity. Nicolson highlights the celebrated Conference of Sparta in 432 BC, perhaps the first account of a diplomatic conference. The Conference was called by the Spartans to decide whether or not to go to war with Athens. However, an Athenian diplomatic mission or delegation was by chance in Sparta on other unspecified business and was invited to address the Assembly and indeed to remain in Sparta even after a vote by Sparta and her allies had been taken to go to war with Athens. Clearly then it had already emerged that diplomats, as we must call these Athenian delegates, enjoyed some protection and were afforded rights which other visitors from Athens are unlikely to have been granted. Some protocol must already have been in place which governed this inchoate diplomatic procedure. Of course not all activity by these early members of a mission or embassy can properly be designated diplomacy. To describe as diplomacy for instance the crude threats of the Athenian envoys to Melos during the Peloponnesian war in exhorting them to surrender to Athenian rule—'the strong do what they can and the weak suffer what they must'[12]—whatever its modern resonances—would be to sell the craft of diplomacy short. In the fourth century BC, Kautilya, a prime minister to the Indian Emperor Chandragupta Maurya, wrote *Arthashastra,* a treatise on statecraft which, besides classifying various diplomatic representatives into categories depending on the power they wielded on behalf of their masters, specified that they were entitled to immunity or protection. 'Kautilya also anticipated Machiavelli in the amoral and ruthless nature of his advice on statecraft to the prince.'[13]

---

[11] G R Berridge, *Diplomacy, Theory and Practice* (5th edn, Basingstoke and New York: Palgrave Macmillan, 2015) 1.

[12] Thucydides, *The Peloponnesian War.* Translation by Richard Crawley, *The Landmark Thucydides,* ed Robert Strassler (Simon and Schuster, 1998) 352.

[13] A F Cooper, J Heine, and R Thakur (eds), *The Oxford Handbook of Modern Diplomacy* (Oxford: Oxford University Press, 2013) 4.

1.7 The Roman contribution to this heritage was characteristic of a people who produced rulers and administrators rather than diplomats, who preferred organization to negotiation, and who sought to impose a universal respect for their own system of law. Yet while their behaviour was often brutal and oppressive, as was perhaps not surprising in the only superpower of their day, they were not entirely without scruple. When one Roman embassy to King Perseus of Macedon duplicitously gulled him into delaying his preparations for war by suggesting that a deal could be struck at Rome, the envoys were criticized by some Romans for their cynical behaviour.[14]

1.8 The Byzantine emperors, on the other hand, although often at pains to elaborate the machinery of diplomatic intercourse, earned this machinery a reputation for complexity and deviousness. And yet as the Byzantine emperors attempted to compensate for their reduced military force by the use of diplomacy, the ceremonial of which was notably ornate, they developed the ancient concept of divide and rule, playing off one group of barbarians against another,[15] often bribing the frontier tribes.[16] They transformed the traditional role of the envoy from a herald or orator who simply set out the emperor's views, threats, or proposals to the beginnings of the role of the modern diplomat, a trained observer and negotiator attempting to interpret what he saw for his master and to negotiate an accord which approximated most closely to the empire's interests. Their success in attracting pagans into the Christian orbit was another means of protecting the empire.

1.9 The Venetians undoubtedly learned much from Byzantine example and it was through them that Byzantine diplomatic practice was passed on to the West, but the diplomacy of the Italian city states was essentially a product of the political conditions of the time. As Garrett Mattingly[17] demonstrated, Italian Renaissance diplomacy did not spring either from a Greek prototype or ready-made from

---

[14] R Lane Fox, *The Classical World: An Epic History from Homer to Hadrian* (London: Allen Lane, 2005) 327.

[15] H Nicolson, *Diplomacy* (3rd edn, London: Oxford University Press, 1963) 25.

[16] Professor T L Hodgkin, in a lecture entitled 'Diplomacy and Diplomats in the Western Sudan', made the following comments about non-resident diplomacy in Arab North Africa from the tenth to the fourteenth centuries:

(i) 'Most of these embassies would fall, so far as their ostensible object was concerned, into the category which Mattingly [see footnote 13], following and adapting Bernard du Rosier, calls "embassies of ceremony", to bring presents and letters of congratulation to a Prince on accession or after conquests, to renew friendship, etc.'

(ii) 'At the same time, from a more practical standpoint, in most cases these embassies also presumably fall into Mattingly's other category as "embassies of negotiation."' (Quoted from K Ingham (ed), *Foreign Relations of African States* (London: Bobbs-Merrill, 1974) 9.)

[17] G Mattingly, *Renaissance Diplomacy* (London: Cape, 1955) chs I–II.

Italian soil. According to his interpretation the Western and Central European world based itself on the triple concept of the Roman Empire and its tradition of civil law; its successor, the Holy Roman Empire, with its system of Germanic feudal and customary law; and the canon law of the ecclesiastical authority. The centre of faith was the Church of Rome, and the centre of doctrine, the Papacy. The whole formed what was termed the *res publica Christiana*. So long as this trinity formed a credible unity, although of course emissaries (whether styled as agents, procurators, or consuls) were sent to transact business in territories other than their own, there was no formal necessity for accredited ambassadors (*legati*) in the sense in which we understand the term today; and certainly not for resident ones. In fact the thirteenth-century canon law authority Gulielmus Durandus gave the definition 'a *legatus* is anybody sent by another'.

Renaissance Diplomacy

Nevertheless, as the Middle Ages proceeded, there was rarely concord between   **1.10** Pope and Emperor; the sovereignty of individual states grew as walled cities found they could defend themselves against quite large imperial or papal forces, and credentials of some kind began to be required if an ambassador was to be received by someone regarding himself as holding sovereign power. Even so, growth was by no means logical or tidy and the move to residential diplomacy is hard to identify with precision. While there were isolated examples—for instance the papal representative at the emperor's court in Constantinople, who was called the *apocrisiarius*, often held the post for a number of years—Gregory the Great held it from 578 to 585, before becoming Pope in 590[18]—the institution of a resident embassy seems to date from the second half of the fifteenth century. Outstanding among early long-term resident diplomatic agents was Nicodemo da Pontremoli, sent by Francesco Sforza, ruler of Milan, not in the first place as his representative to the Florentine State, but as his confidential agent to Cosimo de' Medici, its most powerful citizen. When in 1450 Sforza became Duke of Milan, he furnished his representative with a regular accreditation as 'orator' in the Florentine republic, and Nicodemo held the post for 17 years. One can readily see how in the closely knit but tensely divided polity of fifteenth-century Italy the practice of residential diplomacy, the most important innovation in diplomatic practice, came to be commonly accepted and to evolve its own conventions.

---

[18] The current editor is indebted to Professor Sir Larry Siedentop for drawing his attention to this example.

It was during the Italian Wars (1494–1559)[19] that the practice spread around Europe, not least because the Italian princes and popes needed good intelligence on what was being planned in terms of their own future in the capitals of the countries most prone to intervene in Italy: Paris, Madrid, and Vienna. In the atmosphere of developing nation states, shifting alliances, and the dynastic struggles for power the resident diplomatic agent was invaluable in keeping his master supplied with information and acting as a barometer to register every evidence or portent of impending change.[20] A quarter of a century later 'the earliest major work on diplomatic law'[21] appeared. It was written by Alberico Gentili, a Protestant from Le Marche (Eastern Italy), who fled from the Italian inquisition to find refuge in Queen Elizabeth's Protestant England in 1580 and became Regius Professor of Civil Law at All Souls' College, Oxford seven years later. His book *De Legationibus Libri Tres* (1585)[22] discussed, inter alia, the inviolability of ambassadors and the establishment and conduct of diplomatic missions. Gentili also pointed out what might seem surprising for the time: that it was already common to accept ambassadors from States considered by the receiving State to be infidels or heretics. In this he will have been prompted by the fact that only two years before *De Legationibus* was published 'England's first permanent embassy to the Muslim empire of the Ottoman sultan was created in Istanbul, where it joined two other Christian embassies...those of Venice and France'.[23] However, the wars of religion in the sixteenth and seventeenth centuries so embittered relations between Catholic and Protestant States that for 100 years true diplomacy was well-nigh paralysed by mutual distrust. Ambassadors reported that it was impossible to find out anything, because nobody wanted to talk to them. Christendom appeared to be breaking up and the civilized intercourse essential to good diplomacy suffered a temporary lapse. This very much applied to relations between Catholics and Protestants though channels of communication were still open within the opposing camps.

1.11 It was during this period that the 'Machiavellian' expedients of spying, conspiracy, and deceit brought the reputation of the resident diplomatic agent to its

---

[19] A series of wars originally dynastic but later descending into a general power struggle for territory and control involving most of the Italian city states, the Papal States, and the major European actors.

[20] D Frigo (ed), *Politics and Diplomacy in Early Modern Italy* (Cambridge: Cambridge University Press, 2000) 8–9 and 27–31.

[21] E Young (later Denza), 'The Development of the Law of Diplomatic Relations' (1964) 40 *British Yearbook of International Law* 149.

[22] A Gentili, *De Legationibus Libri Tres*, translated by G L Laing, Classics of International Law (Oxford and New York, 1924; reprinted New York and London, 1964).

[23] G R Berridge, 'Grotius', in G R Berridge, Maurice Keens-Soper, and T G Otte, *Diplomatic Theory from Machiavelli to Kissinger* (Basingstoke, UK: Palgrave, 2001).

nadir. *Raison d'état* or what in English is called 'the end justifying the means' took unquestioned precedence over morality. The French were early leaders in this field, preferring to work with the Ottoman Turks at the expense of their fellow Christian Habsburgs. Another example of this cynical behaviour, particularly notable as it was practised by a prince of the Church, was the work of Cardinal Richelieu of France who saw his country's interests as better served by siding with the Protestants in the Thirty Years' War (1618–48) than allowing the Holy Roman Empire to extend its borders further and so weaken Louis XIII's France. Richelieu was only content when his monarch was as powerful, if not more so, than the Holy Roman Emperor however offensive this was to the universalist tradition of the superiority of morality over expediency. No wonder Pope Urban VIII is said to have commented on hearing of Richelieu's death, 'If there is a God... Richelieu will have much to answer for. If not... well, he had a successful life.'[24] Richelieu was of course providing an early example of balance of power politics which were to underpin European diplomacy until the First World War. He was also among the first (in his *Political Testament*) to call for 'total diplomacy', in other words a wide network of diplomatic representation to reflect the fact that most of Europe was intimately interconnected.[25]

The Origins of Modern Diplomacy

Only in 1648 when the Treaty of Westphalia—which concluded the Thirty   1.12
Years' War—had established a new order of relationships, however precarious at first, could the age of classical European diplomacy (the direct origin of all modern diplomacy) be said to have begun. An observer at that Congress wrote a guide to the diplomatic practice that emerged from it, in some ways an antecedent to the present volume. Abraham de Wicquefort wrote *L'Ambassadeur et ses Fonctions* in prison and published it in French in 1681. Wicquefort's work identifies 'the resident ambassador as the principal institutional device for the conduct of foreign affairs' as Maurice Keens-Soper remarks, and his work provides 'an actualized concept of the seventeenth-century European states-system... at the time of the Congress of Westphalia... [which] set the seal on the transformation of a long divided Christendom into the states-system of the *ancien régime*'.[26] This was diplomacy conducted by members of an avowedly

---

[24] L Auchincloss, *Richelieu* (New York: Viking Press, 1972) 256.

[25] 'J'ose dire hardiment, négocier sans cesse ouvertement en tous lieux, quoiqu'on n'en reçoive pas un fruit présent, et celui qu'on peut attendre à l'avenir ne soit pas apparent, est une chose tout à fait nécessaire.' Cardinal Richelieu, *Testament Politique* (ed. Paris, 1947) 347.

[26] Berridge, Keens-Soper, and Otte, *Diplomatic Theory* 89 and 99–100.

ruling class, who frequently had more in common with each other, across land and sea frontiers, than with the majority of their own people. (The system's elitism helped of course to foster the cohesion of the diplomatic corps.) It proceeded, like the limited wars of the time, according to well-defined rules and civilized conventions. It was personal and flexible, and its style, while not without subtlety, was clear enough for all who took part in it to understand not only what was explicitly said, but what was to be taken for granted. An important contribution to writing on relations between States came from a Swiss lawyer, Emmerich de Vattel, who discussed the application of natural law to international relations in his treatise *Le Droit des Gens* of 1758. The authors of the American constitution were influenced by it, particularly by its focus on liberty and equality, which were echoed in the Declaration of Independence, but also by its defence of neutrality. Vattel too, in discussing the right of maintaining embassies so 'that each Nation possesses both the right to negotiate and have intercourse with the others, and the reciprocal obligation to lend itself to such intercourse',[27] reflected the spirit of the age in his view of embassies as an essential element in the functioning of international society.[28]

1.13   It was however the Congress of Vienna which codified more concretely the new world of diplomacy. Its *Règlement* of 1815 established an agreed basis for diplomatic representation including precedence (see also Chapter 7) and effected the recognition of diplomatic services as a distinct profession within the public service governed by its own internationally accepted codes. The settlement at the Congress of Vienna[29] was remarkable in rebuilding an international order broken by the Napoleonic wars. Europe enjoyed its longest sustained period of peace when, from 1815 to 1914, with the exception of the Crimean War, no general war took place among the major protagonists of the Napoleonic Wars, the so-called Great Powers. It did so by constructing a balance of power which was subtle enough to ensure that the threat from French expansionism was contained, yet in a way which was not sufficiently punitive to lead to France resentfully nursing a grievance. Indeed, France was rapidly admitted (in 1818) to the Congress system which was to prove a form of proto-European government for the period up to the Crimean War. The British were uneasy at any 'system' which might drag them into continental engagement but the Concert of Europe, as this Great Power system of consensus became known, survived as a concept throughout the nineteenth century and was invoked by Gladstone as late as 1879

---

[27] E de Vattel, *The Law of Nations*, Vol 3, 1758, translated by C G Fenwick (Washington, 1916), Book IV, Chapter V, 362.

[28] See also Chapter **8**, paragraph **8.2**.

[29] For a full account of the Congress see A Zamoyski, *Rites of Peace: The Fall of Napoleon and the Congress of Vienna* (London: Harper Perennial, 2008).

during his Midlothian campaign as a principle to be maintained. 'And why? Because keeping all in union together you neutralize and fetter and bind up the selfish aims of each.'[30] Something of the same logic underpinned the creation of the European Communities after the Second World War, some 70 years later. One of the key documents to emerge from the Congress of Vienna was the Quadruple Alliance of Great Britain, Austria, Prussia, and Russia designed to counteract any nascent French aggression with overwhelming force. As Henry Kissinger comments, 'Had the victors convening at Versailles made a similar alliance in 1918, the world might never have suffered a Second World War.'[31]

In post-revolutionary Europe the ascendancy of new objectives began to eclipse earlier values. Acceptance of an established monarchical order gave way to the growing will to overturn the status quo. The international struggle for power brought into play collective national energies which could be more effectively harnessed by constitutional methods and cabinet government than by the rule of Machiavelli's idealized 'Prince'. Although skill in the classical methods continued to command respect and acceptance, it became evident that diplomacy should now be exercised (or at least appear to be exercised) in the interests, not of a dynasty, nor even of an aristocracy, but of the nation as a whole. Much of this arose from statesmen's realization of the importance of public opinion. Two British statesmen, Canning and Palmerston, thought this a positive rather than a negative development. Nicolson reminds us that '[i]t was mainly for this reason that Metternich described him [Canning] as "a malevolent meteor hurled by divine providence upon Europe"'.[32] Palmerston took an excessively optimistic view: 'Opinions, if they are founded in truth and justice, will in the end prevail against the bayonets of infantry, the fire of artillery and the charges of cavalry.' This proved as much a fallacy in Palmerston's time (Prussia in Schleswig-Holstein) as in the last 100 years. Public opinion failed to prevent wars as disparate as the two World Wars, Vietnam, and Iraq though in the case of the latter two it undoubtedly played a role in bringing the wars to an end.

1.14

The End of the Concert of Europe

The First World War was of course the death knell of the Concert of Europe. In truth it had been expiring for 20 years. The system of bipolar military alliances

1.15

---

[30] Extract from Gladstone's third Midlothian Speech, Tuesday 27 November 1879 at West Calder. <http://www.liberalhistory.org.uk/history/extract-from-gladstones-3rd-midlothian-speech-on-foreign-policy/>.

[31] H Kissinger, *Diplomacy* (London: Simon and Schuster, 1995) 83.

[32] Nicolson, *Diplomacy*, 73.

(uncannily mirroring the two power blocs that emerged with the Cold War), which had developed in the last decades of the nineteenth century, exposed Europe to the risk that a single incident could prompt a chain reaction leading to a general war. The rise of Prussian, then German, militarism became the threat which by the end of the nineteenth century had entirely replaced a similar fear of French expansionism a century earlier. The system of alliances and the excessive weight given to military planning and timetables undermined any chance that diplomacy might head off what came to be seen as an almost inevitable clash. Along with the disappearance of old Empires and much of the old order, the First World War also brought an end to old or orthodox diplomacy. The new diplomacy which was to replace it was usually vaguely defined but was clearly predicated on a new openness born of faster communications, the increasing power of the press, and a shift in the balance of forces in the democracies from the ruling elites to the governed.

The New Diplomacy

1.16   Both before and during the First World War, the conviction asserted itself that the time was ripe for diplomacy to be made more open and more accessible to public scrutiny and appraisal. Diplomats like the Cambon brothers, respectively French ambassadors in London and Berlin at the outbreak of the war, articulated this demand as early as 1905[33] as did various pacifist and other anti-war groups. As the cost of the war in terms of millions of dead became clear and as its origins were seen to lie in the failures of the old diplomacy, so the requirement for a new approach became more insistent. The clamour was heard for 'open covenants openly arrived at' in President Wilson's much quoted words. It was natural that electorates claiming to control governments should require to know what agreements were being made in their name and to exercise the constitutional right of accepting or rejecting them (as when the United States Senate in 1919 rejected participation in the League of Nations). Nowadays the openness of agreements is, in principle, guaranteed by the United Nations rule that all agreements concluded by member States must be registered, and their texts deposited, with the Secretary-General.[34] But the problem is that if actual negotiation is carried on entirely in the public eye—as President Wilson at first appeared to think it should be—it quickly turns into a travesty of efficient procedure and runs the risk of betraying any constructive purpose for which it may have been conceived.

---

[33] Ibid, 137.
[34] Art 102 of the United Nations Charter.

By its nature, true negotiation must be confidential, even if broad aims have necessarily been made public. If exhibited, it degenerates into polemic; and this is not diplomacy, it is the continuation of warfare in peacetime by other means. A neat corroboration of this was furnished by Soviet Field-Marshal Shaposhnikov's paradox: 'If war may be said to be the continuation of politics by other means,' [an allusion to the doctrine of Clausewitz] 'then peace, in its turn, is no more than the continuation of conflict by other means.'[35] There is of course nothing new in this. The same thought is implicit in Machiavelli's prologue to his *Art of War*. In such a process of conflict the practice of diplomacy must be presumed to embrace not merely negotiation, but the use of a complex range of moral and psychological weapons. Indeed when Wilson came to negotiate the Treaty of Versailles he clearly abandoned this transparency, the first of his celebrated Fourteen Points (America's war aims, formulated by Wilson before Congress in January 1918), and maintained confidentiality even from lesser allies. All the key decisions were taken by the triumvirate of Wilson, Lloyd George, and Clemenceau (with the Italian prime minister, Vittorio Orlando, the largely ineffective other member of the key body, the Council of Four) who paid scant regard to the views of others. This may be considered an early example of summitry (discussed further in Chapter 2) though the original intentions in assembling such a substantial cast list were very different.[36] The Germans and their allies were, unlike the French at Vienna, completely excluded, as were the Russians. To have excluded the two strongest nations in continental Europe was alone enough 'to have doomed the Versailles settlement'.[37]

The League of Nations

The failings of the Treaty of Versailles have been discussed exhaustively and this is not the place to rehearse them further. But in one area at least it provided the germ of an idea which after a false start would take root. The new diplomacy had, beyond its requirement for openness, a yearning for an international organization to settle disputes and deter those who sought to impose their will by force. In its faltering steps towards world government (the League of Nations), the Versailles Conference changed the nature of diplomacy decisively even if another World War had to intervene before this became apparent. The League of Nations was first proposed—ironically given Britain's obsession hitherto with

1.17

---

[35] Quoted by R L Garthoff in *La Doctrine militaire soviétique* (Paris: Pion, 1956) 4.
[36] For the best account of the Versailles Conference see M Macmillan, *Peacemakers* (London: John Murray, 2001).
[37] Kissinger, *Diplomacy*, 231.

balance of power politics—by the British Foreign Secretary, Sir Edward Grey, to President Wilson's personal adviser, Colonel House, as far back as 1915. Wilson made the idea his own and presented it first in May 1916. It then became one of his Fourteen Points, and Wilson pursued the idea at Versailles with characteristic eloquence and vigour.

1.18 But the League was emasculated by the US failure to ratify the Treaty and by the non-participation of Germany (excluded until 1926, and then withdrawing in 1933) and Soviet Russia (which was a member only for the years 1934–9, when it was expelled). Its limitations were demonstrated by its failure to impose sanctions on Japan in 1931 after its invasion of Manchuria (though Japan withdrew in any case in 1933), its response to Haile Selassie's famously pathetic and personal plea in 1936 to the League for justice and assistance (equally pathetic) in response to Italy's invasion, and its failure to act when Hitler occupied the Rhineland, in direct contravention of the Versailles Treaty. Collective security, the very purpose of the League, was hopelessly undermined. The failure of the League to prevent the slide into the Second World War, as Hitler and Mussolini treated it with rank contempt, marked the temporary eclipse of the new diplomacy. The alliances and pacts, the territorial acquisitiveness, and the suppression of self-determination, all features of the old order, returned with a vengeance. Once the war was over, however, there was a clearly recognized need to create a new international organization to replace the League and to be significantly different in its basic design.

The Cold War, Containment, and Détente

1.19 The shape of the post-war world was however not set by a world forum but by a series of summit meetings of the three Allied leaders, Roosevelt, Stalin, and Churchill (cf Versailles) at Tehran and Yalta and of Truman, Stalin, and Churchill then Attlee at Potsdam. Churchill foresaw that Stalin, the ultimate apostle of *Realpolitik* would never trade the Red Army's gains for abstract principles and proposed instead that each of the Allies should have its sphere of influence. This was anathema to Roosevelt as a return to discredited balance of power and colonial politics which US public opinion would never support. Roosevelt, who famously described the Soviet leader as having something of a Christian gentleman about him, did not live to see the final unmasking of Stalin's bad faith as he took as his sphere of influence the whole of Eastern Europe and Germany to the Elbe. Thus, until the fall of the Berlin Wall and the collapse of the Soviet Union in 1989, new and old diplomacy coexisted. East and West were grouped in two mutually antagonistic alliances while a new world body, the United Nations, struggled to fulfil its potential. The West attempted to deal with the Soviet Empire and Communist China by a policy of containment which lasted 40 years. Containment as a policy was first articulated by the American diplomat George Kennan. In what became known as the 'Long Telegram', Kennan brilliantly analysed Soviet motives and political perspective: they were, he said, an unholy combination of Communist ideology, traditional Russian insecurity, and Tsarist expansionism. To deal with this threat, the West needed 'a policy of firm containment, designed to confront the Russians with unalterable counter-force at every point where they show signs of encroaching upon the interests of a peaceful and stable world'.[38]

But containment was very much a policy for the long haul, reactive and predicated on the eventual collapse or transformation of the Soviet system. The Communist threat was not of course monolithic. When the US began to take advantage of the ideological split between the two Communist mammoths, the Soviet Union and China, in the early 1970s, President Nixon demonstrated his attachment to old balance of power politics by daringly opening up US contacts with Communist China and providing a triangularity among the three major nuclear Powers which had hitherto been absent. At the same time Nixon initiated the policy which became known as détente[39] with the Soviet Union. For Kissinger, the architect of this and so many other aspects of Nixon's foreign policy, 'détente, desirable though it was, could not replace the overall balance of power'.[40] In other words, it flowed from equilibrium and was not a substitute for it. This Sino-Soviet-US geostrategic triangle with the US in pre-eminent position was, as Otte points out, 'precisely the kind of policy for which he [Kissinger] had praised Metternich and Bismarck in his earlier academic writings'.[41] In fact while Kissinger's conceptual approach to diplomacy was traditional, his practice was highly innovative. Given the limitations of nineteenth-century means of transport, neither Metternich nor Bismarck would have been able to follow Kissinger's practice of diplomacy even if they had wanted to. But Kissinger's uses of back-channel and shuttle diplomacy were remarkable. Kissinger as an academic had always been allergic to bureaucracy. His and Nixon's institution of back-channels, early on in the latter's presidency, stemmed from the need for secrecy both to prevent their radical foreign policy initiatives being undermined by State Department leaks and to ensure that opposition to his enthusiasm for linkage,

1.20

---

[38] 'X' (G F Kennan), 'The Sources of Soviet Conduct' (1947) 25(4) *Foreign Affairs* 581.

[39] An easing of tension between the two opposing post-World War II blocs by use of diplomacy and confidence-building measures.

[40] T G Otte, 'Kissinger', in Berridge, Keens-Soper, and Otte, *Diplomatic Theory*, 195.

[41] Ibid, 196.

negotiating on a broad front, was stymied. Kissinger himself put it more prosaically. His use of back-channels was designed to open up potentially blocked channels without completely sidelining the State Department. Once the back-channels 'gave hope of specific agreements, the subject was moved to conventional diplomatic channels. If formal negotiations there reached a deadlock, the Channel would open up again.'[42]

1.21 Kissinger used back-channel or secret diplomacy extensively in his time as US National Security Adviser, initially to implement the policy of détente with the Soviet ambassador in Washington, Anatoly Dobrynin, through what 'Kissinger called "the Channel" used over and over again . . . on every key problem in Soviet-American relations'.[43] Later he used a back-channel with Le Duc Tho of North Vietnam in an attempt to bring the Vietnam War to an end. Kissinger added a new term to the diplomatic lexicon—shuttle diplomacy—whereby the intermediary in a conflict shuttles backwards and forwards repeatedly between the parties in conflict or in dispute to secure the desired result. Of course this type of diplomacy is not guaranteed to succeed, as General Alexander Haig found when attempting to mediate between Argentina and Britain during the Falklands War in 1982, but Kissinger's style and energy often secured results, on occasions because he had worn down the resistance of the opposing sides. As Hamilton and Langhorne put it, 'his mediation in the wake of the [1973] Yom Kippur War constituted a dazzling display of how modern technology could be harnessed to a diplomacy which was at once spectacular, secret and ministerial'.[44] (As an aside, it is hard to gauge how Kissinger's practice would have survived the WikiLeaks era. Kissinger might perhaps have thought that it validated his approach to keep secret negotiations away from official State Department channels where they might be leaked. This whole issue, the impact of often massive deliberate leaks on the conduct of diplomacy, is examined in Chapter 27.)

1.22 Machiavelli in his *History of Florence* remarks that 'Wars begin when you will, but they do not end when you please.' Nor, he might have added, do they always end when you expect. The speed of the ending of the Cold War followed, less than a year after the fall of the Berlin Wall, by the reunification of Germany in October 1990 caught most, if not all, off-guard and, in the case of the reunification of Germany, disconcerted some like Mrs Thatcher (then British prime minister) most adamantly opposed to the post-WWII division of Europe. President Mitterrand of France was also initially opposed but softened his views

---

[42] H Kissinger, *The White House Years* (Boston and London, 1979) 138.

[43] W Bundy, *A Tangled Web: The Making of Foreign Policy in the Nixon Presidency* (London and New York: I B Tauris, 1998) 57.

[44] Hamilton and Langhorne, *The Practice of Diplomacy*, 227.

as he saw early reunification as inevitable. Chancellor Kohl demonstrated considerable diplomatic skills in allaying the nervousness and fears of his allies and resisting the Soviet Union's aim of detaching a unified Germany from NATO. While the end of the Cold War was expected in some quarters to lead to 'the end of history' (to use Francis Fukuyama's phrase[45]) and presumably to the end of diplomacy, this proved to be very wide of the mark: in fact an illusion.

Today's diplomat is the inheritor of a rich history. Diplomacy has evolved and con-   **1.23**
tinues to do so. While bilateral diplomacy remains key, several adjectives qualify other forms of diplomacy—multilateral, summit, public. Each is important as governments address a range of challenges, many stemming from globalization. These include conflict prevention and resolution, international development, trade and investment promotion, human rights, climate change, and many more. Diplomacy is a vital element running through them all, necessitating a set of skills for the diplomat which is even greater than hitherto. This is covered extensively in the following chapters, beginning with the next chapter on the challenges of modern diplomacy, underlining that there will be no limit to the requirements of the role or to the satisfaction from doing a challenging job well and making a difference.

---

[45] Francis Fukuyama, 'The End of History?', *The National Interest* (Summer 1989).

2

THE CHANGES IN AND CHALLENGES OF MODERN DIPLOMACY

Ivor Roberts

2.1 The quarter-century since the end of the Cold War has seen a greater change in the methods if not the aims of diplomacy than in any period since the establishment of permanent diplomatic missions in Renaissance Italy. Yet it is one of the paradoxes of modern diplomacy that in a period when so much of it is conducted at summit level (see paragraph 2.5), the importance attached to establishing diplomatic missions in particular by newly independent countries has not diminished one whit. Nevertheless, summitry and multilateral diplomacy, the emergence of alternatives to conventional diplomacy, the importance of the press and social media, and the speed of communication have, if not negated the traditional diplomat's role, certainly recast it.

Multilateral Diplomacy

2.2 While multilateral diplomacy has flourished in the post-Cold War period, unlikely as it may seem, the practice can be said to have its roots in antiquity. In an attempt to stop the feuding and warfare, the principal Powers in the Eastern

Mediterranean, i.e. the important Greek states and Persia, 'agreed to convene great international political congresses... to discuss a general settlement of outstanding issues'. This general peace, known as the King's Peace, involved eight congresses between 392 and 367 BC and 'not only established a territorial stalemate, with guarantees against an aggressor similar to those which later figured in the Covenant of the League of Nations... they also agreed on certain general principles... and on detailed practical rules of conduct for regulating international affairs'.[1]

In modern times, large-scale conferences took place infrequently in the eight- **2.3** eenth and nineteenth centuries (Vienna and Berlin being major examples from the nineteenth century). In the twentieth century, the Versailles Conference set a precedent which has been followed ever more frequently in recent decades despite the view of some sceptics who see such conferences as largely talking shops. (Paul Cambon believed that 'a conference which includes more than four or five people... can achieve nothing worthwhile'.[2]) This view still has its adherents but there can clearly be advantages to a multilateral conference in terms of efficiency and speed of decision-making. This does not necessarily apply to a standing multilateral conference like the UN or other international organizations which are not time-limited. But a conference will almost certainly be the best forum for decision-making and reaching agreements where it has a deadline, is subject-specific, and/or where technical details are involved and the national experts assembled in one place. Berridge points out that multilateral conferences, particularly major standing ones like the UN, provide an opportunity for principals to meet in the margins to discuss other issues including bilateral ones, a particularly valuable opportunity for those States which have no or very poor diplomatic relations. They can also 'kick start, and then discreetly shroud, a series of essentially bilateral negotiations taking place elsewhere. This was the extremely valuable function performed for the Arab-Israeli bilateral talks by the Geneva Conference of December 1973 and then by the Madrid Conference in October 1991.'[3] A more recent example was President Obama's meeting with President Raúl Castro at the Summit of the Americas in Panama in April 2015, the first meeting between the leaders of the two countries in half a century, which paved the way for the resumption of bilateral diplomatic relations three months later after a gap of 54 years.

The proliferation of international and regional organizations so prevalent in the **2.4** 1960s and 1970s (partly a function of the greatly increased number of inde-

---

[1] A Watson, *Diplomacy: The Dialogue between States* (London: Methuen, 1982) 87.
[2] J-F Blondel, *Entente Cordiale* (London: Caduceus Press, 1971) 40.
[3] G R Berridge, *Diplomacy: Theory and Practice* (4th edn, Basingstoke, UK: Palgrave, 2010) 145.

pendent States who saw in these organizations an opportunity for exerting influence) has levelled off now. But multilateral diplomacy's advantages will ensure that it survives and flourishes despite the frequent echoes of Cambon's put-down. Indeed it is the nation state in its Westphalian form which faces an existential crisis. Are we perhaps seeing the end of traditional geography? In recent years, the nation state has been pulled between post-modern institutions with their orientation towards pooled sovereignty from above and, from below, by secessionist entities. The UK, having voted in favour of so-called Brexit from the EU in a referendum in June 2016, is experiencing both tensions: a withdrawal from pooled sovereignty in the EU and the threat from below of a second independence referendum in Scotland. There is moreover the example, which may prove ephemeral, of the Caliphate claimed by the so-called Islamic State (also ISIL) whose boundaries are indeterminate but whose ambitions are unbounded. And we have the depressingly frequent example of failed States where even when their boundaries are uncontested, their governance is so fraught as often to seem non-existent. (Multilateral diplomacy and international and regional organizations are discussed extensively in **Book IV**.)

Summitry and Modern Diplomacy

2.5 Both bilateral and multilateral diplomacy are increasingly frequently carried out at the highest, that is to say at summit, level. David Dunn refers to summits as meetings between those who 'by virtue of their position...are not able to be contradicted by any other individual'[4] but it would be more exact to the participants in a summit to describe them as persons recognized (including in international law) as having the inherent capacity to bind the State.

2.6 The word 'summit' was first used to describe meetings at this level in a speech in 1950 by Churchill ('a parley at the summit') but the practice, like multilateral diplomacy itself, has ancient roots. In the Middle Ages most diplomacy was carried out at summit level, often by kings and princes of neighbouring States. (A slightly later example was the meeting between Henry VIII and Francis I of France on the Field of the Cloth of Gold (then part of the English Pale of Calais) in 1520 to cement the Anglo-French Treaty of 1514.) The celebrated French diplomat and historian Philippe de Commynes (*c.*1447–1511) disapproved of such meetings not least because of the physical danger involved. (A visiting sovereign if recognized as such would of course enjoy immunity.[5])

---

[4] D H Dunn, *Diplomacy at the Highest Level* (Basingstoke: Macmillan, 1996) 17.
[5] See Chapter **12**, paragraphs 12.23 *et seq.*

He concluded that 'two great princes who wish to establish good personal relations should never meet each other face to face but ought to communicate through good and wise ambassadors'.[6]

With the practice of resident diplomats becoming established in the sixteenth century, so summitry went into relative decline. The practice of summitry enjoyed a renaissance in the nineteenth century and 'underwent a resurgence after 1914, fostered by the democratisation of diplomacy and the belief that issues of war and peace were too important to be left to professionals'.[7] The speed of international travel has seen the practice mushroom in the last 30 years. For some this has been the end of diplomacy, as the makers of foreign policy take it upon themselves to execute it. But that is a superficial assessment to which we shall return.   **2.7**

Summits as originally conceived by Churchill were infrequent and involved only a handful of the most important people on the planet. The practice is now so widespread that it is possible to identify different types.[8] The first category is the serial summit involving several countries, which is part of a regular institutionalized series, examples of which are the European Council, G7/G20 meetings, ASEAN, Arab League, Commonwealth Heads of Government (CHOGM), African Union, Organization of American States, and Franco-German summits. Details of these will be found in Chapters **20–23**. As can be seen many of these are linked to international organizations and can constitute a court of highest appeal when disagreements between members cannot be resolved at a lower level. The second type of summit is an ad hoc summit, which can involve two or many more leaders, often set up to deal with a crisis or break the ice between States whose relations have been poor or non-existent. The meeting in Paris in 1971 between Heath and Pompidou which led the way to British entry into the EEC or Nixon's meeting with Mao in Beijing in 1972 were prime examples as too is the Obama/Castro summit referred to in paragraph **2.3**. Although the substance is often important, the symbolism of such a meeting itself may be even more significant and it will undoubtedly tend to attract more publicity than a serial summit. Or such a summit may arise from a crisis or particular occasion or elevated attendance in an existing institution. The new Millennium was marked by the adoption of a formal Declaration within the framework of the UN General Assembly at summit level in 2000 which included some 150 Heads of State or Government.   **2.8**

---

[6] Quoted by Berridge, *Diplomacy* (5th edn, 2015) 185.

[7] J W Young, *Twentieth-Century Diplomacy* (Cambridge: Cambridge University Press, 2008) 115.

[8] Berridge, *Diplomacy* (5th edn, 2015) 188.

2.9   The third kind is the high-level exchange of views. This least ambitious type of summitry is nevertheless extensively used, particularly by leaders undertaking a tour of a region. They may hope to get to know their opposite number however superficially and may be able to advance some issues which have been blocked.

2.10   The dangers of summitry are not always appreciated by its practitioners. Being high-profile events, expectations of them are often raised and the risk of failure greater. Examples of failed summits or those with negative consequences are legion. Neville Chamberlain's encounter with Hitler in 1938, the notorious Munich agreement on the partition of Czechoslovakia, is an obvious candidate. So too is the Gorbachev-Reagan summit in Reykjavik in 1986 where attempts by the former to reach agreement on the elimination of all nuclear weapons within a decade in exchange for strategic defence initiative research being confined to the laboratory (rejected by Reagan) caused serious alarm among some allies including the British prime minister who believed that President Reagan had come too close to making dangerous disarmament commitments.[9] David Reynolds in his study of key summits of the twentieth century cites the Bush/Blair encounters in the run-up to the Iraq war, the descent into which being 'lubricated by Blair's summitry'.[10] As Dean Acheson, the former US Secretary of State said: 'When a chief of state…makes a fumble, the goal line is open behind him.'[11] Personal chemistry may work to make the occasion a success but if the chemistry works to repel rather than attract the results will at best be meagre and the process best left to the diplomat to pursue. Sometimes they can be dominated by ceremonial and appear to be more exercises in publicity-seeking, all froth and no substance, than breakthroughs in diplomatic negotiations. The most successful summits are those which have been meticulously prepared, a requirement where the professional can be expected to come into his own, and where the outcomes can be far reaching and positive. Many summits are, to continue the metaphor, now prepared by so-called sherpas. Whatever their shortcomings, summits and the accompanying media circus are now a permanent feature of diplomatic topography. A successful summit is one which reinforces the efforts of diplomacy, and appropriately draws upon the expertise and advice of the diplomat.

---

[9] Despite the summit's failure, it improved the atmosphere for disarmament talks more generally and undoubtedly facilitated agreement on the Treaty on Intermediate-Range Nuclear Forces (INF), signed in Washington in 1987.

[10] D Reynold, *Summits: Six Meetings that Shaped the Twentieth Century* (London: Allen Lane, 2007) 389.

[11] Acheson also reflected on the difficulties caused by open or what he called 'new mass' diplomacy. 'The basic anomaly that struck one was the vast separation that existed between the few with the responsibility and capability for taking whatever action might be necessary and the many not only willing but eager to prescribe what that action should be and how it should be managed.' D Acheson, *Present at the Creation* (New York: WW Norton and Co, 1969) 704.

The Diplomat in a Crowded Market Place

While diplomats no longer have a controlling monopoly in carrying out diplo-   **2.11**
matic tasks, part of the competition now comes not just from presidents, prime
ministers, and other ministers and officials in capitals in terms of direct contact
with their opposite numbers in the country to which they are accredited, but
from paradiplomacy and so-called track two diplomacy (track one being the traditional work of and by professional diplomats). Track two diplomacy is always
effected by unofficial and often informal non-governmental actors. Examples
include non-governmental organizations (NGOs), humanitarian organizations
(e.g. Médecins sans Frontières), religious institutions (e.g. the Sant'Egidio community), academics, former government officials (e.g. the Elders founded by
Nelson Mandela, and the Carter Center), and think tanks, and multinational
corporations, among others. (Track two diplomacy is discussed further in
Chapters **28** and **29**.) Paradiplomacy can involve actors from sub-national or
sub-state bodies such as the Canadian provinces, the Australian States, the Basque
country, Catalonia, or the Scottish, Welsh and Northern Irish executives. Track
two actors who assist, support, and complement the work of traditional diplomats may also be described as paradiplomats. But many track two actors may be
in conflict or competition with national representatives. An understanding of
respective roles is desirable, and in many cases the national representative can
work constructively with sub-national representatives.

If the diplomat has to compete in such a busy market place, has the role of a   **2.12**
diplomat been superseded, rendered superfluous? Is a diplomat an endangered
species? Certainly if the market place of diplomacy has become busy, it has also
expanded. States, those basic building blocks of the international order, have
grown in number exponentially. The 1960s and 1970s saw a major growth
linked to the decolonization process. Taken together with the collapse of communism and the continuing vigour of nationalism we have seen a quadrupling
in the number of independent States since 1945. No independent State feels it
has truly reached that status unless it has a network of diplomatic missions to
fly its new flag in foreign countries and at the United Nations. They are as
Berridge puts it 'still the state's first line of defence abroad; daily integrated more
into policy-making by secure, instant communications; the key vehicle for routine negotiations, essential support to special envoys, and nearest thing to a
mind-reader bolted onto the side of a host government'.[12] The growth of international organizations and the need to staff them has also contributed, as has

---

[12] Berridge, *Diplomacy* (5th edn, 2015) 266.

the broadening of many embassies' remit to take in work in economic and trade spheres while traditional consular sections and consulates have had their usefulness rediscovered as they deal with an explosive growth in world tourism, cross-border movements generally (including refugees and people trafficking), and immigration. While summitry has on occasions displaced the ambassador from prime position 'even the most energetic leader could not be in two or more places at once. Prime ministers and special envoys relied on ambassadors to pave the way for successful visits abroad, just as Foreign Ministers needed embassies to keep them informed about other countries' negotiating positions ahead of multilateral talks.'[13] A distinguished British diplomat, Christopher Ewart-Biggs, who was assassinated in Dublin by the IRA, wrote of the Paris embassy's support for an EEC summit: 'one doesn't reach the Summit without a base camp. The base camp was this Embassy.'[14] It is the modern diplomat's task to man that base camp and occasionally perhaps to bask in the reflected glory of those who reach the summit. Less glamour than in diplomacy of old but no lack of fulfilling tasks to execute.[15] Indeed, while globalization leads to many more domestic actors from other ministries on the stage, there is often a real danger of incoherence in the government's message. Hence the important continuing role for the ambassador and the foreign ministry in the capital to ensure consistency and coherence, not to mention the follow-up function: for instance, translating vague commitments from on high into practical action, monitoring the implementation of undertakings given, ensuring that preparatory work for a next high-level meeting is put in train.

Trade and Investment

2.13 In most Western countries, business and government tend to be distinct, in part because of the trend to privatization of state assets, the exceptions often being continued state control of resource industries. This has reduced the possibilities of corrupt practice. In the globalized world, where domestic and foreign policies increasingly intersect, business people travel extensively to pursue their trade interests. Some governments support exporters and may even provide a service, facilitated by their embassies and missions, of publicizing export opportunities in third country markets. In general, business people need little direct help in how to conduct their business, but they will welcome from an ambassador, consul-general, consul, or their (often locally recruited) commercial staff, guidance

---

[13] Young, *Twentieth-Century Diplomacy*, 227.

[14] J Ewart-Biggs, *Pay, Pack and Follow* (London: Weidenfeld and Nicolson, 1984) 161.

[15] For a regularly updated discussion of the theory and practice of diplomacy, see <http://grberridge.diplomacy.edu>.

on who are the key players, the right people to meet, including as appropriate which ministers are likely to be involved in taking key decisions. They will also look to the mission to give general advice on the political lie of the land and any likely or predictable upheavals. Many countries now have legislation which prohibits foreign corruption or bribery by companies located in their State. The commercial staff may well provide the visiting trade mission or individuals with a list of local companies who might be interested in collaborating with the visitors. The commercial staff, including heads of mission for whom trade and investment may make up the bulk of their job description, will also be tasked by home departments to identify opportunities for foreign inward investment. In some countries, the requirement for trade promotion to be closely allied to mainstream diplomatic activity has led to the amalgamation of foreign and trade ministries. Canada, Australia, and New Zealand have all gone down the path of what one Australian foreign affairs officer described as a 'shot-gun marriage, but ultimately well worth it'.[16] In the Canadian experience this has now led to more than half their staff abroad being tasked with trade, economic, and investment affairs.

Public Diplomacy

In an increasing number of diplomatic services, modern diplomats are progressively expected to project their government's message. While they shouldn't become main actors in their host country's affairs, they have no reason to maintain a low profile. The means of delivering their message, what is called public or in some cases digital diplomacy (see Chapter 27), may be modern and indeed shifting constantly as new information technology means are developed but projecting the diplomat's government's message publicly in an attempt to influence mass public opinion is once more an old art (born in a sixteenth-century religious context to propagate the faith). There are those scholars of diplomatic studies who regard public diplomacy as little more than a continuation of this earlier form of propaganda: 'In the hard world of governments, "public diplomacy" is simply propaganda rebranded.'[17] Nevertheless, while public diplomacy can on occasions be guilty of selectivity about the facts, it is now an accepted and established part of the practice of diplomacy not just in Western capitals but globally. From African capitals to the Far East, from the Middle East to Latin America foreign ministries throughout the world have migrated online. As such, all these

2.14

---

[16] Quoted in Greg Mills, 'Trade and Investment Promotion', *The Oxford Handbook of Modern Diplomacy* (2013) 407.

[17] Berridge, *Diplomacy* (5th edn, 2015) 200.

ministries are now struggling to institutionalize the use of social media and digital tools by training diplomats, authoring guidelines, and developing best practices. Public diplomacy is now a major weapon in a diplomat's armoury. To ignore its potential risks diplomacy losing opportunities both to understand and encourage political developments.

2.15 It is moreover worth pointing out one important difference between today's social media and previous forms of communication used to deliver public diplomacy (e.g. radio, television) and that is its interactive nature. Twitter is based on immediate and continuous dialogue between its subscribers. Thus, an ambassador's tweet is immediately commented on by a knowledgeable and opinionated online public, and indeed the uninformed. While this can be risky for diplomats, it also offers many opportunities. Digital diplomacy may now be used to converse with online publics, to stimulate debate on important issues, to foster relations with foreign publics and gauge public opinion in host countries. Thus, Twitter is more than a powerful megaphone: it is a key to the city street or square, and helps avoid the risk of capital/establishment reporting which can present a distorted picture of events, as was the case when the Shah of Iran was deposed (see paragraph 2.20).

2.16 It is, moreover, wrong to think of modern diplomats being put in the shade by travelling ministers. Diplomats have an increasingly public role to play in projecting their government's message locally, not just by media appearances and newspaper articles but by regular use of social media, blogging, Twitter, and evolving techniques. An important statement by the minister can be re-tweeted at the touch of a smartphone but it is the local debate on Google, Facebook, or Twitter which will determine how that policy is perceived, accepted, or rejected. Lord Palmerston on receiving his first telegram in the 1840s is said to have exclaimed 'My God, this is the end of diplomacy.' The modern diplomat must continue to demonstrate the fallacy as a digital interventionist fully engaging with social media because it can amplify the message far more widely and swiftly than can be achieved through traditional rarefied means. A digital démarche carried out with many followers can be far more effective than a traditional démarche through the usual elite channels: the diplomat can mobilize public opinion to change another country's policies. (This can, of course, be a high-risk venture particularly when operating in an authoritarian country or even in a democratic former colony, where attempts to influence public opinion by the former colonial power can be perceived as a form of neo-colonialism or subversion and resented by the government.) It is through embracing new methods of creating and sharing information, delivering services, and networking that the modern diplomat will keep the profession influential and relevant in that crowded market place. It will involve far less co-creation of reports in stark contrast to traditional practice where an initial draft might be seen and commented on by several (usually senior) colleagues; it will use big data not only to determine the overall tone of media and popular debate but also to check the number of the embassy's citizens in country, registered through an embassy app, and their location; and to engage with activists or to counter the efforts of radical groups.

Social media complicates policy-making. Of course, in the wake of Wikileaks **2.17** and Snowden (see Chapter **29**, paragraphs **29.11–29.12**), governments need to convince their publics that they will use the data collected responsibly. Sensible use of digital space will allow the diplomats to take their services to people, not vice versa, so the businessman or tourist arriving in a country will receive on their smartphone information on how to do business, get help if needed, and advice on where to go and not to go. And an invitation to get in touch. But the speed at which information becomes publicly available creates expectations that government should react as quickly, despite having incomplete and undigested information. At another level the confidentiality of negotiations can be difficult to sustain when participants are tweeting the proceedings live. Procedures are required to ensure that wrongful disclosure doesn't inhibit progress.

In the event of a terrorist incident, or other crisis, humanitarian or otherwise, **2.18** given globalization and the speed of modern communications, the diplomat cannot hope to compete with 24/7 news services but it will often fall to the re-sident diplomat to respond to media pressure, sometimes quite unreasonable, not only by addressing the problem in terms of aid supplies or other support but to be seen with a physical presence to be doing so.

State Building

While a traditional diplomatic function has always been conflict resolution, the **2.19** twenty-first-century diplomat may in addition have to help build peace after conflict, support reconstruction work in practical ways, and generally assist in the rebuilding of a State. Three elements of State building are crucial—ending con-flict and sustaining the peace, often through military and police deployment; promoting economic growth and benefit to citizens, especially former fighters; and establishing institutions which respect the rule of law, human rights, and democracy. The government of the State should have the lead role, but other governments and organizations will also be part of the supporting effort. This will involve diplomats getting out of their comfort zone in an embassy or foreign ministry and practising what the US foreign policy analyst, Anne-Marie Slaughter, referred to as networked rather than club diplomacy.[18]

---

[18] Anne-Marie Slaughter, 'America's Edge' (January/February 2009) 88(1) *Foreign Affairs* 94–113.

2.20   Given the complexity of issues, their interdependence, and the diversity of players, the modern diplomat needs to engage not only with the traditional hierarchical 'exclusive' club, e.g. the Foreign Ministry, the Prime Minister's Office, the diplomatic corps, and chambers of commerce etc but also with the network of civil society. Cosy chats to the local chamber of commerce or an international relations institute will no longer suffice. The diplomat will also, with appropriate circumspection depending on local circumstances, want to engage with opposition groups, even those at times who may be planning to seize power by force. The criticism has often been levelled at Western embassies in Tehran at the end of the Shah's regime that they were too optimistic in their analysis of the Shah's position, were insufficiently in touch with the mood on the street and with supporters of Khomeini, and consequently did not anticipate or predict the overthrow of the Shah and the installation of the Ayatollah's regime.

The Changing Profile of the Diplomat

2.21   In another area too tradition is being superseded. The traditional profile of diplomacy right through until the post-WWII era, and in some cases well beyond, was of a male-dominated aristocratic caste. Women's role was often at best secretarial and they were obliged frequently to resign from the foreign service on marriage. It is belatedly the case in most Western countries that diplomacy now increasingly reflects contemporary society in its composition, though in terms of ethnic minority representation and women in senior posts there is still a great deal of ground to make up. Particular problems can be caused by the unwillingness of some, often Muslim, countries to recognize women as valid interlocutors. And same-sex marriages among diplomats may lead to the refusal of a diplomatic visa to the spouse by countries that do not recognize same-sex marriages and/or have anti-homosexuality legislation. In 2015, US State Department officials estimated that 50 per cent of their posts round the world were 'effectively off-limits for Foreign Service officers who would want to move with their same-sex spouses'.[19]

Human Rights

2.22   The traditional geographical concerns of the foreign services of nation states have by contrast not gone away but they have been joined by wider, horizontal

---

[19] Andrew Siddons, *International New York Times*, 19 August 2015, p. 1.

issues such as climate change, pandemics, refugees and their trafficking, international organized crime, modern piracy, disarmament and nuclear proliferation, and, perhaps most notably in the last two decades, the protection and promotion of human rights. (see Chapter 17). The commitment to human rights by virtually every State, enshrined as it is in Article 55 of the UN Charter, has been traduced in many countries that pay scant regard to the declarations to which they have subscribed. If there is a strong emphasis in modern diplomacy on advancing and promoting respect for human rights, it is precisely because of the shortfall between the theory and the practice in so many States. Despite the importance of multilateral diplomacy and the higher profile of NGOs, it is within States that the transgressions occur and it is in relations between States that the greatest pressure can be brought to bear on those who at best pay lip service to their obligations to improve or reform. The tension between actively pro-human rights governments anxious to proselytize and those governments resistant to what they regard as outside interference in their domestic affairs has increased notably in recent years with NGOs playing a key role in pressuring Western democracies to be more robust about raising human rights abuses with the transgressors. This resistance can be a unifying force to bring countries together under the guise of non-interference in the domestic affairs of sovereign States, a term which finds expression in the UN Charter. It also behoves those countries who actively promote human rights abroad to ensure that they practise those same rights at home. But it has often been the case that a country may indulge in megaphone diplomacy (see Chapter 6, paragraphs 6.22–6.23) in criticizing other countries' human rights record or other aspects of their domestic or foreign policies to pander to domestic opinion at home while reassuring the offending government in private that the verbal attacks are not to be taken too seriously. This exercise in *Realpolitik* (Henry Kissinger was a noted practitioner) has become increasingly discredited in recent years as Western democracies have been keen to ensure that their foreign policies have a moral dimension.

2.23 The promotion of respect for human rights has been enhanced by the creation of war crimes tribunals, (generally successful) ad hoc tribunals in the case of the former Yugoslavia (ICTY) and Rwanda (ICTR), and the International Criminal Court (ICC), to try egregious human rights abusers (see Chapter 26). The failure of some major States to ratify the instruments creating the ICC has inevitably attenuated its impact, while its operation has been criticized by certain African States for apparently concentrating on alleged abuses on the African continent.

2.24 The importance of human rights in diplomacy has been highlighted by the progressive development of the doctrine known as Responsibility to Protect (sometimes known as R2P), the title of a 2001 report from the International

Commission on Intervention and State Sovereignty (ICISS), most of the key elements of which were endorsed unanimously by Heads of State and Government at the 2005 UN General Assembly World Summit. It set out a hierarchy of action in response to a crisis involving genocide, war crimes, ethnic cleansing, or crimes against humanity. The first is to remind the State concerned (however paradoxically given its probable primary role as perpetrator) of its responsibility to protect its population; then the international community should help and encourage the State to fulfil that responsibility; and if the crisis persists, the international community has the responsibility consistent with the UN Charter to help protect the citizens involved, and as necessary can take collective action under the Charter's Chapter 7.

2.25 It is not a legal base to authorize action, but a political commitment, case by case, to consider and secure permission to act. All members of the General Assembly signed up to the text, although the political will to act, interests, and circumstances all determine whether there will be action. While it can be prayed in aid of action, it is of only marginal value if the circumstances inhibit agreement. Of course a member State or collection of States can wrap themselves in the cloak of Responsibility to Protect to justify a military intervention not otherwise classically authorized. This would not be dissimilar to the humanitarian intervention used to justify NATO's action against the Federal Republic of Yugoslavia in 1999 in the Kosovo crisis, over which lawyers continue to disagree.

2.26 The doctrine's strongest advocates describe it as 'the most dramatic normative development of our time',[20] which if implemented might have prevented such notorious massacres as occurred in Rwanda or Srebrenica. Its detractors see it as a form of neo-colonialism or as the Nicaraguan diplomat, Miguel d'Escoto Brockmann, when President of the UN General Assembly, put it 're-decorated colonialism',[21] justifying military intervention in sovereign States on not always justified humanitarian grounds (e.g. the US-led invasion of Iraq). Whatever its future, it is an interesting example of how new, networked diplomacy—that is, not just governments and international bodies but think-tanks, academics and NGOs—can be mobilized in the service of human rights.[22]

2.27 Ultimately, the conundrum remains. To what extent are States prepared to see their (often hard-won) sovereignty diluted even in cases where they have failed

---

[20] Ramesh Thakur and Thomas G Weiss, 'R2P: From Idea to Norm-and Action?' (2009) 1(1) *Global Responsibility to Protect* 22.

[21] Statement of the President of the General Assembly at the opening of its 97th Session, 23 July 2009.

[22] See discussion in Luke Glanville, *Sovereignty and the Responsibility to Protect: A New History* (Chicago: University of Chicago Press, 2013) 212–26.

to fulfil the most basic responsibility of a State, to protect its citizens? Who is to judge that failure or the many cases where a State actively oppresses them, if not the UN Security Council? Can unilateral decisions to intervene be justified where agreement on a UN Security Council resolution is unreasonably withheld? The early years of the twenty-first century have posed these questions (and provided conflicting examples). The next decades will determine whether diplomacy has developed dynamically and flexibly enough to answer them.

Conclusion

The contemporary diplomat not only has to possess a range of qualities and skills, but is expected to be familiar with many subjects, issues, and techniques. Moreover, they have to be capable of being applied in a range of countries or organizations depending on circumstances and the wishes of the Ministry. This is a long way from the traditional diplomacy of the nineteenth century and is the essence of the challenge and satisfaction of being a diplomat, bringing together judgement, knowledge, and experience.   **2.28**

This is well encapsulated in the recent history of Kosovo. Post-World War II, Kosovo (with an overwhelming Albanian majority) was an autonomous province of Serbia within the Socialist Federal Republic of Yugoslavia (SFRY). By 1993 the SFRY had dissolved into five different States. Serbia was part of the new Federal Republic of Yugoslavia (FRY) with only Montenegro left as its partner and Kosovo's autonomous status was effectively suppressed by the Milošević regime. By 1997 the traditionally poor relations between Serbs and Albanians had descended into open conflict between Serb security forces and the so-called Kosovo Liberation Army who were pressing for independence from Belgrade. The Dayton Accords of 1995, which had brought to an end the Bosnian war of the 1990s had, to the dismay of the Kosovar Albanians, said nothing about Kosovo. The issue for the observer was what should the international community do to help resolve the abuse of human rights, the worsening humanitarian situation, and the nascent conflict and oppression in Kosovo. What followed drew on the full range of diplomatic instruments, including the use of force. External influences by governments, including a Contact Group[23] of Western powers plus   **2.29**

---

[23] '…sometimes, mediators see numerous advantages in coordinating their actions and, for this purpose, accept the assistance of a self-selecting group of "friends". Such groups—which go by a variety of names—usually have four or five members, as in the case of the Contact Groups on Namibia and Bosnia [later extended to Kosovo] created in 1977 and 1994 respectively, and the "Quartet" [EU, US, Russia, and the UN] on the Middle East formed in 2002.' Berridge, *Diplomacy* (5th edn, 2015) 258.

Russia, the European Union, NATO, and the OSCE had little effect and the situation continued to deteriorate despite the presence of an OSCE mission on the ground. The European Council in June 1998 called for a political solution and in the autumn, the North Atlantic Council issued an ultimatum to President Milošević that the organization was prepared to use force to end what was considered to be the abuse of the Albanian majority and the grave humanitarian situation there. The US diplomat, Chris Hill, carried out shuttle diplomacy between the Albanians and the Serb government. The massacre of some forty-five Kosovo Albanian civilians in the village of Račak in January 1999 brought renewed international focus on Kosovo and an international conference was convened under the joint chairmanship of France and the United Kingdom. This involved the participation of the Yugoslav government and the Albanians, as well as representatives of the US, Germany, Italy, Russia, the UN, EU, and OSCE. It produced the Rambouillet Accords which Milošević refused to accept. As a result, the North Atlantic Council decided to launch a military operation against Yugoslavia, each member State having satisfied itself that such an operation was legally justified by the humanitarian situation in Kosovo, that all other means had failed, and that the means to be deployed were proportional to the ends desired. After 77 days of bombing, the operation ended following intensive negotiations in G8 and the UN, and mediation by President Ahtissari of Finland and former Prime Minister Chernomyrdin of Russia.

2.30   The terms of the future development of Kosovo were set out in UNSCR 1244 which guaranteed the territorial integrity of the FRY, provided for a UN-led administration, UNMiK, to govern Kosovo and a NATO Force, KFOR, to enforce peace. Atrocities committed by both Serbs and Albanians have since come under the scrutiny of the International Criminal Tribunal for the former Yugoslavia (ICTY) and, in 2008, the then Kosovo government declared independence. This was rejected by Serbia, and today sufficient countries have withheld recognition, that Kosovo has been unable to become a member of the United Nations.

2.31   At all stages of this story the diplomacy was intense: bilateral, multilateral, a peace conference, deployment of missions and the threat and eventual use of force, coping with the humanitarian consequences of hundreds of thousands of displaced people, very difficult and contentious legal issues, producing successful resolutions in the Security Council, respecting human rights, establishing a UN Protectorate, ensuring peace through military deployment, delivering justice through the courts and political institutions, and ending with a country moving towards full independence, albeit not universally recognized.

2.32   President Carter's national security adviser, Zbigniew Brzezinski, famously quipped that if foreign ministries and embassies 'did not already exist, they surely would not have to be invented'.[24] Brzezinski may well be right that a world without embassies and diplomats would be an improvement. But that would be a world not immediately recognizable: no wars to end, no conflicts to prevent, no nuclear proliferation threats, no terrorism, no tourists losing their passports or ending up in prison, a world of perfect free trade and all countries so prosperous that development aid wasn't necessary. That world is sadly not on offer. The world a diplomat faces is fraught with problems that leave foreign ministries, embassies. and their diplomats like Sisyphus constantly pushing boulders uphill. Looking far ahead, with the threats from nuclear non-proliferation, climate change, international terrorism, crime and people trafficking, piracy, global financial crisis, widespread poverty, continuing wars and their impact on refugee flows, illegal immigration, and pandemics, diplomacy will not be underemployed.

---

[24] *The Times*, 7 July 1970.

3

INTRODUCTION TO INTERNATIONAL LAW

Elizabeth Wilmshurst

The Relevance of International Law

3.1 The purpose of this chapter is to provide, for those who have not studied the subject, a brief account of what international law is and what are its sources.[1] The relevance of international law to the diplomat is emphasized in this chapter, while being assumed throughout this book.

3.2 In the first place, the whole framework of international relations within which a diplomat operates is predicated on international law. A diplomat represents a 'State': it is international law that defines a State and lays down the criteria used

---

[1] Short and readable introductions to international law can be found in Andrew Clapham, *Brierly's Law of Nations* (7th edn, Oxford: Oxford University Press, 2012) and in Vaughan Lowe, *International Law* (Oxford, 2007). For a longer but accessible treatment, see James Crawford, *Brownlie's Principles of Public International Law* (8th edn, Oxford: Oxford University Press, 2012).

when a new State is created and when one State recognizes the existence of another. A diplomat may be accredited to an international organization, rather than to a State; that organization will have its membership, functions, powers, and responsibilities governed by a treaty binding in international law. A diplomat's status and functions are themselves circumscribed by international law, primarily by a treaty, the Vienna Convention on Diplomatic Relations.[2]

Second, and most importantly, international law is an essential part of the content and conduct of international relations. A whole web of relationships among States has been established by agreements binding in international law. Those agreements are reached by processes of negotiation and collaboration; in those processes diplomats will invariably be involved. Further, state relationships are conducted on the basis of customary international law and the range of international standards laid down in instruments of various kinds. Whether working at home in a ministry of foreign affairs, or in a post abroad, diplomats will frequently be concerned with issues which raise some point of international law. An awareness of the law will enable them to raise an objection where necessary to the assertions of their opposite numbers and to ask the right questions of their own legal advisers. They may have to respond to questions in the media as to the legality of the conduct of their home government. They may have to participate in representations to their home country's courts in a case where a point of international law arises. Within the framework of multilateral diplomacy, the diplomat will wish to be familiar with the network of rights and responsibilities of the international organization concerned and of its members, whether it be the United Nations, the European Union, or one of the many other international institutions. **3.3**

Diplomats thus need to have a basic knowledge of the law governing the subject areas in which they work, and governing relations with the States or international organizations to which they are accredited. This is necessary when relations are going smoothly—and when they are not going well. It is international law that has to be turned to when disputes arise concerning the interpretation of a treaty or the alleged breach of an obligation. It is international law that provides courts and mechanisms for settlement of these disputes, albeit of an incomplete nature. **3.4**

The Nature of International Law

International law may be defined as the law governing relations between States, and between States and international organizations. This is a simplified **3.5**

---

[2] See Chapters 5 and 12–15 for discussion of diplomatic functions and privileges and immunities.

formulation, as we shall see. It ignores theories of international law which focus on processes rather than rules, or which highlight the biases that lie behind the rules or challenge the extent to which the rules in practice govern the behaviour of at least the most powerful States. The discussion of such theories is not the concern of this chapter, however, and would not in any case have much significance to those who use and practise law as diplomats.

3.6 The description of international law as being inter-State also ignores the increasing significance of individuals and non-State entities. In national legal systems the 'subjects' of the law are individuals and groups of individuals, as well as corporations, but in international law the subjects were, traditionally, only States and, later, international organizations. In a movement towards the 'humanization' of international law, however, certain protections and rights are now given directly to individuals, rather than States, by international humanitarian law and international human rights law. International humanitarian law (synonymous with the law of armed conflict) imposes obligations on non-State armed groups in armed conflict, relating to the means and methods of the conduct of conflict and the protection of civilians. International human rights law, by imposing obligations on States in relation to the treatment of all individuals within their jurisdiction, including their own citizens, directly confers rights on persons against their own State. And the conduct of individuals is itself made subject to international criminal law in those areas with which the international community has concerned itself—in particular, genocide, war crimes, crimes against humanity, and aggression, where international courts have been given jurisdiction. Further, non-State entities are now given more of a role in the making of international law: non-governmental organizations may be given some procedural rights in international conferences and in the meetings of international organizations; certain non-State entities have been given the opportunity to make representations before international tribunals. That said, the traditional system of State to State relations, obligations, and rights is still the norm in international law.

3.7 International law is often experienced as much in the framework of a country's national legal system as on the international plane directly. Depending on the terms of a State's constitutional law, international law may either be part of national law, and therefore available to be applied directly by national courts, or have to be specifically incorporated by national legislation. The position may differ depending on whether the international legal rule in question is a treaty provision or one of customary international law.

3.8 It is necessary here to address the old question whether international law is 'really' law. International law is deficient in having no mandatory court system to which all States are subject and no international police to enforce the law;

there is an absence too of a general legislature with worldwide authority. Further there is a huge disparity in the power of States; some governments flout the law with apparent impunity. And while the 'international rule of law' is now an accepted concept, it is very clear that there is not the same respect for the international legal system as exists for the national system in most States; the lack of cohesion of the international community brings with it a reluctance to subject national actions to common international goals.

Despite its differences from the legal systems of the countries of the world, and all of its deficiencies, international law is however a working system of law, as the present book demonstrates. On a wide range of day-to-day matters it enables States to carry on their relations among themselves with stability and predictability. It has for centuries been applied in domestic courts—which are far more numerous than international tribunals—whether as representing a generally recognized principle of law (such as the universal condemnation of piracy) or where the provisions of a treaty are incorporated into a State's own domestic law. **3.9**

In a globalized world the network of international agreements and international organizations, universal or regional, is becoming larger and of more importance to most areas of a State's foreign affairs and to many of its domestic activities. No State, not even the most powerful, can expect to ignore international law. There are some things which can only be done by joint action—whether protecting the environment, regulating air traffic, or introducing shipping lanes, to take uncontroversial examples—and in many instances that joint action is best arranged by international legal rules. **3.10**

When States are accused of breaking the law they very rarely defend themselves by claiming that the system is not really law: they commonly argue that the law has been misinterpreted or misapplied. That is, they defend themselves by reference to the law itself. The words of one international law scholar remain true: 'almost all nations observe almost all principles of international law and almost all of their obligations almost all of the time'.[3] **3.11**

The Sources of International Law

How is international law made? Where do we go to look for the international legal rules which govern a matter? The classic list of sources of law is to be found in Article 38(1) of the Statute of the International Court of Justice: **3.12**

---

[3] Louis Henkin, *How Nations Behave* (2nd edn, New York: Columbia University Press, 1979) 47.

(a) international conventions, whether general or particular, establishing rules expressly recognized by the contesting States;

(b) international custom, as evidence of a general practice accepted as law;

(c) the general principles of law recognized by civilized nations;

(d) judicial decisions and the teachings of the most highly qualified publicists of the various nations, as subsidiary means for the determination of rules of law.

3.13 (a) Chapters **31** to **35** of this book discuss treaties. (The Statute refers to them as conventions; the words are interchangeable.) Treaties are a source of international law for the parties to them, whether those parties are only two States, or many. Treaties that are in principle open to all States may be regarded as the major legislative mechanism of international law.

3.14 Treaties establishing international organizations may provide that the decisions or resolutions of their organs are legally binding. The most notable of these is the Charter of the United Nations, which provides in Article 25 that member States are obliged 'to accept and carry out the decisions of the Security Council in accordance with' the Charter. Resolutions made under Chapter VII of the Charter where the Council has determined there is a 'threat to the peace, breach of the peace, or act of aggression' have required States to adopt and apply economic and other sanctions against States and individuals in order to remedy the situation.[4] These resolutions are binding in international law. In recent years some of the resolutions have taken on a wider law-making character, covering for example a comprehensive approach to terrorism and laying down sweeping obligations regarding non-proliferation of weapons of mass destruction.[5] Security Council resolutions such as these have sometimes been adopted as an alternative to the much slower negotiation and adoption of treaties. It was also by Security Council resolutions adopted under Chapter VII that the two ad hoc tribunals for the prosecution of international war crimes and other atrocities in the former Yugoslavia and in Rwanda were established.[6]

3.15 (b) The second of the sources of international law is practice 'accepted [by States] as law' (customary international law). State practice consists of what States do and say, including in diplomatic acts and correspondence, their

---

[4] See, for example, the series of Security Council resolutions applying sanctions and travel bans in relation to the Democratic People's Republic of Korea, in particular resolution 2270 (2016) adopted following the nuclear test conducted by that country on 5 January 2016.

[5] See, for example, resolution 2178 (2014) which imposes a number of legal obligations on States to prevent their nationals or residents from participating in acts of terrorism in other countries, inter alia requiring States to ensure that their domestic law makes it a serious offence for nationals to travel to other countries for the purpose of participating in, planning, or preparing terrorist acts, or providing terrorist training.

[6] See Chapter 26, paragraphs 26.21–26.29.

conduct in connection with resolutions adopted by an international organization, their legislative and administrative acts, and the decisions of their national courts. In a case which challenged the right of Italian courts to hear claims for reparations against Germany relating to actions in the Second World War, the International Court of Justice had to determine whether there was a rule of customary international law requiring the Italian courts to give Germany immunity from jurisdiction. In deciding whether there was settled state practice sufficient to found such a rule, the Court examined judgments of national courts on the question whether a foreign State is immune, the legislation adopted by States on the subject, claims to immunity advanced by States before foreign courts, and statements made by States in various contexts.[7]

There is also a subjective element to the establishment of customary international law, known as '*opinio iuris*': this means that the practice in question must be not merely usage or habit, but undertaken with a sense of legal right or obligation. So, in the case referred to, the Court stated: **3.16**

> Opinio juris in this context is reflected in particular in the assertion by States claiming immunity that international law accords them a right to such immunity from the jurisdiction of other States; in the acknowledgment, by States granting immunity, that international law imposes upon them an obligation to do so; and, conversely, in the assertion by States in other cases of a right to exercise jurisdiction over foreign States.[8]

The areas covered by customary law have gradually narrowed as a result of the increasing number of treaties. Prior to 1958, for example, most of the law of the sea was of a customary nature; in 1958 treaties were adopted covering much of the subject-matter,[9] and these have now been replaced by the 1982 Convention on the Law of the Sea. **3.17**

A treaty provision may itself form a rule of customary international law if it codifies a rule existing at the time when the treaty was concluded, if it leads to the crystallization of a rule of customary international law, or if it gives rise to a **3.18**

---

[7] *Jurisdictional Immunities of the State (Germany v Italy: Greece intervening)* [2012] ICJ Reports 99. This was a case brought by Germany against Italy claiming that the immunity of Germany had not been respected by the Italian courts; the claims for reparations brought before Italian courts concerned instances of large-scale killing of civilians in occupied Italian territory as part of a policy of reprisals by the Nazi regime and the use of Italian civilians and members of the armed forces as slave labour in Germany.

[8] Ibid, para 55.

[9] 'The 1958 Geneva Conventions'; see Malcolm D Evans, *International Law* (4th edn, Oxford: Oxford University Press, 2014) 651–4; David Harris and Sandesh Sivakumaran, *Cases and Materials on International Law* (8th edn, London: Sweet & Maxwell, 2015) 322–6.

general practice that is accepted as law (*opinio iuris*), thus generating a new rule of customary international law. Many of the provisions of the Geneva Conventions of 1949—the treaties providing for the protection of war victims—were regarded as customary international law, and thus binding on all States, even before their membership became universal.

3.19   There is one category of rules of customary law that cannot be set aside by treaty or other rule of international law. A rule of this kind is termed *ius cogens*, or a 'peremptory' rule, such as the prohibition of genocide, of torture, of aggression, and of slavery and the slave trade.[10]

3.20   (c) 'General principles of law' are those recognized in national legal systems (the reference to 'civilised nations' in the ICJ Statute being now regarded as outmoded). They are of particular importance in the interpretation of provisions of international criminal law by international courts and tribunals.

3.21   (d) Court decisions and academic writings are subsidiary means of determining international law. Unlike court decisions in the English legal system, decisions of the International Court of Justice do not have the status of precedents for future decisions and are not generally binding in international law,[11] but the Court makes an effort to achieve consistency and its decisions may be regarded as evidence of customary international law. The same goes, to a greater or lesser extent, for the decisions of the growing number of other international courts. So also for the decisions of national courts; for example, the Court looked to the decision in the English courts concerning the attempted extradition of former President Pinochet of Chile for evidence of customary international law.[12] Courts can and do refer to academic writings in determining what is the law.

3.22   (e) The list of sources given in the ICJ Statute is not exhaustive. A decision of the International Court of Justice made clear that obligations under international law may also be created by certain *unilateral declarations* made by States. The Court held that a series of statements made by members of the French government that they would refrain from atmospheric nuclear testing created an obligation on France to that effect, binding in international law.[13] Declarations by States will constitute obligations in this way if they demonstrate the intention

---

[10] For the application of *ius cogens* in treaty law, see the reference to Art 53 of the Vienna Convention on the Law of Treaties at Chapter 35, paragraph 35.77.

[11] Art 59, Statute of the International Court of Justice.

[12] *Arrest Warrant of 11 April 2000 (Democratic Republic of the Congo v Belgium)* [2002] ICJ Reports 3.

[13] *Nuclear Tests* case (*New Zealand v France*) [1974] ICJ Reports 457.

by the State to be legally bound and if the authority making the declaration has the power to bind the State.[14]

(f) There is a wide range of international materials, conference declarations, **3.23** standard-setting instruments, and statements of organs of international organizations which are not strictly binding in international law but which are taken into account by States in conducting international relations. This body of so-called '*soft law*'[15] is of growing importance in the making of international law. It contributes to the creation of the law in that it may evolve into customary international law and it contributes to the interpretation of the law by courts and tribunals. It affects the behaviour of States and in that respect it can in some circumstances be considered just as influential as the 'hard' law listed in the Statute of the International Court of Justice.

The Content of International Law

The major areas with which international law deals may broadly be categorized **3.24** thus.

(a) Subjects of International Law

A 'subject' of international law is an entity which has international rights and **3.25** obligations: thus, for example, a State may make a treaty which has effect in international law, but a county or a city cannot do so. International law sets out the criteria for statehood, and governs questions relating to how a State is formed.[16] International organizations may also be subjects of international law under certain conditions.[17]

(b) Territorial Sovereignty

How is a State formed? International law sets limitations on the acquisition of **3.26** territory, and provides the tools to determine disputes as to territorial boundaries. The traditional methods of acquiring territory are adopted from Roman

---

[14] See International Law Commission Guiding Principles applicable to unilateral declarations of States capable of creating legal obligations, 2006.

[15] Examples given in Alan Boyle and Christine Chinkin, *The Making of International Law* (Oxford: Oxford University Press, 2007), at 213 include the 1992 Rio Declaration on Environment and Development; certain UN General Assembly resolutions such as the 1948 Universal Declaration of Human Rights, the 1970 Declaration on the Principles of Friendly Relations among States, FAO Code of Conduct on Responsible Fisheries, and other codes of conduct, guidelines and recommendations adopted by IMO, IAEA, and other such international organizations.

[16] See Chapter 4 for discussion of statehood.

[17] See Chapter 23.

law concepts (occupation, cession, conquest, prescription, and accretion), but these have a faintly outmoded air and there are other principles which are also relevant when a territorial dispute comes before a tribunal for decision.[18] The principle of self-determination, prioritizing the rights of the 'people', may be relevant[19] and the principle of *uti possidetis*, which has as its object the stabilization of boundaries settled by previous colonial administrations in the case of former dependent territories.

(c) State Jurisdiction

3.27 What are the powers of a State? A State has authority in its own territory to make laws, enforce them, and adjudicate on them. In addition, a State may seek to regulate some matters beyond its own territory and to adjudicate on them (taking 'extraterritorial jurisdiction'). While there is little controversy about the right of a State to extend and enforce its law, or at least some of its law, in respect of actions of its own citizens overseas, there is less agreement on a State's right to regulate the actions of people and companies overseas which have an effect in that State's territory. After a long period of argument and litigation, the 'effects' doctrine remains controversial in some areas but has been largely accepted in others (for example in competition law).

3.28 A further question over the exercise of extraterritorial jurisdiction concerns legislating and trying individuals in respect of international crimes, notably war crimes, crimes against humanity, and genocide. 'Universal' jurisdiction—allowing States to legislate and to prosecute international crimes wherever in the world they are committed and by whomever—has been accepted by many countries but its use continues to have the potential to cause political controversy. This was seen in the attempts by Spain to extradite various persons for the commission of international crimes under its own legislation, including former President Pinochet of Chile. The ex-President found himself in the UK, where he was put under house arrest while the extradition request from Spain was litigated in the English courts,[20] giving rise on the one hand to an outcry from those in Chile who insisted on their right to try (or not) their own national, while on the other hand a welcome from the victims of his former regime.

3.29 International law sets limits on a State's legislative and adjudicative jurisdiction within its own territory. There are limits to its powers regarding foreigners and its own citizens, for example in the field of human rights, and its adjudicative

---

[18] See James Crawford, *Brownlie's Principles of Public International Law* (8th edn, Oxford: Oxford University Press, 2012) ch 9.

[19] Ibid, ch 3.

[20] *R v Bow Street Magistrate, ex parte Pinochet (Nos 1 and 3)* [2000] 1 AC 147.

jurisdiction is limited by immunities enjoyed by certain persons such as foreign Heads of State and diplomats.[21]

(d) The Sea and Maritime Zones

International law establishes limits for a State's territorial sea, continental shelf, and other maritime zones, and confines the powers that may be exercised in those areas. For example, a State has full powers in its territorial sea, but must allow the right of 'innocent passage' by foreign ships. Over its continental shelf a State has rights to explore and exploit its natural resources, but must not interfere with rights of other States in the waters concerned; in its exclusive economic zone a State has similar rights in the superjacent waters as well as the seabed and subsoil. The high seas are open to all States, a freedom which is limited only by specified rights such as the seizure of pirate ships. The seabed and ocean floor beyond States' jurisdiction are subject to an international regime, established by the UN Convention on the Law of the Sea 1982, and administered by an international organization, the International Seabed Authority. The seabed and its resources are declared by the Convention to be the 'common heritage of mankind'.

3.30

(e) The Environment and Natural Resources

There is a growing—but still inadequate—body of principles and rules on environmental issues which has evolved gradually, often in reaction to particular incidents. The general principles governing the area can be stated to be: that States have sovereignty over their natural resources and the correlative responsibility not to cause transboundary environmental damage; the principle of preventive action (that is, the duty to reduce, limit, or control activities which might cause damage to the environment); the principle of cooperation; the principle of sustainable development; the precautionary principle; the polluter pays principle; and the principle of common but differentiated responsibility (that is, that while all States have a common responsibility for the protection of the environment, environmental standards may place differing obligations on States depending on their contribution to environmental degradation and their ability to reduce it).[22] The legal status of these principles and their application in practice remain matters of difficulty. There is a growing body of multilateral treaties which concern protection of the marine environment, the atmosphere

3.31

---

[21] For immunities see Chapters 12 to 15.
[22] For discussion of these principles and international environmental law generally, see Philippe Sands and Jacqueline Peel, *Principles of International Environmental Law* (3rd edn, Cambridge: Cambridge University Press, 2012).

and outer space, the polar regions, and biological diversity and deal with hazardous substances and waste. There are treaties on cooperation in the use of natural resources such as energy and transboundary water resources; collective action to combat climate change is also being attempted. The compromises which have been found necessary in some of the international negotiations leading to these treaties have led to the setting of standards less protective than would be desirable.

(f) International Economic Relations, Trade, and Investment

3.32   Regional economic treaties, bilateral and multilateral trading agreements, as well as the many agreements within the ambit of the World Trade Organization make up a substantial body of international law.

(g) International Responsibility

3.33   A State which is in breach of international law is responsible to the State to which the obligation was owed. The law of state responsibility concerns matters such as the attribution of an act to a State, and the consequences of an internationally wrongful act including the obligation to make reparations. Although much of international law is constituted by the rights and obligations of States in respect of other States, some obligations are owed to the international community as a whole (obligations *erga omnes*); all States have an interest in the protection of such rights as those against genocide, slavery, and aggression.

(h) The Protection of Individuals and Groups

3.34   While at one time a State's powers over its own people were a matter for its own domestic jurisdiction, the acceptance of a growing body of international human rights law has led to the imposition of obligations on States both within and outside their own territory. Breaches of human rights have become an international concern and can be examined by courts and other international mechanisms.[23] Certain egregious breaches of human rights which amount to international crimes—genocide, war crimes, and crimes against humanity—have been placed within the jurisdiction of international courts. A growing number of treaties require States themselves to prosecute other crimes of international concern, such as people trafficking, terrorist offences, and enforced disappearances.

3.35   International law also imposes obligations on States regarding the protection of refugees and displaced persons. The UN Convention relating to the Status of

---

[23] See Chapter 17.

Refugees 1951, for example, defines a 'refugee' and establishes the fundamental prohibition of *non-refoulement*: a State may not expel or return a refugee to a territory where his or her 'life or freedom would be threatened on account of his race, religion, nationality, membership of a particular social group or political opinion'.[24]

(i) The Use or Threat of Force by States

No system of law would be adequate if it did not regulate the recourse to force. **3.36** The legality of the use of force against other States is covered by the *ius ad bellum* and is principally drawn from the UN Charter and from customary international law. Article 2(4) of the Charter reads:

> All Members shall refrain in their international relations from the threat or use of force against the territorial integrity or political independence of any State, or in any other manner inconsistent with the Purposes of the United Nations.

A State may use force in self-defence,[25] and force may be used with the authority of the Security Council acting under Chapter VII of the UN Charter. Those are the only two uncontroversial justifications in international law for the use of force in another State without the consent of that State. The *application* of both heads of the law may however be hugely controversial. An example of a disputed claim of self-defence was the argument put forward by Israel in 1981 when it bombed the Osirak nuclear reactor in Iraq; the Security Council condemned the attack as being 'in clear violation of the Charter of the United Nations and the norms of international conduct'.[26] In the case of the 2003 invasion of Iraq by a coalition led by the US, the reliance on past Security Council resolutions as legal justification was criticized by a wide range of governments, scholars, and legal practitioners, as well as the UN Secretary-General.

A disputed exception to the prohibition on the use of force concerns military **3.37** action in humanitarian intervention. Concern to prevent atrocities being committed on the territories of States has led to a call for force to be used when no other way of preventing or stopping humanitarian disaster is available—even when the Security Council has not given authorization for the use of force. An example of force being used in such circumstances was the military action in 1999 by NATO forces in the Federal Republic of Yugoslavia, to avert what was perceived as a threatened humanitarian catastrophe resulting from the activities

---

[24] Art 33(1).

[25] Art 51 preserves 'the inherent right of individual or collective self-defence if an armed attack occurs against a Member of the United Nations, until the Security Council has taken measures necessary to maintain international peace and security'.

[26] SC resolution 487(1981) of 19 June 1981.

of Serb security forces and the Yugoslav army in Kosovo. NATO States contributing to the action had different explanations for their use of force; the UK stated that its action was legally justified 'as an exceptional measure on grounds of overwhelming humanitarian necessity.... The force now proposed is directed exclusively to averting a humanitarian catastrophe, and is the minimum judged necessary for that purpose.'[27] The UK government reiterated its view that there was a 'doctrine of humanitarian intervention' in discussing possible military intervention in Syria in 2013 to prevent the use of chemical weapons (intervention which did not then occur).

3.38   In the aftermath of the Kosovo campaign, the International Commission on Intervention and State Sovereignty, set up at Canadian initiative to consider the whole question of military intervention to prevent humanitarian catastrophe, recommended the use of the term 'responsibility to protect', a term intended to refocus the debate from the rights of States to the interests of victims, while recognizing that the primary duty to protect rests on the State concerned.[28] The matter was taken up by governments in the UN World Summit in 2005; they affirmed that each State has the responsibility to protect its populations from genocide, war crimes, ethnic cleansing, and crimes against humanity but stated that the international community was prepared to take collective action through the Security Council should peaceful means be inadequate and national authorities fail to protect their populations from atrocities. States were clearly not ready to accept that there was a legal basis for using force without Security Council authorization.[29] The protection of civilians and the delivery of humanitarian assistance was given as the reason for the Security Council's authorization of the use of force in Libya in 2011, and there is perhaps less support than at one time for action without such authorization.

(j) The Law of Armed Conflict

3.39   The conduct of armed conflict is regulated by a branch of international law—international humanitarian law, or the law of armed conflict—which applies to

---

[27] Statement in the Security Council, S/PV. 3988, 24.3.1999.

[28] Its 2001 report may be found at <http://responsibilitytoprotect.org/ICISS%20Report.pdf>. See also Chapters **2**, paragraphs **2.24–26** and Chapter **17**, paragraphs **17.8–11**.

[29] Paras 138 and 139; resolution of the General Assembly of 24.10.2005 (A/Res 60/1). This followed the report of the then UN Secretary-General, *In Larger Freedom*, proposing that governments embrace the responsibility to protect as a basis for collective action, while recognizing that the responsibility lies first and foremost with individual States. He also recommended—which did not happen—that the Security Council adopt a resolution setting out the principles for the use of force including in humanitarian cases, to consider before mandating force the seriousness of the threat, the proper purpose of the force used, whether it was necessary and proportionate, and whether there was a reasonable chance of success.

States and to non-State groups, and which forms the *ius in bello*. Although there are humanitarian principles to be found in many older sources, the modern law originated from events following the battle of Solferino in 1859; the horrors of the battle, where it took six days to bring in the wounded from the field,[30] led to the founding of the Red Cross, the first Geneva Convention in 1864 and, after the Second World War, to the adoption of the four Geneva Conventions of 1949 and the two Additional Protocols in 1977. There is also a growing body of customary international law.

Two fundamental principles of the law are those of discrimination and pro- **3.40** portionality. In the conduct of hostilities parties to the conflict must distinguish at all times between civilians (and civilian objects like schools and hospitals) on the one hand and fighters on the other; there is a prohibition against launching attacks on civilians and civilian objects. Nor is it permissible to launch an attack against even lawful military objectives if the attack may be expected to result in civilian harm which is excessive compared with the direct military advantage anticipated.

The law governing international armed conflict (State against State) is more **3.41** detailed and gives higher protection than is the case with non-international armed conflicts. For example, in an international armed conflict, captured combatants have the right to the status of prisoner of war, not available to captured fighters in a non-international armed conflict. But in non-international armed conflict international human rights law has a greater prominence and provides its own protections for victims of conflict.

(k) Settlement of Disputes

When disputes arise between States regarding the interpretation or application **3.42** of international law, the system provides a number of possible means of settlement.[31] Unless States have accepted in advance the methods of settling their disputes, whether by treaty on a specific subject or by acceptance of the jurisdiction of the International Court of Justice, the choice of means of settlement— or whether to accept any means of settlement—is entirely up to the State concerned. Depending on the nature of the dispute, it may be possible to seek action by the UN Security Council. Or there remains for the injured State the possibility of taking countermeasures or of using diplomatic pressure on the offending State. And there is always the court of international

---

[30] See account of H Dunant *A Memory of Solferino* at <https://www.icrc.org/eng/assets/files/publications/icrc-002-0361.pdf>.

[31] See Chapters 24–25.

opinion, which may lead to political consequences for a State which fails to comply with the law.

3.43 Nevertheless, there is a lack of a universal mechanism to enforce the law. One means of enforcement lies in the powers of the UN Security Council under Chapter VII of the Charter in situations where there is a threat or breach of the peace or aggression. Over the years, the Security Council has adopted binding resolutions requiring all States to impose economic sanctions against States in breach of international law in one respect or another, and authorizing the use of force. Security Council resolutions of this nature are subject to the veto power of the five permanent members and this can give rise to accusations of great power impunity and to unremedied injustices, some of long standing.

4

THE STATE

Its Concept as a Legal Person in International Law

Hazel Fox

The State as a Legal Person

Diplomacy is defined in Chapter 1 as: 'the conduct of business between States **4.1** by peaceful means' and the present chapter addresses the State as the prime actor in the conduct of that diplomacy and examines the State's status as a legal person as defined by international law, the nature and scope of which has already been described in Chapter 3.

During the Middle Ages increased communications, trade, and conflicting **4.2** political and religious beliefs confronted and disrupted the regimes of empire or of a single autocrat. In Europe, as described in Chapter 1, after a period of conflict and destruction, the exhausted opponents agreed terms of peace in the Treaty of Westphalia of 1648, and thereafter the State was increasingly accepted as the most practicable means for regulating internal and external relations. The

State, through control of its territory and people, both exercised in fact, and as a legal person in international law, was recognized to be entitled to exercise supreme power—sovereignty, both internally and externally.

4.3 The word sovereignty is used in a number of different ways, but for the diplomat two meanings are of prime importance: internal sovereignty over the control and administration of the State's territory, and the enactment and enforcement of laws over the people and activities within that territory; and external sovereignty, as regards other States, where the sovereignty of the one State is qualified by requirements of equality and non-intervention, that is respect for the sovereign rights of other States and non-interference in the internal affairs of other States.

4.4 To understand the role of the State in international affairs, it is essential to appreciate that it is both a maker and a subject of international law. It has been and continues to be instrumental in the formation, scope, and limits of public international law, a legal system distinct from that administered within individual States, being one which applies to all States equally, and confers on the State a legal personality possessed of capacity, rights, and obligations. The State can act on the international plane—to make treaties with other States, or perform a unilateral act and thus change international law for instance by an act of annexation or surrender of territory. It may share, exploit, or terminate an attribute of its statehood, such as access to its maritime ports or air space, or regulate the transfer of goods, or development of its resources. It may restrict movements of capital or in some respects control its nationals abroad.

4.5 The following four topics may help to explain the nature and scope of the powers and activities of the State in international affairs. They are:

- The qualifications for statehood;
- Recognition of the State as a member of the international community;
- The State compared to an international organization as a legal person and other entities having lesser rights in international law;
- Sovereignty, internal and external, as an attribute of the State.

Each of these will now be examined in turn.

The Qualifications for Statehood

4.6 Since the Peace of Westphalia in 1648, the qualifications for statehood are defined as comprising: first, a people; second, a territory in which that people is settled; third, a government with authority and control over that territory; and fourth, the capacity to enter into relations with other States.

This generally accepted definition of a State[1] takes little account of the size of **4.7** the population or the extent of the territory required to be comprised within the State, a flexibility which has accommodated the increase of the international community to the present global figure in 2016 of some 195 States (193 members of United Nations plus two observer countries).[2]

Though control of territory is essential to the concept of the State, and respect **4.8** for the territorial sovereignty is an essential foundation of international relations, there is no rule that land frontiers must be fully delimited and defined. 'Often in various places and for long periods, they are not, as is shown by the case of the entry of Albania into the League of Nations.'[3] A State's territory includes its subsoil and air space, though the latter is limited; it does not apply to the high seas and exploitation of the deep seabed[4] nor to outer space; areas respectively regulated by the UN Law of the Sea Convention 1982 and, following the development of satellites and remote sensing, the Outer Space Treaty which declared outer space, including the moon and other celestial bodies, not subject to national appropriation.[5]

The third qualification for statehood denotes a stable political organization **4.9** with 'public authorities strong enough to assert themselves throughout the territories without the assistance of foreign troops'.[6] It also requires a government with internal sovereignty, that is, one exercising authority for law-making and for the adjudication of disputes between people and entities within the territory.

The fourth qualification, the capacity to conduct independent international **4.10** relations, describes the external aspect of sovereignty. Cases where statehood was denied due to the lack of this include Japan's attempt to set up a state of

---

[1] Set out in the Montevideo Convention which never entered into force, but came to be accepted in international practice.

[2] The Holy See enjoys an anomalous position as an observer State by reason of its history and the consent of other States, including Italy within whose territory it is located. Recognized as a State, it enjoys diplomatic relations with States, immunity for the Pope as its head, and the capacity to make and be bound by treaty. The other observer State is Palestine.

[3] As explained in the *N. Sea Continental Shelf* case [1969] ICJ Reports 32.

[4] *Corfu Channel Case (Merits)* [1949] ICJ Reports 4, at 35.

[5] 1967 Treaty on Outer Space, 610 UNTS 205.

[6] As accepted by the International Committee of Jurists in the *Aaland Islands Question*, 1921. League of Nations Off. Jo. Sp. Supp. No 3, 1921, p. 3.

Manchukuo in 1931 in Chinese territory,[7] South Africa's grant of 'independence' to the Bantustan enclaves of Transkei and Bophuthatswana, a move towards apartheid which was condemned by the UN General Assembly in 1976,[8] and the Turkish Republic of Northern Cyprus set up with the aid of Turkish troops in 1983 and dependent on continuing support from Turkey.[9] These cases may be contrasted with less controlling events, treated as without effect on a State's separate existence, such as a treaty of protection (as in *Rights of US Nationals in Morocco*[10]), or the setting up of a customs regime between Germany and Austria where certain restrictions of a State's liberty were considered not to affect a State's independence.[11]

4.11   Provided the above four conditions for statehood are met by evidence of an entity exercising control and authority over a people within a territory and demonstrating the ability to conduct independent external relations the essential requirements for statehood will be satisfied, so providing the basis for recognition as a State by other States. Additional qualifications, such as economic or military independence, protection of human rights, and a democratic system shown by the holding of regular elections may be taken into account by another State when appraising a claim to recognition, but they are not included in the international law requirements for a State.

EEC 1991 Guidelines for Recognition of a New State

4.12   The EEC's declaration setting out Guidelines in 1991 for the guidance of members of the EEC in the context of the dissolution of the USSR and of Yugoslavia, tried to go beyond the conditions required for recognition of a State by international law. The 1991 EEC Guidelines, while expressing readiness to recognize new States, qualified it by a list of additional conditions.[12] Thus EEC Members'

---

[7] League of Nations Assembly resolution, 24 February 1933, LNOJ Spec. Supp. No 101/1.87.

[8] UNGA resolution 31/6A, 26 October 1978.

[9] UN Security Council resolution 541, 15 November 1983.

[10] [1952] ICJ Reports 176.

[11] PCIJ, Series A/B Advisory Opinion No 41. The status of Taiwan is a special case: the UK, along with the majority of other governments, has recognized the People's Republic of China as the sole government of China, and 'acknowledges' the position of the PRC that Taiwan is a part of China. Although the government of Taiwan, the Republic of China, remains in de facto control of the island's territory, has relations with many States, and enjoys rights as 'a fishing entity' with regard to law of sea regulations, and a separate customs territory as a WTO member, it does not claim to be a separate State but to be the legitimate government of China.

[12] European Commission's Guidelines on Recognition of New States and the Soviet Union, 19 December 1991, 31 ILM (1992) 1486–7.

recognition was made subject 'to the normal standards of international practice and the political realities in each case', but 'following the historic changes in the region', was restricted to 'those new States... [which] have constituted themselves on a democratic basis, have accepted the appropriate international obligations and have committed themselves in good faith to a peaceful process and to negotiation'.[13]

The lengthy list of commitments to be undertaken by the newly recognized **4.13** States included: respect for the UN Charter and Helsinki Final Act, especially the provisions relating to the rule of law, democracy, and minorities; guarantees for the rights of ethnic and national groups and minorities; respect for the inviol ability of frontiers only to be changed by peaceful means and by common agreement; acceptance of all relevant provisions with regard to disarmament and nuclear non-proliferation as well as to security and regional stability; commitment to settlement by agreement, including where appropriate by recourse to arbitration, all questions concerning state succession and regional disputes. These were unprecedented additional political requirements and have not been followed in later state practice.

Recognition of the State

Recognition is the process by which an entity becomes or is accepted as a legal **4.14** person in international law enjoying relations as a State with existing States. In the absence of an accepted collective process, such recognition involves an appraisal of the factual situation evidenced by an entity's independence and control, and an acknowledgement by existing States of the existence of the entity as a State.

Two theories, the constitutive theory and the declaratory, have been advanced **4.15** as providing an explanation of the process of recognition, but do not greatly assist in understanding its nature. The constitutive theory treats recognition by other States as creating a new State, whereas the declaratory theory treats the action of States as merely acknowledging the factual existence of the entity as a State. Both theories are unsatisfactory; the constitutive overlooks the factual importance of independent existence of the entity whereas the declaratory theory by its reduction of other States' acts to mere acquiescence understates the extent and significance of their participation in the process of recognition.

---

[13] For appraisal see E Denza, 'European Practice on the Recognition of States' (2011) 36 *European Law Review* 321.

4.16 The constitutive theory is closely identified with the positivist view of international law by which States assert control in the shaping of international relations. Some support for the constitutive theory is provided by Shaw in noting that the more overwhelming the scale of international recognition by States, the less may be demanded in terms of the objective adherence to the criteria for a State.[14]

4.17 Crawford, in support of the declaratory theory, maintains forcefully that any constitutive theory (or variation of it subject to a legal duty to recognize) has been disregarded in practice and is unsupported by logic.[15] He argues that, given that the acknowledgement of a State's existence by State conferment of recognition and entering into diplomatic relations is not universal at any one moment in time, in consequence, the constitutive approach results in the impossibility of a legal person both *existing*, and *not existing*, at the same time. Further if, according to the constitutive theory, the acts of the entity prior to States' acknowledgement of its existence have no legal significance, they cannot be treated or ranked as violations of the fundamental norms of international law. Thus, the long-standing refusal of Arab States to recognize Israel as a State while at the same time holding Israel bound by international rules of non-aggression and non-intervention is cited by Crawford as demonstrating the illogicality of the constitutive approach.

4.18 Practice regarding recognition of States (as opposed to changes in government) is diverse, highly responsive to the specific circumstances of each situation, and politically and legally complex. It should be noted that recognition of a State does not mean that all of a new State's claims to territory or jurisdiction are accepted. The circumstances of extinction of a State and its replacement by one or more successors illustrates this diversity in practice: illegal use of force cannot effect change in international law as illustrated by UN member States' refusal to recognize Iraq's invasion of Kuwait in 1990;[16] consent of the State or States concerned will always greatly facilitate the process, as when the two States of the Czech Republic and Slovakia by agreement replaced in 1993 the former State of

---

[14] M N Shaw, *International Law* (6th edn, Cambridge: Cambridge University Press, 2009) 208. See, for modern law and practice, M Craven, 'Statehood, Self-determination and Recognition', ch. 8 in M D Evans (ed), *International Law* (4th edn, Oxford: Oxford University Press, 2014); M Fabry, *Recognizing States* (Oxford: Oxford University Press, 2010).

[15] J Crawford, *The Creation of States in International Law* (2nd edn, Oxford: Oxford University Press, 2008) 264.

[16] UN Security Council resolution 662 (1990).

Czechoslovakia.[17] Similarly, the accession of the Länder of the eastern German Democratic Republic into the western Federal Republic of Germany united in one German State the two parts divided by the Second World War, and was not disputed.[18]

The factual and legal complexities have been well illustrated by the case of **4.19** Kosovo. Following systematic violations of the civil and human rights of the Albanian population in Serbia and prolonged attempts at a negotiated settlement between Serbia and Kosovo, and during the continuance of a UN administration (UNMIK) there, Kosovo representatives unilaterally declared independence on 18 February 2008. On the following day the US and France recognized Kosovo and proceeded to establish diplomatic relations. Many other States followed, but others held back or expressly stated that the secession was illegal and that they would not recognize Kosovo as an independent State in the absence of acknowledgement by Serbia. On the initiative of Serbia, the UN General Assembly sought an Advisory Opinion in October 2008 from the International Court of Justice on the question: 'Is the unilateral declaration of independence by the Provisional Institutions of Self-Government of Kosovo in accordance with international law?' In 2010 the ICJ replied that the Declaration—which had in fact been issued by representatives of the people of Kosovo—was not contrary to any applicable rule of customary law, to Security Council resolution 1244 (which remained in force), or to the constitutional framework for Kosovo and therefore did not violate customary international law. The ICJ made clear that it was not determining whether Kosovo was a State or pronouncing on the legality of recognition or non-recognition by other States. The Opinion had a rather limited effect on the continuing progress of recognition by other States—which can clearly be seen to be conditioned mainly on whether they felt threatened by the 'precedent' of Kosovo in regard to secessionist movements in their own States, rather than by objective appraisals on whether Kosovo met factual or legal qualifications for recognition.[19]

The term 'failed state' is on occasion applied to a recognized State following the **4.20** development of a situation of 'a lack of capacity or factual power . . . the inability

---

[17] See Crawford, *The Creation of States in International Law*, 402; Czech and Slovak Federal Republic Constitutional Act No 54/1992 on the Extinction of the Czech and Slovak Republic, 25 November 1992.

[18] Shaw, *International Law*, ch. 5, 'The Subjects of International Law', 228; State Treaty for the Unification of Germany, 3 October 1990; Keesing's Record of World Events, p. 37466 (1990).

[19] For full analysis, see M Milanović and M Wood (eds), *The Law and Politics of the Kosovo Advisory Opinion* (Oxford: Oxford University Press, 2015), especially chapters by Weller, Pellet, and Crawford.

to run a modern State as a going concern';[20] however, such a situation, if it deteri orates into a State's inability to maintain law and order, may lead to concern on the part of other States with the possibility of forcible intervention. These aspects are examined further in Chapter 2, The Changes in and Challenges of Modern Diplomacy, and Chapter 24, Prevention and Management of Conflict and Settlement of Disputes. As regards the methods by which recognition of a new State and the subsequent establishment of diplomatic relations take place and the distinction between them, see Chapter 5, Functions of Diplomatic Missions and Consulates.

The State Compared to an International Organization and Other Entities

4.21   International personality may now be enjoyed by an international organization as well as a State. In addition, there are a number of situations where inter national law confers some legal status on entities falling short of international legal personality. Thus, protectorates, colonies, trust territories, and areas administered by UN and other international bodies lack the full ability to act, but enjoy limited rights, in international law. Other entities, such as multina tional companies, investors, non-governmental organizations, or armed opposition groups, derive their legal recognition from one or more national legal systems.

International Organizations

4.22   The International Court held the United Nations, following its establishment in 1945, to be:

> intended to exercise and enjoy and is in fact exercising and enjoying functions and rights which can only be explained on the basis of the possession of a large measure of international personality and the capacity to operate upon the international plane,.... [F]ifty States, representing the vast majority of the members of the international community, had the power, in conformity with international law to bring into being an entity possessing objective international personality and not merely personality recognised by them alone, together with the capacity to bring international claims.[21]

---

[20] See the discussion in Crawford, *The Creation of States*, 719–23.
[21] *Reparations* case, Advisory Opinion [1949] ICJ Reports 174.

The perception that more effective action can be achieved by coordination of the decisions and powers of individual States into a collective entity with specified functions, has resulted—in addition to the UN and its Specialized Agencies—in the establishment of many other intergovernmental international organizations, with membership consisting of States and on occasion other international organizations. Thus, dependent on the terms of the constituent treaty, an international organization may enjoy legal personality with the capacity to make treaties, enter into relations with States and other international organizations, sue and be sued, and enjoy privileges and immunities.

Further, to enable it to function in accordance with the purposes set out in its constituent treaty an international organization may also enjoy implied powers, limited always by the function and purposes for which it was created. **4.23**

Other Entities Having Lesser Rights in International Law

From the middle of the seventeenth century onwards, the exploration, and consequent trade overseas, by European States led to the acquisition of overseas territories as colonies or possessions. The title and right to sovereignty exercised by European States over such overseas colonies came to be challenged and gave rise to claims for recognition and statehood, along with nineteenth-century national movements within Europe and elsewhere. Foremost among these claims was the expression of a right to self-determination, which manifested itself in different forms from the nineteenth century onwards.[22] **4.24**

Thus, in the nineteenth-century popular movements inspired by nationalism and historical differences led to demonstrations and rebellions in Europe against monarchs, e.g. the 1848 revolutions in France, Austria, Hungary, and Venice. In the aftermath of the 1914–18 War, President Wilson responded to such claims in proposing, in a speech to Congress, the 'Fourteen Points' to condition the peace settlement, and made reference to 'historically established relations of nationality and allegiance'.[23] **4.25**

Efforts were made to give effect to these aims, by the Minorities Agreements made within the 1919 Peace Treaties conferring collective rights on citizens of newly established States belonging to racial, religious, or linguistic minorities **4.26**

---

[22] See Chapter 2, paragraph 2.20; A Cassese, *Self Determination of Peoples: A Legal Reappraisal* (Cambridge: Cambridge University Press, 1995).

[23] See chapter 12, 'International Dispositive Powers: The World War I Settlements' in Crawford, *The Creation of States in International Law*, 516.

and the setting up of a Mandate system administering the former colonies of the defeated States for the benefit of the inhabitants as peoples' rights to be held in sacred trust.[24]

4.27 After the Second World War, Article 1 of the Charter of the UN explicitly recognized respect for the principle of equal rights and self-determination of peoples as one of the purposes of the UN. Chapter XI entitled 'A Declaration regarding non-self-governing territories' set out an obligation on UN Members, within the system of the Charter, to promote the well-being of their inhabitants. These provisions heralded increased pressure for independence particularly from the overseas colonial territories of European States. Following a series of resolutions in the General Assembly including the 1960 'Declaration of granting Independence to Colonial Territories' and the 1970 Friendly Relations Resolution, the 1960s[25] saw the grant of independence to the majority of the British, French, and Portuguese colonies in Africa.[26]

4.28 Subsequently, in respect of non-colonial administrations, the United Nations' Declaration in 1960 'that all peoples have the right of self-determination' had increasing influence and effect, and in the *Namibia* (1970), and the *W Sahara* (1975) Opinions, 'their right to freely determine their political status' was recognized by the ICJ as a legal right in international law, declared in the *E Timor* (1995) case as an '*erga omnes* right' [that is, a right owed towards all] and further elaborated by UN practice.[27]

4.29 It is worth noting that the holders of the right were described as 'peoples', not a group identified by reference to a particular race, religion, or political ideology. Its fulfilment was seen not only as external—the right for colonial peoples to

---

[24] *International Status of S W Africa*, Advisory Opinion [1950] ICJ Reports 129, separate opinion of Judge McNair, 146 at 150. See H D Hall, *Mandates and Dependencies and Trusteeships* (London: Stevens, 1948); Crawford, *The Creation of States in International Law*, ch 13, 'Mandates and Trust Territories'. The UK evolved an independent system, with the Crown as a symbol of the British Commonwealth, comprising member countries such as Australia, Canada, New Zealand etc. and dependent countries.

[25] 1960 Declaration on the Granting of Independence to Colonial Countries and Peoples, UNGA resolution 1514 (XV), 14 December 1960; 1970 Declaration on Principles of International Law concerning Friendly Relations and Cooperation among States, UNGA resolution 2635 (XXV), 24 October 1970.

[26] See Chapter **18**, paragraphs **18**.74–**18**.79, **18**.88–**18**.90 (The UN and its Charter, the Trusteeship Council).

[27] See Chapter **18**, paragraphs **18**.80–**18**.84 (Non-self-governing Territories); J Dugard *The South West Africa/Namibia Dispute* (Berkeley: University of California, 1973). *Legal Consequences for States of the Continued Presence of South Africa in Namibia (South West Africa) notwithstanding Security Council Resolution 276*, Advisory Opinion [1970] ICJ Reports 4, at 30–1 (para 53); *Western Sahara*, Advisory Opinion [1975] ICJ Reports 12, at 39 (para 79); *Case concerning East Timor (Portugal v Australia)* [1979] ICJ Reports 90, at 102 (para 29).

choose independence if they wished—but also as internal—the enjoyment of the right to vote in free elections with the outcome given effect by the current administration. In this way, a right of self-determination became exercisable within the framework of the territorial sovereignty of the existing State. But many factors, including inability of the internal administration of certain States to control the activity of armed insurrections, have resulted in widespread violation of human rights of the population and demands for humanitarian intervention (see Chapters 2 and 3 on the responsibility to protect).

The Powers of the State as a Legal Person

Internal sovereignty—implying internal control—and authority and external **4.30** sovereignty—implying independent conduct of foreign relations—continue as the prime features of the State as a legal person.

Internal Sovereignty

Internal sovereignty denotes the competence and ultimate authority of a State to **4.31** control matters within its territory and the people within it. Territorial jurisdiction confers the power to regulate and adjudicate on acts within its territory. Control over its people confers the power to grant or withdraw nationality and to regulate the admission of aliens to the country. The disposition and manner of the exercise of these internal powers may take a unitary form with devolved powers granted to identified regions, as currently in the UK, or be organized as a federal system, where powers are divided between geographical units with a central government responsible for foreign affairs, defence, and major economic matters, as in the US. The internal powers of the State will generally be divided into three branches: the legislature, which enacts the laws (which, in a democracy will be adopted by freely elected representatives of the people); the executive, which carries out the laws and decisions of the government; and the judiciary, which enforces the law and determines disputes as to its meaning.

The Head of State (who may or may not also be the Head of Government) serves **4.32** as the prime representative of the State on formal occasions and on occasion as a source of authority and promotion of international Relations. By reason of that office the Head of State enjoys in other States immunity conferred by international law. As an office it may be hereditary, or in a republican State, by election by the legislature or the people. The formal process by which a person is inaugurated as a Head of State, as well as the constitutional scope of the powers when in office and the immunity of the Head before his own national courts, is solely a matter for determination by the internal law of the State. The head of a monarchy or a republic is equally entitled to Head of State status in international law as is the Pope, though he does so as the head of the Holy See rather than of the Catholic Church.

4.33 As a short excursus, it is worth describing the history of titles among sovereigns, although this is largely of historical interest. Originally the title of 'Majesty' belonged to the Emperor alone, who in speaking of himself said: 'Ma Majesté'. Kings were styled 'Highness', or 'Serenity'. Since the end of the fifteenth century other crowned heads assumed the title of 'Majesty', the kings of France setting the example. The Pope's title of courtesy is Most Holy Father, *Très-Saint Père*, also *Vénérable* or *Très-Vénérable Père*. The Emperor of Japan is styled *Tennô* in the Japanese language; the title *Mikado* is antiquated, and never used. In former times the King of France was designated *le Roi Très-chrétien*, and the King of Portugal *le Roi Très-fidèle* since 1748. The King of Spain became *le Roi Catholique* in 1496; the sovereign of Austria-Hungary was 'His Imperial and Royal Apostolic Majesty' from 1758. These titles were conferred by various popes. Leo X bestowed that of 'Fidei Defensor' (Defender of the Faith) on Henry VIII in 1521, and his successors have continued to bear this title. In early times the Russian sovereigns bore the title of Autocrator, Magnus Dominus, Grand-Prince, or Czar (Tsar), the last being the Russian word for 'Emperor' (itself derived from 'Caesar').

4.34 In modern States the ceremonial and political powers of the Head of State may be divided, and in consequence a Head of Government may be accorded the special protection enjoyed by a Head of State in international law; the Institut de Droit International's Vancouver Resolution of 2001 relating to the immunities of a Head of State provides that a Head of Government enjoys the same inviolability and immunity from jurisdiction as a Head of State.[28] A regent appointed to exercise the powers of the State temporarily during infancy, incapacity, or some interregnum may also be accorded the position of Head of State.

4.35 The diplomatic service of a country, headed by the Foreign Minister, a member of the central government, forms part of the executive, charged with the conduct and management of the country's international relations, including the work of its diplomatic missions and the general representation of the country's interests abroad. The Minister for Foreign Affairs will be the senior but far from exclusive intermediary between the State and foreign States, and though his

---

[28] The 2001 Vancouver Resolution of the Institut de droit international on 'Immunities from Jurisdiction and Execution of Heads of State and of Government in International Law' 69 (2000–2001) *ADI*, at 442.

functions and powers may vary according to domestic legislation, and to traditions and political organization of the particular State, in international law he or she is presumed to have the capacity to represent, to conclude treaties, and generally to act for the State.[29]

The relevance of the three senior State officials—the Head of State, Head of **4.36** Government, and Foreign Minister, to the conduct of international relations is recognized in international law by the conferment of immunity from the jurisdiction and the enforcement of the national laws of another State, an immunity also enjoyed in some respects by the State which they represent in its dealings with other States; see further Chapter 12.

Internal sovereignty of a democratic State will be conducted under the rule of **4.37** law. The rule of law includes the absence of arbitrary government, and the rules are set out in a constitution or in recorded practice, but in a broader sense it implies openness (transparency), equality, and freedom of the individual. These requirements may be reinforced by a State's acceptance of international conventions providing for the protection of human rights.

The national laws of the State will be contained in primary statutes (in a demo- **4.38** cratic State, written acts adopted with the approval of the elected representatives of the State's population), subordinate legislation, and judicial decisions, with their form and content being largely a matter for determination pursuant to the internal sovereignty of the State. No State may plead its national law as justification for a breach of international law.

External Sovereignty

External sovereignty implies a State's independence from all other States, with **4.39** the capacity and power to conduct its own affairs within the international community. It is to be emphasized that sovereignty under international law does not imply supremacy over other legal persons, but is qualified by the principles of equality among States and non-intervention.

National law, as stated earlier, provides no defence or justification for a breach **4.40** of international law. Since 1990, the inclusion within international conventions of obligations on States to confer rights with regard to the international community as a whole and to individuals within a State's jurisdiction in respect of the right of access to justice has made the reserved domain of domestic jurisdiction an

---

[29] Vienna Convention on the Law of Treaties 1969, Art 7.2.

increasingly limited concept. Inevitably this change from a bilateral system between States to an international system of law has brought under closer challenge the UN Charter Article 2(7) requirement which prohibits intervention, apart from enforcement measures under Chapter VII, in 'matters essentially within the domestic jurisdiction of the State' (see further under 'Non-intervention' at paragraph 4.43).

Equality

4.41 Equality is a comprehensive principle arising from the interdependence of States, which requires the recognition of mutual rights of other States and compliance on the State's part with the relevant obligations imposed by international law. Although States vary significantly in size, economic wealth, and political influence, the principle of equality as a person in international law requires that mutual respect be accorded to the requirements of other States. The 1970 Declaration on Principles of International Law concerning Friendly Relations and Co-operation among States in accordance with the Charter of the United Nations[30] (commonly called the Friendly Relations Declaration) lists the key elements: juridical equality; respect for the obligation of territorial integrity and independence of other States; freedom to choose and develop its own political, social, economic. and cultural systems; and the obligation to comply in good faith with all relevant international obligations.

4.42 While wide discrepancies in economic and military power have produced compromises, cardinal aspects of equality as a principle include the prohibition on the use of force against the territorial integrity and political independence of any State, and the requirement that the use of armed force without the authorization of the Security Council is permitted solely by way of self-defence (UN Charter Articles 2(4) and 51); also by the rule in the UN Charter of one State, one vote for members of the UN, which however, to accommodate political and practical constraints was qualified by the compromise reserving a right of veto to permanent members of the Security Council, currently the US, Russia, China, France, and the UK.

Non-intervention

4.43 The principle of non-intervention in matters relating to the domestic jurisdiction of the State is both an aspect of a State's enjoyment of its equality with other

---

[30] GA resolution 25/2625.

States and an independent principle in customary international law regarding a State's internal sovereignty as it relates to non-intervention in matters within its domestic jurisdiction. It is affirmed in the UN Charter, the Charter of the Organization of American States, and the Constitutive Act of the African Union. It has also been acknowledged and given effect in decisions of both the Permanent and the International Courts of Justice. The principle operates to bar dictatorial interference by force or similar form of 'imperative pressure'.[31] Oppenheim in defining the term intervention states: 'the interference must be forcible or dictatorial, or otherwise coercive, in effect depriving the State intervened against of control over the matter in question. Interference pure and simple is not intervention.'[32]

In the first 30 years after the Second World War the principle of non-intervention **4.44** was both invoked and refuted in controversies bitterly fought over many areas, constitutional, economic, social, and administrative, of a State's domestic jurisdiction. Thus, the principle was invoked by an aggrieved State in response to challenges relating to the administration and future of its non-self-governing territories;[33] in respect of independent States' internal constitutional or electoral arrangements, for example in Canada when the French President de Gaulle, on an official visit, pledged support for a 'free Quebec',[34] and with regard to US export trade restrictions infringing other States' freedom over trade and investment.[35]

The resort to the principle as a justification during the Cold War by both **4.45** Western and Communist States to prop up failing regimes in disregard of the wishes of their populations[36] prompted the UN General Assembly in referring to the principle of non-intervention to declare that intervention comprised not only 'armed intervention' but also 'other forms of interference or attempted threats against the personality of the State and against its political, economic, and cultural elements'.[37]

---

[31] B Simma (ed), *The Charter of the United Nations: Commentary*, Vol I (2nd edn, Oxford: Oxford University Press, 2002) 152, citing Oppenheim's *International Law* (7th edn, 1948) 378 and H Kelsen, *The Law of the United Nations* (London: Stevens, 1951) 770.

[32] See Oppenheim's *International Law* (9th edn, 1992) 432.

[33] Thus in the UN South Africa walked out during discussion of apartheid, France did so when Algeria was discussed, and the UK was not present during voting on Southern Rhodesia.

[34] *The Times*, 26 January 1967.

[35] See the US export control laws claiming extraterritorial jurisdiction and consequent US proceedings against UK uranium suppliers, the UK Protection of Trade Interests Act 1980, and the *Laker Airways* case.

[36] As regards the USSR. the Hungarian Uprising 1956 and the Prague Spring 1968; as regards the US, its invasion of Dominica 1965, Grenada 1983, and Panama 1989.

[37] The Declaration on Principles of International Law concerning Friendly Relations and Cooperation among States in accordance with the UN Charter, GA resolution 25/2625, 24 October 1970.

4.46 The ICJ's judgment in the *Nicaragua Case* elucidated the scope of member State obligations in respect of the UN Charter, as regards the meaning of 'threat' in Article 2(4) of the UN Charter as it applies to the obligations of state members 'to refrain in their international relations from *the threat* (emphasis added) or use of force against the territorial integrity or political independence of any other State'. In doing so the International Court confirmed the 'forcible or dictatorial' nature of intervention required in the principle of non-intervention.

4.47 In its judgment on the Merits in 1986 relating to the alleged US 'intervention' given by means of support to Nicaraguan guerrillas fighting against the El Salvador government, the International Court provides useful clarification of the extent to which acts that may fall short of a military attack infringe the principle of non-intervention. The Court stated:

> [I]n view of the generally accepted formulations, the principle forbids all States or groups of States to intervene directly or indirectly in internal or external affairs of other States. A prohibited intervention must accordingly be one bearing on matters in which each State is permitted, by the principle of State sovereignty, to decide freely. One of these is the choice of a political, economic, social and cultural system, and the formulation of foreign policy. Intervention is wrongful when it uses methods of coercion in regard to such choices, which must remain free ones. The element of coercion, which defines, and indeed forms the very essence of, prohibited intervention, is particularly obvious in the case of an intervention which uses force...[38]

As regards the second element in the principle of non-intervention—the determining factors which bring matters within a State's domestic jurisdiction, another Court decision—a well-known dictum of the Permanent Court of International Justice (PCIJ) given some 50 years earlier, provides useful guidance. In 1923 in an Advisory Opinion, the PCIJ was asked whether the application of nationality decrees made in Tunis and Morocco by France were matters of domestic jurisdiction in the sense of Article 15(8) of the League of Nations' Covenant. The Court replied in the negative. The PCIJ stated:

> The question whether a certain matter is or is not solely within the jurisdiction of a state is an essentially relative question: it depends upon the development of international relations.[39]

4.48 This analysis of the PCIJ stressing the relativity of the scope of the principle of non-intervention accurately anticipates the reduction of matters to be treated as

---

[38] *Case concerning Military and Paramilitary Activities in and against Nicaragua (Nicaragua v USA) Merits* [1986] ICJ Reports 14, at para 205.

[39] Advisory Opinion in the *Nationality Decrees in Tunis and Morocco* case (1923) PCIJ, Series B, No 4.

exclusive to a State's domestic jurisdiction and hence the principle's operation in maintaining the legal personality of the State in international law in response to political events.

A State may now not object, on the ground of the non-intervention principle, **4.49** to inquiry and discussions being made about the standards of human rights in its territory—although there remain some States which do still so object. But the fact that it has entered into treaty commitments in various areas does not in itself mean that it has handed over the right to other States to enforce those commitments, unless it has agreed to.[40] While the wide ratification of human rights treaties has considerably reduced the number of matters solely within the exclusive jurisdiction of States Parties to them, the element of non-intervention, so long as effective international enforcement is absent, leaves the principle still operative. Today, then, the focus of a State's defence of internal sovereignty and reliance on the principle of non-intervention has shifted away from objecting to matters relating to its domestic jurisdiction or against civil society's support for human rights. The principle of non-intervention is now invoked to restrain proposals for action, without the UN Security Council's authorization, whether by a single State or collectively, to resort to the use of threats or force. The extent to which the principle may no longer be put forward against action by the international community to prevent the commission of egregious human rights violations within a State, under the Responsibility to Protect, is already discussed in Chapters 2 and 3.

By way of conclusion on this topic, it can be said that the principle of non- **4.50** intervention continues to reflect the nature of States as enjoying equal sovereignty in international law. The principle is closely linked to the concept of domestic affairs, which the French call *domaine réservé*, and also to the international legal limits on a State's jurisdiction to prescribe and to enforce.[41] Thus, the principle of non-intervention seeks to express, in terms of the exercise of jurisdiction to the exclusion of outside conflicting challenges, a fundamental concept, based on the elements of people, territory, and effective government which make up a recognized State. Its indeterminacy as to the matters within a State's jurisdiction reflects and is explained by the ongoing shifting nature of controversy and lack of consensus as to the allocation of powers between competing interests.

---

[40] See Chapter 17, paragraph 17.17.
[41] M Wood, Chatham House, Discussion paper 2007, 28 February 2007, at 2.

Conclusion

4.51 Understanding the nature and structure of the sovereign State continues to be essential to understanding the modern world and international relations. The internal sovereignty of the State, particularly as exercised by States which observe democratic principles in their governance, permits the moral values, ability, and energy of the people living within the State to feed into the international system through the exercise of the external sovereignty of the State in accordance with the principles of equality and non-intervention. This process provides the modern State with the capacity and opportunity to join in the shaping of new ideas and collective action in the international community.

Book II

DIPLOMATIC AND CONSULAR RELATIONS

5

FUNCTIONS OF DIPLOMATIC MISSIONS AND CONSULATES

Ivor Roberts

Under long-established principles of international law now codified in Article 2 **5.1** of the Vienna Convention on Diplomatic Relations, the establishment of diplomatic relations between States and the establishment of permanent diplomatic missions take place by mutual consent. The right to send and receive diplomatic agents flows from recognition as a sovereign State and was formerly known as the right of legation (*ius legationis*). The recognition of a new State, the establishment of diplomatic relations with that State, and the establishment of a permanent diplomatic mission in that State are three distinct steps. It may however sometimes happen that two of the three steps occur simultaneously or in immediate sequence, which can give rise to confusion between them.

It is in modern practice highly exceptional for two States to recognize each **5.2** other without formally establishing diplomatic relations—and such a situation usually indicates extreme tension or coolness between them. The United Kingdom for example recognized North Korea as a State some years before the establishment of diplomatic relations between the two in December 2000. The United States also recognized North Korea without establishing diplomatic relations with it.[1] In 1980 the United Kingdom offered to establish relations with Albania, but the offer was accepted only in 1991, while the United States made a similar offer in 1973 which was also rejected by Albania. By contrast, it is now common for two States to establish or to maintain diplomatic relations without having permanent missions in each other's territory.

Recognition of States and Establishment of Diplomatic Relations

5.3 It is common, though not universal practice, for the government of a State to issue a formal statement on recognizing another—usually newly established—State and such a statement may offer to establish diplomatic relations with the new State, or be followed very shortly by such an offer. Sometimes however the stages are merged so that the offer to establish relations, or a jointly released statement by both States of their intention to establish relations, in effect constitutes implied recognition by the old State of the new one. In earlier centuries it was common for States to conclude a treaty formally setting out the right to send and receive diplomatic missions, but this practice is now obsolete.

5.4 Where the birth of the new State takes place without the consent of the State from whose territory it is being formed, premature recognition and establishment of diplomatic relations by other States will be regarded by the parent State as unlawful and in some circumstances as an intervention in its own internal affairs. Thus in February 1991 the Soviet Union protested at a decision by Iceland to recognize Lithuania—then still regarded by Moscow as a constituent Republic of the USSR—and to establish diplomatic relations with it. By September 1991 however constitutional processes had been completed by the USSR State Council recognizing the independence of the former Soviet Republics, and ministers of foreign affairs of the Member States of the European Community met the ministers of foreign affairs of the three Baltic States to mark the restored sovereignty and independence of the Baltic States and to seal the establishment of diplomatic relations with all of them. In 1998, by contrast, Chechnya attempted to assert a claim to independence from Russia by appointing ambassadors, but these were not accepted by other States and were declared by Russia to be illegal.

5.5 Following the secession of Bangladesh from Pakistan in 1971, the new State of Bangladesh was recognized by the United Kingdom, by India, by the Soviet

---

[1] Hansard HC Debs, 20 March 1995 WA, cols 43–45; Department of State Guidance on Diplomatic Relations 1995.

Union, and within a few weeks by numerous other States. In protest at the recognition by Commonwealth governments of Bangladesh, Pakistan on 30 January 1972 withdrew from the Commonwealth. Pakistan did not recognize Bangladesh as a sovereign State until 1974.

Following the unilateral declaration of independence from Serbia by Kosovo on 17 February 2008, the United States on the following day recognized it as a 'sovereign and independent State'. The prime minister of Serbia immediately recalled the Serbian ambassador to Washington, claiming that the US action 'violated international law', and the position of Serbia was supported by other States including Russia, China, India, and Spain.[2] In the absence of a common position among European Union Foreign Ministers on the recognition of Kosovo, a number of Member States including Germany, Italy, France, and the United Kingdom made formal statements of recognition. The UK Foreign Secretary David Miliband said: **5.6**

> The plan is to do it this evening and diplomatic relations will then be established . . . and in the course of the next days and weeks all the terms of full diplomatic representation will be put into place.[3]

In a different category are Montenegro (2006) and South Sudan (2011) as recent examples of States which emerged with the (albeit grudging) consent of the parent State (in the case of the former, the parent was Serbia and Montenegro, the latter Sudan); the emergence of the new States was followed by speedy recognition by other States and entry into diplomatic relations. This is to be contrasted with the position of entities which declare themselves as states but are recognized by few if any others (e.g. Northern Cyprus, Somaliland, South Ossetia, and Abkhazia).   **5.7**

The disappearance of a sovereign State—usually on fusion with another State—is on the same principles followed by the ending of its separate diplomatic relations with other States as they recognize the new situation. On the reunification of Germany in 1989, the separate East German embassies were taken over by the newly reunited Germany. Other States, if they retain former embassy premises in a city which is no longer the seat of government, may transform them into consulates—or perhaps seek the permission of the government of the newly unified State for their transformation into offices forming part of the mission to that State. Once again it is recognition which forms the key to any change in diplomatic relations. When Iraq purported to annex Kuwait in 1990,   **5.8**

---

[2] The legality of recognition turned on the terms of Security Council resolution 1244 (1999) as well as on the entitlement of the people of Kosovo to self-determination.
[3] BBC News Online, Monday, 18 February 2008.

President Saddam Hussein ordered the closure of embassies of other States in Kuwait. Other States however, fortified by a Security Council resolution,[4] refused to comply on the basis that closure would have implied acquiescence in the disappearance of Kuwait as a separate sovereign State. Even where diplomats were withdrawn during the subsequent conflict for reasons of security, other States continued to regard themselves as maintaining diplomatic relations with Kuwait.

5.9   In September 1973, following the recognition by the United Kingdom of North Vietnam as a State, the two governments agreed to enter into diplomatic relations at the level of ambassadors and the former UK consulate-general in Hanoi became an embassy. The government of North Vietnam however refused to accept the credentials of the officer accredited a few months later as ambassador and after a year he was withdrawn. In July 1976 the UK, following the Communist victory in the South, recognized the Provisional Revolutionary Government as the government of South Vietnam and two months later the government of North Vietnam accepted the appointment as ambassador to North Vietnam of the officer who had been acting as British chargé d'affaires in Hanoi. In July 1975 the UK recognized Vietnam following the reunification of North and South Vietnam into a single State having its capital in Hanoi, and the former British embassy in Saigon became a British consulate in what in 1976 was renamed Ho Chi Minh City.

Recognition of New Governments and Diplomatic Relations

5.10   Where a change of government within a State takes place, continuance or otherwise of diplomatic relations between that State and others also depends on whether the new government has been recognized. When the change of government is constitutional, for example as a result of free elections, diplomatic relations with other States will continue as a matter of course. Fresh credentials may be required by ambassadors from other States where the new government results from or entails a different Head of State. Where a change of government results from conflict or revolution, diplomatic relations may continue or there may be a hiatus, and the appointment of new ambassadors is likely. If ambassadors and diplomats from other States remain at their posts pending clarification of the position they are not permitted to have official dealings with the new government since such contacts in the absence of a disclaimer

---

[4] SC resolution 557 (1990).

would imply recognition. Diplomats may however if so authorized have informal dealings with one or other party to a civil conflict particularly on such matters as the safety and the protection of the property of their own nationals.[5]

Under older practice States might expressly recognize a fundamental change in the government of another State. On the death of General Franco in November 1975, for example, the British government immediately and formally recognized the change resulting from the constitutional arrangements in Spain for restoring the monarchy. The Duke of Edinburgh represented the Queen at the service in Madrid seven days later to celebrate the accession of King Juan Carlos to the throne of Spain. **5.11**

In Cambodia, by contrast, the victory in 1975 of the Khmer Rouge resulted in a much more confused situation. Having taken over control of Phnom Penh, the Khmer Rouge warned all foreign diplomatic missions to cease functioning. France closed its diplomatic mission, leaving a consul in charge of French interests although for some weeks the building continued to provide refuge for diplomats and other foreign nationals. Other States also closed their diplomatic missions. Soon afterwards it became clear that the Khmer Rouge were in control of the greater part of the territory of Cambodia, and France, the United Kingdom, and other States formally accorded them recognition as the government of Cambodia and offered to resume diplomatic relations. The new government however ignored these overtures, ignored offers by former Cambodian diplomats to serve the new regime, and ignored offers in foreign capitals to arrange for the protection or the disposal of Cambodian former embassy premises in these capitals. For many years the Khmer Rouge government had no diplomatic relations with Western States. **5.12**

Modern practice is for other States to make no express statement recognizing a new government and for the continuation or resumption of relations—whether through the same ambassador or through a replacement appointment—to take place as inconspicuously as possible. The United Kingdom fell into line with this practice in 1980 following a review of practice in other European States and more generally.[6] A number of States have, however, shown a willingness, in certain insurgency situations, to signal their political approval of particular factions by recognizing them as 'legitimate representatives of the people'. Such 'recognition', while usually falling short of formal recognition as a government, may pave the way for an informal exchange of envoys. The French government **5.13**

---

[5] Oppenheim's *International Law*, ed Jennings and Watts (9th edn, Oxford: Oxford University Press) paras 42–45; 455.
[6] Hansard HC Debs, 25 April 1980 WA, cols 277–79; 23 May 1980 WA, col 385.

for instance declared in 2011 that the Libyan National Transitional Council (NTC) was 'the legitimate representative of the Libyan people'.

5.14 Similar declarations were later made by a number of other States although the UK statement went further. 'We recognise the National Transitional Council as the legitimate representative of the Libyan people.'[7] As Warbrick has argued,

> [t]hese words constitute the revival of the pre-1980 [UK] policy of making decisions on the recognition of governments, although the circumstances which would prompt such a decision in this case appear to have been quite out of line with those which would have had to have prevailed before 1980....We must wait to see whether the incident of Libya and NTC turns out to be an anomalous revival of an abandoned option or whether the attractiveness of the peremptory character of the recognition decision will appeal to future British Governments with the precise object of influencing events in other States.[8]

5.15 With regard to the civil war in Syria, the US took a similar position when, in December 2012, President Barack Obama stated: '[w]e've made a decision that the Syrian Opposition Coalition is now inclusive enough, is reflective and representative enough of the Syrian population that we consider them the legitimate representative of the Syrian people in opposition to the Assad regime.'[9] In the UK, such examples of recognition would not entitle a 'representative of the people' to usual diplomatic immunities and privileges.

5.16 Where a government—even one apparently in control of a State—has not received recognition from other States, it will be unable to establish or to continue diplomatic relations with these other States and its envoys—like those from Chechnya mentioned earlier—will not be received abroad, accorded any diplomatic status, or given control of the financial assets or property such as embassy premises belonging to the State. The Taleban regime, even while in apparent control of Afghanistan, was recognized as a government only by Pakistan, Saudi Arabia, and the United Arab Emirates. Representatives purporting to act as diplomats in European capitals were simply disregarded by the governments of the relevant States, and in October 2001 a Taleban 'embassy' in Frankfurt was closed down by German police who found a list of enemies of the Taleban targeted for killing.[10]

---

[7] Hansard HC Deb, 27 June 2011, Vol 530 c566W.

[8] (2012) 61 *ICLQ* 253 and 263.

[9] 2013 *AJIL* 655 and quoted in *Sovereignty and Legitimacy in the Rule of Law Equation* by David K Linnan, 'Sovereignty and the New Executive Authority Conference', CERL U Penn Law School, 19–20 April 2013, p. 15.

[10] *The Times*, 31 October 2001.

Where Permanent Missions Are not Established between Two States

A State establishes a permanent diplomatic mission in another State with which **5.17** it is in diplomatic relations only where it decides, first, that a permanent mission is necessary for the conduct on its behalf of some or all of the diplomatic functions described at paragraph 5.19, and secondly, that conditions in the receiving State would permit its representatives to exercise such functions safely and effectively. Embassies are financed from the resources of the sending State which are in most cases subject to stringent controls and in some cases to public and parliamentary scrutiny of expenditure. So a sending State which has limited political or commercial interests in another State, and few of its own nationals resident in or visiting that State, may well decide that it does not require a permanent embassy there. Where the receiving State is in the midst of armed conflict, civil disorder, or a high level of terrorist threat, other States will in general not set up permanent missions and may withdraw missions already in existence.

In such situations there is a range of more limited options available to the two **5.18** States for the conduct of their relations:

(1) diplomatic contacts in the capital of a third State or in the margins of international organizations—in particular the United Nations;

(2) occasional special missions sent to discuss specific issues of mutual interest (see Chapter 15);

(3) multiple accreditation—more usually the sending of a single ambassador to two or more receiving States but less frequently the sending by two or more States of a single ambassador to one receiving State. The rules for multiple accreditation are set out in Articles 5 and 6 of the Vienna Convention on Diplomatic Relations. A receiving State may object to receiving an ambassador who is also accredited to another State or who is sent by more than one State;[11]

(4) protection of the interests of the sending State by a third State which is represented in the receiving State. Where a mission has been recalled (perhaps for reasons of economy or security) or diplomatic relations have been broken, the rules are set out in Article 45 of the Vienna Convention and are described in detail in Chapter 10, paragraphs 10.42–10.47. Where the sending State has not previously sent a permanent mission, the arrangement is normally regarded as temporary and the rules are contained

---

[11] In 1825, for example, Canning as British Foreign Secretary rejected a proposal by Argentina to send a minister who was also accredited to France, saying 'Je crois...que ce n'est pas trop pour le cérémonial, d'exiger un ministre pour l'Angleterre seule' and the Holy See will not receive any ambassador also accredited to the Italian Republic.

in Article 46 of the Convention. The consent of the receiving State is required for this arrangement;

(5) consular relations may be continued or established between the two States in the absence of a permanent diplomatic mission and even in the absence of recognition of the receiving government or of diplomatic relations. For many years before 1973 the United Kingdom maintained a consulate in Hanoi without recognizing North Vietnam as a State. This is explained more fully in Chapter **8**, paragraphs **8.7** and **8.28**. Between 1992 and 1995, the UK mission in Belgrade was headed by a chargé d'affaires and consul-general in the absence of formal recognition of the rump Federal Republic of Yugoslavia.

Functions of a Diplomatic Mission

5.19 The functions of a diplomatic mission, which are set out in Article 3 of the Vienna Convention on Diplomatic Relations, are to represent the sending State, to protect its interests and those of its nationals, to negotiate with the government of the receiving State, to report to the government of the sending State on all matters of importance to it, and to promote friendly relations in general between the two States. The mission should seek to develop relations between the two countries in economic, financial, labour, cultural, scientific, and defence matters. Although there have been important changes in the ways in which diplomatic relations are conducted—many due to developments in communications and travel—the basic functions themselves have hardly altered over the past 300 years. The list in Article 3 is however not exclusive, so that novel forms of cooperation, such as police or judicial liaison over extradition, people and drug trafficking, or child abduction, may be accepted as properly diplomatic in character. The functions of diplomatic missions must be distinguished from 'diplomacy'—a broader term discussed in Chapter **1**. In carrying out all of its functions the mission acts on the instructions received from the government of the sending State and on its behalf. The function of 'representing the sending State' is listed first because it describes not merely ceremonial appearances and acts by an ambassador but embraces all of the subsequently named functions. The more specialized functions such as those relating to scientific research or defence cooperation may be carried out by or with the assistance of specially trained members of the diplomatic service or by officers belonging to the armed services of the sending State or to other ministries. The latter are often seconded to the diplomatic service of the sending State and are in any event given diplomatic appointments (such as defence attaché) where they are serving on a long-term basis.

The development of economic and financial relations by a mission is in larger 5.20
posts carried out by a commercial section of the embassy. This work is concerned with the promotion of trade between the two States and with the promotion and protection of direct investment between them. It may not be carried
out with the purpose of generating profit, because of the legal prohibition, now
reflected in Article 42 of the Vienna Convention on Diplomatic Relations, on
the carrying out by diplomatic agents of professional or commercial activity for
personal profit. The distinction between promotional and profit-making activity often gives rise to difficulties with the host State authorities in regard to such
questions as tourist offices, or the selling of tickets for holidays or for cultural or
social events on embassy premises. In addition to the questions of whether such
activities are proper functions of the embassy and proper uses of mission premises there is the further question as to whether they are covered by the immunity
of the sending State which under modern international law does not cover commercial activities. Of course the fact that a particular enterprise—such as an
investment agency or a tourist or medical office—is not accepted by the host
State as carrying out a diplomatic function does not imply that it is not legitimate or governmental in character.

A diplomatic mission is required to carry out all of its functions in accordance 5.21
with international law and also (except where it benefits from a specific exemption) in accordance with the laws and regulations of the receiving State. Article 3
of the Vienna Convention expressly states that, in protecting the interests of the
sending State and of its nationals, the mission acts within the limits permitted
by international law because of the particular sensitivity of the mission's acts
intended to protect its national interests and the need in this context for its
conduct to take account of the duty of diplomats under Article 41 of the
Convention not to interfere in the internal affairs of the receiving State. The
balancing of the right of an embassy to protect the interests of its own nationals
and, more generally, human rights, and its duty not to interfere in the internal
affairs of the host State has in recent years given rise to numerous diplomatic
disputes, particularly, though not exclusively, in countries which strictly limit
freedom of speech and assembly (see also Chapter 17, paragraphs 17.95–17.100
and Chapter 36, paragraph 36.17). An ambassador who offers refuge within his
embassy premises to fugitives from local law enforcement officers may for
example argue that he is justified in giving humanitarian protection, but the
receiving State may take the position that such action amounts to intervention
in its own internal affairs and is not permitted under general international law.
These problems are considered more fully in Chapter 13, paragraphs 13.21–
13.26 and Chapter 17, paragraphs 17.103–17.105.

Performance of Consular Functions
by Diplomatic Missions

5.22 Article 3 of the Vienna Convention on Diplomatic Relations makes clear that the Convention does not prevent the performance of consular functions by diplomatic missions. In modern practice it is very common for embassies to have a consular section performing consular functions and for some of the diplomats and junior staff of the mission also to be given a consular appointment. The existence of diplomatic relations normally implies the existence of consular relations, although, as stated earlier, consular relations do sometimes exist in the absence of diplomatic relations. Some States however do not organize their external services so as to permit their own diplomatic agents to carry out consular functions or do not accept that embassies of other States may perform consular functions in their territory. The position is therefore complex, though it has been clarified to some extent by the 1963 Vienna Convention on Consular Relations.

5.23 There is no clear dividing line between diplomatic and consular functions. Most of the functions of diplomatic missions set out may also be exercised by consular posts. Consular posts also exercise a number of mainly administrative or legal functions (such as registration of births, deaths, and marriages, issuing passports and visas, or assistance to ships and aircraft in transit) which could broadly be regarded as protection of the interests of nationals of the sending State but are not normally carried out by embassies. The key distinction lies in whether the function is carried out through contacts with the central government, the ministry of foreign affairs of the receiving State or other central government ministries (diplomatic functions) or through contacts with local authorities such as regional governments, police, prison, or commercial officials (consular functions).

5.24 In the absence of a specific local bar, diplomatic agents may exercise consular functions on an occasional basis without the specific authority known as an *exequatur*. But a diplomatic agent doing this on a regular basis must be notified to the government of the receiving State and should preferably also be given a consular appointment. Those with a dual appointment will address the appropriate authorities depending on the capacity in which they are acting. Regardless of the capacity in which they are acting they will remain entitled to the diplomatic immunities consequent on their diplomatic status.

5.25 Consular functions are described in greater detail in Chapters 8 and 9.

6

DIPLOMATIC COMMUNICATION

Ivor Roberts

Language: History

Latin, being the written language not only of the Roman Empire, but also of its **6.1** successor the Holy Roman Empire and of the Roman Catholic Church, was not surprisingly the written language of most early European diplomacy. It had the advantage of being a neutral language but the drawback of being little understood in that period beyond the ranks of the clergy.[1] From the Renaissance onward, instructions to diplomatic representatives began to be drafted in the language of the envoy's own country, though the use of Latin was common until the eighteenth century. Latin was also used in conversation between diplomats, where the parties were unable to speak each other's language. French came next in frequency of use after Latin. At the end of the fifteenth century it had become the court language of Savoy and the Low Countries, and also of the Emperor's court.

---

[1] P Chaplais, *English Diplomatic Practice in the Middle Ages* (London: Bloomsbury, 2003) 127–33 and K Plöger, *England and the Avignon Popes: The Practice of Diplomacy in Late Medieval Europe* (London: Legenda, 2005) 189–92.

6.2   The treaties of Westphalia (1648) were in Latin but continental countries increasingly used French from the early eighteenth century onwards. At Aix-la-Chapelle, in 1748, a separate article was annexed to the treaty of peace signed by Great Britain, Holland, and France, to the effect that the use of the French language in the treaty of peace was not to be taken as prejudicing the right of the Contracting Parties to have copies signed in other languages. A similar article was attached to the Final Act of the Congress of Vienna.[2]

6.3   In 1800 Lord Grenville introduced the practice of conducting his relations with foreign diplomats accredited to the Court of St James's in English instead of French, the language previously employed. Lord Castlereagh, when at the headquarters of the Allied Powers in 1814–15, wrote in English to the foreign sovereigns and ministers. Canning, in 1823, discovered that the British representative at Lisbon was in the habit of writing in French to the Minister for Foreign Affairs, although the latter addressed him in Portuguese; he therefore instructed him to use English in future, a practice ratified by Lord Palmerston in 1851.

Language: Modern Practice

6.4   Since the mid-nineteenth century, the right of a British diplomat to use his own language for communications to the government to which he is accredited does not seem to have been contested, the right claimed by Great Britain being recognized by her as belonging to every other State. While this right of the representative of every nation to use the official language of that nation is now generally accepted, there is no universal rule making obligatory the use of one language rather than another, and practice varies. At many posts it is customary to accompany a Note which has been by deliberate preference written in the language of the sender, with a translation into the language of the receiving country, typed on plain paper and bearing the heading 'Courtesy Translation', i.e. that it is strictly without official status. This practice is not merely a courtesy; it may sometimes be advisable in order to avoid on the one hand delay, or on the other the possibility of misinterpretation. Occasionally, when the languages of the sending or receiving State (or both) are not widely known, there may be

---

[2] 'La langue française ayant été exclusivement employée dans toutes les copies du présent traité, il est reconnu par les Puissances qui ont concouru à cet acte que l'emploi de cette langue ne tirera point à conséquence pour l'avenir; de sorte que chaque Puissance se réserve d'adopter, dans les négociations et conventions futures, la langue dont elle s'est servie jusqu'ici dans ses relations diplomatiques, sans que le traité actuel puisse être cité comme exemple contraire aux usages établis.' d'Angeberg, *Le Congrès de Vienne* (Paris, 1864).

mutual agreement to use English or more rarely French as a convenient medium of communication.

As regards treaties, conventions, etc, these, when concluded between two coun- **6.5** tries, are now ordinarily signed in two texts, i.e. in the respective languages of the two countries, though important exceptions occur. The Egypt–Israel Peace Treaty of 1979 was written in Arabic, Hebrew, and English and provided that the English text would be the authoritative one in cases of differences of interpretation. Similarly, in the case of the India–Russia Agreement on Illicit Trafficking in Narcotics of 2007, English was the authoritative third language.[3]

In the case of treaties of a general nature—multilateral treaties—concluded **6.6** between many States, the usual practice was formerly to use French, but after a discussion between French Foreign Minister Pichon, President Wilson, and Prime Minister Lloyd George in January 1919, French and English were generally accepted as having parity; and they were adopted as the official languages of the Versailles Conference and later of the League of Nations. Treaties concluded under the auspices of the United Nations normally have Chinese, English, French, Russian, Spanish, and Arabic texts, all equally authoritative.[4] In the European Union English has now emerged in the last 20 years and in particular since the expanding external dimension of the EU and the accession of Sweden, Austria, and Finland in 1995, as the language most used by officials, though the use of French is very much current. In general, as English has usurped the position of French as the international language (largely as a result of the US's predominant position in international communications through the introduction of the Internet etc) so this has carried through into diplomacy.

Forms and Means: Official Communications

Notes Verbales

The most generally used form of written communication between a head of **6.7** mission and the Minister of Foreign Affairs is called a *Note*. There are a number of possible variations of detail in the drafting and presentation of Notes, to which no universally accepted rules apply. The diplomatic services of different countries have their own standing instructions on matters of drafting and procedure; there is some latitude in the use of terms designating types of docu-

---

[3] G R Berridge, *Diplomacy: Theory and Practice* (5th edn, Basingstoke: Palgrave, 2015) 75.

[4] For a more detailed account of the use of languages in the United Nations, see Chapter **18**, paragraphs **18**.68–**18**.73.

ment; and local custom will be found to vary. The indications given in this chapter can therefore be only of the most general nature. In practice, heads of mission, having taken account of local usage, will ensure that their correspondence is drafted in the manner which they judge most fitting in any given circumstances. Certain formulae are current, but the exact choice of words must always be a matter of discretion.

6.8 Essentially a Note is a formal personal letter but the most common form of exchange between an embassy and the foreign ministry is a third person Note called a *Note Verbale*. The idea originally implicit in this term was that it embodied the substance of an oral communication, or of a conversation, of the wording of which it constituted a formal record, although not designed for publication. The title *Note Verbale* is sometimes written at the top of the paper. It is the customary vehicle for written communications between an embassy and a ministry of foreign affairs and is typed on headed notepaper, beginning with the formula: 'The ... Embassy presents its compliments to the Ministry of Foreign Affairs and has the honour to inform them that ... (or, 'to invite their attention to the following matter'). The usual ending is: 'The Embassy avails itself of this opportunity of assuring the Ministry of its highest consideration.'

6.9 Beside the *Note Verbale*'s standard opening and closing paragraphs, each Note should have an individual number followed by the year of issue. It should also be stamped using the embassy/high commission stamp at the bottom, between the text and the date and the stamp initialled by the issuing officer. All Notes should be registered if on substantive issues. *Notes Verbales* can be used for routine matters, informing the Ministry of a Head of Mission's absence, overflight requests, requests for protocol assistance during a VIP visit, or for serious diplomatic business, e.g. a protest note at the policy of the receiving government, a statement of the sending government's position, or policies on a matter of mutual concern. Such Notes can also be used in conveying information to other diplomatic missions on the arrival of ambassadors, opening of books of condolence, etc.

6.10 At the extreme end of the scale is a Note containing an ultimatum threatening war. A famous example is the Note delivered by the British ambassador in Berlin on 3 September 1939. The text is below.

> Sir,
>
> In the communication which I had the honour to make to you on September 1 I informed you, on the instructions of His Majesty's Principal Secretary of State for Foreign Affairs, that unless the German Government were prepared to give His Majesty's Government in the United Kingdom satisfactory assurances that the German Government had suspended all aggressive action against Poland and were prepared promptly to withdraw their forces from Polish territory, His Majesty's

Government in the United Kingdom would, without hesitation, fulfil their obligations to Poland.

2. Although this communication was made more than 24 hours ago, no reply has been received but German attacks upon Poland have been continued and intensified. I have accordingly the honour to inform you that unless not later than 11 a.m., British Summer Time, today September 3, satisfactory assurances to the above effect have been given by the German Government and have reached His Majesty's Government in London, a state of war will exist between the two countries as from that hour.

Courtesy ending[5]

Collective Note

This is a Note addressed by the Dean of the Diplomatic Corps on behalf of all   **6.11**
missions accredited to a government or by representatives of several States to a government in regard to some matter in which they have been instructed to make a joint representation. The latter involves close relations between the Powers whose representatives sign it. An extension of this procedure, stemming from the development of multilateral diplomacy, is for ministers meeting in some multilateral regional or other grouping (e.g. African Union, EU, various Contact Groups, etc) to issue a public communiqué or statement at the conclusion of their meeting which they would ask to be delivered by some/all of their diplomatic representatives in one or more of the capitals involved in the subject of their communiqué. The representative(s) would be asked to reinforce and perhaps enlarge on the public message in the communiqué and convey any response or reaction. In the EU, Ministerial (Council) and Heads of State and Government (European Council) meetings normally issue public Conclusions which will frequently deal with foreign policy matters. In addition—pursuant to agreed EU policies—the High Representative often issues statements responding to external developments while Heads of EU Delegations, sometimes together with the ambassadors of Member States, may be called on to deliver démarches in third countries.

Treaties are nowadays frequently concluded in the form of an *Exchange of Notes*.   **6.12**
This subject is fully dealt with in Book VII *Treaties and Treaty Making*, Chapter **33**, paragraphs **33.16–33.19**.

Despatches

In British usage, *Despatch* was the name given to a formal letter from the   **6.13**
Secretary of State for Foreign and Commonwealth Affairs to a head of mission abroad, or vice versa; or from one head of mission to another. Despatches are

---

[5] Documents on British Foreign Policy, 1919–1939 Third Series, Vol VII, No 757.

now rarely if ever sent and, where they are, they are sent electronically and are almost invariably from heads of mission to their government not vice versa. First impressions and valedictory despatches in the British diplomatic service are now no longer required. The present editor's valedictory from Rome in 2006 was the last of its kind.[6]

6.14 In addition to special forms of address and styles of correspondence, diplomatic communication has evolved its own characteristic idiom, in which certain set phrases are used to convey, with a certain restraint, statements or warnings which, if delivered more bluntly, would raise tempers. These expressions are widely deployed and their meaning is generally accepted. They are in a sense the counterpart of the parliamentary language employed by legislators and other debaters, and they are preferable to the 'diplomacy by insult' practised by early Byzantine rulers and by like-minded empire-builders of the twentieth century. In matters of language the art of the diplomat, as observed by André Maurois,[7] is that of expressing hostility with courtesy, indifference with interest, and friendship with prudence. When ambassadors, speaking on behalf of their government, say that they 'cannot remain indifferent' to a particular situation or course of action, it is understood to mean that, should that situation arise, they will intervene. If they are said to 'view with concern', or 'with grave concern,' a matter under discussion, this means they are proposing to take a strong line about it. 'My Government will reconsider its position' is a warning that a present state of friendliness may not continue. 'Is obliged to tender grave reservations' means in effect 'will not allow'; while 'will be obliged to consider its own interests' indicates that, however its obligations have hitherto been interpreted, it will claim a free hand, which could result in a severance of relations. 'My Government will regard this as an unfriendly act' means 'will regard this as a threat of armed hostilities'. The ambassador may add 'and will decline to be responsible for the consequences', with the corresponding intention.[8]

Speaking Notes

6.15 The preceding paragraphs have been concerned with the official forms of written communication. An unofficial and personal addition to oral communication

---

[6] M Parris, *Parting Shots* (London: Viking, 2011) 145–50.

[7] *L'éloge du diplomate.*

[8] Lord Trevelyan amusingly caricatured the abuse of diplomatic language in the communiqués issued after conferences to which the press have had no access. '"A frank exchange of views" = "nearly came to blows." "In the spirit of brotherly solidarity" indicates that one side made clear to the other that it was becoming too independent for its future comfort. "An atmosphere of cordiality" may mean that, although one party was on the wrong side of the ideological fence, it was hoped that a little flattery might induce it to do something in the other's interests.' H Trevelyan, *Diplomatic Channels* (London: Macmillan, 1973) 91.

frequently used is a copy of speaking notes. When diplomatic staff make an appointment to discuss some matter with a foreign representative, or in a government ministry, they often have some written notes (taken from their instructions) to jog the memory. They may decide to leave this text (which is much more informal than a Note) with the person to whom they have been speaking, in order to ensure that there will be no room for doubt regarding the main points which they have tried to make. The recipient almost certainly finds this helpful and is grateful for it, especially if the conversation has been in a language in which one or other participant is only moderately proficient. The text usually has no attribution. So while it is both a personal courtesy and a practical convenience, it cannot be claimed by either side to have official status.

In different circumstances a note discreetly passed across the table has saved the **6.16** situation in many a conference which had apparently reached an impasse. Let us suppose that one side has worked out a proposition which it cannot possibly propose on the record, but which, in the interests of a satisfactory outcome, it could agree to recommend to its government, if the other side were to advance it. The anonymous piece of paper might therefore contain language such as 'If you felt able to propose...I should be prepared to try it on my government.' Such a piece of classic give and take can often produce a surprisingly happy result. But if the only response is a shake of the head, at least no word has been spoken and no bones broken. In any case the procedure has to be finely judged and depends, like most good diplomacy, on mutual confidence and respect between negotiators. It would be worse than useless if the opposing delegation were of the kind that aimed not at agreement but at scoring points for the sake of publicity.

Non-Paper and Démarche

A rather similar effect can be achieved by a non-paper, the most unofficial of **6.17** diplomatic documents. It is essentially an off-the-record or unofficial presentation of (government) policy and is used when a government wishes to float certain ideas without prejudice to see how they will be received. It can also be used to good effect in multilateral diplomacy where one government undertakes to draft a non-paper to identify the greatest amount of common ground between the other participants in a negotiation while not accepting to be bound by or taking any responsibility for the positions set out in the non-paper.

On major subjects, Heads of State and Government often send letters to each **6.18** other, either directly or through the ambassador or a member of the mission to the private office of the president or prime minister. This may or may not involve a brief covering letter from the ambassador which might be along the following lines:

Your Excellency

I have been asked by my President to convey to you the enclosed message. I am of course available to convey any response or to attempt to clarify any points in the message.

Courtesy ending

6.19 A less formal way of making diplomatic representations or protests is called a démarche. The following from the most recent US Department of State hand-book sets out the typical procedures and purposes of a démarche.

1. General

A US government démarche to a foreign government is made on the basis of 'front-channel cable'[9] instructions from the Department of State. Although the content of a given démarche may originate in another US government agency, only the State Department may also instruct a post to deliver the démarche. Unless specifically authorized by the State Department, posts should not act on instructions transmitted directly from another post, or from another agency, whether by cable or other means (e.g. email, FAX, or phone).

Any State Department officer or other official under the authority of the chief of mission can make a démarche. Unless the Department provides specific instructions as to rank (for example: 'the Ambassador should call on the Foreign Minister'), the post has discretion to determine who should make the presentation and which official(s) in the host government should receive it.

2. Preparation of the Démarche

Démarche instruction cables from the Department should include the following elements:

- (1) OBJECTIVE: The objective is a clear statement of the purpose of the démarche, and of what the US government hopes to achieve.
- (2) ARGUMENTS: This section outlines how the Department proposes to make an effective case for its views. It should include a rationale for the US government's position, supporting arguments, likely counter-arguments, and suggested rebuttals.
- (3) BACKGROUND: The background should spell out pitfalls; particular sensitivities of other bureaus, departments, or agencies; and any other special considerations.
- (4) SUGGESTED TALKING POINTS: Suggested talking points should be clear, conversational, and logically organized. Unless there are compelling reasons to require verbatim delivery, the démarche instruction cable should make it clear that post may use its discretion and local knowledge to structure and deliver the message in the most effective way. ('Embassy may draw from the following points in making this presentation to appropriate host government officials.')

---

[9] Any official State Department cable, sent from a post or the Department, which could contain substance ranging from policy guidance to a specific instruction or a visa revocation.

- (5) WRITTEN MATERIAL: Use this section to provide instructions on any written material to be left with the host government official(s). Such material could take the form of an aide-mémoire, a letter, or a 'non-paper' that provides a written version of the verbal presentation (i.e., the talking points as delivered). Unless otherwise instructed, post should normally provide an aide-mémoire or non-paper at the conclusion of a démarche. Classified aide-memoire or non-paper must be appropriately marked and caveated as to the countries authorized for receipt, i.e., Rel. UK (Releasable to UK).

3. Delivery and Follow-up Action

Upon receipt of démarche instructions from the Department, post should make every effort to deliver the démarche to the appropriate foreign government official(s) as soon as possible.

After delivering the démarche, post should report to the Department via front-channel cable. The reporting cable should include the instruction cable as a reference, but it need not repeat the talking points transmitted in that cable. It should provide the name and title of the person(s) to whom the démarche was made, and record that official's response to the presentation. As appropriate, the reporting cable should also describe any specific follow-up action needed by post, Department, or the foreign government.

Other Informal Means of Communication

The fax, internet, email, video, or telephone conferencing, and other forms of **6.20** information technology have transformed the means of diplomacy.[10] Busy officers in an embassy will often prefer to email or even text their key contact(s) in host government departments to establish their views as rapidly as possible and without having to visit the ministry concerned. This is particularly useful when eliciting factual information. The well-prepared will anticipate the question in response from the ministry, to which there may be no clear answer 'And what is *your* government's position on this point?' Where diplomats need to persuade the host government of the wisdom of their government's position, they will usually find that this can best be done face to face. Officials in government departments now regularly communicate by telephone or other electronic means directly with their opposite numbers in other capitals, bypassing the embassy. This is now a fact of life in, for example, contacts between opposite numbers in Member States of the European Union. It also arises given the specialization increasingly required to discuss issues like climate change internationally, when it clearly makes sense for the 'experts' to communicate directly. The embassy should be briefed on the substance of exchanges and as appropri-

---

[10] For a very full discussion of this important subject see Berridge, *Diplomacy: Theory and Practice* (5th edn, 2015) 101–13.

ate the foreign ministry. This is not just a question of courtesy, but facilitates the continuing conduct of business by the embassy as well as permitting the well-informed diplomat to put the information received into a broader political context. Examples might be where officials at home needed to be told or reminded that their interlocutor is a political appointee whose career is closely linked to a soon-to-be-departing minister, or that there are other contacts who also need to be consulted.

6.21   At a higher level, Heads of State or Government often speak directly, with or without a video dimension, by secure telephone to discuss and resolve major issues. In the early days of hot-lines between say Washington and Moscow or Washington and London, this was as a diplomatic weapon of last resort. These days such exchanges are fairly routine. Foreign Ministers will often speak to each other by such means several times a day during a crisis. In Western capitals, such conversations will be recorded and a note or record prepared by a private secretary to inform those who need to know of the main points agreed or disagreed. In London, the Prime Minister's Office tends to take a very restrictive view of the number of people who need to see a record of the prime minister's discussions with his principal international interlocutors, sometimes excluding other ministers, senior officials elsewhere, and ambassadors, to their irritation and to the detriment of the smooth working of diplomacy. Ambassadors who are unaware of the fact or the substance of exchanges between their government and their host government at the highest levels cannot be expected to execute their missions effectively.

Megaphone Diplomacy

6.22   While prime ministers, presidents, and foreign and other ministers regularly interact as described above, there is another kind of activity which is essentially the antithesis of diplomacy, viz megaphone diplomacy. The extracts below from an article in the *International Herald Tribune* and from an Australian Broadcasting Corporation report illustrate how such use of public statements and press releases can be counterproductive and how much more preferable is 'quiet' or traditional diplomacy.

> In a direct reference to Russia, the European Commission president, José Manuel Barroso, last week decried 'the use of energy resources as an instrument of political coercion.' Meanwhile, Vice President Dick Cheney on Thursday accused Russia of using its energy resources as 'tools of intimidation or blackmail.'
>
> These have only been the latest examples of a wide-ranging public dressing-down of Russia, including calls for its exclusion from the Group of 8 industrialized nations. Given the reaction that this megaphone diplomacy has caused in Moscow,

it should be abandoned. Western policy makers must recognize that Russia's new-found international clout has fostered a national self-confidence unprecedented in the post-Soviet era.

As a result, Moscow is no longer willing to turn the other cheek when provoked. After the Western comments last week, Gazprom's chief executive, Alexei Miller, ominously warned that 'attempts to limit Gazprom's activity in the European market and to politicize gas issues, which are in fact solely economic, will not produce good results.'[11]

The Federal Opposition says Prime Minister Tony Abbott risks further undermining Australia's relationship with Indonesia after he suggested it was 'high time' Indonesia resumed cooperation on people smuggling operations. Indonesia suspended cooperation after it was revealed that back in 2009, Australian spies had targeted the phones of the Indonesian president, his wife, and inner circle. The revelations were uncovered in documents leaked by former NSA contractor Edward Snowden and reported by The Guardian and the ABC.

During a press conference on his first 100 days in office, Mr Abbott described Indonesia's decision to suspend military cooperation as 'singularly unhelpful' and has urged Indonesia to reverse it. 'Given that people smuggling is a crime in Indonesia, just as it is a crime in Australia, I think it is high time that cooperation was resumed,' he said. 'But I accept that in the end, what Indonesia does is a matter for Indonesia.'

But Opposition Immigration spokesman Richard Marles has accused Mr Abbott of engaging in megaphone diplomacy. 'I think this is another example of a Government certainly with its L-plates on' he said. 'A Government that has no instinct for how to get its diplomatic relations right with Indonesia on the issue of asylum seekers.'[12]

Megaphone diplomacy is often the product of domestic political needs where politicians feel the need for their own domestic political purposes to talk toughly and often roughly even when it will damage their longer term aims. It often falls to the diplomat on the ground to attempt to repair the damage done by resorting to megaphone diplomacy.   6.23

'Rejection' of Diplomatic Communications

The return to the sender of a diplomatic communication occurs only rarely and the reason for the 'rejection' is usually either the objectionable language of the document in question, or that it is a gross interference with the internal affairs of the addressee country, or both.   6.24

---

[11] S Charap and J Hecker in an article 'Enough Megaphone Diplomacy' in the *International Herald Tribune*, 12 May 2006.

[12] <http://www.abc.net.au/news/2013-12-16/opposition-says-pm-risks-australia-indonesia-relationship/5158054>.

6.25 In 1943 Stalin sent a telegram to Winston Churchill about the Arctic Convoys, whose form and substance were so objectionable that the prime minister refused to accept it and, sending for the Soviet ambassador in London, handed it back to him in an envelope. The Ambassador Gousev recognized the document and said that he had been instructed to deliver it. The prime minister 'then said "I am not prepared to receive it" and got up to indicate in a friendly manner that our conversation was at an end'.[13]

6.26 More recently, shortly before the outbreak of the first Gulf War, President George H W Bush sent his Secretary of State, James Baker, in January 1991 to Geneva to deliver via the Iraqi Foreign Minister, Tariq Aziz, a letter to the Iraqi President Saddam Hussein. It contained a blunt final warning to pull back from the brink of war by withdrawing from Kuwait and a particular threat to Saddam about the use of weapons of mass destruction, support for terrorist action, and the destruction of Kuwait's oilfields: 'You and your country will pay a terrible price if you order unconscionable action of this sort.' Aziz read the copy of the letter which was outside the original in a sealed envelope but he was clearly under great strain ('[o]ne member of the American delegation noticed him beginning to perspire and a slight tremble in his hand'). He refused to deliver the letter or take the copy and it was left on the table as the talks broke up after seven hours of meeting.[14]

Correspondence between Sovereigns and Heads of State

6.27 The titles used by sovereigns when addressing each other in correspondence have been described in Chapter 4, paragraph 4.33. The ceremonial observed is less strict than in the case of communications addressed to others; between equals the style is more familiar and less formal and often in French. Such letters begin, Monsieur Mon Frère (et cher Beau-Frère), Sir My Brother (and dear Brother-in-Law); Madame Ma Soeur (et chère Nièce), Madame My Sister (and dear Niece); Monsieur Mon Cousin (Sir My Cousin); etc. In the body of the letter the sovereigns speak of themselves in the singular, and give to their equals the title of *Majesté, Altesse Royale,* etc. Princes of lesser rank speak of crowned heads as *Sire,* both in the body of the letter and its signature. Some friendly expressions, which vary according to the relations or degree of relationship between the two sovereigns, close the letter, such as 'Je saisis cette

---

[13] Winston Churchill, *The Second World War* (London: Cassell, 1950) Vol V, 272.

[14] L Freedman and E Karsh, *The Gulf Conflict 1990–1991* (London: Faber & Faber, 1993) 254–60.

occasion pour Vous offrir les assurances de la haute considération et de l'invariable attachement avec lesquelles Je suis, Monsieur Mon Frère, de Votre Majesté le bon Frère, N.' The signature of the sovereign to such letters is in some countries countersigned by a minister of state. Letters in this form are customarily employed for credentials of ambassadors or ministers accredited between sovereigns, or letters announcing their recall, or expressions of congratulation or condolence conveyed to other sovereigns. (See Chapter 7, paragraphs 7.48–7.50 for examples of credentials.)

Letters addressed by sovereigns to presidents of republics are in a more formal **6.28** and ceremonious style beginning with the name and title of the sovereign, followed by the title of the head of the State to whom the letter is addressed: 'To the President of the Republic of .... Our Good Friend' (or some equivalent). For instance, the Presidents of the United States of America and of the French Republic are addressed by the British Queen as 'Dear Mr President/ Monsieur le Président' and the correspondence is signed 'Your Good Friend Elizabeth R'. These are ordinarily credentials of ambassadors or ministers, letters of recall, announcements of the death of the late sovereign or of accession to the throne, congratulations on election etc, and may end by an expression of the value attached by the sovereign to the maintenance of the friendly relations happily subsisting between the two countries. They are usually countersigned by a minister of state.

Letters addressed by presidents of republics to sovereigns usually begin: 'A.B. **6.29** President of the Republic of .... To His Majesty the King of .... Great and Good Friend' (or some equivalent). These may be credentials of ambassadors or ministers, letters of recall, announcement of election to the presidency, etc. In the case of many republics such announcements of assumption of the office of president are customary.

7

FORMAL ASPECTS OF DIPLOMATIC RELATIONS

Precedence among Heads of State and States, Selection, *Agrément*, Precedence among Heads of Mission, Chargés d'Affaires, Credentials, Full Powers for Heads of Mission

Ivor Roberts

Precedence among Heads of State and States

7.1 While the right of the papacy to fix the order of precedence among sovereigns had been recognized for centuries (though not always accepted without demur),[1] the precedence of the Pope above all other potentates was assumed as a matter of course. Next in order came the (Holy Roman) Emperor; then the King of the Romans, who was the heir-apparent of the latter (by election).

---

[1] The importance of precedence lay in the fact that it conferred a prior entitlement to access to the receiving sovereign. It was not simply a question of vanity and prestige.

The first place being conceded to the Pope, and the second, with universal 7.2 assent, to the Emperor, up to the fall of the Holy Roman Empire in 1806, the question was precedence among the others. Gustavus Adolphus of Sweden asserted the equality of all crowned heads, Queen Christina maintained it at the Congress of Westphalia, and in 1718 it was claimed for Great Britain on the occasion of the Quadruple Alliance. But until the matter was finally settled at the Congress of Vienna in 1815 constant disputes arose.

In 1633,[2] Christian IV of Denmark having proposed to celebrate the wedding 7.3 of his son, the Crown Prince, a dispute arose between the French and Spanish ambassadors, the Comte d'Avaux and the Marqués de la Fuente. The Danish ministers proposed to d'Avaux various solutions of the difficulty, and among these that he should sit next to the King, or next to the Imperial ambassador. To this he replied: 'I will give the Spanish ambassador the choice of the place which he regards as the most honourable, and when he shall have taken it, I will turn him out and take it myself.' To avoid further dispute, de la Fuente, on a plea of urgent business elsewhere, absented himself from the ceremony.

A more serious dispute took place in London on 30 September 1661, on the 7.4 occasion of the state entry of the Swedish ambassador. It was the custom at such 'functions' for the resident ambassadors to send their coaches to swell the cortège. The Spanish ambassador, de Watteville, sent his coach down to the Tower wharf, from where the procession was to set out, with his chaplain and gentlemen, and a train of about forty armed servants. The coach of the French ambassador, Comte d'Estrades, with a royal coach for the accommodation of the Swedish ambassador, were also on the spot. In the French coach were the son of d'Estrades with some of his gentlemen, escorted by 150 men, of whom forty carried firearms. After the Swedish ambassador had landed and taken his place in the royal coach, the French coach tried to go next, and on the Spaniards offering resistance, the Frenchmen fell upon them with drawn swords and poured in shot upon them. The Spaniards defended themselves, mortally wounded a postilion and dragged the coachman from his box, after which they triumphantly took the place which no one was any longer able to dispute with them.[3] Louis XIV, on learning of this incident, ordered the Spanish ambassador in Paris to quit the kingdom, and sent instructions to his own representative at Madrid to demand redress, consisting of the punishment of de Watteville and an undertaking that Spanish ambassadors should in future yield the *pas* to those of France at all foreign courts. In case of a refusal a declaration of war was to be

---

[2] G de R de Flassan, *Histoire générale at raisonnée de la diplomatie française*, 7 vols (2nd edn, Paris, 1811) Vol 3, 15.

[3] *Diary of John Evelyn*, ed Henry B Wheatley (London: Bickers, 1906) Vol 2, 486; *Pepys' Diary* (under date of 30 September 1661).

notified. The King of Spain, anxious to avoid a rupture, recalled de Watteville from London, and despatched the Marqués de la Fuente to Paris, as ambassador extraordinary, to disavow the conduct of de Watteville and to announce that he had prohibited all his ambassadors from engaging in rivalry in the matter of precedence with those of the Most Christian King.[4] The question was finally disposed of by the 'Pacte de Famille' of 15 August 1761, in which it was agreed that at Naples and Parma, where the sovereigns belonged to the Bourbon family, the French ambassador was always to have precedence, but at other courts the relative rank was to be determined by the date of arrival. If both arrived on the same day, then the French ambassador was to have precedence.[5]

7.5   Similar rivalry manifested itself between the Russian and French ambassadors. The latter had instructions to maintain their rank in the diplomatic circle by all possible means and to yield the *pas* to the papal and imperial ministers alone. On the other hand, Russia had not ordered hers to claim precedence over the French ambassador, but simply not to concede it to him. At a court ball in London, in the winter of 1768, the Russian ambassador, arriving first, took his place immediately next to the ambassador of the Emperor, who was on the first of two benches arranged in the diplomatic box. The French ambassador came in late, and climbing on to the second bench managed to slip down between his two colleagues. A lively interchange of words followed, and in the duel which arose out of the incident the Russian was wounded.[6]

7.6   Pombal, prime minister of Portugal, in 1760, on the occasion of the marriage of the Princess of Brazil, caused a circular to be addressed to the foreign representatives, announcing the ceremony and acquainting them that ambassadors at the court of Lisbon, with the exception of the Papal nuncio and the Imperial ambassador, would thenceforth rank, when paying visits or having audiences granted to them, according to the date of their credentials. Choiseul, the French Minister for Foreign Affairs, when the matter was referred to him, maintained that 'the King would not give up the recognised rank due to his crown, and his Majesty did not think that the date of credentials could in any case or under any pretext weaken the rights attaching to the dignity of France'. He added that though kings were doubtless masters in their own dominions, their power did not extend to assigning relative rank to other crowned heads without the sanction of the latter. 'In fact,' said he, 'no sovereign in a matter of this kind recognises powers of legislation in the person of other sovereigns. All Powers are bound to

---

[4] (Baron) J C Dumont, *Corps universel diplomatique du droit des gens* (Paris, 1725–31) Vol 6, Pt II, 403.

[5] Flassan, *Histoire de la diplomatie française*, Vol 6, 314.

[6] Flassan, *Histoire de la diplomatie française*, Vol 7, 376.

each other to do nothing contrary to usages which they have no power to change... Pre-eminence is derived from the relative antiquity of monarchies, and it is not permitted to princes to touch a right so precious... The King will never, on any pretext, consent to an innovation which violates the dignity of his throne.' Nor did Spain accord a more favourable reception to this new rule of etiquette, while the court of Vienna, though the imperial rights had been respected, replied to Paris that such an absurdity only deserved contempt, and suggested consulting with the court of Spain in order to destroy the ridiculous pretension of the Portuguese minister.[7]

Matters remained unresolved until the beginning of the nineteenth century. At **7.7** the Congress of Vienna the Plenipotentiaries appointed a committee which after two months' deliberation presented a scheme dividing the Powers into three classes, according to which the position of their diplomatic agents would be regulated. But as it did not find unanimous approval, especially with the rank assigned to the greater republics, they fell back upon the simple plan of disregarding precedence among sovereigns altogether, and of making the relative position of diplomatic representatives depend, in each class, on seniority, i.e. on the date of the official notification of their arrival. And in order to do away with the last relic of the old opinions that some crowned heads ranked higher than others, they also decided that· '[d]ans les actes ou traités entre plusieurs puissances qui admettent l'alternat, le sort décidera, entre les ministres, de l'ordre qui devra être suivi dans les signatures'.[8] (An English translation would be: 'In acts or treaties made between a number of powers who accept the *alternat,* the order to be followed among ministers [that is, those with authority to sign the instrument] in appending signatures will be decided by lot.')

The *alternat* consisted in this, that in the copy of the document or treaty which **7.8** was to be given to each separate Power, the names of the head of that State and his Plenipotentiaries were given precedence over the others, and his Plenipotentiaries' signatures also were attached before those of the other signatories. Thus each Power occupied the place of honour in turn.[9]

The Holy Roman Empire came to an end in July 1806, as a consequence of the **7.9** establishment by Napoleon of the Confederation of the Rhine, and the precedence over other sovereigns formerly enjoyed by the Holy Roman Emperor

---

[7] Flassan, *Histoire de la diplomatie française*, Vol 6, 193.

[8] But though the *règlement* states that the order of signature shall be decided by lot, the signatures appended to that document followed the alphabetical order of the French language, and the same procedure was adopted for the signature of the *acte final* of the Congress.

[9] For an amusing account of the *alternat*'s former importance see H Nicolson, *The Congress of Vienna* (London: Constable, 1946) 217–20.

disappeared and could not be claimed by the Emperor of Austria, whose title in 1815 was only 11 years old. Nor was France at that time in a position to reassert her claims to rank before the rest of the Powers. From this date the equality in respect of rank of all independent sovereign States, whether empires, kingdoms, or republics, has been universally accepted, and it appears unlikely that there will be any refusals of the *alternat* in connection with treaties, though in the case of multilateral treaties the more convenient method of signing a single instrument in the alphabetical order of the participating countries has more recently replaced former methods of signing several originals according precedence to each in turn. (See Chapter **30**, paragraphs **30.16–30.17** and Chapter **31**, paragraph **31.13** (for signature texts) and Chapter **34**, paragraph **34.4** (for exchange of ratifications).

7.10 In the Treaty of Versailles and other peace treaties resulting from the Peace Conference of Paris in 1919, the five principal Allied and Associated Powers took precedence over all other States ranged against the Central Powers.

7.11 Dr J B Scott[10] relates that at the First Peace Conference at The Hague in 1899 the United States' representatives took their place at the table under the letter É (États-Unis), but at the Second Peace Conference of 1907 under the letter A (Amérique), it having in the meantime been remembered that United States of America was the official title; and he observes that this happy philological discovery enabled the United States delegates at the latter Conference to claim the benefit of the first letter of the alphabet, and to take precedence over other American States.

Classes and Precedence among Heads of Mission

7.12 As with Heads of State, the titles and precedence of heads of mission were topics of great importance in earlier centuries. The reasons were that the choice of title agreed between two States reflected the political importance of the States as well as the diplomatic relations between them and also that the title of the envoy as well as his precedence within that class determined his right of access to the receiving sovereign and therefore his power to influence or to protest. Since 1945 with the growing acceptance, at least in theory, of the sovereign equality of all States as expressed in the Charter of the United Nations, the distinctions between envoys of different rank have largely disappeared and almost all heads of mission are now ambassadors (or have titles of equivalent

---

[10] J Brown Scott, *The Hague Conventions and Declarations of 1899 and 1907* (New York: Oxford University Press, 1915).

rank such as high commissioner in the case of Commonwealth States or nuncio in the case of the Holy See). Precedence retains some importance in protocol and ceremonial contexts but it no longer determines the level of reception of an envoy or the weight accorded to his representations.

The 1815 Vienna Regulation reduced the classes of envoy to three and provided **7.13** that precedence should be determined by the date of arrival in the receiving State. These rules were accepted in international practice and they are now reflected in Articles 13 to 18 of the Vienna Convention on Diplomatic Relations.

Article 14 of the Vienna Convention sets out the three classes of heads of mis- **7.14** sion as:

(a) that of ambassadors or nuncios accredited to Heads of State, and other heads of mission of equivalent rank;

(b) that of envoys, ministers and internuncios accredited to Heads of State;

(c) that of chargés d'affaires accredited to Ministers for Foreign Affairs.

The title of nuncio denotes a permanent diplomatic representative of the Holy See. Formerly the Pope sent a nuncio only where his representative was automatically given the status of dean, or doyen, of the diplomatic corps, but since 1994 this is no longer the case. The term 'heads of mission of equivalent rank' indicates a high commissioner within the Commonwealth. The Pope may also despatch apostolic delegates, but these are not accredited to the Head of State or Minister of Foreign Affairs but to the Church and the Catholic population in a specified region.[11] They may be given diplomatic privileges and immunities as a matter of courtesy but they are not strictly heads of mission.

In the years following the adoption of the Vienna Convention, appointment of **7.15** heads of mission other than ambassadors became very rare and usually resulted from some historical anomaly or coolness in relations. In 1972 the United Kingdom and China, in the context of a wider political settlement, agreed to upgrade their representation from chargés d'affaires to ambassadors and in 1996 the UK and Albania also upgraded their level of representation from that of chargés d'affaires to ambassadors. The last UK Legation sent to the Holy See was, in 1982, replaced by an embassy.

Nowadays, as discussed earlier, no formal precedence is recognized among **7.16** nations. Precedence among heads of diplomatic missions is now determined by the date of their taking up their functions. The taking up of their functions

---

[11] H E Cardinale, *The Holy See and the International Order* (Gerrards Cross: Smythe, 1976) 136–50; J-C Noonan Jr, *The Church Visible: The Ceremonial Life and Protocol of the Roman Catholic Church* (New York: Viking, 1996) 92–3.

may—in accordance with the practice in the receiving State—be determined either by the date of presentation of credentials or by notification of arrival accompanied by presentation of a true copy of the ambassador's credentials to the ministry of foreign affairs of the receiving State. The order of formal presentation of credentials must now be determined by the date and time of the arrival of the ambassador—so that if a receiving State determines the taking up of functions by reference to presentation of credentials it is not permitted to manipulate the date of this ceremony so as to alter precedence. Seniority in post thus determines precedence and the holding of the office of dean of the diplomatic corps, though in some Roman Catholic and other countries, e.g. Italy and Ireland, the representative of the Holy See takes precedence regardless of his date of presenting credentials (see Chapter **10**, paragraph **10**.2). In Washington in April 2008 the position of dean of the diplomatic corps was held by the ambassador of Djibouti who had been in his post for 20 years. In London in 2016, the position of dean was held by the Kuwaiti ambassador who had been in post since 1993 and had been dean since 2003.

7.17 In the case of special representatives sent to attend, for instance, coronations or state funerals, precedence is generally the same as that applying to the resident representatives of their countries. But where there is doubt, the rules of protocol of the host government, or court, are conclusive. The modern law on precedence derives from the Vienna Convention on Diplomatic Relations and in particular Articles 13 and 16.1.

7.18 The precedence of members of the diplomatic staff of each embassy is determined by the sending State and must be notified to the ministry of foreign affairs of the receiving State.

Precedence at the United Nations

7.19 In the United Nations there are two orders of precedence, the precedence between delegates and officials and the precedence between member countries. As regards the first, the President of the General Assembly is held to be the most senior, followed by the Secretary-General and the President of the Security Council in that order. There follow the Chairman of the Economic and Social Council, the Vice-Presidents of the General Assembly, and the Chairmen and Vice-Chairmen of the Assembly Committees. The Secretariat maintains a protocol department to assist delegates, officials, and others with seating arrangements at formal occasions. This department is responsible for determining the general order of precedence for occasions when delegates, officials, and other high dignitaries attend together.

As regards precedence between delegations, this derives from the arrangements agreed for the order of seating and roll-call voting in the General Assembly. Each year, a country is chosen by lot to take the first seat to the left in the front row of the Assembly and the remainder follow in English alphabetical order from left to right in each row of seats. This order of precedence is used in respect of all delegates and advisers of equivalent rank who do not hold any office (e.g. Chairman or Vice-Chairman). The only variation is at Security Council lunches, where representatives are seated in the order of seating which they have in the Security Council itself. The principle of precedence based on the date of presentation of credentials does not apply at the United Nations. **7.20**

The initial selection of its ambassadors and, below them, the members of the staff of a diplomatic mission, is a matter for the law and practice of each State. Most States entrust the conduct of their diplomatic relations with other States, at least below the rank of ambassador, to a professional diplomatic service. The law and practice varies between different States on such matters as whether diplomatic posts are open to persons of other nationalities and on the personal requirements for appointment. Formerly it was common for States to maintain specialized services for consular and commercial matters and the United Kingdom, for example, maintained regional services such as the China Consular Service and the Levant Service for posts in the Middle East. The modern practice however is usually for States to maintain a unified diplomatic and consular service with, at least in theory, complete interchangeability in regard to personnel, functions, and geographical area of work. (Foreign affairs and trade officials have been amalgamated in the same ministry for some years in the Canadian, Australian, and New Zealand departments of foreign affairs and trade.)[12] Requirements as to educational or specialized professional qualifications and as to character are common, but laws against discrimination in many countries ensure that selection to diplomatic posts cannot be limited on grounds of race, religion, or sex. Restricting appointment to nationals of the appointing State however, since it serves as some guarantee of allegiance and loyalty, remains extremely common, and in some States it is a constitutional or legal requirement. In the United States, for example, the Foreign Service Act 1980 provides that only US citizens may be appointed to diplomatic posts abroad.[13] Posts in the British Diplomatic Service are restricted to those who are British citizens, or have dual nationality as long as one of those nationalities is British and have been resident in the UK for at least two of the last 10 years.[14] **7.21**

---

[12] See also Chapter 2, paragraph 2.13.

[13] Public Law 96–465, 22 USC 3901.

[14] The requirements are set out in the Foreign and Commonwealth Office website: <http://www.fco.gov.uk>.

7.22 Beyond these formal restrictions, States are likely to apply tests of aptitude for a diplomatic career in such matters as administrative capability, negotiation and drafting skills, and resilience under stress. Extensive language skills are in some countries no longer a prerequisite, since training can be provided, but aptitude for learning difficult languages may well be assessed and many European diplomatic services continue to require extensive knowledge of two foreign languages, one invariably English. Entry to a diplomatic career is in most States highly sought after so that searching tests may be used for purposes of selecting the best qualified and most suitable candidates. In highly developed countries the process of recruitment for overseas service is kept under almost constant review in the light of the changing needs of the State.

7.23 Bismarck provided a concise summary of what is expected of a diplomat in saying: 'His work consists of practical intercourse with men, of judging accurately what people are likely to do in given circumstances, of appreciating accurately the views of others, and of accurately presenting his own.' And as to the qualities of character sought when selecting from candidates for a diplomatic service it must be stressed that diplomacy is not a career for the compliant. It often imposes on officers the duty of defending the interests of their country in places not of their own choice, where they must be prepared to be resilient both in the face of unhealthy climates and when in the front line of international politics.

7.24 Sir Henry Wotton, ambassador of King James I of England to Venice, is perhaps best remembered among diplomats for his witticism that '[a]n ambassador is an honest man, sent to lie abroad for the good of his country'. The story is an excellent example of the dangers of joking in a language which is not the diplomat's mother tongue (since the ambiguity in the English word 'lie' did not exist in the Latin translation used by Sir Henry). When King James heard a report of the remarks some eight years later, he never again employed Wotton. Sir Henry himself later advised a prospective ambassador that 'to be in safety himself and serviceable to his country, he should always and upon all occasions speak the truth'. Sir Harold Nicolson in his book *Diplomacy* maintained that the qualities of an ideal diplomat were truth, accuracy, calm, patience, good temper, modesty, and loyalty.[15]

Selection of Heads of Mission

7.25 Ambassadors and other heads of mission are in many States selected not only as being the best qualified on personal grounds for appointment to a particular diplomatic post but also for political reasons. This is most apparent in the case

---

[15] (2nd edn, Oxford: Oxford University Press, 1939). See also Chapter 36, paragraph 36.19.

of the United States where Article II Section 2.2 of the Constitution provides that the President 'by and with the advice of the Senate, shall appoint ambassadors, other public ministers and consuls'. There is a long tradition of appointing political supporters of the party whose nominee has been elected President, and the practice has continued at least in regard to senior and hence more desirable appointments such as the main European and other Western posts. Under President Reagan it was said that 40 per cent of senior diplomatic posts were held by political appointees, leaving many senior professionals within the State Department frustrated at being assigned to the most uncongenial posts as ambassador or in playing second fiddle to a political appointee.

In the United Kingdom such political appointments are by contrast rare but not **7.26** at all unknown. In 1940 in the early stages of the Second World War the former Foreign Secretary, Lord Halifax, was appointed as ambassador to Washington and remained in that post for six years. In 1961 Lord Harlech was selected by Prime Minister Harold Macmillan as ambassador to Washington because of his close relationship with President Kennedy and in 1968 Prime Minister Harold Wilson sent Sir Christopher Soames, a former cabinet minister, to Paris. In 1977 the new Foreign Secretary David Owen recalled a career ambassador from Washington and replaced him with the son-in-law of the then Prime Minister James Callaghan and more recently two former UK cabinet ministers have been sent to Pretoria and Canberra.

Given the nature of the duties and functions of an ambassador and the special **7.27** need in many cases to appoint an individual who not only best represents the sending Head of State but has personal links to the head of the receiving State, there can be no standard way for States to select their ambassadors. In different ages and in different countries, advocates and actors, priests and noblemen, merchant princes, cultured scholars, and men of wealth have all been chosen as ambassadors. A modern diplomatic service is staffed with many supporting professionals from linguists and lawyers to cipher clerks and security officers. But at the level of ambassador the flexibility permitted to each State in its choice reflects well the variety of its political relations with other States.

Agrément for Heads of Mission

Article 4 of the Vienna Convention on Diplomatic Relations requires a sending **7.28** State to ensure that the agrément of the receiving State has been given for the person it proposes to appoint as head of its mission to that State. If the receiving State refuses agrément, it is not obliged to give reasons. Both rules reflect longstanding state practice which—with some resistance from the United States and from the United Kingdom—was accepted as customary international law by the 1930s. The requirement is justified by the need for a head of mission, in order effectively to conduct diplomatic relations between two States, to be personally acceptable to both of them.

7.29 The request for approval is normally made confidentially through the most convenient diplomatic channel—most usually by the retiring ambassador to the head of the receiving State's protocol department or foreign ministry, though occasionally by the Minister of Foreign Affairs of the sending State to the ambassador of the receiving State, or rarely and directly by one Head of State or minister to another in a third State or at the United Nations in New York. It is usual for a curriculum vitae to be supplied for the proposed ambassador. Very occasionally a sending State may supply more than one name and leave the choice to the receiving State. Refusals are usually given orally and are not made public, but the receiving State is not legally precluded from making the fact or the grounds of its rejection public.

7.30 Delay in giving agrément or rejection of a proposed appointment may relate to previous postings, conduct, or personal characteristics of the individual; or it may be a sign of strained relations between the two States or occasionally to a combination of both those factors. In 1885 the proposed United States envoy to Rome, Mr Keiley, whose case was important in the establishment of modern practice, was first rejected by the King of Italy on account of the political implications of a speech he had made at a meeting of Roman Catholics in Virginia protesting at the annexation of the Papal States by Italy. Subsequently his appointment to Vienna was rejected by the Austro-Hungarian government as advance agrément had not been sought by the United States, because of his public statements and also because the fact that he was wedded to a Jewish wife by civil ceremony would make his position in Vienna 'untenable and intolerable'. In 1977 Greece delayed agrément for Mr William Schaufele as United States ambassador because of remarks he had made during his confirmation hearing before the US Senate relating to the dispute between Greece and Turkey in the Aegean Sea.[16] Kuwait in 1983 rejected the proposed appointment by the United States of a head of mission who had previously served for three years as consul-general in Jerusalem.[17] Suspicion of involvement in criminal and in particular terrorist activity, in espionage, or in violations of human rights may also be a ground for refusal. The Iranian government declined agrément to David Reddaway, the British nominee for the post of ambassador to Tehran in 2002, accusing him of being 'a Jew and a member of MI6', i.e. a spy. The British

---

[16] (1977) *RGDIP* 827.
[17] (1984) *RGDIP* 244.

government however stated publicly that Mr Reddaway was not Jewish and was not an intelligence officer and responded by downgrading the status of the Iranian ambassador in London—so this rejection should properly be regarded as a sign of the difficult relations between the two States.

Even if agrément has been given, it may be withdrawn if the proposed head of **7.31** mission has not actually arrived in the territory of the receiving State. In 1968, for example, Saudi Arabia withdrew its agrément to the appointment of Sir Horace Phillips as United Kingdom ambassador on grounds of his Jewish origins. The government of Saudi Arabia had in fact been aware of Sir Horace's Jewish origins and its change of heart resulted from these being made public in the British *Jewish Chronicle.*[18]

Appointment of the Staff of the Mission

By contrast with the position of heads of diplomatic missions, the general rule **7.32** is that no advance approval from the receiving State is required for members of the staff of the mission of whatever rank. Article 7 of the Vienna Convention on Diplomatic Relations provides that the sending State may 'freely appoint the members of the staff of the mission'—but there are exceptions in the case of multiple accreditation, in the case of staff who are not nationals of the sending State, and where the staff of the mission exceeds what is 'reasonable and normal'. These exceptions are discussed below. The receiving State may also, under Article 7, require the names of defence attachés (military, naval, or air) to be submitted in advance for approval.

The right freely to appoint diplomatic staff is taken to include the right for the **7.33** sending State to dismiss such staff, and the right of mission staff to challenge dismissal or discriminatory treatment by the sending State is shown by court cases in many countries to be extremely limited.[19] The sending State as a general rule indicates whether each member of its mission staff should be classified as diplomatic staff, administrative and technical staff, or service staff. But since this classification has important implications for the privileges and immunities of individual staff members, some States—in particular the United States—have made efforts to scrutinize individual appointments by reference to the known duties performed and in case of suspected abuse to require that an individual be reassigned to a more appropriate category. In the UK, Protocol Directorate (not

---

[18] J Dickie, *Inside the Foreign Office* (London: Chapmans, 1992) 178–80.
[19] For details of such cases see E Denza, *Diplomatic Law* (4th edn, Oxford: Oxford University Press, 2016) 50–5.

the sending State or its mission) decides whether a mission member should be a diplomatic agent, administrative and technical, or service staff. This determination is made on the basis of the job description supplied by the mission for its member of staff. The sending State is entitled to choose the title accorded to particular members of staff, and although these titles usually conform to standard diplomatic practice (minister; counsellor; first, second, and third secretaries; attachés are the usual ranks among diplomatic staff) there are exceptions. Libya caused particular difficulty when in 1979 it announced that its diplomatic missions would be designated as 'People's Bureaux' and that members of its staff were no longer diplomats. This decision led to prolonged exchanges in a number of capitals as a result of which Libya accepted generally that foreign governments were entitled to make their own determinations, classifying Libyan People's Bureau staff for purposes of conferring appropriate protection, privileges, and immunities on them.[20]

7.34   Under Article 10 of the Vienna Convention on Diplomatic Relations there are extensive requirements to notify the ministry of foreign affairs of the receiving State of the appointment, status, and final departure of members of a diplomatic mission. These notifications are used by the ministry of foreign affairs in the context of establishing entitlement to privileges and immunities for individuals (and are dealt with in Chapter 12) and also in order to compile a local Diplomatic List and in some capitals to issue diplomatic identity cards. Neither entry on the Diplomatic List nor the possession of a diplomatic identity card are conclusive evidence of entitlement to privileges or immunities, but they have social and practical uses for individual members of diplomatic missions.

Nationality of Diplomatic Staff

7.35   As already explained, it is highly unusual for a State to propose for a diplomatic appointment a person who is not one of its nationals, but international law does permit such an appointment. Article 8 of the Vienna Convention on Diplomatic Relations says merely that 'Members of the diplomatic staff of the mission should in principle be of the nationality of the sending State.' The appointment of a diplomat who is a national of the receiving State requires under Article 8 the consent of that State which may be withdrawn at any time. States are also permitted to reserve this right of veto with regard to nationals of a third State who are not also nationals of the sending State—though it is very unusual for this to be done.

7.36   In practice, most appointments of persons having the nationality of the receiving State are of dual nationals who are also nationals of the sending State. This

---

[20] See (1980) *DUSPIL* 286; UK House of Commons Foreign Affairs Committee 1st Report, 1984–5, paras 69–72.

practice is particularly common among States which are members of the Commonwealth. The United Kingdom government has made clear that it sees no problem in such appointments. Appointments of diplomats having only the nationality of the receiving State are by contrast highly exceptional—though this is mainly due to the restrictions usually applied by appointing States rather than to refusal of permission by receiving States. The UK government also permits members of staff of a Commonwealth diplomatic mission or the Embassy of the Republic of Ireland and their private servants who are citizens of the UK *and* are citizens of the sending State to have privileges and immunities to which they would have been entitled had they not also been citizens of the UK.

It is worth underlining that the question of whether such diplomats may be appointed and accepted is a separate question from the privileges and immunities to which they are entitled if appointed, which are described in Chapter 12. It should also be made clear that the limitations on appointment of nationals of the receiving State apply only to diplomatic staff and not to junior staff of the mission. The appointment of local nationals to embassy posts such as administrators, clerks, translators, cooks, and drivers has many advantages in terms of their familiarity with the local language and customs as well as reduced costs for the sending State and it is in practice extremely common. Staff in such positions are not normally dealing with sensitive information or carrying out political functions where their loyalty to the sending State might cause difficulties or risks. **7.37**

Multiple Accreditation

Where permanent missions are not established between two States, one of the alternatives which may be chosen on grounds of security or lower cost is multiple accreditation. This may take the form of sending a single ambassador or diplomat to more than one State (Article 5 of the Vienna Convention on Diplomatic Relations) or the sending by two or more States of a single ambassador to one receiving State (Article 6 of the Convention). When the United Kingdom and Mongolia agreed in 1963 to exchange ambassadors, the UK head of mission to China (then chargé d'affaires *en titre*) was also appointed as British ambassador to Ulan Bator. The Mongolian ambassador to Poland was also accredited as Mongolian ambassador to the United Kingdom. Following the recognition by the United Kingdom in 1992 of a number of former Soviet Republics as independent States, eight of these were initially covered by cross-accreditation of the UK ambassador in Moscow.[21] Both forms of multiple accreditation have **7.38**

---

[21] Hansard HL Debs, 5 February 1992, col 271.

long been in use in diplomatic relations. The first presents no special problems, since ambassadors are not required to reside continuously in the receiving State and are permitted to establish a mission headed by a chargé d'affaires *ad interim* in each capital where they are non-resident. The sending State must under Article 5 give due notification of the proposed arrangement to both, or to all receiving States, and each of them may expressly object. Silence may however probably be taken as an indication of assent.

7.39 It is also permissible for an ambassador or diplomat concurrently to act as representative of his sending State to an international organization and this is common in Rome (where some ambassadors to Italy are also representatives to the Food and Agricultural Organization), in Vienna (concurrent representation to the International Atomic Energy Agency), and in Brussels (concurrent representation to the European Union and/or to NATO). And in London many diplomats are also their country's representative to the International Maritime Organization.

7.40 For practical reasons the second form of multiple accreditation is used much less frequently. The arrangement can only work well where the States sending a single ambassador have close political relations since otherwise the ambassador will find it difficult to act in the interests of both and the diplomatic message sent may be confusing. There may well be problems of confidentiality of archives and of information reported and—except where the arrangement is a merely temporary one—there may be a fear among the participant States of loss of sovereignty or prestige. Sharing an ambassador may however offer advantages of economy in the case of small States which are close both geographically and in political outlook—there is for example in London a diplomatic mission which represents a number of separate Eastern Caribbean States. European Union Member States in a number of capitals outside the Union have what are termed co-location projects in which premises as well as certain functions of reporting and protection are shared, but these do not involve the appointment of a single ambassador. These joint enterprises among Member States are described in Chapter 22, paragraph 22.105. Details of the European Union External Action Service which works in close cooperation with embassies of Member States are described at paragraphs 22.27 *et seq.*

Control of the Size and Location of Diplomatic Missions

7.41 A further possible limitation on the right of a State freely to appoint staff of its diplomatic mission is the right of a receiving State, under Article 11 of the Vienna Convention on Diplomatic Relations, to require that the size of the mission should be limited to what it considers 'reasonable and normal, having regard to circumstances and conditions in the receiving State and to the needs of the particular mission'. Specific agreements between States as to the size of the mission are highly exceptional, and the power to limit the size of a mission is in practice used only where relations with the sending State are strained or there is concern about abuse such as espionage. One well-known case was the ceiling imposed by the United Kingdom in 1971 on the embassy and other agencies of the Soviet Union following the expulsion by Sir Alec Douglas-Home, then British Foreign Secretary, of 105 Soviet diplomats and other officials for 'inadmissible activities' (the standard euphemism for espionage). The UK maintained that the Soviet Union had no 'need' for staff beyond the numbers who were left after the expulsions since those expelled had not been performing diplomatic functions, and on each subsequent occasion when a Soviet official was expelled for 'inadmissible activities' the ceiling was reduced by one. This action was followed by the placing of reciprocal limits on the British embassy in Moscow.[22]

The United States Congress also sought in 1985 to place a ceiling on the Soviet diplomatic mission in Washington so as to achieve parity with the numbers in the US embassy in Moscow. On this occasion however the Soviet Union responded to the US expulsions by requiring the removal of junior staff who were Soviet nationals, so that the US were forced, in order to comply with the new ceiling, to send US nationals as chauffeurs and cleaners to Moscow instead of as diplomatic staff.[23]   **7.42**

The likelihood of retaliation together with the unpredictability of the form which it may take has therefore meant that in spite of publicly stated determination by a number of States to make more use of the power to place ceilings on foreign embassy numbers in order to limit abuse of diplomatic immunity,[24] the power has in fact rarely been used.   **7.43**

A further possible control of foreign embassies lies in the prohibition on the sending State, under Article 12 of the Vienna Convention on Diplomatic Relations, from establishing offices forming part of the mission in 'localities' away from where the mission is established unless prior express consent has been given. The general practice is for embassies to be set up in the capital or seat of government of the receiving State and to follow it if it moves. Where the government of the receiving State is situated in more than one city (for example The Hague and Amsterdam in the case of the Netherlands), embassies   **7.44**

---

[22] See J Dickie, *Inside the Foreign Office*, ch IX 'Spies and Diplomacy', at 203–8.
[23] (1981–8) *DUSPIL* 910.
[24] See in particular the 1985 UK Government Review of the Vienna Convention on Diplomatic Relations, Cmnd 9497, at paras 28–32.

will normally follow the location of the ministry of foreign affairs because of the requirement that they should conduct official business with that ministry unless there is special agreement otherwise. There may be political or geographical restrictions on embassy location (as, for example, with Jerusalem and with the Holy See). There may be local requirements—for example where the receiving State moves its capital as Brazil, Nigeria, Germany, and Burma (Myanmar) have all done in recent decades. The United States permits foreign embassies to maintain in New York a single commercial or financial diplomatic officer in offices forming part of their mission premises. In large States there are of course likely to be foreign consulates in cities outside the capital and there is no bar under international law to other States setting up commercial offices, information offices, tourist offices, cultural centres, or libraries in other cities or towns in the receiving State—but these will not be accepted as part of the diplomatic mission except with express consent.

Chargés d'Affaires

7.45 A distinction must be drawn between chargés d'affaires accredited to ministers of foreign affairs, already mentioned as forming the third class of heads of mission under Article 14 of the Vienna Convention on Diplomatic Relations, and chargés d'affaires *ad interim* who are appointed to act provisionally as head of a mission. The former were sometimes known as chargés d'affaires *en pied* or as chargés d'affaires *en titre* and, as already indicated, they have almost vanished from diplomatic practice as the appointment of ambassadors has become entirely general. An exceptional example of this generally obsolete practice however took place in the Federal Republic of Yugoslavia in 1992 where as a sign of displeasure at that State's role in the break-up of Yugoslavia, many States withdrew their ambassadors from Belgrade and replaced them with chargés d'affaires *en titre*.

7.46 Chargés d'affaires *ad interim*, who are not formally accredited either to Heads of State or to ministers of foreign affairs, are by contrast frequent appointments. Article 19 of the Vienna Convention specifies that they should be appointed when the post of head of mission is vacant or the head is unable to perform his functions. It is usual diplomatic practice for an ambassador to take his leave and for there to be a gap before the arrival of his successor during which a chargé d'affaires *ad interim* will act as head of mission, and a chargé may also be appointed when the ambassador is recalled home for consultations or is abroad on leave, seriously ill, or even held hostage. When in 1971 the British ambassador to Uruguay was kidnapped by the Tupamaros guerrillas, however, the UK government declined for presentational reasons to appoint a chargé d'affaires *ad interim*.[25]

The appointment of a chargé d'affaires *ad interim* must be notified to the ministry of foreign affairs—usually by the departing head of mission but, if he is unable to do so, by the ministry of foreign affairs of the sending State. The post may be held only by a member of the diplomatic staff. If no member of the diplomatic staff is present in the receiving State, the Vienna Convention permits a member of the administrative and technical staff, with the consent of the receiving State, to be in charge of the administrative affairs of the mission (for example securing the embassy premises, property, and archives). Such an individual would however not perform diplomatic functions. An unusual example of this occurred when a member of the administrative and technical staff took over as chargé d'affaires in the British embassy in Tirana in 1997 having sent the memorable telegram to the Foreign Office, 'Chargé has been stabbed. I have assumed charge.' **7.47**

Letters of Credence or Credentials

The form of credentials used in the United Kingdom in the case of foreign sovereigns is that of a *Lettre de Cabinet*,[26] in the following terms: **7.48**

> Sir My Brother and dear Cousin/Madam My Sister and dear Cousin/Your Highness,
>
> Being desirous to maintain without interruption the relations of friendship and good understanding which happily subsist between the two Crowns, I have selected My Trusty and Well-beloved xx to proceed to the Court of Your Majesty in the character of My Ambassador Extraordinary and Plenipotentiary/Envoy Extraordinary and Minister Plenipotentiary.
>
> Having already had ample experience of xx's talents and zeal for My service, I doubt not that he/she will fulfil the important duties of his/her Mission in such a manner as to merit Your approbation and esteem, and to prove himself/herself worthy of this new mark of My confidence.
>
> I request that You will give entire credence to all that xx shall have occasion to communicate to You in My name, more especially when he/she shall express to Your Majesty/Your Highness My cordial wishes for Your Happiness, and shall assure You of the invariable attachment and highest esteem with which I am,
>
> Manu Regia

---

[25] G Jackson, *People's Prison* (London: Faber & Faber, 1973).
[26] The most usual form of communication in a familiar style between monarchs regarding themselves as equals.

Sir My Brother/Sister

Your Majesty's/Your Highness's

Good Sister

ELIZABETH R.

Buckingham Palace

May 2015

To My Good Brother/Sister the King/Queen of [Country]

His/Her Highness [Country]

7.49 Or, in the case of a republic, a *Lettre de Chancellerie*,[27] in such terms as these:

Elizabeth the Second, by the Grace of God of the United Kingdom of Great Britain and Northern Ireland and of Her other Realms and Territories Queen, Head of the Commonwealth, Defender of the Faith.

To His/Her Excellency,

President of the Republic of xxx.

Sendeth Greeting!

Our Good Friend! Being desirous to maintain, without interruption, the relations of friendship and good understanding which so happily subsist between Our Realm and the Republic of xx, We have made choice of Our Trusty and Well-beloved xx. to reside with You in the character of Our Ambassador Extraordinary and Plenipotentiary.

The experience which We have had of xx's talents and zeal for Our service assures Us that the selection We have made will be perfectly agreeable to You; and that he/she will discharge the important duties of his/her Mission in such a manner as to merit Your approbation and esteem and to prove himself/herself worthy of this new mark of Our confidence.

We therefore request that You will give entire credence to all that xx shall communicate to You in Our name, more especially when he/she shall renew to You the assurances of the lively interest which We take in everything that affects the welfare and prosperity of the Republic of xxx.

And so We commend You to the protection of the Almighty.

Given at Our Court of St. James's, the ...... xx .... day of xx .... Two Thousand and Fifteen in the Sixty-Fifth Year of Our Reign.

Your Good Friend,

(Signed) ELIZABETH R.

7.50 The language of such documents is a matter of 'common form'. The heritage of elaborate phraseology has been retained in the formal usage of the United

---

[27] The most formal communication from a monarch preceded by the titles of the sending sovereign, it is often countersigned by the Foreign Minister. The *lettre de chancellerie* has several uses but is most often used for transmitting the credentials or recall of an ambassador. Typically used when the monarch is communicating with the president of a republic.

Kingdom and of some other European countries, where it is felt to express with clarity and due emphasis ideas which have remained basic to diplomacy throughout the centuries. But while each country will tend to evolve its own characteristic style of address and some prefer simpler forms better reflecting contemporary moods and customs, the final phrase asking that credit may be given to all that the agent may say in the name of his sovereign or government is of universal application. This is what constitutes the essential part of a Letter of Credence.

Letters of Recall

Letters of Recall may take the form of a *Lettre de Cabinet* as follows: 7.51

Sir My Brother/Madam My Sister and dear Cousin

Having need elsewhere for the services of My Trusty and Well-beloved xx, who has lately resided at Your Majesty's Court in the character of My Ambassador Extraordinary and Plenipotentiary/Envoy Extraordinary and Minister Plenipotentiary I cannot omit to inform You of the termination of his mission in that capacity.

Having Myself had ample reason to be satisfied with the zeal, ability, and fidelity with which xx has executed My orders on all occasions during his/her Mission, I trust that Your Majesty will also have found his/her conduct deserving of Your approbation and esteem, and in this pleasing confidence I avail myself of the present opportunity to renew to You the assurances of the invariable friendship and cordial esteem with which I am,

Sir My Brother/Madam My Sister,

Your Majesty's Good Sister

Elizabeth R.

Buckingham Palace

July 2015

To My Good Brother/Sister and dear Cousin The King/Queen of [Country]

Or of a *Lettre de Chancellerie*, as follows: 7.52

Elizabeth the Second, by the Grace of God of the United Kingdom of Great Britain and Northern Ireland and of Her other Realms and Territories Queen, Head of the Commonwealth, Defender of the Faith.

To the President of the Republic of xxx.

Sendeth Greeting!

Our Good Friend!

Having need elsewhere for the services of Our Trusty and Well-beloved xx, who has for some time resided with You in the character of Our Ambassador Extraordinary and Plenipotentiary, We have thought fit to notify to You his/her Recall.

We are Ourselves so satisfied with the zeal, ability, and fidelity with which xx. has executed Our orders on all occasions during his/her Mission that We trust his/her conduct will also have merited Your approbation, and in this pleasing confidence

We avail Ourselves of the opportunity to renew to You the assurances of Our constant friendship, and of Our earnest wishes for the welfare and prosperity of the Republic of xxx.

And so We commend You to the protection of the Almighty.

Given at Our Court of St. James's, the .... day of .... Two Thousand and Fifteen in the Sixty-Fifth Year of Our Reign.

Your Good Friend,

(Signed) Elizabeth R.

7.53 A number of concrete examples of credentials etc appearing in earlier editions of this work have been omitted. Their value as guidance to present-day practice has expired and they took up a lot of space. This is also true of the following *Lettre de Chancellerie* but it would be a pity for such a jewel to be lost sight of.

Par la Grâce de Dieu,

Nous Alexandre III, Empereur et Autocrate de Toutes les Russies, de Moscou, Kiow, Wladimir, Novgorod, Tsar de Casan, Tsar d'Astrakhan, Tsar de Pologne, Tsar de Sibérie, Tsar de la Chersonese Taurique, Tsar de la Géorgie, Seigneur de Plescow et Grand Duc de Smolensk, de Lithuanie, Volhynie, Podolie et de la Finlande; Duc d'Estonie, de Livonie, de Courlande et Semigalle, de Samogitie, Bialostock, Carelie, Twer, Jugotie, Perm, Viatka, Bolgarie et d'autres; Seigneur et Grand Duc de Novgorod-inférieur, de Czarnigow, Riasan, Polotzk, Rostow, Jaroslaw, Beloosersk, Oudor, Obdor-Condie, Witepsk, Mstislaw; Dominateur de toute la contrée du Nord; Seigneur d'Ibérie, de la Cartalinie, de la Cabardie et de la province d'Arménie; Prince Héréditaire et Souverain des Princes de Circassie et d'autres Princes montagnards; Seigneur de Turkestan; Successeur de Norvège, Duc de Schleswig-Holstein, de Stormarn, de Dithmarsen et d'Oldenbourg, etc., etc., etc.

A la Très-Haute et Très-Puissante Princesse Victoire Ière, par la Grâce de Dieu, Reine du Royaume-Uni de la Grande-Bretagne et d'Irlande, Impératrice des Indes, etc. salut!

Très-Haute et Très-Puissante Reine, très-chère Soeur et très-aimée parente! Nous avons jugé à propos de rappeler Notre Conseiller Privé et Chevalier Baron Arthur Mohrenheim du poste de Notre Ambassadeur Extraordinaire et Plénipotentiaire qu'il a occupé jusqu'ici près Votre Majesté. En informant Votre Majesté de cette détermination, Nous La prions de vouloir bien congédier gracieusement Notre susdit Ambassadeur, étant persuadé, qu'en se conformant dans l'exercice de ses fonctions aux instructions que Nous lui avons données, il aura déployé tout son zèle pour entretenir les liens qui subsistent entre Nos deux Cours, et aura su meriter la bienveillance de Votre Majesté. Sur ce, Nous prions Dieu qu'Il ait Votre Majesté en Sa sainte et digne garde.

Donné à Pétersbourg, le 8 février, 1884, de Notre Règne la troisième année.

De Votre Majesté l'affectionné Frère et Cousin,

Alexandre.

(Countersigned) N. Giers.

A Sa Majesté la Reine du Royaume-Uni de la Grande-Bretagne et d'Irlande, Impératrice des Indes.

Full Powers

A diplomatic agent to whom a particular negotiation is entrusted for the con- **7.54**
clusion of a treaty or international agreement, or to take other formal action in
respect of the treaty or agreement, requires as a general rule a special authorization, called a Full Power,[28] from the head of the State whom he represents; or,
it may be, from its government, if the proposed treaty arrangement is to be
between governments.

The use of Full Powers has a long history going back through the Middle Ages **7.55**
to the Roman *plena potestas* conferred on a procurator for legal transactions. It
became in due course an established rule that only the bestowal of Full Powers
gave an ambassador authority to commit his sovereign. The object of conferring
them was to be able to dispense, as far as possible, with the long delays needed
in earlier times for referring problems back to higher authority. Their use today
is a formal recognition of the necessity for absolute confidence in the authority
and standing of the negotiator.[29]

In the case of a bilateral treaty, it is usual for the Full Powers of each signatory **7.56**
to be exhibited at the time of signature; in the case of a multilateral treaty, the
duty of examining the Full Powers devolves by default upon the host government, viz, that of the State where the treaty is signed, or upon the international
organization under whose auspices the treaty is concluded. It is not, however,
always the case that an actual exchange or deposit of the original documents will
take place. In some circumstances an inspection will suffice, and certified copies

---

[28] See Chapter 31, paragraph 31.11.

[29] A classic illustration of the importance of a clear definition of full powers and their relation to the instructions given to the negotiator is afforded by the events which led to Cardinal Richelieu's refusal to ratify the Treaty of Regensburg in 1630. His grounds for refusal were that the two French representatives, whose Full Powers had been intended apparently to apply only within the limits of their instructions, had gone far beyond what they were authorized to do, and had thus placed their sovereign in an unacceptable position. But it appeared that the Cardinal's thinking had changed with changed circumstances in the three months between the initial despatch of the negotiators and the opening of the discussions; and that the successive instructions he sent them proved more con-fusing than helpful. For a detailed reconstruction of the whole story and its background, see 'A *Cause Célèbre* in the History of Treaty-Making: The Refusal to Ratify the Peace Treaty of Regensburg in 1630', by D P O'Connell, in the *BYIL* (1968) 71. Professor O'Connell shows how this and other failures to ratify treaties in the first half of the seventeenth century led to greatly intensified scrutiny of the credentials and Full Powers of delegates to negotiations. 'Out of this caution', he concludes, 'was born the modern international law of ratification.'

will be retained, for example where the agent is operating under a general Full Powers not limited to the particular negotiation. Normally Full Powers, where given ad hoc, having served the purpose for which they were intended, are left with the government of the State, or with the international organization, where signature of the treaty takes place, and in this event they are preserved with the signed treaty in the archives of the State or organization concerned.

7.57 Today the Full Powers issued to representatives for such purposes as the negotiation and signature of a treaty vary greatly in form, according to the particular constitution or the settled practice of the country which issues them. The form used in the United Kingdom for the signature of a treaty or convention between Heads of State is that of Letters Patent, as shown in paragraph 7.58, and the wording follows in general that of the past. Many countries adopt a similar formal style; in the case of others it may be simpler, and the phraseology employed may vary considerably, although a template for Full Powers is provided by the United Nations Treaty Secretariat and many States follow this model. Differences may exist also according to the degree of importance ascribed to the treaty, or whether it is to be concluded between Heads of State or, on the other hand, between governments. The essential feature of all such documents is that they should show by their terms that the representative to whom they are issued is invested with all necessary authority on the part of the State concerned to take part in the negotiations pending, and to conclude and sign, subject if necessary to ratification, the treaty instrument which may result from these negotiations.

7.58 An example of the form of special Full Powers issued by the Court of St James's for the purpose of a treaty or convention between Heads of State is as follows:

> Elizabeth the Second, by the Grace of God of the United Kingdom of Great Britain and Northern Ireland and of Her other Realms and Territories Queen, Head of the Commonwealth, Defender of the Faith, &c., &c., To all and singular to whom these Presents shall come,
>
> Greeting!
>
> We hereby invest Paul Spencer Hailston, a Policy Officer in the European Union Department of the Department for International Development with Full Powers to sign, on Our behalf in respect of Our United Kingdom of Great Britain and Northern Ireland, the Agreement amending the Partnership Agreement signed in Cotonou on 23 June 2003 between the African, Caribbean and Pacific Group of States of the one part, and the European Community and its Member States, of the other part.
>
> In Witness Whereof We have caused Our Great Seal to be affixed to these Presents, which We have signed with Our Royal Hand.
>
> Given at Our Court of Saint James's, the first day of July in the Year of Our Lord Two Thousand and Five and in the Fifty-fourth Year of Our Reign.

The following is an example of the form of a general Full Power such as is at **7.59** present held[30] by the Secretary of State for Foreign and Commonwealth Affairs, ministers of State, parliamentary under-secretaries, and the permanent representatives at the United Nations and the European Union in order to enable them to negotiate and sign any treaty on behalf of the United Kingdom:

> Elizabeth the Second, by the Grace of God of the United Kingdom of Great Britain and Northern Ireland and of Her other Realms and Territories Queen, Head of the Commonwealth, Defender of the Faith, &c., &c., To all and singular to whom these Presents shall come,
>
> Greeting!
>
> We hereby invest The Rt. Hon. The Lord Maude of Horsham, Our Minister of State for Trade and Investment, with Full Powers to sign, on behalf of Our United Kingdom of Great Britain and Northern Ireland, subject, if necessary, to ratification, acceptance or approval, all treaties and other international instruments.
>
> In Witness Whereof We have caused Our Great Seal to be affixed to these Presents, which We have signed with Our Royal Hand.
>
> Given at Our Court of Saint James's, the thirty-first day of July in the Year of Our Lord Two Thousand and Fifteen and in the Sixty-fourth Year of Our Reign.
>
> (Signature) Elizabeth R.

In the case of an agreement between governments, an example of the form of **7.60** Full Power issued by Her Majesty's Secretary of State for Foreign and Commonwealth Affairs is as follows:

> Nic Hailey, British High Commissioner to Kenya is hereby granted Full Powers to sign, on behalf of the Government of the United Kingdom of Great Britain and Northern Ireland, the Agreement between the Government of the United Kingdom of Great Britain and Northern Ireland and the Government of the Republic of Kenya Concerning Defence Cooperation.
>
> In Witness Whereof I, Philip Hammond, Her Majesty's Principal Secretary of State of Foreign and Commonwealth Affairs, have signed these presents.
>
> Signed and sealed at the Foreign and Commonwealth Office, London, the thirtieth day of November, two thousand and fifteen.
>
> (Seal)
>
> (Signature of Secretary of State.)

French examples of Full Powers issued for the purpose of a treaty: **7.61**

> *Le Président de la République Française,*
>
> *Vu l'article 52 de la Constitution*
>
> *Autorise*

---

[30] See Chapter **30**, paragraph **30**.10.

Monsieur Pierre Sellal, Ambassadeur, Représentant permanent de la France auprès de l'Union Européenne à Bruxelles,

à signer

l'Accord de partenariat économique APE) entre les Etats de l'Afrique de l'Ouest, la CEDEAO et l'UEMOA, d'une part, et l'Union Européenne

d'autre part,

Fait à Paris, le 6 janvier 2015

(Seal)

(Signed) François Hollande

Président de la République française:

Le Premier Ministre,

(Signed) Manuel Valls

Le Ministre des Affaires étrangères et du Développement international,

(Signed) Laurent Fabius,

And

Le Président de la République Française,

Vu l'article 52 de la Constitution

Autorise

Madame Sylvie Bermann, Ambassadrice de France en Chine,

à signer au nom de la République Française

Le Traité de l'OMPI (Organisation mondiale de la propriété intellectuelle)

sur les interprétations et exécutions audiovisuelles, lors de la Conference diplomatique sur la protection des interprétations et exécutions audiovisuelles,

Fait à Paris, le 25 juin 2012.

(Seal)

(Signed) François Hollande

Président de la République

Le Premier Ministre

(Signed) Jean Marc Ayrault

Le Ministre des Affaires étrangères,

(Signed) Laurent Fabius

7.62 A United States example:

I invest Strobe Talbott, Deputy Secretary of State, or in his absence, John C. Kornblum, Assistant Secretary of State for European and Canadian Affairs, with full power and authority for and in the name of the Government of the United States of America to sign the Treaty Between the United States of America and the Republic of Latvia on Mutual Legal Assistance in Criminal

Matters, together with any related documents, the said Treaty to be transmitted to the President of the United States of America for his ratification by and with the advice and consent of the Senate of the United States of America.

IN TESTIMONY WHEREOF, I have hereunto set my hand and caused the seal of the Department of State to be affixed at the city of Washington, in the District of Columbia, this tenth day of June, 1997.

[signature Madeleine Albright]

Secretary of State

[SEAL]

8

THE APPOINTMENT AND FUNCTIONS OF CONSULS

Joanne Foakes and Eileen Denza

8.1 Consuls have over recent decades become closely assimilated to diplomats in the manner of their appointment and in many of the functions they perform, though not in the methods whereby they carry out these functions. The origins and history of consuls and consular posts are however quite distinct from those of diplomats and diplomatic missions. In modern practice, consuls are appointed by the government of a State to protect the practical, legal, and commercial interests of its own nationals in another State, and their contacts for this purpose with the host State are with regional, local, or police authorities rather than with the ministry of foreign affairs or other departments of central government.

Historical Background

8.2 Consular relations between countries have been established since ancient times and certain aspects of modern consular functions can be traced back to Greek and Roman institutions of that time. The ancient Greek city states applied a system under which foreigners living in Greece were permitted to

120

choose representatives to act as intermediaries between them and local Greek authorities. Greek settlers in Egypt and elsewhere were from the sixth century BC permitted a similar privilege. In the third century BC Rome created the post of *praetor peregrinus* to deal with disputes between foreigners, or between foreigners and Roman citizens, by applying the *ius gentium* (law of nations) which covered both foreign laws and commercial practice. Comparable appointments, for which the term 'consul' came to be used, were devised in Byzantium. At first such appointments entailed for the most part a judicial responsibility for the foreign merchant community exercised by local residents specially appointed for the purpose. Later, *consules missi*, the first of whom were probably Venetians, were appointed and sent from abroad to perform the same function. A similar system operated in China long before the opening of China to the West in the nineteenth century.

In the sixteenth century consuls began to be despatched by national governments, but as representatives of their countries on the national plane they were soon overshadowed by diplomatic missions. Two hundred years later, with the expansion of industry and maritime trade, the usefulness and the separate character of consular functions were reasserted. Commercial and consular treaties and national legislation began to make precise provision for consular functions, privileges, and immunities. A Treaty concluded in 1860 between the United Kingdom and France was based on the principle of free trade and included a 'most-favoured-nation clause' ensuring that privileges given by either party to other States were automatically extended to the other party, and treaties on commerce and navigation on similar lines became widespread. In part through this mechanism, a greater uniformity was gradually established in regard to consular functions and privileges. **8.3**

By the early twentieth century, consular relations, privileges, and immunities were governed by a very limited number of rules of customary international law, by a large network of bilateral consular conventions, and by a few regional conventions such as the Havana Convention of 1928. The Harvard Research Draft of 1932 on the legal position and functions of consuls (1932), based on detailed research into practice, provided a useful basis for the Draft Articles on Consular Intercourse and Immunities submitted in 1957 by Zourek, as Special Rapporteur, to the UN International Law Commission and those in turn formed the starting point for the UN Conference which in 1963 adopted the Vienna Convention on Consular Relations (VCCR).[1] This Convention, like its predecessor the 1961 Vienna Convention on Diplomatic Relations (VCDR), **8.4**

---

[1] 596 UNTS 261.

is now central to international practice. But in comparison to the Diplomatic Convention the provisions of the Consular Convention were less a codification of long-established rules and more progressive development, and the régime it sets out is less uniformly applied. Article 73 of the 1963 Convention permits existing bilateral consular treaties to be kept in force and allows parties to the Convention to conclude new 'international agreements confirming or supplementing or extending or amplifying the provisions thereof'. Parties to the Convention—of which there were 177 in 2016—have taken full advantage of this provision. In the early years of the Convention's operation, for example, bilateral agreements with and between Communist States systematically granted a higher level of personal immunity to consuls.

Consular Relations and Consular Posts

8.5 Article 2 of the VCCR provides that consular relations between States take place by mutual consent and that consent to diplomatic relations implies, unless otherwise stated, consent to consular relations.

8.6 Individual consular posts may be established only with the consent of the receiving State. Article 4.2 specifies that the seat of each consular post, its classification, and the consular district all require the consent of the receiving State, and a change in any of these elements also requires approval. Consular work in the capital is in fact often carried out by a consular section of the embassy, and as both Vienna Conventions make clear, it may be carried out by diplomatic staff. In order to combine flexibility with economy many governments have now unified their diplomatic and consular services administratively in a single overseas service, making it possible for an officer to hold diplomatic or consular appointments alternatively or concurrently, as circumstances may require. An officer may for example hold at one time dual posts as counsellor and consul-general, or as first secretary and consul.

8.7 As discussed in Chapter **10**, the severance of diplomatic relations need not automatically lead to a breach in consular relations, and consular relations may be established as a precursor of full diplomatic relations. Consular functions may also be carried out on behalf of a State which has no permanent mission in another State by a third State as protecting Power and by officers within the Interests Section of the embassy of that Power. Where however either the sending or the receiving State does not recognize the other as a State or does not recognize its government, it is legally possible for existing consular relations to continue because of the fact that the consul deals not with the government but with regional or local authorities. The United Kingdom, for example, continued to maintain a consular post in Taiwan after its recognition in 1950 of the government of the People's Republic of China, and in Hanoi, where it did not recognize North Vietnam as a State. The United States also sought to maintain its consulate in Hanoi, but in their case the Vietminh authorities refused to recognize it on the ground that it violated the sovereignty of the Democratic Republic of Vietnam and it was closed a year later. There are, in the absence of mutual recognition, specific problems in establishing initial consular relations or posts and in replacing the head of a consular post because of the normal practice whereby the head of post is admitted to the exercise of his functions by an authorization from the receiving State usually described as an *exequatur*. This is set out in Articles 11 and 12 of the VCCR which make clear that the head of a consular post is to be provided by the sending State with a Commission or similar instrument which is transmitted through the diplomatic channel and normally leads to issue of an *exequatur* by the receiving State. Clearly this procedure cannot be carried out in the absence of recognition or of diplomatic relations. In the cases of Taiwan and Hanoi, the UK government simply made fresh consular appointments without any request for an *exequatur*. A similar procedure has been followed by a number of States following the invasion of Northern Cyprus by Turkey and the establishment of the Turkish Republic of Northern Cyprus—generally unrecognized as a State. The United States, the United Kingdom, Germany, and others provide services to their own nationals in Northern Cyprus through consular offices based in the Turkish sector of Nicosia, without seeking *exequaturs* either from Turkey or from the Turkish Republic of Northern Cyprus.[2] Such a device, however, requires at least the passive acquiescence of the authorities of the receiving State in order to succeed, and whether this is forthcoming will depend on political considerations.

As a general rule it is necessary to be recognized as a State in order to establish or maintain consular posts abroad. A special case is the Hong Kong Special Administrative Region which, though not claiming to be a State, has by virtue of the Sino-British Joint Declaration of 1984 a high degree of autonomy and in particular the right to independent conduct of its foreign trade and commercial affairs. The Joint Declaration envisaged the establishment of official Hong Kong delegations in foreign countries performing a limited range of commercial consular functions and headed by a Commissioner. The Hong Kong government now operates in places such as Brussels, London, Geneva, Washington, New York, and Tokyo with economic and trade offices (ETOs) carrying out functions of trade promotion and assistance for inward investment in Hong

8.8

---

[2] L T Lee and J B Quigley, *Consular Law and Practice* (3rd edn, Oxford: Oxford University Press, 2008) 102.

Kong. Because Hong Kong is not a State or a party to the VCCR it is necessary for special provision for its status, privileges, and immunities to be made in the national laws of States receiving ETOs, either by specific legislation or in some cases on an administrative basis.[3]

Consular Titles and Appointment

8.9 Consuls are divided into two broad categories: career consuls and honorary consuls. The first contains three classes: consuls-general, consuls, and vice-consuls. Other titles have been used, but are liable to give rise to dispute or not be recognized. Career consuls are generally nationals of the sending State and are salaried, career government servants. Under Article 57 of the VCCR they are debarred from carrying on for personal profit any professional or commercial activity in the receiving State. Honorary consuls may also be appointed in any of the three classes mentioned above. The title of consular agent is generally used in state practice to describe an honorary consul. Honorary consuls are usually resident in the receiving State with business interests of their own, or some other private occupation. They may have no previous consular experience or training and can be nationals of the receiving or the sending State or persons holding dual nationality. But as with diplomatic agents, the express consent of the receiving State is under Article 22 of the VCCR necessary for the appointment of a national of the receiving State (including dual nationals). Honorary consuls perform only limited duties and will receive fees, or an expense allowance, instead of a regular government salary. They may be appointed by the head of the ministry of foreign affairs of the sending State and they may be placed under the supervision of another consular post headed by a career consular officer.[4]

8.10 Under Article 11 of the VCCR, the head of a consular post must be provided by the sending State with a document, usually termed a Commission, which certifies his appointment and category as well as the consular district and the seat of the consular post. This document is transmitted to the government of the receiving State through the diplomatic or other appropriate channel. In contrast to the position for the head of a diplomatic mission it is not necessary under international practice or under the VCCR to seek advance approval for a named individual, although some treaties—in particular those concluded by

---

[3] See statement by the Minister of State, Foreign and Commonwealth Office, introducing the Hong Kong Economic and Trade Office Bill to provide for the status of ETOs in the UK, Hansard HC Debs, 31 October 1996, cols 795–7. See also Chapter **34**.42.

[4] For more detail on the distinction between career consular officers and honorary consuls as applied in practice, see Lee and Quigley, *Consular Law and Practice*, at 32–7 and 505–28.

the Soviet Union and later by Russia—made provision for this. Under Article 12 the head of the consular post is admitted to the exercise of his functions by an authorization from the receiving State usually called an *exequatur*. This may take whatever form the practice or regulations of the receiving State prescribe. The date of the grant of the *exequatur*, or the date on which the officer is provisionally admitted to the exercise of his functions, if this is earlier, determines his seniority in each class of the local consular corps.

Members of the consular staff, other than the head of post, may be freely **8.11** appointed by the sending State, but their names, categories, and class must be notified to the receiving State. The practice of some States is that members of consular staffs should also receive *exequaturs*, although this is not required by the Vienna Convention. In most capitals it is sufficient for notification of new consular appointments to be made on a prescribed form.

The receiving State may, upon notice of the intention to appoint a consular **8.12** officer, refuse to grant an *exequatur*. As in the parallel case of refusal of *agrément* for the head of a diplomatic mission, the receiving State is under no obligation to give reasons. Enquiries even in private are generally avoided, since any statement of reasons is liable to cause further friction. Under Article 23 of the VCCR the receiving State may at any time declare a consular officer to be *persona non grata*, whereupon it is normal for the sending government to recall the officer. The procedures and practices for such an eventuality are the same as those applied under Article 9 of the Vienna Convention on Diplomatic Relations when a diplomatic agent is declared *persona non grata* or another member of the mission declared unacceptable.[5]

While consular functions are carried out by the head of the consular post and **8.13** other consular officers, administrative and technical services for the post are provided by consular employees. Domestic services such as cooking, cleaning, gardening, driving, and security protection are provided by the members of the service staff. All those are members of the consular post. Those employed privately by any member of the consular post are termed members of the private staff, and they are not themselves members of the consular post.[6]

The size of consular staffs may under Article 20 of the VCCR be required by the **8.14** receiving State to be kept within limits considered by it to be reasonable and normal, having regard to circumstances and to the needs of the particular post. The Ethiopian government, for instance, in 1935 voiced its objection at the

---

[5] See Chapter **10**, paragraph **10.18**.
[6] See Art 1 VCCR.

League of Nations Assembly to Italy stationing a consul with a guard ninety-strong in a place where there were no Italian nationals, and suggested that this was not only an abuse of privilege but was also aimed at the penetration and invasion of Ethiopia. In 1961, owing to the sharply deteriorating diplomatic situation, the Cuban government called upon the United States for the mutual reduction, within 48 hours, of diplomatic and consular staff to eleven in the respective capitals. The United States embassy and consulate in Havana employed 300 and had been issuing thousands of visas every month for entry into the United States. The Cuban request was, however, overtaken by a general rupture of relations.

8.15 As to the 'needs' of a particular post there are often differences as to what numbers are required by circumstances. These circumstances will include the number of foreign residents, students, visitors, tourists, businessmen, and ships for which the consulate may have to provide services, as well as the proximity of other consular posts of the sending State. A concept developed by the Soviet Union and applied by other mainly Communist States was that of parity of representation—both as to the number of posts and the number of staff within them, but this notion is now largely discredited as being inappropriate to the proper justification for the maintenance of overseas consular representation. The practices developed within the context of Article 11 of the Vienna Convention on Diplomatic Relations may be applied with due regard to the differences in purposes and functions of diplomatic and consular posts. Where ceilings are called for or unilaterally imposed for wider political reasons—for example against the Soviet Union during the Cold War—they are likely to be applied to both diplomatic and consular missions.

End of Consular Functions

8.16 Chapter **10** described the circumstances in which a diplomatic mission is terminated or withdrawn and the legal framework applicable to each of those cases. Many of those circumstances and legal rules apply also to consular posts, consular officers, and other members of a consular post, although most of the formal and protocol rules do not apply and the terminology is different. There is, for example, no procedure for the appointment of a chargé d'affaires *ad interim* as head of a consular post and it is most unusual to send a consul on a special mission. Article 25 of the VCCR provides that the functions of a member of a consular post come to an end on notification to that effect by the sending to the receiving State, on withdrawal by the receiving State of the *exequatur* (for the head of post), or on notification by the receiving State (for others) that it has ceased to consider them as members of the consular staff. The functions of a member of a consular post, however, also terminate if the consular post is recalled whether on a temporary or a permanent basis, if consular relations are severed or on the disappearance of the sending or the receiving State.

Article 26 of the VCCR imposes obligations on the receiving State to grant, **8.17** even in case of armed conflict, facilities for departure to members of the consular post and members of the private staff (other than nationals of the receiving State) as well as their families. It is closely based on Article 44 of the Vienna Convention on Diplomatic Relations, but resolves some ambiguities in the latter provision. The Consular Convention includes the grant of time and facilities to prepare for departure, and the right to export property does not extend to property whose export was prohibited at the time of departure.

Temporary or permanent closure of an entire consular post, and total severance **8.18** of consular relations between sending and receiving States are regulated under Article 27 of the VCCR. This is closely based on Article 45 of the VCDR, but with the important difference that where a consular post is closed without severance of consular relations and the sending State has no diplomatic mission in the receiving State, provision is made for the protection of premises, property, and archives by another consular post of the sending State in the receiving State. The protecting consulate may—but only with the consent of the receiving State—also take over the exercise of consular functions in the district of the post which has been closed. The requirement for the receiving State to respect and protect consular premises and archives where consular relations are severed, and the possibility of entrusting premises, property, and archives as well as protection of interests to a protecting State acceptable to the receiving State apply as in the case of closure of a diplomatic mission under the VCDR.

The provision of consular services by one State on behalf of another is common **8.19** among countries of the Commonwealth. The United Kingdom, Canada, and Australia, with extensive overseas consular representation, have for many years carried out consular functions on behalf of smaller Commonwealth States, and there are also arrangements between Canada and Australia for the provision by each of consular services on behalf of the other in places where one maintains a consular post while the other does not.[7] Among Member States of the European Union, one aspect of the concept of citizenship of the European Union, established by the Treaty on European Union as amended by the Maastricht Treaty in 1993, was common diplomatic and consular protection arrangements for citizens of

---

[7] Exchange of Notes concerning the Sharing of Consular Services between the Ministers for External Affairs of Canada and Australia, Vancouver, 7 August 1986.

the European Union in third countries. This is now given effect by a Council Directive which provides in Article 1 that

> member states' embassies or consulates shall provide consular protection to unrepresented citizens on the same conditions as to their own nationals.

On proof of nationality, diplomatic and consular representations are required to treat an EU citizen seeking help as if he were one of their own nationals.[8]

8.20 Although as explained earlier the historical origins, the titles, and the status of consuls are different from those of diplomats, the distinction between the functions of consuls and those of diplomats is not clear cut. The essential difference between diplomatic and consular work is that, whereas the diplomat does business with or through the central government of the receiving State, the consul for the most part conducts official business only with local or municipal authorities. The nature of the individual consul's work varies to a much greater degree, as between different posts, than that of the individual diplomat. Consuls in a busy port, for example, may do little else but shipping work; whereas in another place they may be concerned mostly with problems created by fellow nationals in the receiving State as migrant workers, pilgrims, or tourists. Overall, however, it is the function of protection, in its broadest sense, which is the most important consular function, whereas in the case of diplomats the protective function is normally of less importance than the other major functions of negotiating with the receiving State and reporting to the sending State. Of course consuls are concerned with the furtherance of their country's interests and with the maintenance of satisfactory relations between their country and others, but in practical, day-to-day working terms rather than in the political sphere. Their functions quite often overlap with those of the diplomats in the embassy, but they are carried out at a different level and in a different way.

8.21 The distinction is perhaps most easily understood by contrasting the different aspects of the same matter which would fall to the consular and to the diplomatic post. If, for example, a national of the sending State is arrested, it falls to the local consul on being notified of the arrest, to visit him in prison, advise him how best to protect his interests, notify his relatives if he requests it, put him in touch with a local lawyer and an interpreter, attend any criminal proceedings, and perhaps repatriate him if he finds himself released without any funds. But if he complains that he has been held for several months without any charge being brought, or that he has been brutally treated by the police, and that there

---

[8] Council Directive (EU) 2015/637 of 20 April 2015 on the coordination and cooperation measures to facilitate consular protection for unrepresented citizens of the Union in third countries and repealing Decision 95/553/EC, OJ 28.12.95.

is no form of legal redress open to him, then it is likely that the embassy will under its powers of diplomatic protection be called upon to make representations on his behalf to the ministry of foreign affairs. If a merchant ship is detained in a local port because the crew are refusing to work until their arrears of wages are paid, or because the local police wish to conduct an investigation into some minor offence which is alleged to have happened on the vessel, it is for the consul to give assistance to try to settle the dispute, or to persuade the local authorities that proceedings in respect of the offence can better be taken when the ship has returned to its home port. But if such matters are causing repeated difficulty, it may be better to negotiate a consular or a shipping agreement between the sending and receiving States so as to reduce difficulty in the future, and this function will be carried out through the embassy which may propose negotiations to the ministry of foreign affairs. Diplomats protect their nationals in the general or collective sense or where some major issue of principle or possible breach of international law is involved, while the consul gives protection and practical assistance to individuals in a particular case.

Article 5 of the VCCR lists among consular functions 'furthering the develop- **8.22** ment of commercial, economic, cultural and scientific relations'. But now that the promotion of exports and the development of good trading relations is essential for the economic development of all countries, and indeed for the survival of some, a clear distinction can no longer be drawn between 'economic' and 'commercial' work. As a rule, of course, intergovernmental negotiation on general trading matters falls to the embassy, while it is the consul who, in his or her area, will give advice to the particular businessman who wants to meet local contacts such as chambers of commerce or trade associations with a view to exporting goods or setting up a local branch. (In the capital this will be done by the commercial department of the embassy.) But where the deal is of major national importance—for example the sale of European Airbuses to Iranair, US F-15 strike fighter aircraft to Saudi Arabia, or LEAP turbofan engines to China by a GE Aviation/Snecma joint (US/France) venture—the embassy will always be closely involved. Once again the distinction between the diplomatic and the consular function comes down to the level at which contact is made with the authorities of the receiving State.

Apart from the assisting of persons in trouble, reporting and political work, and **8.23** the promotion of commercial interests, most consular functions are basically administrative or legal in character. Among the more important of these administrative functions are:

- issue of passports to nationals of the sending State and visas or other entry documents for others wishing to visit the sending State;

- authentication of documents required under the law of the sending or the receiving State; assistance with repatriation of the body; and on succession and export of property matters on the death of a resident or visitor who is a national of the sending State;
- transmission of various kinds of legal document such as service of process relating to actions begun in the sending State and commissions under which evidence may be taken by courts in the receiving State for use in the sending State; and
- registration of births and marriages in the receiving State of nationals of the sending State.

Most of these functions require some knowledge of the laws and regulations of the sending State and also those of the receiving State, although the difficult or unusual case may have to be referred home for instructions in the light of legal advice, and a local lawyer may have to be consulted on the law of the receiving State. Action following death of a visitor can be particularly sensitive: on one occasion the British consul in Innsbruck was left with responsibility for the body of a tourist who had suddenly died after his widow rejoined her coach tour and could not be contacted to give instructions for repatriation or burial.

8.24 No comprehensive list of consular functions can be drawn up. What functions any particular consul performs depend on two things—on the instructions given by the sending State and on the laws of the receiving State. Consuls in certain cases (such as the representatives exchanged between countries in the Commonwealth)[9] may exercise a much more limited range of functions than is permitted under the local law or accepted under international law. They may, for example, be solely engaged in work relating to prospective immigration into the sending State—a task which may be politically and personally sensitive where for example it involves scrutiny of potentially sham marriages. No consul is entitled to exercise any function which is prohibited under local law, although it may be said that a prohibition which was so wide as to undermine the whole basis of the consular function, such as a prohibition on protecting the consul's own nationals, would probably lead to the breaking of consular relations. More extensive movement of people and modern means of transport have led to new functions in relation, for example, to commercial air services, refugees, child abduction, and forced marriages. Conversely, other functions may diminish in importance. Consuls are now less involved in shipping activities, for example, since local authorities acting under conventions drawn up within the framework of the International Maritime Organization perform many supervisory

---

[9] See Chapter **23**.

and safety functions and seafarer unions may deal with employment matters and disputes between crew and owners. Many States have found it useful to include in a bilateral consular convention a list of permissible consular functions—and indeed the list in Article 5 of the VCCR was drafted on the express wish of newly independent States setting up consular posts abroad for the first time—but such lists are never exhaustive. Article 5 of the VCCR lists the most important consular functions expressly, but also authorizes consuls to perform 'any other functions entrusted to a consular post by the sending State which are not prohibited by the laws and regulations of the receiving State or to which no objection is taken by the receiving State or which are referred to in the international agreements in force between the sending State and the receiving State'. The list in Article 5 is reflected in the consular instructions to their overseas officers issued by many States.[10] Such national instructions, supplementing the training given to most consular officers before they are posted abroad, set out the legal framework and procedures for the discharge of each of their authorized functions.

Consular Protection

The most important of all the functions of a consul is 'protecting in the receiving State the interests of the sending State and of its nationals, both individuals and bodies corporate, within the limits permitted by international law'. These last words were inserted in Article 5 at the instance of those States which recalled with resentment the period when the ill-treatment of nationals of an imperial Power might occasion the despatch of a gunboat or reprisals of a drastic kind. But they remain a useful reminder of the limits of the power of a consul, who must never in his zeal to protect his nationals transgress the local law or intervene in the internal affairs of the receiving State. Protection may involve assisting or repatriating the destitute and victims of robbery, settling disputes and administrative matters arising on visiting ships belonging to the sending State, visiting nationals in hospital if they are injured or become ill on holiday, helping them with their arrangements, and tracing the relatives of victims of an air disaster, storm, or flood in the receiving State. The growth in tourism and in casual travel by the young and impecunious has led to considerable increase in this kind of consular work. Over the past 30 years the United Kingdom has devoted much effort to limiting the need for consular assistance abroad through wide

---

[10] See Lee and Quigley, *Consular Law and Practice*, ch 7 on consular functions and chs 8–20 on specific consular functions.

dissemination of information of what a British Consulate can and cannot do and provision of advice on how to avoid trouble.[11]

8.26 Before consular staff become involved they will of course confirm that the person seeking assistance is one of the consulate's own nationals. Should the individual also possess the nationality of the receiving State, the consul may assist or make informal representations on their behalf to the local authorities, but the consul's right to do so is liable to be challenged. The 'effective' nationality in such circumstances is that of the receiving State. Consular access and protection has become in recent years a matter of such practical importance and legal complexity that it is treated separately in the next chapter.

Reporting and Political Work

8.27 If the consular post is entrusted with reporting or political functions by the sending State, these functions (which do not form part of the traditional consular functions) are in ordinary circumstances exercised in a subordinate capacity to the embassy in the capital. Reports by provincial posts are normally sent to the ambassador or political section of the embassy and will cover any subject of interest to the embassy, whether it is the grass roots of politics, the pattern of agricultural development, or controversy over the building of a new research or nuclear facility. A report addressed to the ambassador may be transmitted, with the embassy's comments, to the home government. If it is addressed elsewhere, for example to the home ministry dealing with commercial or shipping affairs, it may be sent to the embassy under flying seal, so that diplomats there are aware of its contents.

8.28 In ordinary circumstances a consul does not exercise political functions in the broad sense, although a specific task may be delegated to him by the embassy. But there have been many occasions where the circumstances have been highly exceptional and the consul has had to assume a political role. A consul in a remote province or a district unresponsive to the central government may be directed to make political representation to the local civil or military administration. One celebrated case of a consul who found himself by force of circumstances in a political role of the greatest delicacy and importance was that of Bruce Lockhart who,

---

[11] See, for example, the UK government guide *Support for British Nationals Abroad* and the information on the web (<https://www.gov.uk/government/publications/support-for-british-nationals-abroad-a-guide>) about what consuls can do to help, as well as regularly updated travel advice for individual countries (<https://www.gov.uk/foreign-travel-advice>) and downloadable consular publications on specific risks—all of these designed to encourage safer overseas travel.

originally despatched to Russia in a consular role, remained after the 1917 Revolution and the withdrawal of the British Embassy staff from Petrograd (now St Petersburg) in charge of the unofficial relations which were maintained between Britain and the new Soviet government before recognition was accorded in 1921.[12] Daphne Park—later Baroness Park of Monmouth—as consul-general in Hanoi between 1969 and 1970 in the absence of any recognition of North Vietnam by the UK (as explained in paragraph **8.**7) carried out diplomatic functions of considerable sensitivity in addition to the intelligence functions which became public knowledge only after her retirement. The United States, particularly because of its reluctance to recognize governments of which it does not approve, has often conducted business with unrecognized régimes through its consuls. Thus the United States consul-general in Peking was instructed in 1950 to communicate with the authorities of the Chinese People's Republic, and in 1955 the United States consul-general in Geneva was directed to negotiate with the consul-general there of the Chinese People's Republic.[13] The Belgian consul-general in Elizabethville (now Lubumbashi) was instructed to talk to President Tshombe at the time of the latter's secession from the new Republic of the Congo.[14] The assumption of a political role by a consul of course entails the acceptance of political risks, in particular that of expulsion on account of the expression of views or attitudes unacceptable to the receiving State.

A consul who continues to function where diplomatic relations are broken, or where the authorities in his consular area are not recognized by his government, does not necessarily assume any political functions at all. The United Kingdom retained a consul in Taiwan for a number of years after recognizing the government in Peking as the sole government of China, and this consul dealt only with the local provincial authorities and had no contact whatsoever with the authorities of the Nationalist government. The legal reasons for this are described in paragraph **8.**8.   **8.29**

Information and Trade Promotion

Ernest Bevin as British Foreign Secretary after the Second World War circulated an instruction to the British Diplomatic Service to the effect that all members should regard themselves as information officers in addition to their other capacities. At that period, however, and indeed until the adoption of the VCCR,   **8.30**

---

[12] R H B Lockhart, *Memoirs of a British Agent* (London: Putnam, 1932).
[13] *New York Times*, 26 July 1955.
[14] *New York Times*, 11 January 1963.

it was uncertain whether information was a proper consular activity, although it was of major importance throughout the Cold War. The consul will be expected to play a leading role in the community of his or her fellow nationals in the consular district, where the consul will be regarded as spokesperson for his or her country's interests as well as a source of information and advice in times of difficulty. He or she will probably be an honorary member of the local chamber of commerce and should be familiar with the local trade associations. The office may well, if the extent of business justifies it, contain a busy commercial section complementing that of the embassy. The consul will certainly be a useful colleague for the embassy's information officer, or press attaché and be ready to help and advise the cultural attaché in the embassy, or, in the British service, the representative of the British Council. The consulate may contain an information section in the charge of an information officer with consular status. As it is not normally permissible to set up offices forming part of the diplomatic mission in localities other than the seat of government without the government's express consent, it is often convenient for an information officer in the provinces to work under the consular roof, where his or her status will assist the maintenance of direct contact with the public at large.

Privileges and Immunities

8.31 Under customary international law only the most limited immunities, and no privileges, were accorded to consular posts and to consuls. It could broadly be said that only those immunities were required which resulted from the rules of sovereign immunity. Thus the archives of a consulate were generally regarded as inviolable, but this could equally be based on their character as archives of a foreign sovereign State. The consul was entitled to immunity in respect of official acts only. Again these acts were performed as agent for a foreign State and so sovereign rather than consular immunity required that immunity should be accorded in respect of them. The consular premises were not treated as inviolable, consular bags did not enjoy the inviolable status of diplomatic bags, and consuls themselves enjoyed no personal immunity and were given taxation or customs privileges only by courtesy, if at all.[15]

8.32 After the Second World War an increasing number of States began to merge their consular and diplomatic services and to make greater use of career consuls, as opposed to honorary consuls who would be locally engaged and not subject to

---

[15] See W E Beckett, 'Consular Immunities' (1944) *BYIL* 34.

posting at the discretion of the sending State. The same individuals might therefore serve successively in a diplomatic and in a consular appointment. States which maintained extensive consular services abroad found that they would benefit overall from the institution of tax and customs privileges for consuls on a reciprocal basis. The need therefore came to be widely accepted to assimilate career consuls more closely to diplomats and since there was no basis for this in customary law, it was at first done by negotiation of an extensive network of bilateral consular conventions by the major States with substantial consular services. Most of those consular conventions also contained important provisions regarding consular functions. The United Kingdom negotiated a Consular Convention with the United States in 1948 and subsequently concluded broadly similar conventions with fourteen other States, mostly in Western Europe, before the VCCR was drawn up in 1963. These conventions accorded a very limited inviolability to consular premises and gave consuls no additional immunity or inviolability. Career consuls, however, were given extensive tax and customs privileges. Later conventions negotiated during the Cold War with Communist countries in Eastern Europe differed in that, in order to ensure a higher degree of protection, full diplomatic immunities and personal inviolability were conferred not only on consular officers and their families but also on junior staff and on private servants and their families. The United States concluded a similar network of agreements with Communist States, and agreements providing for privileges and immunities at the diplomatic level were also concluded among Communist States themselves.

These bilateral consular conventions remain of considerable practical importance, **8.33** not only because of the provisions they contain in regard to consular functions, but because it was expressly provided in Article 73 of the VCCR that the provisions of the Convention should not affect other international agreements in force as between States Parties to them, and would not preclude States from concluding further agreements confirming, supplementing, extending, or amplifying its provisions. It was clear that the major States attached great importance to continuing their bilateral arrangements—in particular those with Communist States—and that support could not be found for the imposition of a uniform régime designed to supersede these arrangements. The network of consular conventions has indeed continued to grow, though more slowly, and for this reason an account of the provisions of the VCCR does not in many cases provide a full answer to any question of entitlement to privileges or immunities. Even where both States are parties to the VCCR the post must still check whether there is also a bilateral consular convention and if so consult it to learn the applicable rules. Where a bilateral convention accorded a lower standard of privilege or immunity, the United Kingdom proposed to its treaty partners that the Vienna scale of privilege or immunity should be accorded. This was accepted by all the other States concerned. The effect is that where the relevant bilateral convention and the VCCR differ on any point, foreign consuls in the United Kingdom and United Kingdom consuls abroad are entitled to claim the higher of the two standards. They enjoy the higher immunities set out in the VCCR and the higher tax privileges specified in the bilateral consular conventions.

The Vienna Convention on Consular Relations (VCCR)

8.34 It would not be justified in a book primarily concerned with diplomatic practice to examine the Vienna Convention on Consular Relations in detail.[16] A brief account of the provisions of the VCCR regarding privileges and immunities will be given, and this will emphasize those points on which the privileges or immunities accorded by the Vienna *Consular* Convention differ from those accorded under the Vienna *Diplomatic* Convention. The negotiators at the Vienna Conference on Consular Relations in 1963 were heavily influenced by the text of the Vienna Convention on Diplomatic Relations (VCDR) of 1961. Many provisions in the Consular Convention were lifted without change or with only small changes from the Diplomatic Convention and where this is so, it is usually helpful to refer back to the explanation or discussion of the same provision in the diplomatic context. Article 28 of the VCCR on facilities for the work of the consular post and Article 30 on assistance with acquiring premises and accommodation for staff, for example, are identical with the corresponding provisions in the VCDR. With some corresponding articles there is a degree of elaboration in the later VCCR—for example in Article 29 on use of the national flag and coat of arms and in the Definitions Article which contains a definition of 'consular archives' which has no parallel in the VCDR. These later clarifying provisions are in practice assumed to apply also to the earlier Diplomatic Convention.[17] Cases relating to one of the conventions are routinely cited—with due regard to the clear differences in the privilege or immunity accorded—in legal proceedings requiring construction of the other.

8.35 A basic distinction is drawn in the VCCR between consular posts headed by a career officer and consular posts headed by an honorary officer. Posts in the former category, which are given a status much closer to that of a diplomatic mission, are dealt with in Chapter II of the Convention. These posts themselves are, with only two significant exceptions, given the same treatment as to

---

[16] For a comprehensive and up-to-date account, see Lee and Quigley, *Consular Law and Practice*.
[17] See E Denza, *Diplomatic Law* (4th edn, 2016) 160–8.

inviolability of premises, inviolability of archives and documents, freedom of movement, exemption from tax on their premises, and on the fees and charges levied in the course of the work as is given under the VCDR to diplomatic missions. The two exceptions limit the inviolability of consular premises. Where there is a fire or other disaster requiring prompt protective action on the part of the authorities of the receiving State, these authorities may assume that they have the consent of the head of the post to enter the premises. There is no such implied authority in the case of diplomatic premises (see Chapter 13, paragraph 13.9). If expropriation of consular premises is necessary for purposes of national defence or public utility (for example to allow a major road to be widened), it is permissible, provided that all possible steps are taken to avoid consular work being impeded and provided that prompt, adequate, and effective compensation for the property expropriated is paid to the sending State. Such expropriation could not take place in regard to diplomatic premises except with the express consent of the sending State The differences in treatment may be explained by the greater degree of sensitivity and vulnerability of embassies carrying out political work for which guaranteed confidentiality of papers and proceedings is essential. There is also the practical consideration that while embassies are usually detached buildings, consulates often form part of a larger office block so that danger from fire or other emergency is less easily contained. In 1988, the ambassador of Panama to London, a supporter of General Noriega, instructed a private security company to repossess the premises of the Panama Consulate after it was taken over by supporters of the deposed President of Panama, Senor Delvalle. The action was publicly criticized by UK ministers and proceedings were brought against staff of the security company, only to be dropped after it was made clear that the repossession action had been cleared in advance with the Diplomatic Protection Group within the police who had advised that it would be legal, though they would keep a watching brief because of the inviolability of the premises.[18]

As to freedom of communications with the sending State and with its diplomatic missions and other consular posts, wherever situated, there is a difference from the corresponding Article in the VCDR in that Article 35.3 of the Consular Convention permits challenge to a consular bag reasonably suspected of containing something other than the permissible official contents. If the authorities challenge a suspect consular bag they may request that it be opened in their presence by a representative of the sending State, and if the request is refused the bag must be returned to its place of origin. In practice the distinction in   **8.36**

---

[18] *The Times*, 9 and 11 March, 4 June 1988.

treatment is unlikely to be of great significance in that an attempt to smuggle improper contents would almost certainly make use of a diplomatic bag and, as pointed out in Chapter 13, even in such a case it would be possible for the authorities of the receiving State to challenge a bag whose contents posed a threat to human life.

Career Consuls

8.37 Career consular officers are given broadly the same privileges as are given to a diplomatic agent under the VCDR: exemption from taxation subject to similar exceptions, exemption from customs duties and inspection of personal baggage, exemption from social security obligations and from personal, public, and military service. But their immunities are much more limited than those enjoyed by diplomatic agents. Consular officers are under Article 43 of the VCCR immune from the jurisdiction of courts and authorities of the receiving State only in respect of acts performed in the exercise of consular functions. They are not accorded the personal immunity extending to their private acts to which (with limited exceptions) diplomatic agents are entitled. It is emphasized in Article 43 that a consul does not have immunity from a civil action arising out of a contract unless the consul contracted expressly or impliedly as agent of his own State. Thus in *Park v Shin* a US court held that a servant, whose primary role was cooking, cleaning, and child care was entitled to sue her employer, the deputy consul-general of Korea, as a 'personal domestic servant' with the bulk of her duties and time focused on the care of the consular officer and his family not official consular functions.[19] Nor does the consular officer have immunity from a third party claim for damage arising from an accident in the receiving State caused by a vehicle, vessel, or aircraft. It is therefore not relevant in the case of a suit against a consul whether he was driving on duty when the accident leading to the claim occurred. In either case he has no entitlement to immunity. It must however be borne in mind that a diplomat, even when he is exercising consular functions as he is clearly permitted to do, remains entitled to full personal immunity on the basis of his diplomatic appointment. The same is true where an individual concurrently holds both a diplomatic and a consular appointment. The rules for the exercise of consular functions by diplomatic missions are set out in Article 70 of the VCCR.

8.38 A court when required to determine whether a particular act was performed by a consul 'in the exercise of consular functions' should have regard to the list of

---

[19] 313 F 3d 1138 (9th Cir 2992), cited by Garnett in *ICLQ* 64 (2015) 783, at 819–20.

functions set out in Article 5 of the VCCR and in any other applicable international agreement, and to such evidence as may be submitted by the consul or by the sending State. The test is, however, an objective one, so that a statement by the sending State that the act was performed in the exercise of consular functions is not conclusive. There may be immunity for the consul even where the act apparently violated local laws or regulations—for example the issue of a passport to a minor child who was a national of the sending State at the request of her father who had paternal authority, even though the local courts would have awarded custody of the girl to her mother who was a national of the receiving State.[20] On the other hand, where Article 5(a) circumscribes a particular consular function—protecting the interests of the sending State and its nationals—by the words 'within the limits permitted by international law', a national court may take a restrictive construction of the immunity conferred. In the case of *Gerritsen v de la Madrid Hurtado*,[21] the defendants, who were Mexican consuls in Los Angeles, were charged with striking the plaintiff with a metal object, threatening him with a club and a gun, kidnapping him, and seizing his camera and the anti-Mexican leaflets which he intended to distribute outside the Mexican consulate. The United States Court of Appeals held that these actions interfered with the internal affairs of the receiving State and were not 'within the limits permitted by international law'. Nor could they be covered by the words in Article 5(m) ('performing any other functions entrusted to a consular post by the sending State which are not prohibited by the laws and regulations of the receiving State ...'), since it was apparent that many of the alleged acts contravened US penal laws.

A career consul does enjoy under Articles 40 and 41 of the VCCR a degree of 8.39 personal inviolability, although more limited than that of a diplomatic agent. The receiving State is under a duty to respect and protect the consul's person, freedom, and dignity. If a criminal charge is brought, the consul may be arrested or detained only in the case of a 'grave crime'[22] and pursuant to a decision by a judge or court. If the consul is arrested or detained pending trial, the head of the consular post, or the sending State in the case of detention of the head of the post, must be notified of the detention. If criminal proceedings are taken the consul must appear, although the proceedings must be conducted with due respect to the consul's position and so as to hinder consular functions as little as possible. The fact that the consul must appear before the court does not of course prevent a claim of immunity because the act in respect of which proceedings are

---

[20] *In re Rissmann* (1970) 1 *IYIL* 254.

[21] 819 F 2d 1511 (9th Cir 1987), 1987 *AJIL* 949.

[22] The term 'grave crime' was not defined in the Vienna Consular Convention, but is defined in the law of a number of States Parties to the Convention, including the UK Consular Relations Act 1968 (c 18).

brought was an official act. If found guilty, and provided that the sentence is no longer subject to appeal, the consul may be imprisoned. Neither the consul's residence nor property has any inviolability. Where residences for consuls and consular staff are located in the same building as the part of the premises used exclusively for the work of the consular post, the areas used for consular work—which are entitled to inviolability to the extent already described—should be clearly delineated.

8.40 Career consular officers are under Article 44 not exempt from the duty to attend if summoned as witnesses, although if they decline to give evidence no coercive measure or penalty may be applied to them. They are under no obligation to give evidence on official matters or to produce official correspondence or documents, or to give evidence as expert witnesses on the law of the sending State. States however to an increasing extent seek to be helpful by authorizing their consuls to testify in proceedings in other States where there is no special sensitivity in the evidence likely to be sought.

8.41 Career consular employees are accorded broadly similar privileges to those given to administrative and technical staff in a diplomatic mission. Their immunities are, however, strictly limited. They enjoy no personal inviolability whatsoever, and their immunity from jurisdiction is, like that of career consular officers, limited to acts performed in the exercise of consular functions. They are exempt from the obligation to give evidence on official matters.

8.42 Members of the service staff in a career post are accorded only tax exemption on their wages, exemption from social security obligations, and exemption from the obligation to perform personal or public services.

8.43 Members of families in the case of a career consular post enjoy, broadly speaking, the same privileges as the entitled member of the post, but they have no entitlement to immunity or inviolability.

8.44 The rules regarding waiver of privileges and immunities, and regarding the beginning and end of privileges and immunities are virtually the same as those which apply to diplomatic staff. There is, however, one provision—Article 57—which has no parallel provision in the VCDR:

> Consular employees or members of the service staff who engage in private gainful occupations, together with their families and private staff, are excluded from all privileges and immunities and not just in relation to their private gainful activity. Members of families who themselves engage in private gainful occupations suffer a similar exclusion.

8.45 Under Article 71 of the Vienna Consular Convention, consular officers who are nationals or permanent residents of the receiving State are excluded from all privileges and immunities except for immunity from jurisdiction and inviolability in regard to official acts performed in the exercise of their functions. It is possible that this immunity is more limited than that accorded to consular officers who are not nationals or permanent residents of the receiving State because of the requirement that an act, to be covered by immunity, must be 'official' as well as 'performed in the exercise of consular functions'. Their families, other members of the post who are nationals or permanent residents of the receiving State and their families, as well as members of families and members of private staffs who are themselves nationals or permanent residents of the receiving State, are excluded from all entitlement to privileges or immunities.

Honorary Consuls

Chapter III of the VCCR sets out a distinct régime for honorary consular **8.46** officers and for posts headed by such officers. These posts are given very limited privileges and immunities. Many of the obligations relating to posts headed by a career officer are applied—for example the provisions on facilities, acquisition of premises, freedom of movement, and communications. Their premises are however not inviolable, although the receiving State is required to protect them from intrusion, damage, or impairment of dignity. Premises headed by an honorary consul are likely also to be used for his private or business purposes and they are unlikely to contain highly sensitive material. These premises are given tax exemption provided that they are owned or leased by the sending State. Inviolability of consular archives is conditional on their being kept separate from the consul's private and business papers. Only specified articles for office use such as coats of arms, seals, office furniture, and similar articles, are entitled to exemption from customs duty: it is clear that alcohol and other consumables for official entertainment by an honorary post may not be imported free of duty.

Honorary consuls are given the same limited immunity from jurisdiction as **8.47** career consuls. They are not entitled to any personal inviolability although they are entitled to 'such protection as may be required' by reason of their official position. If proceedings are instituted against them, they must be conducted with respect and so as to hinder consular functions as little as possible. Their privileges are limited to tax exemption on their official emoluments and exemption from personal and public services. Their families are accorded no privileges or immunities. If the consul or members of his family are nationals or permanent residents of the receiving State—and this is nearly always the case—they are excluded from almost all privileges and immunities on the same basis as career consuls and their families. The VCCR has not increased the status of honorary consuls and their posts above what was accorded under customary international law. It is only career consuls and their posts whose status was elevated by the Convention.

8.48 As Article 68 of the VCCR makes clear, each State is free to decide whether it will appoint or receive honorary consular officers. Because they are not salaried and do not generally entail the costs of establishment abroad or of posting while they may well have a deep knowledge of local practices and attitudes, they offer distinct advantages for a sending State in certain contexts. This has however to be balanced by the likelihood of their lesser commitment to the interests of the sending State together with the much lower degree of protection and immunity within which they must operate.

9

CONSULAR ACCESS AND PROTECTION

Joanne Foakes and Eileen Denza

As emphasized in Chapter **8**, paragraph **8**.20, protecting in the receiving State **9.1** the interests of the sending State and of its nationals, both individuals and bodies corporate, is the first and most important of consular functions. For many States there has in recent years been enormous growth in the demand for consular protection as businesses increasingly set up subsidiaries and branches overseas and individuals travel abroad as migrant workers, providers, and consumers of services, as students, as tourists, and as refugees. National laws vary greatly not only on such obvious matters as dress and the public consumption of alcohol but also on driving and road safety, photography of sites of cultural or security interest, and entitlement to social benefits and to police protection. In consequence it is easy for the unwary traveller to contravene local laws and to be arrested and detained in police custody without knowledge even of the language, far less of how to secure the services of an interpreter or competent legal representation. In July 2015, a report published by the UK Foreign and Commonwealth Office showed that consular staff had supported more than 17,000 British nationals who had needed serious assistance abroad in 2014/15.[1]

---

[1] Helping British Nationals Abroad 2014/15, 30 July 2015.

Consular Protection and Diplomatic Protection

9.2 A clear distinction must be drawn between consular protection and diplomatic protection—even though consular protection and diplomatic protection may be exercised successively or even on occasion simultaneously in respect of the same events and the lines sometimes become blurred. As explained in Chapter 8, paragraph 8.26, consular protection as well as diplomatic protection may only be exercised on behalf of a national of the sending State, and where the individual or company is also a national of the receiving State, the right to protection may be denied or challenged. Diplomatic protection is defined in the draft Articles drawn up by the International Law Commission as follows:

> For the purposes of the present draft articles, diplomatic protection consists of the invocation by a State, through diplomatic action or other means of peaceful settlement, of the responsibility of another State for an injury caused by an internationally wrongful act of that State to a natural or legal person that is a national of the former State with a view to the implementation of such responsibility.[2]

Before a State may exercise its right of diplomatic protection of its national, it is—with certain exceptions—essential that the national has exhausted all local remedies—that is, legal remedies open to an injured person before judicial or administrative courts or bodies of the State alleged to be responsible. With consular assistance or protection on the other hand, there is no requirement that the national must have exhausted local remedies—indeed the primary purpose of consular protection is usually to provide assistance in the pursuit of local remedies whether with the local authorities or with prison or judicial bodies. Once again this brings out that the essential difference between consular and diplomatic functions is not the objective of the specific task but the method and level at which it is performed.

9.3 The distinction is well illustrated by a case decided in 1999 by the UK Court of Appeal, *R v Secretary of State for Foreign and Commonwealth Affairs, ex parte Butt*.[3] Judicial review proceedings were brought by the sister of one of nine British citizens on trial in Yemen on terrorist charges to require the Secretary of State to make personal representations to the President of the Yemen that the trial be halted, an independent medical examination appointed to examine

---

[2] UN Doc A/CN.4/L.684, 19 May 2006.

[3] Court of Appeal (Civil Division) FC3 99/6610/4. See also *R (on the application of Al Rawi and Others) v Secretary of State* [2006] EWCA Civ 1279, October 2006.

allegations of torture of the accused, and a retrial ordered before delivery of a verdict. It was argued on behalf of the applicants that there had already been intervention by the provision of consular assistance so that it would be irrational to cease now. The UK authorities had insisted on the availability of consular visits, family visits, legal visits, and medical attendance and treatment; had applied pressure to have the allegations of torture investigated; and made some representations to the trial judge and the prosecutor. They had not however made any representations to the judge about the conduct of the trial or brought pressure on the President of Yemen since this would have constituted interference in the internal affairs of Yemen. The Court of Appeal held that the decision by the UK authorities not to make diplomatic representations until the case had concluded and local remedies exhausted was not one which was justiciable by way of judicial review. However, although it is clear that States enjoy a very wide discretion in this area and are under no general international law obligation to provide diplomatic protection, the UK Court of Appeal has now held that there is no reason why the decision of the government in a particular case or its inaction 'should not be reviewable if it can be shown that the same was irrational or contrary to legitimate expectation'.[4] In recent years, governments have shown themselves to be increasingly willing to make diplomatic representations on behalf of nationals subjected to serious human rights violations in foreign States.

General Aspects of Protection

Many of the specific functions already mentioned in Chapter 8—such as issue **9.4** of passports or helping with provision of advice on local law—have in them an element of protection. A consul may take steps to safeguard the rights or interests of a national who is not present in the territory of the receiving State— for example during the local administration of an estate—or may ask for the postponement of legal proceedings, for example on child custody, to enable the national of the sending State to attend in person or make adequate representations to the courts or authorities. Performing marriage ceremonies, settling disputes arising on visiting ships, or making arrangements for the administration of property of a national of the sending State who has died in the receiving State may all in some sense 'protect' the foreign national or ship from the application

---

[4] *R (Abbasi and another v Secretary of State for Foreign and Commonwealth Affairs and Secretary of State for the Home Department)* [2002] EWCA Civ 1598, [2003] UKHRR 76, para 106. For a fuller account of this case and the role of the diplomat in upholding human rights see Chapter 17.

of local laws which they might consider unsuitable. The consul has for such purposes a general right of access to his or her own nationals. This may be expressly safeguarded under the terms of a bilateral consular convention. Article 8.1 of the 1984 Agreement between China and the UK on the Establishment of a British Consulate-General in Shanghai and a Chinese Consulate-General in Manchester,[5] for example, provides:

> Consular officers shall have the right to communicate with nationals of the sending State and to have access to them in the consular district. The receiving State shall not in any way limit the communication of nationals of the sending State with the consular post or their access to it.

Article 36.1(a) of the Vienna Convention on Consular Relations (VCCR) makes similar provision—but on a wider basis in that the right of communication and access is not limited to the consular district. The right of access in ordinary circumstances by consuls to their own nationals is generally regarded as having been established in customary international law.

9.5 Consuls—though protecting their nationals within a generally accepted international framework supplemented by treaty provisions—are also instructed by precise regulations supplied and updated by their sending State as to what they should or may do and on the appropriate procedures. In general, they will not assume functions of a travel agent or investigative functions which belong to the local police. They will lend money only in exceptional circumstances—usually only for purposes of repatriation—and then only with the safeguards of an undertaking to repay and the retention of the traveller's passport while issuing an emergency one-way travel document.

9.6 Whether a consul is under a legal duty to provide any form of protection or to provide specific forms of protection to his or her own nationals is a question to be determined by the law of the consul's sending State. International law gives consuls rights to protect their nationals, but only in the most general sense does international law impose on them a duty to protect them. Consuls are of course appointed, instructed, and paid for the performance of functions of which protection is the most important, and their nationals have a legitimate expectation that consular assistance will be provided to them, but under the law of most States there is a large margin of discretion as to what assistance a consul actually provides.[6] Even where the law of the sending State imposes an obligation it may well be extremely general—under the 1982 Constitution of China, for

---

[5] Signed at Beijing on 17 April 1984, Cmnd 9247; UKTS No 14 (1985).
[6] See paragraph 9.3 and fn 5.

example, 'The People's Republic of China shall protect the legitimate rights and interests of Chinese nationals residing abroad.'[7]

Group Protection

Exercise of consular protection is most crucial and difficult in circumstances **9.7** where some emergency in the receiving State puts many or sometimes even all nationals of the sending State into danger. Examples of disasters include the attacks on the twin towers of the World Trade Center in New York in 2001 in which dozens of British nationals were killed and many more temporarily missing, the Asian tsunami on Boxing Day 2004 which affected areas heavily populated by foreign tourists of many nationalities, and more recently in June 2015 the shooting of thirty-eight people, including thirty British citizens on a Tunisian beach. In such circumstances consuls will find themselves overwhelmed by demands from victims and from their families. With the limited financial and staff resources appropriate to normal circumstances, they will have to set up information and reception centres, help with repatriation of the dead and injured, coordinate distribution of relief, and sometimes also contend with criticism from the press in their own country that more help is not being provided.[8] In 1955, for example, following the shooting down of an El Al aircraft which had strayed into Bulgaria in bad weather, there was press criticism of the allegedly unhelpful response of consular officials and of the Foreign Office who had advised that a visit to the crash site by distraught relatives was not practicable. As Western governments are increasingly sensitive to public criticism of their failure to respond adequately in the event of a disaster, they are often inclined to send out an emergency support team from the home capital to assist the beleaguered consular staff.

Notification to Consul of Arrest or Detention

By contrast with the position regarding the general right of consuls to have **9.8** access to their own nationals, it was not obligatory under customary international

---

[7] Art 50. For the perspective of the six-year-old daughter of a consul see K Hickman, *Daughters of Britannia: The Lives and Times of Diplomatic Wives* (London: Flamingo, 2000) 221: 'My father is a Consel. If any person from England, Scotland, Wales or Irrlang is in trouble in any kind of way my Father has to go and loock after them ... If he doset like eny person he must not say o I don't like yo I don't want to help you. He must be nice and help them.'

[8] On group protection generally, see L T Lee and J B Quigley, *Consular Law and Practice* (3rd edn, Oxford: Oxford University Press, 2008) 118–21.

law for the authorities of the receiving State to inform a consul if one of his or her nationals was detained in prison. Without such notification to the consul, a right of access was often in practice of no value. Many States did in fact notify the consul as a matter of local law or practice if a prisoner requested it, but these were not always the States where concern on behalf of an imprisoned national might be greatest. In consequence, States increasingly made provision in bilateral consular conventions for compulsory notification, and this became established as a general rule in Article 36.1(b) of the Vienna Consular Convention which provides:

> If he so requests, the competent authorities of the receiving State shall, without delay, inform the consular post if, within its consular district, a national of that State is arrested or committed to prison or to custody pending trial or is detained in any other manner. Any communication addressed to the consular post by the person arrested, in prison, custody or detention shall also be forwarded by the said authorities without delay. The said authorities shall inform the person concerned without delay of his rights under this sub-paragraph.

It should be emphasized that the consul must be informed only if the national, having been informed of his or her rights, so requests. If the national prefers that the consul should not be notified—either because he or she does not wish the fact of the arrest or imprisonment to become known to his or her own authorities or because the national is a refugee and wishes to have nothing to do with those authorities—the consul will not be informed. This was a matter of some sensitivity during the Cold War when refugees did not in general want visits from their consuls who might well put pressure on them to return—perhaps through threats to members of their families in their home country. Some bilateral consular conventions did require consular notification regardless of the wishes of the detainee, and it was only after much controversy at the Vienna Conference on Consular Relations that the condition to protect the detainee who did not want his or her consul to be notified was included in Article 36. It remains, however, an important safeguard for protection of foreign nationals and in particular refugees. Some bilateral consular conventions nevertheless—concluded in particular by the United States—require automatic notification of a detention (mandatory notification), the reason being suspicion that the other country concerned might advance the supposed reluctance of the detainee as an excuse for failure to notify the consul.

9.9 The final sentence of Article 36.1(b) which requires foreign nationals to be notified of their rights 'without delay' was added at the Vienna Conference by adoption of a UK amendment, and it is this crucial provision which, when properly applied, sets in motion the entire system of protection. Many foreign nationals are unaware of their rights to consular notification, access, and protection and it has become apparent over recent years in particular that the prison authorities in many States Parties to the Vienna Convention are also insufficiently aware of the requirement. There have been a series of cases before the International Court of Justice[9] and before the United States Supreme Court[10] which brought out clearly the failure at state level within the United States to set up and apply procedures to ensure that foreign prisoners were aware of their rights to consular notification and access. Many of these cases concerned foreign prisoners sentenced to the death penalty without being informed of their rights to consular notification and access. In response to these cases, the US State Department in 1998 published and distributed to arresting and prison authorities a handbook of guidance on consular assistance[11] and a card to be carried by individual arresting officers. Conscious of the need of the United States for reciprocal consular access to its citizens abroad, President George W Bush issued in February 2005 a Memorandum to the US Attorney-General on the need to review cases affected by the judgment of the International Court and the US government has also issued directions to state Attorneys-General and has set up intensive training systems. In the United Kingdom the procedure for notification is contained in a Code of Practice under the Police and Criminal Evidence Act 1984. Other States, such as New Zealand and Ireland, have specific national legal or administrative procedures to guarantee that prisoners are informed of their rights and others are considering their adoption. The question of notification has become a matter of widespread international concern as a result of the cases against the United States and greater emphasis on practical enforcement of human rights. It is clear however that international treaties cannot safeguard the right without detailed procedures at national and local level and consuls should make sure that they are aware of the precise position in any jurisdiction in which they are posted.

The phrase 'without delay' in the context of informing foreign nationals of their rights and also that of informing the consular post is also imprecise and is interpreted differently in different jurisdictions. The Department of State has taken the view that it means 'as quickly as possible and, in any event, no later than the passage of a few days'. Greater precision has been added by the terms of

9.10

---

[9] See in particular *Breard (Paraguay v US)* [1998] ICJ Reports 266; *Lagrand (Germany v US)* [2001] ICJ Reports 466; *Avena (Mexico v US)* [2004] ICJ Reports 12.

[10] For example, *Sanchez-Llamas v Oregon*, No 04-10566; *Medellin v Texas*, No 06-984; 552 and 554 US (2008).

[11] Consular Notification and Access: Instructions for Federal, State and Local Law Enforcement and Other Officials Regarding Foreign Nationals in the United States and the Rights of Consular Officials to Assist Them.

many bilateral consular conventions. The 1972 Consular Convention between the United Kingdom and the Hungarian People's Republic,[12] for example, provided in Article 43 that '[n]otification shall be made without delay and in any event within three days'. Article 8 of the 1984 Agreement between the United Kingdom and China on the Establishment of a British Consulate-General at Shanghai and a Chinese Consulate-General at Manchester[13] requires notification to the consular post 'as soon as possible and at the latest within seven days from the time at which the personal freedom of that national is restricted'. Prompt notification is designed to ensure that persons detained are aware of and can take advantage of their rights before questioning—at which point there is a risk of making self-incriminatory statements—or at the latest before charges are brought. In the *Avena* case Mexico brought proceedings against the United States alleging violations of Article 36 in relation to the treatment of a number of Mexican nationals who had been convicted and sentenced to death in criminal proceedings in the United States. The International Court of Justice in that case[14] held that 'without delay' did not necessarily mean 'immediately and before interrogation', but other tribunals have taken a more rigorous interpretation on the timing of notification because of its importance in the context of safeguarding defence rights. There is also uncertainty as to whether the authorities of the receiving State are required to inform a detainee of the right to consular notification if they are not aware that the detainee is a foreign national. National practice varies on whether all detainees are asked about their nationality, but it is probably acceptable if notification takes place as soon as the authorities are aware, or have reasonable grounds to suspect, that the detainee is a foreign national. The International Court of Justice in the *Avena* case noted the assurance of the United States that routine checks on nationality of detainees were made by some US law enforcement authorities, and described this practice as 'desirable' while stopping short of declaring it mandatory.[15]

Consular Access

9.11 Article 36.1(c) of the Vienna Consular Convention provides some substance to the right of consular access in the following terms:

> [C]onsular officers shall have the right to visit a national of the sending State who is in prison, custody or detention, to converse and correspond with him and to

---

[12] UKTS No 2 (1972).
[13] Cmnd 9247; UKTS No 14 (1985).
[14] [2004] ICJ Reports 12, paras 87–8.
[15] Ibid, para 64.

arrange for his legal representation. They shall also have the right to visit any national of the sending State who is in prison, custody or detention in their district in pursuance of a judgment. Nevertheless, consular officers shall refrain from taking action on behalf of a national who is in prison, custody or detention if he expressly opposes such action.

In addition to legal representation, a consul may also assist with provision of interpretation and with securing bail which is often more difficult for a foreign national—often thought likely to try to return home if released on bail. As with the question of notification, there is a lack of precision in Article 36 as to how frequently a consul is entitled to exercise the right of access to a prisoner. In the 1960s when Gerald Brooke, a London lecturer, was imprisoned in Moscow on a charge of disseminating subversive literature, the British consul in Moscow was given access to him only at very long intervals. Soon afterwards the United Kingdom began negotiation of a Consular Convention with the Soviet Union[16] intended to enhance rights of consular access by requiring access on a regular basis, and such specific requirements were repeated in later conventions concluded by the UK with Communist States and with others, and also in bilateral conventions concluded by the United States. Article 8.2 of the 1984 UK-China Agreement,[17] for example, provides that:

> [a] visit to that national as requested by consular officers shall be arranged by the competent authorities of the receiving State two days after the consular post is notified of the restriction of the personal freedoms of that national. Subsequent visits shall be permitted at intervals not exceeding one month.

The 1985 Consular Convention between the United Kingdom and Egypt[18] in Article 12 requires that the initial consular visit should be permitted 'as soon as possible and at latest within three days from the date on which the national was subjected to deprivation of liberty' and that '[s]ubsequent visits may take place at intervals of no more than one month'.

Following sentence, the purpose of consular visits becomes mainly to ensure 9.12 humane and non-discriminatory treatment for the foreign prisoner,[19] to assist with possible appeals for review of conviction or sentence or for clemency, to assist with provision of adequate food and medicine and, within the limits of the prison rules, communication with family and others outside the prison. The consul should be aware whether there are in force between sending and receiving States bilateral or multilateral treaty provisions permitting prisoners

---

[16] 665 UNTS 259.
[17] Cmnd 9247.
[18] Cmnd 9603.
[19] See also Chapter 36, paragraph 36.17.

under specified conditions to be returned to serve the remainder of their sentence in their home State and if so, should advise the prisoner of the possibility of applying in due course for a transfer. A Council of Europe Convention on the Transfer of Sentenced Persons[20] drawn up in 1983 is open to participation by States outside Europe and now has over sixty parties. Transfer under the 1983 Convention requires the consent of the host State, of the prisoner's home State, and of the prisoner. Such transfers may not only assist in ensuring that the prisoner is suitably treated, kept in touch with family and friends, and prepared for eventual release but also reduce the burden on the consul of regular visits and assistance. It is worth noting that by no means all prisoners welcome the prospect of transfer to the home State. The local prisons where they are held may have a far more liberal regime, for example in terms of hours spent outside the cells, than a 'home' prison.

---

[20] European Treaty Series No 112.

10

THE DIPLOMATIC MISSION, THE CORPS, BREACH OF RELATIONS, AND PROTECTION OF INTERESTS

Joanne Foakes and Eileen Denza

The Diplomatic Corps

The diplomatic body (*corps diplomatique*) comprises the heads and the diplo- **10.1** matic staff of all the missions accredited to a particular receiving State. The *corps diplomatique* has no legal personality or formal constitution. In most major capitals a diplomatic list, based on the notifications of appointments, arrivals, and departures required from missions under Article 10 of the Vienna Convention on Diplomatic Relations (VCDR) is published by the ministry of foreign affairs. The list may also include spouses and members of the families of heads of mission and diplomatic staff. As already explained in Chapter 7, inclusion on the diplomatic list is mainly for protocol and social purposes and is not conclusive evidence of entitlement to privileges and immunities. Where one or more international organizations have their headquarters in a capital there may be additional diplomatic bodies consisting of the permanent representatives to each organization—for example in Brussels there are in addition to the body of ambassadors accredited to the King of the Belgians the body of ambassadors to the European Union and that of ambassadors to NATO.

10.2 The most senior ambassador is the dean or doyen of the diplomatic corps.[1] In most States this seniority is determined by date of arrival. In some capitals, however, particularly in the case of Roman Catholic countries, the representative of the Holy See is automatically accorded the status of dean, and this practice is permitted, though not required by the Vienna Convention on Diplomatic Relations. There have in the past been difficulties over the acceptance as dean of the ambassador of a State whose relations with the receiving State were strained, but given the limited and essentially non-political functions of the dean, such difficulties now appear to be very rare.

10.3 The dean acts as spokesman for his or her colleagues on public occasions and will present the views of the diplomatic corps on matters of ceremony and protocol and may represent them in the event of failure by the government of the receiving State to provide appropriate inviolability, immunities, and privileges. The dean acts as spokesperson on the basis of informal consultation with colleagues and is not expected to become involved in political questions. The dean may be asked by the receiving State to circulate informal information or guidance but the modern practice is for the protocol department of the ministry of foreign affairs to send circular Notes or letters to all embassies on formal matters such as new legislation of particular relevance to diplomatic missions or administrative procedures on such matters as customs clearance or immigration privileges. These circular Notes may be published in national Digests of international law practice, and in the case of the US State Department they are also published on the Internet.[2] There may be informal communication by the government through the dean if there is concern about abuse of privileges but under modern practice problems of abuse are more usually handled by way of representations to particular embassies, sometimes backed up by the threat of sanctions, rather than by complaint to the entire diplomatic corps. There have also been a few examples of representations made to the corps on political matters—for example in 1944 Marshal Pétain summoned the entire corps to protest at his deportation to Germany[3]—but these exceptional events do not reflect modern practice.

10.4 Where difficulties are political rather than administrative in character, collective representations may be made by heads of missions representing political group-

---

[1] The equivalent term for a female dean is 'doyenne' although this title may also be applied to the wife of a male doyen.

[2] At <http://www.state.gov/ofm/31311.htm>.

[3] J A Salmon, *Manuel de Droit Diplomatique* (Bruxelles: Bruylant, 1994) para 130.

ings—which may be groups of which a State particularly affected is a member or groups with a particular interest in the outcome. Collective representations by the ambassadors of European Union Member States, for example, are now very common where a European Union State has grounds for complaint or where the European Union takes the view that it may be able to make effective use of incentives at its disposal, such as aid or trading preferences, and this is further described in Chapter 22. Representations may also be made by one of the United Nations political groups such as the Western European and Others Group or by the Commonwealth. States will take part in such political representations only on the basis of specific authorization from their sending government. The dean of the diplomatic corps will not normally become involved in these representations and even if the dean's own State is a part of the relevant grouping he or she may decline to participate if it is judged that it could prejudice the dean's neutral status.

Because of the neutral status of the dean, he or she may when acting in that **10.5** capacity have dealings with the representatives of States which the dean's own sending State does not recognize or with which it does not have diplomatic relations. These dealings will not carry legal or political implications.

The dean may be consulted on an informal basis by colleagues on matters of **10.6** local protocol and usage, though this does not form part of the dean's official duties. The same advisory function may be carried out by the spouse of the dean—to spouses or partners of diplomatic colleagues.

Communication in the Absence of Diplomatic Relations

Chapter 5 explained the relevance of recognition and the existence of diplo- **10.7** matic relations between sending and receiving States to the sending of permanent diplomatic missions. As between embassies and diplomats in the same receiving State, relations between their sending States may also limit the contacts which they maintain. The representative of a State which does not recognize another or does not recognize its government may not communicate with the representative of the unrecognized entity and may not formally acknowledge a communication received from it, since under such circumstances either communication or acknowledgement of a communication may be evidence of implied recognition.[4] A communication received by a mission may be retained

---

[4] The Bosnian Serb war criminal, Radovan Karadžić (convicted in 2016) sent condolences (by fax) on the death of Princess Diana to the British embassy in Belgrade in 1997 in his claimed capacity as President of the unrecognized statelet of Republika Srpska. The communication was not acknowledged.

without acknowledgement (for example when it is expected that recognition will shortly be forthcoming) or may be returned to the sending mission. If communication is for some reason essential it may be effected through the ministry of foreign affairs of the receiving State or through another embassy which does recognize the sending mission.

10.8 Where there are no diplomatic relations between the two sending States the rules are somewhat less rigorous, since diplomatic relations cannot be established by implication or inadvertence. As explained in Chapter 5, States which recognize one another almost always establish diplomatic relations even without setting up permanent missions, so absence of relations is much more likely to result from a deliberate breach by one State. The constraints on contact in such cases are political, and in many cases the sending State will issue instructions to its representatives abroad, either by way of general guidance or with particular reference to the individual State or States. There are no rigid bars on informal, private, or secret contacts—which sometimes occur in the context of efforts at mediation. Humanitarian considerations may be overriding—even as between representatives of States at war. Callières relates the story of Sieur de Grenonville, French representative at Rome during hostilities between France and Spain, who, learning of a plot to kill the Spanish ambassador, warned the intended victim and earned much praise for his action.[5]

National Days

10.9 On the date chosen for the celebration of its National Day, it is customary for the head of each diplomatic mission to receive the congratulations of representatives of the host government and of the heads of all other diplomatic missions accredited in that capital. Usual practice is for the head of the celebrating mission to give a reception—usually in the embassy or in the residence of the ambassador. All heads of mission invited are in theory expected to attend and if unable to do so, should ensure that he or she is represented by a senior member of the diplomatic staff. At most embassies a visitors' book is kept in the entrance hall and is open for signature by all who call on the head of mission—whether on business, for expressing thanks, congratulations, or condolences, or on a courtesy call on first arrival or departure from the receiving State. Heads of mission will normally sign the visitors' book on attending a National Day and this gesture of goodwill is sufficient to make it unnecessary to send an individual letter of thanks later.

---

[5] F de Callières, *De la manière de négocier avec les souverains* (Paris and Amsterdam, 1746).

Flags

Article 20 of the Vienna Convention on Diplomatic Relations states that a **10.10**
diplomatic mission and its head have the right to use the flag and emblem
of the sending State on the premises of the mission, including the residence of
the head of mission and on his or her means of transport. The right under the
Convention is unlimited, but there may be local practices limiting the flying of
the flag on the chancery building to special occasions—which would include as
a minimum the National Day and principal public festivals of the sending State
and the National Day and the birthday or accession anniversary of the Head of
State of the receiving State. If these practices take the form of local laws or regulations, diplomats are required to respect them under Article 41 of the Vienna
Convention—provided of course that they do not fundamentally undermine
the basic right of the embassy to display its flag and emblem. The flag is customarily flown at half mast on the death of the head of the sending State and on the
death of the head of the receiving State and may be flown at half mast in the
event of some other tragedy or disaster in the sending or the receiving State.

The symbolic character of the flag implies a particularly high duty on the **10.11**
authorities of the receiving State to protect it from insult or damage, since such
attacks would obviously infringe the dignity of the sending State. At the same
time the flag and emblem present a particularly attractive target for political
demonstrators. In 1968, for example, North Vietnamese students in protest at
the war in Vietnam tore down the flag and shield from the United States
embassy in Prague. Although later on that same day Czech students returned
the shield together with a new flag to the Embassy, with apologies for the conduct of their fellow students, the US nevertheless made a formal protest and
received an apology from the Czech government.[6]

The privilege of flying the flag on means of transport is limited to the personal **10.12**
conveyance of the head of mission. It does not extend to public conveyances
used by the head of mission or to the means of transport of the mission, and an
acting head of mission or chargé d'affaires *ad interim* should probably fly the
flag only when making an official call. The use of the privilege is now often
limited by considerations of security which mean that anonymity of the ambassador's car is more important than visible signs of status which might identify
the ambassador as a target.

---

[6] (1969) *RGDIP* 177.

Endings to Appointments and Missions

10.13 The mission of a diplomatic agent may be brought to an end in any one of the following ways:

(i)   recall by the sending State or termination of appointment at the end of the period for which the diplomatic agent was posted, or on completion of the task for which he or she was sent;

(ii) in the case of a chargé d'affaires *ad interim,* on the return or arrival of the permanent head of mission;

(iii) the ending of the appointment of the head or a member of a special mission on the conclusion of the task for which the mission was appointed (special missions may come to an end in other ways, as is made clear by Article 20 of the New York Convention on Special Missions,[7] and formal recall of a special mission is not necessary);

(iv) on the death of the diplomatic agent;

(v)   where the receiving State asks for the recall of the diplomat or formally notifies the sending State that the diplomat is *persona non grata;*

(vi) where the sending State recalls the diplomatic mission, whether on a temporary or on an indefinite basis;

(vii) where diplomatic relations are broken off between sending and receiving States; and

(viii) on the disappearance of the sending or the receiving Head of State.

Recall

10.14 The first of these is of course the most usual. A diplomat may be recalled for the purpose of a further appointment in the home State or elsewhere, on retirement from the service, or on his or her resignation being accepted by the sending government. Although a diplomat's functions come to an end with the notification by the sending to the receiving State—as is made clear by Article 43 of the VCDR—the diplomat is entitled to personal privileges and immunities by virtue of Article 39 of the Convention until he or she leaves the receiving State or has had a reasonable period in which to do so, as described more fully in Chapter 14. An ambassador who is about to leave post for any of the above reasons may ask for a farewell audience with the Head of State, at which letters of recall may be presented if he or she has received them. This audience is usually private. It

---

[7] See Chapter 15.

is now more usual for an arriving ambassador to present the letters of recall of the predecessor together with his or her own letters of credence. When about to leave post, whether temporarily or finally, the head of mission should write to the appropriate official in the ministry of foreign affairs (in London, the Vice-Marshal of the Diplomatic Corps) giving the exact date of departure and nominating a chargé d'affaires *ad interim*. Under Article 19 of the Vienna Convention on Diplomatic Relations, the appointment of a chargé d'affaires *ad interim* cannot properly be made after the departure of the head of mission except by the ministry of foreign affairs of the sending State. Notification of the departure of other members of the mission and their families is also required by Article 10 of the VCDR, but this is normally done through the protocol department of the ministry of foreign affairs and no special formalities are prescribed.

Death of a Head of Mission or other Member of the Mission

On the death of the head of a diplomatic mission, it will be necessary for the sending State to notify the receiving State of the name of a chargé d'affaires *ad interim*, if one has not been previously appointed. If the death takes place in circumstances where ordinarily an inquest would be held, the authorities in the receiving State should if necessary be reminded that it has been general international practice[8] not to hold an inquest where a diplomatic agent or other member of a mission dies in office, whether in inviolable premises or not. This practice may be based on the continuing immunity from jurisdiction and inviolability now reflected in Article 39 of the VCDR. The sending State may waive immunity and allow an inquest to take place, although this would be highly unusual. The privileges and immunities applicable to family members and to property in the event of the death of a member of a mission are described in Chapter 14, paragraph 14.30.
  10.15

If the mission terminates by the death of an ambassador at post, the receiving State may wish to mark the occasion by some ceremonial mark of respect in view of the ambassador's representative character. The nature of such a ceremony would be for agreement between the sending and receiving States as well as the ambassador's own family. Alternatively, a memorial service or a similar ceremony of honour and respect to the deceased ambassador might be arranged.[9]
  10.16

---

[8] See Chapter 14, paragraph 14.21.

[9] On the death of the Netherlands ambassador in London in 1952 a ceremonial procession was arranged from the embassy to Knightsbridge Barracks, where there was a guard of honour and the coffin was transferred from a gun carriage to a motor hearse for conveyance to the airport. In 1958 full military honours were also accorded when the body of the Iranian ambassador was taken from the embassy to Northolt airport.

An early example occurred on the death of the British ambassador, Sir Julian Pauncefote in Washington on 24 May 1902. The ambassador and doyen of the diplomatic corps had been held in such respect and affection that President Roosevelt himself attended the funeral ceremony in Washington and broke with precedent by flying the American flag at half-mast on the White House. As a further courtesy the ambassador's body was conveyed to Southampton on the USS Brooklyn for interment in the family graveyard in Nottinghamshire. More recently on the sudden death of the Czech ambassador to the UK in 2009, his body was flown from Northolt Airport to Prague for his funeral, and the Marshal of the Diplomatic Corps in London attended the airport on behalf of the Queen as a mark of respect.[10]

10.17   In place of the farewell audience it is practice that the Head of State of the receiving State should convey his sympathy to the acting head of mission and the family of the deceased ambassador and should be represented at any funeral or memorial service. In London, the Marshal of the Diplomatic Corps calls on the acting head of mission to convey the Queen's sympathy. The Queen is represented, normally by the Marshal of the Diplomatic Corps, at the funeral or memorial service in the United Kingdom and by her ambassador at the funeral or memorial service in the home country of the deceased ambassador. The Marshal of the Diplomatic Corps attends the departure of the body from London.

Persona Non Grata

10.18   The process by which an ambassador or other diplomatic agent who is personally unacceptable to the receiving government is removed has been known under varying descriptions at different periods. Under modern practice the usual procedure is for the receiving State to 'request the recall of a diplomat' and for the sending State to comply. Only if compliance is delayed or refused does the receiving State proceed to a formal notification of *persona non grata* under the procedure set out in Article 9 of the VCDR. 'Png' and 'to png' are the standard colloquial terms. Whatever terminology is employed, the characteristic feature of the *persona non grata* procedure is that it is the diplomat personally who has offended the receiving government. Where the displeasure is not with the diplomat personally but with the policies or actions of the sending State, one course for the receiving State is to break diplomatic relations, or in a less serious case to 'recall its ambassador for consultations'. One consequence might be retaliation by the sending State, expelling one or more of the diplomatic staff in the sending State's capital. Nor should a declaration or declarations of *persona*

---

[10] Court Circular, 25 February 2009.

non grata be used for the purpose of reducing the number of diplomatic staff in the mission of the sending State. The correct procedure for that purpose is now set out in Article 11 of the VCDR. When the British government in 1971 expelled 105 Soviet diplomatic and other staff for 'inadmissible activities', (see paragraph **10.**25) they established a ceiling which was reduced by one whenever any other Soviet official was expelled. 'This was justified under Article 11 on the basis that the "needs of the particular mission" did not include those "diplomats" whose activities were not properly diplomatic.'[11]

An early example of correct use of the *persona non grata* procedure was the **10.19** expulsion of the Spanish Ambassador de Mendoza by Queen Elizabeth I of England. In 1584 one Francis Throkmorton was arrested in England, in consequence of a letter he had written to Mary Queen of Scots, which was intercepted, and the investigation showed that Don Bernardino de Mendoza, the Spanish Ambassador, was party to a plot which aimed at the deposition of Queen Elizabeth I. Camden[12] records:

> But yet lest the Spaniard should thinke, that not Mendoza's crimes were punished, but the privileges of his Embassadour violated, William Waad Clerke of the Councell, was sent into Spaine, to inform the Spaniard plainly how ill he had performed the office of his Embassie; and withal to signifie (lest the Queene by sending him away might seeme to renounce the ancient amity betwixt both kingdomes) that all offices of kindnesses should be shewed, if he would send any other that were desirous to preserve amity, so as the same kindnesses might in like sort be shewed to her Embassadour in Spaine.

Waad, however, was refused an audience of the Spanish King and 'returned' home unheard. This account illustrates the practice that became general: the offence was a personal—indeed a serious criminal one—and the receiving sovereign tried to make it clear that her quarrel was with the ambassador personally and not with the sending sovereign.

Later examples from the nineteenth century confirmed the practice of asking for **10.20** recall of an envoy whose conduct was regarded as unacceptable. In 1846 the United States chargé d'affaires at Lima, became involved in a dispute with the Peruvian Minister for Foreign Affairs, and was recalled in consequence of a reiterated request from the Peruvian government. The Secretary of State laid it down that 'if diplomatic agents render themselves so unacceptable as to produce a request for their recall from the government to which they are accredited, the instances must be rare indeed in which such a request ought not to be granted. To refuse it would be to defeat the very purpose for which they are sent abroad, that

---

[11] E Denza, *Diplomatic Law* (4th edn, Oxford, 2016) 81. See also Chapter 7, paragraph 7.41.
[12] *Annales Rerum Anglicarum et Hibernicarum, regnante Elizabetha*, translated by R N Gent (3rd edn, London, 1635) 263–4.

of cultivating friendly relations between independent nations. Perhaps no circumstances would justify such a refusal unless the national honour were involved.'[13]

10.21　Other cases may, however, be noted where a request for withdrawal of a diplomat who was no longer acceptable to the receiving State was not met and the matter led to some dispute between the two governments. In most of the cases where this occurred it is clear that the conduct of the diplomat was authorized or at least sanctioned by his government, and the incident could not appropriately be dealt with by means of the *persona non grata* procedure, since it reflected a real difference on substantive matters between the governments concerned.[14] A good example was the dispute between France and Venezuela in 1905 which eventually led to the recall of the French minister and expulsion of the Venezuelan chargé d'affaires. Diplomatic relations between the two countries were suspended for several years.[15]

10.22　At this period, however, a few governments and in particular the British government expected reasons to be given when asked to recall one of their diplomats abroad, and reserved the right to examine these reasons and not to recall the diplomat unless satisfied that the reasons were adequate.[16] In 1888 the legal views of Britain and the United States clashed over the affair of Lord Sackville.[17] The United States Government, insisting on their right to have Lord Sackville recalled without giving reasons for their request, quoted Calvo as authority for their position:

> When the government near which a diplomatic agent resides thinks fit to dismiss him for conduct considered improper, it is customary to notify the government which accredited him that its representative is no longer acceptable, and to ask for his recall. If the offence committed by the agent is of a grave character, he may be dismissed without waiting the recall of his own government. The government which asks for the recall may or may not at its pleasure, communicate the reasons on which it bases its request; but such an explanation cannot be required.[18]

---

[13] J W Foster, *A Century of American Diplomacy* (Boston, 1900) 433. See also an account of a case in 1871 involving the Russian head of legation in Washington where the United States government reaffirmed its view that an official statement that a diplomatic agent had ceased to be *persona grata* 'is sufficient for the purpose of obtaining his recall'.

[14] In 1852 the US government asked for the recall of the Nicaraguan minister which was refused. Ibid, 497.

[15] C de Boeck, 'L'Expulsion et les difficultés internationales qu'en soulève la pratique' (1927) *RdC* 502.

[16] See Lord Palmerston's assertion that 'it must rest with the British Government in such a case to determine whether there is or is not any just cause of complaint against the British diplomatic agent, and whether the dignity and interests of Great Britain would be best consulted by withdrawing him or maintaining him at his post'. J B Moore, *Digest of International Law*, Vol 4 (Washington: Govt Print Office, 1906) 538–9; Correspondence Presented to Parliament (1848).

[17] C Calvo, *International Law* (4th edn, Paris, 1888) Vol 3, 213; Moore, *Digest*, Vol 4, 536.

[18] Ibid.

The position then taken by the United States and by most other States is now **10.23** set out in Article 9 of the VCDR which states that:

1. The receiving State may at any time and without having to explain its decision, notify the sending State that the head of the mission or any member of the diplomatic staff of the mission is *persona non grata* or that any other member of the staff of the mission is not acceptable. In any such case, the sending State shall, as appropriate, either recall the person concerned or terminate his functions with the mission. A person may be declared non grata or not acceptable before arriving in the territory of the receiving State.
2. If the sending State refuses or fails within a reasonable period to carry out its obligations under paragraph 1 of this Article, the receiving State may refuse to recognize the person concerned as a member of the mission.

These procedures are intended to ensure that when a diplomat becomes personally unacceptable to the receiving State, the matter is handled with as little embarrassment to the diplomat as possible and in the way least likely to lead to protracted and unprofitable dispute between sending and receiving States. In most cases the reasons for the recall are known both to the sending and the receiving State, but they are not discussed in diplomatic correspondence or in public. The diplomat may have committed a serious criminal offence, such as espionage or fraud, may have taken some action which is resented by the receiving State as interference in its internal affairs, or may simply have given offence by his or her personal manner, attitudes, or conduct. If both States agree, the matter may be handled so quietly that it does not become public knowledge at all that the diplomat concerned has left before the end of the normal tour of duty.

The Vienna Convention makes clear that a diplomat may be declared *persona* **10.24** *non grata* before arrival and in that event need not be granted a visa or admitted on arrival. There is no *agrément* procedure for diplomats other than the head of mission (and in some States for defence attachés) and so this possibility may be of importance if the receiving State finds that it has been notified of the imminent arrival of someone newly appointed to a diplomatic mission and is aware that serious criminal charges have been made against the diplomat or suspects that he or she is a spy.

The rules, however, do not lead to the avoidance of dispute or political tension **10.25** between sending and receiving States in all cases. Probably the most dramatic use of the *persona non grata* procedure occurred in 1971 when the British government requested the withdrawal of 105 Soviet government officials, many of them on the diplomatic staff of the embassy of the Soviet Union in London. On the instructions of the Foreign Secretary Sir Alec Douglas-Home, Mr Ippolitov, the Soviet chargé d'affaires, was asked to call on Sir Denis Greenhill, Permanent

Under-Secretary. He was handed an aide-mémoire which contained the government's request for the withdrawal of the officials in the following terms:

> inadmissible activities by Soviet officials in Britain have continued. During the last twelve months a number of Soviet officials have been required to leave the country after being detected in such activities. During the same period it has been decided not to issue visas to a number of officials nominated to Soviet establishments in the United Kingdom on account of their previous activities.
>
> The staffs of the Soviet Embassy and the Soviet Trade Delegation, which form the two largest elements in the Soviet official establishment in Britain, far outnumber the British officials working in the Soviet Union.
>
> Her Majesty's Government have tolerated the growth of these establishments.... Evidence has however been accumulating that this tolerance has been systematically abused.
>
> The abuse is a matter of serious concern to Her Majesty's Government as a direct threat to the security of this country. Moreover the recurring need to request the withdrawal of Soviet officials from this country, or to refuse visas to certain officials selected for service in this country, imposes strains on Anglo-Soviet relations. So do unjustified acts of Soviet retaliation...
>
> The Soviet Embassy is therefore requested to arrange for the persons named on the attached list, all of whom have been concerned in intelligence activities, to leave Britain within two weeks from the date of this aide-memoire. Henceforth:
>
> (a) The numbers of officials in (i) the Soviet Embassy (ii) the Soviet trade delegation and (iii) all other Soviet organisations in Great Britain will not be permitted to rise above the levels at which they will stand after the withdrawal of the persons named in the attached list;
>
> (b) If a Soviet official is required to leave the country as a result of his having been detected in intelligence activities, the permitted level in that category will be reduced by one.[19]

The officials concerned were recalled within the time limit set and the affair led to a prolonged coolness in the relations between Britain and the Soviet Union. The drastic measure did however lead to a significant drop in espionage activity in Britain and it was some years before the provision for reduction of the overall ceiling on embassy numbers had to be invoked by the UK in response to espionage by Soviet agents.

10.26 In October 1976, evidence of widespread smuggling and illegal sales of drugs, alcohol, and cigarettes by North Korean diplomats in Scandinavia led to a series of declarations of *persona non grata*. The first country to act was Denmark, which gave the North Korean ambassador and his entire diplomatic staff six days to leave on the grounds that they had turned their embassy into a front for the

---

[19] The text of the aide-memoire was printed in *The Times*, 25 September 1971.

illegal import and sale of drugs, liquor, and cigarettes. This followed the seizure of 385 pounds of hashish, estimated at about £200,000. The North Korean ambassador initially denied all the charges. A few days later the government of Finland disclosed that Finland had been used as a transit station for drugs destined for other Scandinavian countries, and declared *persona non grata* the North Korean chargé d'affaires and three other diplomats. The chargé d'affaires at first refused to go and demanded that the Finnish government should review 'the illegal decision'. The following day the North Korean ambassador to Norway and Sweden was declared *persona non grata,* together with four of his diplomatic staff. On this occasion however the diplomats concerned were recalled and returned home immediately. The Swedish Foreign Minister said that her government was 'deeply disturbed by the fact that officials at a foreign embassy had so seriously misused their diplomatic immunity in committing such obvious criminal activity'.[20]

In its 1985 Review of the VCDR which followed the shooting from the Libyan **10.27** People's Bureau described in Chapter 13 and an enquiry and report by the House of Commons Foreign Affairs Committee, the United Kingdom government set out in detail its policy regarding the expulsion of persons entitled to diplomatic immunity who were alleged to be involved in serious criminal offences as follows:

> As a general rule espionage and incitement to or advocacy of violence require an immediate declaration of *persona non grata*. Those involved in violent crime or drug trafficking are also declared *persona non grata* unless a waiver of immunity is granted. In addition the following categories of offence normally lead to a request for withdrawal in the absence of a waiver:
>
> (a) firearms offences;
> (b) rape, incest, serious cases of indecent assault and other serious sexual offences;
> (c) fraud;
> (d) second drink/driving offence (or first if aggravated by violence or injury to a third party);
> (e) other traffic offences involving death or serious injury;
> (f) driving without third party insurance;
> (g) theft including large scale shoplifting (first case);
> (h) lesser scale shoplifting (second case);
> (i) any other offence normally carrying a prison sentence of more than 12 months.
>
> The criteria for dealing with alleged offences are applied with both firmness and discretion, but not automatically. Full account is taken of the nature and seriousness of the offence and any inadequacies in the evidence.[21]

---

[20] *The Times*, 16, 21, 22, and 23 October 1976.
[21] Review of the Vienna Convention, 1985, Cmnd 9497, paras 60–71.

10.28   The United States has in Guidance for Law Enforcement Officers in 1988 stressed that although it is by the terms of Article 9 of the VCDR under no legal obligation to give reasons for a request for withdrawal or declaration of *persona non grata*, it will take this step only if there is reasonable certainty that a criminal act has been committed. To act in an arbitrary or prejudiced way in invoking such an extreme tool would not serve the reputation of the United States as a society governed by the rule of law, and if it could not be defended to the other government concerned could lead to a reciprocal measure against an innocent American diplomat.[22] By contrast, the United Kingdom has in a few exceptional cases required recall of diplomats without suggesting that they were personally involved in unlawful activity. These included its response to the failure of the Russian government to extradite Andrey Lugovoy to stand trial in Britain for the murder by poisoning with polonium-210 of the dissident and former Russian security service officer Alexander Litvinenko or to cooperate in the search for a solution.[23] In all States, where a retaliatory expulsion of diplomats takes place, the diplomats required to leave are also selected without regard to their own personal conduct. There are occasions when a receiving government without going so far as to declare the person concerned *persona non grata* may intimate to an embassy that the behaviour of one of its diplomats has caused it such displeasure that he will no longer receive any assistance or cooperation from the host government and that it would be in the best interests of both countries if the sending government were to withdraw him. Such an incident occurred in the 1960s in Paris when, after a Western diplomat was overheard making disobliging remarks about the then French President, Charles de Gaulle, the French government took the action described above. In 1997 the Yugoslav government of Slobodan Milošević threatened the British ambassador with expulsion for interference in internal affairs during the mass demonstrations against the Yugoslav government's vote rigging and again a few months later for importing decoders via the diplomatic bag to distribute to opposition radio stations to help them relay news broadcasts. When the ambassador responded that the cause of the protest was not alleged misuse of the diplomatic bag but attempt at censorship of the opposition media and that he would recommend that recently granted trade concessions to Yugoslavia be withdrawn, the government backed down and the ambassador remained.

---

[22] Department of State Guidance for Law Enforcement Officers with regard to Personal Rights and Immunities of Foreign Diplomatic and Consular Personnel, 27 ILM (1988) 1617, at 1633.
[23] Hansard, HC Debs, 16 July 2007, cols 21–8.

Withdrawal of a Diplomatic Mission

The recall of an entire diplomatic mission, whether on a temporary or on an   **10.29**
indefinite basis, without breach of diplomatic relations between sending and
receiving States is now a relatively frequent procedure. Recall may take place for
political, economic, or security reasons. In all cases the two States remain formally
in diplomatic relations and there are no constraints in their contacts at international conferences or organizations or in third States. Normally it is hoped that a
permanent diplomatic mission may be re-established under more favourable circumstances, and this is more straightforward when no formal breach of relations
has taken place. A formal breach is usually very difficult to reverse quickly, even if
the reason for it has disappeared. In 1956, for example, Saudi Arabia broke relations with the United Kingdom and France on 6 November, one day before the
cease-fire which brought an end to their intervention in Suez, but relations were
not restored between Saudi Arabia and either State until 1962.

An example of recall of a mission for political reasons took place in 1981 when   **10.30**
in response to Libya's support for international terrorism the United States
closed its embassy in Libya and asked Libya to close its mission in Washington,
saying that the action 'reduces our relations with Libya to the lowest level consistent with maintenance of diplomatic relations'.[24] In 2011, the Holy See
recalled its nuncio from Ireland following the Irish prime minister's strong criticism of its handling of sexual abuse allegations against some of its priests. Later
that year Ireland announced the closure of its mission to the Holy See. It was
claimed by the government that the closure was for reasons of economy, a claim
that was widely questioned.[25] (The mission to the Holy See was reopened in
2014.) Closure of diplomatic missions for reasons of economy is carried out
even by highly developed States following review of their overseas representation and of the justification for individual posts in terms of the extent of business to be carried out. In Chapter 5, it was explained that financial constraints
often lead to a decision not to establish a permanent mission and the same
reasons also lead to closures. In 1998, following the bombing by Al Qaeda of US
embassies in Kenya and Tanzania, the United States closed its embassies in
those States and in a number of other States in Africa because of fears as to their
physical security.[26] A mission may be recalled where, because of serious civil
disturbance or armed conflict, it has become difficult or impossible for it to

---

[24] (1981) *AJIL* 957.
[25] *Catholic Herald*, 29 July 2011; *The Times*, 4 November 2011.
[26] *The Times*, 25 and 28 August 1998, 25 June 1999.

carry out its functions safely or effectively.[27] In 1990, during the military action to liberate Kuwait from occupation by Iraq, many Western States withdrew their diplomatic missions while stressing that this was not acceptance of the demand by Saddam Hussein for their closure on the ground that Kuwait had become a province of Iraq and that they remained in full diplomatic relations with Kuwait.[28] In all these cases, it is normal for arrangements to be set up for protection of interests.

Breach of Diplomatic Relations

10.31　The mission of a diplomatic agent comes to an end on a break in diplomatic relations between the sending and receiving States. The functions of the diplomatic staff concerned terminate on notification by the State which initiates the breach since—as explained in Chapter 5—the existence of diplomatic relations depends on agreement by the two States concerned. Privileges and immunities of all members of the mission subsist in the normal way until they leave the country, or have had a 'reasonable period' of opportunity to do so, or are reaccredited as diplomatic agents of the protecting Power should they stay on in that capacity. Arrangements for protection of interests are explained in paragraphs 10.43–10.48. In addition, the receiving State is bound to permit diplomatic agents (with the exception of its own nationals) to leave the country, and Article 45 of the VCDR requires the receiving State to respect and protect the premises of the mission, together with its property and archives. As is emphasized by Articles 44 and 45, a rupture of diplomatic relations, whether or not followed by hostilities, does not in itself affect the obligations of the receiving State to protect members of the mission, as well as its premises, property, and archives. When the diplomatic agent's functions terminate on account of a breach in relations, the courtesies associated with normal recall described in paragraph 10.14 are not observed.

10.32　Until the First World War the breaking of diplomatic relations was very often the prelude to war or to some form of military action, but this is no longer the case. Since 1945 it may occur that two States are involved in war or in some form of armed conflict without diplomatic relations being broken (as was the case with India and Pakistan in 1965 and again in 1971), and it also happens that diplo-

---

[27] Between 2012 and 2014 many diplomatic missions in the Middle East were closed as a result of the unrest following the Arab Spring including the United States and United Kingdom missions in Syria, Egypt, Yemen, and Libya.

[28] This response was required by SC resolution 664.

matic relations are broken between two States without any intention on either side to resort to military action. Breach of relations is however an extreme action usually taken by the initiating State in response to a severe injury to its own perceived interests. The United Kingdom, for example, broke diplomatic relations with Libya in 1984 following the fatal shooting from the Libyan mission premises of a policewoman protecting these premises in the context of a demonstration by Libyan dissidents and the failure of the Libyan government to take any realistic steps to permit the murder to be investigated. In 1986 the UK broke diplomatic relations with Syria on the basis of evidence of active involvement of the Syrian embassy in a plot—discovered in time by the Israeli security authorities—to sabotage an El Al airliner and kill all the passengers on board. For many years during which Germany was divided, the government of the Federal Republic of Germany under the Hallstein doctrine broke diplomatic relations with any State (with the sole exception of the Soviet Union) which recognized East Germany as a separate sovereign State. In 2008 Serbia withdrew ambassadors from any country which recognized Kosovo as an independent State.

Relations may also be broken by way of strong protest at some action by another **10.33** State not directed against the State initiating the breach but affecting an issue of widespread concern. In 1965, for example, seven African States broke diplomatic relations with the United Kingdom in protest at its handling of Rhodesia's unilateral declaration of independence.

Disappearance of the Head of the Sending or the Receiving State

Following the disappearance of the Head of State, either of the sending State or **10.34** of the receiving State, it is normally quickly apparent whether or not diplomatic appointments will be renewed as a matter of course. Only very exceptionally (for example when the Royal Government of National Union of Cambodia replaced the government of the Khmer Republic in May 1975)[29] is there an interval before it becomes evident whether diplomatic appointments are being renewed.

Where in either State a monarch or other hereditary ruler is replaced by his **10.35** successor, whether constitutionally or otherwise, or where in either State changes not provided for in the constitution lead to the emergence of a new Head of State, it is general practice that ambassadors who remain at their posts

---

[29] See Chapter 5, paragraph 5.12.

are provided with fresh credentials. Under Article 16 of the VCDR, ambassadors' order of precedence is unaffected when this occurs. On the other hand, the replacement in either State of a president or other elected or appointed Head of State, whether on death, resignation, or expiry of his term of office, has never been regarded as making fresh credentials necessary. It is sometimes difficult to determine whether the constitutional change which has occurred is of a nature to make fresh credentials necessary, and the modern tendency is, in cases of doubt, neither to seek nor to issue fresh credentials. This is particularly the case when for political reasons it is desired not to draw attention to the change which has occurred.[30]

10.36 Where the change in the Head of State of a sending or receiving State takes place as a result of violent revolution or armed conflict, it is more usual that diplomatic appointments are not confirmed. A radically new government will wish to replace former ambassadors by appointing new ones sympathetic to their own views. If the sending State has merged with or been absorbed by another State it will—as explained in Chapter 5—no longer have the right to send or receive ambassadors at all. Where the government changes in the receiving State, other States may not recognize the new government in control of the capital, or may withdraw ambassadors to indicate displeasure with the new régime. The new government itself may not wish to remain in diplomatic relations with all the States which formerly sent ambassadors to it, or may wish fresh appointments to be made simply in order to indicate its distaste for persons who did business with its predecessor.

10.37 Where the government in the receiving State falls as a consequence of armed conflict, it is likely that ambassadors and their staffs will for security reasons—as explained earlier—have been withdrawn in advance. The diplomatic missions of all Western States were withdrawn before the fall of Saigon in 1975, and the French mission to Cambodia was alone in remaining staffed until after the fall of Phnom Penh a few weeks earlier. Where, however, some violent or unconstitutional change has occurred and ambassadors remain at their post, they may not enter into any form of official contact with the newly established authorities until instructed by their governments that recognition is being accorded to the new government in the capital. When a new government establishes itself by means of a *coup d'état*, revolt, or revolution, it is customary for a circular Note to be sent to the heads of the diplomatic missions remaining in the capital, informing them of the establishment of the new government and expressing the wish that diplomatic relations should continue between that State and the

---

[30] See Chapter 5, paragraph 5.10.

States which have accredited the ambassadors receiving this Note. Since to acknowledge this Note could imply recognition of the new government, it should not be acknowledged until instructions authorizing this are received from the home capital.[31] There may be delay due to consultations among groups of closely associated States (for example the European Union or the African Union), regarding the policy and timing of any recognition. The acknowledgement of a Note of this kind is now the most common way in which a new government is recognized and the intention to continue diplomatic relations is confirmed, and the procedure was used, for example, on the emergence in 1972 of Bangladesh as an independent State following its secession from Pakistan.

Following the deposition of Saddam Hussein by military force in 2003 and the establishment of a Coalition Provisional Authority as the interim government of Iraq, the United States stated that ambassadors and other diplomats remaining in post in Baghdad were not regarded as exercising diplomatic functions.[32] Some governments sent special representatives to the Coalition Provisional Authority. After the interim Iraq government assumed sovereign powers one year later, relations with it were established on a normal basis.   **10.38**

Where the government in the sending State disappears in some violent conflict, ambassadors and their staffs abroad will have to assess their position in the light of the circumstances. An ambassador retains diplomatic and representative status up to the moment when the receiving State makes clear that it has withdrawn recognition from the government which accredited the ambassador. After the fall of the government of President Allende of Chile in 1973 the new government in Santiago, before it had been recognized by the United Kingdom, dismissed the Chilean ambassador in London and appointed a member of the diplomatic staff as chargé d'affaires. The Chilean diplomats were divided in their loyalties, some being willing to serve the new government and some preferring to resign. Those willing to serve the new government assumed control of the chancery building while the ambassador remained in his official residence, which was separate. In this situation the Foreign and Commonwealth Office made clear that, since they had not withdrawn recognition from the government of President Allende, they continued to regard the ambassador accredited by him as the ambassador of Chile and did not regard his functions as having terminated. The government therefore refused to cooperate when the unrecognized chargé d'affaires asked for assistance to evict the ambassador from his residence. Shortly afterwards, however, the United Kingdom recognized the   **10.39**

---

[31] See also paragraph **10**.7 regarding contacts in the absence of recognition.
[32] State Department Press Briefing 29 May 2003.

new government in Chile and from that time regarded the chargé d'affaires appointed by that government as head of the mission of Chile. In 2011, the Libyan ambassador in London was given 24 hours to leave the country and this was followed a short time later by the expulsion of the remaining embassy staff after a decision by the United Kingdom government to recognize the Libyan National Transitional Council as the 'sole governmental authority in Libya'.[33]

10.40　An ambassador may on the other hand prefer to resign on the fall of the government which accredited him, without waiting for the receiving State to withdraw recognition of that government. On the fall of the government of the Republic of Vietnam in 1975 the Ambassador in London notified the Foreign and Commonwealth Office of his resignation and that of his entire staff nine days before the recognition by the United Kingdom of the Provisional Revolutionary Government of South Vietnam. The Foreign and Commonwealth Office accepted that this resignation terminated his functions as ambassador and at his request assumed temporary custody of the premises and property of the embassy. These were later returned to the chargé d'affaires of North Vietnam, which was—during the period before reunification of North and South Vietnam a year later—protecting the interests of South Vietnam in the United Kingdom. On the collapse of the government headed by Saddam Hussein in 2003, ambassadors appointed by him to posts abroad for the most part burnt or shredded documents and quietly left their posts.[34]

10.41　The receiving State must in the conduct of its diplomatic relations with the State undergoing violent change have regard only to the statements or communications of whichever government it recognizes at the relevant time as the government of that State. It is, however, entitled to presume, when it recognizes a new government, that unless that new government has made clear by direct communication or by public announcement that its country's previously appointed ambassador has been recalled or dismissed, the ambassador continues to exercise his functions on behalf of the new government.

Facilities for Departure

10.42　Regardless of the circumstances in which the diplomatic mission comes to an end a diplomat or other member of a diplomatic mission who is not a national

---

[33] See announcement by the Foreign Secretary, William Hague, 28 July 2011; also C Warbrick 'British Policy and the National Transitional Council of Libya' (2012) 61 *ICLQ* 247 and Chapter 5, paragraph 5.14.

[34] *The Times*, 11 April and 24 July 2003.

of the receiving State must be given under Article 44 of the VCDR facilities to leave the receiving State and in case of need provided with the necessary means of transport. Members of their families—irrespective of their nationality—must also be permitted to leave. These rights apply in addition to continuing privileges and immunities under Article 39 (described in Chapter 14) and apply even in case of armed conflict. These facilities for departure were uniformly granted in many States in Europe on the outbreak of the Second World War. In 1984, when the United Kingdom broke diplomatic relations with Libya, all those remaining in the diplomatic mission were transported under guard to Heathrow Airport and simultaneously the entire staff of the British embassy in Tripoli with their families were transported to the airport. Even the take-off of the two aircraft from London and Tripoli was synchronized.

Protection of Interests

Chapter 5 explained the reasons why a State may choose not to enter into diplomatic relations with another State or not to establish a permanent diplomatic mission there. Paragraphs 10.29–10.33 set out the circumstances in which a diplomatic mission may be recalled either on a temporary or on an indefinite basis while formal diplomatic relations continue, or in which diplomatic relations may be broken. In any of these cases a sending State may ask another State to protect its interests in a receiving State where, for whatever reason, it is not represented by a permanent diplomatic mission. Arrangements under which one State protects the interests of another sovereign State in a third State are increasingly frequent and sophisticated. Such arrangements may offer to a sending State many of the advantages of a permanent diplomatic mission at less risk and cost to itself, and the functions to be carried out on behalf of the State whose interests are protected as well as the modalities of protection may vary considerably. **10.43**

The basic framework for protection of interests is set out in Articles 45 and 46 of the VCDR. Article 45 covers the situation where diplomatic relations are broken off or a mission is permanently or temporarily recalled, and entitles the sending State both to entrust the custody of its mission premises, property, and archives to a third State acceptable to the receiving State and to entrust the protection of its interests and those of its nationals to a third State acceptable to the receiving State. It is not necessary for the receiving State to give express approval of a specific protecting State, and the notification and implied acceptance are normally carried out informally. It is not however permitted under the Vienna Convention for a receiving State to withhold its consent to any protecting **10.44**

State so as to nullify the right of the unrepresented State to have its interests protected. Such a course was taken by Indonesia in 1961 following its breach of relations with The Netherlands, but was even then—before the VCDR—widely criticized as contrary to international practice.[35]

10.45 By contrast, where there are no pre-existing diplomatic relations, prior consent of the receiving State is required before another State may set up any form of protection of its own interests there. Article 46 provides that:

> [a] sending State may with the prior consent of a receiving State, and at the request of a third State not represented in the receiving State, undertake the temporary protection of the interests of the third State and of its nationals.

The reason for the discrepancy between Article 45 and Article 46 is that the protection of interests option, where there have been no previous relations, was seen when the Convention was drafted as an interim step to establishment of full relations or permanent diplomatic missions, both of which under Article 2 require the consent of both States. It is, however, no longer the case that the option is usually only temporary, and it is significantly more common than in 1961. Luxembourg, for example, a small State with limited capacity for external representation, normally has its interests protected by Belgium. Many other small States accredit an ambassador to several States, as permitted by Article 5 of the VCDR, and in capitals where the ambassador is non-resident and there is no permanent mission, it is frequent for another State to be asked to act as protecting Power.

10.46 When a diplomatic mission is recalled or relations broken, a sending State is entitled in the receiving State, first, to a reasonable period for withdrawal of the head and members of its mission, and during this period its premises will continue to be entitled to inviolability. The Vienna Convention does not define what is 'reasonable' in this context and in practice much will depend on the circumstances leading to the withdrawal of the mission or breach in relations. Where withdrawal is low-key and due, for example, to economic circumstances, the receiving State will normally grant more than the one-month period usual in the case of departure of an individual diplomat to allow the sending State to dispose of premises and property or possibly to conclude protection arrangements. On the other hand, where the breach is acrimonious, the receiving State may require a speedier withdrawal. When the United Kingdom broke relations with Libya in 1984 following the shooting from the Libyan People's Bureau of a British policewoman protecting the premises during a demonstration, seven days only were permitted for withdrawal, and until that period had elapsed the

---

[35] (1961) *RGDIP* 611.

police did not enter the premises—even after they were in fact empty—to search for evidence relating to the murder. The premises were left empty under the custody of the embassy of Saudi Arabia as protecting Power and it was made clear that the Libyans would never again be permitted to use them as a diplomatic mission in view of the public outrage at the events leading to the breach in relations.[36]

After the 'reasonable period' has elapsed, the premises are no longer regarded as 'used for the purposes of the mission' (the definition of mission premises under Article 1 of the Convention) so that full inviolability lapses. The authorities may enter them to check that they are secure and, if leased, the landlord may recover possession to the extent permitted under local law. The receiving State is however still bound by paragraph 1 of Article 45 to 'respect and protect the premises of the mission, together with its property and archives'. This duty to 'respect and protect' falls short of what is required in the case of inviolability, but normally precludes expropriation of the premises so long as title remains with the former sending State. If the premises are simply left empty, perhaps with valuable moveable property inside, the duty of protection may be an onerous one for the receiving State, which may well take the view that it cannot provide 24-hour security protection on an indefinite basis in the absence of any reimbursement of expenses by the sending State. Such was the experience of the United Kingdom in the years following the assumption of power in Cambodia in 1975 by the Pol Pot regime which made no response to an express invitation from the United Kingdom government to resume diplomatic relations, gave no instructions for custody or disposal of its former embassy premises or property, but simply left their abandoned premises open to occupation by squatters. These difficulties were one reason why the UK made provision some years later, in the Diplomatic and Consular Premises Act 1987,[37] for a system of control of mission premises, provision for precise dates of commencement and termination of their status in accordance with rules of international law, and powers for the Secretary of State to expropriate and sell former premises 'if he is satisfied that to do so is consistent with international law'. The exercise of these powers in the case of the former Cambodian embassy was challenged in the Case of *R v Secretary of State for Foreign and Commonwealth Affairs, ex parte Samuel.*[38] The court there held that the action taken by the UK government to evict the squatters (who would otherwise have acquired title to the premises), take title to the premises, sell them, and hold the proceeds in trust for the Cambodian government,

10.47

---

[36] *The Observer*, 20 September 1987.

[37] c 46. A circular Note to diplomatic missions in London describing the provisions of the Act is printed in (1987) *BYIL* 541.

[38] Times Law Reports, 17 August 1989, 83 ILR 231.

was not in breach of the duty of the UK government to 'respect and protect' the premises and could not be reviewed by an English court unless it was unreasonable or taken in bad faith.

10.48　The United States have similar powers[39] to preserve and protect premises of a former diplomatic mission where there is no protecting State and, one year after mission functions have come to an end, to dispose of them and remit the proceeds to the former sending State, and these powers were used in 1996 in regard to the former embassy of Somalia.

Express Arrangements for Protection of Interests

10.49　Situations such as those just described are obviously also unsatisfactory from the point of view of sending States with a long-term interest in the preservation of their embassy property and in many cases in restoration of a normal diplomatic presence at some later date. The sending State may in some cases also be responsible for a large community of expatriates living or working in the receiving State and in need of advice, political protection, and consular services. It is therefore much more common for an unrepresented State to entrust the protection of its interests in the receiving State to a third State and to take advantage at the least of the provisions of Articles 45 or 46 of the Vienna Convention described earlier. The choice of the third State asked to undertake this responsibility will depend on political as well as on practical considerations. Formerly Switzerland and Sweden were popular as protecting Powers because of their perceived neutrality. A State will wish to select a protecting Power sympathetic to itself, but also with reasonable working relations with the receiving State. Canada, on suspending its diplomatic relations with Nigeria in 1997 and recalling its high commissioner in Lagos, asked the United States to protect its interests there.[40] The United Kingdom when it broke relations with Libya in 1984 chose Italy as its protecting Power, while Libya chose Saudi Arabia. The close links among Member States of the European Union developed under the Common Foreign and Security Policy now make it standard for one EU Member State to request another to act as protecting Power, but this may be impracticable where all EU Member States are involved in the reason for the breach of relations or join in a collective decision to break relations. From a practical perspective, the State chosen should have a reasonably solid diplomatic presence in the receiving State so that it will have sufficient staff to discharge the

---

[39] Foreign Missions Act 1982, s 205(c).
[40] *The Times*, 14 March 1997.

administrative, consular, and perhaps some limited political functions which are likely to be requested.

The negotiation of express and detailed arrangements for the protection of interests and for the reimbursement of expenses incurred became general practice during the later part of the twentieth century. In 1965, nine African States—Algeria, Congo Brazzaville, Ghana, Guinea, Mali, Mauritania, Sudan, Tanzania, and the United Arab Republic—broke diplomatic relations with the United Kingdom in protest at its response to the Unilateral Declaration of Independence by Southern Rhodesia.[41] In that context the United Kingdom developed a form of protection of interests arrangement which has since become widespread. The arrangements between the State seeking protection, the protecting Power, and the receiving State involve the retention of a few junior diplomatic, administrative, and technical staff belonging to the State seeking protection and their notification to the receiving State as members of the diplomatic mission of the protecting Power. The premises whose use for the purposes of the former mission has been discontinued are notified and accepted as premises of the mission of the protecting Power and in this capacity they will enjoy not only the 'respect and protection' described earlier but full inviolability.   **10.50**

Similar arrangements were set up on an informal basis in 1967 when Egypt broke diplomatic relations with the United States in the context of the Six-Day War and Spain assumed the responsibility of protecting US interests in Egypt. The US embassy formally became the American Interests Section of the Spanish embassy and was staffed originally by only a single United States administrator but later by six or seven staff led by a US diplomat of counsellor rank. In 1976 when Iceland broke relations with the United Kingdom during the 'cod war', a British Interests Section was established in Reykjavik within the embassy of France which became the protecting Power. This consisted of all the members of the former UK embassy other than the ambassador, and they were instructed so far as possible to continue normal business. The Swiss government was from 1961 to 2015 the protecting Power for the Cuban Interests Section in Washington and from 1991 to 2015 (when diplomatic relations between the United States and Cuba were restored), for the US Interests Section in Havana. In both cases the Interests Sections were staffed by their own diplomatic staff.   **10.51**

The advantage of this kind of arrangement to the sending State is that many basic functions such as reporting on conditions in the receiving State and carrying out administrative and consular functions may be performed by members of its own service who are familiar not only with its general instructions to   **10.52**

---

[41] For details, see L Sfez, 'La Rupture des relations diplomatiques' (1966) *RGDIP* 359, at 386.

overseas officers but sensitive to the political and cultural requirements of the sending State for information. There is no need to reimburse a protecting Power for expenses incurred for functions carried out by staff in the Interests Section, although arrangements for protection of interests normally make provision for reimbursement of expenses incurred by the protecting Power. The tripartite arrangements will normally make clear what functions may be performed by the 'Interests Section' within the mission of the protecting Power. Political representations, for example, are not normally made by diplomats forming part of the Interests Section, and indeed the protecting Power may itself be unwilling to perform these in sensitive cases. When Westminster City Council brought proceedings against Iran for recovery of the expenses they had incurred in making the former Iranian embassy safe, after its violent liberation from siege by the Special Air Service led to its total destruction by fire, English law required service of the writ on the ministry of foreign affairs in Tehran before proceedings could validly continue. Sweden however, which was at the time protecting British interests in Iran, regarded this task as too controversial and outside its duties as protecting Power (which were set out in the Agreement quoted in paragraph **10.54**). In the absence of valid service on the government of Iran, the case against them as defendants could not proceed.[42]

10.53   Early international practice was to draft arrangements between the protecting Power and the State receiving protection of its interests, or tripartite arrangements involving the receiving State, as non-binding arrangements which did not require to be published. Recently, however, a number of them have been published. In 1986 the United Kingdom published the diplomatic Notes setting out the arrangements under which, following the breach of relations by the United Kingdom in response to the proven involvement of Syria in the attempted sabotage of an El Al airliner, Syrian relations were to be protected by Lebanon and UK interests by Australia, with Interests Sections in the Lebanese embassy in London and the Australian embassy in Damascus.[43]

10.54   Sweden is now required by national legislation when accepting responsibility as protecting Power to conclude a binding international agreement with the State whose interests it is to protect, and such agreements must be published. An Agreement with the United Kingdom regarding protection of UK interests in Iran was concluded in 1989.[44] Article 1 of the Agreement provided:

---

[42] *Westminster City Council v Government of the Islamic Republic of Iran* [1986] 3 All ER 284, 108 ILR 557.

[43] (1986) *BYIL* 554 and 625.

[44] UKTS No 45 (1989) also printed in (1990) *ICLQ* 472.

(1) Sweden undertakes to represent the United Kingdom as protecting power in the Islamic Republic of Iran.

(2) The commission as protecting power comprises administrative, humanitarian and consular matters. If the commission is to be extended to cover other matters a separate agreement to that effect is required.

(3) In dealing with protection matters, the protecting power may avoid taking action that could damage its position or good name in the receiving country, or in relation to any other country. In case of doubt in dealing with a matter, the Ministry of Foreign Affairs in Stockholm shall take the decision. This always applies to letters and other messages from the commissioning country to the receiving country.

It is possible, though unusual, for States to be in consular relations without also **10**.55 being in diplomatic relations, and in such cases there is no need for special arrangements to enable the protecting Power to exercise consular functions on behalf of the State whose diplomatic interests it has agreed to protect. Some years after the Falklands War in 1982 between the United Kingdom and Argentina, consular relations between the two States were resumed as an interim step towards the resumption of full diplomatic relations a year later, in 1990.[45]

---

[45] *The Times*, 16 February 1990.

11

TERRORISM AND DIPLOMACY

Ivor Roberts

General

11.1 Although it has not proved possible to reach an international consensus on a legal definition of terrorism, the motivations and international character of modern terrorism are addressed in the definition of that term in section 1 of the UK's Terrorism Act.[1] Despite the lack of consensus, the UN General Assembly has made clear that terrorism is contrary to the principles of the UN Charter, and States have addressed specific activities (e.g. hijacking, bombing, financing) in a number of conventions (see also paragraphs **11.35–11.36**). As far as diplomacy is concerned, attacks on diplomatic and consular missions and on diplomats are attacks on institutions which on the one hand enjoy inviolability under

---

[1] The Act defines terrorism as the use or threat of action which is designed to influence a government or an international governmental organization, to intimidate the public or a section of the public anywhere in the world, and the use or threat is made for the purpose of advancing a political, religious, racial or ideological cause and where the action (a) involves serious violence against a person; (b) involves serious damage to property; (c) endangers a person's life, other than that of the person committing the action; (d) creates a serious risk to the health or safety of the public or a section of the public anywhere in the world; or (e) is designed seriously to interfere with or seriously to disrupt an electronic system.

international law but on the other offer attractive targets simply because of their representative character. There can be no a priori definition of procedure to be applied if such attacks take place, although experience shows that capitulation leads only to an escalation in terrorist demands. The only way to work out any guidance on best practice is by taking examples and deducing from them such general advice as one can.

Some of the attacks described later in the chapter imply an aroused public— 11.2 aroused possibly by the receiving government—as well as a degree of political instability. In a stable situation, these incidents should be rare; if they are at all likely to arise, police protection should, in accordance with international law and practice, be available and sufficient.

In an unstable political situation, an alert and well-informed mission in an earlier 11.3 era should have been able to sense when disorder and perhaps violence were to be expected. Global terrorism makes such anticipation very much more diffi-cult, and can create a very real threat even in stable situations. The present edi-tor enjoyed for instance round-the-clock protection in his last two posts, Dublin and Rome. Where disorder or violence is a possibility, a pre-emptive request in advance to the government of the receiving State, underlining its responsibility as the host government, for it to provide special protection is a wise precaution in itself, and will strengthen the position of the mission and the sending govern ment in any later argument about compensation. If there is prolonged distur-bance or civil conflict, the mission will probably ask its own government for enhanced security or other special assistance, clearing, where feasible, with the host government such matters as the carrying of weapons by security forces sent to protect the embassy.

Whatever doubt there may be about facts and cases, the 'victim' government 11.4 should ask the local government (whether the established one or a new one) to accept responsibility for any failure in the duty to protect diplomatic premises, and also responsibility for paying compensation. As shown in many of the cases described here, there is an overwhelming body of international practice in which—at least after passions have cooled—full compensation is paid by receiv-ing States irrespective of fault for damage sustained by foreign embassies and injuries received by diplomatic personnel (see Chapter 13, paragraph 13.18).

In the event of an attack, an official request should be addressed immediately to 11.5 the host government on behalf of the victim government for an assurance of effective protection both for the official representation of the victim country, and for its local community. The right to claim compensation should also at once be reasserted even where the host government is as much a victim as the diplomatic mission, e.g. an attack by a suicide bomber which kills local staff working in the foreign mission, or simply bystanders, or both as in the attack on the British consulate-general in Istanbul (see paragraph 11.17). This kind of diplomatic action should be taken without delay (i.e. without waiting for instructions) by the mission affected.[2] In the case of the burning of the British embassy in Beijing in 1967 (see paragraph 11.24) this was done by the British chargé d'affaires, who in the absence of other facilities sent a letter typed by himself through the ordinary post! These days an email with scanned attachment would no doubt be the preferred route.

11.6 It is a great help in such cases to have developed good working relationships between the missions of countries friendly to each other in the wider context. These would naturally include fellow-members of political organizations pursuing similar policies, such as the Member States of the EU, NATO, the Commonwealth, or regional groups such as the Organization of American States and the African Union. Each individual country must be cautious of involving itself politically in the causes leading to violent attacks. But where the threat is not against one mission only, collective representations may be more effective than representations by one ambassador only. These may be led by the dean or doyen of the diplomatic corps (see Chapter 10, paragraph 10.2) or in more political cases by the senior ambassador of the embassies of a regional grouping. A camaraderie among members of the diplomatic corps can be very helpful and supportive of the members of a 'victim' mission's morale in a situation which can often be extremely frightening and dangerous.

Kidnappings and their Implications

11.7 Attacks on embassies such as those presuppose either a degree of complicity on the part of the host government or more likely the activity of a terrorist group who are able to counter the security arrangements put in place by the host government and the foreign mission. In the late 1960s and early 1970s, however, attacks were very often effected by the kidnappings of senior diplomats. There was no need to storm and wreck an embassy in order to kidnap the head of it. Whereas the purpose of a mass demonstration might be to give vent to a natural or stimulated national emotion (e.g. the destruction of the British embassy in Dublin after Bloody Sunday (see paragraph 11.34), the purposes of the

---

[2] The question whether this immediate request should be made on instructions or on the responsibility of the head of mission may well depend on the possibility of immediate communication with the mission's own foreign ministry; if there is any doubt about this at all, immediate action by the head of mission is the wise course.

kidnappings of individual diplomats were far more calculated and coldblooded. The object was nearly always to extract a particular concession from a government, under the threat that, if the concession were not granted, a human life would be lost and the government refusing the concession would be to blame, both generally and in the eyes of the country which the victim represented.

Nor, when the technique was new, could the security authorities of the country **11.8** of the crime be specially blamed. Kidnappings of this kind were always carefully planned and the security authorities could hardly be expected to provide protection for all diplomats, whether at home or during their comings and goings.

The first case of attempted kidnapping which really startled world opinion **11.9** occurred in Guatemala City on 28 August 1968. The American ambassador, John C Mein, was returning normally to his office from lunch at the embassy residence when his official car was blocked in a down-town street. Seeing a number of young men in fatigue uniform bearing down on the car, the ambassador jumped out and ran, and was shot dead. The next day an organization called Fuerzas Armadas Rebeldes announced that he had been killed 'while resisting political kidnapping'. Seven months later, on 21 March 1969, in very similar circumstances, the Federal German ambassador, Count Karl von Spreti, was forced from his car by members of the same organization, who held him captive and demanded as the price for his freedom the release of seventeen political prisoners. While the diplomatic corps were discussing the situation with the Guatemalan government and the German government were pressing for release on the conditions proposed, the price was raised to twenty-five prisoners and US$700,000, which the Germans offered to pay. The Guatemalan government insisted that some of the prisoners had already been convicted of crimes and that the verdict of the courts could not be set aside by executive order. While the discussion was still in progress the deadline set by the kidnappers passed and on 5 April the body of Count von Spreti was found with a bullet-hole in the temple. The Federal German government claimed that the Guatemalan government had failed to meet its obligations under the Vienna Convention and virtually broke diplomatic relations with them.[3]

Other such events include the kidnapping in 1970 of James Cross, British Trade **11.10** Commissioner in Montreal; the kidnapping in 1971 of Geoffrey (later Sir Geoffrey) Jackson, British ambassador in Uruguay;[4] the kidnapping and murder of the Israeli consul-general in Istanbul by Turkish terrorists in May 1971; and the

---

[3] E Denza, *Diplomatic Law* (4th edn, Oxford: Oxford University Press, 2016) 215.
[4] For an account from his wife's perspective of his ordeal see K Hickman, *Daughters of Britannia* (London: Flamingo, 2000) 247–9.

appalling sequel to the occupation in March 1973 of the Saudi-Arabian embassy in Khartoum by the Arab 'Black September group', during which the American ambassador, his counsellor, and the Belgian chargé d'affaires were murdered. Over twenty-five such kidnappings or attempted kidnappings took place in the years 1968–73.[5]

11.11   The basic purpose of kidnapping and holding as hostages people of diplomatic status was to cause the sending State to exercise pressure on the receiving State, which is responsible for their protection, to 'purchase' their release. The purchase price can be very precise, for instance the release by the receiving State of certain people held in prison—people probably of no direct interest to the 'victim' State at all. Or the purpose could be political but less precise, as in the kidnapping of the British ambassador to Uruguay, where the motive appeared to have been a determined desire by the Tupamaros organization, a young revolutionary group, to establish itself as the recognized second power within the State. A kidnapping operation could also be the expression of something more fundamental still, a violation of law in pursuit of a doctrinal 'war of nerves', described by the infamous Brazilian terrorist Carlos Marighela in the following words: 'The object of the war of nerves is to misinform, spreading lies among the authorities—thus creating an air of nervousness, discredit, insecurity, uncertainty and concern on the part of the Government.'

11.12   It is clear that diplomatic kidnapping, although an event concerning international diplomacy, is not amenable to diplomatic method as between, for instance, the government employing the kidnapped diplomat and the kidnappers. The victim government will indeed use the diplomatic channel to urge a government in whose territory a diplomatic kidnapping takes place to intensify its search for kidnappers and kidnapped and to assure better protection in the future. But any 'negotiation' should be between the territorial government and the kidnappers. If the diplomat's sending State embarked on its own direct negotiations with the kidnappers, this could be resented by the territorial government as an intervention in an affair which was its responsibility.

11.13   Underlying the governmental decisions in such cases is the fundamental political and ethical question as to whether the paramount consideration is to preserve the life of a human being, or to discourage recurrent kidnapping by refusing to accede to the kidnappers' demands. A life may well be risked by a refusal to pay the price demanded. An interesting comment on this, quoted by

---

[5] Sources include *Political Kidnappings*, Committee on Internal Security. US House of Representatives, 93rd Congress, 1 August 1973, and Professor C E Baumann, *The Diplomatic Kidnappings* (The Hague: Martinus Nijhoff, 1973).

Professor Baumann,[6] was made by Burke Elbrick, a US ambassador kidnapped in 1969 and subsequently released, when he said that, although such a refusal would have resulted in his own 'disappearance from the scene', it would in general be unwise for a government to negotiate with terrorists and to give in to any of their demands. Sir Geoffrey Jackson, who had suspected that the Tupamaros might seek to kidnap him, had made it clear in advance to the British government that he did not wish to be ransomed. Knowledge of this by his captors may have helped to save his life. But where governments have taken a weaker line with kidnappers or been willing to do indirect deals with governments which had influence over the kidnappers to see their citizens released (as happened in the mid to late 1980s when there was a spate of hostage-taking in Beirut), there has usually been a corresponding increase in those taken hostage.

Although, therefore, diplomats are deeply concerned in this aspect of terrorism, **11.14** since any one of them might suddenly become a victim, diplomatic activity as such remains that of seeking to persuade governments in countries where kidnapping has taken place to act in accordance with the wishes of the victim government if it proves not to be possible to secure the release of the individual on terms acceptable to both governments. This was most demonstrably not carried out at the time of the siege of the Japanese embassy in Lima in 1996 (see Chapter 13, paragraph 13.16) although in the light of the success of the rescue operation Japan made no formal protest. The wishes of the victim government do not always align themselves with the victims themselves who must in their minds always be balancing the desirability of being rescued with the high risk usually involved in the attempted rescue. They will naturally be fearful of being killed during the rescue attempt or by retribution at the hands of the terrorists/kidnappers/hostage-takers. Failed attempts do not always impact mainly on the hostages. The fallout from the failure of the attempt to rescue the US embassy personnel in Tehran was largely political and the damage was done to the Carter administration (see paragraph **11.27**).

Although each case is individual there are certain actions which involve diplo- **11.15** matic procedures. First, it has to be accepted that as terrorism is increasingly global, security precautions need to be reviewed regularly and tightened up as appropriate in all countries receiving diplomatic and consular missions. There can be no mathematical rule of thumb about this. For instance, some countries are more vulnerable to terrorist attack than others if they hold in prison persons who can be described credibly, whether correctly or misleadingly, as political prisoners. The spate of kidnappings in Beirut in the 1980s by Hizbollah was

---

[6] C E Baumann, *The Diplomatic Kidnappings* (The Hague: Martinus Nijhoff, 1973).

thought to have been prompted by Kuwait's imprisonment of Islamists known as the Dawa 17, some of whom were related to Hizbollah leaders, including the chief hostage-taker, Imad Mugniyah. Experience is at best an uncertain guide in any attempt to forecast the occurrence of an attack on a mission or a kidnapping, or its timing; though reasonably good intelligence about the strength, vitality, and mutual relationships of terrorist groups will obviously be helpful. In this context, a State with an effectively repressive regime is more likely to be able (if willing) to control access to embassies than a freer regime.

11.16　Although it remains the duty of the receiving Power to protect the lives of members of diplomatic missions and of course the missions themselves, security forces are often—owing to the considerable rise in terrorist and criminal activity in recent years—too tightly stretched to give the diplomatic community the full protection that the threat warrants. The receiving Power, in these circumstances, can reasonably expect all missions to take measures to protect themselves and there is a self-serving responsibility on diplomats themselves to take reasonable precautions and behave with due regard to potential risks. Some missions on occasion employ armed security guards, but a number of countries object to arms being carried officially within their territory by anyone other than their own security forces. Where possible, therefore, armed intervention against terrorists should be left to the receiving Power, which should of course have the means to intervene quickly and effectively against armed terrorists attacking diplomatic missions.

11.17　Some countries, especially those which feel themselves threatened, have adopted what are now well-known defensive precautions. Their embassies have often been turned into fortresses where access is heavily controlled and sometimes discouraged. Moreover, apart from reinforcement of security personnel, there are variations of times and routes of official (increasingly armoured) cars (a notably vulnerable target), temporary abandonment of official flags and number plates, and the use of cars of any colour provided it is not black. But these useful secondary measures in turn have their limitations. For instance, depending on relative locations there may be very limited possibilities of varying the route taken between residence and office, and a determined group can sometimes rush the defences. By and large, however, diplomatic kidnapping has now become much rarer as governments both of the sending and of the host State have invested, in many cases substantially, in physical security measures. Those countries whose diplomats are seen to be most at risk (e.g. the US, UK, Israel, Turkey) have unsurprisingly invested the most. Sometimes there is a displacement risk where one diplomat is so well protected that a terrorist group will target someone from the same or another mission considered more vulnerable. It was thought that Brigadier Saunders may have been murdered in Athens (see paragraph 11.34) because his US opposite number, the original target, was too well protected. Similarly, in the case of Roger Short (see paragraph 11.5), he may well have been targeted because the US consul-general in Istanbul had recently moved to a purpose-built post on the top of a hill overlooking the Bosphorus.

There is little doubt that, at least for Al Qaeda, the UN represents as high a value **11.18** target as the representatives of those nations most at risk mentioned in the previous paragraph. Personnel of the UN and prominent NGOs no longer enjoy the protection which the nature of their work formerly afforded. However, unlike those nations, and despite the murderous suicide bombing of its headquarters in Iraq and Algeria, the UN appears to lack the capacity and funds to offer the same level of protection to its staff. For example, in mid-December 2008, Bob Fowler, the UN Secretary-General's special envoy to Niger (former Canadian deputy minister of defence, ambassador to the UN and Italy), together with his assistant, Louis Guay (former ambassador to Gabon), and their UN driver, were captured by 'Al Qaeda in the Islamic Maghreb' (AQIM) on the outskirts of Niamey, and held for four and a half months in the remoteness of the Sahara Desert. While Fowler is the first under-secretary-level UN employee to be kidnapped, with well over 50,000 employees worldwide, given the security threat, the UN face a challenge in continuing to recruit and retain high-quality staff.

Destructive Attacks on Missions

The following case studies of attacks on diplomatic premises are mere exemplars **11.19** and make no attempt to be exhaustive.

China

An early and particularly notorious example was the attack on the British mis- **11.20** sion in Beijing in 1967 during the Chinese 'Cultural Revolution'. This mass movement led to widespread turmoil throughout the year, involving both demonstrations against domestic authorities and attacks, marked by a recrudescence of anti-foreign sentiments, on a number of diplomatic missions. The Chinese Foreign Ministry had been temporarily taken over by members of extreme left-wing groups. Harassment was directed particularly at British diplomats because of events in the then British Crown Colony of Hong Kong. Severe restrictions were imposed on the movements of British diplomats in Beijing, which made it impossible for them to carry out their diplomatic duties. The Chinese authorities also from time to time withheld exit permits for diplomatic personnel. The mood in China seemed to vary from week to week and the harassment of British officials led to restrictions on Chinese movements in Britain and to demonstrations by British crowds outside the Chinese mission in London. The diplomacy of the period moreover was highly unorthodox, the Chinese chargé d'affaires[7] in London, for instance, refusing to accept four written protests delivered to him.[8]

11.21   The Cultural Revolution had spread to Communist supporters in Hong Kong, where there was a bomb campaign and a menacing succession of riots directed against the Hong Kong government. Legal action was taken to restore public order, which involved acting against, among others, certain Chinese journalists and representatives in Hong Kong of the official New China News Agency. These measures sometimes resulted in imprisonment and entailed the prohibition of the publication of at least three newspapers. They were described in Beijing as 'fascist atrocities'.

11.22   The first actual attack on British representation in China was not in Beijing, but in Shanghai where a crowd in May 1967 invaded the large British consulate-general compound in Shanghai. The consul-general and his family were subjected to indignities and furniture was wrecked. This resulted in an immediate representation to the Chinese chargé d'affaires in London, in which the British government reserved the right to claim compensation for the damage done to British property.

11.23   Next month there were officially inspired anti-British demonstrations in Beijing, under pretext of alleged British support for the Israelis in the 1967 Middle East war. An intrusion, without exception by non-Chinese, mostly Arab nationals resident in Beijing, was made into the premises of the British mission.

11.24   The most serious incident, however, occurred in August 1967, immediately following the expiry of a Chinese government ultimatum to the British government, demanding that they release certain journalists imprisoned in Hong Kong or 'accept all the serious consequences'. At the moment when this ultimatum expired, a very large crowd of Chinese demonstrators (10,000 according to the New China News Agency), who had surrounded the British mission throughout the day and prevented the staff from leaving, entered the compound and set fire to and sacked the chancery building, which was completely destroyed. The British chargé d'affaires, Donald (later Sir Donald) Hopson, and his staff, including five women, on leaving the building were physically attacked and beaten by the crowd before being eventually rounded up by detachments of the Chinese Army who had been present throughout.

---

[7] Mr Shen P'ing, who was appointed in 1975 Director of the Chinese Foreign Ministry's Asian Affairs Department.
[8] See Chapter 6, paragraphs 6.24–6.26.

The response of the British government was an immediate protest in London **11.25** delivered by a minister, in which an assurance of future protection was demanded and the right to full compensation was asserted. A number of severe restrictions were placed on Chinese officials in Britain, notably a ban on moving more than 5 miles (8 kilometres) from the centre of London, or leaving the country without specific permission. Tension continued, and there was a demonstration in London by the staff of the Chinese embassy against the restrictions placed on them. However, at no time were diplomatic relations broken off.

On 30 August a further hostile demonstration was directed against the British **11.26** chargé d'affaires and his staff, who were obliged to appear publicly before the demonstrators. It was only after Donald Hopson had been physically manhandled by the Red Guards in an effort to get him to abase himself that soldiers intervened to prevent further developments. An attempt to obtain protection from the Chinese foreign ministry resulted only in advice to meet the demonstrators' requests. At the beginning of September, the Chinese prime minister, Chou-En-Lai, was reported to have issued a directive, with a clear wish by both governments to lessen tension, to Red Guards that they should be content to 'demonstrate but not penetrate' foreign diplomatic missions. A number of restrictions on both sides were removed in succeeding months. After prolonged negotiations for compensation, the Chinese government in 1971 agreed to bear the cost of rebuilding the British diplomatic premises.

Iran

Perhaps the most egregious violation of diplomatic immunity came with the **11.27** seizure of the US embassy in Tehran in November 1979 by a group of Iranian students in retaliation for US support for the deposed Shah. He had recently been admitted to the US for medical treatment and the US and the UK had in 1953 been heavily implicated in the removal of the democratically elected Mossadeq government and the imposition of the then young Shah. Fifty-two of the original sixty-six American diplomats were held hostage for 444 days and were released only after the inauguration of the new US President, Ronald Reagan. The defeat in the US election of his predecessor, Jimmy Carter, was in part attributed to the hostage crisis and the abortive attempt by the US military to rescue the hostages in April 1980 when helicopter failures and a crash led to several fatalities and the abandonment of the mission.

The end of the crisis was negotiated through the Algerian government as inter- **11.28** mediary. Under the Algiers Accords signed in January 1981,[9] the US released

---

[9] See also Chapter 31, paragraph 31.4.

$8 billion of frozen Iranian assets which were used for the settlement of claims by United States citizens—private investors as well as the hostages themselves—and undertook not to intervene in Iran's internal affairs. Unlike other incidents described earlier in the chapter, the students' action received enthusiastic support from the highest level of authority, Iran's Supreme Leader Ayatollah Khomeini, thus making the government responsible for the numerous breaches of international law. The relatively moderate government of Prime Minister Mehdi Bazargan resigned within a few days. While the affair created internal political shockwaves within the two countries directly affected, it was regarded with outrage by the international community as infringing the most basic tenets of international law: the inviolability of diplomats and other embassy staff as well as the inviolability of the premises and archives of a diplomatic mission. Sanctions were imposed against Iran not only by the United States but in solidarity by European Community Member States and by others (see Chapter **13**, paragraph **13**.17). One further aspect of the incident deserves to be highlighted. At the time of the takeover of the embassy, six US diplomats avoided capture and took refuge in the Canadian and Swedish embassies. Meeting in secret for the first time in peacetime, the Canadian Parliament passed the appropriate legislation allowing Canadian passports (with forged Iranian exit visas) to be issued to the US diplomats who were thus able to escape from Iran in January 1980 by taking a flight to Switzerland using their Canadian documents.[10]

11.29   In the course of the crisis, another incident took place in London when the Iranian embassy was taken over by Arab separatists demanding autonomy for Khuzestan in southern Iran. Twenty-six hostages were taken initially including a policeman on diplomatic protection duty although five were released over the first few days. On the sixth day of the siege, one of the diplomats was executed by the hostage-takers and his body thrown out of the embassy, with threats of further killings of hostages. This led to the immediate deployment of waiting British counter-terrorist forces, the Special Air Service (SAS), and the storming of the embassy. Five of the six terrorists were killed by the SAS and one of the remaining hostages was killed by the terrorists during the assault. The rest were safely released. Notwithstanding their own concurrent behaviour towards the US embassy in Tehran, the government of Iran vigorously insisted on their rights to diplomatic protection in London, claiming that the police protection had been inadequate and claiming compensation for the burnt-out premises. An agreement for compensation for claims and counterclaims was ultimately reached, as explained in Chapter **13**, paragraph **13**.19.

---

[10] L C Green, 'Trends in the Law Concerning Diplomats' (1981) 132 *CYIL* 144–7 and various obituaries (15 October 2015) of Ken Taylor the Canadian ambassador in Tehran at the time.

Lebanon

In April 1983, a suicide bomber drove a van into the US embassy in Beirut **11.30** destroying a large part of the premises and killing over sixty members of the embassy staff and visitors. It was the worst attack on an embassy in terms of casualties seen up to that time and marked the first use of a suicide bomber in a terrorist attack on a diplomatic target. The attack is thought to have been perpetrated by Hizbollah, the pro-Iranian Shiite militia in Lebanon. Further attacks followed largely linked to the Western presence in the Middle East, and in particular the arrival of US troops in Saudi Arabia where some of the holiest shrines of Islam are to be found at Mecca and Medina. In December 1983, there were coordinated attacks on the US and French embassies in Kuwait with limited casualties. The US government responded to these outrages by commissioning a report into diplomatic security, which recommended 'a substantial relocation and rebuilding program'[11] to put security on an altogether higher plane.

Al Qaeda and so-called Islamic State

Despite the programme of rebuilding being approved and given an initial **11.31** budget of $366 million, in August 1998 the US embassies in Nairobi and Dar es Salaam were simultaneously attacked by car bombs which killed over two hundred and injured several thousand people, mostly passers-by outside the premises. It appeared that both buildings had been completed prior to the implementation of the report.[12] The claim of responsibility by the terrorist organization, Al Qaeda, brought it to widespread international attention for the first time, some three years before the 9/11 attacks in New York and Washington DC. In November 2003, Al Qaeda claimed responsibility for a series of suicide bomb attacks on two synagogues in Istanbul and, five days later, on the British consulate there and the HSBC bank. Some thirty people were killed in the second wave of attacks including the consul-general, Roger Short.

As was mentioned earlier in connection with kidnappings (paragraph 11.18), **11.32** for Al Qaeda, the UN is a high-value target. In 2003, just five days after it had been set up, the United Nations Assistance Mission in Iraq was bombed resulting in the death of over twenty people, including the UN Special Representative in Iraq, Sergio Vieira de Mello. De Mello, a distinguished long-serving Brazilian UN diplomat, widely admired and sometimes spoken of as a future UN Secretary-General, was a specific target of the group who claimed responsibility. Al Qaeda

---

[11] J Craig Barker, *The Protection of Diplomatic Personnel* (London: Ashgate, 2006) 91–2.
[12] Ibid, 97.

in Iraq, the parent organization of so-called Islamic State or ISIS or ISIL, led by the notorious Abu Musab al-Zarqawi, justified the attack on the UN mission as it saw the UN as protector of Jews and having been involved in the creation of Israel at the expense of the Palestinians.[13] De Mello was moreover singled out as being responsible, as UN transitional administrator, in East Timor for the territory successfully detaching itself from Indonesia and therefore from the Islamic Caliphate. Within weeks most of the 600 UN staff were withdrawn from Iraq.

Libya

11.33 In September 2012, a year after the downfall of Colonel Qaddafi and on the eleventh anniversary of 9/11, the US ambassador, Christopher Stevens, was killed in an attack on the US consulate in Benghazi. One other Foreign Service officer and two CIA contractors were also killed that day. The attack was premeditated and apparently carried out by an Islamist militia, an Al Qaeda affiliate, Ansar al-Sharia. Initial reports, echoed by President Obama and Secretary of State, Hillary Clinton, suggested that the attack was prompted by a video, '*The Innocence of Muslims*', which attracted widespread hostility in the Islamic world for its anti-Muslim message. But subsequent investigation indicated that the attack was calculated and well-organized by attackers who were armed with heavy weaponry. The Obama administration came under sustained criticism (including Hillary Clinton at the time and subsequently after she left the administration) not least because of its unwillingness to abandon the thesis that the attack was a spontaneous demonstration as a result of the hateful video and the revelation that the State Department had denied requests from the consulate before the attack for enhanced security measures.

European Terror Groups

11.34 Although many of the attacks on diplomatic premises and diplomats have had a Middle East connection, several attacks had quite different motives. A prime example was the burning of the British embassy in Dublin in 1972 by an angry crowd after Bloody Sunday when thirteen civil rights demonstrators were shot dead by British soldiers. The Irish government took the view that it was safer to allow the crowd to burn down the embassy—which was empty at the time—than to try to prevent it happening. The British government demanded and received compensation for the damage caused. Two British ambassadors, one in Dublin[14] and one in The Hague, were subsequently assassinated by the IRA in

---

[13] Audio tape by Zarqawi reproduced in the TV programme *Frontline*, 21 February 2006.

[14] See Hickman, *Daughters of Britannia*, 253–62 for a graphic diary account of the day of Christopher Ewart-Biggs' assassination and subsequent events.

1979. Turkish diplomats have been regular targets of Kurdish separatist terrorists and of the '17 November' terrorist group in Greece though most of the latter's targets have been US diplomats or Greek political or business figures. After the assassination of the British defence attaché, Brigadier Saunders, in Athens in 2000, the British government exerted considerable pressure on the Greek government to find the perpetrators. In 25 years and over a hundred attacks, no individual had ever been charged. Finally, in 2002, nineteen arrests were made, including the group leader and the chief of operations. Fifteen convictions were secured in 2003, since when there have been no further attacks by '17 November'.

The Legal Position

Given the increasing globalization of terror, diplomats can anticipate being cen- **11.35**
trally involved not only in the negotiation of international conventions on the suppression of terrorism (see paragraphs **11.36–11.37**) but in the establishment of networks of multilateral cooperation and intelligence-sharing, activity which they can expect to share with colleagues in security and intelligence services and in interior ministries. The key international document is the Vienna Convention on Diplomatic Relations of 1961. Under it, diplomatic agents and premises enjoy inviolability under customary international law. The receiving State is under a special duty to take all appropriate steps to prevent any attack on the person, freedom, and dignity of diplomats and to protect diplomatic premises.[15] International cooperation is clearly essential both in the prevention of crimes against diplomats and in the punishment of offenders. To this end, it was felt increasingly desirable to conclude an international convention (similar to those on hijacking and sabotage of aircraft) concerning legal measures aimed at the prevention and punishment of crimes against diplomats.[16] The Organization of American States adopted a regional convention on the subject in 1971, and later that year the United Nations General Assembly asked the International Law Commission to prepare draft articles. On the basis of the Commission's draft, the Sixth (Legal) Committee of the Assembly elaborated the Convention on the Prevention and Punishment of Crimes against Internationally Protected

---

[15] See Chapters **13** and **14**.

[16] UKTS No 3 (1980). See Michael Wood in (1974) 23 *ICLQ* 791. This desire was intensified by the kidnapping of James Cross in Canada (see paragraph **11.10**). A fascinating account of this episode, with all the complexities of a situation in which a federal government and a state government were dealing simultaneously with more than one terrorist group, will be found in Baumann, *The Diplomatic Kidnappings*, ch VII, 111–38.

Persons, including Diplomatic Agents, adopted by the General Assembly in 1973.

11.36 This Convention,[17] which entered into force in 1977, provides that persons alleged to have committed certain attacks against diplomatic agents and other internationally protected persons should either be extradited or have their case submitted to the authorities of the State Party where they are, for the purpose of prosecution. It contains, in addition, provisions concerning cooperation, the transmission of information, and the treatment to be accorded to alleged offenders. However, extradition could still be refused on the traditional, but increasingly discredited, ground of the so-called 'political' character of the alleged offence.

11.37 The European Convention on the Suppression of Terrorism, adopted in 1977 by member States of the Council of Europe,[18] imposes an obligation on Contracting States not to regard specified offences (including crimes against internationally protected persons) as political offences for the purpose of extradition. (The Convention has been replaced in so far as it relates to extradition procedures as between Member States of the European Union by the tough provisions of the European Arrest Warrant (EAW).[19] This was used expeditiously by the Italian government to extradite a bomber fleeing from his part in the abortive terrorist attacks on London transport in July 2005, two weeks after the attacks which had killed fifty-two people. Similar bilateral arrangements to the EAW, for instance between the United Kingdom and India and the United States, and between the United States and India and Jordan, now exist to make comparable provision.

Diplomacy and Negotiation

11.38 Not all diplomacy relates of course to physical and legal prevention of terrorism. Using killing and violence for political ends is always to be condemned. Most countries have individual measures in place to prevent and deal with terrorist attacks. The nature of terrorism requires cooperation between countries and many international bodies and organizations adopt policies to combat the

---

[17] Cmnd 6176; 13 ILM (1974) 41.

[18] States outside the Council of Europe can accede to the Convention.

[19] Council Framework Decision of 13 June 2002 on the European arrest warrant and the surrender procedures between Member States (2002/584/JHA [2002] OJ L190/1). Also Michael Wood, 'The European Convention on the Suppression of Terrorism' (1981) *Yearbook of European Law* 307, UKTS No 93 (1978).

scourge. This is all the more necessary because terrorism will identify the weakest defence and act there. Solidarity against terrorism is vital. The diplomat is therefore likely to come across the negotiation of anti-terrorism measures or the implementation of such measures in a multitude of fora. UN action is described in paragraphs 11.35–11.36. But the EU and AU for example have adopted such measures. Negotiation is always complicated by the frequent failure to define terrorism, and the different political perspectives to acts of violence.

Diplomacy can and should play a key part in trying to resolve (where possible) the grievances which are used by perpetrators as their justification for acts of terrorism. (The Arab-Israel conflict is the most egregious example of unresolved grievances where 60 years of failed diplomacy have left a toxic residue which continues to poison relations within the region and between the countries of the region and the West.) But the prospects of any agreement are much diminished by the actions of extremists and terrorists. Rabin, the assassinated prime minister of Israel, famously addressed the issue. 'We shall negotiate as though there is no terrorism, and we shall pursue the terrorist as though there were no negotiation.' Louise Richardson identifies different kinds of terrorist groups and divides them into ethno-nationalist, who are looking for traditional territorial concessions like the IRA, PLO, ETA, and the PKK; social revolutionary groups, who look to overthrow capitalism, like the Baader-Meinhof Gang or the Red Brigades; Maoist groups like Sendero Luminoso in Peru who want to refashion society; lastly, the fundamentalist groups who want to replace secular with religious (usually sharia) law and/or 'want to bring about the millennium',[20] in the case of Al Qaeda and Islamic State, the return of the Caliphate. The last have used killings and the savagery of the act specifically as acts of terror, to intimidate and subjugate populations. They have no interest in any negotiation. **11.39**

The extent to which terrorists' demands are negotiable and the support they enjoy from within their communities are both key considerations. It is important to differentiate between negotiation with terrorists over a particular situation, and a political negotiation with a terrorist organization. The former, for example a kidnapping, raises real issues for a government. To negotiate and yield may serve to encourage more kidnappings. Hence initiatives such as the declaration by the G7 in 1995 which called on the member States to condemn kidnapping, not to accede to kidnappers' demands, to stop kidnapping being profitable for the perpetrators, and to secure the punishment of kidnappers. **11.40**

---

[20] Louise Richardson, *What Terrorists Want: Understanding the Terrorist Threat* (London: John Murray, 2006) 100.

11.41 The policy of 'no concessions to terrorists' is sensitive and can be controversial. 'Governments always resist talking to terrorists for fear that it confers legitimacy on them, or rewards their terrorism.'[21] Yet, if their demands are negotiable, then it pays to negotiate not least as there is considerable intelligence advantage in knowing the terrorists and their demands better 'to establish…the nature of their goals and second, to isolate them from their community of support'.[22] The British government had secret talks with the IRA from the early days of 'The Troubles' (as detailed in Chapter **29**, paragraph **29.5**) and ultimately a peace accord was reached in 1998 after years of direct and indirect or secret talks, on terms which had essentially been on offer more than 20 years earlier.

11.42 It is far more difficult to embark on a negotiation secret or otherwise with those whose demands are non-negotiable. The best that contact may be able to achieve could be a realistic assessment of how much community support the terrorists enjoy and what might be needed to detach the community from the terrorists. Sometimes the terrorists may themselves alienate their own community by their barbarism, though sometimes, as appears to be the case with Islamic State, their excesses attract recruits rather than repel them. On other occasions, engagement, however politically risky, may point the way towards actions governments can take domestically to weaken terrorist support. And with more 'moderate' terrorists, engagement may allow the terrorists' grievances, not all of which may be unreasonable, to be analysed and partly at least to be addressed. Not rejecting all terrorist demands out of hand (for example conceding political prisoner status to captured terrorists in exchange for a meaningful cease-fire), far from being an example of negotiating weakness may be an effective part of a counter-terrorism strategy to undermine the terrorists' support. The best recruiting sergeant for terrorism can often be an obdurate and inflexible attitude to demands which do not in themselves seem wholly unreasonable. The deaths in 1981 of ten IRA hunger strikers, who were demanding the right to wear their own clothes in prison, and which became an almost personal stand-off between the British Prime Minister Margaret Thatcher and the hunger strikers, boosted IRA recruitment and increased paramilitary activity just at a time when the IRA's campaign seemed to be faltering. An ostensible win for the British government thus became a very Pyrrhic victory.

---

[21] Ibid, 257.
[22] Ibid, 258.

Book III

PRIVILEGES AND IMMUNITIES

12

PRIVILEGES AND IMMUNITIES OF THE STATE, THE HEAD OF STATE, STATE OFFICIALS, AND STATE AGENCIES

Hazel Fox

Introduction

This chapter provides an account of the immunities of the State, its officials, **12.1** and state agencies in international law. After a general description of the plea of state immunity and a brief historical account of the development of the law of state immunity it will briefly set out the law relating to the immunities of the State itself as a legal person followed by the law applicable to its officials and to state agencies, including the Central Bank. In addition, in the absence of any written formulation of the rules, an account based on customary international law will be provided of the immunities of senior state officials, in particular, of the Head of State, the Minister for Foreign Affairs, and the Head of Government.

12.2 The rules relating to the privileges and immunities of the diplomatic mission and the members of the mission are of first importance in the conduct of diplomacy, and in particular to the State which sends the diplomatic mission (the sending State) and to the State (the receiving State) in whose territory the mission is established. These rules are set out in general terms in the 1961 Vienna Convention on Diplomatic Relations (hereafter the 1961 Vienna Convention) and they are described in some detail in this and other chapters.[1] By way of conclusion some note is made of the extent to which the practice of diplomatic missions at the present time accords with the requirements of state immunity law as now set out in written form in the 2004 UN Convention on the Jurisdictional Immunities of States and their Property with reference in particular to the two exceptions to state immunity for commercial transactions and employment contracts where some continuing differences and uncertainty continue.

12.3 To complete the account of the special provisions which relate to agencies of a foreign State in respect of their acts before national courts, mention should be made of the procedure which provides protection for a State's armed forces when stationed with the consent of another State in that State's territory. In place of the conferment of immunities by the receiving State, bilateral agreements between sending and receiving States have been adopted, allocating the exercise of jurisdiction between the two States, in respect of visiting armed forces within the receiving State's territory. This allocation of jurisdiction seeks to achieve a balance between the local interests of the receiving State, and the functional needs of the visiting State for the exclusive command and internal administration of its military force. Multilateral agreements, such as the NATO, UN, and EU Status of Forces Agreements (SOFA), based on a similar allocation of jurisdiction, are also common.[2]

---

[1] Chapters **13**, Privileges and Immunities of Diplomatic Missions, **14**, Privileges and Immunities of Diplomatic Agents, and **15**, Special Missions.

[2] See Chapter 18, paragraph **18.43–18.47** (Use by the United Nations of Armed Forces).

The Nature of the Plea of Immunity

The State's exercise of internal sovereignty over its people and territories includes **12.4**
the judicial power to exercise jurisdiction over all who seek to bring claims in its
national courts arising from damage or loss suffered to the person, or property,
or by conduct of business. The exercise of this territorial jurisdiction, however,
unless consented to by the foreign State, conflicts with the equality of States in
international law which all States including the territorial and foreign States
enjoy as legal persons. In consequence, one State is required by international
law to impose a bar of immunity on the exercise of its territorial jurisdiction in
its national courts in respect of proceedings brought against another State. The
imposition of this bar of immunity prevents the subjection of a foreign State to
the adjudication of its disputes in another State's courts.

The plea of immunity is one of immunity from suit, not of exemption from law. **12.5**
In the words of the International Court of Justice in the Jurisdictional
Immunities case:

> [T]his law of immunity is essentially procedural in nature . . . It regulates the exercise
> of jurisdiction in respect of particular conduct and is entirely distinct from the
> substantive law which determines whether the conduct is lawful or unlawful.[3]

In effect, as shown in the above case where the ICJ held the plea barred the
adjudication by the Italian national courts of claims for reparation brought
against the Federal Republic of Germany for violations of international humanitarian law committed in the Second World War by the German Reich between
1943 and 1945, immunity bars the exercise of national courts' jurisdiction
against a foreign State.

The consent of the foreign defendant State, either by appearance by an author- **12.6**
ized representative of that State before the national court, or by the State's consent in writing, even where given in advance of proceedings, to the national
court's exercise of jurisdiction will remove the bar of immunity. Where the
defendant State gives such a consent, proceedings in the national court may
continue in the same way as for a private person.

Persons Enjoying Immunity

Not only the State may claim this immunity from another State's jurisdiction, **12.7**
but also the Head of State, the agencies of the State, in particular the diplomatic

---

[3] *Jurisdictional Immunities of the State (Germany v Italy, Greece Intervening)* [2012] ICJ Reports 99,
at para 58. See Chapter 3, paragraph 3.13.

service, and State officials when performing acts on behalf of the State. The scope of immunity varies according to the nature of the act and the extent of the authority exercised. All state officials, when acting on the State's behalf in the performance of official duties, enjoy immunity; acts performed by them in the course of official functions are treated as acts of the State itself. Described as functional, this functional immunity (*ratione materiae*) is to be distinguished from acts relating solely to the state official's own private affairs for which no immunity is granted. Additional to this functional immunity for acts performed on behalf of the State, personal immunity is provided in respect of a select group of senior state officials—the Head of State, Head of government, Minister for Foreign Affairs, and the diplomatic agent in the receiving State; this personal immunity (*ratione personae*) covers acts of a private nature performed by these senior officials for their own private purposes while in office, but terminates on leaving office.

12.8 With regard to the position when out of office, the 1961 Vienna Convention Article 39.2 expressly provides in relation to diplomatic agents that, when their functions have come to an end, immunity enjoyed shall cease save in respect of such acts performed in the exercise of their functions as members of the mission. Analogous with this treaty rule, both the senior group of officials and all other state officials on leaving office lose all personal immunities, though immunity continues in respect of official acts, performed while in office by them on behalf of and in the name of the State.

12.9 As later discussed in respect of the Head of State, Head of Government, and Minister for Foreign Affairs, this continuance of immunity has been challenged with regard to acts alleged to be committed by them while in office on behalf of the State amounting to international crimes such as genocide, torture, war crimes, and crimes against humanity.

Privileges

12.10 In addition to the imposition of immunities which impede the exercise of another State's jurisdiction and are negative in effect, privileges may also be conferred by the territorial State. Privileges have a positive nature conferring on the diplomat or representative of the foreign State a special status or benefits free from national requirements. Such privileges may relate, for example, to freedom from national requirements of compulsory public service or exemption from import and export charges.[4]

---

[4] See Chapter 14, paragraph 14.34 (Privileges of Diplomatic Agents).

History

The need for protection from the commands of another and consequent exemption from their observance is demonstrated by the earliest recorded accounts relating to the exchange of envoys between despots. From time immemorial the protection of an envoy when present in another State's territory, conducting negotiations on behalf of a recognized sovereign, has been universally observed; similarly for many centuries it has been well established in customary international law that a sovereign, or Head of State, when present in the territory and at the invitation of another sovereign, is entitled to wide privileges and to ceremonial honours appropriate to his or her position and dignity, and to full immunity from the criminal, civil, and administrative jurisdiction of the State which he or she is visiting.[5]   **12.11**

Watts explains well this early relationship between the Head of a State and the State itself: **12.12**

> Until the French revolution ushered in the modern era of republics, the States which were the active participants in the international community which gave rise to modern international law were monarchies whose rulers were regarded as possessing personal qualities of sovereignty. In many respects the State could almost be seen as the property of the ruler, and it was to a considerable degree the ruler's personal attributes of sovereignty which gave his State the quality of being a sovereign State, rather than the other way round...Perhaps not surprisingly, the older law not only treated Heads of State as entitled to very special legal consideration, but also frequently made no clear distinction between the Head of State on the one hand and the State itself on the other.

With the establishment of the nation State in the late nineteenth century, and increasing cross-border communication and trade, the historic privileges and immunities enjoyed by the Head of State and its ambassador became centred in the legal person of the State, with the plea of state immunity, adopted with particular rigour by States of common law jurisdiction, barring the exercise of jurisdiction in civil proceedings in other States' national courts in respect of every type of state activity, whether commercial or of a public nature.   **12.13**

In civil law systems, however, particularly in Italy, Belgium, and the mixed courts of Egypt, and, after the Second World War in Austria and Germany, there was a greater diversity of court decision, in large part by reason of the State's increasing engagement in trade with growing support for a restrictive   **12.14**

---

[5] A Watts 'The Legal Position in International Law of Heads of States, Heads of Governments and Foreign Ministers', 247 Hague Recueil (994-III) 9. See further H Fox and P Webb, *The Law of State Immunity* (3rd edn, Oxford: Oxford University Press, 2015) ch 18, 544–64; ch 19, 587–600.

doctrine, and a readiness to distinguish acts of a commercial nature relating to business or of a private nature *de iure gestionis*, from acts performed of a public governmental nature *de iure imperii*.

12.15 This move towards greater restriction of state immunity was furthered by the issue of the Tate letter of 19 May 1952 in which the US State Department, after noting that 'the increasing practice on the part of governments of engaging in commercial activities makes necessary a practice which will enable persons doing business with them to have their rights determined in the courts', announced that it 'will hereafter be the Department's policy to follow the restrictive theory of sovereign immunity in the consideration of requests from foreign governments for a grant of sovereign immunity'.[6]

12.16 In 1972 the Council of Europe adopted the European Convention on State Immunity setting out a list of exceptions (including the State's waiver) to State immunity and this was followed by the enactment in the United States (1976), UK (1978), and a number of other States of national legislation introducing a range of exceptions to state immunity for commercial transactions and proceedings for personal injuries caused in the territory of the State where the claim was brought.[7]

12.17 At the same time as these developments were curtailing, by the adoption of the restrictive rule, the scope of the immunity of the State, the state practice of granting over centuries many favours and exemptions from local laws to the diplomatic representatives of other States, culminated in the successful conclusion in 1961 of the Vienna Convention on Diplomatic Relations (the 1961 Vienna Convention). Its preamble describes its purpose as 'the promotion of friendly relations among nations irrespective of their differing constitutional and social systems', but adds a qualification 'realising that the purpose of such privileges and immunities is not to benefit individuals but to ensure the efficient performance of diplomatic missions'.

12.18 Finally, to complete the historical account, at the beginning of the twenty-first century a codification of the law was adopted by the UN General Assembly in

---

[6] 'Changing Policy Concerning the Granting of Sovereign Immunity to Foreign Governments', Letter to US Acting Attorney-General, 19 May 1952, 26 *US Department of State Bulletin* (1952) 984 ('the Tate letter').

[7] Foreign Sovereign Immunities Act 1976 (USA); State Immunity Act 1978 (UK); Foreign States Immunities Act 1985 (Australia); State Immunity Act 1982 (Canada); Immunities and Privileges Act 1984 (Malaysia); State Immunity Ordinance 1981 (Pakistan); State Immunity Act 1979 (Singapore); Foreign States Immunities Act 1981 (South Africa); Immunities and Privileges Act 1984 (No 16 of 1984) (Malawi); other common law jurisdictions have enacted similar legislation, e.g. St Kitts 1979.

the UN Convention on the Jurisdictional Immunities of States and their Property 2004 (the 2004 UN Convention on State Immunity).

The State

Applicable Law

Based largely on state practice, extensively examined in 20 years' work of the **12.19** International Law Commission and 10 years' discussions in the UN General Assembly's Sixth (Legal) Committee, the 2004 UN Convention consolidates the restrictive approach to state immunity with regard to the exercise of civil jurisdiction by the national courts of States. The 2004 UN Convention on State Immunity states in Article 1 that it applies to 'the immunity of a State and its property from the jurisdiction of the courts of another State'. The preamble of the Convention states that 'the jurisdictional immunities of States and their property are generally accepted as a principle of customary law', and that the purpose of setting out these immunities in the 2004 UN Convention on State Immunity is to 'enhance the rule of law and legal certainty, particularly in dealings of States with natural or juridical persons', taking into account 'developments in State practice with regard to the jurisdictional immunities of States and their property'. The preamble further affirms that the rules of customary law continue to regulate matters not regulated by the Convention.

Immunity from Criminal Jurisdiction of the State

As regards the criminal jurisdiction of the State itself, the adoption in the last 50 **12.20** years of the restrictive doctrine limiting the extent of a State's immunity from the civil jurisdiction of other States' national courts left untouched the position in international law relating to criminal proceedings. Broadly that position is that there can be no exercise of criminal jurisdiction by way of criminal prosecution and imposition of arrest and punishment of the State as a legal person in another State's national courts. The imposition of any such measure of constraint unavoidably infringes international law's requirements of respect for the equality of States and non-intervention.[8] The 2004 UN Convention on State Immunity

---

[8] In the commentary to the ILC Articles on State Responsibility, the Special Rapporteur commented that 'the law of international responsibility is neither civil nor criminal' and that 'it is purely and simply international' a view confirmed by the ICJ in the *Case concerning the Application of the Genocide Convention (Bosnia-Herzegovina v Serbia and Montenegro)* [2007] ICJ Reports 43 at paras 167–79, holding that international crimes committed through state organs or by persons over whom they have control sufficient to attribute their conduct to the State in international law, are in consequence under the obligation solely in international law to prevent such crimes.

contains no express exclusion of criminal proceedings, and its provisions regarding the immunity of the State from the jurisdiction of other States' national courts and provision for exceptions to such immunity are restricted solely to civil loss incurred by parties to proceedings in the national courts of another State.[9]

Immunity from Civil Jurisdiction of the State

12.21 In setting out the rules relating to state immunity from the civil jurisdiction of national courts, the UN 2004 Convention on State Immunity first states a general rule of immunity, and then after stating a provision for waiver by express 'agreement in an international treaty, or written contract, or by a declaration before the [national] court or by a written communication in a specific proceeding', the Convention sets out the exceptions to the rule. These exceptions to state immunity in the Convention are formulated broadly in the same terms as in the UK 1978 State Immunity Act. They effect a considerable reduction of the scope of immunity removing the bar in respect of some eight types of transaction including commercial transactions, contracts of employment, ownership of property, and personal injuries.[10] Procedurally, it is to be noted that, as with all the treaty and legislative formulations of state immunity, the Convention first states the general rule of immunity to be observed, leaving the occasions when it is not to be applied to be set out in exceptions to that rule. Thereby it preserves a continuing bias in favour of a foreign State's special treatment when made a litigant in national proceedings.

12.22 Despite the continued coolness of the United States and China towards accepting its provisions as law, the UN Convention on State Immunity provides a useful written statement of international law relating to state immunity at the present time. In setting out extensive exceptions to a State's immunity from a State's immunity from adjudication, but, at the same time, affirming the continuance of the State's immunity from enforcement by attachment of State property (save by consent or where the state property is in commercial use), the Convention also provides an overview of state practice at the present time, as currently largely observed worldwide in respect of business and commercial dealings involving States.

---

[9] The 1989 ILC Commentary and the Understandings in the Annex to the Convention itself make no reference but the GA resolution adopting the 2004 UN Convention referred to the general understanding reached in the ad hoc committee that the Convention did not cover criminal proceedings. Switzerland and Liechtenstein in their ratifications of this Convention have made an interpretative declaration that they understand the Convention not to include criminal proceedings.

[10] The exceptions to state immunity in the UN Convention relate to commercial transactions (Art 10), contracts of employment (Art 11), personal injuries (Art 12), property (immovable situated in the territorial State or movable) (Art 13), intellectual property (Art 14), companies (Art 15), ships (Art 16), and arbitration relating to commercial matters (Art 17).

The Head of State

Applicable Law

In the absence of any international convention in force,[11] the position of the Head   **12.23**
of State and the personal privileges and immunities which attach to that office
remain largely based on customary international law.[12] As the principal representative of the State, and to enable the performance of the functions of the office and
the promotion of international relations, customary international law confers on
the holder of the office both the functional immunities *ratione materiae* enjoyed
by all state officials, and the immunities *ratione personae* for private acts performed while in office conferred on senior state officials.[13] A former Head of
State, on his or her office ceasing for whatever reason, whether by death or retirement, will, as court decisions indicate, enjoy less immunity than that enjoyed
when in office.[14] Immunity *ratione personae* is lost but immunity *ratione materiae*
continues, that is in respect of acts, whether of criminal intent or civil nature,
performed in the course of official functions during the tenure of office.

The practice of the United States, other common law countries of the Com-   **12.24**
monwealth courts, and civil law States provides support for these rules of international customary law relating to the immunities of a Head of State.[15] In the
USA, US federal courts, in reliance on State Department suggestion, treat the
Head of State as unique and afford the holder of the office immunities, based
on common law and customary international law, distinct from that of other

---

[11] The Vienna Convention on Diplomatic Relations of 1961 makes no express reference to the office of Head of State. The express distinction made between the privileges and immunities enjoyed by a Head of State from that of diplomatic agents or other high-ranking officials in the 1969 New York Convention on Special Missions and in the 1972 Convention on Internationally Protected Persons provides support for the Head of State's primacy and separate status. The extent of such immunities, however, is not stated and consequently uncertain. Some States equate a Head of government with a Head of State, but as with the position of ministers, comity rather than customary law may determine both their grant and extent. See further Chapter 15.

[12] See Fox and Webb, *Law of State Immunity* (3rd revised paperback edn, 2015) 553–61. The Institut de Droit in 2002 adopted the only set of rules in writing relating to the Head of State; the Vancouver Resolution on the Immunities from Jurisdiction and Execution of Heads of State and Government in International Law, ADI Vol 69 (2002), 742–55. See Fox and Webb, *Law of State Immunity*, 555.

[13] The 1994 UN Convention on State Immunity, Art 3, Privileges and immunities not affected by the present Convention, provides at paragraph 3 that 'the present Convention is without prejudice to the immunities accorded by international law to heads of State *ratione personae*'.

[14] The UK and Australian legislation, as referred to later in the chapter, expressly so provides by applying the provision, 'subject to any necessary modifications', of a head of diplomatic mission as set out in the 1961 Vienna Convention on Diplomatic Relations.

[15] Fox and Webb, *Law of State Immunity* (3rd revised paperback edn) 552–6.

state officials. The member countries within the Commonwealth, which has a hereditary monarch as its head, similarly recognize in their national legislation the entitlement of the office of Head of State to immunities from the jurisdiction of the national courts of other States. South Africa alone goes further and confers immunity in its national law on a Head of State from criminal and civil jurisdiction as well as 'such privileges as a head of State enjoys in accordance with customary international law'.[16]

12.25 Thus the UK and Australia apply in their national legislation a rule of immunity to the Head of State, 'subject to the necessary modifications', as provided in the 1961 Vienna Convention on Diplomatic Immunity for a head of a diplomatic mission.[17] This UK provision equating the position of a Head of State to a head of a diplomatic mission provides some guidance but, as its construction in the Pinochet case illustrates,[18] the addition of the words 'subject to any necessary modifications' in the English provision both misconceived the nature of a head of mission's immunities—relating to a single mission in a single receiving State—and overlooked the wide range of governmental duties—applicable to all States and regardless of whether the Head is located abroad or in his or her home State—for which the immunity of a Head of State is afforded.

Immunity from Criminal Jurisdiction

12.26 Wherever located, a serving Head of State enjoys absolute immunity from criminal jurisdiction before the courts of another State. In the Djibouti/France case the ICJ held that 'the determining facts in assessing whether there has been an attack on the immunity of the Head of State lies in the subjection of the latter to a constraining act of authority'.[19] Every type of act, regardless of its gravity, is covered by this personal immunity from criminal jurisdiction, whether official or personal, committed during office or prior to its assumption, performed in an official capacity or a private capacity, when present in the territory of another State or outside. Since, as stated with regard to the Minister for Foreign Affairs 'even the mere risk that, by travelling to or transiting another State a Minister

---

[16] The South African Diplomatic Immunities and Privileges Act 2001, s 4(1) provides: 'A head of State is immune from the criminal and civil jurisdiction of the courts of the Republic and enjoys such privileges as … a) Heads of State enjoy in accordance with the rules of customary international law…' See further *The Minister of Justice and Constitutional Development v The Southern African Litigation Centre* (867/15) [2016] ZASCA 17, casenote Akande EJILTalk 29 March 2016.

[17] The UK State Immunity Act 1978, s 20(1), applied in *Al Saud v Apex* [2014] 1 WLR 493. The same Act, however, applies the restrictive rule applicable to the State to the Head of State in respect of acts performed in a public capacity, UK Act, ss 14(a) and 20(5).

[18] *R v Bow Street Metropolitan Magistrates, ex parte Pinochet (Amnesty intervening) (No 3)* [2000] 1 AC 147; 119 ILR 135.

[19] *Certain Questions of Mutual Assistance in Criminal Matters (Djibouti v France)* [2008] ICJ Reports 177, at para 170.

[for Foreign Affairs] might be exposing himself or herself to legal proceedings could deter the Minister from travelling internationally when required to do so for the purposes of the performance of his or her official functions'.[20] Thus, the French Court of Cassation overruled a lower court and held Colonel Qaddafi as the serving Head of State of the Libyan Arab Jamahiriya immune in respect of alleged complicity in acts of terrorism leading to murder and the destruction of a French civilian aircraft on 19 September 1999 over the desert.[21]

International Crimes

Since the establishment of the International Criminal Courts for the former **12.27** Yugoslavia and Rwanda in 1993 and 1984 pursuant to the Security Council resolutions under Chapter VII of the UN Charter, and the codification in the Statute of the International Criminal Court of the international crimes of genocide, war crimes, and crimes against humanity, the continued enjoyment of immunity by a Head of State, ministers, and senior officials accused of international crimes, whether in office at the time or retired, has been questioned.

In the *Arrest Warrant* case, the ICJ was asked to consider whether the issue by a **12.28** Belgian court of an international arrest warrant for a serving Minister for Foreign Affairs of the Congo, accused of the commission of international crimes, amounted to a breach of international law. The ICJ ruled that the international circulation of the arrest warrant constituted a breach of the Foreign Minister's immunity. In addition at paragraph 60 of its judgment, the ICJ, in considering the extent of the immunity claimed by the Foreign Minister, indicated four situations where immunity claimed by the Foreign Minister would not apply; first in respect of a criminal prosecution in the Minister's own home country according to the relevant rules of domestic law; second, with waiver by the State which the Minister represents or had represented; third, as regards the former Foreign Minister, prosecution in respect of acts performed in a private capacity;[22] and fourth, both a serving and a former minister might 'be subject to criminal proceedings before certain international criminal courts, where they

---

[20] *Arrest Warrant of 11 April 2000 (Democratic Republic of Congo/Belgium)* [2002] ICJ Reports 1, at para 55. In this case which related to a Foreign Minister, the ICJ stated that 'a Head of State enjoys full immunity from criminal jurisdiction and inviolability' which protects him or her 'against any act of authority which would hinder him or her in the performance of his or her duties'.

[21] *In re Ghadafi, SOS Attentat and Castelnau d'Esnault v Ghadafi, Head of the State of Libya*, France, Court of Cassation, criminal chamber, No 00-87.215, 13 March 2000, 125 ILR 490.

[22] 'Provided that it has jurisdiction under international law, a court of one State may try a former Minister for Foreign Affairs of another State in respect of acts committed prior or subsequent to his period of office, as well as in respect of acts committed during the period of office in a private capacity.' *Arrest Warrant*, Judgment, para 61.

have jurisdiction',[23] such as the international criminal courts for the former Yugoslavia and Rwanda, established pursuant to Security Council resolutions under Chapter VII of the UN Charter, or the ICC, established by the 1998 Statute of the International Criminal Court.

12.29   This ruling has been accepted as also applying to the immunity of a serving Head of State, and indeed was so recognized by the ICJ itself.

12.30   As regards the former Head of State, in contrast to the above view, supported by the ICJ ruling, a body of state practice provides some support for the view that, once office is left, a former Head of State should enjoy no such functional immunity for criminal prosecution for the commission of international crimes committed during the time when in office as Head of State. The Statute of the International Criminal Court, which in general only binds parties to it,[24] expressly states that not only is the office of a Head of State no defence but that official status cannot be pleaded as a bar to the ICC's exercise of its jurisdiction (Article 27(1) and (2)).

12.31   It has been argued with regard to national courts that the same rule of removal of immunity should apply so as to permit the criminal prosecution of anyone, regardless of any immunity enjoyed, who is alleged to have committed an international crime. In 2000 the English courts at the highest level declared immunity to be no bar to the extradition of General Pinochet, a former Head of the Republic of Chile, on a charge of torture committed while in office, a crime which by the 1974 UN Convention on Torture, the relevant States—Chile, Spain, and the UK—had undertaken to prosecute.[25] This ruling, which has been widely quoted (including by the International Court of Justice), provides support for the removal of immunity where States are placed under an obligation, either by a binding Security Council resolution or by treaty, to prosecute a former Head of State who might otherwise enjoy immunity.

12.32   The subsequent proceedings in the Habré case go some way in support of this approach and of the fourth situation described by the ICJ. The former Head of the State of Chad, Hissene Habré, was overthrown on 1 December 1990, accused of serious crimes committed while in office. With Mr Habré at the present time living in Senegal, Belgium, as a party to the 1974 UN Torture Convention, invoked before the ICJ the responsibility of Senegal, as another State Party, to

---

[23] *Arrest Warrant*, para 61.

[24] A Security Council resolution adopted under Chapter VII of the Charter binds non-parties to the ICC Statute and can remove immunity, explicitly or impliedly.

[25] *Pinochet (No 3)* [2000] 1 AC 147; 119 ILR 135. The international crime of state torture, as defined in the 1984 UN Convention on Torture, was given effect in UK law by the UK Criminal Justice Act 1988, s 134(i).

comply with its obligations to extradite or to prosecute a person accused of the international crime of torture who might otherwise enjoy immunity.

The International Court held Senegal, by its delay in adopting the necessary **12.33**
legislative measures or in instituting proceedings against Habré in its national courts, to be in breach of the 1974 Torture Convention and ordered it without further delay, if it did not extradite Mr Habré, to submit the case to the competent authorities for prosecution.[26] Subsequently an Extraordinary African Chamber of the Senegal judicial system, inaugurated by the African Union and Senegal, convened in 2015. Mr Habré was forcibly brought to court, and having refused to appoint his own lawyers, was represented by lawyers appointed by the Chamber. On 30 May 2016 the Extraordinary African Chambers (EAC) found Hissene Habré guilty of crimes against humanity, war crimes, and torture in Chad between 1982 and 1990 and sentenced him to life imprisonment; lawyers acting on behalf of Mr Habré have stated an appeal will be lodged.[27, 28]

In sum, save where by order of the UN Security Council or by treaty, States are **12.34**
under an obligation to surrender to the ICC or to prosecute in their national courts in respect of the commission of international crimes, it would seem that the present position continues, namely that, for all practical purposes, the functional immunity of a Head of State survives after vacating office for all acts performed in the course of official functions including the commission of international crimes.[29]

Immunity from Civil and Administrative Jurisdiction
of the Head of State

A Head of State enjoys immunity from the exercise of civil and administrative **12.35**
jurisdiction of the courts of another State in respect of acts performed as acts of the State in the course of official duties.

Official Visits in the Territory of Another State

The occasion of an official visit peculiarly celebrates the representation of a State **12.36**
in the person of the visiting Head although a State which does not recognize

---

[26] *Questions relating to the obligation to prosecute or to extradite (Belgium v Senegal)*, the Habré case, [2012] ICJ Reports 422.
[27] AU Press Release No 210/2016. See Amnesty ITC 30.05.2016.
[28] AU Press Release No 190/2015,13.08.2015.
[29] *The Minister of Justice and Constitutional Development v The Southern African Litigation Centre* (867/15) [2016] ZASCA 17, See Fox and Webb, *Law of State Immunity* (3rd revised paperback edn, 2015) 556–61 and the authorities there cited.

another State or its head is under no obligation to consent to such a visit. Hence, Slovakia was held by the ECJ as entitled to refuse permission to the President of Hungary to enter Slovak territory, on the basis that the particular status of a Head of State distinguishes him or her from all other EU citizens.[30] A bar is generally recognized on civil proceedings against a Head in the courts of a State during the period of an official visit to that State although no immunity will apply in respect of a counterclaim relating to proceedings initiated by the Head of State. And civil proceedings in respect of private unpaid debts of a Head of State or relating to private premises or property may be allowed in some foreign courts (subject always to nothing being done in respect of such proceedings where the Head of State is present in the territory of that State in exercise of official functions).[31]

12.37   When present in a State's territory on an official visit, the protection and total exemption of Heads of State from the local jurisdiction covers their persons, the premises in which they reside, their personal baggage and other accompanying property, and the means of transport used in coming into and leaving the State and travelling within it; inviolability means that the police or other officials of the visited State may not enter the premises or detain or inspect the property without the consent of the Head of State nor arrest or detain the Head against his or her will.

The Obligation of Due Respect

12.38   A serving Head of State is also to be treated with all due respect: a balance is here required to be struck between the respect due to the Head of State and the interests of justice and the rights of individuals. Presence in the territory of another State may require closer observance of the duty; thus the citizen's right to freedom of expression was held to be no defence to prosecution for a scurrilous

---

[30] Judgment in Case C-364/10, *Hungary v Slovakia,* 16 October 2012. Slovakia refused to allow the President of Hungary to enter Slovak territory to participate in a ceremony on 21 August, a sensitive date in Slovak history. The ECJ observed that 'under international law the Head of State enjoys a particular status in the international law of diplomatic relations,' distinguishing [the Head of State] from all other EU citizens with the result that that person's access to the territory of another member State is not subject to the same conditions, namely freedom of movement, applicable to other citizens. EU law thus did not oblige Slovakia to guarantee access to the President of Hungary.

[31] Article 3 of the 2001 Vancouver Resolution of the Institut de Droit International on 'The Immunities from jurisdiction and execution of Heads of State and of Government in international law' provides: 'In civil and administrative matters, the Head of State does not enjoy any immunity from jurisdiction before the courts of a foreign State, unless the suit relates to the acts performed in the exercise of his or her official functions. Even in such cases, the Head of State shall enjoy no immunity in respect of a counterclaim. Nonetheless, nothing shall be done by way of court proceedings with regard to the Head of State while he or she is in the territory of that State, in the exercise of official functions', 69 *Annuaire de l'Institut de droit international* 743 at 744.

attack on a foreign visiting Head of State in the local press[32] and the ICJ has indicated that the sending of an email inviting a Head of State to give evidence, and setting, without consultation, an extremely short deadline to appear in a judge's office, constitutes a failure 'to act in accordance with the courtesies due to a foreign Head of State'.[33] Where an act of disrespect is alleged when the Head is not personally present in the State, the observance of respect may be less demanding and a distinction may be drawn between offensive conduct by an official representative of the State and conduct by a private party.

In proceedings before the English court between a former wife and a fortune **12.39** teller, directions were sought by the Sultan of Brunei to anonymize all reference to the intimacies of his married life on the basis that, as a serving Head of State, he was entitled under the UK State Immunity Act section 20, to the same inviolability as an ambassador, and consequently, by virtue of the 1961 Vienna Convention Article 29, the UK (including its courts) was required to 'treat him with due respect . . . and take all appropriate steps to prevent any attack on his dignity'. Lawrence Collins LJ distinguished there between the right that a Head of State has to be protected from attacks on his dignity on the one hand and the uniform practice of host States of extending courtesy or comity to a foreign Head of State 'as a matter of diplomatic courtesy rather than as a recognition of a legal responsibility' on the other.[34] The English court held there to be 'no supervening right in a foreign sovereign to complete protection irrespective of the interests of justice; but the courts will do all that can be done consonantly with the interests of justice to protect any third party, a foreign sovereign included, from the fallout of other people's litigation'.[35]

Immunity from Execution

The law of State immunity affords a general bar to the forcible seizure, attach- **12.40** ment, or sale by national authorities of the property of the State. Property owned

---

[32] *JAM v Public Prosecutor*, Netherlands Supreme Court, 21 January 1969, *YBIL* (1970) 222; 73 ILR 387.

[33] *Certain Questions of Mutual Assistance in Criminal Matters (Djibouti v France)* Judgment [2008] ICJ Reports 177 at paras 170–3.

[34] Immunities accorded to a Head of State 'under international law in a personal capacity' are expressly excluded by the 2004 UN Convention on State Immunity, Art. 3.2.

[35] *Aziz v Aziz & Sultan of Brunei* [2007] EWCA Civ 712 (11 July 2007), per Sedley LJ, at para 132a. Lawrence Collins LJ, at para 90, in considering whether the obligation on States to prevent offensive conduct by private individuals against foreign Heads of State is 'rather more a matter of etiquette or comity than of law', cited Stowell 'Courtesy to our Neighbours' (1942) 36 *AJIL* 99, in which the US Secretary of State, Cordell Hull, is reported as making an apology to Japan in 1935 for a cartoon of the Mikado published in *Vanity Fair*, and President Roosevelt an apology in 1941 to Chile for a reference to the President of Chile 'as spending more and more time with the red wine he cultivates'.

by the State in use by the Head of State will clearly be immune from enforcement. Private property of Heads of State located in another State may not be immune from execution in pursuance of a valid judgment given against them but no such enforcement is to take place whilst the Head of State is present in the territory where such execution is to be carried out.

Taxation and Other Privileges

12.41 Visiting Heads of State are entitled to exemption from national and local taxation though not necessarily in respect of private immovable property owned by them or income from private activities. If the foreign sovereign engages in a trading venture or in speculative investment, it may be justifiable to subject the Head to civil suit or to deny tax exemption on the profits. But state practice in regard to the taxation of the personal investments of foreign Heads of State is in fact very varied. Other privileges of a ceremonial nature derive more from comity and goodwill between the two countries than strict law.

Obligation on Head of State to Respect the Local Law of Receiving State

12.42 The enjoyment of personal immunity does not authorize the Head of State to disregard the local law. The duty imposed by Article 41 of the Vienna Convention on Diplomatic Relations 'to respect the laws and regulations of the receiving State' obliges the diplomat to honour his contractual promises as well as to provide funds to discharge them. The same may be argued to apply to Heads of State.

The Minister for Foreign Affairs

12.43 Similar protection and immunities to those enjoyed by the Head of State have now been recognized by the International Court of Justice as regards a serving Minister for Foreign Affairs of a State. The International Court of Justice noted three characteristics that entitled the Minister for Foreign Affairs of a State to special protection in international law: responsibility for the conduct of the government of the State's diplomatic activities; representation of that government in inter-State negotiations and at intergovernmental meetings and generally to act for the State—there being a presumption simply by virtue of the office of full powers to act on behalf of the State without letters of credence (the 1969 Vienna Convention on the Law of Treaties (VCLT) Article 7, para 2(a)); and an ability to travel internationally freely and without hindrance on government business.

12.44 Declaring that 'a Minister for Foreign Affairs, responsible for the conduct of his or her State's relations with all other States, occupies a position such that, like the Head of State or the Head of Government, he or she is recognized under international law as representative of the State solely by virtue of his or her office', the Court held Belgium to be in breach of international law by the mere circulation of the warrant against the serving Foreign Minister of the Republic of Congo, even though no action was taken by any other State and no Red Notice was issued by Interpol at the relevant time consequent on such circulation.[36]

Other Ministers of the Central Government of a State

The conduct of government business with other States is no longer confined to the Minister of Foreign Affairs. As the International Court has noted 'with increasing frequency in modern times other persons representing a State in specific fields may be authorized by that State to bind it by their statements in respect of matters falling within their purview. This may be true, for example, of holders of technical ministerial portfolios exercising powers in their field of competence.'[37]   **12.45**

Similarly, while until relatively recently all communications by diplomats with the government of the State to which they are accredited were addressed to the ministry for foreign affairs, whether in seeking or furnishing information, these days it is often more convenient, when dealing with specialized subjects, such as the detail of financial, commercial, or scientific activities, or questions concerning development, technical cooperation, etc for a diplomatic officer to establish direct contact with the appropriate department or expert, especially if he or she has made personal acquaintance with them already. Ideally, the ministry of foreign affairs should be kept informed in general terms of communications between an embassy and other government departments.   **12.46**

The Criteria for Immunities of other Ministers

The criteria for extension of the personal immunity of the Head of State to ministers of central government other than the Minister for Foreign Affairs remain uncertain, though the International Court has indicated that Djibouti's minister responsible for internal national security would not so benefit.[38] On the basis of the present authorities, it is suggested that any extension of such personal status to ministers other than the Minister for Foreign Affairs is best arranged by   **12.47**

---

[36] *Arrest Warrant of 11 April 2000 (Democratic Republic of the Congo v Belgium)* Judgment of 14 February 2002, para 70; Cassese 13 EJIL (2002) 853.

[37] *Armed Activities on the Territory of the Congo (Democratic Republic of the Congo/Rwanda)* ICJ Jurisdiction and Admissibility of the Claim [2006] ICJ Reports 6, at para 47.

[38] *Djibouti v France* [2008] ICJ Reports 244, at para 196. See further Fox and Webb, *Law of State Immunity* (3rd revised paperback edn, 2015) 566–7.

agreement between the States concerned for a special mission in respect of the named individual. See Chapter 15 as a means for the receiving State to extend immunity *ratione personae* to high-level missions.

12.48   It should not, however, be overlooked that in any event State immunity may provide some protection to a high-ranking state official. Any minister, as in the case of any state official, enjoys functional immunity in respect of acts which he or she performs on behalf of and in the name of the State.

Agencies and Other Instrumentalities of the State

12.49   Modern States employ agencies and other instrumentalities to carry out the different aspects of their exercise of internal sovereignty. In a federal State some of these powers may be exercised by separate geographical units to a large extent independent of the central government which carries out defence and control of the economy, with specific immunities provided by treaty as in the 1961 Vienna Convention on Diplomatic Relations relating to foreign diplomats, or in the shared jurisdiction provided in Status of Forces agreements regarding military personnel. In a single State the different departments of administration may be carried out by departments, public corporations created by charter or decree, or private companies under private law in which the government may be the principal shareholder. The Minister for Foreign Affairs will be the head of one of these departments and is likely to be responsible to the government for the management of diplomatic missions.

12.50   Agencies or instrumentalities that are entitled to perform and are actually performing acts in exercise of sovereign authority come within the definition of the State in Article 2.1(b)(iii) of the 2004 UN Convention on State Immunity and are entitled to enjoy the immunities of the State set out in that Convention. To qualify for such immunity, the two requirements of entitlement and performance are governed by different systems of national law. Entitlement to perform acts of sovereign authority is conferred by the law of the State creating the agency and the provision of evidence supporting the proof of performance of such acts including their designation as of a contractual, proprietary, or delictual nature is determined by the application of the law of the receiving forum State in the territory where such acts are performed.

12.51   This conferment of immunity on a state agency is of particular value in conferring immunity from execution in respect of its assets, and hence preserving the general revenue of a State from commercial attachment. Unlike the assets of a trading company which are available to meet any failure in its business undertakings, the assets of a state agency enjoy immunity from execution unless the agency has consented to their attachment or evidence is shown that they are in use for commercial purposes.[39]

The Central Bank

A central bank of a State serves as its monetary authority with 'the duty of being **12.52** the guardian and regulator of the monetary system and currency of that State both internally and externally'. Central banks may be departments of a government or given independent personality as a separate entity by a State's local law.

As a separate entity, a central bank will enjoy immunity under the 2004 UN **12.53** Convention on State Immunity Article 21(c) and national legislation, as with the UK State Immunity Act, section 14(1), if, and only if, the proceedings relate to anything done by it in the exercise of sovereign authority and the circumstances are such that the State itself would be immune. Article 21(c) of the 2004 UN Convention thus gives special treatment to 'the central bank or other monetary authority of the State' with such property not being subject to attachment in respect of commercial liabilities, or judgments of local courts given in respect of them, without express consent in writing or allocation of specific assets to meet such liabilities.

The Common Purpose Underlying State and Diplomatic Immunity

This chapter, in giving an account of the immunities of the State, state entities, **12.54** and state officials, particularly the Head of State and the Foreign Minister, has sought to describe the role which immunity serves in the conduct of foreign relations with other States by protecting the State and its diplomats, when present in another State, from the difficulties and misunderstandings which inevitably arise from the unfamiliar local administration and its regulations and impede the work of the diplomatic mission. The chapter is intended as an introduction to the following chapters which set out the immunities of the diplomatic

---

[39] Claims relating to 'piercing the corporate veil' are relevant to the sourcing of funds and management of an agency as well as its immunity from the jurisdiction of local courts, see Lord Mance's speech in *La Générale des Carrières et des Mines (Gecamines) v Hemisphere Associates LLC (Jersey)* [2012] UKPC 27; Robert Walker, Denning Society, 'Metaphors and Metaphysics' Lincoln's Inn lecture, 24 November 2015.

mission and of the diplomats and other members of the mission. Broadly its theme throughout is that state immunity is now restricted to the protection of the acts of a public nature relating to the administration of the State when performed by the sending State, its officials, and agencies.

12.55 This same restriction to acts of a public nature, that is acts of a non-commercial and non-private nature, underlies and applies to the immunities enjoyed by a diplomatic mission and its members. Although described as a separate branch of law, the fundamental functions for which the grant of immunity to diplomatic missions is made—the representation, protection, and promotion of the sending State's interests, negotiation with the receiving State, and the ascertainment of that State's conditions and interests—are all by their nature 'acts of a public nature' which promote 'the efficient performance of the functions of diplomatic missions' as stated in Article 3 and the preamble of the 1961 Vienna Convention.

12.56 It is, therefore, no surprise that many of the rules now set out in written form in the 2004 UN Convention on State Immunity have the effect of clarifying the extent of the immunities which diplomatic missions apply and enjoy today.[40] Thus, both the 2004 Convention and modern diplomatic law treat the State as the proper party to be named in any proceedings brought in the national courts of another State. Similarly, although waiver of the foreign State was required by a long-established rule to be express, Article 7 of the 2004 UN Convention on State Immunity makes prior written consent of the State given in advance of proceedings sufficient to constitute waiver of immunity in respect of commercial transactions of the diplomatic mission.[41]

12.57 However note should be taken that the restrictive doctrine of immunity which applies in the twenty-first century as set out in the 2004 UN Convention on State Immunity has effected a certain reduction of the scope of immunity now available to a foreign State in proceedings before national courts. This reduction of the scope of a foreign State's immunity has particular relevance to the immunities of the diplomatic mission in respect of its business transactions and employment of service staff in diplomatic premises. Thus, while the activities of 'developing economic relations' is a function of a diplomatic mission as set out in Article 3.1(f) of the 1965 Vienna Convention, the activities of a diplomatic mission which make use of diplomatic premises by, for example, the selling of

---

[40] See generally Fox and Webb, *Law of State Immunity* (3rd revised paperback edn).
[41] Compare Art 32 of the 1961 Diplomatic Convention, to the liberal terms of Art 7 of the 2004 UN Convention, which provides that immunity may be invoked where a State 'expressly consents … (a) by international agreement; (b) in a written contract; or (c) by a declaration before the court or by written communication in a specific proceeding'.

tickets for travel and air flights or the provision of cultural or educational services may be challenged as the performance of 'commercial transactions', the purpose of which is to generate profit, and which accordingly comes within Article 10 of the 2004 UN Convention which renders such activities unprotected by immunity.[42] In consequence the mission will be exposed to their examination and review by the local courts of the receiving State.[43]

Similarly, by reason of the application of the restrictive rule of immunity which now applies in the law of state immunity an employment contract made 'between the State and an individual for work performed, or to be performed... in the territory of another [that other] State' no longer comes within the bar of state immunity.[44] Proceedings may accordingly be brought against a sending State in the national courts of the receiving State for breach of an employment contract made by the sending State for work to be performed in the receiving State's country.   **12.58**

Terms of employment, however, are no longer solely a matter of concern between employer and the employed. Many States now have in force labour laws providing compulsory conditions relating to employment within their countries with legal sanctions for their non-observance.[45] In addition, States, in particular member States of the Council of Europe, are under legal obligations in human rights conventions regarding affording access to court and the right of non-discrimination in respect of alleged violation of internationally adopted employment requirements.[46] Accordingly, claims relating to service staff, who are nationals of the receiving or of a third State, employed as service staff for work in the premises of the diplomatic mission, may no longer enjoy immunity   **12.59**

---

[42] Art 10 of the 2004 UN Convention on State Immunity describes the proceedings for commercial transactions for which state immunity cannot be invoked as one for a 'commercial transaction' between a State and a foreign natural or juridical person which falls within the jurisdiction of the national court of another State; and Art 2.1(c) comprehensively defines such 'commercial transactions' as including any contract for the sale of goods or supply of service, loan or other transaction of a financial nature, and contract of a commercial industrial, trading, or professional nature (but excluding contracts of employment of persons).

[43] The scope of the commercial exception to state immunity, in the 2004 UN Convention on State Immunity, Arts 2.1(c) and 10, is broader in scope than the narrowly construed exception in Arts 31(3) and 45 of the 1961 Vienna Convention for 'professional or commercial activity exercised by the diplomat outside his official functions'. See further Chapter 13, paragraphs 13.12–13.13.

[44] Art 11 of the UN Convention on State Immunity.

[45] *Park v Shin* 313 F 3d 1138 (4th Cir 2002) where a domestic employee pursuant to the 1963 Vienna Convention on Consular Relations brought proceedings against the Deputy Consul General of Korea as her employer. See further R Garner 'State and Diplomatic Immunity and Employment Rights: Europe to the Rescue?' (2015) 64 *ICLQ* 783, at 822–3.

[46] *Reyes and another v Al-Malki and another* [2015] EWCA Civ 32; *Benkharbouche v Embassy of Republic of Sudan* [2015] 3 WLR 301 (under appeal to the UK Supreme Court).

and their complaints may be adjudicated by national courts located in the receiving State.

12.60 These two areas relating to commercial transactions and contracts of employment made by States, which in many instances are already familiar to States by reason of their operation in the private and commercial sector of their own countries, should present no difficulty to the sending State and its head of mission in the application of the exceptions to immunity set out in Articles 10 and 11 in the 2004 UN Convention on State Immunity and in ensuring the observance of similar standards in their diplomatic missions in the territory of other States.

12.61 Overall, despite these two areas, the clarification of the rules applicable in state immunity are of considerable benefit to the diplomatic mission as well as the protection from the jurisdiction of national courts which the 2004 UN Convention affords by the plea of immunity.

12.62 Thus considerable protection is afforded to the diplomatic mission by the immunity from the enforcement jurisdiction of national courts set out in Part IV, Articles 18 to 21 which bars pre-and post-judgment measures of constraint, except with express consent,[47] against the property of the foreign State including the embassy bank accounts of the mission.[48] The provisions of the 2004 UN Convention on State Immunity protect the bank account of the mission by expressly stating in Article 21.1(a) that 'property, including any bank account, which is used or intended for use in the performance of the functions of the diplomatic mission of the State or its consular posts, special missions, missions to international organizations or delegations to organs of international organizations or to international conferences' is to be treated as 'property in use or intended use...for government non-commercial purposes'. Consequently, despite the absence of any immunity granted in the 1961 Vienna Convention, the embassy bank account is protected by state immunity and is not to be frozen or seized in the event of debts incurred by the mission remaining unpaid. This immunity in respect of the embassy bank account applies, even where the failure to pay relates to goods supplied or services rendered of a commercial nature. A similar protection is granted by the 2004 UN Convention on State Immunity, Article 21.1(c) to the 'property of the central bank or other monetary authority of the State' and provides an essential element in the regulation

---

[47] Appearance in court of a state representative is insufficient: express consent to measures of constraint. or earmarking or allocation of embassy or state property is required: *Alcom Ltd v Republic of Columbia* [1984] AC 580, *NML v Argentina* [2013] France, Cour de Conseil, Judgments Nos 394, 395, and 396 of 23 March 2013.

[48] The *Philippine Embassy* case, 46 BverfGE 342; 63 ILR 146.

of the monetary policy of a State and the system of secure deposit abroad of a sending State's national reserves in a receiving State.

In similar fashion the 2004 UN Convention on State Immunity clarifies the **12.63** position of state enterprises whose trading abroad contributes an important part of the conduct and prosperity of a State's economy. The 2004 Convention distinguishes the status of the organs and representatives of a State from the legal position of trading corporations. Whilst the latter enjoy no immunity, state agencies which undertake state projects and engage in trade continue to enjoy immunities in respect of acts which they are entitled to perform and are actually performing in the exercise of acts of a public governmental nature.[49] Contrary to the protection of these state agencies, commercial companies are liable and all their assets enforceable in respect of their business commitments.

Thus, to a considerable extent as shown, the practice of diplomatic missions **12.64** today accords with the requirements of state immunity law as now set out in the provisions of the 2004 UN Convention on State Immunity. In consequence, to a large extent, state and diplomatic law now are in conformity in respect of the extent to which a foreign State's immunity today restricts the jurisdiction of the receiving State and its national courts.

Conclusion

Finally, it should be recorded that the protection from enforcement powers of **12.65** the national courts of the receiving State in Part IV of the 2004 UN Convention relating to state immunity from measures of constraint considerably strengthens the position of the diplomatic mission of the sending State and the observance of the immunities of the mission by leaving in place the immunity from enforcement and the absolute bar relating to all measures of constraint against state property. No judgement can be enforced against the mission or the diplomat in post, save where consented to by the sending State itself or by that State's direct engagement in the commercial undertaking for which enforcement is sought. Disputes relating to the operation of the diplomatic mission are solely for settlement between the sending and receiving States by the application of international law and its procedures.

---

[49] The 2004 UN Convention of the Jurisdictional Immunities of States and their Property, Art 2, para 1(b)(iii) and para 2.

13

PRIVILEGES AND IMMUNITIES OF DIPLOMATIC MISSIONS

Joanne Foakes and Eileen Denza

Justification for Diplomatic Privileges and Immunities

13.1 Two fundamental rules of diplomatic law—that the person of the ambassador is inviolable and that a special protection must be given to the messages which are sent to and received from the ambassador's sovereign—have been recognized from time immemorial among civilized States.

13.2 The broad outlines of customary international law regarding the privileges and immunities of diplomats, their property, premises, and communications were established by the middle of the eighteenth century, and were described by Vattel in *Le Droit des Gens*. Vattel explained why the nature of the ambassador's function made these immunities necessary. The law of nations—now known as public international law—required States which accepted foreign diplomats to guarantee rights necessary to enable them to exercise their functions including independence from local jurisdiction. It was important that ambassadors should not be afraid of traps or distracted by legal trickery.[1] Montesquieu also emphasized

---

[1] E de Vattel, *Le Droit des Gens* (London, 1758) Vol IV, Book VII, Sect 92.

the need for the ambassador to be independent of the receiving sovereign.[2] Modern practice and theory have adopted this explanation of 'functional need' as the correct justification for diplomatic privileges and immunities.

With immunities founded on the customary practice of many centuries, ambas- **13.3** sadors and their staffs were enabled to act independently of any local pressures in representing the sending State while being themselves under protection from attack or harassment. Such immunities are thus essential to the conduct of relations between independent sovereign States given on a basis of reciprocity, and have proved a most effective guarantee of observance of the rules. Every State is both a sending and a receiving State. Any government which fails to accord privileges or immunities to a diplomat within its territory knows that it risks not only collective protest by the *corps diplomatique* in its own capital but also reprisals for its violation by the injured sending State against its own diplomats.[3]

Although the broad rules regarding the privileges and immunities of ambassa- **13.4** dors and the staff of their missions continued unchanged from the eighteenth century, there was considerable variation in the detailed practice of individual States. Some States admitted exceptions to the rule of immunity from civil jurisdiction in regard, for instance, to real property, or where the action related to the diplomat's commercial activities, while others, in particular the United Kingdom and the United States, admitted no exceptions. Some States refused to accept their own nationals as diplomatic representatives of another State, others accepted them provided that they enjoyed no privileges or immunities, others again allowed them privileges and immunities. Some States gave full privileges and immunities to all members of the ambassador's staff—known as his suite—from senior diplomats such as counsellors and first secretaries down to chauffeurs and cleaners; others accorded immunity to clerks and typists in regard to official acts only and no privileges or immunities to domestic servants; while most drew the line at intermediate points. The twentieth century led to new forms of diplomatic communication, such as wireless transmitters in missions and carriage of diplomatic bags by ad hoc couriers, or by hand of the pilot of an aircraft, and no clear agreement emerged as to whether these new methods were permissible or entitled to equal protection with the traditional diplomatic bag. There was a series of codifications of the rules of diplomatic law, of which the two most important were the Havana Convention on Diplomatic Officers, signed in 1928,[4] and the Harvard Research Draft Convention on

---

[2] C L de Secondat de Montesquieu, *De l'Esprit des Lois* (Geneva, 1748) xxvi, ch 21.
[3] Sir Cecil Hurst, 'Les Immunités diplomatiques' (1926) 2 *HR* 123.
[4] *UN Legislative Series*, Vol 7, 419.

Diplomatic Privileges and Immunities, published in 1932.[5] Although the latter had great persuasive authority, neither Convention attracted widespread acceptance nor caused States to modify the provisions of their domestic law where these diverged.

13.5 The successful conclusion in 1961 of the Vienna Convention on Diplomatic Relations (VCDR), to which by 2016 there were 190 States Parties, placed the law on diplomatic privileges and immunities on a clear legal basis which is now virtually universal. The text of the Convention was carefully prepared for several years by the International Law Commission of the United Nations,[6] and was submitted to a Conference to which all members of the United Nations, members of the Specialized Agencies, and parties to the Statute of the International Court of Justice had been invited. The Convention therefore from the outset carried great authority as a codification of those areas of diplomatic law where the customary rule was clear, or the weight of state practice could be ascertained by research. Equally important, the text took careful account of the sometimes conflicting interests of governments on those few but important issues where, in the interests of progressive development of the law, it was necessary to negotiate a compromise solution. The overwhelming acceptance of the Convention by the international community as a whole as well as the limited number and importance of reservations made to it by parties is clear testimony to the soundness of its provisions. The instances of serious breach of its provisions by governments, although usually very well publicized when they do occur, have, in practice, been very rare. In short, the Vienna Convention constitutes modern international law in regard to the privileges and immunities of diplomats.

13.6 The Convention justifies privileges and immunities by reference to functional need. The preamble sets out 'that the purpose of such privileges and immunities is not to benefit individuals but to ensure the efficient performance of the functions of diplomatic missions as representing States'. The result of this approach was that a greater degree of protection than under customary law was given to the mission itself—to its premises and to its communications in particular—whereas for diplomatic agents and for the subordinate staff of the mission privileges and immunities were generally restricted below what had been accorded under customary law or national practice. This restrictive approach to individual privileges and immunities relates particularly to matters outside

---

[5] (1932) 26 *AJI Supplement* 19. For evaluation of its long-term significance see E Denza 'Diplomatic Privileges and Immunities', in J P Grant and J C Barker (eds), *Harvard Research in International Law: Contemporary Analysis and Appraisal* (New York: Hein, 2007).

[6] For a summary of the debates and successive drafts of the International Law Commission see *ILC Yearbook*, 1957 and 1958.

diplomatic functions, such as commercial activities or the private ownership of real property within the receiving State.

Following the arrangement of the text of the Vienna Convention, diplomatic **13.7** privileges and immunities will be described in this chapter and Chapter 14 under the following headings: the status of the mission itself as regards its premises, archives, and communications; the privileges and immunities of diplomatic agents together with the position of their families and junior staff and of nationals and permanent residents of the receiving State; and the position of diplomatic agents in third States will also be considered.

The Premises of the Mission

The inviolability of the ambassador's residence—which was normally also his **13.8** place of work and the residence of members of his suite—was generally established in customary international law by the eighteenth century. Before then the extent of protection and immunity from law enforcement accorded to diplomatic residences varied from capital to capital. Grotius remarked that ambassadors were, by legal fiction, deemed to be outside the territory of the State where they were residing;[7] but when this fiction came to be popularly misunderstood as meaning that embassies were small enclaves of foreign soil, it was seen to be misleading and dangerous. The term 'extraterritoriality', is sometimes used to denote the totality of privileges and immunities accorded to diplomatic agents, their families, and subordinate staff, or to describe the status of embassy premises. But it is now everywhere accepted that it does not mean that the diplomat is not legally present in the receiving State or that the embassy is deemed to be foreign territory. Marriages, or crimes, occurring on diplomatic mission premises are regarded in law as taking place in the territory of the receiving State.

Article 22 of the VCDR lays down that '[t]he premises of the mission shall be **13.9** inviolable'. The term 'inviolability' has two distinct aspects in modern international law. The first is immunity from any legal process or any action by the law enforcement officers of the receiving State. This is spelt out in paragraphs 1 and 3 of Article 22. Without the consent of the head of mission, the premises may not be entered by the police, by process servers, by building safety or health inspectors—even by the fire brigade if the premises are on fire. The absence of an exception in case of emergency on the premises of the mission was seen to be justified when a fire in the United States embassy in Moscow was tackled by

---

[7] H Grotius, *De Jure Belli ac Pacis* (Paris, 1625) II. XVIII. iv.5.

'fire-fighters' who were in fact KGB agents more interested in taking secret documents than in extinguishing the flames. No right of entry is given to the receiving State, even where it believes that inviolability is being abused and the premises used in a manner 'incompatible with the functions of the mission' (which is prohibited under Article 41). But on one occasion the Pakistan government told the ambassador of Iraq that it had evidence that arms imported under diplomatic cover into Pakistan and intended for rebel tribes in Baluchistan were being stored in the embassy of Iraq, and asked permission to search the premises. The ambassador refused, but the police were authorized to carry out a search in his presence and large quantities of arms were found to be stored in crates. The Pakistan government protested strongly to the government of Iraq, declared the ambassador *persona non grata* and recalled their own ambassador.[8] Entry in such circumstances of threat to national security can only be justified, if at all, as a measure of self-defence.

13.10 In London in 1984, during a demonstration by Libyan dissidents outside the Libyan diplomatic mission (which was then styled the Libyan People's Bureau) a policewoman on duty protecting the mission was fatally shot by a gunman within the building. The Libyan government of Colonel Qaddafi refused permission for police to enter and search the building. The British government upheld the inviolability of the premises, but in the face of continued refusal to cooperate by the Libyan authorities they broke diplomatic relations with Libya and all those within the mission were required to leave the United Kingdom. The House of Commons Foreign Affairs Committee later carried out an enquiry into these events and concluded that under circumstances in which there was no continuing threat from the mission to the public, the authorities would not have been justified on grounds of self-defence in forcibly entering the premises of the mission.[9] In 1989 the United States carried out an armed intervention in Panama in order to seize General Noriega who was acting as Head of State of Panama though not recognized as such by the US. He took refuge in the mission of the Holy See to Panama and US troops did not infringe the inviolability of its diplomatic premises—though their search of the residence of the ambassador of Nicaragua which formed part of the embassy of Nicaragua would, but for a US veto, have been condemned by a Security Council resolution.[10]

13.11 Even for a bona fide public purpose, such as the widening of a road, the receiving State has no power to expropriate any part of the premises of the mission.

---

[8] *The Observer*, 11 February 1973.
[9] House of Commons Foreign Affairs Committee 1st Report, 1984–5, paras 88–95; UK Government Review of the Vienna Convention, Cmnd 9497, para 83.
[10] (1990) *RGDIP* 495, 803; *The Times*, 28 and 30 December 1989.

Thus, when the British authorities wished to construct a new underground railway line running underneath the premises of several embassies, the general compulsory powers of acquisition were not used and the express consent of each embassy to the tunnelling underneath its building was sought and granted.[11]

It is clear that Article 22 prohibits any personal service of legal process whether such attempt at service occurs at the door of the mission or inside and whether it is directed at the sending State itself or members of the mission; for example an Irish court has held that service of proceedings on the British ambassador in Ireland was a breach of Article 22.[12] The question of whether service of process by post is a breach of inviolability was less clear but gradually the view that such service is prohibited began to prevail and was reflected in State practice. The preferred route for serving legal documents on a foreign State is through transmission by the forum State's ministry of foreign affairs, via its diplomatic mission in the defendant State to the defendant State's ministry of foreign affairs. Accordingly, the United Kingdom State Immunity Act 1978[13] provides for a writ against a foreign State to be sent via the Foreign and Commonwealth Office to the ministry of foreign affairs of the defendant State. Practical difficulties may, of course, arise where there are no diplomatic relations between the two States concerned and no permanent mission in the foreign State through which the writ may be transmitted. In 1986 proceedings were brought against Iran by Westminster City Council. The Swedish Embassy, which was then protecting British interests in Tehran, had refused to effect service of the proceedings on the ministry of foreign affairs and the English court concluded that it could not proceed in the absence of valid service. It is perhaps the existence of such difficulties which led the English Court of Appeal to decide in 2015 that Article 22 can permit the service of process by post to the mission (or to the private residence of a diplomatic agent).[14] This decision has given rise to some confusion and uncertainty and would appear to put UK practice at odds with the approach taken in many other States. **13.12**

It must be emphasized that the inviolability of diplomatic premises which precludes personal service of legal process on the sending State via its diplomatic mission does not mean that the State itself is immune from the legal proceedings in question. It is now widely accepted that there are a number of important **13.13**

---

[11] More recently the proposed basement extension of a private individual living next door to the French embassy has prompted protests based upon Art 22 from the French ambassador and other diplomats with residences in the same road. *The Sunday Times*, 10 January 2016.

[12] *Adams v Director of Public Prosecutions* [2001] 2 ILRM 401, [2000] IEHC 45.

[13] C33.s 12.f.

[14] *Reyes v Al-Malki* [2015] EWCA Civ 32.

exceptions to the immunity of a foreign State most notably in regard to its commercial activities but also in regard to breaches of employment contracts in respect of work performed or to be performed in the forum State. Article 11 of the 2004 UN Convention on the Jurisdictional Immunities of States and Their Property[15] expressly excludes the application of the employment exception to the diplomatic staff of a mission but it seems highly doubtful that this exclusion would extend to service staff engaged in work of a non-governmental nature.[16]

13.14   Immunity from legal process is extended by Article 22.3 of the Vienna Convention to property on mission premises and to the means of transport of the mission. Embassy cars are protected from 'search, requisition, attachment or execution', but it is accepted in many major capitals that a car which is causing serious obstruction and whose driver cannot be traced may be towed away provided that no charges or fines in respect of the incident are imposed on those involved. Embassy bank accounts to fund diplomatic operations in the receiving State are not held on mission premises so that they are not directly covered by the terms of Article 22, but a series of cases in national courts has established that such accounts cannot be made subject to attachment or execution on the basis that they serve sovereign purposes of a foreign State.[17] The embassy account is treated in this context as a whole even if the funds in the account are used for commercial purposes (such as payment for supplies of goods or services) as well as for strictly governmental purposes. These cases have established a rule of customary international law. The rule has been explicitly confirmed in Article 21 of the 2004 UN Convention on State Immunity, which provides that 'property, including any bank account, which is in use or intended for use in the performance of the functions of the diplomatic mission of the State or its consular posts, special missions, missions to international organizations or delegations to organs of international organizations or to international conferences' is not to be considered as coming within the general exemption from immunity for state property used or intended for use for commercial purposes.[18]

13.15   The second aspect of the inviolability of embassy premises is the duty of protection laid on the receiving State. Under Article 22.2 of the Vienna Convention

---

[15] UN Doc A/RES/59/38.

[16] *Benkarbouche v Embassy of Republic of Sudan* [2015] 3 WLR 301 (under appeal to the UK Supreme Court).

[17] See in particular *Philippine Embassy Bank Account Case*, 65 ILR 146; *Alcom v Republic of Colombia* [1984] AC 580, 74 ILR 170; *Liberian Eastern Timber Corporation v The Government of Liberia*, 89 ILR 360.

[18] See further Chapter 12, paragraph 12.61 as to the protection of the bank account etc of the diplomatic mission of a foreign State from all measures of constraint in connection with proceedings in the national courts of States—2004 UN Convention on Jurisdictional Immunities of States and Their Property, Art 21(a).

'[t]he receiving State is under a special duty to take all appropriate steps to protect the premises of the mission against any intrusion or damage and to prevent any disturbance of the peace of the mission or impairment of its dignity'. 'Appropriate' steps imply that the extent of protection provided must be proportionate to the risk or threat to the premises. If the authorities know of an impending hostile demonstration, or if the ambassador informs them of an intrusion or an impending attack, then they are obliged to provide protection proportionate to the threat or to remove the intruders on request.

Attacks on or threats to embassies do not as a general rule involve breach of its **13.16** duties by the receiving State when they are instigated by terrorists or dissidents seeking payment or political concessions for the release of diplomatic hostages. They do however give rise to special difficulties for the authorities of the receiving State who may be unable to secure the consent of the head of the mission to any operation to end the siege if the ambassador is himself held hostage. In 1980 the Iranian embassy in London was occupied by commandos hostile to the Islamic regime in Tehran and diplomats were held hostage. The British government secured the consent of the government of Iran, as well as that of the most senior Iranian diplomat not held within, before authorizing the Special Air Service to carry out a relief operation which led to the rescue of all surviving hostages and the death of all but one of the terrorists.[19] The hostage-takers holding the embassy may also make political or financial demands on the government of the receiving State. Evidence from a number of embassy sieges shows that capitulation to these unlawful demands leads only to further sieges and escalation of demands, but the sending State may sometimes refuse to authorize forcible rescue. In December 1996 guerrillas from the Tupac Amaru Revolutionary Movement seized the residence of the Japanese ambassador to Peru, making extensive demands for money, release of prisoners, rejection of foreign investment, and safe conduct to the Amazon jungle. After four months the Peruvian government ended the siege through trickery and force without securing the consent of the government of Japan—which however expressed understanding after the rescue operation was successfully completed.[20]

Most States take their responsibilities under this provision very seriously indeed **13.17** and deliberate breaches by the receiving State are rare. The seizure in November 1979 of the United States embassy in Iran—originally effected by militant 'students' but condoned over the subsequent 15 months by the government of

---

[19] 1980 *RGDIP* 1134.
[20] *The Times*, 20 and 21 December 1996; 23 and 24 April 1997; 2 and 14 May 1997; *Japan Times*, 23 April 1997; Eileen Denza, *Diplomatic Law* (4th edn, Oxford: Oxford Univesity Press, 2016) 134–5.

Iran, who failed entirely to take any 'appropriate steps' either to prevent it or to bring it to an end, was a rare exception in this regard. The US took proceedings against Iran before the International Court of Justice, and the International Court first ordered the release of the hostages as an interim measure and in its final judgment in the *Hostages Case* condemned Iran for repeated and multiple breaches of the Vienna Convention on Diplomatic Relations. The government of Iran made no serious attempt to justify these breaches before the International Court and sanctions were imposed against Iran by Member States of the European Communities and by other States as well as by the US.[21]

13.18 It is not obligatory, nor is it universal practice, for national law to provide especially severe penalties for attack or trespass on embassy premises, or to make mere insult to the premises or the flag of the embassy a criminal offence. But provisions of this kind are not uncommon. For example legislation in the United States makes it an offence to display a flag or placard intended to intimidate or ridicule foreign diplomatic representatives, to interfere with performance of diplomatic duties within 500 feet of embassy premises except under a police permit, or even to congregate within that area and refuse to disperse on police orders.[22] Political demonstrations outside foreign embassies are however now a fashionable form of protest with regard to the policies of the sending State—or sometimes against the policies of the receiving State. In democratic countries with constitutional guarantees of freedom of speech and assembly or party to human rights treaties, the police and government authorities and sometimes the national courts must try to balance the rights of the demonstrators to protest with the rights of the embassy to carry out its functions and to have its inviolability and also its dignity protected. The US Supreme Court held in 1988 in the case of *Boos v Barry* that under Article 22 of the Vienna Convention 'the prohibited quantum of disturbance is determined by whether normal embassy activities have been or are about to be disrupted'.[23]

13.19 The duty of protection in Article 22 does not make it a matter of legal obligation to pay compensation in respect of any damage that may be inflicted on embassy premises by terrorists or by protesters in the absence of failure on the part of the receiving State to accord the appropriate protection. But both before

---

[21] *Case concerning United States Diplomatic and Consular Staff in Tehran* [1980] ICJ Reports 3. See also *Case concerning Armed Activities on the Territory of the Congo (DRC v Uganda)* [2005] ICJ Reports 168, at paras 306–45 3; J Craig Barker, *The Protection of Diplomatic Personnel* (Aldershot UK: Ashgate, 2006) 8–9 and ch 4.

[22] *UN Legislative Series*, Vol 7, 375; (1938) 32 *AJIL* 344 and Supplement, 100. *Frend et al v US Annual Digest* (1938–40), No 161.

[23] 458 US 312; 121 ILR 499, at 551. For other national cases on demonstrations outside embassies see Denza, *Diplomatic Law* (4th edn, 2016) 140–5.

and after the Vienna Convention (when attacks on mission premises have become more frequent in many parts of the world) British practice has been to pay on an *ex gratia* basis all claims for damage to inviolable premises in London, while claiming reciprocally for all damage deliberately inflicted on British missions and diplomatic residences abroad. Many other countries follow this practice and, generally speaking, there has been little difficulty in arriving at satisfactory settlements of these claims. One instance where payment was made for damage which did not result from any deliberate attack on mission premises related to the damage to the Nigerian High Commission in London resulting from a car bomb explosion in March 1973. This attack by the Irish Republican Army was directed against the British authorities and not against the Nigerian High Commission and there was no suggestion of any failure on the part of the police to take appropriate steps to protect the mission. But the British government met the full cost of the damage. The siege of the Iranian embassy in London described in paragraph 13.16 resulted in the total destruction by fire of the building, and the United Kingdom government at other times suffered extensive damage to its embassy in Tehran—these claims and counterclaims were finally settled by an Exchange of Notes between the two governments in 1988.[24] Notwithstanding this widespread practice of paying compensation on an *ex gratia* basis, the modern tendency among those States more vulnerable to terrorist or politically motivated damage is to increase the level of their physical protection, perhaps to employ private security firms for this purpose, and also to take out insurance. The use of public or private security forces by a sending State for protection has become more common in recent years in the face of an increasing terrorist threat. The Vienna Convention does not prohibit such additional protection although any such personnel are obliged to comply with the laws and regulations of the receiving State in carrying out their functions. The existence of such additional protection does not remove or affect the duty of the receiving State under Article 22. The UK government has taken the view that individuals carrying out security functions for a diplomatic mission, even if employed by private security companies, can legitimately be notified to the receiving State as members of the administrative and technical staff.[25] There can be disadvantages in such enhanced physical security with the risk, in particular, that it may turn the embassy into a fortress cut off from the surrounding city and thereby prevent the mission from carrying out its functions effectively.

---

[24] Exchange of Notes concerning the Settlement of Mutual Claims in respect of damage incurred to the Diplomatic Premises of the United Kingdom in Iran and the Islamic Republic of Iran in London, 6 July 1988, Cm 480.

[25] Response of the Secretary of State for Foreign and Commonwealth Affairs to the Foreign Affairs Committee Report on Human Rights Session 2008–9 Cm 7723, [2009] *BYIL* 835–6.

13.20 The premises of the mission are defined in Article 1 of the Convention as 'the buildings or parts of buildings and the land ancillary thereto, irrespective of ownership, used for the purposes of the mission including the residence of the head of the mission'. The functions of a diplomatic mission are set out in Article 3 of the VCDR although it is clear that the list is not exhaustive. These include developing economic relations between sending and receiving States and, in determining whether or not particular premises should be accorded diplomatic status, it may be important to distinguish between this function and the performance of commercial activities, the purpose of which is to generate profit such as selling flight tickets or the provision of educational or cultural services. In its 1985 Review of the VCDR, the United Kingdom stated that diplomatic status would be withdrawn from premises not being used for purposes compatible with diplomatic functions.[26] At the same time, it withdrew diplomatic status from separate tourist offices. Neither the sending nor receiving State has a right unilaterally to identify specific buildings as embassy premises. They have to reach agreement in borderline cases such as cultural institutes under the direction of a cultural attaché, tourist offices, embassy reading rooms, or information offices open to the public. But in practice most problems usually arise in determining the time when the status of premises of the mission begins and ends. The Vienna Convention has clear provisions regarding commencement and termination of personal privileges and immunities, but not in regard to mission buildings. It is settled that ownership of property by a sending State, perhaps with a remote intention to use it for diplomatic purposes, is not enough to make these premises inviolable.[27] But if the sending State has notified the receiving State of its acquisition of premises for use as an ambassador's residence or embassy offices, and has secured any consents which may be needed under local law (for the character of a building as embassy premises does not exempt it from local building or planning laws), then those premises are generally regarded as premises of the mission while they are being prepared for occupation and use. In the opposite case, where a diplomatic mission has vacated buildings, they continue to enjoy inviolability for a 'reasonable period' of a few months, just as the diplomat is entitled to privileges and immunities for a reasonable period after his appointment ends. When the United Kingdom broke diplomatic relations with Libya in 1984 following the shooting from the mission premises described earlier, the premises were treated as inviolable for a further seven days before police entered to search for evidence related to the

---

[26] Cmnd 9497, para 39.
[27] *Tietz et al v People's Republic of Bulgaria, Weinmann v Republic of Latvia, Bennett and Ball v People's Republic of Hungary, Cassirer and Geheeb v Japan*, 28 ILR 369, 385, 392, 396.

killing. (The 'reasonable period' was very short in this case because of the conduct which had led to the mission being vacated.) After diplomatic relations have been broken off or a mission has been recalled, the receiving State will still be obliged under Article 45 of the Vienna Convention to 'respect and protect' the premises of the discontinued mission, along with the property and archives in them.

National laws or regulations may prescribe that consent of the receiving State is   **13.21** required before particular premises are accepted as 'premises of the mission', provided always that any system requiring notification or consent is not used to prevent a mission from acquiring appropriate premises. Receiving States may for example require embassies to be located in a diplomatic compound or at least in an area suited to diplomatic use in terms of security and traffic or parking control. The United Kingdom under the Diplomatic and Consular Premises Act 1987 and the United States under the Foreign Missions Act 1982[28] both require notification of and consent to any proposal to use premises for purposes of a diplomatic mission. Receiving States may be required under Article 21 of the Vienna Convention to assist in the acquisition of suitable premises, and systems of notification before consent to diplomatic use is given are helpful in this context. States on occasion have concluded special international agreements for the mutual provision of suitable embassy sites. The United States, for example, concluded successive agreements with the Soviet Union and, more recently, with China, and the United Kingdom has also concluded agreements relating to construction of embassy buildings in London and Moscow.

Diplomatic Asylum

A right to give asylum in diplomatic missions to refugees from the authorities   **13.22** of the receiving State has often been claimed, but it has not always been accepted and there is as yet no universal agreement among States on the circumstances in which the right may be exercised. When the International Law Commission was charged with formulating the rules of diplomatic privileges and immunities, it was agreed that the question of diplomatic asylum should be left aside and it was not expressly considered either in the context of the ILC's work or by the subsequent Conference which negotiated the Vienna Convention on Diplomatic Relations. The preamble to the Convention provides 'that the rules of customary international law should govern questions not expressly regulated by the provisions of the present Convention'. It is therefore necessary to consider

---

[28] Public Law 97–241, 22 US Code 4301.

the extent to which customary international law admitted a right to give asylum in diplomatic missions. Many of the older cases involved bitter disputes between the States directly concerned and it is difficult to claim that any clear rule emerged from these controversial incidents.

13.23   Among Latin American countries a right of diplomatic asylum has as a matter of local usage been generally accepted, and international agreements were concluded between those countries establishing rules for the exercise of the right. The International Court of Justice carefully considered the nature and scope of one of these agreements—the Havana Convention on Diplomatic Asylum in 1950 in the *Asylum Case*[29] and in 1951 in the *Haya de la Torre Case*.[30] In the first of these related cases they observed that:

> asylum as practised in Latin America is an institution which, to a very great extent, owes its development to extra-legal factors. The good neighbour relations between the republics, the different political interests of the Governments, have favoured the mutual recognition of asylum apart from any clearly defined juridical system. Even if the Havana Convention, in particular, represents an indisputable reaction against certain abuses in practice, it in no way tends to limit the practice of asylum as it may arise from agreements between interested Governments inspired by mutual feelings of toleration and goodwill.

The International Court held that neither general international law nor the Havana Convention entitled Colombia—which had extended asylum within its embassy in Lima to Haya de la Torre who was accused of military rebellion against Peru—unilaterally to qualify him as a political refugee. The grant of asylum should be brought to an end, but this did not mean that Colombia was under a duty to surrender him to the Peruvian authorities. An agreement was eventually reached between the two States under which Haya de la Torre left Peru.

13.24   Under general international law, however, diplomatic asylum is regarded as a matter of humanitarian practice rather than a legal right, and it is accepted that it may now be accorded only for the purpose of saving life or preventing injury in the face of an immediate threat to the refugee. As such any right is exercised and belongs to the sheltering State, not to the 'refugee' who does not necessarily fall within the term 'refugee' as defined by the 1951 Convention relating to the Status of Refugees and its 1967 Protocol.[31] Even then diplomatic asylum should, in the absence of an established local usage, be accorded only on a temporary basis

---

[29] [1950] ICJ Reports 266.
[30] [1951] ICJ Reports 71.
[31] See *R (on the application of 'B' and Others) v Secretary of State for the Foreign and Commonwealth Office* [2004] EWCA Civ 1344, [2005] QB 643 where the UK Court of Appeal held that to have given the applicants refuge against the demands of the Australian government would have been 'an abuse of the privileged inviolability accorded to diplomatic premises'.

and the fugitive should be surrendered on the basis of a lawful demand by the local authorities unless an agreement for his safe passage out of the country can be secured. It is therefore during war and violent revolution that diplomatic asylum is most commonly extended. In this context the United States and European States which do not accept a general right to grant diplomatic asylum except for essentially humanitarian reasons, have on a number of occasions granted short-term diplomatic asylum to political refugees—for example during the civil war in Chile in 1891, following the suppression of the uprising in Hungary in 1956, and following the fall of the regime of President Allende in Chile in 1973. The political character of the offence alleged is in theory not relevant when temporary asylum is accorded for humanitarian motives, but in practice those who benefit from asylum are often in danger because of their involvement in political disturbances. Proposals regarding diplomatic asylum were made in 1957 to the International Law Commission[32] but no provisions on the matter were included in the Vienna Convention. Later discussion of the question in 1974 at the request of Australia by the Sixth Committee of the United Nations General Assembly was also inconclusive.[33]

Although there are no provisions in the Vienna Convention expressly regulating **13.25** diplomatic asylum two provisions are relevant. First, Article 41.1 requires diplomats and all others enjoying privileges and immunities to respect the laws and regulations of the receiving State, meaning that in the absence of any special custom or entitlement under local law, the ambassador has no right to offer asylum indefinitely to anyone whose surrender is lawfully requested by police or other authorities. Secondly, even if asylum is granted without permission or entitlement, the surrender of a refugee may not be enforced by means of entry to an embassy or other inviolable premises. These two provisions reflect the customary law as set out by the International Court of Justice in the *Haya de la Torre* case mentioned earlier. In 2012, the Wikileaks founder Julian Assange took refuge in the Ecuador Embassy in London. Assange was wanted for questioning by the Swedish authorities on charges of sexual assault and was the subject of extradition proceedings. He claimed to fear onward transfer from Sweden to the United States where he might face prosecution on charges related to his leaking of various diplomatic documents. Although these claims were greeted with some scepticism by many legal and political commentators, Ecuador granted him 'asylum' and to date he remains in the Embassy despite protest

---

[32] *ILC Yearbook* (1957) Vol 1, 54.
[33] See GA resolution 3321 (XXIX). See also chapter on Diplomatic Asylum by Eileen Denza in *The 1951 Convention Relating to the Status of Refugees and its 1967 Protocol*, ed A Zimmermann (Oxford: Oxford University Press, 2011).

from the United Kingdom government that such a grant, combined with its failure to facilitate any questioning by the Swedish prosecutor, constitutes 'a stain on the country's reputation'.[34]

13.26 The ambassador of a State Party to the European Convention on Human Rights must also be aware that the obligation of his sending State not to surrender a refugee to authorities likely to inflict on him torture or inhuman treatment applies to conduct on overseas embassy or consular premises since these are under the jurisdiction and control of the sending State.[35]

13.27 A distinction may be drawn between the grant of diplomatic asylum to individual refugees and the grant of collective shelter. The latter may be traced to the custom which existed in Persia in former times of taking 'bast' or shelter in a foreign legation as a means of asserting grievances. The principles of hospitality prevailing there precluded the denial of hospitality under these circumstances, whatever inconvenience might be caused. One incident of the kind is recounted in the biography of Sir Mortimer Durand, British Minister at Tehran:[36]

> One day a royal eunuch came galloping into the legation in great haste to see me on most important business. The message was that the Shah's wives had taken umbrage at his decision to marry a girl who was sister of one of his wives. The new favourite was a daughter of a gardener whom the uxorious monarch had seen in one of his many gardens and loved, to the great indignation of her sister, and against Persian custom.
>
> The other wives took up the matter hotly, and issued an ultimatum that if the Shah would not forgo his purpose, they would all leave the Palace, and take *bast* at the legation, which was, they declared, a place of refuge for slaves like themselves, and a sanctuary for the oppressed.
>
> I expressed myself as being highly honoured at this proof of their confidence, and declared that the legation was at the service of the ladies. Upon enquiring the size of the party, I was somewhat staggered to learn that there would be about three hundred in all. I said that the legation would hardly hold so many, but with a sweep of his hand towards the lawn, the eunuch replied that a tent was all that was required and, as for food, a few sheep and some bread would suffice.
>
> The eunuch then galloped off and returned two hours later, by which time tents had been pitched on the lawn, sheep had also been purchased, together with the entire contents of a baker's shop. He declared that the arrangements were excellent, that the Shah was furious, and that the ladies were getting into their carriages. He again galloped off, and we awaited the arrival of the refugees with keen interest,

---

[34] *The Times*, 13 and 14 August 2015. In 2016 it was reported that the Ecuador Foreign Minister had announced that Swedish prosecutors will be allowed to question Assange at the Ecuador embassy in London. See *The Guardian*, 15 January 2016.

[35] *B v Secretary of State for Foreign and Commonwealth Affairs* [2004] EWCA 1344.

[36] P. M. Sykes, *The Right Honourable Sir Mortimer Durand: A Biography* (London: Cassell, 1926) at 233.

when the eunuch reappeared like a whirlwind and shouted out, wild with excitement, 'The Shah has yielded, the ladies are getting out of their carriages and send you their grateful thanks!'

Collective shelter, or mass asylum, has been used to powerful political effect in recent years. In August 1989, following the new entitlement of East Germans to travel without visas to Czechoslovakia and Poland, hundreds of East Germans took refuge in West German embassies in Prague and Warsaw, claiming entitlement to be transported to the Federal Republic of Germany where they would be accepted automatically as citizens. At first the West German authorities tried to stem the inflow, even by temporarily closing their diplomatic missions, and to negotiate safe passage only for refugees already on embassy premises. But when the refugees departed under guarantee of safe passage they were at once replaced with others. It soon became apparent that the East German prohibition on travel to the West could no longer be sustained and within a few weeks the Berlin Wall began to be dismantled.[37] Similar tactics were employed in Albania in 1990 when refugees in foreign embassies refused to leave until granted passports enabling them to leave Albania[38] and again in Beijing in 2002 when some North Korean defectors took refuge in foreign embassies and were ultimately through the good offices of several sympathetic countries taken to South Korea.[39]

Exemption of Mission Premises from Taxation

Article 23 of the Vienna Convention exempts the sending State and the head of **13.28** the mission from all taxes in respect of the premises of the mission, with the exception of taxes which 'represent payment for specific services rendered'. It is for each State Party to give a precise interpretation of this exception in terms of its own local taxation system, but the general effect is that the embassy, in addition to being obliged to pay for commodities or utilities actually supplied, where charges are normally levied for these, is expected to pay any tax, or element of a tax, which relates to a supply or a service from which the embassy benefits. For example, the embassy would be expected to pay taxes which related to road maintenance and cleaning or street lighting. It would not be obliged to pay rates or taxes which related to national defence, or education, or administration. Under the practice of many States embassies are not expected to pay any element of local taxes or charges which relates to police protection, although they do benefit significantly from police protection, because the obligation to

---

[37] *The Times*, 20 October and 11 November 1989; 1990 *RGDIP* 123.
[38] *The Times*, 6 July 1990.
[39] *The Times*, 15 March 2002; 2002 *RGDIP* 650.

provide such police protection to foreign missions is part of the duty which falls on the receiving State to protect inviolable premises and persons.

13.29   For the exemption to apply, the tax must in law fall on the sending State or on the ambassador. If a private landlord lets his property to a diplomatic mission he cannot claim exemption from rates or taxes which under the local law fall on him.

Inviolability of Mission Archives

13.30   Article 24 of the Vienna Convention provides that the archives and documents of the mission shall be inviolable at any time and wherever they may be. Clearly the archives may not be seized or detained for examination by the executive authorities of the receiving State but the provision has also been interpreted to mean that they may not be used as evidence or their production compelled for the purposes of any legal proceedings in that State. In the case of *Rose v The King*[40] a Canadian court held that documents which had been stolen by a defector from the embassy of the Soviet Union were admissible evidence in the trial of a Canadian citizen for espionage, but this decision turned on the absence of any intervention or protest either from the Canadian government which had supplied the documents to the court, or from the Soviet Union. The Vienna Convention extended the protection accorded to mission archives in that it was previously regarded as uncertain whether archives were inviolable when they were neither on embassy premises nor in a diplomatic bag. The Convention by contrast protects archives 'wherever they may be', in contrast to other property of the mission which is only inviolable when it is on embassy premises.

13.31   The term 'archives' is not defined in the Vienna Convention, but it is normally understood to cover any form of storage of information or records in words or pictures and to include modern forms of storage such as tapes, sound recordings and films, or computer disks. The Vienna Convention on Consular Relations provides that 'consular archives' includes all the papers, documents, correspondence, books, films, tapes, and registers of the consular post, together with the ciphers and codes, the card-indexes, and any article of furniture intended for their protection or safe-keeping and this wider definition would apply by analogy to diplomatic archives, but without being exclusive of other methods of information storage. On the other hand, documents which no longer belong to the mission but have been sent to third parties outside the mission (such as

---

[40] 3 DLR (1947) 618, *Annual Digest* (1946) No 76.

letters to members of the public) are not regarded as being archives.[41] The status of documents held outside the mission premises by professional consultants to an embassy was considered in 2002 by the US House of Representatives Committee on Government Reform in the context of an enquiry it held into abductions of children of dual US and Saudi Arabian nationality but in the event there was no firm guidance on the question either from the US State Department or through a court ruling.[42] If inviolability for such documents is important (for example in the case of architects' plans for the construction of embassy buildings) it may be better to retain them on mission premises or to mark them specially as mission archives.

The English Court of Appeal considered the extent of the protection conferred **13.32** on the archives and documents of a diplomatic mission in *R (Bancoult) v Secretary of State for Foreign and Commonwealth Affairs (No 3)*.[43] The applicants sought to rely on a document which purported to be a record of a meeting in the US embassy in London which had been sent to Washington. It had already been published by Wikileaks and several UK newspapers after it had allegedly been leaked by Private Bradley Manning from a US base in Iraq. The case was unusual in that it was not the sending State which was trying to exclude the document but the receiving State. It was argued that the words 'wherever they may be' was limited to territory within the receiving State and, secondly, that the term 'inviolability' did not automatically require such archives or documents to be treated as inadmissible in judicial proceedings. Instead it was intended to prevent direct interference or compulsion by the receiving State. The Court did not express any firm conclusion on the first argument. It did, however, accept the second argument concluding that where a document has become available to a third party, even as a result of an earlier breach of inviolability, it should be *prima facie* admissible in evidence. One consideration was that the person seeking to rely on the document had not been in any way complicit in its disclosure. Finally, the Court noted that the central object and purpose of the Vienna Convention was to 'ensure the efficient performance of the functions of the diplomatic mission'. Where a document has already been disclosed to the world the damage has been done and it would be pointless to prevent an innocent third party from relying on it in legal proceedings. It is notable that, as in *Rose v King*, the sending State made no intervention or protest in the case. There is also some force in the argument that admitting the document would not breach

---

[41] According to the judgment of the UK House of Lords in *Shearson Lehman Bros Inc v Maclaine Watdon & Co Ltd and Others (International Tin Council Intervening)* [1988] 1 All ER 116, 77 ILR 145.

[42] The State Department response is in 2002 *Digest of UK Practice in International Law* 567.

[43] [2014] EWCA Civ 708.

the inviolability of the US embassy archives because it had already been so widely published. However, any implication that inviolability cannot be breached unless the sending State or the party seeking to rely on it committed the original violation could seriously undermine the protection conferred by Article 24.

Freedom of Communications

13.33 The right of the diplomatic mission to free and secure communication for official purposes is guaranteed by Article 27 of the Vienna Convention. Special protection for its communications is in practical terms probably the most important of all diplomatic privileges and immunities. Without the right to send messages in code and without being able to rely on the inviolability of the diplomatic bag an embassy cannot properly perform its function of observing and reporting to the sending government and it will be seriously hampered in the conduct of negotiations on any matter of importance if it cannot receive confidential instructions. But because of the uncertainty of the previous international law on a few points and fear of abuse of wireless transmitters and of the diplomatic bag, Article 27 was one of the most controversial at the Vienna Convention.

13.34 International law had long recognized the right to secure diplomatic communications, although the practice has sometimes fallen short of the ideal. On the rare occasions where interception was detected and complained of, the State challenged would usually claim that it had not been authorized. If the interception revealed evidence of some conspiracy against the receiving State, that State could claim to be acting exceptionally in defence of its vital interests. Adair recounts the frequent interceptions of despatches authorized by Parliament during the period of the English Civil War which Parliament believed to be justified by the disturbed state of the country. He notes that in this regard the Portuguese envoy was particularly suspect.[44]

13.35 Improvement in methods of cipher and the development of wireless transmission made really secure communication possible. But at the Vienna Conference, States differed in their approach to diplomatic wireless. Only the richer States could afford it and took the view that the inviolability of diplomatic premises, together with the right to free communication, implied that they were under no obligation to seek the consent of the receiving State in order to install wireless transmitters. If the frequency selected caused difficulty, they would cooperate in changing it. Less developed States, which often could not afford such installation

---

[44] E R Adair, *The Extraterritoriality of Ambassadors in the 16th and 17th Centuries* (London: Longmans, 1929) 175.

and were also nervous that transmitters could be used for propaganda against them, eventually succeeded in including in the Vienna Convention the provision that 'the mission may install and use a wireless transmitter only with the consent of the receiving State'. Under subsequent practice, if a transmitter is installed, it is the responsibility of the sending State to observe international telecommunication regulations. The receiving State, by contrast, is not responsible. Some States, including the United Kingdom, do not require diplomatic missions to notify or seek permission for installation of a transmitter, while others, including the United States, do confer express authorization and in this context agree with diplomatic missions the frequencies they will use.

Article 27.1 entitles a diplomatic mission to communicate with its sending government and with other diplomatic and consular missions of the sending State anywhere in the world by 'all appropriate means'. This includes telephone, fax, electronic mail, and other methods which may be devised—and interception of any of these is prohibited regardless of whether the interception involves placing physical equipment such as a bug on mission premises. During the Cold War covert listening devices were discovered on numerous occasions on the mission premises of the principal adversaries. On such occasions the authorities of the receiving State would usually deny complicity even suggesting that the bugs had been placed there by the victims themselves. More recent events suggest that covert surveillance continues to be routinely carried out by some States even against allies and fellow delegations to the United Nations in New York. In 2003 Katharine Gun, a translator at the UK Government Communications Headquarters, leaked evidence of surveillance of the communications of delegations whose votes were important in the context of securing a further Security Council resolution authorizing the use of force against Iraq. When arrested and charged with breach of the Official Secrets Act, she defended her actions on the basis that they had exposed illegality on the part of the US government in the interception of diplomatic communications and in regard to its justification for the use of force. The case was dropped in 2004, following UK ministers' refusal to confirm or deny that bugging had taken place or even to confirm that UN premises and communications were protected by international agreement from interception.[45]   **13.36**

This unusual disregard for a rule of diplomatic law is likely to be due to two reasons—first that most violations are not detected and secondly that the prohibition on interception is, unlike other diplomatic rules, not fully underpinned   **13.37**

---

[45] *The Observer*, 15 and 29 February 2004; *The Guardian*, 26 and 27 February 2004; *The Times*, 27 February 2004.

by reciprocity, since many States do not have equal technical capacity for interception. States which discover that their communications have been compromised rarely resort to the normal remedies of downgrading or breaking relations but instead try to improve their own security defences.

13.38   The official correspondence of a diplomatic mission is under Article 27.2 of the Convention accorded inviolability—but as in practice this inviolability cannot be guaranteed if the letters are sent through the public post rather than through a sealed diplomatic bag, this provision is seldom relied on or publicly invoked.

The Diplomatic Bag

13.39   The diplomatic bag is accorded under the Vienna Convention a more absolute protection than was given under previous customary law. Under the latter it was generally accepted that the receiving State had a right to challenge a bag which it reasonably believed contained unauthorized articles. If challenged, the sending State could elect either to return the bag unopened or to open it in the presence of the authorities of the receiving State. This practice of challenge to a suspect bag is permitted in the case of a consular bag under Article 35 of the Vienna Convention on Consular Relations. But it is no longer permitted in the case of a diplomatic bag. The bag may contain only diplomatic documents or articles intended for official use, but the authorities of the receiving State may not demand that it be returned or opened even if they suspect that it is being used to smuggle arms or other illegal imports or exports. States were fully aware of the dangers of abuse but even more aware that any right to challenge could be abused by officials claiming to suspect any bag they wished to impede or investigate. A bag may, however, be subjected to detector devices designed to show the presence of explosives, metal, or drugs since this does not involve opening or detaining it. If such tests disclosed grounds for suspicion, airlines could decline to carry it. In extreme cases, States have been prepared to go further and in one incident the customs authorities in Rome noticed that a large diplomatic bag destined for Cairo was emitting moans. They seized and opened it and found that it contained a drugged Israeli who had been kidnapped. Some members of the Egyptian embassy were declared *persona non grata* as a result of this discovery.[46]

13.40   In 1984 customs officers at Stansted airport in the United Kingdom became suspicious that two large crates equipped with air holes, originating from the Nigerian High Commission in London and addressed to the Ministry of

---

[46] *The Times*, 18–20, 23–25, and 27 November 1964.

Foreign Affairs in Lagos, contained a former Nigerian Minister, Umaru Dikko, who had been abducted earlier that day. The crates did not have lead or wax seals (the 'visible external marks of their character' as required by Article 27.4 of the Vienna Convention) and did not therefore constitute a diplomatic bag but only property or baggage of the mission. As such they could be inspected and inspection confirmed the suspicions of the customs officers. The diplomats directly involved were declared *persona non grata* and required to leave the UK.[47] Following this incident some suggestions were put forward for the systematic recording of the size and weight of bags, for seeking a restrictive amendment to Article 27 to enable challenge to suspect bags, or to negotiate a protocol setting out additional rules for the treatment of bags (on the basis of draft Articles elaborated by the International Law Commission) but all came to nothing.[48]

Article 27 of the Convention provides that the bag 'may contain only diplomatic documents or articles intended for official use'. It is well established that suspicions of disregard of this requirement do not give rise to an entitlement to open or search a suspect bag, except perhaps in the event of a manifest threat to human life such as might have been the case had the crate containing Umaru Dikko been labelled and sealed so as to constitute a diplomatic bag. Regulations of a number of diplomatic services, however, offer some guarantee that the restrictions on use are respected even though they cannot be enforced through inspections on behalf of other States. Because diplomats are also required to respect the laws and regulations of the receiving State, such items as guns (for protection of diplomats and mission premises) and alcohol (for consumption at official receptions) may not be carried in the bag even for official use if this would contravene local law, although there is a good deal of evidence to suggest that this has been regularly ignored by many Western missions in Muslim countries. There are no limits imposed on the size of bags, so that bulky items such as cipher equipment and even building materials for embassy premises may lawfully be carried in packages forming diplomatic bags.[49] **13.41**

Although as stated earlier diplomatic bags may be subjected to tests not involving opening or detaining them in order to detect unauthorized contents, it is now generally accepted that they may not be electronically screened. Although such screening may not involve opening or detention of the bag, modern **13.42**

---

[47] For a vivid account of events, see C R Ashman and P Trescott, *Outrage* (London: WH Allen, 1986).

[48] See Report of the House of Commons Foreign Affairs Committee, 1984–5 on the Abuse of Diplomatic Privileges and Immunities; UK Government Review of the Vienna Convention 1985, Cmnd 9497; ILC Yearbook 1989, Vol II, Part 2; Denza, *Diplomatic Law* (4th edn) 194–207.

[49] The government of Iran has imposed a rule restricting bags to 15 kilogrammes which has hampered the UK government's efforts to install equipment in the newly reopened embassy in Tehran. *The Times*, 21 August 2015.

screening methods are capable of compromising the security of contents such as cipher equipment and even of reading documents. Their use, therefore, violates the basic entitlement to free communication which is fundamental to Article 27 of the Convention. On those few occasions where customs authorities, whether on a general or on a particular basis, have claimed entitlement to challenge and screen a diplomatic bag accompanied by a courier, the practice is for the courier to refuse permission and to return with the bag unscreened.

13.43 Article 27 of the Convention does not distinguish between a bag accompanied by a diplomatic courier and an unaccompanied bag, but in practice those States who have the resources do employ professional couriers or couriers ad hoc (usually diplomats or other public officials travelling on some special mission). Even an unaccompanied bag, because of the seals which prevent its being opened without detection, is more secure than a letter sent through the ordinary post, or possibly any form of electronic communication which may be 'hacked' or leaked. But a bag accompanied by a courier, who will always refuse to be physically parted from his bags on whatever pretext, cannot be screened, detained, or opened without the courier protesting at violation of the rules and its contents can, therefore, be guaranteed to be secure. Just as the diplomatic bag must be clearly identified as such, usually by official seals in lead or wax and labels indicating the official source and destination of the bag, so the diplomatic courier must carry identifying documents, usually a courier's passport and a document identifying the packages which constitute his bag. This is important because the courier's own baggage is not exempt from search in the ordinary way. The only privileges or immunities given to the courier are those which are essential to ensure the unimpeded transit of the bag, namely personal inviolability and immunity from arrest and detention. Otherwise he enjoys none of the personal immunity from suit or the tax and customs privileges of a diplomatic agent. In the case of an ad hoc courier it is even clearer that his limited inviolability derives from his function as carrier of the bag, since his inviolability ceases as soon as he has delivered the diplomatic bag. The Vienna Convention also authorizes the modern practice of sending a diplomatic bag 'by hand of the pilot' of a commercial aircraft. The captain who carries a diplomatic bag in this way is not regarded as a courier ad hoc, but a member of the mission is entitled to access to the aircraft and the captain in order to take charge of the bag directly from him.

Freedom of Movement

13.44 The freedom of diplomats to travel without restriction within the territory of the receiving State was widely accepted during the eighteenth and nineteenth centuries. Within Europe at least there were until the twentieth century no frontier controls over immigration or transit and no systematic police supervision of the movement of aliens within the territory of a State. It was, therefore, unnecessary for States to claim or writers on diplomatic law to assert any special right of diplomats to move freely within the receiving State. But during the twentieth century the position changed. After the Second World War, the Soviet Union issued regulations prohibiting travel by members of diplomatic missions more than 30 kilometres from Moscow without express permission. Other Communist countries in Eastern Europe, and later China, imposed similar restrictions. Many Western countries, including the United States, France, and the United Kingdom responded by imposing reciprocal limits on travel within their territories for Soviet and other relevant diplomats while making it clear that these would be lifted as soon as the original restrictions were removed.[50]

Article 26 of the Vienna Convention obliges the receiving State to ensure freedom of movement and travel in its territory for all members of a diplomatic mission. This obligation is '[s]ubject to its laws and regulations concerning zones entry into which is prohibited or regulated for reasons of national security'. But it is clear that the intention of those who drew up this provision was that while it would permit the closing of limited areas of military significance it would not authorize laws and regulations so sweeping in their effect as to undermine the right of free movement for diplomats. The restrictions already referred to severely limit the effectiveness with which diplomatic functions such as the protection of the sending State's nationals and observing and reporting on conditions in the receiving State can be carried out.   **13.45**

When the Cold War came to an end, restrictions on travel by diplomats were largely discontinued on both sides. In a few cases this was done by express agreement[51] and in others the system for control simply withered away. However, the right of unrestricted travel for diplomats remains of practical importance in some States.[52]   **13.46**

---

[50] G Perrenoud, 'Les Restrictions à la liberté de déplacement des diplomates' (1953) 57 *RGDIP* 444.

[51] See, for example, a joint press release by the UK and Ukraine of 15 September 1992, printed in (1992) *BYIL* 685.

[52] The issue arose, for example, in the negotiations leading to the reestablishment of diplomatic relations between the United States and Cuba in July 2015 where the US government reportedly accepted some restriction on the freedom of movement of most of the members of its embassy in Havana whereby prior notification of travel would need to be given to the receiving State.

14

PRIVILEGES AND IMMUNITIES OF DIPLOMATIC AGENTS

Joanne Foakes and Eileen Denza

14.1   The immunities accorded to a diplomatic agent personally, as distinct from those dealt with in Chapter 13, which belong to the mission, include personal inviolability and immunity from criminal, civil, and administrative jurisdiction. The distinction between an immunity and a privilege is not easy to define precisely, and the terms have often been used interchangeably, but in general a privilege denotes some substantive exemption from laws and regulations such as those relating to taxation or social security, whereas an immunity does not confer any exemption from substantive law but rather a procedural protection from the enforcement processes in the receiving State. Unless entitled to some specific exemption by international agreement or by national law, a diplomatic agent is legally bound by the laws and regulations of the receiving State. Diplomatic agents are not exempt from the obligation to obey the local criminal law, or from the duty to pay debts, or to seek local planning permission before rebuilding their residences, or from local regulations regarding the maintenance and insurance of vehicles when driving. But if they break any of these laws, immunity means that they cannot be arrested or detained by the executive authorities of the receiving State and cannot be subjected to criminal trial or sued in civil proceedings before the judicial authorities of that State.

Personal Inviolability

Personal inviolability is, of all the privileges and immunities of missions and **14.2** diplomats, the oldest established and the most universally recognized. In Europe the inviolability of diplomats can be traced back to the religious protection accorded among the Greeks to the heralds who were the emissaries of the States in war and later to the envoys who undertook peacetime missions.[1] Similar customs can be seen in the earliest history of ancient peoples in India and in China.[2] The inviolability of ambassadors is clearly established in the earliest European writings on diplomatic law[3] and from the sixteenth century until the present one can find virtually no instances where a breach of a diplomat's inviolability was authorized or condoned by the government which received him. The seriousness with which an infringement of personal inviolability was viewed by both governments is clearly illustrated by the well-known incident of the arrest of the Russian ambassador in London in 1708, which led directly to the enactment, by way of expiation, of the Diplomatic Privileges Act 1708 (often known as the Act of Anne). In 1708 M. de Mathveof (Matveev) the Russian ambassador, who was about to present his letters of recall, was arrested, with some degree of violence, in the streets of London, at the instigation of certain merchants, to enforce payment of debts. He was shortly afterwards released, on bail being offered by his friends. On hearing of the incident, the Queen commanded the Secretary of State to express regret to the ambassador, who was informed that the offenders would be brought to trial, and punished with the utmost rigour of the law. He was, however, in no way satisfied with this apology,

---

[1] G Ténékidès, 'Droit international et communautés fédérales dans la Grèce des cités' (1956) II *RDC* 552; C Phillipson, *The International Law and Custom of Ancient Greece and Rome* (London: Macmillan, 1911) Vol 1, ch XIII.

[2] H Chatterjee, *International Law and Inter-State Relations in Ancient India* (London and Calcutta, 1958) 66.

[3] e.g. A Gentili, *De Legationibus Libri Tres* (1585).

and hurriedly left the country, without presenting his letters of recall, or availing himself of any of the courtesies placed at his disposal. To make amends, Lord Whitworth, the British envoy at St Petersburg, was accredited as special ambassador, for the purpose of conveying to Peter the Great at a public audience the expression of the Queen's regret for the insult offered to his ambassador, and it is recorded that the Tsar's carver and cupbearer proceeded to his residence in a court carriage to fetch him to the audience, followed by twenty other coaches conveying court personages and gentlemen of the embassy.[4]

14.3 Personal inviolability of a diplomatic agent is now guaranteed under Article 29 of the Vienna Convention. This inviolability has two aspects: first the immunity from any action by law enforcement officers of the receiving State who must not subject the diplomat to any form of arrest or detention: and secondly the special duty of protection of the receiving State which must treat the diplomat 'with due respect and shall take all appropriate steps to prevent any attack on his person, freedom or dignity'.

Protection from Arrest or Detention

14.4 The first aspect of inviolability, protection of a diplomat from arrest or detention, has been very generally observed even under extreme circumstances. An extraordinary exception to this pattern was the detention of the diplomatic and consular staff of the United States embassy in Tehran in November 1979 by militant students. The government of Iran made no attempt to prevent this attack on the embassy or those within it and subsequently made clear that they approved it, so incurring international responsibility for numerous breaches of inviolability. The International Court, in an interim Order of 15 December 1979 requiring release of the hostages, emphasized the importance of the rules which had been broken. There is no more fundamental prerequisite for the conduct of relations between States than the inviolability of diplomatic envoys and embassies, so that throughout history nations of all creeds and cultures have observed reciprocal obligations for that purpose.[5]

14.5 A diplomat who is suspected of an offence may be invited to accompany a police officer to a police station so that identity and status may be verified, but he or she cannot be taken there under arrest, detained, or otherwise compelled to attend. Although a diplomat may not be compelled to submit to a breath test or other medical examination, it is practice in some countries including the United States and Canada to invite a suspect diplomatic driver to submit voluntarily to

---

[4] Baron C de Martens, *Causes Célèbres du Droit des Gens* (Leipzig, 1827) Vol I, 68.
[5] [1979] ICJ Reports 19. See J C Barker, *The Protection of Diplomatic Personnel* (Aldershot: Ashgate, 2006) 76–87.

a breath test on grounds of safety. A diplomat who is obviously incapable of driving may on grounds of self-defence or protection of the public be restrained from further driving and alternative arrangements offered for his safe transport. On similar grounds, the Swedish police in 1988 disarmed the Yugoslav ambassador to Sweden who was observed lying under a blanket in a sandpit and brandishing a loaded pistol.[6] A diplomat cannot be compelled to undergo screening or physical search before boarding an aircraft, but in practice diplomats do in general submit to X-ray screening before air travel on a voluntary basis, and it is permissible for an air carrier to deny boarding to any diplomat who refuses screening.

Duty of Special Protection

As to the second aspect of inviolability—the duty of special protection—many **14.6** States have created special offences under national law in regard to attacks on diplomats, or have imposed especially severe penalties. The Vienna Convention, however, does not make the creation of special offences or penalties compulsory; nor does the Convention on the Prevention and Punishment of Crimes against Internationally Protected Persons, including Diplomatic Agents,[7] which does however oblige States Parties to 'make these crimes punishable by appropriate penalties which take into account their grave nature'. 'These crimes' include murder, kidnapping, other violent attacks, and threats and attempts to commit such attacks.[8] Many States, including the United Kingdom, do not have special offences in regard to diplomats, and so although violent attacks are punishable under the ordinary criminal law, and the courts would take into account the fact that they took place against a diplomat, offensive comments and criticisms in the press are usually only punishable if they are obscene or constitute a criminal libel[9] which is seldom the case. But sending States which exercise strict control over their own media will often expect that a receiving State where wide latitude is given in the interests of freedom of expression should censor press material which they find offensive to their diplomats. It is clear, however, that Article 29 prohibits personal service of legal process on a diplomat and in 2000 an Irish court held that the service of proceedings on the British ambassador to Ireland was a breach of his inviolability and was ineffective.[10]

---

[6] *The Times,* 17 May 1988.

[7] Art 2, 1035 UNTS 167.

[8] Ibid.

[9] Criminal libel has become a controversial offence in many States and was abolished in the UK in 2010.

[10] See *Adams v DPP* [2001] 2 ILRM 401, [2000] IEHC, 45; also *Reyes v Al-Malki* [2015] EWCA Civ 32, at para 84.

14.7 The extent of the duty of the receiving State to protect the dignity of an ambassador was considered in the United Kingdom by the Court of Appeal in 2007 in the
case of *Aziz v Aziz and Others, Sultan of Brunei intervening*.[11] The Sultan of Brunei,
entitled under UK law to the same inviolability as an ambassador, claimed that in
order to protect his dignity the court should in publishing a report of legal proceedings brought against a fortune teller by his former wife suppress facts which
would lead to his own identification and, he claimed, loss of his dignity. The
court, however, rejected the claim that international law required him to be protected to a greater extent than any other third party to legal proceedings from the
consequences of conduct by others which was simply offensive or insulting. As in
the case of embassy premises, a balance must be struck by the receiving State
between its duty to protect foreign ambassadors and Heads of State and its own
constitutional guarantee of free speech.[12]

14.8 What 'appropriate steps' the receiving State must take to protect diplomats and
other inviolable persons in its territory must be determined in the light of many
relevant circumstances by agreement between the sending and the receiving
States. The negotiators of the Vienna Convention deliberately added the word
'appropriate' to make it clear that there must be limits to the obligations of the
receiving State. Major capitals will have several thousand diplomats, together
with their families, and members of the administrative and technical staffs of
embassies and their families, all entitled to inviolability, and clearly it would be
an impossible burden for each of these to have special police protection for
person and residence. But where there is evidence of a threat to the safety of a
diplomat, such as a likely mob attack or indications that a kidnapping is being
planned, the sending State can demand that the receiving State should provide
special protection such as an armed guard. States where conditions are unusually dangerous, such as Colombia, may provide armed guards for all ambassadors and their secretaries.[13] A sending State which is well equipped with
resources may prefer to provide special protection itself for vulnerable diplomats, and it should do this in agreement with the receiving State. States whose
diplomats are particularly vulnerable to kidnapping or attack (such as the
United States) provide or organize their own security to an increasing extent
even though the primary obligation to protect belongs to the receiving State.
Bodyguards provided by the sending State are not, of course, exempt from the
laws of the receiving State regarding the carrying of firearms, or the use of force.

---

[11] Judgment of Collins LJ, 11 July 2007 [2007] EWCA Civ 712.
[12] See also *Case concerning Questions of Mutual Assistance in Criminal Matters (Djibouti v France)*
[2008] ICJ Reports 177, at para 178 where the ICJ adopted a similarly restrictive interpretation of the
obligation to protect the dignity of a foreign Head of State.
[13] (1982) *AFDI* 1099.

It is now settled among parties to the Vienna Convention that the 'appropriate **14.9** steps' which the receiving State must take to protect personal inviolability do not include surrendering to demands made by hostage-takers when kidnapping of a diplomat has taken place. When the German ambassador to Guatemala, Count von Spreti, was kidnapped in 1970 the government of Guatemala refused to accept the illegal demands made by his kidnappers, and the Count was murdered.[14] The German government accused the Guatemalans of failing in their duty to protect the Ambassador, but the Guatemalan government did not accept that they had in any way fallen short of their legal obligations. It soon became apparent through a series of kidnappings of diplomats, particularly in Latin America, that bargaining with the kidnappers seizing diplomats led merely to inflation of the political and financial demands made as the price for release of the hostages. Western governments took a collective stand in refusing to capitulate to unlawful demands, and the United Kingdom in particular resisted temptation when its ambassador to Uruguay, Sir Geoffrey Jackson, was kidnapped by Tupamaros guerrillas and held captive for eight months.[15] The fact that governments agreed that a diplomat's inviolability did not require a surrender to illegal demands made by kidnappers in exchange for his release probably did as much as the tightening of security measures and the conclusion of the Convention on the Prevention and Punishment of Crimes against Internationally Protected Persons, including Diplomatic Agents, to dissuade terrorists from regarding diplomats as particularly attractive targets. The incidence of this particular form of hostage-taking—though not of other forms of terrorist attacks against diplomats—declined soon afterwards.[16]

Inviolability of Diplomatic Residences and Property

The Vienna Convention defines 'premises of the mission' so as to include the **14.10** residence of the ambassador only, but Article 30 provides that the private residence of a diplomatic agent is entitled to the same inviolability and protection. Whether premises are in fact the 'residence' of a diplomatic agent may sometimes be a difficult question of fact, for example if they are being prepared for occupation but he has not moved in. In the English case of *Agbor v Metropolitan*

---

[14] *The Times*, 17 April 1970; J A Salmon: *Manuel de droit diplomatique* (Bruxelles: Bruylant, 1994) para 390.

[15] Sir Geoffrey Jackson published an account of his captivity in *People's Prison* (London: Faber & Faber, 1973).

[16] For a comprehensive account and analysis, see Barker, *The Protection of Diplomatic Personnel* especially 316, 67–70, and 87–96.

Police Commissioner[17] the question in issue was whether the London police, relying on Article 30 of the Vienna Convention, were entitled to evict without a court order a family identified with the side in the Nigerian Civil War opposed to the government, who had taken possession of a flat which was claimed to be the residence of a Nigerian diplomatic agent. The Court of Appeal found as a fact that he had moved out without the intention of returning and that the flat was therefore no longer his residence. The new occupants were in possession, and the court held that even had the premises been the residence of a diplomatic agent, the executive were not entitled to evict them without the authority of a court order. This situation was not thought adequate to enable the government to fulfil its duty of protection; section 9 of the Criminal Law Act 1977[18] was adopted making it a criminal offence to trespass on premises which are the residence of a diplomatic agent and giving the police power to arrest offenders. Whether the intruders into diplomatic residences are 'squatters' or political demonstrators the police must, however, have the consent of the ambassador, or in his absence the consent of the sending State, before they may enter the premises to carry out any eviction.

14.11   Article 30 also gives inviolability to the papers, correspondence, and property of a diplomatic agent. The inviolability of his papers and correspondence is unqualified and implies that they may not be searched or screened. In the event of a threat to members of a mission, as for example in 1972 when letter bombs were dispatched to several Israeli diplomats, it is likely that a mission so threatened will give consent to surveillance. In the case of a diplomat's property, inviolability does not apply where there is an exception (as described at paragraphs 14.16–14.18) to his immunity from civil jurisdiction, provided that execution can be levied without infringing the inviolability of his person or residence. The United Kingdom authorities interpret this Article as permitting them to tow away an obstructing vehicle belonging to a diplomat under the same conditions as an official embassy car.[19] It is common practice, at least in major capitals, for diplomatic cars to be easily identifiable by police or other traffic authorities by means of special plates.

14.12   The inviolability of a diplomat's property does not mean that he is exempt from the laws and regulations of the receiving State regarding exchange control. He must, in accordance with Article 41 of the Convention, respect these like other laws. But in practice most States apply their regulations to foreign diplomats in such a way that they do not experience practical difficulties. If any State did not

---

[17] [1969] 1 WLR 703, [1969] 2 All ER 707.
[18] C 45.
[19] See Chapter 13, paragraph 13.14.

do so, it could be argued that it was failing in its duty under Article 25 of the Convention to 'accord full facilities for the performance of the functions of the mission'.

Immunity from Jurisdiction

If a diplomatic agent commits a crime in the country to which he is accredited, **14.13** he cannot be tried or punished by the local courts. No case can be cited where, without his consent or that of his government, such a course has been followed. During the sixteenth and seventeenth centuries the writers on diplomatic law often asserted that where an ambassador was detected in a criminal conspiracy or in treason against the receiving State, the receiving State could in self-defence try and punish him.[20] Many cases of charges of treason against an ambassador can be cited, and in all of them the result was that the ambassador was expelled or (as it would now be put) declared *persona non grata*.[21]

The immunity of a diplomatic agent from the criminal jurisdiction of the **14.14** receiving State is set out, without any exceptions whatever, in Article 31 of the Vienna Convention. The receiving State may, however, take certain actions if it learns of evidence of a criminal offence by a diplomat. A minor offence may be drawn to the attention of the head of mission in the expectation that a reprimand or disciplinary action will be taken by the head of mission. It is customary in London, for example, to bring to the attention of heads of mission and to publicize to Parliament the numbers of parking offences which appear to have been committed by members of the mission and for which proceedings could not be taken. Since their Review of the Vienna Convention in 1985[22] it has been UK government policy to request from their sending States the withdrawal of offenders incurring more than a set number of unpaid parking tickets. The use of the procedure of *persona non grata* for the purpose of controlling abuse of immunity from jurisdiction in regard to parking offences was then without precedent, but was reluctantly accepted by the diplomatic corps and led to a dramatic drop in the number of parking tickets incurred by diplomats and others entitled to immunity. The United States now withhold driving privileges from diplomats regarded as persistent violators of traffic laws and regulations—suspensions are notified to the relevant embassy which is asked to

---

[20] A McNair, *International Law Opinions* (Cambridge: Cambridge University Press, 1956) Vol 1, 186.
[21] The case of Prince de Cellamare was one example. See Martens, *Causes Celebres du Droit des Gens*, 139.
[22] Cmnd 9497.

guarantee that the violator will not drive for any period of suspension.[23] In more serious cases such as a firearms offence, drink driving, or driving without insurance, the receiving State is likely to ask for immunity to be waived so that a trial may take place, and if this request is refused, it is likely that the diplomat will be withdrawn. In 1988, for example, a diplomat in the Vietnamese embassy was required by the UK government to leave London on 24 hours' notice after he was observed brandishing a handgun at a crowd of protesters outside his embassy.[24] If the suspect is not withdrawn, the receiving State may declare him *persona non grata* and the sending State will then be obliged to withdraw him. States do not have set rules as to when they will ask for a waiver of immunity or declare an offender *persona non grata*, or when they will withdraw a diplomat against whom serious accusations have been made. It has, however, become more common in recent years for a waiver of immunity to be granted in respect of drugs charges.

14.15 Immunity from civil jurisdiction was established somewhat later than immunity from criminal jurisdiction, and came under challenge during the seventeenth century in several European States. The magnificence then expected in the style of life of an ambassador was not supported by allowances from the sending sovereign, and ambassadors were often obliged to incur debts, or to engage in trading to obtain money to pay for the necessary display. Embarrassing incidents led to the enactment of legislation to put the position beyond doubt. In England the Diplomatic Privileges Act 1708 was enacted in order to appease the Tsar of Russia whose ambassador had been dragged from his coach and detained for several hours at the instance of his irate creditors.[25] The Act provided that all 'writs and processes that shall at any time hereafter be sued forth or prosecuted, whereby the person of any ambassador, or other publick minister of any foreign Prince or state, authorised and received as such by Her Majesty, Her Heirs or Successors, or the domestick, or domestick servant of any such ambassador, or other publick minister, may be arrested or imprisoned, or his or their goods or chattels may be distrained, seized or attached, shall be deemed and adjudged to be utterly null and void, to all intents, constructions, and purposes whatsoever'.[26]

14.16 The immunity from civil and administrative jurisdiction of a diplomatic agent is restated in Article 31 of the Vienna Convention. This immunity is subject to

---

[23] State Department Circular Notes to Chiefs of Mission in Washington of 2 July 1984, 17 December 1984, and 22 December 1993.
[24] *The Times*, 7 and 8 September 1988.
[25] Denza, *Diplomatic Law* (4th edn, 2016) 233–4.
[26] 7 Anne, c 12.

three important exceptions which were not previously admitted in common law countries but which were established in many civil law countries. The first exception relates to a real action relating to private immovable property situated in the territory of the receiving State, unless he holds it on behalf of the sending State for the purposes of the mission. A real action is an action where ownership or possession of immovable property is claimed. It is not, however, clear from the records of the Vienna Conference whether the words 'unless he holds it on behalf of the sending State for the purposes of the mission' merely exclude from the exception the case of the diplomat in whose name the mission premises are placed or whether their scope is wider and they exclude from the exception the private residence of a diplomat, which he can be said to hold 'on behalf of the sending State for the purposes of the mission'. Since the rationale of this exception to immunity is to make possible the trial of actions affecting title to real property, which the diplomat's home State would lack jurisdiction to determine, it may be argued that the exception should be narrowly construed and that it should be possible to bring an action to enable the courts of the State of the forum to determine the legal question of the ownership of a house in which a diplomat is living. Cases in several countries have tended to confirm this interpretation of Article 31.1(a). Any judgment against the diplomat would, of course, be unenforceable under Article 30 of the Convention so long as he continued to live in the property.

14.17 The second exception relates to an action relating to succession in which the diplomatic agent is involved as executor, administrator, heir, or legatee as a private person and not on behalf of the sending State. It is quite common for diplomats, particularly when exercising consular functions, to be involved in succession matters in an official capacity, since if a national of his own State dies in the receiving State leaving money to other nationals in his home State, the diplomat may become involved in the distribution of the estate. He may also be involved in the estate through claiming on behalf of his government either for taxes owed, or as 'bona vacantia' if there are no heirs either by will or intestacy. In such cases the diplomat enjoys immunity in the ordinary way. His involvement in a private capacity in a succession, on the other hand, is not part of his functions and here the interest of the receiving State in asserting jurisdiction over all the parties involved in a succession question is regarded as paramount.

14.18 The third exception to immunity is an action relating to any professional or commercial activity exercised by the diplomatic agent in the receiving State outside his official functions. Article 42 of the Convention prohibits a diplomat from exercising in the receiving State for personal profit any professional or commercial activity. But an exception to immunity is still needed as well. A diplomat may disregard the prohibition on professional or commercial activities. The sending and receiving State may agree that the bar should be waived in an exceptional case where the individual is unusually well-qualified for the post, and in such a case the diplomat would not be immune in regard to his business activities. In 1984, for example, when President Reagan appointed Mr William Wilson as ambassador to the Holy See, he was permitted to retain his position in two US commercial companies.[27] The exception is, however, most important in regard to members of the diplomat's family, who enjoy the same immunity from civil jurisdiction but are not obliged to abstain from professional or commercial activities. The fact that immunity from civil jurisdiction does not extend to professional or commercial activities makes it easier for the spouse or child of a diplomat to practise their own profession or to take a job in the receiving State. The receiving State cannot object to this on the grounds that they would be unfairly protected if, for example, he or she could not be sued as a doctor for professional negligence. Some States do discourage members of diplomatic families from taking employment, sometimes in order to reserve scarce employment for their own nationals, and sometimes for social reasons. This will be further considered later.

14.19   Cases in a number of States have clarified the meaning of this exception from diplomatic immunity. It is clear that it does not cover a single transaction by the diplomat but rather a continuous activity and that it does not cover a contract for goods or services incidental to daily life in the receiving State. In the case of *Tabion v Mufti*,[28] for example, the US Court of Appeals held that a contract of employment between a diplomat and a Philippine national for performance of domestic services was not covered by the exception to immunity. It is worth noting, however, that a possible expansion of this exception may be anticipated at least so far as the embassies of European States are concerned following decisions of the European Court of Human Rights (ECtHR) which have adopted a restrictive interpretation of the immunities enjoyed by a foreign State and its diplomatic mission as employers of service staff.[29] Although a single loan or investment by a diplomat might well be regarded as covered by his general immunity from jurisdiction, a continuous investment of personal assets would be covered by the exception. Diplomatic service regulations of some States prohibit investment by their own diplomats in companies or enterprises in countries where they are posted.

---

[27] *International Herald Tribune*, 13 July 1984; (1985) *RGDIP* 141.
[28] 4th Cir 73 F 3rd 535; 1996 US App. LEXIS 495; 107 ILR 452.
[29] See e.g. *Cudak v Lithuania* Application No 15869/02, Judgment of 23 March 2010 and *Sabeh el Leil v France*, Application No 34869/05, Judgment of 29 June 2011. See also the decision of the English Court of Appeal in *Benkharbouche v Embassy of the Republic of Sudan* [2015] 3 WLR 301.

A diplomatic agent is immune from any measures of execution. Even if his gov- **14.20**
ernment waives his immunity from jurisdiction, the resulting judgment cannot
be enforced in the receiving State unless there is a separate waiver. But in the case
of the three exceptions to jurisdiction already discussed, there is also an exception to immunity from execution. So if an action were brought against a diplomat in respect of a private business activity and judgment obtained against him,
the judgment could be enforced so long as the enforcement did not infringe his
personal inviolability or that of his residence. His business stocks might be seized,
but his house could not be entered. Although this means that the possibilities
of enforcing a judgment against a diplomat are limited, a serious view would be
taken by the government of the receiving State of a failure to comply with a judgment of a national court, and would be likely to lead to a request to the sending
State for his recall.

The immunity of a diplomatic agent from civil and administrative jurisdic- **14.21**
tion covers family proceedings involving divorce or matters of custody and
also means that bankruptcy proceedings cannot be instituted against him personally. In the event of a diplomatic agent dying, whether on embassy premises or not, in circumstances which would normally necessitate the holding of
a coroner's inquest, it has become established practice, where immunity is
claimed by the diplomatic mission, to waive the proceedings. On the suicide
of the butler of the British embassy at Madrid in 1921, the ambassador
received the examining magistrate of the district at the embassy, and the evidence given by him and some of the servants was embodied in a *procès-verbal*,
which stated that he had waived those rights for the occasion. In February
2009, Jan Winkler, ambassador of the Czech Republic to the UK, died suddenly at his London home, and although a post-mortem examination proved
inconclusive as to the cause of death, on the request of his family, and of the
governments of the Czech Republic and of the UK, the coroner agreed that
no inquest would be held.[30]

Exemption from Giving Evidence

A diplomatic agent is not obliged to give evidence as a witness in any legal pro- **14.22**
ceedings in the receiving State. This position was established very much later
than the diplomat's immunity from jurisdiction, and the position was still
uncertain during the nineteenth century.[31] The Vienna Convention makes clear

---

[30] *Hampstead and Highgate Express*, 26 February 2009.
[31] See John B Moore, *Digest of International Law* (Washington, 1906) Vol 4, 662.

that the diplomat is not merely immune from compulsion in regard to the giving of evidence; he is exempt from any legal obligation in the matter. The receiving State would thus not be justified in using his refusal as a reason to declare him *persona non grata*. Many States take a helpful attitude and are occasionally prepared even to permit a diplomat to give evidence in the normal way. The British government, for instance, not only waived the immunity of their ambassador in Dublin, Sir Ivor Roberts, in 2002 to allow him to give evidence in the Special Criminal Court against the head of the Real IRA, but also permitted him to be cross-examined. In the alternative, States sometimes authorize their diplomats to make statements on condition that they are not cross-examined, to submit written statements, or to make oral statements on embassy premises. Such evidence was formerly of little use in common law jurisdictions, but written evidence is now admissible in many countries to a greater extent and so statements made under special conditions are increasingly acceptable. A receiving State may, however, still refuse to admit evidence if it is offered on condition that it may not be subject to cross-examination or not given in open court. In effect any special arrangements must be decided between the sending and the receiving State for each request, and there are no exceptions to the diplomat's absolute freedom from any legal duty in the matter. Many States make clear to their own diplomats that they may not give evidence in local proceedings without express authorization from their own government.

Procedure When Immunity Is Raised

14.23   The procedure by which a claim to immunity is asserted varies from country to country. In some States a diplomat may simply inform the ministry of foreign affairs of the proceedings, or a writ served through the ministry of foreign affairs may be returned with the information that the defendant is entitled to immunity. In most cases, of course, proceedings are simply never instituted because the plaintiff is aware of the defendant's entitlement to immunity. In many States it is practice for the executive to guide or direct the courts on the question of immunity. In the United States, for example, provision is made in the Diplomatic Relations Act 1979[32] for the establishment of immunity by motion by the defendant or his government or by 'suggestion' which would come from the State Department. Such 'suggestions' may cover applicable law as well as relevant facts. In others, such as the United Kingdom, diplomatic immunity must be

---

[32] PL 95–393.

decided by the courts as a matter of law. The function of the executive is confined to issuing to the court or to the parties a certificate on relevant matters of fact within the knowledge of the Secretary of State for Foreign Affairs. Thus the Foreign and Commonwealth Office's certificate might state that the Secretary of State had been notified on a certain date of the appointment of the defendant as Second Secretary in the embassy of Utopia, and that he continues to be received in that capacity. The court would, under the Diplomatic Privileges Act 1964,[33] be obliged to accept as conclusive these facts which indicate the status of the defendant. But if the plaintiff argued that this action related to a commercial activity of the defendant, or that the defendant was not entitled to immunity because he was a permanent resident of the United Kingdom, the court would decide this issue itself as a question of law.

Waiver of Immunity

The rules on waiving the immunity of diplomats, subordinate staff, and their families are set out in Article 32 of the Vienna Convention. It is made clear that the immunity belongs to the sending State and must therefore be waived by that State. Previous state practice had been conflicting as to whether immunity could be waived by the individual concerned, particularly as regards the family and servants of a diplomat. But the usual practice was to ensure that the waiver was made only with the authority of the sending State.[34] **14.24**

The fact that the immunity belongs to the sending State does not preclude that State from delegating authority to waive it. The instructions given to diplomatic service officers of the United States and the United Kingdom are that immunity from jurisdiction must never be waived without instructions from the home government. But not all States require reference back before waiver and whether such reference is necessary or not is a matter for internal regulation not international law. The receiving State is therefore not obliged to enquire whether the sending government has in fact been consulted. It is customary for a State to assume that acts or statements made by an ambassador are made with the authority of the sending State. Thus the United Kingdom has provided in section 2(3) of the Diplomatic Privileges Act 1964,[35] that '[f]or the purpose of Article 32 a waiver by the head of mission of any State or **14.25**

---

[33] 1964, c 81, s 4.
[34] See *The Waddington* case, 14 *RGDIP* 159.
[35] C 81.

any person for the time being performing his functions shall be deemed to be a waiver by that State'.

14.26   The Vienna Convention requires that waiver must always be express. Previously there were cases in which it was held that entering an appearance or contesting an action or charge could be deemed to constitute a waiver of immunity. But a court which is aware of the diplomatic status of a defendant cannot now safely proceed without a waiver in express terms. The requirement for express waiver does not, however, imply that it must relate to particular proceedings. The tendency at least in common law countries has been to regard a waiver as valid only if it relates to particular proceedings,[36] and to treat as null and void an undertaking made in advance to submit to the jurisdiction. This means, for example, that where a landlord is unwilling to let to a diplomat because of diplomatic immunity, the diplomat cannot get around the problem by agreeing in the lease to waive immunity in regard to any disputes which may arise under that lease. Under the Vienna Convention such undertakings would not necessarily be invalid, provided that they were authorized by the sending State, but the safer course is for a waiver to be sought for proceedings about to be instituted or already begun. The modern law on state immunity now makes clear provision for advance waiver by a State of its immunity, and such advance waivers are now common in the context of substantial contracts for loans and guarantees.[37] But this rule cannot simply be extended to apply to waiver of diplomatic immunity where different considerations may apply.[38]

14.27   If the diplomatic agent chooses to bring proceedings before the local courts, he or she is obliged to comply with the rules of the court and cannot plead immunity in regard to any set-off or counterclaim which may be pleaded by the defendant, provided that it is directly connected with the principal claim. If successful in the action, and the defendant appeals, the diplomatic agent cannot plead immunity in regard to the appeal. For these reasons, many States require their diplomats to seek permission before bringing any proceedings in States where they are serving. But execution of a judgment and the carrying out of penalty or sentence following criminal proceedings are regarded as separate from

---

[36] See *Empson v Smith* [1966] 1 QB 426, [1965] 2 All ER 881, 41 ILR 408.

[37] See e.g. Art 7 of the United Nations Convention on the Jurisdictional Immunity of States and Their Property, 2004.

[38] But see Denza, *Diplomatic Law* (4th edn, 2016) 280 where it is noted: 'provided that the undertaking was in clear terms and given for consideration, there seems no reason of principle why the State, which has the sovereign power to waive immunity, should not be held to its agreement'.

the issue of liability or guilt, and a separate waiver by the sending State is required before they may be carried out.

Commencement and Termination of Immunities

Article 39.1 of the Vienna Convention lays down that personal privileges and **14.28** immunities begin when the person entitled enters the receiving State on the way to take up the posting. If already in the territory of the receiving State when appointed, privileges and immunities begin when the appointment is notified to the ministry of foreign affairs. This provision ends the previous uncertainty in state practice as to whether the critical date for the beginning of immunities was the date of notification of appointment, the date of formal presentation of credentials (in the case of a head of mission), or the date of arrival in the territory. If legal proceedings have already been begun when the entitlement to immunity arises, the immunity may be raised as a bar to their continuing (in contrast to the position regarding waiver where proceedings begun on the basis of a waiver cannot be stopped by a withdrawal of the waiver by the sending State). This may occasionally cause difficulty for the receiving State if it is notified of the appointment as a diplomatic agent of a person against whom criminal proceedings are pending, or if it suspects that the appointment may have been engineered in order to obstruct pending civil proceedings. On one occasion where the United Kingdom government was informed of the appointment in a diplomatic capacity of a person against whom serious criminal charges had been laid, they asked the State in question to withdraw the notification, and this was done. If a State declined to withdraw a notification in such circumstances, the receiving State could, of course, declare the individual *persona non grata*, but it would also have to argue that the procedure constituted an abuse of diplomatic immunity such that it was not obliged to accord the normal period of immunities which might enable the person to leave the country with impunity.

The UK Court of Appeal in 1990 in the case of *R (Bagga and Others)*[39] confirmed **14.29** the above interpretation of Article 39.1 of the Vienna Convention which had been thrown into doubt by a number of earlier UK cases, particularly in the field of immigration. It is now clear that immunity begins on entry into the receiving State and does not depend on notification to or acceptance by the receiving State except in the case where the member of a diplomatic mission is already in the receiving State when appointed.

---

[39] [1991] 1 All ER 777, [1990] Imm AR 413.

14.30   The position regarding termination of immunities, on the other hand, has long been established—that immunities subsist until the diplomatic agent leaves the country on termination of his or her mission, or for a reasonable period to enable departure. In 1859, in the case of the *Magdalena Steam Navigation Company v Martin*, in the English courts, Lord Chief Justice Campbell observed:

> There can be no execution while the ambassador is accredited, nor even when he is recalled, if he only remains a reasonable time in this country after his recall.[40]

Although the principle of the 'reasonable period' to leave the country is now laid down in Article 39.2 of the Vienna Convention, no guidance is given on what constitutes a 'reasonable period'. A few States have defined in precise terms in their internal law the duration of this 'reasonable period'.[41] Others have preferred to retain a flexible approach which allows their courts or administrative authorities (in the case of privileges) to have regard to the facts of each case. For example an ambassador who was winding up the affairs of the mission as a whole might claim to be entitled to a longer 'reasonable period' than one merely leaving for another posting. The United Kingdom, in general, prescribes a period of one month for administrative purposes such as tax exemption, but this could be varied in special circumstances and would not bind the courts if immunity were in issue. When an appointment is terminated in notorious circumstances, such as when the United Kingdom in 1984 broke diplomatic relations with Libya following the shooting of a policewoman by a gunman within the mission, the receiving State is likely to allow only a few days for members of the mission to leave the country. Even in such a case, however, the receiving State may extend a longer 'reasonable period' to members of the family of the diplomat expelled on short notice. If a member of a diplomatic mission dies, members of his or her family are also entitled to a reasonable further period of entitlement to privileges and immunities. Article 39.4 of the Vienna Convention also makes special provision to permit the withdrawal of property of a deceased diplomat or family member and for exemption from succession or inheritance tax on that property.

14.31   The immunity of a diplomatic agent for official acts—acts performed in the exercise of his or her functions as a member of the mission—is on the other hand unlimited in time. It therefore subsists even when the diplomat's immunity for personal acts has ended along with his or her mission. This rule was

---

[40] 121 ER 36, 2 El & El 94.
[41] e.g. Switzerland (six months maximum), Venezuela (one month minimum): *UN Legislative Series*, Vol 7, 305, 403.

reaffirmed by the English Court of Appeal in the case of *Zoernsch v Waldock*, where Diplock LJ explained the position as follows:

> In respect of acts done by an envoy in his private capacity the purpose of his immunity from suit or legal process is so that he may perform his duties to his government without harassment while en poste. The immunity is from legal process, not from liability, and its purpose is fulfilled when he has ceased to be en poste and has had a reasonable time to wind up his affairs in the country to which he is accredited. The English cases show that in English law an envoy's immunity from suit and legal process in respect of acts done in his private capacity endures only so long as he is en poste and for a sufficient time thereafter to enable him to wind up his affairs: *Magdalena Steam Navigation Co v Martin* (23); *Musurus Bey v Gadban* (24). Quite different considerations, however, apply to acts done by him in his official capacity. Such acts are done on behalf of his government. His government being a foreign sovereign government, under principles of English law which are so well known that I refrain from citing authority, is immune from the jurisdiction of the English courts. The propriety of its acts cannot be examined in a municipal court unless it consents to waive its immunity. A foreign sovereign government, apart from personal sovereigns, can act only through agents, and the immunity to which it is entitled in respect of its acts would be illusory unless it extended also to its agents in respect of acts done by them on its behalf. To sue an envoy in respect of acts done in his official capacity would be, in effect, to sue his government irrespective of whether the envoy had ceased to be en poste at the date of the suit.[42]

The actions in this case were clearly official acts performed by Sir Humphrey Waldock as a member of the European Commission of Human Rights and entitled in that capacity to diplomatic immunities. In the German case of *Tabatabai*[43] in 1983, by contrast, the charge was one of possession of opium, and the provincial court of the Federal Republic made clear that such unauthorized possession could not be classed among official diplomatic functions. More controversially, the District Court of Columbia in the case of *Knab v Republic of Georgia*[44] accepted that a diplomat who caused a fatal car crash on his way home from a diplomatic reception had acted in the course of his official duties and was therefore entitled to continuing immunity from civil jurisdiction following a waiver by the Government of Georgia of his immunity from criminal jurisdiction and his dismissal from office. This finding was, however, agreed between the two parties with a view to opening the way to legal action against the sending State which was, in effect, accepting responsibility for the conduct of its diplomat. In *Wokuri v Kassam*[45] an English court held that a former Ugandan

---

[42] [1964] 2 All ER 265–6.
[43] 80 ILR 389.
[44] 97 CV 03118 (TPH) dc, 2 May 1998.
[45] [2012] EWHC 105 (Ch).

diplomat did not enjoy continuing immunity in respect of an employment claim brought by her privately employed chef.

Other Remedies Where Immunity from Civil Jurisdiction Bars a Claim

14.32   A person who has a civil dispute with a diplomat or other person entitled to diplomatic immunity has, if it is clear that immunity will preclude proceedings before the courts of the receiving State, three alternative channels through which satisfaction may be attempted:

1. Institution of proceedings before the courts of the diplomat's home State. Although Article 31 of the Vienna Convention makes clear that the immunity from jurisdiction of a diplomatic agent in the receiving State does not exempt him from the jurisdiction of the sending State, there are many practical obstacles to such a course. The prospective plaintiff must seek legal advice in the sending State. If he commences proceedings it may be impossible to serve process on the diplomat while he is entitled to inviolability in the receiving State, and the diplomat may leave his post only to proceed directly to another. Even if proceedings are validly instituted in some way it will be difficult to persuade witnesses to travel to another State to give evidence, and there will be many matters, such as disputes over real property in the receiving State, where the sending State has no jurisdiction. For some kinds of action, however, such as family proceedings, resort to the courts of the sending State is likely to be the best course.

2. Laying the matter before the ambassador of the sending State hoping to gain his assistance in obtaining a settlement. A member of a mission who has been dilatory in settling a debt or a claim for damages may be reluctant to have the matter reported to his government with possible adverse comment on his behaviour by the ambassador.

3. Laying the matter before the home government, usually before the ministry of foreign affairs, asking them to intervene with the head of mission concerned. There are no legal rules as to what action may be taken in such a case. Practice of the Foreign and Commonwealth Office is to intervene only when three conditions are satisfied. The complaint must first produce satisfactory evidence of a *prima facie* legal case. Secondly, other methods of obtaining settlement (by drawing the matter to the attention of the member of the mission concerned and the head of that mission) should have been exhausted. Thirdly, there must be evidence that the defendant is sheltering behind diplomatic immunity (so that, for example, the Foreign

and Commonwealth Office will not intervene if there appears to be no immunity because the diplomat's appointment has ended or the matter relates to a claim against a member of the administrative and technical staff which is clearly of a private nature).

In many cases taken up by a ministry of foreign affairs the representations **14.33** will be sufficient to obtain satisfaction for the claimant. If there are important differences between the parties, the ministry of foreign affairs may use its good offices to a limited extent to assist towards a settlement, but it will normally be reluctant to put itself in the position of arbitrator, because of the difficulty in testing evidence from the two sides and possible damage to its relations with the other government concerned. It may press for a waiver to enable the issue to be tried. It may suggest that the question be referred to arbitration and even assist in the arrangements to set up such an arbitration. If there are persistent complaints in regard to a particular member of mission as regards conduct or apparent evasion of legal liabilities, the sending State may be asked to withdraw that member of the mission and if it refuses, the individual concerned may be declared *persona non grata*.

Privileges of Diplomatic Agents

Five privileges are specifically set out in the Vienna Convention—exemption **14.34** from taxation, exemption from customs duties and baggage inspection, exemption from social security obligations, exemption from personal and public services, and special treatment under the laws of the receiving State regarding the acquisition of nationality. The right to freedom of movement, which has already been discussed in Chapter 13, may also be characterized as a personal privilege. In addition a diplomat may also be granted special privileges under the law of the receiving State in the absence of international obligation. For example, exemptions from local requirements regarding immigration formalities or registration by aliens are quite common, although there is no reference to them in the Convention. Unlike an immunity, a privilege gives substantive exemption from national law, and not merely protection from judicial or executive enforcement. Privileges are justified in principle by the peripatetic nature of the diplomatic career which would make it difficult as well as inappropriate for a diplomat on each new posting to have to grapple with the complexities of national laws on tax and social security. Reciprocity means that overall States neither gain nor lose from exemption. Some privileges, for example exemption from jury or military service, are justified by the fact that diplomats owe allegiance to the sending State and not to the receiving State.

Exemption from Taxation

14.35 Exemption from taxation is probably one of the most important of the diplomat's personal privileges. The principle was clearly established under customary international law, but States varied in the exceptions which they admitted to the general principle. Article 34 of the Vienna Convention now provides that a diplomatic agent shall be exempt from all dues and taxes, personal or real, national, regional, or municipal, and then sets out a list of exceptions to this general rule. There appear to be three types of taxation where a diplomat is *not* entitled to exemption.

14.36 The first category consists of taxes where it would be administratively impractical to make arrangements for exemption or refund. Taxes of this kind include purchase tax, value-added tax, sales tax, and airport tax (where this forms part of the ticket price). These are described in the Vienna Convention as '(a) indirect taxes of a kind which are normally incorporated in the price of goods or services'. Some countries do in fact make arrangements under which a diplomat may escape paying sales tax or its local equivalent. A special card may be issued to diplomats to show in shops in order to claim exemption from the tax element in the price of what is purchased. Such a system is applied in the United States and (for petrol) in Belgium. In many countries coupons are issued to privileged persons for the purchase of petrol at tax-free prices. Alternatively, refunds may be made by the authorities on presentation of receipts. The United Kingdom authorities make refunds in respect of value-added tax or car tax on only three categories of purchase—cars, alcohol and tobacco products purchased from bonded warehouses, and fine furnishings. In each case the article must have been manufactured in the United Kingdom. The purpose of such an approach is to encourage diplomats to buy British-made goods rather than take advantage of their exemption from customs duty by importing foreign equivalents more cheaply.

14.37 The second category of tax which the diplomat must pay relates to activities which are extraneous to his or her proper activities in the receiving State. Diplomats must pay taxes on private immovable property in the receiving State unless they hold it 'on behalf of the sending State for the purposes of the mission'. If a diplomat acquires a holiday cottage, or flats which are then let to tenants, any rates and property tax imposed on those premises must be paid. If, however, a diplomat holds embassy premises in his or her own name as may be required by the regulations of the sending State, he or she is not obliged to pay rates or taxes on them. The words of the Vienna Convention clearly imply that no taxes are payable on embassy premises held in the name of a member of the mission but it is less clear whether their effect is to take a diplomat's principal residence out of the scope of the exception. As with the corresponding words in Article 31.1(a) the records of the Vienna Conference leave room for argument on this point, and not all States have adopted the same interpretation in regard to diplomatic residences. The general principles applied in the formulation of Article 34 suggest that residences should be exempt from tax, since the occupation of a residence is essential to living in the receiving State in order to perform diplomatic functions. The United Kingdom regard the diplomat's residence (whether privately owned or leased or forming part of government-owned or leased premises) as held by the diplomat 'on behalf of the sending State for the purposes of the mission'. They therefore accord relief from local taxes on such residences and British diplomats receive reciprocal treatment from the majority of other States. This does not mean that all such States share the same interpretation of the Convention. Some believe that principal residences are not covered by the term 'private immovable property'; others do not impose any tax on residences, while others may grant relief purely on the basis of reciprocity.

Another exceptional case where a diplomat is liable to tax is 'estate, succession or inheritance duties levied by the receiving State, subject to the provisions of paragraph 4 of Article 39'. Article 39.4 in the special context of the death of a member of the mission deals with the question of export of the personal property of the deceased (which must be permitted, with the exception of property acquired in the country the export of which was prohibited at the time of the diplomat's death) and with estate or inheritance duty. It provides that '[e]state, succession and inheritance duties shall not be levied on movable property the presence of which in the receiving State was due solely to the presence there of the deceased as a member of the mission or as a member of the family of a member of the mission'. These provisions reflect a functional approach to the question of tax exemption by which a diplomat should not pay tax in respect of matters which are a necessary part of his living and working in the receiving State. On the other hand if a diplomat chooses to hold property in the receiving State which has no relation to his functions, estate or succession duty is payable on it. **14.38**

A further exception relates to 'dues and taxes on private income having its source in the receiving State and capital taxes on investments made in commercial undertakings in the receiving State'. If the diplomat lets property privately or makes profits from investing on the stock exchange in the receiving State, tax is payable on these profits. **14.39**

The final category of tax which the diplomat is liable to pay is tax which is in reality a charge for a service. Article 34 lists among the exceptions 'charges levied for specific services rendered'. The most frequent application of this exception is to local taxes and charges. Just as under Article 23 the embassy is made liable to that part of local rates or taxes which relate to services rendered to the property such as street cleaning and lighting, so under Article 34 the diplomat must pay such charges in relation to his residence. He may also be required to pay road and bridge tolls, where the proceeds are used for the upkeep of the particular road or **14.40** bridge. In 1985 however diplomats refused to pay a general 'surtax' imposed by the Swiss government on users of motorways and on heavy vehicles.[46] Many diplomatic missions, following the lead of the United States, have also insisted that the congestion charge imposed by Transport for London is not a 'charge for a specific service rendered' but a tax. They have pointed in particular to a lack of proportionality in that the scheme imposes a flat charge regardless of the time spent driving in the zone, the impossibility for most diplomats—given the nature of their duties—of staying outside the zone or of using public transport, and the fact that the primary purpose of the scheme is not to raise revenue but to influence the conduct of drivers and reduce traffic congestion.[47]

14.41 Also within this category of exception in Article 34 is 'registration, court or record fees, mortgage dues and stamp duty, with respect to immoveable property, subject to the provisions of Article 23'. The dues described are, in general, designed to cover the administrative cost of providing the service of registration of immovable property. Embassy premises are, however, exempt from these dues.

14.42 Article 34 is of necessity cast in very general terms, and to ascertain the precise position it is often necessary to examine the tax laws and practice of each State Party to the Convention. There are sometimes difficulties in applying the Convention to a new tax and differences between States as to whether a particular tax has been correctly classified, as may be seen from the example of the London congestion charge.

Exemption from Customs Duties and Baggage Search

14.43 Although it had for several centuries been the practice to grant diplomats exemption from customs duty on import of their personal effects and articles for their personal use or consumption, this was regarded as a matter of usage and not of binding customary law.[48] Exemption from customs duty has always been a privilege susceptible to abuse. One notorious instance of abuse is described by Bismarck, speaking of Charles, Duc de Mornay:[49]

> When he was appointed ambassador at St Petersburg, he arrived with a whole string of fine, elegant carriages, and a host of trunks, boxes and chests full of laces, silk-stuffs and ladies' dresses, for which as ambassador he had no duties to pay. Each servant had his own coach, each attaché or secretary two at least, and he himself quite five or six; and, as he was there, for a few days, he auctioned the lot—carriages

---

[46] (1985) *RGDIP* 177, 807.

[47] For a fuller analysis of the arguments see Denza, *Diplomatic Law* (4th edn, 2016) 303–6.

[48] E de Vattel, *Le Droit des Gens* (London, 1758) Vol IV, Book VII, Sect 105; P Pradier-Fodéré, *Cours de Droit Diplomatique* Vol 2 (Paris, 1899) 50–62; McNair, *International Law Opinions* Vol I, 204; Harvard Research, 26 *AJIL* (1932) (Supplement) 107.

[49] Duc de Mornay (1811–1865) sent to St Petersburg in 1856 as French Ambassador Extraordinary to attend the coronation of Tsar Alexander II.

and laces and wearing apparel. He must have made eight hundred thousand roubles. He was unscrupulous but amiable, he could really be most amiable.

Article 36 of the Vienna Convention, however, obliges the receiving State to **14.44** grant exemption from customs duties and taxes on articles for the official use of the mission and on articles for the personal use of a diplomat or a member of his family, including articles intended for his establishment (such as furniture or a motor car). But it is made clear that such exemption is to be granted in accordance with such laws and procedures as the receiving State may adopt. Missions therefore need to consult the laws of the receiving State and any guidance issued by that State in order to ascertain what procedure should be followed in order to clear baggage or official consignments of goods through customs, whether any limits are imposed on quantities of goods such as alcohol or tobacco, and what rules will apply if a diplomat wishes to dispose of goods he has brought in duty free. Regulations on such matters—either to prescribe procedures or prevent abuse—are imposed by most countries and are clearly permitted under Article 36. But regulations imposed in bad faith or so restrictive as to obstruct the exercise of the right to duty-free imports, may be challenged. In one country, for example, the *corps diplomatique* challenged a local restriction on the import of duty-free official cars on the grounds that its purpose was primarily protectionist and that it undermined the right to import articles duty free.

Where the ambassador certifies that a particular consignment is 'of articles for **14.45** official use', the receiving State will ordinarily accept the duty-free import even of highly unusual items; for example, the United Kingdom during the construction of new embassy premises in the Soviet Union imported building materials free of duty into the Soviet Union. Article 36 imposes a duty to permit entry, as well as to exempt from duty, and so the sending State, provided that the articles are genuinely required for official use, can import items which would normally require special licence or permission under the law of the receiving State. On the other hand diplomats cannot import for personal use articles the import of which is prohibited under local law, unless they have specific authority from the receiving State. The powers given in Article 36.2 to search a diplomat's baggage when there are serious grounds to suspect that it contains 'articles the import or export of which is prohibited by the law or controlled by the quarantine regulations of the receiving State' imply that the receiving State need not admit such articles.[50] In one incident illustrating this

---

[50] During Prohibition, the United States made it clear that diplomatic missions were not entitled to bring alcohol into the country and the import of alcohol into Muslim countries remains a shadowy area for diplomats. The import of firearms—whether for personal protection or sporting purposes—is also subject to complex and changing national rules which must be checked by diplomats on each new posting.

exceptional right of search, the Indonesian ambassador to Tanzania was found on inspection of his baggage to be about to export an illegal load of ivory weighing more than 3 tons.[51] The right to inspect the personal baggage of a diplomat in these exceptional circumstances is an important exception to the general inviolability of a diplomat's property in the receiving State. On a separate issue, it should be added that if a diplomat declines to allow his or her baggage to be inspected or tested by agents of an air carrier, the carrier is under no obligation to carry that diplomat.

14.46   No specific provision is made in Article 36 limiting the right to search incoming or outgoing consignments of articles for the official use of the mission. The absence of any such prohibition made it easy for UK customs authorities in 1984 to investigate the suspect official crates which were found to contain the Nigerian ex-minister Umaru Dikko (described more fully in Chapter 13, paragraphs 13.40–13.41). It is of course always open to the sending State to send any particularly sensitive items with the seals and labels which give it the character of a diplomatic bag thus rendering it inviolable.

Exemption from Social Security Obligations

14.47   Article 33 of the Vienna Convention provides that diplomatic agents shall be exempt from any social security provisions in the receiving State with regard to their work for the sending State. This exemption was not established in international custom, although some States expressly exempted diplomats in their legislation. In others there was no exemption and, in practice, the diplomat could choose whether or not to participate, relying on immunity from jurisdiction if choosing not to do so. Embassies were not pressured to comply except in regard to staff recruited in the receiving State. The Convention still permits voluntary participation by the diplomat if this is permissible under the local law (although under the law of the United Kingdom such participation is not permitted). It is also open to sending and receiving States to make more liberal or more restrictive social security arrangements in bilateral social security agreements.

Exemption from Personal and Public Services

14.48   Exemption from compulsory services such as jury service and military service, including military obligations such as requisition and billeting and from duties to assist in public emergencies, has traditionally been accorded to diplomats. In most

---

[51] *The Times*, 21 January 1989.

cases, they would not in any event, because of their nationality, be subject to civic duties. Exemption is now required under Article 35 of the Vienna Convention.

Nationality

As a general rule, those States which confer nationality automatically on children **14.49** born in their territory make an exception in regard to the children of diplomatic agents of other States (other than those diplomats who are their own nationals). States also make provision to ensure that children born to their own diplomats serving abroad acquire the nationality of their home State. However, the precise details as to how this is achieved can vary considerably from one State to another. The Vienna Conference attempted to formulate a provision on the question for inclusion in the Convention but none of the drafts produced secured the necessary two-thirds majority for inclusion, and so it was agreed to formulate the draft prepared by the International Law Commission as an Optional Protocol concerning Acquisition of Nationality. Those States which had supported that draft could then become parties to the Protocol.

Article II of the Optional Protocol provides that '[m]embers of the mission not **14.50** being nationals of the receiving State, and members of their families forming part of their household, shall not solely by the operation of law of the receiving State, acquire the nationality of that State'. There were two main objections to this provision. The first was that it did not take account of the degree of connection between the child born and the receiving State. For example a child born to parents both of whom were permanently resident in the receiving State and whose father was a national (if the mother was a member of the mission and not a national) would not acquire automatically the receiving State's nationality. The second was the possibility that in some cases the provision could give rise to statelessness—for example in the case of an illegitimate child born to a woman member of a diplomatic mission. The Protocol also has the effect of excluding the possibility of nationality automatically being acquired on marriage to a member of a diplomatic mission. The Protocol does not of course exclude the acquisition of nationality by naturalization, or by some other voluntary action.

Because of these problems on the text, the parties to the Protocol form a limited **14.51** proportion of the parties to the Vienna Convention and do not for example include France, the United Kingdom, or the United States. States which are not parties to the Protocol continue, in general, to apply local laws which accord with the broad principle established under customary international law. Where the matter may be of importance it is however essential for members of diplomatic missions to seek advice on local nationality laws.

Duties of a Diplomatic Agent

14.52   Certain duties laid on a diplomatic agent under customary international law may be said to be the corollary of the immunities enjoyed by the diplomat in the receiving State. These duties are now set out in Article 41 of the Vienna Convention. The most important is the duty to respect the laws and regulations of the receiving State. A Memorandum on Diplomatic Immunity sent to all new diplomats taking up posts in London makes clear that:

> [i]n accordance with Article 41 of the Vienna Convention on Diplomatic Relations members of diplomatic missions and their families are expected to respect the laws and regulations of the United Kingdom. Diplomatic immunity in no way absolves members of diplomatic missions or their families from their duty to obey the law.

Although a diplomat's immunity from jurisdiction does not imply any exemption from liability, special provision is sometimes made in local law to provide that diplomats shall be exempt from certain obligations—for example rules under local labour law—which may be inappropriate to their special circumstances or incompatible with their status. In the absence of such special provision or privilege the diplomat is bound by local laws even if they cannot be enforced because of immunity. For example, it is of the greatest importance that the diplomat observes local motor traffic regulations, maintains a vehicle to the standard legally required, and takes out third party insurance where this is compulsory. In the United Kingdom it was established in *Dickinson v Del Solar*[52] that an insurer cannot take advantage of the position of a client entitled to diplomatic immunity in order to avoid making payment on a third party claim, since the client is liable in the event of causing damage.[53]

14.53   The obligation to respect the laws and regulations of the receiving State applies to the official as well as the private activities of diplomats. For example, a diplomat may only properly exercise consular functions on embassy premises if this is permitted under local law. Some States prohibit this and others require special permission and Article 3 of the Vienna Convention was intended to make it clear that a diplomatic mission had no inherent right to perform consular functions regardless of the wishes of the receiving State. In particular, diplomats should not perform consular marriages on embassy premises unless permitted

---

[52] (1930)1 KB 376.

[53] The Foreign and Commonwealth Office avoids argument on this by asking all insurers in this field to provide an assurance that they will not seek to take advantage in this way. A list of insurers who have provided such an undertaking is circulated to missions in London and their attention drawn to the requirements of UK law. For United States practice in this field see Foreign Missions Amendments Act 1983, Public Law 98–164, 97 Stat 1017.

under local law. United Kingdom diplomats are instructed not to perform such marriages unless two conditions are satisfied—such marriages are permitted under local law and the local law will regard the marriage as valid.[54]

A second duty laid upon diplomatic agents, and restated in Article 41, is the duty not to interfere in the internal affairs of the receiving State. There have been a number of notorious instances where flagrant or unluckily discovered breach of that rule has led to the diplomat in question being declared *persona non grata*.[55] It remains generally the case that diplomatic agents while informing themselves in regard to forthcoming elections and probable outcomes thereof must avoid public statements or actions which would be construed as supporting one candidate or party. Thus, for example, the US embassy in London in 2001 disassociated itself clearly from a fund-raising appeal by the Conservative Party which suggested that previous donors had through their generosity gained access to the outgoing US ambassador, explaining that to link the ambassador to a fund-raising drive by any political party was incorrect and inappropriate.[56] The application of the general rule has, however, given rise in recent years to difficulties in many countries for two principal reasons. First, some States object to conduct on the part of foreign diplomats which overtly supports and encourages democratic freedoms, for example seeking to meet or to listen to opposition candidates, and argue that this amounts to interference in their own internal affairs. The government of Burma, for example, repeatedly condemned as intervention in its domestic affairs attempts by foreign diplomats to make contact with the then opposition leader, Aung San Suu Kyi.[57] In 2008 a convoy of British and US diplomats on their way, during the extended elections in Zimbabwe, to investigate allegations of violence against members of the opposition Movement for Democratic Change were harassed and accused of 'trying to effect regime change in Zimbabwe'.[58] In 2012 the US ambassador to Russia participated in talks with leaders of street protests organized against Vladimir Putin's plan to resume the Presidency. He was accused by the Russian Parliament of 'fomenting revolution'.[59] Secondly, international law now requires States to defend and actively protect human rights abroad, and the existence of multilateral commitments to respect human rights implies that breach of these commitments is no

14.54

---

[54] Unless such conditions are satisfied, the marriage would be unlikely to be regarded as valid in any country other than the diplomat's sending State.

[55] See e.g. *Papers Relating to the Foreign Relations of the US*, 1888, pt. Ii, B.F.S.P., Vol 81, 479; Moore, *Digest of International Law*, Vol 4, 536.

[56] *The Times*, 28 February 2001.

[57] *The Times*, 6 September 2000.

[58] *The Times*, 6 June 2008.

[59] *The Times*, 25 January 2012.

longer a matter of exclusive domestic jurisdiction but a matter of legitimate international interest. A diplomat is properly entitled to protect the interests of his sending State even where the receiving State may claim that this is improper interference, and the scope for protective action covers not only a case where a national of the sending State has suffered breach of his human rights but also where obligations to respect human rights are owed to the sending State through a multilateral treaty on human rights.

14.55 The third general obligation set out in Article 41 of the Vienna Convention is procedural in nature: 'All official business with the receiving State entrusted to the mission by the sending State shall be conducted with or through the Ministry for Foreign Affairs of the receiving State or such other ministry as may be agreed.' The general rule reflects the need for the ministry of foreign affairs to be aware of all aspects of relations between sending and receiving States so that particular problems and requests may be set within the wider context of overall relations. It has, however, long been the practice for specialist attachés to deal directly with the relevant specialist ministry. As international relations have become more technical in character and methods of communication more informal, it has become increasingly frequent that States agree between themselves to vary this rule in their daily business. It is still, however, highly advisable to ensure that the ministry of foreign affairs is kept generally aware of the substance of direct exchanges between an embassy and a specialist ministry.

Families, Junior Staff, and Nationals

14.56 The previous paragraphs set out the immunities and privileges which are accorded under the Vienna Convention on Diplomatic Relations to diplomatic agents who are not nationals or permanent residents of the receiving State. A majority of the individuals who are entitled under the Convention to some immunities or privileges do not, however, come into this category, and they receive privileged treatment on a lesser scale. Families of diplomatic agents, junior staff of the mission, and private servants of members of the mission are, generally speaking, ancillary to the conduct of diplomatic functions, although their presence and proper protection is essential to enable these functions to be carried out effectively. Article 37 of the Convention sets out in precise terms the immunities and privileges to be accorded to families of diplomatic agents, to members of the administrative and technical staff of the mission and their families, to members of the service staff of the mission, and to private servants of members of the mission. Nationals of the receiving State are entirely excluded from the provisions of Article 37. Permanent residents of the receiving State are excluded also unless they are members of the family of a diplomatic agent. Article 38 sets out the immunities to be accorded to diplomatic agents who are nationals or permanent residents of the receiving State. As explained in what follows, in the application of those two articles, it is essential to understand the distinction made there between acts done in or outside the course of a person's duties, and official acts performed in the exercise of a person's functions.

Families of Diplomatic Agents

The members of the family of a diplomatic agent forming part of his household, **14.57** unless they are nationals of the receiving State, enjoy the entire range of diplomatic privileges and immunities. If they are nationals of the receiving State they have no direct entitlement to personal privileges or immunities at all, although the diplomat may use his exemption from customs duty to import free of duty articles for their personal use. Continuing immunity in regard to official acts is, of course, irrelevant in the case of a family member who does not carry out official acts. In evidence to the UK House of Commons Foreign Affairs Committee enquiry into *The Abuse of Diplomatic Privileges and Immunities* the Diplomatic Service Wives Association justified immunities and privileges for diplomatic families in these terms:

> Families are regarded essentially as extensions of the persons of the diplomats themselves. The protection of diplomatic dependants has, therefore, been regarded as quite as necessary as that of the diplomats, to ensure the diplomats' independence and their ability to carry on their governments' business however unpopular their country, their mission or their instructions.[60]

The expression 'member of the family forming part of the household' is not **14.58** defined anywhere in the Convention. Considerable effort was devoted during the Vienna Conference to the formulation of a definition, but none of those proposed obtained the necessary majority. The question of who may quality as a 'member of the family', although ultimately a question of law, is thus in practice often a matter of negotiation between sending and receiving States, and there is no set procedure for determining differences of opinion. But States may establish reasonable guidelines for the interpretation of the term,

---

[60] 1st Report, 1984–5, Appendix 4 to Evidence. For a lively and fascinating account of the experiences of British diplomatic families from 1661 onwards, see K Hickman, *Daughters of Britannia: The Lives and Times of Diplomatic Wives* (London: Flamingo, 2000).

and these will normally be applied in practice in the receiving State. Most States have not set out rigid rules on the matter and have preferred to retain sufficient flexibility to deal with unusual cases (such as polygamous diplomats arriving *en poste* with more than one wife) as and when they arise. For the most part, unusual cases are addressed at the time of notification of arrival rather than left for later resolution in the context of privileges or of legal proceedings. All States accept the spouse of a diplomatic agent as a member of the family. Spouse includes the husband of a woman diplomat, and such appointments have in the years since the Vienna Convention become frequent. In some States an unmarried partner is in this context accepted as a 'spouse', and more than one spouse may also be accepted as a member of the family. Same-sex civil partners have also been accepted as members of the family at least in States which make provision in their national law for civil partnership. The United Kingdom is among those countries, and 'members of the family' in its practice includes same-sex partners from other States provided that the relationship satisfies precisely defined criteria. More recently the Marriage (Same Sex Couples) Act 2013 has made the marriage of same-sex couples lawful and has made it possible for civil partnerships to be converted into marriages, thereby extending the interpretation of the term 'spouse' for the UK.[61] All States also accept the minor child of a diplomat as a member of the family, although there may be differences between sending and receiving State as to whether a child is still a 'minor'. Most receiving States apply their own national law to determine this question. Beyond these two categories state practice varies. The United Kingdom for the purpose of the administration of privileges (a claim to immunity would under UK law be determined by the courts) normally accepts as members of the family persons in the following categories; (i) a child between 18 and 25 clearly resident with the diplomat, financially dependent on him or her, in full-time education at a recognized educational establishment, and not engaged in paid full-time employment; and (ii) in certain cases, a dependent parent of the diplomat normally resident with him or her. But these categories are not exclusive, and other claims to privileges as a member of the family of a diplomatic agent will be considered by the Foreign and Commonwealth Office in the light of the particular facts. A broadly similar approach is taken by Canada, Australia, New Zealand, Germany, Belgium, and the US, with exceptional cases being discussed between sending and receiving States.

---

[61] For details of current UK practice, see Denza, *Diplomatic Law* (4th edn, 2016) 320–4.

Members of the family of a diplomatic agent are not barred by the Vienna **14.59** Convention from exercising professional or commercial activities in the receiving State, and in exercising such activities they are not entitled to immunity from civil or administrative jurisdiction. In many receiving States, however, family members have been faced with obstacles to their working which may be social or cultural, political or economic intended for example to reserve scarce employment opportunities for local nationals. Sending States where dual-career families are normal seek to enhance the mobility of their diplomatic services by making it easier for spouses, in particular, to continue their careers while living abroad, and, of course, a working spouse can contribute significantly to the diplomat's own understanding of the receiving State. It has therefore, in recent years, become frequent for States to conclude bilateral agreements which guarantee on a reciprocal basis that family members may carry on remunerated activity during a diplomatic posting, provide for an authorization procedure, stress the need for compliance with local requirements on qualifications, and (in some cases) contain express exclusions of tax privileges and immunity in regard to such employment. Given the clear exclusions in the Vienna Convention, this last provision is highly undesirable unless it is clearly drafted as being no more than a restatement of these exclusions, since it could suggest that in the absence of express bilateral provision the exclusions in the Convention were ineffective. In 1987 the Council of Europe drew up a model agreement to facilitate engagement in gainful occupation by family members of a member of a diplomatic mission or consular post.[62] This model also contains provision designed to encourage waiver of any immunity from criminal jurisdiction regarding acts carried out in the course of gainful occupation. Many European States have concluded bilateral agreements based on the Council of Europe model. The US State Department also drew up a model agreement, and the United States has concluded over 100 agreements with the objective of enhancing employment opportunities for family members of diplomats posted abroad.

Administrative and Technical Staff

The question of the privileges and immunities to be extended to the 'suite', as **14.60** the family and junior staff of the mission were formerly called, was one on which there was no consistent practice among States. Some States, notably the

---

[62] Recommendation No R(87)2 adopted by the Committee of Ministers of the Council of Europe and Explanatory Memorandum.

United Kingdom, the United States, and Germany, extended the entire range of diplomatic immunities down the scale to domestic servants working in the embassy and private servants of the ambassador. Most States limited the privileges and immunities of junior staff in some way, but there were no consistent rules in regard to the limitations which might be imposed. The matter might be determined by reciprocity. The United Kingdom, for example, from the enactment in 1955 of the Diplomatic Immunities (Restriction) Act,[63] limited on a precisely reciprocal basis the immunity which it extended to junior staff in diplomatic missions in London. The most restrictive States accorded to junior staff only the immunities which flowed from their status as agents of a foreign sovereign government, namely immunity in regard to official acts and exemption from taxation on their official emoluments. In the Vienna Convention, however, a clear distinction is drawn between those staff, termed the administrative and technical staff, whose work is highly responsible, who may be dealing at a lower level with diplomatic matters, and who whether as personal secretaries, as cipher clerks, or as wireless operators have access to diplomatic secrets, and on the other hand those staff whose functions are essentially domestic and who are not in direct contact with official matters, namely the service staff.[64] The first category require on functional grounds a greater protection than is afforded by immunity for official acts alone, whereas the second are not likely to be harassed or attacked for political reasons and, therefore, do not need the special protection of inviolability or immunity from jurisdiction in regard to their private acts. The distinction itself was readily accepted and the terms have quickly become standard diplomatic usage. But it proved difficult to agree on the exact treatment to be accorded to administrative and technical staff. The formulation in Article 37 resulted from compromise. It constituted progressive development in this area, and it has not been universally accepted.

14.61 There are no precise rules in the Convention or in practice as to which tasks are properly to be performed by 'administrative and technical staff' and which by 'service staff'. Members of the administrative and technical staff are defined simply as the members of the staff of the mission employed in the administrative and technical service of the mission. 'Members of the service staff' are the members of the staff of the mission in the domestic service of the mission. It is for the sending State to notify the receiving State of the appointment of

---

[63] 4 & 5 Eliz 2 c 21.

[64] Service staff in the Vienna Convention does not refer to the defence attachés (generally known in English as service attachés), or to other naval, military, or air force members of the mission. These are diplomatic staff.

mission staff in the various categories, and it must therefore decide borderline cases, such as security guards and embassy teachers, for itself, while acting in good faith. For example, it is clearly improper to appoint staff to a staff category which is not justified by the work they do, simply to give them greater privileges and immunities. But the receiving State is not under the Convention given power to challenge a classification of staff or unilaterally to demand that they be assigned to a lower staff category. It can, of course, ask the sending State to reclassify particular staff, and some States do now challenge notifications which they regard as placing staff in categories inappropriate to their actual functions. But if the sending State refuses, or claims that special training or functions assigned for example to security officers justify a high grading, the receiving State, if unwilling to acquiesce, can only declare the individuals *persona non grata* or not acceptable, or use its powers under Article 11 of the Convention to limit the number of staff appointed to a particular category.

Members of the administrative and technical staff, and members of their families forming part of their households, unless they are nationals or permanent residents of the receiving State, enjoy the same privileges and immunities as diplomatic agents, with two important exceptions. They do not enjoy immunity from civil and administrative jurisdiction in regard to acts performed 'outside the course of their duties'. They can never be tried on a criminal charge in any circumstances (unless their immunity is waived by the sending State), but they may be sued on personal matters, for example, if they write a libellous article in a local paper, or fail to pay their children's school fees, or keep wild animals which escape and cause damage. The immunity given to administrative and technical staff in regard to acts performed in the course of their duties is wider than the immunity which is given to a diplomatic agent who is a national of the receiving State and which covers only 'official acts performed in the exercise of his functions'. The former expression includes acts performed during the working day which are reasonably incidental to employment with the embassy, for example driving to an official appointment. 'Official acts performed in the exercise of his functions', on the other hand, properly includes only those acts which are performed on behalf of the sending State. The expression 'outside the course of their duties' was construed in the English case of *Re B*[65] where the Family Division of the High Court decided that they could continue an interim care order made in respect of the child of a member of the administrative and technical staff of a foreign mission found to have suffered serious non-accidental

14.62

---

[65] [2002] EWHC 1751 (Fam), [2003] 1 FLR 241.

injuries consistent with repeated hitting, on the basis that beating his child was not within the scope of the father's duties.

14.63 The second limitation on the privileges and immunities of administrative and technical staff as compared with diplomatic staff is that the former enjoy exemption from customs duty only in regard to those articles which they import when they arrive to take up their post. They cannot later import items free of duty, and in particular they cannot import wines, spirits, and tobacco duty free on a continuing basis as diplomats can. Each receiving State has exact regulations concerning 'first arrival privileges' (*première installation*), as the privilege given to administrative and technical staff is often called. Some countries may allow only one car to be imported on arrival in the receiving State. All countries have a period during which articles must be imported if they are to qualify as being 'imported at the time of first installation'. Some countries (including the United Kingdom) require articles to be imported within three months after the arrival of the staff member himself. Others are more generous and grant exemption from duty even where the articles are imported up to six, nine, or twelve months later. Most will allow an extension if there are special circumstances such as an unexpected delay in the shipment. The United Kingdom also expects items to be in the ownership or possession of the staff member when he arrived, or at least to have been ordered by then. A staff member travelling to a different climate who wishes to import suitable clothing duty free after his arrival must at least place his order before travelling to the receiving State.

14.64 Four States, Egypt, Morocco, Cambodia, and Qatar, entered reservations which remain in effect to the provision in the Vienna Convention which regulates the privileges and immunities of members of the administrative and technical staff. They wished to accord to those staff only the much lower scale of privileges and immunities which under the Convention is given to service staff. A number of other States, mainly European, objected to those reservations but made clear that they nevertheless regarded the reserving States as parties to the Convention. Other States made reservations which were later withdrawn, or made clear that they would accord Vienna Convention treatment to administrative and technical staff only on a basis of reciprocity. China, which acceded to the Convention in 1975, stated in its instrument that it 'holds reservations...on the provisions of paragraphs 2, 3 and 4 of Article 37'.[66] This reservation applied to all junior staff and private servants; many States lodged objections to it and it was later withdrawn. Generally speaking, however, the reservations entered to the Vienna

---

[66] CN 354, 1975, Treaties 8.

Convention have gradually become of limited importance as provisions which originally formed 'progressive development' of customary law have become universally accepted.

Service Staff

Service staff, defined as members of the staff of the mission in the domestic service of the mission, include embassy drivers, cooks, door-keepers, and cleaners. They differ from 'private servants' of members of the mission in being employed by the sending State and not by any individual member of the mission. They receive under the Vienna Convention only immunity *in respect of acts performed in the course of their duties*; exemption from tax on their wages, which may equally be regarded as an exemption for the sending State which pays these wages; and exemption from social security provisions. They are entitled to no immunities or privileges of a purely personal character. Service staff who are local nationals or permanent residents receive nothing. It is clear that immunity can arise only in respect of acts performed in the actual exercise of official duties or as a natural consequence of those duties and would not cover a charge of murder, even though the accused embassy driver was at the time on embassy premises, within his hours of duty, and at the disposal of the mission.[67]

14.65

The limited privileges and immunities accorded under the Vienna Convention may, of course, be supplemented by more generous provisions under local law or practice, or by bilateral agreement between sending and receiving States. Article 47 expressly sanctions the giving of more favourable treatment than is required by the Convention where this is based on custom or agreement. The United Kingdom accords more generous treatment to junior staff in foreign missions only on the basis of agreements or arrangements already in force when it became a party to the Vienna Convention. It maintained in force a number of such agreements or arrangements providing for more generous exemption from customs duty for junior staff, and three agreements, with the Soviet Union, Bulgaria, and Czechoslovakia, which accorded inviolability of person and residence and personal immunity from jurisdiction on the diplomatic scale to junior staff.[68] Even where there is no explicit provision for according greater privileges and immunities to junior staff, it may also happen in many countries that administrative

14.66

---

[67] *Ministère Public and Republic of Mali v Keita*, 1977 Journal des Tribunaux 678; 77 ILR 410, Brussels Court of Appeal.

[68] Details or arrangements and agreements were published in the *London Gazette* of 1 October 1964, and amended on 1 September 1966 (by the removal of Hungary on termination of the relevant arrangement).

discretion will be used in their favour. For example, if a member of a foreign mission is detected shoplifting or driving while unfit through drink, the executive, if it has discretion over the initiation of criminal proceedings, may prefer, in order not to damage relations with the sending State, to send a private account of the matter to the ambassador rather than institute criminal proceedings. The United States also has power under the Foreign Missions Act 1982[69] to provide, on a basis of reciprocity, more generous treatment than required by the Vienna Convention and this power is used to implement bilateral agreements with former Soviet Republics and with China. Information as to special agreements or arrangements will normally be made available to embassies by the ministry of foreign affairs.

Private Servants

14.67   In traditional diplomatic practice, the private servants of the ambassador were regarded as members of his 'suite' and entitled to at least some privileges and immunities on that basis. The Vienna Convention, however, distinguishes between service staff, employed by the sending State, and the private servants of members of the mission. No distinction is made between the private servants of the ambassador and the private servants of other members of the mission. Private servants who are not nationals or permanent residents of the receiving State enjoy two privileges only (both of which are in reality for the benefit of their employers). They are exempt from tax on the emoluments of their employment, and, on condition that they are covered by social security in another State, they are exempt from the social security provisions of the receiving State. The employer diplomats do not therefore have to pay such high wages as they would if subject to tax and social security deductions by the receiving State and do not have to master the intricacies of local tax and social security law. A private servant who has accompanied a diplomat will usually continue to contribute to a social security scheme in his or her own country and may also be liable to tax there—though the exact position will depend on the terms of any double taxation agreement.

14.68   The Vienna Convention also provides that jurisdiction over private servants must be exercised 'in such manner as not to interfere unduly with the performance of the functions of the mission'. In practical terms this means that the local authorities including the police should try to exercise their powers in such a way that the diplomatic employer is not too seriously inconvenienced. If the

---

[69] Public Law 97–241; 22 US Code s 4301 *et seq.*

private servant is living with the diplomatic employer, proceedings cannot be begun by service of process or a judgment executed in such a way as to infringe the inviolability of the residence of the diplomat.

Nationals and Permanent Residents of the Receiving State

The exclusion of nationals of the receiving State from privileges and immunities **14.69** was common, although not universal, under customary international law. The writers on international law were conscious of the special problems posed if a national of the receiving State was accepted in the capacity of a diplomatic agent, but they were not consistent in the conclusions they drew.[70] Some States avoided the problem by refusing altogether to accept their own nationals as diplomats representing another State, and of those who were willing to accept them some gave them full privileges and immunities, some gave them no privileges and immunities (or only immunity for official acts), and some regulated the matter expressly at the time of receiving the diplomatic agent, usually by reserving the right to withhold immunities and privileges.

The Vienna Conference, however, was firmly in favour of excluding nationals **14.70** of the receiving State from all personal privileges and immunities. Junior staff are not even accorded immunity in regard to official acts, though this would not prevent the sending State in appropriate cases from arguing that these acts were in reality acts of a foreign sovereign and therefore for reasons of sovereign immunity not within the jurisdiction of the receiving State. Diplomatic agents who are nationals or permanent residents of the receiving State enjoy under Article 38 of the Convention *only* immunity from jurisdiction, and inviolability, in respect of official acts performed in the exercise of their functions. The wording makes clear that both the inviolability and the immunity are limited to official acts. The acts covered are only those which are in some sense performed on behalf of the sending State. It is irrelevant that incidental acts performed during the working day, or necessary for the conduct of life in the receiving State, such as the renting of living accommodation, or driving to an appointment, may be said to be 'in the course of duties' (the expression used in Article 37). They are not 'official acts performed in the exercise of his functions'. While the embassy chauffeur, who is a national of the receiving State, would be acting in the course of his duties when driving the ambassador to an appointment, if he caused an accident he would have no immunity

---

[70] See the account of de Wicquefort's changes of opinion given by E R Adair in *The Extraterritoriality of Ambassadors in the 16th and 17th Centuries* (London: Longman, 1929) 312.

under Article 38. The same would apply to a diplomat who is a national of the receiving State if he or she chose to drive to an appointment and caused an accident.

14.71 Among Commonwealth countries, dual nationals of sending and receiving States are treated, for the purpose of privileges and immunities, as though they held only the nationality of the sending Commonwealth State. This is an example of the 'more favourable treatment' which is permitted under Article 47.2(b) of the Vienna Convention where it is based on custom.

14.72 The exclusion of 'permanent residents' as well as local nationals from virtually all privileges and immunities has given rise to difficulty. Whether a person is a national of the receiving State is under general principles of law to be determined by the law of that State. But the exclusion of 'permanent residents' from privileges and immunities was not common in national legal systems before the Convention. 'Permanent residents' were added to the text of the Convention at a very late stage and without much discussion, and the term is not defined nor a procedure for resolving differences over its application prescribed in the Convention. Disputes arose and in the light of several years' experience of administering the regime under the Convention, and in an effort to avoid the arguments over particular cases which wasted time and caused friction, the United Kingdom government elaborated working criteria which they circulated on 27 January 1969 to all diplomatic missions in London for their guidance. The guidance read, in part, as follows:

> When determining whether or not a particular member of your staff should be regarded as a permanent resident of the United Kingdom the test should normally be whether or not he would be in the United Kingdom but for the requirements of the sending State. In applying this test I suggest that you should be guided by the following considerations:
>
> (i) the intention of the individual; a person should be regarded as permanently resident in the United Kingdom unless he is going to return to his own country or proceed to a third country as soon as his appointment in the United Kingdom ends. It is suggested that points which may be relevant to this question include the links of the individual with the State which he claims as his home, e.g. payment of taxes, participation in social security schemes, ownership of immovable property, payment of return passage by the sending State.
>
> (ii) the prospect of the individual being posted elsewhere as a career member of the service; he should be regarded as permanently resident in the United Kingdom if his appointment in the United Kingdom is likely to continue or has continued for more than five years, unless the Head of Mission states that the longer stay in the United Kingdom is a requirement of the sending State and not a result of personal considerations.

   (iii) local recruitment of the individual; a person who is locally engaged is presumed to be permanently resident in the United Kingdom unless the Head of Mission concerned shows that he is going to return to his own country or to proceed to a third county immediately on the termination of his appointment in the United Kingdom; and

   (iv) marital status of the individual; a woman member of the Mission who is married to a permanent resident of the United Kingdom is presumed to be herself permanently resident in the United Kingdom from the time of her marriage unless the Head of Mission shows that in addition to her satisfying the other criteria, there remains a real prospect in view of the special circumstances of her case that she will be posted as a normal career member of the service.

If a review in the light of this guidance leads Your Excellency to conclude that any of your staff should henceforward be regarded as permanent residents of the United Kingdom for the purposes of the Diplomatic Privileges Act, I suggest that any change in status should take effect from 1st April 1969 and would request that such cases be notified to this Office by that date. Thereafter it would be helpful if Your Excellency could arrange for prompt notification to this Office of any change in the residential status of members of your staff. Should a difference of opinion arise between a Mission and Her Majesty's Government as to whether an individual is permanently resident in the United Kingdom, I suggest that consultation should take place between the two sides and that each side should inform the other of any relevant evidence which may be in their possession.

This guidance has been followed by the UK in administering privileges since 1969 and, although consultations as envisaged have sometimes taken place, it has not been generally challenged by missions in London. In 2004 it was judicially considered by a Special Tax Commissioner for the UK in the case of *Lutgarda Jimenez v Commissioners of Inland Revenue*.[71] It was held in that case that the guidance followed since 1969 constituted 'subsequent practice in the interpretation of the application of the treaty which established the agreement of the parties regarding its interpretation' and now reflected customary international law.[72] The key test in the Circular was whether the individual was resident in the receiving State for a purpose unconnected with the holding of the status of membership of the mission.

A number of other countries have since 1969 drawn up practice guidelines on   **14.73** the meaning of 'permanently resident in the receiving State' which are broadly similar to those applied by the United Kingdom (though without the discriminatory limitation to 'a woman member of the mission' in the context of marriage

---

[71] [2004] UKSPC 00419 (23 June 2004).
[72] See Art 31.3 of the Vienna Convention on the Law of Treaties.

to a local national). The United States when it first became a party to the Convention defined 'permanent resident' in the sense which it had in US immigration law, but in 1991, in a Circular Note to Chiefs of Mission in Washington, set out revised criteria similar to, but more restrictive than, the criteria applied in other capitals. The United States asserts more strongly a right to make a unilateral determination of whether an individual is permanently resident in the receiving State, though it does this in the light of evidence and assurances from sending States. It also offers the possibility of more favourable treatment on a basis of reciprocity, as permitted under Article 47 of the Vienna Convention.

14.74   Most States accept the possibility of a change in residence status during a diplomatic posting, but France is an exception in this regard and determines residence status on an indefinite basis at the time of original appointment and notification. The difference in approach between France and the United Kingdom was settled in 1987 by a compromise agreement whereby the UK authorities would accept the original determination for a period of ten years in post. At this point the status would be reviewed and, for non-permanent resident status to continue, an assurance would be required from the relevant ambassador that continuation in the post was the result of a decision by the sending State (rather than the personal wish of the individual).

Diplomatic Agents in Third States

14.75   Two questions arise for diplomatic agents who wish to cross a third State on their way to or from the State where they have been appointed. Does international law owe them an automatic right of passage, at least in time of peace, and are they entitled to any special privileges and immunities while passing through? Practice on both matters varied considerably at different periods.

14.76   During the sixteenth and seventeenth centuries it was the custom for diplomats who wished to cross foreign territory on the way to their post, and indeed for private persons, to seek the assurance of a safe-conduct from the ruler of the foreign territory concerned. States might provide in general terms for the safe passage of their ambassadors in transit, as did Britain and Russia in a Treaty of 1623, which protected:

> Ambassadors, Messengers or Posts through the Countries and Dominions of the other unto and from Germany, France, Spain, Denmarke, Sweathland and Netherland, or unto and from Persia, Turkey and other Partes of the East, which are not in open Hostilities with either of their renowned Majesties...[73]

---

[73] De intercursu mercandisarum cum imperatore Russiae, Rymer, *Foedera*, Vol 17, 506.

Gradually the practice of seeking safe-conduct fell into disuse but States until the nineteenth century accepted that the ambassador had a right of innocent passage through third States on his way to his post. It was clearly to the advantage of all States that this should be the position and legal restrictions on immigration or on the movement of aliens within a territory were still uncommon.

During the late nineteenth and early twentieth centuries, however, controls on **14.77** travel became general and States became more restrictive, requiring foreign diplomats to obtain a prior visa if such a visa was necessary for an ordinary traveller of the same nationality. The reaction of the French government to the transit of M. Soule indicates this new attitude:

> In 1854 he French Government refused to M. Soule, United States minister at Madrid (of French origin, but naturalised in the United States, and said to have been 'of a fiery temperament') permission to stay in France on his way to his post, on the ground that his antecedents had attracted the attention of the authorities charged with public order; they had no objection to his merely passing through, but as he had not been authorised to represent his adopted country in his native land, he was for the French Government merely a private person, and as such subject to the ordinary law.[74]

In the vast majority of cases a visa, or permission to transit on production of **14.78** a diplomatic passport, was granted as a matter of course, but where the diplomat was not acceptable to the third State, or the third State had no diplomatic relations with either the sending or the receiving State, he would find that the 'right of innocent passage' was of little practical significance. Article 40 of the Vienna Convention is clearly based on the assumption that the diplomat has no right of transit across a third State, and that he is not exempt from obtaining a visa for such passage in the ordinary way. The old right of passage has, in fact, become of much less practical significance now that air travel has become general, since diplomats usually do not need to enter third States in order to proceed to or from their posts. Such transits do however still occur, whether in the context of changing aircraft or otherwise, and in such cases the immigration authorities are entitled to require a transit visa or a passport inspection.

On the question of whether an ambassador in transit was entitled to privileges **14.79** and immunities the early writers were unanimous that he had no such entitlement. His special position, if any, depended on the terms of a safe-conduct, or on a special bilateral agreement, or on courtesy. But later practice was more

---

[74] Moore, *Digest of International Law*, Vol 4, 557; J W Foster, *The Practice of Diplomacy as Illustrated in the Foreign Relations of the United States* (Boston: Houghton, Mifflin, 1906) 53.

varied. A few States, such as the Netherlands, in their ordinance of 1679,[75] and France, under the decree of 13 ventose, an II (of the Revolution), made provision in their legislation to treat diplomats in transit in the same way as diplomats accredited to the State. A series of United States cases, *Holbrook v Henderson*,[76] *Wilson v Blanco*,[77] and *Bergman v De Sieyes*,[78] established in that country that the diplomatic agent in transit to or from his post was entitled to immunity from jurisdiction. The view was taken in these cases that such immunity was necessary for the free and unimpeded exercise of diplomatic duties, and that to oblige a diplomatic agent to attend the trial of an action in a third State was more inconvenient than to oblige him to attend one in the receiving State. Where difficulty might be caused by the uncertain state of the law, matters could be regulated by agreement as was done in the Lateran Treaty between Italy and the Holy See of 11 February 1929, which provided:

> Article 12: Italy recognises the right of the Holy See to active and passive legation in accordance with the general rules of international law. Envoys of foreign governments to the Holy See shall continue to enjoy in the Kingdom all the privileges and immunities appertaining to diplomatic agents in virtue of international law, and their headquarters may remain in Italian territory and shall enjoy all the immunities due to them in accordance with international law, even if the states to which they belong maintain no diplomatic relations with Italy. It is understood that Italy undertakes always and in every case to leave free the correspondence from all states, including belligerents, to the Holy See, and *vice versa....* In virtue of the sovereignty recognised, and without prejudice to the provisions of Article 19 below, diplomatists of the Supreme Pontiff shall enjoy in Italian territory, even in time of war, the treatment due to diplomatists and carriers of despatches of other foreign governments, in accordance with the rules of international law.

> Article 19: Diplomatic officers and envoys of the Holy See, diplomatic officers and envoys of foreign governments accredited to the Holy See.... possessing passports issued by their state of origin and visas by Papal representatives abroad, shall be admitted without further formality to the City across Italian territory. The same shall apply to the above-mentioned persons, who, being furnished with regular Papal passports, are proceeding abroad from the Vatican City.

14.80 Article 40 of the Vienna Convention adopts a strictly functional approach to the question of the privileges and immunities to be given to a diplomatic agent passing through a third State to or from his post. The third State is obliged only to accord him 'inviolability and such other immunities as may be required to ensure his transit or return'. The same inviolability and immunities are required

---

[75] UN Laws and Regulations regarding Diplomatic and Consular Privileges and Immunities *(UN Legislative Series*, Vol 7, 201).
[76] (NY 1839); 4 Sandf 619.
[77] (NY 1889); 4 NY Suppl 714.
[78] 71 F Suppl 334; 170 F 2d 360; *AD* (1947), No 73.

in the case of members of his family enjoying privileges or immunities who are accompanying him or travelling separately to join him or return to their country. The diplomat and his family in transit are therefore entitled to the special protection and freedom from arrest or detention implied in inviolability, but any civil proceedings may be brought against them provided that these do not involve their arrest, and they have no privileges such as exemption from baggage search. In 1972 in the Netherlands (at that time not yet party to the Vienna Convention but applying most of its provisions) a search of the luggage of an Algerian diplomat in transit to Brazil found that it contained letter bombs, grenades, other explosives, and pistols. They confiscated the luggage but allowed the diplomat to continue his journey since they took the view that they were unable to arrest or charge him.[79]

A diplomatic agent is entitled to these limited immunities irrespective of the **14.81** relations between his sending and receiving State on the one hand and the third State on the other. The obligations in Article 40 apply even where the presence of the diplomat (or other entitled person, or diplomatic bag) is due to *force majeure*, such as the forced landing of an aeroplane, but it is not entirely clear whether it would override the traditional rules and practice which apply during a state of war. Armed conflict is specifically mentioned in relation to the general right of a diplomat to leave the receiving State and in relation to breach of diplomatic relations, but not in regard to transit of a third State. To benefit from the immunities in Article 40 a diplomat must be accredited to a specific receiving State. In the case of *R v Governor of Pentonville Prison, ex parte Teja*[80] in 1971 a United Kingdom court refused to allow immunity from extradition proceedings to Dr Teja, a Costa Rican 'roving envoy' who carried a diplomatic passport, but was neither accredited to nor received by the government of any particular country. It is also essential that the diplomat should be appointed by a government which is recognized as such by the third State. Emissaries of 'national liberation movements' or of other unrecognized entities such as the regime illegally set up in Rhodesia in 1965, for example, would not be entitled to immunity in third States under the Vienna Convention.

Under the Vienna Convention a diplomat who is in a third State for recrea- **14.82** tional or other private purposes, or who pauses during his transit to or from his post for a prolonged private holiday, is entitled to no immunity. This reflects the position as it was under customary international law. As Rivier pointed out: 'If he is there solely for his own pleasure, or in pursuit of some merely private

---

[79] UN Doc S/10816; (1974) *RGDIP* 247.
[80] [1971] 2 QB 274, [1971] 2 All ER 11.

object, he is merely a distinguished personage, neither more nor less.'[81] It is not however necessary for Article 40 protection to apply, that the diplomat or family member should be travelling directly between the sending and the receiving State, provided that he or she is either proceeding to post or returning to his or her own country. This was illustrated by the UK case of *R v Guildhall Magistrates' Court, ex parte Jarrett-Thorpe*.[82] Jarrett-Thorpe was the husband of a diplomat in the embassy of Sierra Leone to Italy who travelled to London to help his wife with official purchases for her embassy in Rome, found that she had already left, and was arrested while awaiting a flight to rejoin her in Rome. The court held that he was immune from UK jurisdiction even though he was not accompanying his wife and was not in direct transit between sending and receiving States. By contrast, a Belgian Court of Cassation in *Vafadar*[83] denied immunity to the wife of the ambassador of Afghanistan to India who was arrested while passing through Belgium in order to visit her sick mother in Moscow, as she was neither travelling to her husband's post nor returning to her own country.

14.83 Third States are also obliged not to 'hinder the passage' through their territories of members of the administrative and technical staff of a mission and members of their families proceeding to or from their posts. Such persons do not have immunity but the third State must not inconvenience or delay them without good cause. Service staff and private servants are not entitled to any special treatment. Diplomatic agents who are nationals or permanent residents either of the receiving State or of the third State are not specifically excluded from the terms of Article 40; but it is unlikely that such persons would be passing through or in the territory of the third State en route to their post or returning to their own countries.

14.84 Official correspondence and other official communications, diplomatic couriers, and diplomatic bags in transit through third States are entitled under Article 40 to the same inviolability and protection as the receiving State is bound to accord under Article 27.

14.85 Under customary international law a State was entitled to arrest the diplomatic agent of a hostile State during war with that State and treat him as a prisoner of war.[84] It was therefore invariable practice for diplomatic relations to be broken

---

[81] A Rivier, *Principes du Droit des Gens* (Paris, 1896) Vol I, 508.
[82] Times Law Reports, 6 October 1977.
[83] 82 ILR 97.
[84] W E Hall, *A Treatise on International Law* (Oxford: Clarendon, 1924) 365.

before a formal declaration of war. Where transit through another country at war was necessary, it was necessary to seek a safe-conduct.[85]

Such practice presupposes the existence of a formal state of war but since 1945 **14.86** the formal declaration of war between States has become a rare event, and conflicts between States are usually described as 'armed conflicts'. It remains uncertain whether States involved in an 'armed conflict' are entitled to exercise in regard to diplomats in transit what are essentially belligerent rights. Article 40 of the Vienna Convention is not expressly limited to peacetime passage by diplomats, nor does it refer to 'armed conflict' although other Articles of the Convention clearly deal with the contingency of armed conflict between the sending and receiving State. In the Preamble to the Convention it is affirmed 'that the rules of customary international law should continue to govern questions not expressly regulated by the provisions of the present Convention'. However, the matter may probably now be regarded as of limited importance, since general air travel means that it is rarely necessary for a diplomat to traverse hostile territory on the way to or from post.

---

[85] See Oppenheim's *International Law* (8th edn, Lauterpacht, 1955) Vol I, 398; and R Genet, *Traité de diplomatie et de droit diplomatique* (Paris: Pédone, 1931) Vol I, 596.

15

SPECIAL MISSIONS

Hazel Fox and Joanne Foakes

15.1 From the twentieth century onwards to the present day the sending and receiving of representatives on short-term missions has become a regular practice. Not only do Heads of State, prime ministers, and ministers of all kinds visit their opposite numbers with a frequency previously unthinkable, but business exchanges at the ordinary diplomatic and technical level have steadily increased. The cost of maintaining permanent missions abroad, and speed of travel have made it more practicable to send the expert in a particular subject to negotiate, meaning that a special mission has become essential to the discussion and resolution of issues and protection of States' interests in others' capitals.

15.2 The Vienna Convention on Diplomatic Relations of 1961 (VCDR) set aside the question of special missions for separate consideration and, following the preparation of a draft treaty, and discussions in the ILC and the UNGA Sixth Committee (the Legal Committee), the New York Convention on Special Missions was adopted in 1969, and entered into force in 1985. The United Kingdom signed in 1970, but has not ratified the Convention. Most other major European States have also chosen not to become parties with the exceptions of Switzerland, Austria, Spain, and Poland. The United States is not a signatory.

15.3 The small number of States Parties to the Convention—thirty-eight—is largely explained by an unwillingness on the part of Western European States, many of which already had substantial numbers of diplomatic missions in their capitals, to extend tax and customs privileges accorded in the New York Convention to the multiplicity of foreign officials who come and go on government business. These European States were prepared to guarantee diplomatic status including inviolability to high-level missions led by a Head of State, Head of Government, minister, or senior official, but more routine missions should, they believed, be content with the immunities to which their character as emissaries of a sovereign State entitled them, together with a lower level of privilege which could be defended on grounds of functional need. The majority of governments, however, did not accept this approach. The smaller countries took the view that they were much more likely than the European countries to send a special mission to a capital where they had no permanent diplomatic mission, with its additional possibilities of protection, and that to a certain extent special missions were the form of diplomacy best suited to the poorer countries. To give their ad hoc representatives an inferior status to ambassadors of the richer countries would thus amount to discrimination against them. This view prevailed and, as a consequence and as succinctly described by one commentator, the Convention confers 'a higher scale of privileges and immunities upon a narrower range of missions than the extant customary international law'.[1]

A 'special mission' is defined in Article 1(a) of the New York Convention on   **15.4**
Special Missions as a 'temporary mission, representing the State, which is sent by one State to another State with the consent of the latter for the purpose of dealing with it on specific questions or of performing in relation to it a specific task'. 'Temporary' distinguishes the special mission from the permanent diplomatic mission; 'representing the State' distinguishes the special mission from a parliamentary delegation, a football team, or a visiting orchestra carrying on a cultural exchange, since, whatever their sponsorship, they are not authorized to speak for the State, even when the State may assist in financing them; and 'specific questions' or 'specific task' defines the purpose of the special mission. The functions of the special missions are determined by mutual consent (Article 3) with the consent being 'previously obtained through the diplomatic or another agreed or mutually acceptable channel' (Article 2).

Despite the small number of States Parties, the Special Missions Convention   **15.5**
has had a significant impact on the development of rules of customary international law and there is now widespread acceptance of some of its basic principles. Nevertheless, it remains the case that not all of its provisions reflect customary international law.[2] As Wood explains, the customary rules have developed by analogy with permanent diplomatic missions, which have similar functional needs, while taking into account the temporary duration of the special mission.[3]

Consent of the receiving State is essential to conferment of immunity by means   **15.6**
of the procedure of a special mission. In the *Khurts Bat* case an English court held that a senior security officer sent by the State of Mongolia on a special

---

[1] J Crawford, *Brownlie's Principles of Public International Law* (8th edn, Oxford: Oxford University Press, 2012) 414.

[2] This was confirmed by a German court in the case of *Tabatabai*, 80 ILR 389.

[3] M Wood. 'The Immunity of Official Visitors', in A von Bogdany and R Wolfrum (eds), *Max Planck Yearbook of United Nations Law*, Vol 16, 2012, 35–98.

mission to the United Kingdom was not entitled to immunity; and ruled to that effect in reliance on a letter to the District Court from the Director of Protocol and Vice-Marshal of the Diplomatic Corps proving conclusively that the Foreign and Commonwealth Office (FCO) did not consent to the visit as a special mission: 'no invitation was issued, no meeting was arranged, no subjects of business were agreed or prepared'.[4] At the same time the FCO of the UK circulated a Note to diplomatic missions and international organizations in London stressing that 'under customary law a special mission is a temporary mission representing a state which is sent by one state to another with the consent of the latter in order to carry out official business. In this context "official business" will normally involve official contact with the authorities of the United Kingdom, such as a meeting with officials of her Majesty's Government, or attendance at a ceremonial occasion, for example a Royal Wedding.'[5] The Note also drew attention to the introduction of a new formal procedure designed to clarify the circumstances in which the UK consents to an official visit as a special mission. This procedure has been applied in subsequent cases where the UK has given special mission status to official visits by several controversial figures.[6] While there is still some uncertainty as to the precise content of the privileges and immunities under customary international law to which persons on special mission are entitled, it is generally accepted and now confirmed by the English Divisional Court that inviolability and immunity from criminal jurisdiction for the duration of the special mission are included.[7]

15.7   The Dutch government, in consultation with the Netherlands Advisory Committee on Public International Law (CAVV), has set out in a letter a useful summary of the four conditions which it requires to be met both by members of foreign official missions visiting the Netherlands and by members of Dutch official missions visiting other countries.

15.8   The four conditions to be met by such 'temporary' diplomats are:

(a) the official mission to be temporary in nature, (generally for 'a relatively short time, ranging from part of a day to a period of several weeks');

---

[4] *Khurts Bat v The Investigating Judge of the German Federal Court* [2011] EWHC 2028 (Admin), [2013] QB 349, (2012) 147 ILR 633 at paras 55–63, Moses LJ.

[5] Written Ministerial Statement (William Hague), House of Commons, 4 March 2013.

[6] e.g. Mahmoud Hegazy, the Egyptian Military Chief of Staff (*The Guardian*, 2 November 2015) and Tzipi Livni, the Israeli Justice Minister and Benny Gantz, the Israeli Military Chief of Staff (*The Guardian*, 13 May 2014).

[7] *R (Freedom and Justice Party and Others) v FCO, DPP, and Commissioner for the Metropolitan Police (Redress and Amnesty International as Interveners)* [2016] EWHC 3010 (Admin) Lloyd Jones LJ, Jay J.

(b) the mission to be 'from one state to another'. But 'this does not mean that all the members of an official mission must be government officials. They may include, for example, parliamentarians or representatives of the business community';

(c) 'an official mission must be a mission to the government of the receiving state';

(d) 'the receiving state must have consented to receive the mission in question'.

15.9 US practice on special missions (called 'special diplomatic missions') is similar to that of the UK and the Netherlands, with the US State Department submitting 'suggestions of immunity' for such missions to which the US has consented.[8]

15.10 The scale of facilities, privileges, and immunities provided for in the Convention (Articles 22 to 49) follows, with only relatively minor modifications, that provided in relation to permanent diplomatic missions by the VCDR. This includes, most importantly, inviolability of the person and immunity from criminal jurisdiction of members of special missions (Articles 29 and 31, para 1). It also includes immunity from civil and administrative jurisdiction, subject to the same exceptions as members of a permanent diplomatic mission plus an additional exception for 'an action for damages arising out of an accident caused by a vehicle used outside the official functions of the person concerned' (Article 31, para 2). This reflects general concerns about immunity in regard to motor accident claims particularly in capitals where there are substantial numbers of persons entitled to diplomatic immunity. Immunities and privileges are extended to subordinate staff and to nationals and permanent residents of the receiving State.[9]

15.11 Members of special missions enjoy transit rights across third States but only where the transit State has been informed in advance, either in the visa application or by notification and has raised no objection to it. This emphasizes that, as in the case of members of the diplomatic mission, there is no right of passage through a third State and that the third State must consent to the transit before being required to accord any special privilege to members of special missions.

---

[8] Restatement (Third) of US Foreign Relations Law, 1987, Vol 1, para 464, cmt i.

[9] Family members, however, receive privileges and immunities only if they accompany members of the special mission and provided they are not nationals or permanent residents of the receiving State.

Book IV

MULTILATERAL DIPLOMACY, HUMAN RIGHTS, AND INTERNATIONAL ORGANIZATIONS

16

THEORY AND PRACTICE OF MULTILATERAL DIPLOMACY

Emyr Jones Parry

As well as the legal aspects of multilateral diplomacy, dealt with in the preced- **16.1**
ing chapter, how it works in practice and theories about its role—shaping the
public perceptions of its institutions—need to be considered. The multilateral
approach to diplomacy became increasingly common post 1945. It was partly a
generic consequence of the modern state system, and partly a response to the
challenges of the post-war period when the Bretton Woods institutions and the
United Nations were finding their place. United States leadership was influential as a means of addressing economic, financial, and collective security challenges. The multilateral approach became increasingly common, not just in
formal organizations within the UN system, but as regional/global efforts grew
to address issues which concerned many countries, and were not confined to the
territory of one State. The realization that comprehensive solutions to certain
challenges for a State could not be met by that State acting alone, but required
cooperative action by several States, fuelled the need for multilateral approaches.
Indeed, the responses required cooperative action by many. Paradoxically, this
evolution of cooperative action was firmly anchored on the territorial integrity and the equality of States, while nevertheless helping to facilitate peaceful
change.

There are many examples, beginning with the United Nations itself. In 1949, **16.2**
the North Atlantic Council was established as a binding arrangement of collective defence among its members. The trend to establish organizations of States
for collective cooperation developed through geographic groupings and through
arrangements for functional cooperation in areas such as trade, human rights,
energy, and many more. This phenomenon accelerated quickly as the effects of
globalization became more apparent and countries were pushed to cooperate

together if its consequences were to be mitigated. Two examples suffice to make the point. Money laundering can only be combatted effectively if all States adopt common procedures to prevent it. Otherwise money, like water, will find the weakest point and enter. Similarly, an effective response to climate change requires commitment by most countries, and especially the largest economies. The outcome is that all States belong to several multilateral organizations, beginning with the universal membership of the United Nations, and then participation in geographical or functional arrangements depending on their interests. The obligations of membership of each organization are *sui generis*.

16.3   There is no single definition of multilateralism and yet it is easily recognizable when at least three countries are seen to be working together diplomatically to solve a supranational problem. It involves the importance of rules, institutionalized collective cooperation, and inclusiveness among the members of the group, who in turn decide who should belong. According to Keohane,[1] a truly global multilateral organization is open to States meeting specified criteria, embodied in publicly known rules that constrain activity and shape expectations of members, and allocate roles. While Ruggie[2] has defined it as 'action among three or more states on the basis of generalised principles of conduct… which offers members a rough equivalence of benefits in the aggregate and over time'. In essence too, multilateralism was seen as an effective, efficient technique to foster cooperation between independent States when the transaction costs of a multiplicity of bilateral agreements would be high, and when States are prepared to negotiate a beneficial outcome, often with no particular result favoured in advance. The saving in transaction costs is simply illustrated. A European Union of twenty-eight States would require a network of 378 bilateral agreements to replace the provisions of the Treaties which bind the twenty-eight. In general, multilateral institutions do not supersede States as the most important actors. After all they have been created by States and States dominate their decision-taking. They do reduce the costs of making and enforcing agreements, help share information about other States' policies, and encourage States to live up to their commitments. The result benefits international law and often encourages domestic reforms leading to better governance.

16.4   The process of getting to agreement in a multilateral forum is by necessity invariably more complex then a bilateral negotiation between two States. Negotiations require a member State to be very clear about its objectives, to understand and take account of the interests of many other parties, and frequently to be prepared

---

[1] R O Keohane, *Garnet Working Paper,* University of Warwick, 09/06 (1992).
[2] J Ruggie, 'Multilateralism' (1992) 46(3) *International Organization* 561–98.

to compromise to obtain an agreement acceptable to all. Obviously each party needs to be satisfied with the overall outcome and to derive some national advantage and/or believe that there is a wider benefit. The multilateral diplomat will by definition spend much time with the colleagues from other States represented in the organization. Relations with those colleagues is a vital element of multilateral work, as is the trust engendered by working cooperatively for shared objectives. That cooperation can be fostered, or indeed impeded, by contacts between ministries in the capitals of the States concerned. All international organizations have some secretariat. Its role can be helpful as a source of knowledge and advice, and it is invariably useful to be on good terms with the secretariat.

Multilateralism began more as cooperation in defined areas, mutual undertak- **16.5** ings by a group of States to implement agreements, sometimes with a degree of enforcement but not governance. Over the years, the architecture of multilateralism has become more varied, more comprehensive, and an element of governance has emerged. This last dimension raises the acceptability of process to justify actions. Multilateralism therefore exhibits different forms:

- institutionalized, where rules-based international organizations are established. The World Trade Organization is an example.
- arrangements which may include a forum for discussion, accompanied by an element of choice as to whether to accede to elements which become binding on appropriate national ratification. Examples would be Conventions adopted in the United Nations General Assembly and which are then open to accession by individual States, or the European Convention of Human Rights, within membership of the Council of Europe;
- emerging areas, where new international rules and organizations are being established, often driven by events. Examples are the International Criminal Tribunal for the former Yugoslavia, the International Criminal Court, and the continuing efforts to deal with climate change;
- aspirational recommendations, where in the absence of binding rules, norms should inform foreign policy behaviour. The Responsibility to Protect doctrine, included in the agreed conclusions of the 2005 General Assembly Summit, has no legal authority, but represents a set of principles which should influence States' response to a crisis;
- a system of supranational law and multilateral governance, as in the European Union. This can involve a transfer of some sovereignty from the member State to permit agreement to binding provisions in a specific area. The justification is that the Union is then able to act to the benefit of all of its members, an advantage which would not be as available to the State acting alone. Similarly, the United Nations Security Council can adopt certain resolutions which,

because of their legal base and language, are binding on each of the member States of the United Nations, regardless of their national law.

16.6 The routes by which States come to favour multilateralism are varied.[3] Some States are individualistic, entering into contractual relations in a rational, self-interested way. They may want to discourage unilateralism and see the multilateral forum as giving the smaller State a voice which might otherwise not be possible. For others it may stem from the identity/power of the State, its beliefs and norms, capacity to persuade and be persuaded. At times, powerful States choose not to participate in agreements, thus much reducing their potential effectiveness—the United States chose to stay outside the Kyoto Protocol on climate change and the International Criminal Court. Still others favour an approach which gives primacy to institutions and processes and where state sovereignty is more a relational concept than an absolute.

16.7 Legitimacy is a crucial element in the acceptability, and indeed durability, of a multilateral organization. This can stem from a normative process where practices and aims meet a set of defined values and standards that have been defended and furthered. Or it can result sociologically, a matter-of-fact legitimacy when the organization's actions are accepted as appropriate and worthy of being respected by relevant audiences. These coincide naturally when the relevant audience endorses the normative aspect too. Achievement of legitimacy can be assessed in two ways. Firstly, if the results of action by the organization achieve its purposes, for example if the United Nations Security Council produces improved international peace and security in a given crisis. Secondly, if the process of decision-taking is accepted by the audience, which is itself sufficiently representative, diverse, and inclusive.

16.8 Discussion of legitimacy relates more to the action of States than it does to the responses of individuals. International organizations often fail to meet today's expectations of democracy and accountability in the way that governments aim to do. This challenge to the multilateral approach is in part a challenge to the State. Security problems are often more intra- than inter-State. Trade and economic activity is predominantly private-sector and less easy to regulate. Civil society and non-governmental organizations are more international, drive global norms, and monitor performance. Human rights and governance issues intrude on state sovereignty. Against that background, multilateral organizations tend to justify their actions by arguing that their individual member governments act according to their own national procedures and that the organization's

---

[3] J A Caporaso, International Relations Theory and Multilateralism: The Search for Foundations 599–632.

legitimacy stems from effective collective decisions of a diverse membership. The organization seldom has any direct accountability to the public in the member States. But the governments participating in the decision are themselves accountable to their own public by those national procedures.

Today's United Nations has a particular legitimacy, stemming from universal **16.9** membership of 193 States, founded on the basis of sovereign equality rather than democratic principles. It tackles challenges that no one State can solve, taking its decisions by agreed processes, often based on obtaining a consensus of members, that is to say, with no State objecting. Hopefully, the results too justify the action. The Security Council can provide legitimacy for the use of armed force in circumstances going beyond the right of a State to self-defence, including collective defence. Ultimately, the justification of the United Nations is that it reflects an imperfect real world which sits between unconstrained power politics and Panglossian peace and harmony. As Dag Hammarskjöld, the second Secretary-General, put it: 'it was created not to take humanity to heaven, but to save it from hell'.

How then does multilateral performance rate? Critics point to failures in many **16.10** conflicts, and an inability by the Security Council to agree measures to tackle them. The efficiency of service delivery is easily criticized. There are persistent abuses of human rights, civil wars, failed States, post-conflict recidivism as fighting again breaks out, and continuing threats from weapons of mass destruction. The United Nations seldom acts with the efficiency of a single State, and is often portrayed as slow and bureaucratic. Sometimes effective multilateral action follows unilateral state action, for example UN action in Bosnia followed that of the United States. Again, critics argue that many of the States taking decisions are themselves either undemocratic or only partially democratic. None of this is surprising as decisions of the Council have to carry the requisite majority and ensure that there is no veto by a Permanent Member. This requires decisions to be compatible with the interests of those Members.

In an imperfect world advantages and disadvantages of the multilateral approach **16.11** are evident. Daily, international organizations and the UN family demonstrate the good that results from their work. The goal is to agree and implement effective policies to cope with the myriad of challenges which confront the world. Judgment is made on the basis of successful action, but also on those cases where the international community failed to act.

Multilateralism in the twentieth century provided institutionalized collective **16.12** action to deal with security threats, development, human rights, and so on. Legitimacy demands were modest and action was seldom intrusive against the wishes of an individual Member State. This century's challenges are greater, more diverse, and in many ways more difficult, demanding, and intrusive. It is not only to combat weapons of mass destruction, but to eliminate terrorism and the risk of terrorists obtaining such weapons. How are the weak and vulnerable to be protected when their own government cannot protect them, or worse, is itself the agent for their oppression? The Responsibility to Protect doctrine described in Chapter 2 offers some comfort. Policy prescriptions are likely to be more intrusive of state sovereignty and therefore more difficult to agree and implement. The contradiction between respecting national sovereignty and approving action which would impinge on that sovereignty is an enduring challenge to getting agreement.

16.13　History shows that multilateralism, its forms and institutions, have evolved, although not sufficiently. Kohler[4] has pointed out that historically States have sought to protect their interests by insisting on unanimity for decisions. Obviously this makes agreement more difficult, especially as membership of the organization grows. This has produced a trend of decision-making by some form of qualified majority, which in turn produces a tension for those States who are reluctant to countenance the possibility of being outvoted. On the other hand it can be argued that the decline of the practice of unanimity has led to an increase in non-binding declarations.[5] As challenges and priorities change, as external and internal dynamics move, as independence in the financial world becomes even more limited, as civil society and global multinational corporations flex muscles, and as the norms and values of what constitutes international society become more relevant, so multilateral institutions must adapt and change further if they are to be capable of taking the decisions necessary to meet the serious problems they confront. That in essence is the test for the multilateral diplomat. Conferences, a principal mechanism for multilateral diplomacy, are dealt with in Chapter 30.

---

[4] M Kohler, *Multilateral Organization* (Massachusetts: Massachusetts Institute of Technology, 1992) 681–708.

[5] P Sands and P Klein, *Bowett's Law of International Institutions* (6th edn, London: Sweet and Maxwell, 2009) ch 11.

17

HUMAN RIGHTS

Amal Clooney

Introduction

Every State that is a member of the United Nations has made a commitment to **17.1** uphold human rights.[1] Today, a State's human rights record is routinely scrutinized by the UN and in the media, and compliance with human rights obligations can define a State's reputation and relations with other States. Diplomats are also increasingly involved in speaking out on behalf of their State about human rights abuses, whether or not these are committed against the State's

---

[1] See paragraph **17.13**.

own citizens. They are also expected to respond to allegations of human rights abuses levelled against their government.

17.2 The idea that there are rights that all humans inherently possess is not new. In the English-speaking world, a written charter of rights has existed since at least 1215, when the King of England agreed to sign Magna Carta, guaranteeing that '[n]o free man shall be taken or imprisoned, or be disseised of his freehold or liberties...but by...the law of the land'.

17.3 When the United Nations was created, such principles became international. The UN's founding Charter, adopted in 1945, refers to the promotion of respect for human rights as one of the Organization's purposes. The Universal Declaration of Human Rights was adopted three years later, recognizing certain global human rights in thirty numbered articles. These include civil and political rights such as the right to free speech and protest, but also economic, social, and cultural rights like the right to food, housing, work, health, and education. Its drafters hoped that it would 'become the international Magna Carta of all men everywhere'.[2]

17.4 The Universal Declaration is not a binding treaty, but it was proclaimed by the General Assembly and provides the first definition of the concept of 'human rights' that appears in the UN Charter. Many of its provisions also served as the foundation for the UN human rights treaties that came to be adopted in subsequent decades.

17.5 Before the United Nations was created, it was generally accepted that the rulers of sovereign States could do as they wished to their citizens within their own borders, without challenge on the international plane. But the atrocities of the Second World War challenged this assumption. As French jurist René Cassin, one of the Universal Declaration's framers, argued in 1947: 'we do not want a repetition of what happened in 1933, where Germany began to massacre its own nationals, and everybody...bowed, saying "Thou art sovereign and master in thine own house"'.[3]

17.6 Today, all States have ratified treaties that define their human rights obligations and the ability of individuals under their jurisdiction to seek redress outside the State's borders. This reflects a relinquishment of sovereignty, but it is voluntary, and States still control the extent of their human rights obligations

---

[2] Eleanor Roosevelt, 'Statement to the United Nations General Assembly on the Universal Declaration of Human Rights', quoted in Mary Ann Glendon, *The Forum and the Tower: How Scholars and Politicians Have Imagined the World, from Plato to Eleanor Roosevelt* (New York: Oxford University Press, 2011) 217.

[3] Mary Ann Glendon, *A World Made New: Eleanor Roosevelt and the Universal Declaration of Human Rights* (New York: Random House, 2002) 60.

by deciding which treaties to ratify and which enforcement mechanisms to be a party to. The continuing relevance of state sovereignty is also reflected in Article 2.7 of the UN Charter, which provides that 'nothing contained in the present Charter shall authorize the United Nations to intervene in matters which are essentially within the domestic jurisdiction of any state'.

The reach of Article 2.7 is however limited to matters that are 'essentially' within **17.7** the domestic jurisdiction of a State, and it is increasingly accepted that human rights are issues of global concern.[4] Article 2.7 also states that the principle of non-intervention 'shall not prejudice the application of enforcement measures [taken by the Security Council] under Chapter VII' of the UN Charter to maintain or restore international peace and security.

Some take the view that the UN Security Council not only has a right but also **17.8** a *duty* to intervene in the case of egregious human rights violations because the Council has a 'responsibility to protect populations from genocide, war crimes, ethnic cleansing and crimes against humanity'.[5] The elements of this doctrine of 'responsibility to protect'[6] or 'R2P' were endorsed by the UN Secretary-General and 150 Heads of State and Government at the 2005 World Summit[7] after the UN Secretary-General called for States to agree to 'the principle that massive and systematic violations of human rights...should not be allowed to stand'.[8]

Advocates of the responsibility to protect doctrine point to its invocation as a **17.9** basis for two Security Council resolutions authorizing military force to protect civilians in Libya in 2011.[9] These were described by the UN Legal Counsel as the 'first fully-fledged "R2P resolutions"'.[10] But the Council's inaction in other human rights crises since then, including in Syria, shows that for the time being Security Council members do not consider the doctrine to be a legal requirement for action or a legal basis alone to authorize such action.

---

[4] Human Rights Committee, 'General Comment 31' (29 March 2004) UN Doc CCPR/C/21/Rev.1/Add.13; See also *Barcelona Traction, Light and Power Company, Limited (Belgium v Spain)* (Second Phase) [1970] ICJ Reports 3.

[5] GA resolution 60/1 (24 October 2005) UN Doc A/RES/60/1.

[6] See Chapter 2, paragraphs 2.21–2.24.

[7] See GA resolution 60/1 (n 5).

[8] Kofi A Annan, 'Annual Report to the General Assembly' (20 September 1999) UN Doc SG/SM/7136.

[9] See SC resolution 1970 (26 February 2011) UN Doc S/RES/1970; SC resolution 1973 (17 March 2011) UN Doc S/RES/1973.

[10] Patricia O'Brien, 'The Responsibility to Protect—Inception, conceptualization, operationalization and implementation of a new concept' (Opening statement at the Human Rights Committee of the Association of the Bar of the City of New York, 7 February 2012), available at <http://legal.un.org/ola/media/info_from_lc/4_POB%20at%20ABCNY%20Human%20Rights%20Cttee.pdf>.

17.10 The United Kingdom has also argued that there is a doctrine of 'humanitarian intervention' according to which it is not unlawful for a State to use force against another State, without Security Council authority, in cases of serious human rights violations amounting to an 'overwhelming humanitarian catastrophe'. This is provided that there is convincing and generally accepted evidence of extreme humanitarian distress; that it is objectively clear that there is no practicable alternative to the use of force if lives are to be saved; and that the proposed use of force is necessary and proportionate to the aim of relief of humanitarian need.[11]

17.11 The UK has invoked this doctrine to justify limited uses of force for the establishment of safe havens and no-fly zones to protect Kurds and other civilians in Iraq, and the subsequent, more extensive use of force in Kosovo in the 1990s.[12] However, like the 'responsibility to protect', the status of the doctrine of humanitarian intervention as a legal basis for unilateral military action to protect human rights remains disputed.

Sources of International Human Rights Law

17.12 States' international human rights obligations are derived from both treaties and customary international law.

Core International Human Rights Treaties

17.13 The UN Charter was the first treaty to call for the protection of human rights in peacetime. It refers in its preamble to 'faith in fundamental human rights, in the dignity and worth of the human person, in the equal rights of men and women and of nations large and small'. Articles 1 and 55 of the Charter refer to one of the purposes of the UN as 'promoting and encouraging respect for human rights and for fundamental freedoms for all without distinction as to race, sex, language, or religion'. And, under Article 56, '[a]ll Members pledge themselves to take joint and separate action in co-operation with the Organization for the achievement of the [these] purposes'.

---

[11] See UK Prime Minister's Office, 'Chemical weapon use by Syrian regime: UK government legal position' (29 August 2013), available at <http://www.gov.uk/government/publications/chemical-weapon-use-by-syrian-regime-uk-government-legal-position/chemical-weapon-use-by-syrian-regime-uk-government-legal-position-html-version>.

[12] See Defence Committee, *Intervention: Why, When and How?: Government Response to the Committee's Fourteenth Report of Session 2013–14* (HC 2014–15, 581) 12–15.

It took another two decades of negotiations before specialized human rights **17.14** treaties entered into force.[13] In 1966, two of the UN's 'core' international human rights treaties—the International Covenant on Civil and Political Rights (ICCPR) and the International Covenant on Economic, Social and Cultural Rights (ICESCR)—were adopted. Together with the Universal Declaration they form a trio of documents known collectively as the 'International Bill of Human Rights'.[14]

The two covenants added flesh to the bare-bones descriptions of human **17.15** rights in the Universal Declaration and both treaties have since been widely ratified. A total of 168 States are parties to the ICCPR and 164 States are parties to the ICESCR.[15]

The ICCPR is arguably the most significant human rights treaty as it focuses on **17.16** individual rights and includes a number of explicit prohibitions on government conduct across a broad range of subjects. Under the treaty, a government cannot impose slavery, use torture, or discriminate between individuals based on race, religion, or gender. It cannot impose criminal laws *ex post facto* or interfere with freedom of thought, conscience, and religion. Nor can it restrain free speech, movement, assembly, association, or privacy except on defined grounds set out in the treaty.

The ICESCR sets out a different type of obligation. A State that is a party to the **17.17** ICESCR is required 'to take steps...to the maximum of its available resources, with a view to achieving progressively the full realization of the rights recognized' in that treaty. This 'best efforts' obligation is different to the specific undertakings and prohibitions that characterize the ICCPR, and as a consequence the scope for identifying and remedying a violation of the ICESCR is more limited.[16]

In addition to the two covenants, eight other 'core' international human rights **17.18** treaties have been concluded.[17] Two of these, the 1984 Convention against

---

[13] Although the Genocide Convention, considered at paragraph 17.20, came into force on 12 January 1951.

[14] See UN Office of the High Commissioner for Human Rights, 'Fact Sheet No 2 (Rev 1), The International Bill of Rights', available at <http://www.ohchr.org/Documents/Publications/FactSheet2Rev.1en.pdf>.

[15] As of 20 February 2016.

[16] See Committee on Economic, Social and Cultural Rights, 'General Comment No 3' (14 December 1990) UN Doc E/1991/23.

[17] UNOHCHR, *The Core International Human Rights Treaties* (United Nations Publications, 2006).

Torture[18] and its 2002 Optional Protocol,[19] prohibit States from subjecting individuals to torture and other forms of cruel, inhuman, and degrading treatment. The other six deal with enforced disappearance,[20] racial discrimination,[21] women's rights,[22] children's rights,[23] migrant workers,[24] and the disabled.[25] The most recent treaty, on enforced disappearance, was adopted in 2006. The most widely ratified, on children's rights, requires only one more ratification (that of the United States) to become universal.

Other International Human Rights Treaties

17.19 Most human rights treaties have one or more protocols supplementing the obligations contained in it. Some of these protocols impose further substantive obligations: the second Optional Protocol to the ICCPR, for example, outlaws the death penalty. Other protocols allow individuals to take their case to an international committee that can determine whether there have been violations of the treaty once domestic remedies have been exhausted. For example, the first Optional Protocol to the ICCPR grants individuals the right to bring their case to the UN Human Rights Committee,[26] and similar protocols allow individuals to file complaints before corresponding committees monitoring compliance with the other core treaties.

17.20 There are also treaties dealing with international criminal law, refugee law, and employment law that protect human rights in different ways. For instance, the Genocide Convention requires States to prevent and punish genocide[27] and the Rome Statute of the International Criminal Court sets out rules on criminal

---

[18] Convention against Torture and Other Cruel, Inhuman or Degrading Treatment or Punishment (adopted 10 December 1984, entered into force 26 June 1987) 1465 UNTS 85.

[19] Optional Protocol to the Convention against Torture and Other Cruel, Inhuman or Degrading Treatment or Punishment (adopted 18 December 2002, entered into force 22 June 2006) 2375 UNTS 237.

[20] International Convention for the Protection of All Persons from Enforced Disappearance (adopted 20 December 2006, entered into force 23 December 2010) 2716 UNTS 3.

[21] International Convention on the Elimination of All Forms of Racial Discrimination (adopted 7 March 1966, entered into force 4 January 1969) 660 UNTS 195.

[22] Convention on the Elimination of All Forms of Discrimination against Women (adopted 18 December 1979, entered into force 3 September 1981) 1249 UNTS 13.

[23] Convention on the Rights of the Child (adopted 20 November 1989, entered into force 2 September 1990) 1577 UNTS 3.

[24] International Convention on the Protection of the Rights of All Migrant Workers and Members of their Families (adopted 18 December 1990, entered into force 1 July 2003) 2220 UNTS 3.

[25] Convention on the Rights of Persons with Disabilities (adopted 13 December 2006, entered into force 3 May 2008) 2515 UNTS 3.

[26] See paragraph 17.55.

[27] See e.g. *Application of the Convention on the Prevention and Punishment of the Crime of Genocide (Bosnia and Herzegovina v Serbia and Montenegro)* [2007] ICJ Reports 43.

accountability of individuals for genocide and other international crimes. The Convention relating to the Status of Refugees guarantees the right of refugees not to be forced to return to a country where their lives or freedom would be threatened on account of their national, racial, religious, social, or political identity. And the treaties promulgated by the International Labour Organization protect the rights of employees.

Regional Treaties

Regional human rights treaties governing Europe, Africa, and Latin America exist in parallel with international human rights treaties. Each of the regional treaties sets out the human rights obligations of governments and establishes a court or commission, or both, to deal with individual complaints.   **17.21**

The European system is the oldest and most developed, with a mandate to supervise compliance by the forty-seven countries that make up the Council of Europe with the European Convention on Human Rights.[28] The Convention was adopted in 1950 and, like the UN human rights treaties, was based on the Universal Declaration. The list of civil and political rights in the original treaty has been supplemented over the years by additional protocols, and the Strasbourg-based European Court of Human Rights has issued thousands of detailed judgments interpreting the provisions of the Convention as a 'living instrument'.[29] In most European States the Convention has also been incorporated into domestic law and can be invoked in national courts.   **17.22**

The Inter-American system consists of three human rights instruments. The first is the 1948 Charter of the Organization of American States (OAS)—an organization that comprises thirty-five States[30]—which includes some general references to human rights.[31] The second is the 1948 American Declaration on the Rights and Duties of Man, a high-level document focused on human rights that predated even the Universal Declaration.   **17.23**

The third human rights treaty within the OAS system is the American Convention on Human Rights,[32] a detailed charter of rights that entered into force in 1978, to which twenty-three of the thirty-five OAS member States are parties.[33] Most of the rights in the American Convention are derived from the ICCPR   **17.24**

---

[28] As of 20 February 2016.
[29] *Johnston and Others v Ireland* (1987) 9 EHRR 203, para 53.
[30] As of 20 February 2016
[31] See Chapter 23 for further information about the OAS.
[32] American Convention on Human Rights (adopted 22 November 1969, entered into force 18 July 1978) 1144 UNTS 144.
[33] As of 20 February 2016.

but some of them are expressed in terms distinctive to the Americas. For instance, there is a guarantee that the right to life 'shall be protected by law and, in general, from the moment of conception'.

17.25 The Inter-American Court of Human Rights adjudicates cases arising under the Convention. Its case law has grown significantly in the last two decades and States are increasingly amending national legislation to bring it into conformity with the Convention and avoid negative rulings. The system is however held back by the fact that the US and Canada, as well as some Caribbean States, are not parties to the Convention.

17.26 There is also an African Charter on Human and Peoples' Rights,[34] which was adopted three years after its inter-American counterpart entered into force, in 1981. It sets out human rights obligations for the fifty-four States[35] that make up the African Union.[36] Although the Charter provides that interpretation of its terms should 'draw inspiration from international law on human and peoples' rights',[37] it frames certain rights in a more limited fashion than its European and Inter-American counterparts. For instance, there is no explicit right to privacy or prohibition on forced labour. The provisions concerning arrest and fair trial, political participation, and freedom of conscience are also less comprehensive than those in the ICCPR.

17.27 In other ways, the African Charter is more expansive than its regional counterparts. It protects economic and social as well as civil and political rights. It is also the first human rights convention to explicitly recognize 'peoples' rights' in its title. These are defined in the treaty as including rights to self-determination, to sovereignty over natural resources, to peace, and to 'a generally satisfactory environment favourable to their development'.[38] And unlike the European and Inter-American treaties, the African Charter does not contain a derogation clause, leaving open the question of whether any rights in the African Charter are derogable when there is a public emergency.[39]

17.28 Asia does not currently have a regional human rights treaty, but there is an Arab Charter on Human Rights[40] which was adopted in 2004 and subsequently rat-

---

[34] African Charter on Human and Peoples' Rights (adopted 27 June 1981, entered into force 21 October 1986) 1520 UNTS 217.

[35] As of 20 February 2016. All but one of the fifty-four States have ratified the Charter. The newest African State, South Sudan, has not yet done so.

[36] See Chapter 23 for further information about the AU.

[37] African Charter (n 34) Art 60.

[38] Ibid, Art 24.

[39] See paragraphs 17.33–17.37.

[40] Arab Charter on Human Rights (adopted 22 May 2004, entered into force 15 March 2008) (2005) 12 IHRR 893.

ified by thirteen States. This treaty has been criticized on the basis that its terms are more restrictive than its regional or international counterparts, though there is a guarantee under Article 43 that '[n]othing in this Charter may be construed or interpreted as impairing the rights and freedoms protected by the . . . laws . . . set forth in the international and regional human rights instruments which the states parties have adopted or ratified'.

There is currently no court with jurisdiction to interpret the Arab Charter's **17.29** provisions or resolve individual claims and the committee overseeing implementation of the Arab Charter has been largely inactive. Although the establishment of an Arab Court of Human Rights was approved 'in principle' by the Arab League in March 2014, the Court has not been established.[41] The draft of the Court's Statute was also criticized on the basis that there is no individual right to petition the Court (i.e. cases can only be filed by States) and insufficient guarantees of judicial independence.[42]

In addition to the Arab Charter, a Human Rights Declaration was adopted on **17.30** 18 November 2012 by the Association of Southeast Asian Nations (ASEAN).[43] This details the human rights commitments made to the 600 million people living in the region by the ten ASEAN member States.[44] The ASEAN Declaration was inspired by the Universal Declaration and covers economic and social rights as well as civil and political ones. It includes some rights not explicitly recognized in other instruments such as 'the right to a safe, clean and sustainable environment', protection from discrimination for 'people suffering from communicable diseases, including HIV/AIDS', and the right to peace. But like the Arab Charter, the Declaration has been criticized for failing to include several key rights. The ASEAN Declaration also includes a sweeping caveat that 'the realization of human rights must be considered in the regional and national context'.

Non-State Actors

The human rights obligations that are defined in international treaties apply **17.31** explicitly to States. States ratify the treaties and the obligations contained within them are addressed to organs of the State including the executive, legislative, and judicial branches. But under some treaties, the State is required not only to

---

[41] As of 20 February 2016. See Decision No 539 of the League of Arab States Summit Council of 26 March 2014.

[42] See International Commission of Jurists, 'The Arab Court of Human Rights: A Flawed Statute for an Ineffective Court', available at <http://icj.wpengine.netdna-cdn.com/wp-content/uploads/2015/04/MENA-Arab-Court-of-Human-Rights-Publications-Report-2015-ENG.pdf>.

[43] See Chapter 23 for further information about ASEAN.

[44] As of 20 February 2016.

respect the rights of individuals but also to protect them and ensure that they can be exercised. This has been interpreted to mean that States Parties must also see to it that the human rights of their inhabitants are not violated by others, including by private parties subject to the State's jurisdiction or authority.[45]

17.32 Some international instruments also describe the human rights obligations of non-State entities. For instance, the United Nations' Guiding Principles on Business and Human Rights call directly on business enterprises to 'respect' human rights.[46] The Security Council also often refers in its resolutions to the human rights obligations of actors other than States. Resolutions have for instance addressed human rights violations by 'all parties', 'factions', and 'armed groups', as well as specific terrorist organizations such as ISIL.[47] Outside these contexts, the extent to which non-State entities have human rights obligations is controversial.

Derogations and Reservations

17.33 Most human rights are not absolute and can accordingly be restricted under certain circumstances. For instance, a State must permit free expression under Article 19 of the ICCPR, but this can be restricted to the extent necessary to protect the rights of others, national security, public order, or public health and morals.

17.34 There are a small number of human rights that are absolute under international law, meaning that they cannot legally be restricted under any circumstances. For example, under the ICCPR, the right to be free from torture and enslavement and the right not to be prosecuted under *ex post facto* laws are absolute. They are also 'non-derogable', meaning that States cannot suspend the obligation to uphold them in times of emergency.

17.35 Some rights are not absolute, but still cannot be subject to derogation. These are sometimes identified in a treaty. For instance, Article 4(2) of the ICCPR lists a number of non-derogable rights including the right to life and the right to freedom of thought, conscience, and religion.

17.36 Rights that are 'derogable' can lawfully be suspended if a State is facing a public emergency 'which threatens the life of the nation', such as aggression by another

---

[45] See e.g. Committee on Economic, Social and Cultural Rights, 'General Comment No 14' (11 August 2000) UN Doc E/C.12/2000/4, para 35; Human Rights Committee, 'General Comment No 31' (29 March 2004) UN Doc CCPR/C/21/Rev.1/Add.13, para 8.

[46] See UNOHCHR, 'Guiding Principles on Business and Human Rights: Implementing the United Nations "Protect, Respect and Remedy" Framework' (2011) UN Doc HR/PUB/11/04.

[47] See e.g. SC resolution 2249 (20 November 2015) UN Doc S/RES/2249.

State or a major natural disaster. Derogations may also need to be notified to a specified body. For instance, there must be notification to the UN Secretary-General in accordance with Article 4 of the ICCPR or to the Secretary General of the Council of Europe under Article 15 of the European Convention if rights under those treaties are to be subject to a valid derogation.

Rights may be derogated from only to the extent required by the circumstances. **17.37** In the past, some governments—such as that of President Mubarak in Egypt—sought to declare permanent states of emergency lasting several decades. Although there is no time limit on a derogation as such, the UN Human Rights Committee has questioned the validity of such a long-term derogation.[48]

States can also seek to amend their treaty-based human rights obligations by **17.38** entering declarations or reservations to treaties that they ratify. But like derogations, reservations declared by a State will not necessarily be legally valid.

Many human rights treaties do not specifically address the issue of reservations **17.39** and much of the law relating to the impact of reservations is unsettled.[49] It is however clear that a reservation to any treaty cannot be valid if it is incompatible with the object and purpose of the treaty. A State could not, for instance, validly enter a sweeping reservation to a human rights treaty stating that the treaty only applies to the extent that it is compatible with domestic law. Reservations that offend peremptory norms would also by definition be incompatible with the object and purpose of a human rights treaty and consequently be invalid.[50]

Customary International Law

Some of the rights guaranteed by the principal human rights treaties are now **17.40** also protected under customary international law. This means that these rights must be respected even by States which are not party to those treaties.

The International Court of Justice (ICJ) has established that customary inter- **17.41** national law prohibits genocide[51] and torture.[52] The Human Rights Committee

---

[48] UN General Assembly, 'Report of the Human Rights Committee' (7 October 1993) UN Doc A/48/40 (Part I), para 704.

[49] See Chapter 35, paragraphs 35.42–35.45.

[50] Vienna Convention on the Law of Treaties (adopted 22 May 1969, entered into force 27 January 1980) 1155 UNTS 331, Art 19. See also Human Rights Committee, 'General Comment No 24' (4 November 1994) UN Doc CCPR/C/21/Rev.1/Add.6.

[51] See e.g. *Application of the Convention on the Prevention and Punishment of the Crime of Genocide (Bosnia and Herzegovina v Serbia and Montenegro)* (n 27), para 161.

[52] See *Questions relating to the Obligation to Prosecute or Extradite (Belgium v Senegal)* [2012] ICJ Reports 422, para 99.

has also identified a number of ICCPR provisions which, in its view, represent customary international law. These include the prohibitions on slavery and arbitrary detention and the guarantee of freedom of thought, conscience, and religion.[53]

Enforcement Mechanisms

17.42 Human rights are enforced by domestic and international courts, a host of UN bodies, and a system of bilateral, regional, and international sanctions. These methods of enforcement vary widely in their scope and effectiveness.

UN Human Rights Council

17.43 The UN Human Rights Council is one of the principal UN bodies tasked with monitoring and enforcing international human rights law.[54] It was established on the recommendation of the UN Secretary-General in 2006 to replace its predecessor, the controversial Commission on Human Rights, which had become so politicized that it 'cast a shadow on the reputation of the United Nations system as a whole'.[55] The new body was designed to have tighter entry requirements and function more objectively.

17.44 The Council is a subsidiary body of the UN General Assembly. It is based in Geneva and made up of forty-seven UN member States. It meets for at least three sessions each year, for a total of at least ten weeks. Its member States are elected by a majority of the General Assembly and voting takes place by secret ballot. All regional blocs are represented on the Council, and no State may have more than two consecutive three-year terms. Members may be suspended for gross and systemic human rights violations by a vote of two-thirds of the UN General Assembly present and voting. This led to Libya's temporary suspension in 2011.

17.45 The Council's main function is to investigate and report on States' human rights performance. It issues public resolutions condemning violations of human rights law by States and suggests appropriate remedies. It establishes fact-finding mechanisms to report on gross human rights violations around the world, such

---

[53] Human Rights Committee, 'General Comment No 24' (n 50), para 8. See also Restatement (Third) of the Foreign Relations Law of the United States, s 702 (1987). See paragraph 17.55 for further information about the Human Rights Committee.

[54] See also Chapter 19.

[55] Kofi A Annan, 'Secretary-General's Address to the Commission on Human Rights' (Geneva 7 April 2005), available at <http://www.un.org/sg/STATEMENTS/index.asp?nid=1388>.

as the Commission of Inquiry on Syria and its counterpart on Gaza. It coordinates the work of the UN treaty bodies and other human rights experts. And it supervises the Universal Periodic Review (UPR) process, a public assessment of the human rights record of all 193 UN member States that takes place every four years. The Council also has a complaints procedure whereby individuals and civil society actors can bring allegations of human rights violations to it directly, but since this takes place entirely behind closed doors its value is difficult to discern.

National human rights institutions and non-governmental organizations that **17.46** hold consultative status with the UN Economic and Social Council can submit written statements to the Council and speak in debates. This is a useful means by which the Council is informed about human rights developments at the national level. It also contributes to the value of the UPR process.

Although it is facilitated by the Council, the UPR is essentially a peer-review **17.47** system, meaning that every State has the right to comment on the human rights compliance of every other State and make recommendations for reform. At the end of the review, which includes the compilation of reports on a State's performance by the UN and an oral hearing in Geneva, each State receives a list of recommendations from other States and must report at the next review on its progress in implementing the recommendations that it has accepted to take on board.

The horizontal nature of the review process means that in some cases States with **17.48** poor human rights records criticize the human rights records of other countries that are considered to be more advanced in this area. For instance, in April 2013, the Democratic People's Republic of Korea expressed 'concerns regarding violations of the rights to peaceful assembly and freedom of expression, torture, racial discrimination and xenophobia' in Canada.[56] Meanwhile, Iran urged the United States to 'put on trial its gross violators of human rights and its war criminals and accede to [the International Criminal Court]', a court to which Iran itself has not acceded.[57] States have also complained that having over a hundred recommendations can be unwieldy and lead to difficulties in monitoring compliance.

The Council has attracted some of the same criticisms as its predecessor, the **17.49** most serious being that since many of its members have been States with unimpressive human rights records, it is still the case that 'the firefighters' are

---

[56] UN Human Rights Council, 'Report of the Working Group on the Universal Periodic Review—Canada' (28 June 2013) UN Doc A/HRC/24/11, para 23.
[57] UNHRC, 'Report of the Working Group on the Universal Periodic Review—United States of America' (4 January 2011) UN Doc A/HRC/16/11, para 92.175.

also 'the arsonists'.[58] Nevertheless its mandate has been renewed by the General Assembly and there are no significant proposals for reform under discussion.

UN Office of the High Commissioner for Human Rights

17.50   The Office of the High Commissioner for Human Rights was established in 1993 by the UN General Assembly and is based in Geneva. It is staffed by UN employees and its mandate is to coordinate human rights protection throughout the UN system and provide staff to support the work of the Human Rights Council and associated bodies. The High Commissioner also has eleven country offices and eight regional offices monitoring and reporting on human rights abuses on the ground.

17.51   The Commissioner has become the principal UN spokesperson on human rights issues: the 'human rights policeman' who issues statements that name and shame States that violate international human rights norms. The impact of the Office is therefore shaped to a large extent by the personality and skills of the incumbent.

17.52   The Commissioner also provides technical assistance to States. Recent practice includes training Tunisian law enforcement officials on prison reform and advising Sri Lanka on establishing a judicial process to establish accountability for human rights violations spanning several decades.[59]

UN Treaty Bodies

17.53   The UN treaty bodies are committees of unpaid experts who monitor national implementation of the core international human rights instruments. States that are parties to a treaty can nominate their nationals to serve on a committee, and all States Parties may then vote to elect the members. Once elected, experts serve in their personal capacity.

17.54   The committees monitor compliance with UN human rights treaties in two main ways: through periodic country reports issued by the committee describing the compliance by a member State with a treaty; and through the adjudication of individual complaints filed by persons residing in these States.

17.55   The Human Rights Committee is the most established of the treaty bodies and its mandate is to monitor compliance with the ICCPR. States must report on their compliance with this treaty every five years, usually in the form of responses

---

[58] Rudy Boschwitz, 'Remarks at the 61st Session of the UN Commission on Human Rights' (Geneva 31 March 2005), available at <http://2001-2009.state.gov/p/io/rls/rm/44151.htm>.

[59] UNOHCHR, 'Report 2014', available at <http://www2.ohchr.org/english/OHCHRReport2014/WEB_version/index.html>; 'Comprehensive Report of the Office of the United Nations High Commissioner for Human Rights on Sri Lanka' (28 September 2015) UN Doc A/HRC/30/61.

to specific questions posed by the Committee during the previous review. The Committee also poses questions to that State orally following the submission of the report, and a record of the discussion as well as the report are made available on the Committee's website. Non-governmental organizations have played an increasingly important role in bringing attention to human rights concerns, and Committee review sessions can provide an otherwise rare opportunity to hear a State's formal policy on salient human rights questions.[60]

Most treaty bodies can also receive individual complaints regarding violations of treaty rights if a State has accepted their jurisdiction to do so, and they have an active and growing caseload.[61] For instance, the Human Rights Committee, over three sessions in 2014–15, considered eighteen reports from States Parties to the ICCPR and processed 126 communications from individuals alleging violations of their rights.[62]   **17.56**

Once it has reviewed an individual communication, a treaty body may decide that a State has violated an individual's human rights and, in such cases, it can recommend that specific action be taken. In cases that come before the Human Rights Committee, suggested remedies can include paying compensation, reforming laws, retrying a case and releasing an individual from detention. The treaty bodies do not have the power to compel compliance with their recommendations, but their decisions represent a public and objective assessment of the facts and in high-profile cases there can be significant public pressure on a State to implement a decision.   **17.57**

The Human Rights Committee considers that a decision of a treaty body represents 'an authoritative determination' of the treaty provision in question with which States must comply.[63] The ICJ, however, has stated that although it will 'ascribe great weight' to the Committee's understanding, it 'is in no way obliged, in the exercise of its judicial functions, to model its own interpretation' on that of the Committee.[64]   **17.58**

UN Special Procedures

The Human Rights Council's 'special procedures' are a group of unpaid independent human rights experts who are appointed by the Council to report and   **17.59**

---

[60] See also Chapter **28**.
[61] UNOHCHR, 'Strengthening the United Nations human rights treaty body system' available at <http://www2.ohchr.org/english/bodies/HRTD/docs/HCReportTBStrengthening.pdf>.
[62] UNGA, 'Report of the Human Rights Committee' (11 August 2015) UN Doc A/70/40.
[63] Human Rights Committee, 'General Comment No 33' (5 November 2008) UN Doc CCPR/C/GC/33, paras 13–15.
[64] *Ahmadou Sadio Diallo (Guinea v DRC)* (Merits) [2010] ICJ Reports 639, at para 66. See also *Jones v Saudi Arabia* [2006] UKHL 26, paras 23 and 57.

advise on human rights from a thematic or country-specific perspective. Some serve alone, in which case they are usually known as Special Rapporteurs.[65] There are also six procedures organized as 'working groups' made up of five members drawn from each of the UN regional blocs: the African Group, the Asia-Pacific Group, the Eastern European Group, the Latin American and Caribbean Group, and the Western European and Others Group.

17.60 There are fifty-five special procedure mandates, either assigned by the Human Rights Council or, in a few cases, the UN Secretary-General.[66] Fourteen are dedicated to the state of human rights in particular countries, such as Belarus and Iran. The rest are thematic, focusing on issues such as the right to safe drinking water and sanitation, or the independence of judges and lawyers.

17.61 Special Rapporteurs are expected to conduct visits to relevant States, communicate with States about alleged violations, report to the Human Rights Council and General Assembly, and help to articulate and develop human rights standards. Many also accept individual complaints about alleged human rights breaches.

17.62 Special Rapporteurs usually play a limited role in adjudicating individual complaints compared to treaty bodies: they will generally forward a complaint to the appropriate national authorities for a response and then issue a brief public comment. Some special procedures do however issue detailed opinions dealing with individual cases.[67] For instance, the Special Rapporteur on Torture complements the work of the Committee against Torture by issuing 'urgent appeals' to governments who are accused of torture in individual cases. The Working Group on Arbitrary Detention also issues detailed findings and has argued that these are authoritative interpretations of the Universal Declaration and the ICCPR that are binding due to 'the collaboration by States in the procedure, the adversarial nature of its findings and also by the authority given to the [Working Group] by the UN Human Rights Council'.[68] However, the Human Rights Council does not have the power to enforce compliance.

17.63 Special Rapporteurs generally have discretion to tackle the issues linked to their mandate that they deem to be the most salient and significant. For instance, the

---

[65] Some are known as Special Representatives or Independent Experts.

[66] As of 1 December 2015: see UNOHCHR, 'Directory of Special Procedures Mandates Holders' (June 2016) UN Doc HRC/NONE/2016/75.

[67] UNHRC, 'Report of the Working Group on Arbitrary Detention: A compilation of national, regional and international laws, regulations and practices on the right to challenge the lawfulness of detention before court' (30 June 2014) UN Doc A/HRC/27/47, para 1.

[68] Working Group on Arbitrary Detention, 'Julian Assange arbitrarily detained by Sweden and the UK, UN expert panel finds', available at <http://www.ohchr.org/EN/NewsEvents/Pages/DisplayNews.aspx?NewsID=17013&LangID=E>.

Special Rapporteur on the promotion and protection of human rights and fundamental freedoms while countering terrorism has reported on the legality of drone strikes in Pakistan, Yemen, and Libya. In doing so, he conducted extensive on-site investigations, interviewed government officials, and reported on the legal and factual lacunae in this evolving area of law. The same Rapporteur also conducted an inquiry into whether the use of mass surveillance is compatible with human rights, making a number of recommendations to governments about how their terrorism laws should be reformed.[69]

Although the special procedures have been called the 'crown jewel' of the UN human rights system by a former UN Secretary-General,[70] the impact of rapporteurs depends to a large degree on the person who occupies the role, and there has been some criticism in recent years about the proliferation of mandates with varying levels of effectiveness. **17.64**

General Assembly

The General Assembly is the body that promulgated the Universal Declaration of Human Rights in 1948 and it has maintained a role in human rights monitoring since then. The General Assembly exercises supervisory powers over the Geneva-based human rights bodies and approves key human rights appointments such as that of the UN High Commissioner for Human Rights. **17.65**

The General Assembly also hears reports from the High Commissioner as well as many Special Rapporteurs. And it votes on resolutions on human rights issues, taking into account the recommendations of its 'Third Committee', a group comprised of a representative from each UN member State which handles social, cultural, and humanitarian matters on behalf of the broader body. **17.66**

Like the Geneva-based bodies, but unlike the Security Council, the General Assembly has no coercive powers. It is also technically unable to make any recommendation on a dispute or situation that is actively being considered by the Security Council, except by request of the Council itself.[71] **17.67**

Security Council

The Security Council has primary responsibility under the UN Charter for the maintenance of international peace and security, but it also plays an increasingly **17.68**

---

[69] See HRC, 'Report of the Special Rapporteur on the promotion and protection of human rights and fundamental freedoms while countering terrorism' (10 March 2014) UN Doc A/HRC/25/59.

[70] Kofi A Annan, 'Secretary-General's message to the Third Session of the Human Rights Council' (Geneva 29 November 2006), available at <http://www.un.org/sg/statements/?nid=2333>.

[71] Charter of the United Nations (adopted 25 June 1945, entered into force 24 October 1945) 1 UNTS XVI, Art 12(1).

important role in the human rights arena. It could be said that the most serious human rights violations will often, if not always, affect international peace and security, and the Council itself determines when this threshold is met.

17.69 The Council's modern practice includes routinely issuing statements expressing its views on specific human rights situations, including through resolutions, presidential statements and public communications by individual members of the Council. For example, in 2014–15 the Council issued resolutions '[d]emand[ing] that all parties to the Syrian domestic conflict, in particular the Syrian authorities, immediately comply with their obligations under international humanitarian law and international human rights law'.[72] It also called during this time frame for the governments of Ukraine, South Sudan, and the Democratic Republic of Congo to uphold their human rights obligations.

17.70 The Council can also initiate international investigations and prosecutions of grave human rights violations. The Council kick-started the system of international criminal justice when it created the ad hoc tribunals for the former Yugoslavia and Rwanda dealing with genocide, war crimes, and crimes against humanity in those countries.[73] It has since referred the situations in Libya and Darfur to the International Criminal Court.[74] It was instrumental in establishing a special tribunal for terrorist offences in Lebanon including the assassination of the prime minister.[75] It has created investigative commissions for Lebanon and Sudan, and has sent human rights observers to Syria. Its power to impose binding international trade and economic sanctions under Chapter VII of the Charter can also be used to obtain compliance by States with the most fundamental of their human rights obligations.[76]

17.71 Although potentially the most robust mechanism for enforcing international human rights law, the Council has frequently been criticized for failing to take coercive action in situations involving the most egregious violations of human rights law and international humanitarian law due to the use of the veto power by its permanent members. This criticism has been most pronounced in relation to the situation in Syria after 2011.

International Courts

17.72 A State may be able to file a case on behalf of one of its citizens whose human rights are violated by another State before the ICJ, so long as both States have

---

[72] SC resolution 2191 (17 December 2014) UN Doc S/RES/2191.
[73] See Chapter 26.
[74] See Chapter 27.
[75] SC resolution 1757 (30 May 2007) UN Doc S/RES/1757.
[76] See paragraphs 17.86–17.91.

accepted the jurisdiction of the Court.[77] Seventy-two States currently recognize the compulsory jurisdiction of the Court—the principal judicial organ of the United Nations—to resolve international law disputes with other States that have accepted the Court's jurisdiction on the same terms.[78] States can also agree to send a dispute to the Court on an ad hoc basis. In addition, approximately 300 treaties, including those dealing with human rights, such the Genocide Convention, provide that disputes arising under the treaty may be resolved by the Court if a State Party to the treaty requests that the Court intervene.[79]

The ICJ deals with questions of public international law and many of its cases **17.73** concern territorial and maritime issues. But the Court has also dealt with cases concerning human rights. In one case, Guinea brought proceedings against the Democratic Republic of Congo to protect the rights of a Guinean national who had been arbitrarily arrested, detained, and subsequently expelled by the Congolese authorities. The Court found that this treatment violated the DRC's human rights obligations under the ICCPR and the African Charter and ordered the DRC to pay US$95,000 in compensation.[80]

In another case, the Court found that the US had violated its obligation under **17.74** the Vienna Convention on Consular Relations to notify fifty-one Mexican nationals held on death row in the United States of their right to consult a Mexican consular officer upon detention. The Court ordered that the US 'provide, by means of its own choosing, review and reconsideration of the convictions and sentences'.[81] The Court found in another case that Senegal had violated its obligations under the Convention against Torture by failing to investigate, prosecute, or extradite Hissène Habré, the former Chadian dictator who had been granted asylum by its authorities.[82] When assessing the conflict in the Democratic Republic of Congo, the Court found, among other things, that Uganda had violated its obligations under international human rights law when its armed forces committed acts of killing, torture, inhumane treatment, and violence against civilians.[83] The Court has issued a series of judgments concerning allegations of genocide during the war in the Balkans.[84] And in a

---

[77] See Chapter 25.

[78] As of 20 February 2016. The terms of the declarations often include reservations, however.

[79] Convention on the Prevention and Punishment of the Crime of Genocide 1948 (adopted 9 December 1948, entered into force 12 January 1951) 78 UNTS 227, Art 9.

[80] *Ahmadou Sadio Diallo (Guinea v DRC)* (Compensation) [2012] ICJ Reports 324.

[81] *Avena and Other Mexican Nationals (Mexico v USA)* (Merits) [2004] ICJ Reports 12, at para 153.

[82] *Questions relating to the Obligation to Prosecute or Extradite* (n 52).

[83] *Armed Activities on the Territory of the Congo (DRC v Uganda)* [2005] ICJ Reports 168.

[84] *Bosnia and Herzegovina v Serbia and Montenegro* (n 27); *Application of the Convention on the Prevention and Punishment of the Crime of Genocide (Croatia v Serbia)*, available at <http://www.icj-cij.org/docket/files/118/18422.pdf>.

landmark Advisory Opinion, the Court concluded that the construction of a wall by Israel in the Occupied Palestinian Territory violated the right of the Palestinian people to self-determination as well as their rights to liberty, health, education, and an adequate standard of living.[85]

17.75   The International Criminal Court and the other international criminal tribunals—including those established for the former Yugoslavia, Rwanda, Sierra Leone, and Cambodia—have jurisdiction over international crimes, which include the most severe human rights violations.[86] Unlike the International Court of Justice, which determines the legal responsibility of States and may impose civil penalties, international criminal courts determine the culpability of individuals for specific crimes. These courts have the power to impose sentences of life imprisonment (but not capital punishment) for the gravest offences.[87]

Regional Courts

17.76   There are three regional courts with jurisdiction over human rights cases: the European, African, and Inter-American courts.[88] A plan to establish an Arab court was recently discussed but ultimately abandoned, and currently there is no supranational court that deals with human rights cases anywhere in Asia.[89]

17.77   The European Court of Human Rights is the most robust regional court established to date. The Court, based in Strasbourg, considers violations of the European Convention on Human Rights and its jurisdiction is recognized by all forty-seven States that form part of the Council of Europe, a group of countries larger than the European Union. Adherence to the European Convention on Human Rights is a condition of membership of the Council of Europe,[90] and both Belarus and Kazakhstan have been hindered in their attempts to join as a result of human rights concerns.[91] The judges come from all the member States and sit in panels of up to seventeen judges. The Court has so far issued almost 20,000 judgments, compared to the roughly three hundred judgments issued by the Inter-American Court and eight merits judgments issued by the African Court.[92]

---

[85] *Legal Consequences of the Construction of a Wall in the Occupied Palestinian Territory* (Advisory Opinion) [2004] ICJ Reports 136.

[86] See Chapter **26**.

[87] See Chapter **31** for further information on international and internationalized courts applying international criminal law.

[88] See paragraphs 17.21–17.30.

[89] See paragraphs 17.28–17.30.

[90] See e.g. Guy de Vel, *The Committee of Ministers of the Council of Europe* (Council of Europe Press, 1995) 50.

[91] See e.g. Paul Bayley and Geoffrey Williams (eds), *European Identity: What the Media Say* (Oxford: Oxford University Press, 2012) 121.

[92] As of 1 January 2016.

The European Court's judgments are generally well respected and trigger a high **17.78** rate of compliance. There have however been a number of judgments which have not been complied with by member States.[93] In such cases the Committee of Ministers, a body made up of the Foreign Ministers of the States comprising the Council of Europe, monitors the situation and can issue statements condemning non-compliance.[94] Although rates of compliance vary among member States and judgments of the Court can create controversy at the domestic level, no State has withdrawn from the Convention or sought to enter a reservation to the obligation to implement the Court's judgments set out in Article 46.

The Inter-American Court of Human Rights is based in Costa Rica and consid- **17.79** ers alleged violations of the American Convention on Human Rights by the OAS States. Unlike its European counterpart, it cannot consider cases brought directly by individuals within these States; cases must instead be referred to the Court by the Inter-American Commission on Human Rights or by one of the twenty-four States that have ratified the American Convention.

States within the OAS that have ratified the American Convention without **17.80** making a declaration recognizing the jurisdiction of the Inter-American Court cannot be brought before it. These States are instead subject to 'recommendations' from the Inter-American Commission—a group of seven independent experts elected by the general assembly of the OAS—based on complaints of alleged violations brought by individuals.

A few OAS Member States, including the United States, have not ratified the **17.81** American Convention at all. These States remain subject to recommendations by the Inter-American Commission if they are found to have violated the American Declaration of the Rights and Duties of Man, an instrument similar to the Universal Declaration of Human Rights.

The newest regional court (in existence since 2004) is the African Court on **17.82** Human and Peoples' Rights. This court is based in Tanzania and has a mandate to hear cases against African Union (AU) States alleging violations of the African Charter on Human and Peoples' Rights. Like the Inter-American Court, it has a tiered jurisdiction. Of the fifty-four States that make up the AU, twenty-six have accepted the jurisdiction of the Court to hear human rights cases brought by the African Commission or a State, but only seven have made the optional declaration that enables individuals and NGOs to file complaints. The Court

---

[93] See e.g. *Mammadov v Azerbaijan* (2014) 58 EHRR 18; *Greens and MT v United Kingdom* (2011) 53 EHRR 21.
[94] Council of Europe, 'About the Committee of Ministers', available at <http://www.coe.int/t/cm/aboutCM_en.asp>.

has so far issued eight judgments on the merits dealing with issues such as freedom of expression.[95]

17.83 There are also several sub-regional courts. Although it is not principally a human rights court, the Court of Justice of the European Union (CJEU) in Luxembourg often rules in its cases on alleged violations of fundamental rights and in particular the EU Charter on Fundamental Rights, an instrument of EU law that covers some of the same rights as the European Convention on Human Rights but applies only to the smaller number of States that make up the EU. The Luxembourg Court can consider questions referred to it by national courts, Member States, or the EU institutions, or in some cases by individuals, but the alleged violations must relate to the implementation of EU law. This has led to a number of decisions by the Court on human rights issues and some of the decisions, for instance on sanctions, have been more far-reaching than the comparable jurisprudence of the Strasbourg-based European Court of Human Rights.[96]

17.84 Other sub-regional courts include the East African Court of Justice, the Court of the Economic Community of West African States, the Caribbean Court of Justice, and the Court of Justice of the Andean Community. These courts deal with human rights issues in a relatively small number of cases. The Judicial Committee of the Privy Council, a British institution, is also a form of regional court as it exercises final appellate jurisdiction over Crown Dependencies and British Overseas Territories as well as certain independent States within the Commonwealth.[97] The Judicial Committee's jurisprudence has helped define the scope of human rights standards in these States and, together with the Privy Council and the Caribbean Court of Justice, it deals with a significant number of cases involving prisoners on death row.[98]

17.85 Regional enforcement mechanisms can be a more robust alternative to the Geneva-based UN mechanisms when it comes to upholding human rights in individual cases, and they have seen a marked increase in their workload over time. For example, the number of valid applications to the European Court of Human Rights grew from 10,500 in 2000 to 65,800 just over ten years later.[99]

---

[95] As of 1 January 2016. On 1 July 2008, at the African Union Summit in Sharm El Sheikh, Egypt, Heads of State and Government signed a Protocol on the merger of the African Court of Human Rights with the still non-operational African Court of Justice. As of September 2014, only five countries had ratified the Protocol out of fifteen needed for its entry into force. The new court will be known as the African Court of Justice and Human Rights.

[96] See e.g. *Dereci (Case C-256/11)* [2012] 1 CMLR 45, para 72.

[97] For further information regarding the Commonwealth, see Chapter **23**.

[98] See e.g. *Pratt and Morgan v Attorney-General for Jamaica* [1994] 2 AC 1.

[99] ECtHR, 'Annual Report 2014' (Registry of the ECtHR 2015) 170.

There were nearly twice as many judgments issued in the year 2006 alone (1,560) than there were in the four decades leading up to 2000.[100] The Court has also heard seventeen inter-State cases[101] and now has jurisdiction to issue Advisory Opinions directly to national courts.[102]

Sanctions

In parallel with international and regional courts and UN human rights bodies, **17.86** sanctions are an increasingly important tool used by States, regional organizations, and the United Nations to bring about compliance with international human rights obligations.

At the Security Council, country-wide sanctions such as economic embargoes, **17.87** trade bans, or the suspension of diplomatic relations have been imposed in order to influence the behaviour of countries perceived to represent a threat to international peace. These include sanctions for violations of human rights, particularly in the context of armed violence. Sanctions are also sometimes imposed on leaders and other individuals within a State.

States and regional bodies can also impose sanctions and, like the Security Council, **17.88** are moving towards reliance on 'smart' or targeted sanctions rather than more sweeping measures. At the regional level, the European Union has issued asset freezes and travel bans against many individual State officials who were responsible for grave human rights abuses in recent years. For instance, in 2012 it imposed such targeted sanctions on 'persons responsible for serious violations of human rights or the repression of civil society and democratic opposition' in Belarus.[103] This followed a finding that the Belarus authorities were responsible for manipulating elections, using violence against peaceful protestors, and convicting and detaining political prisoners. It also issued sanctions against those 'responsible for serious human rights violations in Iran, and persons, entities or bodies associated with them' following the arrest of demonstrators and sham trials against political opponents.[104]

Sanctions for human rights violations can be imposed on members of the judi- **17.89** ciary and business community, as well as government officials. Targets have included presidents, heads of intelligence, judges who sentenced human rights

---

[100] ECtHR, 'Annual Report 2008' (Registry of the ECtHR 2009) 12.

[101] ECtHR, 'Inter-States Applications', available at <http://www.echr.coe.int/Documents/InterStates_applications_ENG.pdf>.

[102] Under Protocol No 16 to the Convention for the Protection of Human Rights and Fundamental Freedoms.

[103] Council Decision 2012/642/CFSP of 15 October 2012 (EU).

[104] Council Regulation No 359/2011 of 12 April 2011 (EU).

defenders in unfair trials, and prison directors who ordered ill-treatment or unlawful solitary confinement of prisoners.[105]

17.90 Sanctions can also be applied bilaterally by one State in response to human rights violations committed by another. For example, the United States has imposed travel bans and asset freezes on Russian officials 'responsible for extra-judicial killings, torture, or other gross violations of internationally recognized human rights' against whistle-blowers and human rights defenders.[106] This led Russia to issue its own sanctions banning certain US citizens from entering Russia and freezing their assets, as well as preventing American citizens from adopting Russian children.[107]

17.91 Other States impose measures short of sanctions that make cooperation with their partners contingent on a good human rights record. For instance, the UK government has adopted a policy of refusing entry to the UK to non-European nationals where 'there is independent, reliable and credible evidence that [they have] committed human rights abuses'.[108] The government does not release data on the implementation of this policy, but at least two people were denied entry and accreditation to the 2012 London Olympics on this basis.[109]

The Role of a Diplomat in Upholding Human Rights

17.92 Although diplomats are expected to maintain good relations with their receiving State and should not in principle interfere in the internal affairs of that State[110] they have throughout history played an important role in upholding human rights.

17.93 During the Second World War Ambassador Raoul Wallenberg and his fellow Swedish diplomats saved thousands of Hungarian Jews from genocide by providing them with protective passports during the German occupation of Budapest. Today, diplomats around the world are increasingly involved in

---

[105] See e.g. Council Decision 2012/739/CFSP of 29 November 2012; Council Decision 2012/642/CFSP of 15 October 2012; Council Decision 2011/235/CFSP of 12 April 2011 (EU).

[106] Russia and Moldova Jackson-Vanik Repeal and Sergei Magnitsky Rule of Law Accountability Act 2012 (USA).

[107] See Patrick Ventrell, 'Statement on Russia's Yakovlev Act' (28 December 2012), available at <http://www.state.gov/r/pa/prs/ps/2012/12/202401.htm>.

[108] UK Foreign and Commonwealth Office, 'Human Rights and Democracy' (Cm 8339, 2011) 53.

[109] UK FCO, 'Human Rights and Democracy' (Cm 8593, 2012) 52.

[110] See Vienna Convention on Diplomatic Relations (adopted 18 April 1961, entered into force on 24 April 1964) 500 UNTS 95, Art 41(1); Vienna Convention on Consular Relations (adopted on 24 April 1963, entered into force on 19 March 1967) 596 UNTS 261, Art 55(1). See also the discussion of human rights in Chapter 2.

human rights issues when their own citizens, but also others, need assistance in the countries in which they are working.

Support for Nationals

Diplomats routinely engage with human rights issues through consular assistance   **17.94**
to their nationals. For instance, if a UK citizen is arrested abroad, the UK embassy's consular staff will be on hand to provide basic professional advice, put the detainee in touch with a support network and appropriate legal advisers from whom to choose, issue emergency travel documents, and conduct regular prison visits.[111]

In recent years, officials from some countries have taken an increasingly active   **17.95**
role in ensuring that the rights of their nationals are respected in the receiving State. For example, the UK has abandoned its policy of refraining from making diplomatic representations in individual court cases except in situations where all local remedies had been exhausted. The modern policy commits the government to act instead in all those 'cases where fundamental violations of the British national's human rights had demonstrably altered the course of justice. In such cases, [the government] would consider supporting their request for an appeal to any official human rights body in the country concerned, and subsequently giving advice on how to take their cases to relevant international human rights mechanisms.'[112] This commitment to espouse the case of a British national to a foreign government is however subject to the State's national security and foreign policy interests.[113]

Even the most senior officials of a State routinely complain publicly about viola-   **17.96**
tions of their citizens' human rights by another State, particularly in cases involving unfair detentions, the rights of women, and freedom of religion. For instance, in 2015 the UK Foreign Secretary publicly intervened to secure the release of an elderly British citizen who had been sentenced by a court in Saudi Arabia to a public flogging as punishment for the possession of alcohol.[114]

Support for Non-nationals

In certain cases, diplomats negotiating aid packages or commercial contracts   **17.97**
may also make them conditional on human rights compliance. For example,

---

[111] See UK FCO, 'Support for British Nationals Abroad', available at <http://www.gov.uk/government/publications/support-for-british-nationals-abroad-a-guide>. See also Chapter **8**.
[112] *R (Abbasi and Another) v Secretary of State for Foreign and Commonwealth Affairs and Secretary of State for the Home Department* [2002] EWCA Civ 1598, para 90.
[113] Ibid, para 99.
[114] 'Foreign Secretary statement on the return of Karl Andree to the UK' (London 11 November 2015), available at <http://www.gov.uk/government/news/foreign-secretary-statement-on-the-return-of-karl-andree-to-the-uk>.

the British government indicated that it had cancelled a £5.9 million contract to provide a training programme for prisons in Saudi Arabia following objections raised in Parliament on the basis of human rights concerns.[115] The European Union, in concluding an agreement with a non-member State, also routinely includes an article introducing a degree of conditionality to that State's human rights record.[116]

17.98 And the US made a $750m aid package for three Central American countries conditional on the requirement that recipient governments must 'investigate and prosecute...members of military and police forces who are credibly alleged to have violated human rights' and 'cooperate with...regional human rights entities'.[117]

17.99 Diplomats may well also become involved in individual cases in which the treatment of prominent local figures in the State in which they are posted is seen to violate international standards. Areas of concern on which diplomats are often expected to comment include women's rights, sexual violence, torture, freedom of religion and belief, freedom of expression, the rights of migrant workers, and capital punishment.[118] Most frequently, diplomats will be involved when individuals face execution or are alleged to be unfairly detained.

17.100 Diplomats all over the world called, on behalf of their governments, for the release of Aung San Suu Kyi in Burma and Nelson Mandela in South Africa.[119] More recently, the US Embassy in Kuala Lumpur expressed 'serious concerns regarding the Anwar [Ibrahim] case' after the prominent Malaysian opposition leader was convicted of sodomy following a flawed trial.[120] American, British, and other foreign government officials expressed similar concern over the detention of the former President of the Maldives following a trial 'conducted in a manner contrary to...the minimum fair trial guarantees and other protections under the [ICCPR]'.[121]

17.101 Diplomats' involvement in human rights cases is not limited to those involving prominent political figures. In one month (October 2015), Ambassador Samantha

---

[115] HC Deb, 13 October 2015, Vol 600, col 180.

[116] Lorand Bartels, 'The EU's Human Rights Obligations in Relation to Policies with Extraterritorial Effects' (2014) 25(4) *EJIL* 1071, 1079–80.

[117] Consolidated Appropriations Act 2016 (HR 2029).

[118] See UK FCO, 'Human Rights and Democracy' (Cm 9027, 2015).

[119] See also Chapter 36.

[120] US Embassy in Malaysia, 'U.S. Embassy Statement on the Conviction of Anwar Ibrahim' (Kuala Lumpur 10 February 2015): <http://my.usembassy.gov/u-s-embassy-statement-on-the-conviction-of-anwar-ibrahim/>.

[121] US Embassy in Sri Lanka, 'U.S. Statement On Trial and Sentencing of Former Maldives President Mohamed Nasheed' (Colombo 14 March 2015): <http://srilanka.usembassy.gov/st-14march15.html>.

Power, the US Permanent Representative to the United Nations, made public statements at least eight times about unfair trials involving non-US lawyers, bloggers, and human rights activists around the world.[122] When three journalists from Canada, Australia, and Egypt working for Al Jazeera television were convicted on charges of aiding terrorism in a widely condemned trial in Cairo, States from all over the world issued diplomatic statements criticizing the conviction and suggesting they should be released.[123]

In dealing with human rights issues, diplomats and consular officials will often **17.102** work with local human rights organizations. The UK Foreign and Commonwealth Office (FCO) advises that officials meet with local human rights defenders regularly and 'establish a visible presence' by attending trials, visiting activists in prison, as well as conducting '[l]obbying, demarches, or public statements on individual cases'.[124] Officials are also encouraged to include human rights defenders in meetings with senior officials and to use social media to 'maintain contact and show support' for their work.[125]

Diplomatic Premises

Perhaps the most dramatic type of diplomatic intervention in human rights **17.103** cases arises when individuals are given refuge in an embassy in an attempt to prevent a further violation of their rights. The granting of 'diplomatic asylum' to fugitives whose fundamental human rights are under threat is controversial.[126] However, the International Court of Justice has made it clear that a State may under certain circumstances have a right to do so if the 'administration of justice [is] corrupted by measures clearly prompted by political aims'.[127]

Diplomats throughout history have granted temporary refuge to individuals **17.104** in imminent danger. During the Cold War, Cardinal József Mindszenty, a prominent Hungarian anti-Communist who had been subjected to torture and a show trial, was granted refuge at the United States embassy in Budapest, and ultimately remained there for 15 years. In the 1980s, a group of six American diplomats were taken in by the Canadian ambassador in Tehran after their

---

[122] See <https://twitter.com/AmbassadorPower>.
[123] Egyptian Ministry of Foreign Affairs, statement of 30 August 2015, available at <http://www.facebook.com/MFAEgypt/posts/917941704944443>.
[124] UK FCO—Human Rights and Democracy Department, 'How To …Work With Human Rights Defenders at Post'. See also Chapter **36**.
[125] Ibid.
[126] See Chapter **8**.
[127] *Asylum Case (Colombia/Peru)* [1950] ICJ Reports 266, 284. The Court made this statement in the context of a claim under the 1928 Havana Convention on Asylum.

embassy was attacked, and the 'Canadian Six' remained there for two months until they made a dramatic escape.

17.105 More recently, Ecuador gave refuge at its London embassy to Julian Assange, an Australian who faced extradition to the US following the publication on his 'Wikileaks' website of classified US government cables, based on his 'well-founded fear of political persecution'.[128] The United States gave refuge to its citizen, Sam LaHood, at the US embassy in Cairo after he faced criminal charges for working for a non-governmental organization in Egypt in 2012. He remained at the embassy for four weeks until he was allowed to leave the country.[129] In 2012, the Canadian embassy in Ukraine also offered shelter to anti-government protesters (some but not all of whom were Canadian) for approximately a week. Switzerland similarly sheltered an Azerbaijani journalist, Emin Huseynov, who feared reprisals in Azerbaijan following political persecution.[130]

A Duty to Act?

17.106 Much of the work of a diplomat in the human rights arena is based on discretion and government guidance, and there is no requirement under international law that a State exercise diplomatic protection on behalf of its citizens.[131] However, there are times when the diplomat has a legal duty to act to protect human rights. In the United Kingdom, despite the wide discretion accorded to the FCO, it has been accepted that there is 'scope for judicial review of a refusal to render diplomatic assistance to a British subject who is suffering violation of a fundamental human right as the result of the conduct of the authorities of a foreign State'.[132]

17.107 The English courts have found—on the basis of evidence such as published advice given to British travellers on government websites—that 'it must be a normal expectation of every citizen that, if subjected abroad to a violation of a fundamental right, the British Government will not simply wash their hands of

---

[128] Ministry of Foreign Affairs, Trade and Integration of Ecuador, 'Declaración del Gobierno de la República del Ecuador sobre la solicitud de asilo de Julian Assange' (16 August 2012), available at <http://www.webcitation.org/69xdGRSLN>. However, the United Kingdom has refused to recognize Assange's asylum status: see UK FCO, 'UK disputes UN working group opinion on Julian Assange', available at <http://www.gov.uk/government/news/uk-disputes-un-working-group-opinion-on-julian-assange>.

[129] US Department of State, 'Daily Press Briefing' (Washington, 30 January 2012), available at <http://www.state.gov/r/pa/prs/dpb/2012/01/182732.htm#EGYPT>.

[130] Swiss Federal Department of Foreign Affairs, 'Emin Huseynov arrives in Bern after 10 months at Swiss embassy in Baku' (Bern 12 June 2015): <https://www.admin.ch/gov/en/start/documentation/media-releases.msg-id-57667.html>.

[131] *Barcelona Traction* (n 4), para 78.

[132] *R (Abbasi)* (n 112), para 80.

the matter and abandon him to his fate'.[133] If the UK were to do so, 'it would be appropriate for the court to make a mandatory order to the Foreign Secretary to give due consideration to the applicant's case'.[134]

Even as regards the granting of diplomatic asylum at an embassy, a concept **17.108** whose legal contours are disputed, the English Court of Appeal has stated that officials of States Parties to the European Convention on Human Rights 'may well' be subject to 'a duty... to afford diplomatic asylum' in circumstances where it is clear 'that the receiving state intends to subject the fugitive to treatment so harsh as to constitute a crime against humanity'.[135]

The requirements of the European Convention on Human Rights may apply to **17.109** diplomats from Council of Europe countries no matter where they are posted in the world. This is because the agents of a State, including diplomatic or consular officials, remain under that State's jurisdiction when abroad, and they may also bring other persons or property within the jurisdiction of the State, and therefore the European Convention, to the extent that they exercise authority over such persons or property.[136] The mere provision of 'advice and support' to a national, or the making of diplomatic representations on her behalf, 'cannot [however] be regarded as any kind of exertion of authority or control by agents of [a State]'.[137] In such circumstances, 'international law has not yet recognized that a State is under a duty to intervene by diplomatic or other means to protect a citizen who is suffering or threatened with injury in a foreign State'.[138]

Challenges for Human Rights Protection

An elaborate system of human rights protection has been created since the end **17.110** of the Second World War. Many treaties govern States' obligations in this area, and compliance is overseen by a patchwork of courts, committees, and experts at the international and regional levels that publicly pronounce on human rights violations by States. It is now commonplace for States to have to answer to other States for their human rights record in public. And issues such as aid

---

[133] Ibid, para 98.

[134] Ibid, para 104.

[135] *R (B and Others) v Secretary of State for Foreign and Commonwealth Affairs* [2004] EWCA 1344, [88]. See also Chapter **8**.

[136] *Cyprus v Turkey* (1975) 2 DR 125, para 8; See also *Legal Consequences of the Construction of a Wall in the Occupied Palestinian Territory* (n 85), paras 107–111.

[137] *R (Sandiford) v Secretary of State for Foreign and Commonwealth Affairs* [2014] UKSC 44, para 19.

[138] *R (Abbasi)* (n 112), para 69.

and trade can be directly affected by the human rights performance of a State. This represents a major overhaul of the old world order where state sovereignty meant that a government could do as it wished to its citizens inside its own borders, without legal consequences on the international plane.

17.111　But the universal acceptance of human rights standards on paper has not been matched by governments' conduct on the ground. Some governments have sought to limit their obligations by refusing to ratify treaties or adopting sweeping reservations or derogations. More often, governments accept obligations on paper but ignore them in practice. Most of the UN bodies that monitor compliance lack enforcement powers and many States do not allow their citizens access to such bodies or to international courts. Powerful States can escape sanction much more easily than others, especially if they have veto power at the Security Council. And although some bodies, such as the ECtHR and the ICJ, have developed a rich jurisprudence and commanded a high rate of compliance with their judgments, some of the UN human rights bodies have struggled to inspire confidence and compliance with their decisions.

17.112　In the absence of a global human rights court with coercive powers and universal jurisdiction, financial sanctions imposed by individual States, regional groups, or the UN have become an increasingly important tool when it comes to promoting human rights compliance. Public and private advocacy by diplomats also remains essential in putting pressure on States to respect their human rights obligations towards their citizens and other individuals who fall under their jurisdiction.

18

THE UNITED NATIONS—I THE CHARTER AND ITS OPERATION

Emyr Jones Parry

It would be idle to pretend that the UN is an uncontroversial body, though **18.1** widespread ignorance of its workings and its complexity contribute to this. Some knowledge of its history facilitates understanding of the UN's present situation.[1] Its principal predecessor, the League of Nations, established in 1919, had been unsuccessful, failing to have any significant impact on the events leading to the outbreak of the Second World War in 1939. With the end of the

---

[1] For a perceptive insider's view see Lord Hannay, *New World Disorder* (London: I B Tauris, 2008).

Second World War the formation of the United Nations in 1945 replaced the League of Nations which bequeathed certain of its less political responsibilities to the new body.

18.2 The term 'United Nations' derives from the 'Declaration by United Nations' of 1 January 1942, in which the twenty-six nations then fighting against the German-Italian-Japanese Axis affirmed their resolve to cooperate in winning the war and their adherence to the Atlantic Charter. That Charter, proclaimed on 14 August 1941 by the President of the United States, Franklin D. Roosevelt and the prime minister of the United Kingdom, Winston Churchill, looked forward to a peace affording to all peoples freedom and security from aggression.

18.3 Before any formal steps were taken internationally to set up a new world political and security organization, a conference in the name of the United Nations was held in May and June 1943 at Hot Springs, Virginia, USA, at the invitation of President Roosevelt. It was called under the title 'United Nations Conference on Food and Agriculture' and it was attended by representatives from forty-four countries. Its mandate was purely advisory, but the Conference led directly to the establishment in October 1945 of the Food and Agriculture Organization of the United Nations (FAO).

The Charter

18.4 The first formal international discussions with the objectives described in paragraph **18.2** were held at Dumbarton Oaks, Washington, DC, in the summer of 1944, between representatives of the United States, the United Kingdom, and the Soviet Union. They were followed by similar talks between the United States, the United Kingdom, and the Republic of China, represented by the Nationalist Chinese, which caused the Soviet government to refuse to participate in these preliminary meetings. Further discussions took place at the Yalta Conference in February 1945, attended by President Roosevelt, Marshal Stalin, and Prime Minister Churchill. Those talks resulted in a text of a draft Charter[2] for presentation to the forthcoming United Nations Conference on International Organization which opened in San Francisco on 25 April 1945.[3] Extensive argument also took place between the greater and smaller Powers over the Dumbarton

---

[2] It is generally accepted that the word 'charter' originated in the group in the United States State Department engaged, under the supervision of Dr Leo Pasvolsky, in the preparation of documents and drafts for the Dumbarton Oaks talks. The alternative word 'covenant' was rejected as reminiscent of the failure of the League of Nations. See Chapter 36, paragraph **36.4**.

[3] See Chapter 23, paragraph **23.37**.

Oaks proposals as modified at Yalta; some concessions were thereby achieved by the smaller Powers, but in the main the major Powers' proposals stood. The Charter was signed on 26 June by representatives of all the fifty-one nations taking part in the Conference, except Poland, which signed on 15 October. The requisite number of ratifications having been received, the Charter went into force on 24 October 1945.

Membership

The names of the original membership of fifty-one are below.[4] By 2016 there   **18.5**
were 193 members and the list of current members will be found at <http://www.un.org/en/member-states/>.

Members are admitted under Article 4.1 of the Charter, which reads as follows: **18.6**

> Membership in the United Nations is open to all other peace-loving states [i.e. other than original members] which accept the obligations contained in the present Charter and, in the judgment of the Organisation, are able and willing to carry out these obligations.

Admission is effected by a decision of the General Assembly upon the recommendation of the Security Council. This means at least unanimous acquiescence by the permanent members. As the number of members has grown, so membership of States widely recognized as sovereign and applying pursuant to Article 4.1 has become more or less automatic. Hence the concept of universality of membership of the UN.

Principal Organs

The principal organs of the United Nations are: **18.7**

The General Assembly
The Security Council
The Economic and Social Council
The Secretariat
The Trusteeship Council
The International Court of Justice.

---

[4] Argentina, Australia, Belgium, Bolivia, Brazil, Byelorussian Soviet Socialist Republic, Canada, Chile, China, Colombia, Costa Rica, Cuba, Czechoslovakia, Denmark, Dominican Republic, Ecuador, Egypt, El Salvador, Ethiopia, France, Greece, Guatemala, Haiti, Honduras, India, Iran, Iraq, Lebanon, Liberia, Luxembourg, Mexico, Netherlands, New Zealand, Nicaragua, Norway, Panama, Paraguay, Peru, Philippines, Poland, Saudi Arabia, South Africa, Syrian Arab Republic, Turkey, Ukraine, Union of Soviet Socialist Republics, United Kingdom of Great Britain and Northern Ireland, United States of America, Uruguay, Venezuela, Yugoslavia.

The International Court of Justice is considered in Chapter 25. Comments on the operations of the other organs are given in the following paragraphs.

The General Assembly

18.8 The General Assembly is the only organ in which all members of the United Nations are directly represented. The Assembly is charged to discuss and make recommendations about any matter within the scope of the UN Charter. This has included the development of international law and its codification, as well as promoting international cooperation in the economic and social areas, and human rights. It also receives and notes reports from the Security Council and other bodies, and it is the Assembly which approves the budget of the organization. While the Assembly's sphere of activity is thus as wide as the Charter itself, in essence, apart from household questions (budgets, elections, appointments, etc) and affirmations of corporate views (e.g. on racism), it is a recommending and not a deciding body. Under Article 11.1 the General Assembly

> may consider the general principles of cooperation in the maintenance of international peace and security, including the principles governing disarmament and the regulation of armaments, and may make recommendations with regard to such principles to the Members or to the Security Council or to both.

But even this broad function is circumscribed by Article 12.1, which lays down that:

> [w]hile the Security Council is exercising in respect of any dispute or situation the functions assigned to it in the present Charter, the General Assembly shall not make any recommendation with regard to that dispute or situation unless the Security Council so requests.

However, this limitation,[5] intended in the main to avoid confusion, has not been difficult to circumvent by procedural devices.

18.9 The preceding paragraph has placed necessary emphasis on the limitations imposed by the Charter on the General Assembly in the matter of taking decisions. The corollary is that if the Assembly discusses and adopts a resolution which it is known in advance will be unacceptable to the Security Council then there will be no prospect of the Council, as the competent organ, authorizing action on the basis of that resolution. But there can nevertheless be a significant political impact by the passage by a large majority in the Assembly of resolutions on a major or highly topical matter.

---

[5] The effect of the limitations on the powers of the Assembly to act in a situation in which the Security Council may not be able to do so is referred to in paragraphs 18.9 *et seq.*

The Assembly is bound by the 'non-intervention' section of the Charter. Article **18.10**
2.7 reads:

> Nothing contained in the present Charter shall authorise the United Nations to
> intervene in matters which are essentially within the domestic jurisdiction of any
> state or shall require the Members to submit such matters to settlement under the
> present Charter; but this principle shall not prejudice the application of
> enforcement measures under Chapter VII.[6]

Meetings

The Charter provides (Article 20) that the Assembly shall meet in regular annual **18.11**
sessions and in 'such special sessions as occasion may require'. Such sessions can
be convoked at the request of the Security Council or by a majority of members. In practice a session of the General Assembly now begins at United
Nations Headquarters in New York each September, beginning with a ministerial element starting on the third Tuesday of the month. The Assembly remains
in session until the next session opens a year later, thus making redundant the
provisions of the 'Uniting for Peace' resolution (1950) which had made specific
provision for meetings at short notice.[7]

Structure of the General Assembly

Main Committees

The final authority within the General Assembly is the Plenary Meeting which **18.12**
can be called at any time during a session. At the next level the Assembly has set
up six main committees on which each member country may be represented by
one person. (No limit beyond that of space is placed on the number of advisers
present.) The committees are:

First Committee: Disarmament and International Security
Second Committee: Economic and Financial
Third Committee: Social, Humanitarian and Cultural
Fourth Committee: Special Political and Decolonization
Fifth Committee: Administrative and Budgetary
Sixth Committee: Legal.

Procedural Committees

These are two in number. **18.13**

---

[6] See paragraph **18.29**.
[7] See paragraph **18.41**.

The General Committee. This Committee consists of twenty-eight members, namely the President of the Assembly, who presides, and the twenty-one vice-presidents, together with the chairmen of the six main committees.[8] It occupies a position in the structure which gives it some influence, since it assists the President of the Assembly over the arrangement of the agenda, including additional items presented for admission over and above those originally accepted.[9] It can also in theory tender general advice to the President on the handling of the sessions: in practice, its advice covers procedural issues rather than political questions.

18.14   *The Credentials Committee.* This is a committee of nine members, appointed at the beginning of each session by the General Assembly on the proposal of the President. It examines the credentials presented by the leaders of the delegations to the particular session and reports on them to the Assembly. It has a particular responsibility to report in those cases where the admission of a delegation has been challenged.

18.15   In such cases the function of the committee may no longer be routine. For instance, a question of accreditation can arise if, during a civil war, both sides seek to send delegations to United Nations headquarters. This happened in the case of the Democratic Republic of Congo, and the question overhung for many years the membership of China.[10] Questions of official acceptability have arisen also when international opinion has moved very strongly against a member country, as it did when pressure developed for exclusion of South Africa from the United Nations.[11]

Standing Committees

18.16   This title is applied to two committees only, the Advisory Committee on Administrative and Budgetary Questions (ACABQ) and the Committee on Contributions. The former has its origin in the Advisory Group of Experts whose quiet, expert work at the San Francisco Conference subsequently laid the

---

[8] Selection of Vice-Chairmen of the Assembly and Chairmen of Committees is carried out by negotiation, first within and then between 'blocs'. The electoral process starting with the President may be protracted. The Assembly specified in resolution 33/138 of 19 December 1978 that the number of vice-presidents should in future be twenty-one, distributed in agreed proportions between African, Asian, Eastern European, Latin American, Western European, and other Groups, and permanent members of the Security Council. A comparable system has also been worked out for the choice of the six chairmen of the Main Committees.

[9] The Soviet Draft Resolution on non-self-governing territories of 1960 was a case in point.

[10] For the sequel see paragraph **18.34**.

[11] The United Nations Assembly records are full of examples of the mutual influence of politics, law, institutional theory and practice, etc. A classic instance is the debate on the position of South Africa recorded in A/PV 2281 of 12 November 1974.

foundation for a rational structure for the United Nations. It examines and reports on the regular and peacekeeping budgets and the accounts of the United Nations and the administrative budget of the Specialized Agencies and advises the General Assembly on other administrative and financial matters referred to it. In the selection of the sixteen members of this committee, provision is made not only for broad geographical representation, but also for personal qualifications and experience.

The second standing committee, the Committee on Contributions, advises the General Assembly on the division of the expenses of the UN among its members, the assessments for new members, appeals by members for a change of assessment, and application of Article 19 in cases of arrears. Its membership stands at eighteen and it seeks to avoid entanglement with the politics of arrears. This particular matter is dealt with by Article 19 of the Charter which reads in part: **18**.17

> A member...in arrears in the payment of its financial contributions to the Organisation shall have no vote in the General Assembly if the amount of its arrears equals or exceeds the amount of the contributions due from it for the preceding two full years...

At the time of the Congo crisis of 1960, there was disagreement within the United Nations about paying for the United Nations Emergency Force in the Middle East and for peacekeeping operations in the Congo. The Soviet Union and its Communist associates had taken the line from 1956 onwards that only the Security Council had the authority to establish United Nations forces and decide how their operations should be financed. The Soviet Union in 1960 opposed peacekeeping activities in the Congo.   **18**.18

The Assembly failed to resolve the dispute between the two organs and the Soviet Union and, in respect of the Congo, France began to withhold payments. The Assembly in 1961 decided by a majority to refer to the International Court of Justice the question whether peacekeeping activities in the Middle East and the Congo constituted 'expenses of the Organisation' under Article 17 of the Charter.[12] The Court took, by majority vote, the view that these operations were properly authorized to serve the purposes of the Organization and were thus legitimate expenses. In 1964, when Soviet payments were seriously in arrears, the United States raised the possibility of action under Article 19 to suspend the Soviet vote in the Assembly. There was naturally relief when crisis was averted by a so-called 'non-objection procedure' which enabled the United   **18**.19

---

[12] Art 17.2 reads: 'The expense of the Organisation shall be borne by the Members as apportioned by the General Assembly.'

States to withdraw its pressure. But this procedural device thinly concealed a major concession of principle proving the non-effectiveness of rules and committees when a leading Power decides not to comply.[13]

Subsidiary and Ad Hoc Bodies

18.20   The remaining committees, boards, commissions, and working groups are grouped by the United Nations under the title Subsidiary and Ad Hoc Bodies. In 2016 there were sixty-two of them. This total divides itself into four almost equal groups: political and disarmament, individual problems and crises, administration, and the remainder, notably legal, social, and economic. They vary greatly in activity and performance; their scope extends from the 124 members of the Special Committee on Peacekeeping operations, the sixty-three-nation Committee on Disarmament, and the sixty-seven members of the Committee on the Peaceful Uses of Outer Space, through the International Law Commission, to the Joint Inspection Unit which continually inspects the functioning of the United Nations machinery.[14] There is one characteristic of almost all of these committees. They are the classic field of modern collective diplomacy conducted by mixed national teams that contain specialist and diplomatic skills, increasingly through individuals knowledgeable in both areas.

18.21   General policy speeches, often made by Heads of Government and if not, by Foreign Ministers are delivered in plenary session during the first two or three weeks of the regular Assembly session. Since most speakers work out their speeches carefully in advance and devise them at least in part to satisfy audiences at home, there is not much actual debate at this stage. From then on, practically every item on the agenda is considered in the appropriate committee which will, if necessary, refer them, generally between sessions, to an existing or ad hoc subcommittee. This permits detailed and specialized work in a group smaller than the main committee of anything up to 193 people. Recommendations on each item will come back from committee to the Plenary Assembly where it will be voted on, sometimes without discussion and generally with much briefer discussion than that in committee.

---

[13] The discussions, voluntary initiatives, and expedients accompanying this main question were of immense length and complexity and can only be studied completely by reference to United Nations documents. A good background can be obtained from S D Bailey, *The General Assembly of the United Nations* (rev edn, New York: Praeger, 1964) and S C Xydis in *The United Nations, Past, Present and Future*, ed James Barros (New York and London, 1972).

[14] The best way to approach a more detailed knowledge of this subject is undoubtedly to use the latest edition of the *United Nations Yearbook* as a starting-point. Research into the more detailed or more controversial activities can then follow.

Decisions are taken in committees by a simple majority of those present and **18.22** voting. The same rule applies in plenary meetings of the Assembly, except in respect of 'important' questions on which, as required by the Charter, decisions are taken by a two-thirds majority of those present and voting. 'Important' questions include automatically recommendations concerning the maintenance of peace and security, elections to the Councils, admission, suspension, and expulsion of members, and budgetary questions: other questions may be ruled to be 'important' by a simple majority vote. The overwhelming majority of substantive decisions are taken in this way. Those wishing to oppose a draft resolution can choose to make approval more difficult by advocating the more difficult hurdle of a two-thirds requirement.[15] Thus a preliminary quasi-procedural vote (or decision by consent) can in fact anticipate the final, formal vote itself.

Order of Roll-call Voting

Rule 89 of the Rules of Procedure of the General Assembly reads in part as follows: **18.23**

(a) The General Assembly shall normally vote by show of hands or by standing, but any representative may request a roll-call. The roll-call shall be taken in the English alphabetical order of the names of the Members, beginning with the Member whose name is drawn by lot by the President...[16]

In the early meetings of the General Assembly, the roll-call was conducted in alphabetical order starting at the beginning of the alphabet. This meant that when roll-call votes were declared publicly, the first vote on a difficult question on which voting lines had not yet become clearly defined could have an influence on subsequent voting. Nowadays the General Assembly usually votes by mechanical means which replaces the show of hands or standing. The outcome and each member State's vote are publicly visible. Any member State may call for a recorded vote, which replaces a roll-call vote, and the result of the mechanical vote is then inserted in the formal record of the meeting.

The Security Council

The Security Council has the primary responsibility for the maintenance of **18.24** international peace and security.

Membership

Originally the Security Council had eleven members, five permanent and six **18.25** non-permanent. The permanent members were the Republic of China, France,

---

[15] The Soviet Union applied to this 'thesis' the term 'hidden veto'.
[16] *Rules of Procedure of the General Assembly, United Nations* (New York, 1970) 18: Rule 128 prescribes the same procedure for the Main Committees of the Assembly.

the Union of Soviet Socialist Republics, the United Kingdom of Great Britain and Northern Ireland, and the United States of America. The six non-permanent members were to be elected by the General Assembly for two years, a provision in Article 23.2 ensuring that three would be elected each year. Since that time there have been two important changes, one in the number of members and the other in the identity of one of the permanent members.

18.26 In the election of non-permanent members, due regard should be paid to the contribution of members to the maintenance of international peace and security and to the other purposes of the organization. In practice regard is seldom paid. Each year, candidates for election to the Council are elected by the full membership of the UN from each of the geographic groupings, thus ensuring equitable geographical distribution. Frequently each group nominates the same number of candidates as there are places available for that group.

Procedure

18.27 The Security Council is organized so as to be able to function continuously at a few hours' notice. Every member of the Council has to be represented at all times at the seat of the organization. The position of president is held for a month at a time by each of its members in turn, in the alphabetical order of their English names.

Functions

18.28 The main functions of the Security Council are dealt with in Chapters VI and VII of the Charter. Under Chapter VI of the Charter, entitled the 'Pacific Settlement of Disputes', the Council may call on the parties to a dispute to settle it by peaceful means; may investigate any dispute or any situation which might lead to international friction or give rise to a dispute, in order to determine whether the continuance of the dispute or situation is likely to endanger the maintenance of international peace and security; or, at any stage of such a dispute or situation, may recommend procedures or methods of adjustment. Any member of the United Nations or the Secretary-General may bring such a dispute or situation to the attention of the Council, or of the General Assembly. Theoretically, any State not a member of the United Nations may bring to the attention of the same bodies any dispute to which it is a party, if it accepts for the purposes of the dispute the obligations of pacific settlement provided in the Charter.

18.29 Chapter VII of the Charter is entitled 'Action with respect to Threats to the Peace, Breaches of the Peace and Acts of Aggression'. Under it the Council is given extensive powers, including the power to authorize the use of armed force. Chapter VII sets out a hierarchy of potential action by the Council if it determines the existence of any threat to the peace. It can make recommendations to the parties concerned, or decide on measures intended to maintain or restore international peace and security. Under Article 25 of the Charter, member States are obliged to comply with decisions of the Security Council (whereas resolutions of the General Assembly can, as a rule, only have the force of recommendations). Not all conclusions of the Council are decisions, and only decisions are binding on member States. Under Article 41 of the Charter the Council may decide measures not involving the use of force, effectively sanctions, to give effect to its decisions. If such measures are considered inadequate or have proved to be inadequate, the Council may take action under Article 42 which can include the use of armed force. The use of these articles evolved slowly, owing to the power of veto of the permanent members of the Security Council, and the Council rarely exercised the powers granted to it by the provisions of Chapter VII. An early example was resolution 217 which in 1965 called upon member States to do their utmost to break all economic relations with the then Southern Rhodesia, including imposing an oil embargo. This was followed in 1966 by resolution 221 which called upon the United Kingdom to prevent, by force if necessary, the delivery of oil destined for Southern Rhodesia. Since 1989, the Council has increasingly adopted resolutions which have been mandatory in nature, and involved sanctions and even the use of force. But the Military Staff Committee, for which Article 47 provides and which was intended to assist the Security Council in making plans for the application of armed force, has had from the beginning a purely formal existence. Mandates for peacekeeping forces invariably authorize the use of force, both to protect the troops themselves and to protect civilians. There have been few cases where the Council has authorized the use of force by nations in order to maintain international peace and security. Examples include resolution 678 which in 1990 authorized member States to use all necessary means to secure the withdrawal of Iraqi forces from Kuwait; resolution 1973 which in 2011 authorized member States to take all necessary measures to protect civilians under threat in Libya; and resolution 2085 which in 2012 authorized the deployment of an African led International Support Mission to Mali.

18.30 While thus vesting primary responsibility for the maintenance of peace in the Security Council, Article 51 of the Charter also provides that nothing contained in it shall impair the inherent right of individual or collective self-defence, if an armed attack occurs against a member of the United Nations, until the Security Council has taken measures necessary to maintain international peace and security. A debate continues as to whether this legitimizes pre-emptive action against what is perceived as an imminent threat of attack. It is under this provision of the Charter that the establishment of the North Atlantic Treaty Organization (NATO) was justified (see Chapter 23).

18.31 The Charter also allows (in Chapter VIII) for the establishment of regional arrangements for dealing with such matters relating to the maintenance of international peace and security as are appropriate for regional action. But no enforcement action can be taken under regional arrangements or by regional agencies without the authorization of the Security Council. Both the African Union and the European Union favour only deploying military forces for peace-keeping operations when the Council has adopted a resolution giving specific authorization.

Enlargement of Membership

18.32 With the achievement by a large number of former colonies, particularly in Africa, of national independence, it had become clear that a Security Council of eleven members would not satisfactorily accommodate the views of the various regions of the world on a basis of equitable geographic distribution. It was accordingly decided in 1963 (ratified in 1965) that the membership of the Security Council should be raised to fifteen, the number of permanent members remaining at five.[17] The geographical distribution of the ten non-permanent seats was laid down as follows:

Africa and Asia	5
Eastern Europe	1
Latin America and Caribbean	2
Western Europe and other States	2

18.33 This change had a consequence which was more than mathematical. When the Security Council numbered eleven members, a resolution required seven affirmative votes, so that one such vote had to come from one of the five permanent members. When the membership was raised to fifteen, it was decided to fix the number of affirmative votes required to carry resolutions at nine. As a result, provided that no permanent member exercises a veto, resolutions can be passed without an affirmative vote from any of the permanent members, and even with the support of the five permanent members a resolution also requires the positive votes of four non-permanent members if it is to be approved. To put it differently, any seven of the ten non-permanent members can collectively exercise a 'sixth veto'. Therefore, on a matter on which the permanent members are not enthusiastic but on which no permanent member wishes to vote negatively, whether alone or in company with others, a proposition can be carried by

---

[17] General Assembly resolution 1991 (XVIII) of 17 December 1963. The resolution came into force on 31 August 1965 on receipt of the necessary ratifications.

the votes of non-permanent members only. This procedure was used in a vote in 1973 in regard to the holding of a Peace Conference in Geneva.[18] The veto of permanent members of the Council cannot be applied to procedural decisions. Subsequently, and especially in the period 2000–10, debate on a further enlargement of the Council continued, the main focus of discussion being an enlargement in the number of permanent members. There was notably strong support for the membership of Japan, India, Brazil, and Germany and representatives of Africa, on whose identity there is no clear consensus within African States. Other States also have claims to membership. Agreement to enlarge the permanent membership is proving very difficult, the more so if it is proposed that the new members should also be able to exercise a veto. Since any amendment of the Charter would require the formal ratification of each of the five existing permanent members as well as an affirmative vote by two-thirds of the General Assembly, there is little prospect of a package amendment to enlarge the Council membership.

Replacement of the Republic of China by the People's Republic

At the San Francisco Conference China was represented by the Republic of **18.34** China. On the initiative of the United States, China was accepted as one of the original sponsors of the San Francisco Conference and one of the permanent members of the Security Council. As a result the Republic of China (which after the Chinese revolution in 1949 existed only as the Chiang Kai-shek administration in Taiwan) occupied the seat until its replacement by the People's Republic of China on 25 October 1971.[19]

Voting in the Security Council

Article 27 of the Charter which deals with voting in the Security Council orig- **18.35** inally read as follows:

1. Each member of the Security Council shall have one vote.
2. Decisions of the Security Council on procedural matters shall be made by an affirmative vote of seven members.
3. Decisions of the Security Council on all other matters shall be made by an affirmative vote of seven members including the concurring votes of the permanent members; provided that in decisions under Article VI and under paragraph 3 of Article 52, a party to a dispute shall abstain from voting.

(The Articles specifically referred to in subparagraph 3 above concern the Pacific Settlement of Disputes, whether in a general or regional context.)

---

[18] In 1976 Angola was admitted despite abstention by the United States.
[19] General Assembly resolution 2758 (XXVI) of 25 October 1971: 'Restoration of the lawful rights of the People's Republic of China in the United Nations.'

18.36 Under the amendment to the Charter already mentioned in paragraph **18.32**, which entered into force on 31 August 1965, the number of votes required for affirmative decisions was raised from seven to nine.

18.37 The effect of Article 27.3 of the Charter is to create the so-called 'veto', exercisable by any of the permanent members. Not unnaturally this was strongly attacked at the San Francisco Conference by both 'middle' and smaller Powers, but it was a proposition from which the sponsoring Powers and France were not prepared to move, maintaining that it was only by a measure of this kind that the constitution of the United Nations could be made to conform with the realities of world power. The only modification agreed later (1946/7) by the permanent members, and confirmed by the ICJ, was that a veto by a permanent member required the exercise of a negative vote. Thus, if a permanent member abstained, such an abstention would not imply failure of a draft resolution provided that there were sufficient affirmative votes to make up seven or, after August 1965, nine.

18.38 On 25 June 1950, troops from North Korea crossed the boundary into South Korea and met resistance from South Korean forces. The matter was at once brought to the attention of the Security Council. In the debate the Secretary-General, Mr Trygve Lie, intervened to give his opinion that the attack was a violation of the United Nations Charter. It was to be presumed, however, that any proposal for United Nations preventive action would be vetoed by the Soviet representative.

18.39 But the Soviet Union was at that time boycotting the Security Council and other organs of the United Nations on the ground that, given the victory of the Communist forces on the Chinese mainland the year before, China was no longer properly represented at the United Nations by a Nationalist delegation. Accordingly, when a draft of resolution 82 was put to the vote in June 1950 calling for a cease-fire and a withdrawal of forces, there was no veto. Four subsequent resolutions were also passed in 1950. Of these, resolution 83 recommended that members of the United Nations, implicitly under the rubric of self-defence, furnish such assistance to the Republic of Korea as may be necessary to repel the armed attack and resolution 84 welcomed such support and recommended that forces should be made available to a unified command under the United States of America, which persisted throughout the subsequent war. This was to be one of the very few resolutions dealing with the use of military force until resolution 678 in 1990.

18.40 Hostilities were eventually and formally brought to an end by an armistice signed in Korea on 27 July 1953 by the Commander-in-Chief, United Nations Command, the Supreme Commander of the (North) Korean People's Army, and the Commander of the Chinese People's Volunteers. The Armistice agreement provided for the setting up of a Military Armistice Commission, consisting of five members from each side, whose instructions were 'to supervise the implementation of this armistice Agreement and to settle through negotiation any violations of the Armistice Agreement'. Nearly a quarter of a century then passed without change in this military and political arrangement. The absence of the Soviet delegate from the relevant meeting permitted the Security Council to adopt resolutions not only condemning aggression in Korea, but also recommending and welcoming action to repel it. The 'Uniting for Peace' resolution, accepted by the General Assembly on 3 November 1950[20] provided principally that, if the Security Council were prevented by lack of unanimity among its permanent members from taking action in a case involving a threat to the peace, breach of the peace, or an act of aggression, the Assembly might be called within 24 hours at the request of seven members of the Security Council, or of a majority of Member States, to meet in emergency special session for the purpose of making recommendations for collective measures to maintain or restore peace.

The 'Uniting for Peace' resolution also provided for a Peace Observation Commission of fourteen members which could observe and report on the situation in any area where international tension existed; a Panel of military advisers to be available to advise Member States on the formation of military units which they would be asked to keep ready for service upon the recommendation of the General Assembly or the Security Council; and a Collective Resources Committee of fourteen members to study and report to the Security Council and the Assembly on methods of maintaining and strengthening international peace. In fact, none of these provisions was ever put into effect. But what had been done was the best that could be achieved in the absence of a Security Council decision and an effective United Nations Military Staff Committee as intended under Article 47 of the Charter.[21] **18.41**

No situations involving the procedural complications produced by the Korean crisis arose in the following years. But the proceedings just described enabled a Special Session of the General Assembly to be convoked in November 1956 at the time of the Suez crisis, and which authorized the formation of a United Nations Emergency Force to secure and supervise the cessation of hostilities. **18.42**

Use by the United Nations of Armed Forces

The sequels of this episode ran along two lines, the use of military forces by the United Nations, and the use of the veto. It was not unreasonable to expect that, **18.43**

---

[20] Resolution 377 of 3 November 1950.
[21] On how the 'Uniting for Peace' procedure has operated in practice, see D Zaum, 'The Security Council, the General Assembly, and War: The Uniting for Peace Resolution', in V Lowe, et al. (eds), *The United Nations Security Council and War* (Oxford: Oxford University Press, 2008) 154–74.

as a result of what happened over Korea, no permanent member of the Security Council would again be absent on a comparable occasion and no further use of armed forces would be made by the United Nations. The first judgment has been correct. The second judgment would be wrong. It is true that with the tacit approval of at least two permanent members of the Security Council, machinery for organizing action under Article 47 of the Charter through the Office of the Military Adviser had been allowed to run down. However, this did not happen to the use of the armed forces of the United Nations in the cause of peacekeeping.

18.44 Two years before the Korean War, the Security Council had on 29 May 1948 authorized the United Nations mediator in Palestine to use military observers for truce supervision; but at that stage these observers did not constitute an 'interposition' force between possible combatants. Later, after the Suez crisis, a United Nations Emergency Force was placed on the border between Israel and Egypt between the forces of the two countries. In 1967, however, in a tense political situation, the withdrawal of the force was demanded by President Nasser of Egypt. The then United Nations Secretary-General, U Thant, acceded to this demand on the grounds that Egypt was not consenting to the presence of the UN force. His immediate acquiescence and failure to consult the Security Council provoked controversy. At the end of the subsequent hostilities, the passage five months later of Security Council resolution 242 resulted in the truce supervision organization assuming responsibility for maintaining the cease-fire in the Suez Canal Zone. When in 1973 war broke out again, the Security Council in resolutions 338 and 339 of 21 and 23 October set up a new UNEF with the instruction to 'supervise the immediate and complete implementation and observance of the cease-fire...and to use its best efforts to prevent a recurrence of the fighting'.

18.45 The use of United Nations forces in a peacekeeping capacity has not been confined to the Middle East. In 1960 in the former Belgian Congo (Zaire), now the Democratic Republic of the Congo, the employment of forces in the name of the United Nations was wholly different from the other two referred to earlier. A few days after independence day (20 June 1960) the Congolese army revolted against the Belgian forces still stationed there. Tensions were high and the then Secretary-General, Dag Hammarskjöld, put the matter urgently to the Security Council under Article 99 of the Charter. He couched his initiative in language which was based on the setting up of the UNEF in Sinai and avoiding the concept of 'enforcement'. The Secretary-General persuaded the Security Council to accept his plan[22] and at one time there were contingents from eleven members

---

[22] UN Security Council resolution 143 (1960) adopted on 14 July 1960.

of the United Nations in the Congo for the purpose of promoting the peace and unity of the country. In the wake of the Soviet and French complaints about the Congo operation, a Special Committee on Peacekeeping Operations was set up by General Assembly resolution 2006 (XIX) of 18 February 1965 to draw up guidelines on peacekeeping operations. As of 2016 the UN peacekeeping operation in what is now the Democratic Republic of Congo is the UN's largest such operation.

Yet another variation in the use of United Nations forces for peacekeeping was the Security Council's resolution 186 of 4 March 1964, designed to keep the Greek and Turkish protagonists in a near-civil war in Cyprus from actual hostilities. Under this resolution there was established, in consultation with the governments of Cyprus and the three guarantor Powers, Greece, Turkey, and the United Kingdom, a United Nations Force in Cyprus (UNFICYP). Drawn from seven Commonwealth and European countries (including, for the first time, a permanent member of the Security Council, the United Kingdom), the force became operational on 27 March 1964, initially for three months. It remains there in 2016. **18.46**

Peacekeeping and the presence of UN blue helmets or blue berets in conflict areas has become a key UN role and one of the most recognizable aspects of the UN. Conventionally the United Nations only deploys a peacekeeping presence in support of a peace agreement or cease-fire between the protagonists, and with the consent of the parties. By the beginning of 2016 there were sixteen UN peacekeeping operations. One, a joint operation with the African Union, is in Darfur. There are also some separate non-UN peacekeeping operations, carried out by regional organizations, but with authorization from the UN Security Council, for example the NATO-led force in Kosovo and the African Union Mission in Somalia. In approving a UN peacekeeping operation, the Council resolution spells out its mandate, authorizes the use of force necessary to defend the troops and civilians in the area of deployment, and the size of the deployment. It is then for the UN Department of Peacekeeping to generate the Force consistent with the mandate from the offers made by UN Member States. The cost of deployment is a charge on the UN's peacekeeping budget, and in practice the General Assembly's Fifth Committee ensures that the funding is provided. The key to this budget places a particular responsibility on permanent members. The nature of the Security Council resolution adopted has evolved to embrace a comprehensive peace support operation, covering the economic, political, and human rights aspects, as well as taking account of the work of UN agencies and others. **18.47**

The Veto after Korea

The unique experience of the Korean debate and its sequel did not immediately change the spirit or practice of the Security Council in the use of the **18.48** veto. In general, the custom was to bring disputes and situations involving possible dangers to peace rapidly before the Security Council (as indeed appeared to be the intention of the Charter) with the resultant risk of veto occurring soon after.[23]

18.49   The hundredth Soviet veto was applied in 1961. At the end of that year the total number of vetoes cast since 1945 was as follows:

China (Nationalist)	1	
France	4	(2 jointly with the United Kingdom)
USSR	104	
United Kingdom	3	(2 jointly with France)
United States	nil	

18.50   Although many of these vetoes had to do with potential new members, it was damaging to the UN organization to face an international crisis and take no decision at all, or worse still, not even to face it, despite the words of the Charter in Article 1.1:

> The Purposes of the United Nations are:
>
> 1. To maintain international peace and security, and to that end: to take effective collective measures for the prevention and removal of threats to the peace…[24]

18.51   A classic example of successful diplomacy to avoid the veto was the handling of the diplomatic situation after the Six-Day Arab–Israel War of 1967. A cease-fire was followed by the calling of a Special Assembly of the United Nations at which the Soviet Union prompted a draft resolution wholly favourable to the Arab view. This was not adopted, and deadlock appeared complete. However, early in August there emerged the first signs that there could be the possibility of compromise. This possibility was pursued over the next three months, particularly by two leaders of delegations in New York, Lord Caradon (United Kingdom) and Arthur Goldberg (United States), and by V V Kuznetsov (Soviet Union), who arrived for the 1967 General Assembly. The end of this intensive 'conference diplomacy' was Security Council resolution 242 of 22 November

---

[23] Any serious study of the question owes the highest debt to Sydney D Bailey, both for his general work on the United Nations, and, in this present context, for his careful, informative, and sensitive work *Voting in the Security Council* (Bloomington: Indiana University Press, 1969), and his later work *The Procedure of the Security Council* (Oxford: Clarendon, 1975).

[24] There was, for instance, criticism of the failure of the Security Council in 1976 to take active cognizance of the intervention of Cuban troops in the civil war in Angola; and of the civil war in the Lebanon in the same year.

1967, which remains an essential element of any proposal for the final settlement of the Arab–Israel conflict.[25]

In the later years of the Cold War, from the mid-sixties to the late eighties, there **18**.52 was a notable decrease in the overall number of vetoes used. The US became the principal user of the veto in this period—reflecting the fact that it had become relatively isolated in the Security Council due to the degree of understanding between the Soviet bloc and many of the UN's post-colonial member States. The numbers of vetoes cast in this period was:

Country	Vetoes cast in 1964–90
China	2
France	14
USSR	15
United Kingdom	29
United States	69

The proportionate increase in Western as opposed to Communist vetoes **18**.53 reflected among other things the careful choice by the Soviet Union of initiatives which, in the view of that government, might secure the support or non-resistance of the non-aligned countries while arousing at least anxiety in the Western world. Since 1990 the USA has been the most frequent user of the veto. Neither France nor the UK has used the veto since 1989. The USA has used it most often to veto resolutions critical of Israel. Indeed, the so-called Negroponte doctrine is attributed to the US ambassador who is said to have told the Council that the US would oppose any resolution which condemned Israel without also condemning terrorist groups. A particularly controversial use of the veto was China's opposition in 1999 to the renewal of the mandate for a UN peacekeeping operation in the Former Yugoslav Republic of Macedonia because of that country's diplomatic relations with Taiwan. In 2007 and 2008 Russia and China both vetoed resolutions on the situation in Burma/Myanmar and Zimbabwe respectively, on the grounds that they represented an unjustified interference in the domestic affairs of a sovereign State.

---

[25] The resolution left behind one ambiguity for which, in the view of the Israelis and some others, a solution is required. The English text of the first 'affirmation' in the resolution contains the following principle: '(i) withdrawal of Israeli armed forces from territories occupied in the recent conflict...' The French text ('*des* territoires') does not admit the narrow distinction between 'territories' and 'the territories' implied in the English, and this distinction may require final compromise—and statesmanship. The interpretation of the formula by the majority of delegations was that the text meant a wholesale restoration of occupied territories qualified only by small agreed modifications where experience and good sense indicated that these would help secure agreement.

18.54   Overall up to the end of 2015 the number of vetoes cast was as follows:

China	11
France	18
USSR/Russia	127
United Kingdom	30
United States	83

18.55   The work of the Council has broadened to cover the changing threats to international peace and security. Article 41 of the Charter empowers the Council to impose measures if it considers this necessary for the maintenance of international peace and security. Initially this power was little used but by the early 1990s the Council began to turn to this approach. Faced with threats and judging that military action was not appropriate and when diplomatic and political pressures had not succeeded, sanctions of a nature binding on all States were agreed. Early examples were those imposed on Iraq following its invasion of Kuwait, and on the Federal Republic of Yugoslavia (Serbia and Montenegro). More sanctions followed, including those against Somalia, Liberia, Cote d'Ivoire, Sudan, North Korea, and Iran. Early sanctions were often criticized as ineffective and as penalizing ordinary citizens, the weak, and unintended targets. As a result, sanctions became much more focused, targeted more precisely to seize assets, to impose arms embargoes, and to subject named individuals to bans on international travel. The outcomes tend to be more effective, but still of limited impact. Resolutions imposing sanctions are adopted under Chapter VII of the Charter so as to be mandatory and usually set up a sub-committee to oversee the implementation of the sanctions, often assisted by experts. Regional organizations, for example the EU, often act to give effect to UN sanctions, or act in parallel or even separately from the UN.

18.56   As terrorism became a more immediate threat, so the Security Council reacted to it. In 1999 the Council adopted resolution 1267 aimed at imposing asset freezes, travel bans, and arms embargoes against named individuals judged to be connected to Al Qaeda and the Taliban. Immediately following the 9/11 attacks in 2001, the Council in resolution 1373 set up the Counter Terrorism Committee and imposed obligations on States to prevent terrorism, to deny safe haven to terrorists, and to cooperate in combating terrorism. States were encouraged as necessary to sign the twelve international anti-terrorism conventions agreed by the General Assembly. In 2004 resolution 1540 addressed the proliferation of weapons of mass destruction and prohibited their transfer to or holding by terrorists. Each of these resolutions set up committees to ensure their implementation. A further resolution 1673 (2005) prohibited incitement to commit terrorist attacks. None of the resolutions sought to define terrorism and more generally, neither in the Security Council nor in the General Assembly has it proved possible to reach agreement on what constitutes terrorism. The search stumbles on the difficulty of covering action by States and acts in resistance to foreign occupation.

The agenda of the Security Council has evolved to include issues which are less **18.57** an immediate threat to international peace and security as a longer-term or indirect threat. Sometimes termed thematic or horizontal issues, they include consideration of the conflict spectrum including prevention, the role of Special Tribunals, ongoing situations in countries like Sudan and South Sudan, and HIV/Aids. A significant resolution was 1325 (2000) which addressed 'Women, Peace and Security' and recognized the role of women as disproportionate victims of conflict and their contribution to ending conflict and creating stable States. There is now an annual debate on this subject, often accompanied by a further resolution. In May 2007 the Council held a debate on the security threats posed by climate change, again pushing the boundary of competence.

A key tension within the United Nations is that between the advocates of Article **18.58** 2.7 who attach overriding importance to non-intervention in what they consider to be the domestic affairs of a sovereign State and those who want action. This has stopped the Council taking action in response to crises in Burma/Myanmar and Zimbabwe. The issue was addressed in the 2005 World Summit. It set out a doctrine on the responsibility to protect populations from genocide, war crimes, ethnic cleansing, and crimes against humanity. It held that each individual State had the primary responsibility to protect its citizens. The international community has a responsibility to assist the State, but if the threat persists the international community, through the authority of the UN Security Council, then has the responsibility to act to protect the population from these threats.[26] The principle of 'responsibility to protect' as adopted requires Security Council authorization for any military action to give effect to the principle in a specific case. It is therefore distinct from those doctrines of 'humanitarian intervention' that claim that individual States, or groupings of States, have a right to intervene in situations of urgent humanitarian necessity. The latter was invoked by a number of NATO Member States in 1999 to justify the military operation in defence of the Kosovars. Although all States at summit level agreed the principle of responsibility to protect, it remains to be seen whether, case by case, States are prepared to act and can secure agreement for action in the Security Council.[27]

---

[26] '2005 World Summit Outcome', General Assembly resolution 60/1 of 16 September 2005.
[27] See Chapter 2, paragraph 2.24 and Chapter 3, paragraph 3.38.

Economic and Social Council

18.59 Under the heading 'International Economic and Social Cooperation', Article 55 of the Charter sets out the objectives of this side of the organization's work as follows:

> With a view to the creation of conditions of stability and well-being which are necessary for peaceful and friendly relations among nations based on respect for the principle of equal rights and self-determination of peoples, the United Nations shall promote:
>
> (a) higher standards of living, full employment, and conditions of economic and social progress and development;
> (b) solutions of international economic, social, health, and related problems; and international cultural and educational cooperation; and
> (c) universal respect for, and observance of, human rights and fundamental freedoms for all without distinction as to race, sex, language, or religion.

18.60 Authority for carrying out the above functions is vested in the General Assembly and, under its authority, in the Economic and Social Council (Article 60). The Council may make or initiate studies on the matters referred to, and may make recommendation upon them to the General Assembly, to member States, and to the Specialized Agencies concerned. It may also make arrangements for consultation with non-governmental organizations. The Council enters formal relationships with the Specialized Agencies by negotiating special agreements with each of them, subject to approval by the General Assembly.

Membership and Procedures

18.61 Originally the Economic and Social Council consisted of eighteen members, of which one-third retired each year but remained eligible for immediate re-election. The number was increased to twenty-seven in 1963 and to fifty-four in 1971. Decisions of the Council are made by a majority of members present and voting, each member having one vote.

18.62 Why, given the importance of the economic and social aims of the United Nations and the progress made since 1945 in respect of many of them, does the Economic and Social Council not enjoy significant prestige? In the United Nations' formative years of 1945–6, while economic and social objectives were accepted as very important, the main interest of governments and peoples lay in organizing the preservation of peace and the prevention of future war: that is why the Charter gave the Security Council strong potential powers. But there was also a basic difference between the two Councils. The Security Council had no competitors—at least not within the UN system; the Economic and Social Council had competition existing already in the International Labour Organization (1919), the International Bank for Reconstruction and Development, and the International Monetary Fund (Articles approved in 1946), and later in the World Health Organization (1948) and, on the economic analysis side, the Organisation for Economic Cooperation and Development (OECD) (1961) and the United Nations Conference on Trade and Development (UNCTAD) (1964). Of these 'competitors', all but the OECD have since become Specialized Agencies of the UN. Thus, while the Economic and Social Council has initiated such enterprises as the GATT (General Agreement on Tariffs and Trade) now the WTO (see Chapter **20**) and encouraged progress on economic and social developments, including in later years work designed to assist the developing countries, it has never succeeded in establishing for itself a place of world authority.

The Secretariat

In the opening words of Article 97, 'The Secretariat shall comprise a secretary-general and such staff as the Organisation may require'. **18.63**

The Secretary-General

The same Article continues: 'The Secretary-General shall be appointed by the General Assembly upon the recommendation of the Security Council. He shall be the chief administrative officer of the Organisation.' Article 98 states that the Secretary-General '[s]hall act in that capacity in all meetings of the General Assembly' [and of all the Councils of the Organisation] 'and shall perform such other functions as are entrusted to him by these organs'. **18.64**

The functions of the Secretary-General are up to this point somewhat modestly described. But Article 99 is of a different quality. It reads: 'The Secretary-General may bring to the attention of the Security Council any matter which in his opinion may threaten the maintenance of international peace and security.' It was realized by those who devised the Charter that one of the difficulties which obstruct international peacemaking and peacekeeping is a situation in which national or group sensitivities are so touchy, or moods so tense, that none of the States concerned wish to invoke or provoke third party intervention, national or international. Article 99 contains the strong implication that in such circumstances the Secretary-General has some moral obligation to have the position discussed in the Security Council. Such a decision would need both judgement and courage. If the Secretary-General acted too hastily, he might make matters worse; if he hesitated too long or did not act at all, he might be failing to exercise on behalf of the organization established as the guardian of the world's security a most important faculty provided explicitly by the Charter. Different secretaries-general have taken different views. In any case the political arguments in favour of a Security Council discussion of a particular situation come to the fore. **18.65**

The Staff

18.66 The staff of the Secretariat is appointed by the Secretary-General under regulations established by the General Assembly. The paramount consideration in their employment and in the determination of their conditions of service is, according to Article 101.3, the 'necessity of securing the highest standards of efficiency, competence and integrity. Due regard shall be paid to the importance of recruiting staff on as wide a geographical basis as possible.' In practice, all these conditions are seldom fulfilled. Indeed, they are hardly self-consistent, since the choice of the most competent candidate cannot be expected regularly to coincide with the widest possible selection on a geographical basis.

18.67 In the performance of their duties the Secretary-General and staff may not seek or receive instructions from any government or from any other authority external to the organization. They are to refrain from any action which might reflect on their position as international officials responsible only to the organization. According to Article 100, each member of the United Nations undertakes to respect the exclusive international character and responsibilities of the Secretary-General and his staff and not to seek to influence them in the discharge of their responsibilities.[28] This is an undertaking observed more in the breach than in its implementation.

Languages

18.68 On 1 February 1946, during the first part of its first session, the United Nations General Assembly adopted a resolution entitled 'Rules of Procedure concerning Languages' of which the Annex, paragraph 1, reads as follows: 'In all the organs of the United Nations, other than the International Court of Justice, Chinese, French, English, Russian and Spanish shall be the official languages, and English and French the working languages.' This meant in effect that speeches made in one working language were interpreted into the other, and speeches made in the official languages were interpreted into both working languages. Any representative might make a speech in any other language, but in that case he would be responsible for providing interpretation into one of the working languages; the Secretariat would then provide interpretation from that working language into the other. Apart from this, a fuller documentation would be furnished in the working languages than in any other.

18.69 At that time simultaneous interpretation was in a very early technical stage, but by 15 November 1947, the General Assembly had decided[29] that simultaneous interpretation should be adopted as a permanent service, either as an alternative

---

[28] Full text in Arts 100 and 101.
[29] Resolution 152 (II) of 15 November 1947.

to, or in connection with, consecutive interpretation. In fact, this was the end of consecutive interpretation in the Assembly.

Consecutive interpretation has some merit if there are only two languages in use **18.70** at a Conference, since it gives delegates whose own language is other than either of these two a little more time and opportunity to make sure they understand what has been said. But the increase in the number of working languages has made the consecutive procedure impossibly lengthy, and made simultaneous interpretation essential.[30]

Meanwhile the number of working languages increased. In 1948 Spanish was **18.71** added. Twenty years later the Assembly decided to add Russian. Five years after that in 1973, Chinese was included for all purposes, together with Arabic for the Assembly and its Committees. The terms 'official' and 'working' languages were retained in the title of Rule 51, the text of which reads:

> Chinese, English, French, Russian and Spanish shall be both the official and the working languages of the General Assembly, its Committees and the subcommittees. Arabic shall be both an official and a working language of the General Assembly and the main Committees.[31]

Thus the simultaneous interpretation system, with its six booths containing **18.72** interpreters, enabled the assimilation of working and official languages to progress, and various national and group claims on behalf of particular languages to be met. A limited addition to the language services was made when, to respond to the needs of Austria and the then two Germanys, it was decided that written German translation services (as opposed to oral interpretation) should be furnished in respect of basic documents, provided that the three countries collectively covered the cost.

As a result the annual budget provision for the aggregated expenditure of the **18.73** Translation Division, Interpretation and Meeting Division, and the Editorial and Records Division now amounts to substantial sums.

The Trusteeship Council

The United Nations Charter devotes three chapters to the subject of dependent **18.74** territories. Chapters XII and XIII, entitled respectively 'International Trusteeship

---

[30] It is, however, pleasant to record that the end of the era of consecutive system in the United Nations had its glorious moment. The noted Latin-American statesman and orator Señor Fernando Belaúnde of Peru made at the General Assembly a long political speech in Spanish which was translated into French by one of the famous Kaminker brothers. M. Kaminker reproduced every significant phrase, every telling pause, every emotional tone and even every dramatic gesture, and, having used no notes at all, sat down amid a thunder of applause.

[31] Resolutions 3189 (XXVIII) and 390 (XXVIII). See also Chapter 7, paragraph 7.9.

System' and 'The Trusteeship Council', deal with a special task inherited from the Permanent Mandates Commission of the League of Nations as modified by the changes in the world military and political situation brought about by the Second World War. Chapter XI, under the title 'Declaration regarding Non-Self-Governing Territories', presents a declaration under which '[m]embers of the United Nations which have or assume responsibilities for the administration of territories whose peoples have not yet attained a full measure of self-government'[32] accept certain obligations. The scope and limits of these obligations are discussed in the following section of this chapter. But before the two methods of approach are described separately, it is important to note a degree of common origin.

18.75   Throughout history, stronger States or other groups have for a range of motives occupied through force or threat of the use of force, territories 'belonging to' or administered by others or barely administered at all. From the late sixteenth century onwards, European countries sought first trading posts and later sovereign territory in other parts of the world, notably Asia, Africa, and Central and South America, often in competition with each other.

18.76   At the end of the First World War, strong pressure by the United States, under the leadership of President Woodrow Wilson, led to a change in the world order. Colonies of the defeated colonial Powers (Germany and Turkey) were placed not under the sovereignty of individual victorious Powers, but under mandate exercised by individual Powers or groups of Powers on behalf of the world community embodied in the League of Nations, and in accordance with obligations laid down in the Covenant of the League. (The failure of the United States itself to become a member of the League did not affect the adoption of the new system.) This brought a new dimension into international law and diplomatic practice.

18.77   It was natural that the drafters of the United Nations Charter should have made provision for the continuation of the Mandate or, under its new name, Trusteeship system. Eleven territories were placed under the Trusteeship Council through agreements approved by the General Assembly. Of these, ten had become independent by 1975. With the termination of the Trusteeship Agreement for the Trust Territory of the Pacific Islands in 1994 and Palau's admission as a member of the UN, the Trusteeship Council had completed the tasks entrusted to it in respect of the last of the eleven territories placed under the Trusteeship system. One territory, South-West Africa (later Namibia), for-

---

[32] See Art 73, Chapter XI of the UN Charter.

merly a League mandate administered by South Africa, was not transferred by the administering State to the United Nations Trusteeship system.

By the early 1990s the constitution and proceedings of the Trusteeship Council **18.78** had become irrelevant to the main stream of United Nations policy and action in respect of dependent territories. On 1 October 1994, with the termination of the status of Palau it completed its task and on 1 November 1994 it suspended its operation. The Trusteeship Council having thus fulfilled its purpose, the Secretary-General in both his report in 1994 on the work of the organization and in his 2005 report 'In Larger Freedom' recommended the elimination of the Trusteeship Council in accordance with Article 108 of the Charter. The 2005 Summit endorsed this recommendation. However, no Charter amendment has yet followed from that decision of the Summit. The Trusteeship Council continues in existence but is non-operational.

Two points may, however, be briefly noted. Article 76(b) of the Charter describes **18.79** as a 'basic objective' of the trusteeship system:

> To promote the political, economic, social, and educational advancement of the inhabitants of the trust territories, and their progressive development towards self-government or independence as may be appropriate to the particular circumstances of each territory and its peoples and the freely expressed wishes of the peoples concerned, and as may be provided by the terms of each trusteeship agreement.

Thus in careful language, bearing every sign of negotiation and compromise, the Trusteeship system looked forward to independence for those territories which had been committed to Trusteeship.

Non-self-governing Territories

During the Second World War various Allied declarations spoke in terms of **18.80** freedom, and in the case of India a highly serious, if unsuccessful, effort was made in 1942 to advance this progress beyond the provincial self-government already achieved. India had in any case been a member of the League of Nations while not yet independent of Britain, and it was accepted internationally that India would be independently represented not only at politico-technical conferences such as the Chicago Civil Aviation Conference in 1944 but also at the San Francisco Conference itself. American opinion, official and unofficial, was strongly opposed to the return of French and Dutch rule in Indo-China and Indonesia respectively, where strong nationalist movements had developed during Japanese occupation. It was thus inevitable that the question whether there should be an Article in the United Nations Charter about non-self-governing territories should be raised and hotly debated in San Francisco. The majority of the Conference, containing as it did Asian, Arab, and Latin-American States, many of which had had colonial pasts, favoured the inclusion of such an article. Against this the proponents of the emerging Article 2.7, the non-intervention clause, could and did argue that the two concepts were inconsistent.[33] When both Article 2 and Chapter XI—the latter dealing with non-self-governing territories—became part of the Charter as ratified, their coexistence raised obvious difficulties. Administering States in due course sought to use Article 2.7 to prevent discussion of items concerning non-self-governing territories, but the Assembly could, if the majority so wished, vote by majority to undertake such discussion.

18.81   The wording of Chapter XI is cautious. It is described as a 'Declaration', and its introductory paragraph, in Article 73, reads as follows:

> Members of the United Nations which have or assume responsibilities for the administration of territories whose people have not yet attained a full measure of self-government recognise the principle that the interests of the inhabitants of these territories are paramount, and accept as a sacred trust the obligation to promote to the utmost, within the system of international peace and security established by the present Charter, the well-being of the inhabitants of these territories...

18.82   Article 73(b) opens with a commitment 'to develop self-government' but does not contain a commitment to political independence. On the other hand, the phrase 'have not yet attained a full measure of self-government' has an implication of progress towards independence, and a much stronger implication is to be found in Article 1.2 of the Charter which, under the introductory phrase 'The purposes of the United Nations are—' reads in part: '2. To develop friendly relations among nations based on respect for the principle of equal rights and determination of peoples...'[34] Yet here again interpretation has to be made carefully.

18.83   And, as if in the early stages of the United Nations this matter were not ambiguous enough, reference may be made back to Article 73(e), in which administering Powers accept the obligation to 'transmit regularly to the Secretary-General for information purposes... statistical and other information of a technical nature relating to economic, social and educational conditions in territories for which they are respectively responsible'. The equivalent provision in Article 22 of the

---

[33] Art 2.7 reads in part: 'Nothing contained in the present Charter shall authorise the United Nations to intervene in matters which are essentially within the domestic jurisdiction of any state or shall require the Members to submit such matters to settlement under the present Charter...' (The remaining language removes this limitation in cases arising under Chapter VII which deals with threats to the peace, etc.).

[34] This Article of course excluded Trusteeship territories for which provision is made in Chapter XII of the Charter.

League of Nations Covenant had been weaker: 'In every case of mandate, the Mandatory shall render to the Council an annual report in reference to the territory committed to its charge.' Although it is stronger, Chapter XI of the Charter does not provide for the furnishing by the administering Power of political information.[35]

The limitations in Chapter XI of the Charter are important. But the essential change from previous practice is that the administering Powers accepted the proposition that they had a degree of obligation, sustained by international Charter, to report in detail to the international community on a wide range of matters regarding non-self-governing territories. **18.84**

A third consideration, to become later of great importance, was that, no doubt because Chapter XI is a 'declaration', no specific organ of the United Nations was created with power to supervise its operation. The information under Article 73(e) was to be furnished to the Secretary-General. But the Secretary-General was not told what to do with the information. In the event, he transmitted it to the General Assembly, which created a committee to examine it. This committee, like the Trusteeship Council, was constituted on the basis of parity between administering and non-administering States. The colonial Powers resisted attempts by the committee or the General Assembly to issue guidance or directives on colonial policy, and also took refuge in the fact that there was no obligation on them to transmit political information on certain territories, on the grounds that these had already attained the 'full measure of self-government' referred to in the Charter. The committee to examine information submitted under Article 73 was dissolved in 1963, as part of the major changes of attitude and pace in the handling of these matters in the early 1960s. **18.85**

In the early years after the ratification of the Charter a number of expected developments occurred. India and Pakistan became independent from Britain in 1947 and Ceylon (Sri Lanka) and Myanmar (Burma) in 1948: the first three within the Commonwealth and Burma outside. The Dutch, under pressure from the United Nations, accepted similar developments in the Dutch East Indies (Indonesia) in 1950. In 1956, Morocco and Tunisia declared independence from France, and Sudan emerged from a nominal Anglo-Egyptian condominium. In 1957, the Gold Coast (Ghana), under the leadership of Dr Kwame **18.86**

---

[35] Professor David A Kay, University of Wisconsin, in his essay 'Colonisation and Decolonisation', in James Barros (ed), *The United Nations, Past, Present and Future* (New York: The Free Press and London, 1972), writes (at 168, n 20) 'significantly for later developments, this provision was sponsored at the San Francisco Conference by the Soviet Union'.

Nkrumah, became the first British African colony to gain independence, and in South-East Asia the same step was taken by Malaya (Malaysia).

18.87 History had now taken charge. Achievement of independence by a number of non-self-governing territories encouraged others to follow suit. The conspicuous failure of the United Kingdom and France, the two leading European colonial Powers, in their Suez enterprise in 1956; developments towards Algerian independence (1962); the speech by Harold Macmillan, the British prime minister, on 3 February 1960 while on a visit to South Africa, which launched the famous phrase 'the wind of change is blowing through the continent', all pointed this way. There was now no stopping the momentum to independence.

18.88 This was briefly the historical and constitutional picture in 1960 when over and above the many new admissions in the 1950s, seventeen more colonial countries were due to attain independence and, therefore, to become eligible for membership of the United Nations. The next episode is a classic example of a political tactic applied with appropriate timing to a foreign policy and diplomatic situation. On 23 November 1960 the Soviet Delegation requested that an additional item be added to the Assembly agenda, namely, a 'declaration on granting of independence to colonial countries and peoples'.[36]

18.89 The text was considered so important that it was moved by the chairman of the Soviet Council of Ministers (Nikita Khrushchev) himself. Apart from the main theme of the resolution, perhaps the most penetrating phrase of the document as finally adopted was that 'inadequacy of... preparedness should never serve as a pretext for delaying independence'.

18.90 There were objections from some delegations to the tone of the language, notably from those Latin-Americans who maintained that there had been some accomplishments in the colonial periods for which credit must be given to the colonizers. The Soviet draft, with minor modifications, was carried by 89 votes to nil with nine abstentions (the administering Powers).[37] By abstaining from voting the administering Powers can be said to have conceded the proposition.

18.91 As explained in paragraph 18.8, a policy resolution by the General Assembly is not binding; but by a two-thirds majority vote, the Assembly can endorse a declaration which would include the establishment of a subordinate body. On 27 November 1961 the Assembly passed a resolution[38] setting up a special

---

[36] In the original Soviet draft, the introduction was violent in tone, containing old-fashioned phrases such as: (in the colonial territories) 'the swish of the overseer's lash is heard; there heads fall under the executioner's axe'. (Ibid, 149). The declaration as adopted by the General Assembly was of course less intemperate.

[37] General Assembly resolution 1514 (XV) of 14 December 1960.

[38] General Assembly resolution 1654 (XVI) of 27 November 1961.

Committee on the Situation with regard to the Implementation of the Declaration on Decolonization, to make suggestions and recommendations on the progress and extent of the implementation of the Declaration and to report to the Assembly at the next session. The original committee consisted of seventeen members of the United Nations but was increased in 1962 to twenty-four, a figure which has caused it to be known as the Committee of Twenty-four. No provision was made for parity between administering and non-administering countries among the first seventeen members; seven were from formerly non-self-governing countries in Africa and Asia, and three from Communist countries, if Yugoslavia is included. The procedure included a provision that the Committee would resort to voting procedures 'whenever any member felt that procedure was necessary'.

The proceedings of the Committee of Twenty-four evolved over subsequent years. There were some difficulties, including the withdrawal of Australia[39] in 1969, and later, in 1971 that of the United States and the United Kingdom. The United Kingdom now has a working relationship with the Committee. **18.92**

These events left behind important questions of procedure.[40] One, affecting delegations, especially those on the defensive, was by whom public argument should be conducted. Many of the meetings of the Committee of Twenty-four were conducted in an atmosphere of emotion, sometimes attended with abusive nagging, a challenge to reasoned argument and moderate language. **18.93**

The handling of non-self-governing or dependent territory matters was inevitably caught up in East–West rivalries during the Cold War. This eased as more countries became independent. Post 1990, thirteen States from the former Soviet empire and eight from central Europe became new members of the UN. **18.94**

Contemporary United Nations

These sections have sought to show how over more than 60 years a number of events and developments have affected the character and practices of the United **18.95**

---

[39] As a minor example, a sub-committee of the main committee visited Aden (South Yemen) in 1967. They correctly called in London on their way and saw the Foreign Secretary, George Brown, who explained the local situation to them. When they reached Aden, the situation was disturbed; the sub-committee stayed in their hotel and refused even to meet members of the local administration. After a few days they went back to New York and (with the tacit acquiescence of the Secretary-General, U Thant) did not return to Aden.

[40] In this connection William Wallace's observations are valuable. See *The Foreign Policy Process in Britain* (London: Oxford University Press for Royal Institute of International Affairs, 1975), especially 261 *et seq.*

Nations. Processes which may appear complicated and even frustrating may be more readily understood when their origins and history are examined. Undoubtedly, the most important single development has seen the total membership grow to nearly fourfold (50 to 193) in number. Of this latest number, a majority are former dependent territories.

18.96 Immediately after the drafting and ratification of the Charter in 1945, hopes of government and public opinion were naturally high, perhaps too high. The system set out in the Charter was anchored on agreements between sovereign States. But thereafter, nations did not cease to behave like nations, parties like parties, or politicians like politicians. Successes and failures were mixed. But at least, remarkably, membership of the United Nations has proved universal. No country wishing to become independent thought in terms of independence outside the United Nations and the only nation so far to suspend its participation (Indonesia) came back (see Chapter 35).

18.97 It is natural that the question of the revision of the United Nations Charter should often arise. The rules governing amendments of the Charter are set out in Article 108. They are precise and read as follows:

> Amendments to the present Charter shall come into force for all Members of the United Nations when they have been adopted by a vote of two-thirds of the members of the General Assembly and ratified in accordance with their respective constitutional processes by two-thirds of the Members of the United Nations, including all the permanent members of the Security Council.

Permanent members of the Security Council have different views on the merits of changing their number or identity. National interest, history, and the reality of power play a part in these attitudes. Mustering the necessary majority within the General Assembly is also proving elusive as any suggested enlargement package seems to attract a blocking opposition. However, it is worth recalling that the Charter as it is at present has not worked too badly.

18.98 The United Nations system touches most aspects of global economic activity and of course international peace and security. It suffers most of the disadvantages of a massive spreading bureaucracy where change is very difficult to agree. The case for reform is long-standing but creating the conditions to amend the status quo has proved largely elusive. Vested interests, both within and outside the organization, inhibit change. But in Hammarskjöld's words 'the United Nations was designed, not to create heaven on earth but to prevent hell'. With all its limitations, the United Nations seeks to do good consistent with its Charter.

18.99 The United Nations system represents the principal multilateral bodies, with the Security Council pre-eminent. Increasingly the major issues confronting governments are global in nature, often requiring multilateral agreements. As an organization of States this presents problems for decision-making, not least if the apparent sovereignty of States is to be challenged. The organization will need to respond to the myriad challenges facing the United Nations. These include putting in place effective policies to cope with contemporary issues such as poverty and development, climate change, a sustainable environment, terrorism, and so on, not to mention effective peacekeeping, the peaceful settlement of disputes, conflict prevention, and peacebuilding. Members will need to meet their obligations and confront the difficulties. The individual organs of the UN for their part must be prepared to undertake reform, to modernize their processes, to focus on results, and generally become much more efficient, delivering value for the annual subscription by States.

Diplomats working within the UN system usually belong to a national mission **18.100** in New York and elsewhere. This entails a specialized role, invariably concentrating on a particular topic or committee, and being the basic source of advice to the ambassador, and hence to the capital. The range of issues is almost infinite as all challenges, one way or the other, impact on the Organs of the UN or its funds, programmes, and agencies. Obviously the diplomat's interest is in the organization and not in the host country. The diplomat will spend more time with colleagues from other member States rather than in the mission. The crucial skills needed include the ability to present arguments orally and in writing, negotiate and draft outcomes with representatives of other countries, and concert results and agreements. A capacity to engage across traditional groupings and blocks is a great asset. Representatives of Member States of the European Union will spend much time concerting EU positions in the General Assembly and its committees, where usually the External Action Service of the European Union will speak for all twenty-eight EU Member States.[41] Similarly, African States increasingly discuss issues within the context of the African Union. Indeed most countries set their policies within some form of regional grouping.

---

[41] See K V Laatkainen, 'Multilateral Leadership at the UN after the Lisbon Treaty' (2010) 15 *European Foreign Affairs Review* 475, at 479–80.

19

THE UNITED NATIONS—II SPECIALIZED AGENCIES, FUNDS AND PROGRAMMES, REGIONAL COMMISSIONS, AND SPECIAL BODIES

Emyr Jones Parry

19.1 The Charter established the six organs of the United Nations (Chapter **18**, paragaraph **18**.7). But the reach of the United Nations 'family' is extensive. Hardly a branch of economic activity is not touched in some way by a body associated with the United Nations. The Security Council, General Assembly, and Economic and Social Council have each created bodies and committees. The result is a wide collection of bodies, coming loosely under the headings Specialised Agencies, Funds and Programmes, Other Entities, and Related Organizations. The United Nations website <http://www.un.org> is an entry point into this maze. A simple and readable guide is the handbook produced by the New Zealand Ministry of Foreign Affairs and Trade, <http://www.mfat. govt.nz>un-handbook>.

Specialized Agencies

As Aust[1] has noted, '[t]he UN specialized agencies are not part of the United   **19.2**
Nations... But they all have "relationship agreements" with the United Nations
and are regarded as part of the "UN family"', one of the purposes of which is to
provide for them to respect decisions of the Security Council. On important
political matters, such as recognition of statehood, they generally follow the
lead given by the United Nations. Specialized Agencies are independent international organizations funded by both voluntary and assessed contributions.

Article 57 of the United Nations Charter reads as follows: **19.3**

1. The various specialized agencies, established by inter-governmental agreement
and having wide international responsibilities, as defined in their basic instruments, in economic, social, cultural, educational, health, and related fields, shall be
brought into relationship with the United Nations in accordance with the provisions of Article 63.

Article 63, paragraph 1 states that:

[t]he Economic and Social Council may enter into agreements with any of the
agencies referred to in Article 57 ...

and adds that:

[s]uch agreements shall be subject to approval by the General Assembly.

In paragraph 2 of the same Article it is laid down that the Economic and Social   **19.4**
Council (ECOSOC) 'may coordinate the activities of the specialized agencies
through consultation with and recommendations to such agencies and through
recommendations to the General Assembly and to the Members of the United
Nations'. The Council has yet to realize its potential for coordination, particularly in terms of global economic policy where it has little influence on the work
of the Bretton Woods Institutions.

At the time of the signing of the Charter in June 1945, there was in existence   **19.5**
only one Specialized Agency of the broad politico-social kind covered by these
Articles—the International Labour Organization. Two other important organizations, the International Postal Union, as it then was, and the International
Telecommunications Union, soon became Specialized Agencies. Moreover,
activity in the direction of creating international agencies to cover Food and
Agriculture, Finance, Civil Aviation and Education, Science, and Culture had

---

[1] A Aust, *Handbook of International Law* (2nd edn, Cambridge: Cambridge University Press,
2010) 189–90.

already reached an advanced stage, and it was clear that this portended an unprecedented growth of intergovernmental cooperation through agencies organized not as periodic conferences, but as bodies with permanent staffs and continuous international work between conference meetings.

19.6　The nature, volume, and authority of such work could not be clearly foreseen; hence the prudent wording of the first sentence of Article 63.2, quoted in paragraph **19.4**. Both the concepts and the constitutions of a number of Specialized Agencies had reached an advanced stage before the United Nations Charter had been approved. By 2016, there were fifteen Specialized Agencies, working with the United Nations and with each other through the coordinating mechanism of ECOSOC at the intergovernmental level, and in turn often reporting to the General Assembly. The aim is to deliver at least a measure of compatibility, coherence, and mutual help enhanced by practical coordination through the Chief Executives Board for Coordination at the inter-secretariat level. There are also five Specialized Agencies within the World Bank Group. A schedule of Agencies, with brief descriptions of their origins and purposes, appears in Appendix IV.

19.7　The basic structures of such Agencies are generally similar. They consist of an Assembly or Conference of all members to receive reports and determine the broad orientation of policy, a smaller Executive Board to meet regularly between Assembly meetings to steer and ensure implementation of policy and to prepare Assembly meetings, and a Secretary-General or Director to deliver the work of the agency, approve, and put in place programmes and projects, and manage the overall operation under the control of the Board.

19.8　At the beginning of 2016, there were 193 member States of the United Nations, and membership of key agencies tends to be close to that figure; for example, the International Telecommunications Union, the Universal Postal Union, and the World Health Organization each have 193 members. Other more technical agencies may have a slightly smaller membership; for example, the World Intellectual Property Organization has 188 members and the International Labour Organization 185. Each agency has an executive body, usually with a membership of between thirty-five and fifty, chosen with due regard to the equitable distribution of seats among the five world regions of the United Nations (Americas, Western Europe and others, Africa, Asia, and Eastern Europe). The degree of political as opposed to technical influence varies with each organization.

19.9　At the time of the establishment of the United Nations, there was a widespread view that it would be natural and useful also to set up United Nations regional organizations to handle economic problems under the auspices of ECOSOC. Their regional nature differentiated them from the Specialized Agencies organized on a world scale; their basis in the United Nations differentiated them from independent regional intergovernmental organizations such as the future Organization of American States or the African Union.

Each regional economic Commission was set up by ECOSOC and the present list is as follows: **19.10**

	Established	*Headquarters*
Economic Commission for Europe	28 March 1947[2]	Geneva
Economic and Social Commission for Asia and the Pacific (ESCAP) (formerly the Economic Commission for Asia and the Far East—(ECAFE))	29 March 1947[3]	Bangkok
Economic Commission for Latin America (ECLA)	8 March 1948[4]	Santiago de Chile
Economic Commission for Africa	29 April 1968[5]	Addis Ababa
Economic Commission for Western Asia (ECWA)	9 August 1973[6]	Beirut

Broadly each is charged with supporting the economic and social development of the member States in the region and fostering regional economic cooperation and trade.

Funds and Programmes

Funds and Programmes are usually set up by decisions of the General Assembly or the Economic and Social Council, or both. They are funded by voluntary contributions and have their own elected Executive Boards which report to the organ which created them. They have no separate international legal personality. In 2015 there were eleven such bodies.   **19.11**

UNCTAD

The Bretton Woods Institutions (the International Monetary Fund and the World Bank family) together with the GATT (General Agreement on Tariffs and Trade) were intended as the primary global promoters of economic growth. By the 1960s, the depth of the problems facing developing countries had become   **19.12**

---

[2] ECOSOC resolution 36 (IV) of 28 March 1947.
[3] ECOSOC resolution 37 (14) of 28 March 1947.
[4] ECOSOC resolution 106 (VI) of 28 February and 5 March 1948.
[5] ECOSOC resolution 671 (XXV) of 29 April 1968.
[6] ECOSOC resolution 1818 (LV) of 9 August 1973.

clear, and at the call of the General Assembly, the first United Nations Conference on Trade and Development met in Geneva from 23 March to 16 June 1964.[7] By resolution 1995 (XIX) of 1964, the General Assembly established UNCTAD as an entity of the Assembly.

19.13 UNCTAD has subsequently held conferences every four years, the most recent being UNCTAD XIII in Doha in 2012. The first item in the official statement of UNCTAD's purposes reads: '(a) To promote international trade, particularly between countries of different stages of development, with a view to accelerating the economic growth of developing countries.' Its aim is to encourage policies to end global economic inequalities and to promote people-centred sustainable development.

19.14 As a body of the Assembly UNCTAD did not appoint a Secretariat after the form of a Specialized Agency, but entrusted to a Trade and Development Board the task of carrying out the functions of the Conference between these formal sessions. The Board meets regularly each autumn for 10 days.

United Nations High Commissioner for Refugees (UNHCR)

19.15 After the First World War, machinery was set up in Geneva, under the auspices of the League of Nations, to deal with the problem of refugees. This organization continued in operation after the Second World War, and the General Assembly decided in December 1950 to appoint a United Nations High Commissioner for Refugees for a three-year term. This appointment has since been renewed at five-yearly intervals. From its beginnings as a non-operational organization, by 2015 a staff of 9,300 was helping 51 million refugees and internally displaced persons in 123 countries with an annual budget of $7 billion. The main purpose is to afford international protection to refugees and other persons of concern, and safeguard their rights and well-being. The UN High Commissioner for Refugees also monitors the operation of the Geneva Convention and Protocol on the Status of Refugees and issues guidance on its interpretation.

UNICEF

19.16 An allied and, in United Nations terms, older body, the United Nations Children's Emergency Fund was set up as an emergency body in 1946[8] and

---

[7] ECOSOC resolutions 917 (XXXIV) of 3 August 1962 and 963 (XXXVI) of 18 July 1963, endorsed by General Assembly resolution 1785 (XVII) of 8 December 1962.

[8] General Assembly resolution 57 (I) of 11 December 1946. (The terms of reference were amended in resolution 417 (V) of 1 December 1950.)

became a permanent organization in 1953, when it was renamed the United Nations Children's Fund but its acronym remained unchanged.[9] UNICEF work is set out in a strategic plan, addressing young child health, development, nutrition, water and sanitation, education and equality, and child protection, including combating disease. UNICEF has the special feature of accepting subscriptions from both governments and private organizations as well as from individuals. It is one of the most widely respected members of the UN family working in more than one hundred countries and devoted to improving the quality of children's lives. UNICEF reports through its Executive Board, thirty-six members each elected for three years, to the Economic and Social Council, which in turn reports to the General Assembly. For further details see <http://www.unicef.org>.

United Nations Development Programme (UNDP)

UNDP began operations in 1966 under General Assembly resolution 2029 (1965)[10] which combined relevant programmes and made it the main body responsible for coordinating UN development work. It has a presence in more than 170 countries and territories, is the largest provider of development grant assistance within the UN system, and seeks to coordinate global and national efforts to implement the Sustainable Development Goals, in particular to eradicate extreme poverty and improve democratic governance. The UNDP representative in a developing country tends to be the resident coordinator for the activities of the UN family in that country. UNDP has co-financing arrangements with donor and recipient governments, as well as with multilateral financing institutions. It has an Executive Board which is responsible for supervising both UNDP and the United Nations Fund for Population Activities. Its Annual Human Development Report focuses on key development issues, providing measurement tools, and often involving controversial policy proposals; for example, the 1992 Report examined progress on political freedom and human development as well as developing country access to global markets: see <hdr.undp.org/en/global/hdr1992>.

19.17

United Nations Environment Programme

UNEP was established by the General Assembly in 1972[11] following the Stockholm Conference on the Human Environment and is based in Nairobi. In

19.18

---

[9] UNICEF/UK Agreement of 7 October 1953 (Cmd 8981).
[10] General Assembly resolution 2029 (XX) of 22 November 1965.
[11] General Assembly resolution 2997 (XXVII) of 15 December 1972.

1977, the Nairobi Declaration established its mandate which includes analysis of the global environment, provision of policy advice on environmental threats, furthering the development of international environmental law and sustainable development, and advancing the implementation of international norms and policies. This is a rapidly evolving area of work. Climate change is now recognized as the major threat to developed and developing countries alike and environmental concerns have much increased importance. It supports the work of the UN Framework Convention on Climate Change which is key to securing global agreement on reducing gaseous emissions. Meanwhile debate continues on how UNEP should evolve institutionally. It is funded by regular budget allocations from the UN, the Environmental Fund, and voluntary contributions—see <http://www.unep.org>.

Human Rights

19.19   In December 1948, the General Assembly adopted the Universal Declaration on Human Rights. Rights are inherent to all human beings, regardless of any grouping to which they may belong, and are indivisible and embrace political, civil, economic, and legal rights. Member States of the UN have a duty and obligation to promote and protect these rights. In 1993, the General Assembly established the post of High Commissioner for Human Rights to promote and protect the enjoyment by all peoples of the comprehensive rights set out in the Declaration (<http://www.ohchr.org>). Additionally, the General Assembly has adopted numerous conventions on different rights and set up various bodies to safeguard rights. Special Rapporteurs are frequently appointed to review implementation of an individual right generically or its abuse. There is now a substantive body of law, exposition of rights, and relevant norms. But the implementation and respect for rights in States has not matched these provisions and the continued violation of rights remains all too apparent.

19.20   Frustration at the lack of progress on the ground, and with the then institutional arrangements in Geneva for reviewing human rights, led the General Assembly on 15 March 2006[12] to create the Human Rights Council (<http://www.ohchr.org/EN/HRBodies/HRC/Pages/HRCIndex.aspx>). It is composed of forty-seven member States elected by a majority of the General Assembly, is responsible for strengthening the promotion and protection of human rights around the globe, and is mandated to investigate violations of human rights. Its

---

[12] General Assembly resolution 60/251 of 15 March 2006.

procedures include the universal periodic review, a mechanism to assess the human rights situation in all 193 member States. The Council has a number of subsidiary and advisory groups and meets in three sessions each year. Again concern at infringement of national sovereignty inhibits many member States from criticizing what are often flagrant abuses in individual countries. A full treatment of human rights is set out in Chapter 17.

Apart from those already summarized, there are eight other Funds and Pro- **19.21**
grammes. Full details are available on the UN website <http://www.un.org> and in the handbook produced by the New Zealand Ministry.

Other United Nations Entities and Bodies

Apart from those summarized earlier, there are numerous other bodies associ- **19.22**
ated with the United Nations and which form part of the wider family. Other entities include the Joint UN Programme on HIV/AIDS, the UN Office on Drugs and Crime, and the UN University. There are some nine Treaty and Related Bodies such as the Committee Against Torture and the Committee on the Rights of the Child. The Law of the Sea Treaty has produced bodies, as has the Environment programme. Secretariats have been established to monitor and implement decisions. Additionally, there are autonomous organizations linked to the United Nations through special agreements. The International Atomic Energy Agency (IAEA) is an example. In total there are too many and too diverse family members all to be mentioned individually but they can be identified as in paragraph **19.21**.

Postscript

It would be remiss not to underline the role of the Office for the Coordination **19.23**
of Humanitarian Affairs (OCHA), part of the United Nations Secretariat, created in 1998, which coordinates the delivery of humanitarian assistance to the victims of disasters and other emergencies, bringing together the UN response, and that of governments and non-governmental organizations. Humanitarian advocacy is also a function, as is the promotion of disaster preparedness and prevention. The Office coordinates responses to crises and frequently launches appeals for funding for individual countries in crisis. It operates the Central Emergency Response Fund of the United Nations, using a standing fund to dispense humanitarian assistance immediately as required. Following the Asian tsunami of 26 December 2004, its role as the coordinator for a global humanitarian crisis came to the fore.

20

THE G8/G7, G20, BRICS, WTO, OECD, IMF, AND THE WORLD BANK

Ivor Roberts

The G8/G7

20.1 Given the effect of globalization and multinational enterprises on the global economy, it is no surprise perhaps that many States have concluded collectively and individually that the global economy cannot be left entirely to steer itself. To this end, a variety of financial institutions has emerged, the most important of which are covered in this chapter. The Group of Eight (G8), currently known as the Group of Seven (G7), is an informal international forum and as such has no permanent headquarters, secretariat, or budget. The G8 comprises seven of the world's leading industrialized nations (US, Japan, Germany, France, UK, Italy, Canada) and Russia (which was suspended after Russia's annexation of Crimea in March 2014). The leaders of these countries meet annually at summits to coordinate loosely their economic and financial policies, in particular to encourage global economic growth and adopt conclusions on major financial and related issues. The venues for their meetings have increasingly become the focus of often violent protest against the G7/G8's perceived endorsement of and support for globalization.

The Group's origins go back to the oil crisis and global economic recession   **20.2** of the early 1970s. In 1973, these challenges led the US to form the Library Group—an informal gathering of senior financial officials from the US, Europe, and Japan. At the instigation of Valéry Giscard d'Estaing, the then French President, the 1975 meeting encompassed Heads of State or Government in what was originally intended to be an informal gathering, 'a fireside chat'. The delegates agreed to meet annually. The presidency of the group rotates annually among the member countries, with each new term beginning on 1 January. The country holding the presidency is responsible for planning and hosting a series of ministerial level and expert meetings, leading up to a mid-year summit attended by the Heads of Government. Each leader has a personal representative, a 'sherpa', and it is the sherpas who prepare the summits and are the informal consultation mechanism between summits. The Presidency is also responsible for handling the increasingly onerous security arrangements for G7/8 meetings.

The six nations originally involved became known as the G6, and later the G7   **20.3** and G8 after the respective entries of Canada (1976) and Russia (1998). Though the G8 was originally conceived as a forum for discussing economic and trade matters, politics intruded, despite French resistance, as early as the late 1970s. The G8 relies for its influence on the economic strength of its members whose agreements carry no legal weight. The workings of the G8 are far removed from the 'fireside chats' of the early 1970s and summit conclusions carry weight across an increasing range of issues. Security has become a major concern after violent protests in recent years and the leaders now tend to meet in remote or isolated locations. There is still an attempt to keep some of the original informality, with advisers excluded from the room, ties and jackets discarded, and an effort made to keep the agenda flexible.

The European Union is represented at the G8 by the President of the European   **20.4** Commission and the President of the European Council but the EU as such does not take part in G8 political discussions. Critics of the G8 have accused the body of representing the interests of an elite group of industrialized nations, to the detriment of the needs of the wider world. In an effort to reach out to others, important countries with fast-growing economies, notably China, Brazil, India, Mexico, and South Africa, and selected African leaders have been invited to attend special 'outreach' sessions during summits. Sessions with these +5 (or G5) leaders have taken place at all summits since the Evian Summit in 2003, with the exception of the Sea Island Summit in 2004. In recent years, notably at the Gleneagles Summit of 2005, the G8 has launched initiatives on debt relief and disease, including malaria and HIV/Aids, and its members pledged to reach 0.7 per cent of GNP for official developmental assistance. Recent summits have taken place in Deauville (2011), Camp David (2012), County Fermanagh (2013), Brussels (2014), Schloss Elmau (2015), and Shima (2016). G8 ministerial meetings bring together ministers responsible for issues as wide-ranging as health, law enforcement, labour, economic and social development, energy, environment, foreign affairs, justice and internal affairs, terrorism, and trade.

20.5 In August 2008, in response to Russia's invasion of Georgia, Foreign Ministers from the other seven members took the unprecedented step of issuing a strongly worded statement criticizing Russian action. In 2014, the original G7 States voted to suspend Russia in response to the latter's annexation of Crimea and the Group has reverted to being known as the Group of Seven. The door is, however, open for Russia's eventual return.

The G20

20.6 The G20, which originally grouped finance ministers and central bank governors from nineteen of the world's twenty largest national economies, plus the European Union (EU), was set up by the G7 finance ministers meeting in 1999 and held its first meeting in Berlin that year. Its aim was to expand the G8 in response to criticism of its elite and increasingly unrepresentative status and provide a broader forum to discuss and consult on international financial questions and to promote international prosperity and stability. In November 2008 in response to the dramatically worsening economic circumstances of that period, the G20 met at Heads of State and Government level in Washington DC and has held further summit meetings in London and Pittsburgh both in 2009, Toronto (Canada) 2010, Seoul (South Korea) 2010, Cannes (France) 2011, Los Cabos (Mexico) 2012, St Petersburg (Russia) 2013, Brisbane (Australia) 2014, Antalya (Turkey) 2015, and Hangzhou (China) 2016. It will be held in Germany in 2017. At its Pittsburgh meeting, the G20 was designated the premier forum for international economic cooperation where it is replacing the G7/G8 in importance. It now holds annual summits.

20.7 Collectively, the G20 economies account for about 85 per cent of global GNP and 80 per cent of world trade. The G20 has no permanent secretariat or staff. The country holding the chairmanship in any particular year organizes the meetings and provides secretarial support. The chairmanship rotates annually among the members on a regional basis. Membership, which has remained unchanged since inception, comprises Argentina, Australia, Brazil, Canada, China, France, Germany, India, Indonesia, Italy, Japan, Mexico, Russia, Saudi Arabia, South Africa, South Korea, Turkey, the United Kingdom, the United States, and the European Union, which is represented by the President of the European Council and the European Central Bank. (Spain, although not a member of the G20 is a permanent invitee to summits.) In addition to these twenty members, the chief executives of the International Monetary Fund and World Bank participate in meetings as do the Chair of ASEAN; two African countries (the chair of the African Union and a representative of the New Partnership for Africa's Development (NEPAD)); and a country or countries invited by the presidency, usually from its own region.

20.8 The G20 receives support from international organizations, which provide advice and help identify policy gaps where actions will have the most impact. Representatives of certain international organizations are invited to relevant G20 meetings, including meetings of sherpas, finance deputies, and working groups. These organizations include:

- the Financial Stability Board (FSB). The FSB, which was established by G20 leaders following the onset of the global financial crisis, coordinates the work of national financial authorities and international standard-setting bodies to develop and promote effective regulatory, supervisory, and other financial sector policies.
- the International Labour Organization (ILO). The ILO promotes rights at the workplace, encourages decent employment opportunities, enhances social protection, and strengthens dialogue on work-related issues.
- the International Monetary Fund (IMF). See paragraphs **20.26–20.30** and **20.34**.
- the Organisation for Economic Co-operation and Development (OECD). See paragraphs **20.13–20.20**.
- the United Nations (UN). See Chapters **18** and **19**.
- the World Bank. See paragraphs **20.31–20.34**.
- the World Trade Organization (WTO). See paragraphs **20.22–20.25**.

See also <http://www.g20.org>.

The BRICS

20.9 The acronym 'BRICs' was coined in 2001 by the economist, Jim O'Neill, in a report on growth prospects for the economies of Brazil, Russia, India, and China, who between them represented a sizeable percentage of the world's population and rapidly growing economies, as well as developing or newly industrialized States.

20.10 In 2006, the four countries decided on a regular informal coordination, through annual meetings of Foreign Ministers in the margins of the September UN General Assembly (UNGA). In 2009, these meetings were promoted to the level of summits of Heads of State and Government. The first summit, held in Yekaterinburg in 2009, broadened the scope of the BRICs (BRICS in 2011 after the inclusion of South Africa) beyond its original aim into a significant new political as well as economic grouping. Since then summits have been held in Brasilia, 2010; Sanya, 2011; New Delhi, 2012; Durban, 2013; Fortaleza, 2014; Ufa, 2015; and Panaji, 2016. The BRICS have promoted reform of the structures of global financial governance, particularly in the economic and financial fields—e.g. G20, IMF, and the World Bank which receive a special emphasis—and in the political structure of the UN.

20.11 At its Fortaleza Summit, the BRICS established a New Development Bank (NDB), aimed at financing infrastructure and sustainable development projects in the BRICS and other developing countries. Its initial subscribed capital is US$50 billion. See also <http://www.ndb.int>.

20.12 The five BRICS countries represent over 3 billion people, or 42 per cent of the world's population. In 2015 the BRICS GDP (based on purchasing power parity) as a percentage of world GDP (30.8 per cent) was close to matching that of the combined GDP (32.8 per cent) of the EU and US (IMF figures). See also <http://www.en.brics2015.ru>.

The Organisation for Economic Cooperation and Development or OECD (previously the Organisation for European Economic Cooperation or OEEC)

Origin and Purpose

20.13 The formation of the OEEC to organize post-World War II self-help and mutual and external aid on the European economic front owes its origin to the historic speech made at Harvard University on 5 June 1947 by the United States Secretary of State, George C Marshall, in which he referred to the need for positive action to help Europe towards economic recovery, but stressed the need for the countries of Europe to reach agreement on the requirements of the situation before the United States could consider how it could aid a joint European programme.

The speech produced a prompt and positive response from Western Europe but 20.14
not from the Soviet Union nor from other countries under Soviet influence. Accordingly, the French and United Kingdom governments invited all European States (with the temporary exception of Spain) to participate in a Conference for the drawing up of a European programme. The invitation was accepted by the majority of European governments but declined by the governments of Finland and of those countries under Soviet influence.

In 1947, at a conference in Paris of most Western European countries, it was 20.15
agreed to form a Committee of European Economic Cooperation (CEEC). On the basis of the Committee's report covering estimates of production, requirements, and future plans, the US President presented to Congress the outline of a European Recovery Programme, the Marshall plan, which provided for economic aid to Europe during a four-year period ending in 1952, and set up a United States Economic Cooperation administration to manage this aid.

On the initiative of the governments of France and the United Kingdom, a 20.16
working party prepared proposals for a new intergovernmental body and drew up a draft multilateral agreement which led in Paris in April 1948 to the signature of the Agreement and the inaugural meeting of the Organisation for European Economic Cooperation (OEEC). Including Germany (originally represented by Allied Commanders-in-Chief), there were seventeen members.

In 1950, the United States and Canada became associate members of the organ- 20.17
ization. In practice, all the participants took part in the work of the organization from its inception.

The central aim of the organization was 'the achievement of a sound European 20.18
economy through the economic cooperation of its members'. Rapid and dynamic progress was made and a report was presented annually to the governments, including those of the United States and Canada. Perhaps the most notable feat was the conclusion in 1950 of the European Payments Union. Under this agreement resources made available under the Marshall Plan were used to support European currencies in liberating trade and payments from the tightly controlled bilateral channels in which they had had to operate and developing an increasingly free-flowing multilateral system.

The European Recovery Programme ended in June 1952, but the United States 20.19
continued economic aid to Europe. By the end of the 1950s, however, the main purposes of the OEEC had been accomplished. The financial problems of Europe were no longer localized. In terms of industrial supplies, scarcity had been succeeded by plenty and the ordinary channels of trade were operating freely under the rules of the GATT (see paragraphs **20.22–20.25**).

20.20   Accordingly, in December 1959 the Federal Republic of Germany, France, the United Kingdom, and the United States agreed that the next steps should be:

(a) furthering the development of the less developed countries, and

(b) pursuing trade policies directed to the sound use of economic resources and the maintenance of harmonious international relations.

At a meeting the following April, nominees of the governments of the United States, France, the United Kingdom, and Greece proposed the setting up of a new body to be called the 'Organisation for Economic Cooperation and Development'. This new name and the future foreseen for the organization took its work outside the confines of Europe and North America and its main task was to become an authoritative centre of research and initiative in economic thought and development on the economic performance and prospects of the world as a whole. The OECD duly took over from the OEEC in 1961. Since then, in its own words, its mission has been to help its member countries to achieve sustainable economic growth and employment and to raise the standard of living in member countries while maintaining financial stability—all this in order to contribute to the development of the world economy. Its membership now totals thirty-three countries and its activities are wide ranging. They include the Development Assistance Committee and the adoption of guidelines on a myriad of subjects affecting member governments and companies. The OECD's focus has progressively broadened to include cooperation with a growing number of other countries. It now shares its expertise and accumulated experience with more than seventy developing and emerging market economies. For a full list of its current membership and partners see <http://www.oecd.org>.

The International Energy Agency (IEA)

20.21   The International Energy Agency was established in 1974 in response to the 1973 oil shock. It is separate from but associated with the OECD (membership of OECD is a prerequisite). The IEA has four main areas of focus: energy security, economic development, environmental awareness, and engagement worldwide. For most of its history its members (as of 2016, they are twenty-nine in number) have constituted the major consumers of oil, although with the emergence of countries such as China as global economic players this is changing. Members coordinate their mandatory policies on oil stocks through the IEA, which has become the leading authority on analysis of global oil markets and is developing its analytical capabilities in other energy markets. See also <http://www.iea.org/>.

WTO previously GATT

The World Trade Organization's predecessor, the General Agreement on Tariffs **20.22** and Trade (GATT), was conceived as an interim agreement with the objective of reducing (and ultimately eliminating) barriers to free trade rather than as an organization. It was established after the Second World War in the wake of other new multilateral institutions dedicated to international economic cooperation—notably the Bretton Woods institutions known as the World Bank and the International Monetary Fund. A comparable international institution for trade, named the International Trade Organization, was successfully negotiated. The ITO was to be a United Nations Specialized Agency and would address not only trade barriers but other issues indirectly related to trade, including employment, investment, restrictive business practices, and commodity agreements. But the ITO treaty was not approved by the United States and never came into effect. In the absence of an international organization for trade, the GATT treaty was left as the principal instrument to promote trade liberalization.

The GATT was the only multilateral instrument governing international trade **20.23** from 1948 until the WTO was established in 1995. Despite attempts in the mid 1950s and 1960s to create some form of institutional mechanism for international trade, the GATT continued to operate for almost half a century as a semi-institutionalized multilateral treaty regime on a provisional basis with a small secretariat in Geneva. Nevertheless, it evolved into a de facto international organization and expanded from twenty-three original signatories to over 120 by the time it was replaced by the WTO in 1995. By that time there had been eight Trade Rounds which increasingly liberalized trade and involved more countries each time. Left outstanding at the end was the Doha Round which should have improved developing country access to industrialized markets.

In 1993 the GATT was updated (GATT 1994) to include new obligations upon **20.24** its signatories. One of the most significant changes was the creation of the World Trade Organization (WTO). Seventy-five existing GATT members and the European Communities became the founding members of the WTO on 1 January 1995. The other fifty-two GATT members joined the WTO in the following two years. As of December 2015, there were a total of 161 member countries in the WTO. China became a member in 2001. For a current membership list see <http://www.wto.org/>.

Whereas the GATT was a set of rules agreed upon by nations, the WTO is an **20.25** institutional body and while the GATT had mainly dealt with trade in goods, the WTO and its agreements now cover trade in services, and in traded inventions, creations, and designs (intellectual property), and have a binding dispute settlement mechanism. While the current WTO Doha Round of trade liberalization begun in 2001 has made only limited progress and is effectively stalled, a key objective of the organization—lowering barriers to trade—is now carried forward outside the WTO, via bilateral or regional trade treaties, e.g. the ASEAN–China Free Trade Area (ACFTA)—2010, Japan–Thailand Economic Partnership Agreement (JTEPA)—2010, and US–Morocco Free Trade Agreement—2004. These further the goal of increased liberalization but are not of course global. It is vital that such agreements are consistent with WTO principles.

The IMF and the World Bank

20.26 The International Monetary Fund was created in July 1944, when representatives of forty-four allied governments meeting in the town of Bretton Woods, New Hampshire, in the United States, agreed on a framework for international economic cooperation with the aim of avoiding a repetition of the disastrous economic policies that had contributed to the Great Depression of the 1930s.

20.27 During that decade, attempts by countries to shore up their economies—by limiting imports, devaluing their currencies to compete against each other for export markets, and curtailing their citizens' freedom to buy goods abroad and to hold foreign exchange, the so-called 'beggar thy neighbour' policy—proved to be self-defeating. World trade declined sharply, and employment and living standards plummeted in many countries.

20.28 In their attempt to restore order to international monetary relations, the IMF's founders charged the new institution with overseeing the international monetary system to ensure exchange rate stability and encouraging countries to eliminate exchange restrictions that hindered trade. The IMF came into existence in December 1945, when the first twenty-nine member countries signed its Articles of Agreement. Since then, the IMF has adapted itself as often as necessary to keep up with the expansion of its membership—188 countries as of 2016—and changes in the world economy. For current membership see <http://www.imf.org/external/np/sec/memdir/members.htm>. The headquarters of both the IMF and the World Bank are in Washington.

20.29 The IMF's membership rose significantly in the 1960s, when a large number of former colonies joined after gaining their independence, and again in the 1990s, when the IMF welcomed as members the countries of the former Soviet bloc after the dissolution of the USSR. The IMF's role in promoting better economic policies is reflected in the growth of international trade—which has increased from about 8 per cent of world GDP in 1948 to about 20 per cent today—and, until the 2008–9 credit crunch and accompanying financial and economic crises, the smoothing out of boom-and-bust cycles. But the benefits have not flowed equally and while poverty has declined dramatically in many countries it remains a particularly entrenched problem in Africa, partly as a result of long-running wars, debt burdens, and economic mismanagement.

Since 2010, the IMF has been involved in administering economic reform pro-   **20**.30
grammes in eurozone countries: Greece, Ireland, Portugal, and Cyprus. Forming a tripartite structure with the European Commission and the European Central Bank, this so-called Troika has overseen the economic adjustment efforts in these eurozone members, heavily affected by the global financial crisis that started in 2008. In particular, the economic wisdom of the IMF's policy pre-scriptions for Greece has been questioned by influential observers inside and outside the organization. Overall, the IMF's role in these high-income countries has attracted criticism due to purported double standards in the organization's handling of financial assistance requests from European countries, compared to its regular low- and middle-income country clientele. This trend has been accentuated by the membership and voting rights enjoyed on the Executive Board by the large economies, whose representatives also cover the interests of groupings of States. Pressure has grown to dilute those voting shares and give more to the BRICS and developing countries.

The World Bank was also established at the Bretton Woods Conference in 1944.   **20**.31
Its purpose was to help the war-devastated countries of Europe and Japan to rebuild. By the early 1960s, these countries no longer needed World Bank assist-ance, and its lending was redirected to the newly independent and emerging nations of Africa, Asia, Latin America, and the Middle East and, in the 1990s, to the transition countries of Central and Eastern Europe.

Since its birth in 1944, the World Bank has expanded from a single institution   **20**.32
to a closely associated group of five development institutions. It has developed from the International Bank for Reconstruction and Development (IBRD) as facilitator of post-war reconstruction and development to take responsibility for worldwide poverty alleviation in conjunction with its affiliate, the International Development Association (IDA).

While poverty reduction is at the core of the World Bank's work, reconstruction   **20**.33
retains an important role, given the natural disasters and post-conflict rehabili-tation needs that affect developing and transition economies.

The IMF and the World Bank complement each other's work. While the IMF's   **20**.34
focus is chiefly on macroeconomic and financial sector issues, the World Bank is concerned mainly with longer term development and poverty reduction. Its loans finance infrastructure projects, the reform of particular sectors of the

economy, and broader structural reforms. Both organizations have constitutional arrangements drawing inspiration from the UN Charter.

Countries must join the IMF to be eligible for World Bank membership. For details of current membership see <http://www.worldbank.org/>.

20.35 Because both the IMF and the World Bank have come under intense criticism for failing to reform their governance structures and for being seen as too Western-centric, in 2014 and 2015 the so-called BRICS nations—Brazil, Russia, India, China, and South Africa, see paragraphs **20.9–20.12**—have established new international organizations, both headquartered in China, that parallel some of the core tasks of the IMF and the World Bank. The New Development Bank (NDB) (see paragraph **20.11**) provides development financing and balance-of-payments support to countries in need, and the Asian Infrastructure Investment Bank (AIIB) supports infrastructure upgrading in the Asia-Pacific region and aims to complement the NDB. The AIIB has thirty-one founding members, including several Western countries who joined the Bank against the wishes of the US administration, and opened for business in January 2016. See its website <http://www.aiib.org>.

21

THE EUROPEAN UNION—I DEVELOPMENT, STRUCTURE, AND DECISION-MAKING

Paul Berman

Of all the international and regional arrangements to emerge in the aftermath **21.1** of the Second World War, the European Union is perhaps the most difficult to classify. More than a classic intergovernmental organization, and less than an embryonic State, the EU's wide-ranging responsibilities and byzantine structures can make it a challenging prospect for diplomats from within the Union as well as for those engaging with its work from other countries.

The Origins and Development of the European Union

Post-War Europe and the ECSC

21.2 The origins of the European Union lie in the 1951 Treaty of Paris concluded by 'the Six' (Belgium, France, Italy, Luxembourg, the Federal Republic of Germany, and the Netherlands) which established the European Coal and Steel Community (ECSC).[1] This followed an initiative by the French Foreign Minister, Robert Schuman, who the previous year had issued a declaration proposing that 'Franco-German production of coal and steel as a whole be placed under a common High Authority, within the framework of an organization open to the participation of the other countries of Europe'. This, he urged, would make war between France and Germany 'not merely unthinkable but materially impossible' as well as establishing 'common foundations for economic development'.[2]

21.3 The ECSC was only one of a number of regional arrangements set up in Europe in the years after the Second World War. The Organisation for European Economic Cooperation (OEEC), the precursor of the Organisation for Economic Cooperation and Development (OECD), had already been established in 1948. The following year the Council of Europe was established providing the forum for the elaboration of the European Convention on Human Rights signed in 1950. 1948 also saw the conclusion of the Brussels Treaty whose mutual defence and security cooperation arrangements provided the basis for the Western European Union set up in 1954 (see also Chapter 23).

21.4 All these regional arrangements had their roots in the efforts to address the challenges facing post-war Europe—the prevention of future conflict, economic recovery and development, promoting political and social stability, and dealing with the security demands of the Cold War. They also reflected debates across Europe about the nature of the cooperation and integration needed to address these challenges. Most of these new organizations retained an essentially intergovernmental character based on collective decision-making by the constituent Member States. In contrast, the ECSC, while operating within a limited field, was endowed with some *supranational* characteristics. Alongside a Council

---

[1] On the origins and development of the European Union, see D Dinan, *Europe Recast: A History of the European Union* (2nd edn, London: Palgrave Macmillan, 2014). For the wider historical and political context, see T Judt, *Postwar: A History of Europe since 1945* (London: William Heinemann, 2005).

[2] For text of the Schuman Declaration see P Stirk and D Weigall (eds), *The Origins and Development of European Integration: A Reader and Commentary* (London: Pinter: 1999).

of Ministers (composed of representatives of Member States) its institutional framework comprised an executive High Authority, a Court of Justice, and a Common Assembly (composed of nominated members of national parliaments).

This framework itself represented a compromise between those advocating that **21.5** power should be vested in supranational institutions and those concerned that control should rest with the governments of Member States. The Schuman Declaration had referred to the common foundations for economic development 'as a first step in the federation of Europe' and the debate between those regarding the regional structures as a stepping stone to deeper political integration and those supporting the maintenance of what de Gaulle advocated as the *Europe des patries*,[3] in which States remain the pre-eminent constituents, has persisted throughout much of the subsequent development of the European Union.

Euratom and the EEC

Plans for an integrated European military force, the European Defence Community, had been put forward in parallel to those for the ECSC. But following **21.6** their rejection, the Six, meeting at the Messina Conference in 1955, focused on closer economic cooperation. This led to two further treaties signed in 1957— one establishing the European Atomic Energy Community (Euratom) and the Treaty of Rome establishing the European Economic Community (EEC), subsequently renamed the European Community (EC).[4] These three regional organizations—ECSC, Euratom, and EEC (collectively termed 'the European Communities')—had similar institutional frameworks and supranational characteristics. While they each initially had their own Council of Ministers and Commission (or High Authority in the case of the ECSC), the 1965 Merger Treaty created a single institutional framework under which a single Council of Ministers, Commission, Court, and Assembly served all three Communities.

Like the ECSC, Euratom was limited in its scope focusing on the 'conditions **21.7** necessary for the speedy establishment and growth of nuclear industries' and reflecting both the confidence of the period in the potential of atomic energy and concerns about the security of fissile material. Conversely the EEC proved significantly wider in its scope and provided the main vehicle for the subsequent expansion in the activities of the European Communities.

---

[3] See J Touchard, *Le Gaullisme 1940–1969* (Paris: Seuil, Collection Points, 1978).
[4] The Treaty of Rome, or Treaty Establishing the European Community. Following the entry into force of the Lisbon Treaty this has been renamed the Treaty on the Functioning of the European Union ('TFEU').

21.8   Central to the Treaty of Rome was the creation of a European common market—a customs union within which barriers to economic activity between its Member States would be removed. This comprised several key elements: the removal of barriers to the free movement of goods, labour, business, and capital between Member States (the 'four freedoms'); the creation of a common customs tariff (CCT) and common trade or commercial policy (CCP) in relation to third countries; and common rules regulating competition and government subsidies. In addition, separate provision was made for common policies in relation to transport and agriculture. The Common Agricultural Policy (CAP) reflected concerns, particularly in France, to protect domestic production, with the financing of agriculture subsidies becoming a particularly significant area of EC expenditure.

21.9   While these areas remain core to the work of the European Union, the establishment of the European Communities in the 1950s was only the beginning of a continuing process of development marked by a significant increase in membership, important changes to the institutional framework, and expanding areas of activity.

Expansion in Membership

21.10   In 1973 the membership of the European Communities increased for the first time with the admission of Denmark, Ireland, and the United Kingdom. From the early 1950s, the participation of the United Kingdom in particular had been a focus of political discussion and diplomatic activity. Within the United Kingdom itself this reflected debates about the country's position in the post-war world and ambivalence about the Communities' supranational elements. It is claimed that the British observer at the Messina Conference left with the words: 'Gentlemen, you are trying to negotiate something which you will never be able to negotiate. But if negotiated, it will not be ratified. And if ratified, it will not work.'[5] However by 1961, and again in 1967, the UK had applied to join the Communities. On each occasion this was effectively vetoed by the French President de Gaulle—who was concerned about British and French differences on the CAP, trade, and relations with the US—and it was only with his departure in 1969 that accession negotiations could be opened.

21.11   The expansion of membership from six to nine States in 1973 was followed by the admission of Greece in 1981; Spain and Portugal (1986); Austria, Finland, and Sweden (1995); Cyprus, the Czech Republic, Estonia, Latvia, Lithuania,

---

[5] Quoted in P M W Thody, *Europe Since 1945* (London and New York: Routledge, 2000) 171. The words attributed to the official, Russell Bretherton, are probably apocryphal.

Malta, Hungary, Poland, Slovakia, and Slovenia (2004); Bulgaria and Romania (2007); and Croatia (2013). This expansion has been dictated by various factors: the extent to which existing Member States have been ready to admit new countries, the domestic, political, and economic assessments underlying individual governments' decisions to apply for membership, and—in relation to those admitted in the 1980s and the first decades of the twenty-first century—a desire to support new democracies emerging from military and Communist dictatorship and in so doing to reinforce stability and security in Europe.

Membership is open to all European States which respect key principles such as **21.12** democracy and fundamental rights[6] and the process of enlargement is continuing, focusing in particular on the Western Balkan countries.[7] In addition, accession negotiations were launched with Turkey in 2005 and are expected to extend over several years.[8] Not all expansion has arisen from the accession of new members. In 1990, the territory of the former German Democratic Republic was absorbed into the European Communities as a result of German reunification. Conversely, Greenland, which had previously been covered by Denmark's membership, ceased to be part of the Communities in 1996.

The increase in membership from six to twenty-eight States inevitably changed **21.13** the character of the organization. It has increased its global significance in terms of population, economic importance, and the diplomatic and military weight of its membership. At the same time resources have had to be committed to absorb less economically developed countries while the increase in national perspectives and interests and sheer number of delegations has placed additional pressures on the decision-making process.

Some European States have decided not to join, reflecting in particular domes- **21.14** tic concerns about control over national resources and the autonomy of national decision-making. Norway actually completed two accession negotiations in 1972 and 1994 which were both then rejected in referendums. In 1960, a European Free Trade Association (EFTA) was established by States remaining outside the European Communities but subsequent accessions left only four EFTA

---

[6] Art 49 of the Treaty on European Union. The 'Copenhagen criteria', laid down by the European Council in Copenhagen in 1993, also set out political and economic criteria for accession such as a functioning market economy.

[7] States which the EU considers ready to start the process of accession are given candidate status leading on to the opening of formal membership negotiations. As of 2016, in the Western Balkans, Albania, the former Yugoslavia Republic of Macedonia, Montenegro, and Serbia had all been granted candidate status.

[8] Iceland also applied to join the European Union in 2009. Accession talks were formally opened in 2010 but, following a change in government, were suspended in 2013. In March 2015 Iceland formally requested that it should no longer be considered as a candidate country.

States—Iceland, Lichtenstein, Norway, and Switzerland. Of these, Iceland, Lichtenstein, and Norway concluded the European Economic Area (EEA) Agreement in 1992 with the European Communities and its Member States creating a single free trade area across their respective territories.

21.15   Any existing Member State may decide to leave the Union. The Lisbon Treaty established a procedure for negotiating such a withdrawal which is set out in Article 50 of the Treaty on European Union.[9] Following years of political debate within the United Kingdom about the country's relationship with the European Union, the Conservative Government elected in May 2015 undertook to hold a referendum on British membership of the Union.[10] This took place in June 2016 and supported leaving the Union—'Brexit'—by a margin of 51.9% to 48.1%. Taking office after the referendum, Prime Minister Theresa May underlined her intention to withdraw from the EU[11] and established a Department for Exiting the European Union. The departure of a Member State is unprecedented in the history of the Union. As well as the intensive work required in negotiating the UK's withdrawal and its future relationship with the EU, and the impact that the departure of one of the its largest Member States is likely to have on the Union's policies and decision-making, the prospect of UK withdrawal has also heightened discussions about the future direction of the Union. In responding to the referendum result, the leaders of the other twenty-seven Member States noted that the outcome 'creates a new situation in the Union', underlined their determination to 'work in the framework of the EU to deal with the challenges of the 21st century', and decided to start 'a political reflection to give impulse to further reforms'.[12]

Amending Treaties

21.16   In parallel to the expansion in membership, the European Union has continuously evolved both in its activities and in its structures and decision-making procedures. This has been reflected above all in a succession of agreements revising the original Treaties which have both reformed the institutional framework and provided for new areas of responsibility.

---

[9] On the Lisbon Treaty see paragraph **21.22**.

[10] The 2015 Conservative Party Manifesto (at p 73) committed to holding an 'in-out' referendum after negotiating 'a new settlement for Britain in the EU' and a package of measures intended to address the concerns of the British government, to be applied in the event that the United Kingdom voted to remain in the EU, was agreed at the European Council in February 2016.

[11] 'I am very clear that Brexit does mean Brexit.' Prime Minister May speaking in the UK Parliament, July 2016 (Hansard, House of Commons, Vol 613, col 820, 20 July 2016).

[12] Statement, Informal Meeting of Heads of State or Government of 27 Member States and the Presidents of the European Parliament and Commission, Brussels 29 June. <http://www.consilium. europa.eu/en/press/press-releases/2016/06/29-27ms-informal-meeting-statement>.

The first substantial amending treaty was the Single European Act signed in **21.17** 1986. This significantly extended majority voting, in particular to facilitate the completion of an internal single market, and made other changes including increasing the powers of the European Parliament, setting out new powers for the EEC in areas such as the environment, research, and economic and social cohesion, and formalizing procedures for cooperation on foreign policy issues (European Political Cooperation). The most significant modifications to the structure of the founding treaties were however made by the next agreement, the Treaty on European Union (TEU—also known as the Maastricht Treaty) signed in 1992.

The Treaty on European Union followed parallel negotiations between Member **21.18** States on closer economic and political integration. It introduced into the Treaty of Rome new provisions and institutional arrangements paving the way for Economic and Monetary Union (EMU) and the introduction of the European single currency, the euro, in 1999. It also established, as free-standing chapters in the TEU itself, two new areas of intergovernmental cooperation, distinct from the decision-making procedures of the European Community treaties: the Common Foreign and Security Policy (CFSP) and Justice and Home Affairs (JHA) covering cooperation on civil and criminal justice matters and immigration.[13]

The TEU made a range of other changes. These included both changes to the **21.19** institutional framework—creating new bodies such as a Committee of the Regions and again increasing the powers of the European Parliament, notably through the new co-decision procedure—and conferring new powers on the EEC in areas such as social policy, culture, education, development aid, consumer protection, and industry policy. In recognition of the fact that the EEC had clearly expanded beyond its original economic remit, its name was changed simply to the 'European Community'. A new overarching term, 'European Union', was also introduced as a collective name for the European Communities and the intergovernmental areas of CFSP and JHA.

The changes made by the following treaties—the Amsterdam Treaty, signed in **21.20** 1997, and the Nice Treaty, signed in 2001—were less ambitious. The Amsterdam Treaty brought into the Treaty of Rome both civil justice and immigration—leaving police and criminal justice cooperation in the intergovernmental area of JHA—and the Schengen arrangements[14] which had developed outside the EU framework. It also provided for some new EC activities in areas such as energy

---

[13] See also paragraph 21.37.

[14] The Schengen Agreement (1985) and Convention (1990), were originally concluded and developed by some Member States outside the framework of the European Communities and provided for abolition of internal frontier controls.

and tourism, and made some further institutional changes including enhancing the role of the Commission President and reinforcing CFSP decision-making. The Nice Treaty was largely confined to relatively small institutional changes in anticipation of the admission of a significant number of new members from Central and Eastern Europe. It also marked a milestone by winding up the affairs of the ECSC, which had been established for a fixed period of 50 years, and transferring them to the EC.

21.21　These changes fell far short of the reforms which many considered were needed both to ensure the effective operation of a much-expanded European Union and to make the Union more accessible to its citizens and better able to address twenty-first-century challenges such as globalization, terrorism, and migration. A 'Convention' of representatives of Member States, national parliaments, and the EU institutions was therefore set up and drew up a draft 'Constitution for Europe', signed in 2004, repealing the existing treaties in their entirety and replacing them with a single text. Following rejection of this Constitutional Treaty in referendums in 2005 in France and the Netherlands many of its innovations were taken up in a new amending treaty, the Treaty of Lisbon, which was signed in 2007 and entered into force in December 2009.[15]

21.22　The Lisbon Treaty kept the existing Treaties but sought to simplify matters by merging the previous structures into a single European Union. It brought the remainder of the intergovernmental JHA provisions into the Treaty of Rome; gave legal status to the Charter of Fundamental Rights, a text reaffirming the fundamental rights previously applicable under Community law; and made a number of other changes. But its main focus was on institutional reform— including providing for a single individual to exercise external relations functions across the European Communities and CFSP, creating an elected President of the European Council, introducing new voting rules in the Council, and extending the areas of majority voting.[16]

The Ongoing Development of the European Union

21.23　The Lisbon Treaty was presented as completing, at least for some time, the process of treaty and institutional change. Certainly after only limited changes to

---

[15] This was after an initial rejection of the Treaty in a referendum in Ireland in 2008, the negotiation of additional guarantees for Ireland, and separately the Czech Republic, and the approval of the Treaty in a second Irish referendum. On the negotiation of the Lisbon Treaty see P Berman, 'From Laeken to Lisbon—The Origins and Negotiation of the Lisbon Treaty', in A Biondi, P Eeckhout, and S Ripley (eds), *EU Law After Lisbon* (Oxford: Oxford University Press, 2012) 3–39.

[16] See J-C Piris, *The Lisbon Treaty: A Legal and Political Analysis* (Cambridge: Cambridge University Press, 2010).

the Communities' framework during the first 30 years of their existence, the period since the Single European Act had seen an ever-accelerating process of treaty change. This was driven in part by enlargement and the need to reform decision-making to deal with an enlarged Union. It was also driven by the European Union's internal dynamics as the elaboration and implementation of its policies and closer cooperation between Member States led to work in new areas which were then formally recognized in subsequent treaties. Many apparently new responsibilities conferred by amending treaties—such as the environment, development aid, and cooperation on justice and home affairs—simply reflected activities previously done under existing powers[17] or on the basis of ad hoc cooperation between governments.

The original core concept of a common market itself provided a catalyst for the extension of the Union's activities. While the EC's original remit was clearly economic in character, the creation of a single market in which goods and people can travel freely brought with it the need both to ensure the removal of all barriers to free movement and to avoid a 'race to the bottom' in which those with the lowest standards gain an economic advantage. This led to the establishment of Union-wide rules in such diverse areas as manufacturing standards, environmental protection, professional qualifications, and working conditions. **21.24**

External factors also clearly played a key role in the development of the Union. Increased concerns about international migration, transnational crime, and terrorism were an important catalyst in the rapid development of Justice and Home Affairs. Increasing sensitivity to issues such as protection of the environment, protection of fundamental rights, and combating discrimination were all reflected in the EU's work. Concerns to ensure greater transparency and democratic accountability also prompted internal institutional changes and, in part at least, the increase of the European Parliament's powers in each successive treaty. **21.25**

The EU's development was equally influenced by the divergent views of its Member States both on key issues such as balancing free market principles and social and economic protection and on the fundamental question, extending back to the establishment of the ECSC, of the appropriate level of integration and the balance between Member States' powers and those of the EU institutions. The latter has been an explicit, or implicit, issue in every stage of the Union's development and the compromises which it has engendered account for much of the complexity of the EU's structure. **21.26**

---

[17] Including what is now Art 352 TFEU providing for the adoption of measures 'necessary to attain, in the course of the operation of the common market, one of the objectives of the Community' where the Treaty has not provided the necessary powers.

21.27 These internal and external factors have continued to exert an important influence on the development of the Union in the period following the entry into force of the Lisbon Treaty in 2009. In particular, the Eurozone (or European debt) crisis beginning the same year led to the creation of new structures and arrangements to shore up both the stability of the Union's financial systems and the solvency of vulnerable Member States in the Eurozone.[18] In addition to a raft of significant legislation using existing treaty powers, the EU Treaties were themselves amended yet again in 2013 to permit the creation of an intergovernmental fund to support Eurozone Member States, the European Stability Mechanism (ESM).

21.28 As well as the ESM, other intergovernmental agreements, separate from the EU Treaties, were concluded to reinforce economic stability and budgetary discipline amongst Member States and in particular the Eurozone—notably the Fiscal Compact Treaty concluded in 2012. While closely linked to the arrangements under the EU Treaties, the fact that these were intergovernmental agreements was necessitated in part by divergences within the Union. The ESM reflected the approach that only Member States whose currency was the euro should be responsible for ensuring, and funding, the financial stability of the Eurozone. Equally the Fiscal Compact Treaty was concluded as an intergovernmental treaty after the British prime minister opposed further changes to the EU Treaties without obtaining safeguards on the regulation of the financial sector.

21.29 Some observers have regarded these developments as indicative of an increasing tendency after the entry into force of the Lisbon Treaty to address new challenges through ad hoc intergovernmental arrangements—not least to avoid the lengthy and often difficult procedures needed to ratify changes to the EU Treaties. Others have commented that the effective governance of the Eurozone will require yet deeper integration among Eurozone Member States with a corresponding need to deal with the position of non-Eurozone countries. Debates about 'variable geometry' and a 'two-speed' Europe frequently recur in discussions on the future of the Union.[19] Such catalysts for change are not limited to the Eurozone and other crises, such as the significant influx of migrants beginning in 2015, have also raised questions about the capacities of the Union's current structures. What is certainly clear is that there will continue to be pressure in the future for yet further changes to the arrangements governing the Union.

---

[18] On the governance and structure of the Eurozone see paragraph 21.98.

[19] See in particular J-C Piris, *The Future of Europe: Towards a Two-Speed EU?* (Cambridge: Cambridge University Press, 2012).

The Legal Framework

The Legal Character of the European Union

While the European Union may be classified as an international organization 21.30
the nature of its powers and procedures mean that it is usually regarded as a *sui
generis* entity. There are a number of elements which taken together distinguish
it from other organizations which extend back to the Treaties establishing the
original European Communities in the 1950s.[20]

Legal Powers

Under the Treaty of Rome, Member States conferred on the then European 21.31
Community legal powers or 'competences' to act both within the EC ('internal
competence') and in relation to third countries and organizations ('external
competence') across a wide range of areas. This included the power to adopt
detailed legislation and legal instruments which can in many cases apply directly
as part of the laws of each Member State ('direct effect/applicability') and prevail over any conflicting national laws ('primacy'). Moreover, where the Community acted (or in some cases simply had the power to act), Member States
were generally precluded from acting themselves.

The Lisbon Treaty introduced for the first time an explicit list of these compe- 21.32
tences[21] indicating those areas where what is now the Union could act to support the action of Member States ('supporting competences'), where either it or
Member States[22] could act ('shared competences'), where only the Union was
entitled to act ('exclusive competence'), or *sui generis* competences such as the
Common Foreign and Security Policy.[23]

As early as 1963, the European Court of Justice concluded that the above char- 21.33
acteristics meant that the 'Community constitutes *a new legal order of international law* for the benefit of which the States have limited their sovereign
rights, albeit within limited fields, and the subjects of which comprise not only

---

[20] On the EU's legal framework, and EU law generally, see A Dashwood, D Wyatt, et al., *European
Union Law* (6th edn, London: Sweet & Maxwell, 2011); A Arnull and D Chalmers, *The Oxford
Handbook of European Law* (Oxford: Oxford University Press, 2015); and P Craig and G de Búúrca,
EU Law: Text, Cases and Materials (6th edn, Oxford University Press, 2015).

[21] Arts 2–6 TFEU.

[22] But not both together—Member States being able to act to the extent to which the Union has
not, or no longer, exercised its competence—save in the specific areas of research and development
and humanitarian assistance (see Art 4(3), (4)).

[23] The Lisbon Treaty also reinforced references to the principle that the Union could only
act within the limits of the powers conferred on it by the Treaties—the 'principle of conferral' (see
Arts 4(1) and 5(2) TEU).

Member States but also their nationals' (emphasis added).[24] Like other international organizations, it remained open to Member States, as the parties to the Treaty of Rome, to modify the Community's powers or indeed to withdraw from the Community altogether. But subject to these limits, and within its areas of responsibility, the Community exercised extensive powers which closely circumscribed those of its Member States.

The Community Method and Intergovernmentalism

21.34 The Community's powers were reinforced by the supranational characteristics of its institutions. As discussed later in the chapter, significant powers were vested in a number of institutions—the Commission, European Parliament, and European Court of Justice—which operate independently of the constituent Member States. In addition, the development of the Community saw a considerable increase in majority voting among States' representatives in the Council reducing their ability to block the adoption of legislation.

21.35 These elements were often referred to collectively as the 'Community (or supranational) method'. They undoubtedly played a key role in the Community's success in establishing, and enforcing, a common market and other policies which might otherwise have become bogged down in competing national interests and conflicting national laws. However by the same token they represented a significant constraint on the powers of Member States. For this reason many governments were wary about extending the Community's powers, and the Community method, to new areas of activity.

21.36 This was dramatically demonstrated in the early years of the Communities by the 'empty chair' crisis of 1965. For several months France boycotted the Council of Ministers in a dispute focusing on President de Gaulle's opposition to the introduction of majority voting for agricultural matters. De Gaulle, an outspoken critic of the Communities' arrangements, declared: 'On peut faire des discours sur l'Europe supranationale. Ce n'est pas difficile: il est facile d'être un Jean-foutre.'[25] The dispute was only resolved by a political understanding, the 'Luxembourg Compromise', that a State would not be outvoted where very important national interests were at stake.

The Pillar Structure

21.37 In the negotiations leading to the conclusion of the Maastricht Treaty in 1992, there was particular reluctance to subject the sensitive areas of the Common

---

[24] Case C26/62, *Van Gend en Loos v Nederlandse Administratie der Belastingen* [1963] ECR 1 at 12.

[25] 'One can readily make speeches about a supranational Europe; it's not difficult—it's easy to be a jackass' (author's translation). De Gaulle was speaking at a reception at the Elysée Palace, 10 June 1965. Cited in Touchard, *Le Gaullisme 1940–1969*, 218.

Foreign and Security Policy (CFSP) and Justice and Home Affairs (JHA) to the Community's powers. It was for this reason that these areas were kept outside the remit of the European Community and made subject to 'intergovernmental' decision-making.[26] This did not mean traditional government-to-government diplomacy—decision-making still took place within an institutional framework laid down by the TEU—but rather maintaining governments' control through the Council of Ministers and curtailing many of the elements of the Community method: a predominance of unanimity voting, a smaller role for the Commission, no joint decision-making with the European Parliament, and the exclusion or limitation of the jurisdiction of the European Court of Justice and with it the application of legal principles and concepts developed in relation to the European Community.

This complex arrangement, characterized by the then Commission President **21.38** Jacques Delors as 'organized schizophrenia',[27] was referred to as the 'three pillars'. The first pillar comprised the original European Communities each established by its own treaty: the European Community, the European Atomic Energy Community (Euratom), and the later defunct European Coal and Steel Community. Each was a separate international organization with its own legal personality and areas of responsibility but sharing the same institutions and similar, albeit not identical, decision-making procedures and legal powers. The second and third pillars referred to the separate intergovernmental areas of CFSP and JHA.

While the term 'European Union' was introduced by the Maastricht Treaty to **21.39** refer to this three-pillar structure there was much debate as to whether it was to be regarded as an international organization in its own right. Unlike the Communities, legal personality was not expressly conferred on the European Union. However, as the Maastricht Treaty did provide for the European Union to conclude international agreements with third States and organizations in the areas of CFSP and JHA it was regarded as having the functional capacity necessary to conclude such agreements in its own name. But in doing so the European Union did not replace the European Communities which continued to exercise their own powers.

After the Lisbon Treaty

To simplify this confusing situation, in which third countries and organizations **21.40** might find themselves having to deal with both the EU and EC, the Lisbon

---

[26] See E Denza, *The Intergovernmental Pillars of the European Union* (Oxford: Oxford University Press, 2002).
[27] 'Delors Calls Latest EC Plan Crippling', *International Herald Tribune*, 21 November 1991. Also quoted in D Buchan, *Europe—The Strange Superpower* (Vermont: Dartmouth, 1993).

Treaty abolished the distinction between the European Union and the European Community. The European Union was given express legal personality and took over the responsibilities of the European Community which has ceased to exist. Thus it is now the European Union which has all the legal powers and characteristics which previously vested in the European Community. Euratom however remained a separate international organization based on its own treaty although continuing to share the same institutions.

21.41   Moreover, in addition to areas previously within the remit of the European Community, criminal justice—the remaining area of Justice and Home Affairs in the third pillar[28]—also became subject to the supranational method, leaving only CFSP as a distinct area of intergovernmental decision-making subject to 'specific rules and procedures'.[29]

The Treaties

21.42   Following the entry into force of the Lisbon Treaty there are now two key treaties underlying the European Union: the Treaty on European Union and the renamed Treaty establishing the European Community (i.e. the Treaty of Rome) now called the Treaty on the Functioning of the European Union.[30] As already noted, the Treaty establishing the European Atomic Energy Community also continues in force but as a separate agreement distinct from those relating to the European Union. All the other treaties providing for institutional changes, new powers, or enlargement have largely operated by amending these founding treaties.

21.43   These treaties are fundamental. They are the basis for the Union's powers, they set out its tasks and objectives, and they establish its institutional structures and decision-making procedures. For those working within the European Union, the treaties are an everyday reference tool relied upon and cited in negotiations and meetings. All activities of the Union must be grounded, expressly or implicitly, in the Treaties and all legal instruments must cite the treaty provision ('the legal base') authorizing their adoption. For the Court of Justice of the European Union, the Treaties, or 'primary law', are the ultimate source of authority against which legislation and executive action must be judged.

21.44   The objectives of the Union are set out in the Treaty on the European Union together with general provisions on, e.g. institutional framework, fundamental

---

[28] As noted at paragraph **21.20**, under the Amsterdam Treaty the areas of immigration and cooperation on civil justice were made subject to the supranational method leaving criminal justice subject to 'intergovernmental' decision-making.

[29] Art 24(1) TEU.

[30] For the full texts of the Treaties see <http://eur-lex.europa.eu/collection/eu-law/treaties.html>.

rights and enlargement, and the articles relating to CFSP. Other policy areas and the detailed provisions on the Union's institutional arrangements are in the Treaty on the Functioning of the European Union which as previously noted[31] also sets out a list of the EU's competences. Some key provisions, particularly those providing for special arrangements applicable to particular States, are also set out in protocols which form an integral part of the Treaties themselves (see also Chapter 32, paragraph 32.14).

Amendment of the Treaties is subject to procedures set out in Article 48 of the   **21.45** Treaty on European Union and in particular requires the convening of an Intergovernmental Conference (IGC) of representatives of Member States who must unanimously agree any changes which are then subject to ratification 'in accordance with national constitutional requirements'. For most States this involves some form of approval or legislation by national parliaments and for some the holding of a referendum. IGCs frequently adopt declarations clarifying or commenting on treaty provisions which are not binding but might in principle serve as aids to interpretation of the treaty provisions themselves. The Lisbon Treaty provides for a Convention of representatives of Member States, national parliaments, and the EU institutions to be held prior to an IGC; it also allows in certain limited cases for the Treaties to be amended by 'simplified revision procedure' without an IGC.[32]

Legislation

The Treaties give the Union powers to adopt legislation and other legal instru-   **21.46** ments across a wide range of policy areas. The negotiation, adoption, and implementation of these instruments is the main focus of much of the work of the EU's institutions as well as being a key vehicle for the delivery of many EU policies. All these legal instruments are binding on those to whom they apply— whether States, companies, or individuals—and save where jurisdiction is limited (for example in relation to CFSP instruments) are subject to application and interpretation by the Court of Justice of the European Union and, where they take effect in national law, by Member States' own courts.

The TFEU provides for three main types of legislation—Regulations, Directives,   **21.47** and Decisions.[33] Regulations and Directives are the principal instruments used to implement policies across all Member States. Regulations automatically apply as part of Member States' national laws. Directives require Member States

---

[31] Paragraph 21.32.
[32] The simplified revision procedure was used for the first time to amend the EU Treaties in 2013 to allow for the establishment of the ESM see paragraph 21.27.
[33] See Art 288 TFEU.

to implement their provisions through their own legislation (but where States fail to do so may take effect directly in national law). Decisions are used for matters addressed to a particular company or person (for example in relation to a competition or State aid matter). Decisions are also used for internal matters which have legal effect—for example to authorize the opening of the negotiation of an agreement with a third country and subsequently to approve its conclusion.[34]

21.48 The Lisbon Treaty introduced a distinction between 'legislative' and 'non-legislative acts'—the former simply being those measures which the Treaties stipulate shall be adopted by a 'legislative procedure'.[35] The adoption of legislative acts always involves both the Council and the European Parliament and must always be sent in draft to the national parliaments of Member States which may in certain circumstances require that the draft is reviewed.[36] The Lisbon Treaty also revised the arrangements for conferring on the Commission the power to adopt the large and often significant range of technical legislation distinguishing between 'delegated' and 'implementing' acts.[37]

21.49 All these legal acts, together with the Treaties and a diverse range of other instruments, principles, and practices established within the framework of the Union, collectively constitute what was termed the *acquis* which all new Member States must accept on acceding to the Union.

Derogations and Opt-outs

21.50 A further complexity in the EU's legal framework has arisen from the variations in the ways in which its arrangements apply to different Member States. The general presumption is that the same rules and procedures apply across all States. That is inherent in the notion of creating a common market and common policies. While it was largely possible to maintain this approach in the early years of

---

[34] Prior to the Lisbon Treaty different instruments were used in the intergovernmental areas of CFSP (including Common Positions, Joints Actions and Decisions) and Police and Criminal Justice Co-operation (Common Positions, Framework Decisions, and Decisions). These were binding on Member States but did not take effect directly in national law. Decisions are now used for CFSP matters (on which the European Council may also define 'general guidelines') while Police and Criminal Justice Co-operation is implemented by the same instruments used for all other areas of the Treaties.

[35] See Art 289(3) TFEU.

[36] See Protocol 1 on the Role of National Parliaments in the European Treaties and Protocol 2 on the Application of the Principles of Subsidiarity and Proportionality.

[37] See Arts 290 and 291 TFEU. Delegated and implementing are subject to varying degrees of control by the European Parliament and the Council or Member States; the former are intended to supplement or amend, and the latter to implement, the principal legal acts to which they relate but making the distinction has proven difficult and contentious.

the Communities, with the increase in membership and the extension of the Communities' and Union's activities into new and more sensitive areas, it has been necessary to find ways of accommodating the divergent circumstances of different States.

States acceding to the EU are frequently given transitional periods during which **21.51** the application of rules in certain sectors is suspended to allow them time to adjust. States may occasionally secure permanent derogations to address specific areas of sensitivity. Thus, for example, Ireland's constitutional provisions on abortion and Danish national rules on second homes are excluded from the application of the EU Treaties. Special provision may also be needed for a State's particular circumstances—such as the suspension of the application of Community law to northern Cyprus—or for territories having a particular relationship with a Member State—such as the United Kingdom's Crown Dependencies and Sovereign Base Areas (which are outside the European Community but subject to some Community laws) and Gibraltar (which is part of the Community but outside its common customs area).

However, beginning with the Treaty of European Union's extension into areas of **21.52** particular sensitivity, it has also been necessary to find ways of accommodating States' divergent views. At the time of the TEU, both Denmark and the United Kingdom secured exemptions from the obligation to adopt the single currency. The United Kingdom also remained outside new provisions on social policy (the 'Social Protocol') although this was later reversed. Under the Amsterdam Treaty, the United Kingdom and Ireland secured a series of special arrangements to protect their national positions in relation to frontier controls, the Schengen arrangements,[38] and JHA. These included the right to choose whether to opt into civil justice and immigration matters and subsequently extended to cover criminal justice and police cooperation matters.[39] Denmark also secured opt-outs in relation to both JHA and defence matters.[40] Yet further arrangements applicable to particular Member States were agreed in relation to the Lisbon Treaty.[41]

The recognition of the need for greater flexibility led at the time of the **21.53** Amsterdam Treaty to the introduction of an 'enhanced cooperation' procedure

---

[38] See n 14.

[39] Under the Lisbon Treaty, the UK also secured the right to opt out *en bloc* of all existing criminal justice and police cooperation measures before they became subject to the supranational arrangements already applicable to civil justice matters. It exercised this right with effect from December 2014 while at the same time opting back into thirty-six individual measures.

[40] In December 2015 a referendum in Denmark rejected a proposal to convert this bloc opt-out into a case-by-case opt-in akin to that exercised by the UK and Ireland.

[41] Protocols were agreed on the application of the Charter of Fundamental Rights to the United Kingdom and Poland and subsequently on the concerns of the Irish People (see n 15).

allowing smaller groups of Member States to take forward legislative proposals[42] and a further arrangement under which certain Member States could commit to reinforce their defence capabilities—'permanent structured cooperation'—was introduced by the Lisbon Treaty.

21.54　To date these derogations, opt-outs, and other arrangements for flexible participation in EU measures have managed to accommodate the divergences in the positions of Member States. However, as already noted, these divergences, perhaps most significantly in relation to the euro, have led to debates about 'variable geometry' and the possibility of different Member States committing themselves to varying degrees of integration and reflected in treaty and institutional arrangements.

The Institutional and Decision-Making Framework

21.55　Article 13 of the Treaty on European Union provides for seven institutions to carry out the Union's tasks: the European Parliament, the European Council, the Council, the European Commission, the Court of Justice of the European Union, the European Central Bank, and the Court of Auditors.[43] The Parliament, European Council, Council, Commission, Court of Justice, and European Central Bank are discussed in detail later in the chapter while the role of the European Central Bank is covered in examining the particular arrangements relating to the Union's budget.

21.56　In addition, while not classified as institutions, there are a number of other bodies created under the Treaties. The Economic and Social Committee, comprising representatives of 'economic and social components of organized civil society' and the 'Committee of the Regions', comprising representatives of regional and local authorities, are both consultative bodies, have the right to be consulted on some issues, but have no legislative powers.

---

[42] This procedure has been used or approved for use in relation to divorce law, a unitary patent, and a financial transaction tax.

[43] On the EU's institutions and decision-making process see Y Devuyst, *The European Union Transformed: Community Method and Institutional Evolution from the Schuman Plan to the Constitution for Europe* (rev edn, Brussels: PIE-Peter Lang, 2006); J Peterson and M Shackleton (eds), *The Institutions of the European Union* (3rd edn, Oxford: Oxford University Press 2012); H Wallace, M Pollack, and A Young (eds), *Policy-making in the European Union* (7th edn, Oxford: Oxford University Press, 2014); and M Cini and N Pérez-Solórzano Borragán (ed), *European Union Politics* (4th edn, Oxford: Oxford University Press, 2013). The European Union portal at <http://www.europa.eu/index_en.htm> provides links to detailed information and documentation on the operation, policies, and structures of the EU institutions.

Other bodies established by the Treaties include the European Investment Bank **21.57** and the Ombudsman. An increasing number of separate agencies have also been created by legislation exercising executive functions across a range of important areas such as food safety, medicines, fundamental rights, chemicals, and the environment. By 2016 over forty such agencies had been established.[44]

The European Council and the Council

The Council, composed of ministers from each Member State, has a pivotal role **21.58** in the Union's legislative and decision-making procedures.[45] Its agreement is required for all legislation (except where it has delegated this role to the Commission), CFSP measures, and the conclusion of international agreements. From the time of the ECSC it has represented the governments' counterbalance to the role of the other supranational institutions.

While formally a single entity, the Council meets in ten sectoral configurations **21.59** each composed of ministers with responsibility for that particular area—General Affairs; Foreign Affairs; Economic and Financial Affairs; Justice and Home Affairs; Employment, Social Policy, Health and Consumer Affairs; Competitiveness; Transport, Telecommunications, and Energy; Agriculture and Fisheries; Environment; and Education, Youth, and Culture. Councils meet regularly throughout the year to agree both policy and legal measures, with debate often focusing on the text of Conclusions published after each meeting. Meetings are held in Brussels and Luxembourg (but may exceptionally take place elsewhere, e.g. for trade negotiations) and may be supplemented by 'informal' Councils hosted by the State holding the Council Presidency.

All Councils, other than the Foreign Affairs Council which since the entry into **21.60** force of the Lisbon Treaty is chaired by the High Representative,[46] are chaired by the Member State holding the Presidency. This rotates on a six-monthly basis among all Member States and gives the incumbent a powerful role in setting the agenda of the Council and more generally the Union as a whole. Since the entry into force of the Lisbon Treaty, each successive group of three Presidencies also

---

[44] For a list of these agencies and their responsibilities see <http://europa.eu/about-eu/agencies/index_en.htm>. These include those classified as executive agencies, as decentralized agencies, and those established under CFSP. See also A Ott, 'EU Regulatory Agencies in EU External Relations: Trapped in a Legal Minefield between European and International Law' (2008) *EFAR* 515.

[45] See U Puetter, *The European Council and the Council* (Oxford: Oxford University Press, 2014); F Hayes-Renshaw and H Wallace, *The Council of Ministers* (2nd edn, Basingstoke: Palgrave Macmillan, 2005); P de Boissieu, et al., *National Leaders and the Making of Europe—Key Episodes in the Life of the European Council* (London: John Harper Publishing, 2015).

[46] See paragraph 21.63 and Chapter 22. When the Foreign Affairs Council meets to discuss trade matters it is as a matter of practice chaired by a minister from the rotating Presidency.

coordinates as a 'trio' to establish a common agenda and to provide continuity over their 18 months in office.

21.61 The work of the Council is prepared by two Committees (Corepers I and II)[47] composed of Member States' Permanent Representatives, i.e. ambassadors, to the European Union, and chaired by the ambassador of the Member State holding the rotating Presidency. The Permanent Representatives themselves, generally appointed from States' foreign ministries, constitute Coreper II which deals with general affairs, external relations, financial matters, and justice and home affairs. The Deputy Permanent Representatives, often appointed from other ministries, meet in Coreper I which deals with the other sectors and in contrast to Coreper II can often be highly technical in its work. Where, as often occurs, agreement is reached on a proposal within either Coreper it is referred to the Council as an 'A' point for formal approval by ministers without debate. The EU Treaties also established other groups meeting at ambassadorial or senior official level, but without prejudice to Coreper's role, including the Political and Security Committee covering CFSP matters (see Chapter 22) and the Standing Committee on Operational Cooperation on Internal Security (COSI).[48]

21.62 The work of Coreper is itself prepared by an extensive network of working groups[49]—covering everything from fruit juices to military operations—meeting at varying intervals and staffed by officials coming from capitals or based in the States' missions to the European Union, the Permanent Representations. The latter are themselves composed of officials drawn from across each Member State's ministries with each State's internal arrangements determining both the size of the mission and the degree of autonomy that it is allowed in responding to often fast-moving negotiations. As well as supporting the work of ministers, ambassadors, and officials in the various Council bodies, the Representations also act as the principal conduit for Member States' relations with the Commission, Parliament, and other EU bodies.

21.63 The work of the Council is also supported by a permanent General Secretariat whose size and influence have grown with that of the Union. The Secretariat is headed by a Secretary-General appointed by the Council whose functions were previously combined with the role of High Representative for CFSP, created by the Amsterdam Treaty. However, under the Lisbon Treaty this has been replaced

---

[47] 'Coreper' is one of the numerous acronyms to be found across the European Union. It comes from the French name for the Committee—Comité des représentants permanents.

[48] Art 71 TFEU. Also see the Economic and Finance Committee at paragraph 21.102.

[49] Working groups are similarly chaired by the rotating Presidency with some exceptions such as those relating to CFSP which are chaired by representatives of the High Representative from the External Action Service.

by the post of High Representative of the Union for Foreign Affairs and Security Policy with new responsibilities and a concurrent role as Vice-President of the Commission and supported by a separate European External Action Service. (For the institutional arrangements applicable to external action see Chapter **22**.)

The dynamic of negotiations within the Council is heavily influenced by the **21.64** relevant voting procedure. While there is always strong pressure to reach consensus, and formal voting is therefore relatively rare, whether or not opponents to a proposal can ultimately block it is always an implicit factor in the conduct of discussions. The Council acts by qualified majority voting (qmv) in all cases[50] save where the Treaty provides otherwise. Under the rules as amended by Lisbon Treaty qmv requires a 'double-majority' with the support of 55 per cent (or in some cases 72 per cent) of States whose combined populations constitute at least 65 per cent of the population of the Union.[51] This can make the arithmetic complicated but means, for example, that opposition by three of the largest States (Germany, France, United Kingdom, Italy, Spain) and one medium-sized State would usually be sufficient to block a proposal.

In areas of particular sensitivity or significance, including most aspects of CFSP, **21.65** certain areas of justice and home affairs, harmonization of legislation on indirect taxation and social security, and key decisions on the Union's financing, the Council continues to act by unanimity. Conversely, for simple procedural matters, the Council can act by simple majority. Where it is not acting formally under treaty procedures, for example in drawing up general political Conclusions, the Council operates by consensus. In addition, as described at paragraph **21.36**, a political understanding, the 'Luxembourg Compromise', was reached in the 1960s that a State would not be outvoted where very important national interests are at stake.

Arguably one of the Council's, and the EU's, great strengths, and one of the **21.66** great challenges and opportunities for those working within the Council at all levels, is the absence of fixed voting blocs and coalitions which so often characterize other organizations. States will align themselves differently depending on whether they tend to be more or less integrationist, liberal, or protectionist in their approach to trade; a large or a small State; more or less in favour of social protection and of free markets; a centralized or federal State; a net contributor to or recipient from the EU budget; Atlanticist or Euro-centric in their approach to defence; socially conservative or liberal; and so on. The picture is further complicated by the various opt-outs and derogations described at paragraphs

---

[50] As of 2016, qmv applies to about 80 per cent of the legislation adopted by the Council.
[51] Art 238(3) TFEU.

21.50–21.54. While some States generally find themselves always in the same (or opposing) camps, coalitions can shift rapidly meaning that ministers and officials may themselves be opposed and allied on different issues in the course of the same meeting.

21.67 Heads of State and Government, and the President of the Commission, also meet at least four times a year in the configuration known as the European Council (not to be confused with the Council of Europe described in Chapter 23). It is charged under the EU Treaty with providing 'the Union with the necessary impetus for its development' and defining 'its general political directions and priorities'. It sets the strategic agenda for the Union, generally acting by consensus, and delivering the outcome of its meetings by way of Conclusions.

21.68 While the European Council's focus is necessarily on high-level issues, under the Lisbon Treaty it also acquires extra formal decision-making responsibilities and is now defined as a separate institution. Previously chaired by the Head of State or Government of the rotating Presidency, it is now chaired by the President of the European Council—a post created by the Lisbon Treaty to give the role greater focus and continuity—who is elected by its members by qmv for a period of two and a half years.

21.69 A distinctive feature of European Council and Council business is the frequency with which it brings Heads of State and Government and ministers together face-to-face. While much ground-clearing work is done in working groups and Coreper, there are still a wide range of substantive discussions and negotiations—often on technical and detailed issues—which are conducted in person by prime ministers, and presidents and ministers. Such negotiations can often be prolonged and fatiguing—and tempers can occasionally fray[52]—but they provide a far greater degree of direct contact between government members than is found in traditional diplomatic fora.

The European Commission

21.70 The European Commission[53] is sometimes described as the Union's civil service but its powers are much more extensive. It is the 'guardian of the Treaties'

---

[52] There were widespread reports of an exchange at the October 2002 European Council between UK Prime Minister Blair and French President Chirac. Blair asked 'How can you defend the common agricultural policy and then claim to be a supporter of aid to Africa? Failing to reform the CAP means being responsible for the starvation of the world's poor.' Chirac responded 'You have been very badly brought up. No one has ever spoken to me like that before.' Quoted in *The Guardian*, 29 October 2002.

[53] See H Kassim, et al., *The European Commission of the 21st Century* (Oxford: Oxford University Press, 2013).

charged with ensuring that Treaties' provisions, and measures adopted under the Treaties, are respected. In this capacity it regularly brings infringement[54] actions against Member States. It has the power to adopt legally binding decisions in key areas such as competition and State aids. It also has delegated to it extensive powers to adopt technical legislation comprising both implementing acts—subject to a system of supervision by committees of Member States experts known as 'comitology'—and delegated acts.

In most areas under the Treaties, the Commission has the sole right to bring forward proposals for legislation—the so-called 'right of initiative'. While the enactment of such legislation is a matter for the Council and European Parliament, the Commission's control over which proposals are brought forward gives it significant powers in shaping the legislative agenda. This is reinforced both by the Commission's ability to withdraw a proposal once it has been tabled and submit a revised alternative which is more likely to secure approval in the Council and by the requirement that, even in areas where majority voting applies, the Council can only amend Commission proposals by unanimity. In addition, the Commission is represented at all Council meetings, from working group to ministerial level, and the Commission President is a member of the European Council, and thus it also has an ongoing input into the Council's, and European Council's, own deliberations **21.71**

In the intergovernmental areas of CFSP the Commission's role is more curtailed. Under the Lisbon Treaty it can no longer make proposals in this area, which is limited to Member States and the High Representative.[55] It is also the High Representative who is responsible for the conduct of CFSP, as mandated by the Council, and for representing the Union in this area. **21.72**

The Commission, appointed for five years, is composed of nationals from each Member State 'chosen on grounds of their general competence' and whose independence is 'beyond doubt'.[56] Both the Nice and Lisbon Treaties had envisaged the reduction of the number of Commissioners reflecting concerns that enlargement had made the size of the Commission unwieldy. However this remained a point of sensitivity for certain States and the arrangement of one Commissioner per Member State has been maintained. **21.73**

The appointment of the President of the Commission is of key importance in setting the direction of the in-coming Commission. Under the Treaties, the European Council initially proposes a candidate for President of the Commission **21.74**

---

[54] Sometimes referred to by the French term, 'infractions'.
[55] Art 30 TEU. The Commission may 'support' the High Representative in making proposals.
[56] Art 17(3) TEU.

by qualified majority 'taking into account the election to the European Parliaments' who is then 'elected' by the European Parliament. The proposed list of other Commissioners as a whole is then adopted by the Council by common accord with the nominee for President. The President, High Representative, and other Commission members are then submitted for a vote of consent by the European Parliament before finally being appointed by the European Council by qualified majority.

21.75 In practice the initial choice of Commissioner from each Member State is largely a matter for the government concerned and appointees are usually experienced national politicians. However, the Commission President has an important role in the process—reinforced by his responsibility for allocating portfolios amongst the Commission appointees—and, as outlined below and at paragraph 21.88, the European Parliament can also assert significant influence in relation to both the appointment and dismissal of members of the Commission.

21.76 In 2014, the main political parties in the European Parliament, citing the requirement to take account of the Parliament elections, nominated their own candidates for Commission President (known by the German terms '*Spitzenkandidaten*'). The European Council did then propose the *Spitzenkandidat* of the party which had secured the largest vote in the European Parliament elections, Jean-Claude Juncker from the EPP. This was seen by some as a usurpation of the treaty rules and the role of the European Council and both the United Kingdom and Hungary opposed the appointment.[57] Concerns have also been expressed that appointing a President on the basis of political affiliation was inimical to the Commission's executive and regulatory responsibilities.

21.77 Formal decision-making is done by the body of Commissioners as a whole— known as the College of Commissioners—acting by majority. The Treaties stress that Commissioners 'shall neither seek nor take instruction from any government or any other body'[58] and Commission members do not act as representatives of their respective governments. At the same time they can provide an informal conduit both to enable the Commission to understand the perspective and circumstances of a particular government and for a government to appreciate the approach of the Commission. To improve coordination, the portfolios of the Commissioners appointed in 2014 have been organized into five 'project teams' each headed by a Vice-President. Each Commissioner is supported by a

---

[57] On the *Spitzenkandidaten* episode see de Boissieu, et al., *National Leaders and the Making of Europe*. Acknowledging the concerns about the procedure, the June 2014 European Council which proposed J-C Juncker also stated that it 'will consider the process for the appointment of the president of the European Commission for the future, respecting the European treaties'.

[58] Art 17(3) TFEU.

cabinet, a private office, whose officials—and particularly the head of cabinet—play an important role in advising and representing their Commissioner.

In its wider sense, the Commission also refers to the officials—thirty-three, **21.78** in 2015—responsible for carrying out the institution's functions under the direction of the College of Commissioners. These staff are organized in some thirty-three Directorates General each responsible for a particular subject area, headed by a Director General and answerable to the Commissioner with the relevant portfolio.[59] In addition there are a series of Services with horizontal responsibilities including an influential Commission Legal Service as well as a Secretariat General ensuring overall coordination.

The Commission's supranational structure and its range of powers and preroga- **21.79** tives—including in relation to the initiation of legislation and the enforcement of the treaties—have made it emblematic of the Union's distinctive character and a key element in the latter's development. Some have argued that the role of the Commission over the past three decades has decreased relative to both the Council and the European Parliament. Nevertheless it maintains a central position in the Union's institutional machinery.

The European Parliament

During the development of the European Union, the role and powers of the **21.80** European Parliament[60] have changed more significantly than those of any other institution. It also remains the first and only directly elected international body.

Established as the ECSC's Common Assembly, it was originally composed of **21.81** representatives nominated by the national parliaments of Member States and had only limited 'supervisory' powers. Its name was subsequently changed to the European Parliament but the critical stage in its development was the first direct election held in 1979. This marked the start of the period in which the Parliament increasingly asserted its role beginning the same year with the use for the first time of its power to block the EC budget. From the Single European Act, which introduced the assent and cooperation procedures giving the European Parliament important new powers, successive amending Treaties have significantly increased both the Parliament's decision-making and legislative powers and the range of issues to which they apply. The European Parliament's

---

[59] For a list of the Directorates General see <http://ec.europa.eu/about/index_en.htm>.
[60] See R Corbett, F Jacobs, and M Shackleton (eds), *The European Parliament* (8th edn, London: John Harper, 2011); and D Judge and D Earnshaw, *The European Parliament* (2nd edn, Basingstoke: Palgrave Macmillan, 2008).

principal legislative powers are now exercised through the co-decision procedure, introduced by the Maastricht Treaty.

21.82   As from the 2014 elections, the European Parliament is composed of 751 members allocated among the Member States in relation to population size (ranging
from ninety-six MEPs for Germany to six each for Cyprus, Estonia, Luxembourg,
and Malta) but with proportionately greater representation for the smaller
States. MEPs are elected for a period of five years by direct universal suffrage on
the basis of proportional representation (using the list system or single transfer-
able vote). Within Parliament they sit by political grouping, rather than Member
State, the largest groups including the European People's Party, the Alliance of
Socialists and Democrats, the European Conservatives and Reformists, and the
Alliance of Liberals and Democrats for Europe—each grouping comprising
MEPs from national political parties sharing broadly similar principles.

21.83   The size of each grouping determines in particular the allocation of the influential
chairs of the committees.[61] There are twenty-two Standing Committees covering
the full range of the European Union's work including for example the budget,
foreign affairs, agriculture, industry, internal market, legal affairs, women's rights,
and the environment.[62] The committees—which meet, usually in Brussels, once or
twice a month—prepare the work for the European Parliament's plenary sessions,
considering and proposing amendments to legislation which has been referred
to the Parliament and preparing detailed reports on issues within their remit.

21.84   The relative size of the political groupings also determines the selection of the
President of the European Parliament who is elected by absolute majority for a
two-and-a-half-year period. Amongst other tasks, he or she is responsible for
chairing the plenary sessions and addresses the opening session of each European
Council. Plenary sessions are held monthly in Strasbourg. The diverse location
of the EU institutions, important symbols of reconciliation in the early years
of the Communities, has been an increasing focus of debate—above all in relation to the cost created by the split between the Parliament's plenary seat in
Strasbourg and its committee work in Brussels.

21.85   It is the plenary sessions which exercise the European Parliament's formal
decision-making powers, usually by a simple majority of votes cast—or in some

---

[61] Chairs are elected by committee members who in turn roughly represent the representation of
their parties in the Parliament. In practice the d'Hondt system—the formula devised by the nineteenth-century Belgian political scientist Victor d'Hondt to ensure an equitable distribution of posts
reflecting the weight of the largest groups while also protecting smaller groups—has been used for
the allocation of posts.

[62] For a list of committees see <http://www.europarl.europa.eu/committees/en/home.html>.

cases by a vote of two-thirds or an absolute majority of its component members. There are four main aspects to the Parliament's powers and influence: as a legislator, as a budgetary authority, in exercising oversight of the Commission, and in the adoption of resolutions.

On some matters, such as the conclusion of some international agreements or the admission of new Member States, the European Parliament has a veto under the consent procedure. A few areas are still subject to the consultation procedure under which the Parliament has the right to give its opinion but the Council is not bound by its position. However, as noted earlier, the Parliament's principal legislative powers are now exercised through the co-decision procedure under which it adopts legislation jointly with the Council.[63] The areas in which the Treaties are subject to co-decision have steadily increased and under the Lisbon Treaty it has become the default 'ordinary legislative procedure'. Co-decision entails a three-stage procedure. The Parliament and the Council can seek to agree a legislative proposal, and each other's amendments, at a first or second reading. However if agreement cannot be reached the proposal is referred for intensive (and often late-night) negotiation by a conciliation committee comprised of representatives of the Parliament and Council. In practice much legislation is now agreed at the first reading stage. **21.86**

The budget and oversight of the Commission are the other areas in relation to which the European Parliament enjoys important powers. The Parliament and the Council together constitute the joint budgetary authority. In the past, the Council had the last word on 'compulsory expenditure', matters on which the Community was legally obliged to incur expenditure, and Parliament had the ultimate decision on 'non-compulsory expenditure'. The Parliament could also 'for important reasons' decide to reject the budget as a whole[64]—a power which it exercised in 1980, 1982, and 1985. Under the Lisbon Treaty these arrangements have been replaced by a new procedure in which both the European Parliament and the Council are involved in deciding the budget as a whole. In addition the Parliament must give its consent to the Multiannual Financial Framework (see paragraph **21.107**). **21.87**

In relation to the Commission the European Parliament must elect the President of the Commission and approve the appointment of the Commission as a whole. In doing so it submits Commission nominees to detailed scrutiny in hearings and, as noted previously,[65] European political parties have sought to extend their **21.88**

---

[63] The co-decision procedure is set out in Art 294 TFEU.
[64] Formerly Art 272(8) TEC.
[65] Paragraph **21.76**.

role in relation to the choice of Commission President through *Spitzenkandidaten*. The European Parliament can also require the Commission to resign by adopting a motion of censure: powers which influenced the resignation of the entire Santer Commission in 1999 and delayed the appointment of the Barroso Commission in 2004. The former in particular was seen as the Parliament's 'coming of age'[66] in asserting its place in the EU's institutional framework. The episode arose from accusations of financial mismanagement and fraud against one Commissioner, Edith Cresson. To avoid a motion of censure, the Commission agreed to the appointment of a committee of experts and resigned en bloc in response to the committee's criticism of the Commission as a whole.[67]

21.89 Commissioners regularly appear before the European Parliament and the Commission must submit an annual report to, and answer questions from, the Parliament. Council Presidencies have similarly developed the practice of appearing before the Parliament during their term in office reflecting the Parliament's increasing influence.

21.90 The European Parliament regularly adopts resolutions and reports setting out its position across the whole range of issues of interest to the European Union. These may be seen as being reinforced by the Parliament's authority as the only *directly* elected EU body although, as the Treaties recognize, members of the Council are also democratically accountable at the national level.[68] At the same time, there remain some areas under the Treaties where the Parliament's decision-making role is limited and its participation in the areas of intergovernmental decision-making is even more restricted. While the European Parliament's role has grown significantly over the past 60 years it still remains in a number of respects less powerful than the Council or Commission.

The Court of Justice of the European Union

21.91 The Court of Justice of the European Union[69] (also known as the European Court of Justice or ECJ) played a significant role in shaping the character and development of the Communities and, as the final arbiter on the interpretation

---

[66] 'This entire debate has represented a coming of age, a new maturity in understanding its [the EP's] democratic rights and in its capacity to empower itself to act in the public interest.' Pat Cox, leader of the ELDR and later EP Parliament speaking in the March 1999 debate on the Commission's resignation. Quoted in *The Independent*, 16 January 2002.

[67] On this episode, see P Craig, 'The Fall and Renewal of the Commission: Accountability, Contract and Administrative Organisation' (2000) 6 *ELJ* 6.

[68] A point which is explicitly underlined by new provisions introduced by the Lisbon Treaty (Art 10 of the TEU).

[69] See A Arnull, *The European Union and Its Court of Justice* (2nd edn, Oxford: Oxford University Press, 2006).

and application of the Treaties, is one of the most powerful elements of the institutional framework.

Under Article 19(1) of the Treaty on European Union, the Court's function is to 'ensure that in the interpretation and application of the Treaties the law is observed'. It was set up at the time of the establishment of the ECSC and its workload has continued to grow significantly throughout the development of the Union. To address this, a second court, a Court of First Instance (now renamed the General Court), was established in 1989 while the Nice Treaty provided for the creation of specialist judicial panels. On this basis a Civil Service Tribunal, to deal with cases brought by staff of the institutions, was constituted in 2005 but its functions were absorbed back into the General Court in 2016. The term Court of Justice was used to refer to both the judicial institution as a whole and to what has become the highest court but the Lisbon Treaty now distinguishes the former by referring to the *Court of Justice of the European Union*. Its workload continues to grow: in 2014 there were 622,912, and 157 new cases before the Court of Justice, the General Court, and Staff Tribunal respectively.[70]   **21.92**

Both the Court of Justice and General Court are currently constituted of one judge per Member State appointed, by the common accord of all Member States, from persons 'whose independence is beyond doubt and who possess the ability required for appointment to the highest (or high) judicial office'. The Court of Justice itself also comprises eleven Advocates General, shared amongst the larger Member States and by rotation amongst the smaller States, whose role it is to prepare an opinion to aid the Court's deliberations. Members of the Court are assisted by legal clerks or '*référendaires*'. In practice each Member State proposes the judges and Advocates General of its own nationality—usually drawn from the judiciary, academia, or public service—who, under arrangements introduced by the Lisbon Treaty, are scrutinized by a committee of senior judges from national jurisdictions and former members of the Court, before being submitted for appointment by the common accord or all Member States. The Civil Service Tribunal marked an important change from this practice with only seven judges, appointed by the Council on the basis of recommendations made by an advisory panel of experts.   **21.93**

The workload of the Court has continued to grow. To address this, the Court brought forward proposals in 2011 for a partial increase in the size of the General Court. However, following failure among Member States to agree on how these new posts would be allocated, it was finally decided in 2015 progressively to   **21.94**

---

[70] See the Courts' annual reports at <http://www.curia.europa.eu>. The Courts' judgments, opinions, and other decisions are also available at this site.

double the size of the General Court including judges transferred from the Civil Service Tribunal in 2016.

21.95   Cases can reach the Courts by two principal routes: by direct actions against the EU institutions and Member States and by preliminary references. Direct actions can be brought challenging the decisions or legislation of EU institutions on various grounds including acting outside their powers, failing to comply with procedural requirements or principles of EU law, and misuse of powers. Such challenges are frequently brought both by Member States, and by EU institutions against each other, and form an important part of the process of defining the parameters of their respective powers. They can also be brought, under strictly defined limits,[71] by companies and individuals who may be particularly affected by a decision or legislative act.

21.96   The Commission frequently brings infringement (or 'infraction') cases against Member States for failure to comply with the Treaties and in particular for failure to implement legislation. This has proven to be one of the most important elements in enforcing the common market, and EU law generally, and was reinforced by the power to fine Member States which failed to comply with Court judgments, introduced by the Maastricht Treaty.[72] Member States may also launch enforcement actions against each other but this is rarely done. As EU legislation forms part of Member States' own domestic law, national courts also play an important key role in its application but can (and sometimes must) refer to the Court of Justice for definitive interpretative rulings. These preliminary references form an important part in ensuring the uniform application of EU law across all Member States.

21.97   While the Court is based in Luxembourg away from the EU's centres of political and legislative activity, it has played a key role in developing many of the concepts which have been fundamental in the development of the European Union—primacy, direct effect, fundamental rights, exclusive competence for external action, and many of the key principles regulating the common market were all established by Court judgments. Concerns have been expressed by some, and rejected by others, both about an 'activist' court relying extensively on purposive (or teleological) interpretation and about its powerful position as the ultimate judicial authority on matters within its jurisdiction.[73] Sensitivities

---

[71] See Art 263 TFEU.

[72] Art 260 TFEU.

[73] See e.g. G Beck, *The Legal Reasoning of the Court of Justice of the EU* (Oxford: Hart Publishing, 2013); H Rasmussen, *On Law and Policy in the European Court of Justice* (Dordrecht: Martinus Nijhoff, 1986); J Weiler, 'The Court of Justice on Trial' (1987) 24 *CMLR* 555; P Neill, *European Court of Justice: A Case Study in Judicial Activism* (London: European Policy Forum, 1995); and T Tridimas, 'The Court of Justice and Judicial Activism' (1996) *ELR* 21. See also the Report of the House of Lords Select Committee on the European Union on 'The Future Role of the European Court of Justice', 6th Report, 2003–04, HL 47.

about the Court's role meant that its jurisdiction has been largely excluded from CFSP. Limitations in relation to its jurisdiction over Justice and Home Affairs were phased out under the Lisbon Treaty.

The European Central Bank and the Eurozone

Detailed legal provisions on the establishment of economic and monetary union (EMU), including institutional arrangements, were introduced by the Maastricht Treaty. This was followed by a preparatory process, including greater economic convergence and monetary coordination between participating Member States, leading up to the establishment of the European Central Bank (ECB) and the European System of Central Banks (ESCB—comprising the ECB and national Central Banks)[74] in June 1998 and the introduction of the euro in January 1999.[75] **21.98**

The progression to Economic and Monetary was divided into three 'stages' with the third stage being the adoption of the euro. With the exception of Denmark and the United Kingdom which secured opt-outs at the time of the Maastricht Treaty, all Member States which meet the necessary convergence criteria are obliged to move the third stage and adopt the euro.[76] As of January 2016 sixteen Member States had adopted the euro and were part of the 'Euro area' or 'Eurozone'.[77] **21.99**

The ECB based in Frankfurt is responsible for conducting the monetary policy of the Eurozone. Its main decision-making body is the Governing Council comprising the President and the five other members of the Executive Board, all appointed by the European Council, and the national governors of the Central **21.100**

---

[74] The ESCB includes the Central Banks of all Member States including those not using the euro. Responsibilities in relation to the euro are exercised by the Eurosystem which comprises the ECB and Central Banks on Member States using the euro.

[75] Euronotes and coins were introduced in 2002. The design of Euronotes is common across the Eurozone while Member States can place their national emblems on one side of coins. This can ruffle diplomatic sensitivities as Belgium found in June 2015 when it minted a €2 coin to commemorate the 200th anniversary of the Battle of Waterloo. It had to withdraw the coins after France objected. Instead it issued a €2.50 coin which being in a non-standard denomination did not require approval at the EU level. The Belgian finance minister, Johan Van Overtveldt was at pains to stress 'that the goal is not to revive old quarrels. In a modern Europe, there are more important things to sort out.' Quoted in *The Guardian*, 8 June 2015.

[76] However non-euro Member States are still generally subject to the arrangements relating to the earlier stages of Economic and Monetary Union, such as those relating to budgetary and fiscal discipline.

[77] As of January 2016, apart from the UK and Denmark, Sweden, Poland, Czech Republic, Hungary, Romania, Bulgaria, and Croatia had not adopted the euro. Sweden has voluntarily not met one of the third-stage criteria—joining the exchange rate mechanism—indicating that it will not join the euro unless approved by a national referendum.

Banks of the Eurozone.[78] As well as the conduct of monetary policy—the primary objective of which is to ensure price stability—the Bank is charged with ensuring the implementation of other tasks including conducting foreign-exchange operations, holding the foreign reserves of participating Member States and operating payment system; it also has responsibility for the issuing or approval of Euronotes and coins and for the oversight of certain financial institutions.

21.101 Given the global economic significance of the euro and the Eurozone economy, and monetary powers of the ECB, the Bank can wield enormous economic and political influence. The Bank played a key role in seeking to address the Eurozone debt crisis from 2009 onwards, using a range of instruments at its disposal including cutting interest rates and a policy of buying back bonds, demonstrated in particular by ECB President Mario Draghi's high-profile intervention in July 2012 declaring that 'within our mandate, the ECB is ready to do whatever it takes to preserve the euro. And believe me, it will be enough.'[79]

21.102 Alongside the ECB and ECSB are other institutional arrangements dealing with the economic and financial matters and specifically with the governance of the Eurozone. These include the Economic and Financial Committee (EFC), charged with monitoring the economic and financial situation in Member States and including officials from all Member States, the Commission, the ECB (and sometimes National Central Banks), and the Eurogroup bringing together Ministers from Eurozone countries to discuss informally specific issues relating to the euro and electing a permanent President.[80] The EFC also meets as the Eurogroup Working Group, just with representatives from the Eurozone, to prepare the Eurogroup's work.

21.103 As noted in paragraph **21.27** the Eurozone crisis created unprecedented strains and led to the adoption of new arrangements and legislation to safeguard financial stability and the solvency of Member States. It highlighted differences between Member States, generated concerns about the possibility of sustaining

---

[78] Since January 2015, a new system was introduced to increase the efficiency of decision-making under which fifteen voting rights rotate amongst the nineteen Member States' representatives with those from larger economies and financial systems getting the right to vote more frequently.

[79] Speech at the Global Investment Conference in London. In the same speech, President Draghi recalled 'something that people said many years ago and then stopped saying it: The euro is like a bumblebee. This is a mystery of nature because it shouldn't fly but instead it does. So the euro was a bumblebee that flew very well for several years ... Now something must have changed in the air, and we know what after the financial crisis. The bumblebee would have to graduate to a real bee. And that's what it's doing.'

[80] Under the Lisbon Treaty the arrangements for the Eurogroup and Eurogroup President were formally enshrined in a Protocol to the EU Treaties.

monetary union across diverse national economies without yet greater integration, and has led to calls for yet further changes to institutional arrangements for economic and monetary union.[81]

The Budget

Finally, separate mention should be made of the EU's budgetary arrangements which straddle the responsibilities of a number of institutions and can be the focus of some of the most intensive and politically charged negotiations within the Union.   **21.104**

The budget—set at €155 billion for 2016[82]—funds expenditure across nearly all areas[83] of the Union's work including agricultural subsidies, funds for less advantaged regions, development aid, and the EU's own running costs. A detailed draft annual budget is prepared by the Commission and submitted for adoption by both the Council (acting by qmv) and European Parliament in accordance with the procedure laid down in the TFEU.[84] This includes, in the case of differences between the two institutions, the convening of a joint Conciliation Committee tasked with reaching agreement on a joint text. In the event that agreement cannot be reached on the budget, the previous year's budget continues to be applied on a monthly basis.[85] With very limited exceptions, expenditure can only be incurred by the Union where provision has been made in the budget and the frequent disagreements over the budget usually reflect broader differences between the institutions regarding the EU's work and the priorities.   **21.105**

The Treaties stipulate that expenditure must be balanced by revenue in each budgetary year.[86] The Court of Auditors, based in Luxembourg and composed of one member appointed from each Member State, is responsible for auditing the accounts of all revenue and expenditure accounts of the Union. Revenue   **21.106**

---

[81] See e.g. the so-called 'five Presidents' report on 'Completing Economic and Monetary Union' produced by the Presidents of the Commission, European Council, ECB, Eurogroup, and Parliament in June 2015.

[82] This is the 'commitment appropriation'. The EU budget differentiates between 'commitment appropriations'—the spending commitments which may be undertaken and 'payment appropriations', the funds which may actually be paid out. The former is generally greater than the latter as not all spending commitments may not actually result in actual expenditure, e.g. due to changed circumstances. Payments appropriations for 2016 were set at €143.89 billion. For the detailed breakdown of the budget see <http://www.eur-lex.europa.eu/budget/www/index-en.htm> and on the budget more generally <http://www.ec.europa.eu/budget>.

[83] Separate financing arrangements have been established in a very few cases, notably the European Development Fund for funding cooperation with African, Caribbean, and Pacific countries.

[84] See Arts 313–316 TFEU.

[85] Art 315 TFEU. Under the arrangement known as 'provisional twelfths', a sum not greater than one twelfth of the previous year's budget may continue to be spent in each month.

[86] Art 310(1) TFEU.

originally came from Member States' direct contributions but was later replaced by financing from the Communities' (now the Union's) 'own resources'. These are determined by a decision,[87] adopted by the Council acting unanimously and subject to ratification by Member States, and currently comprise revenue from agricultural levies and customs duties, a fixed percentage of Member States' national revenue from value-added tax, and contributions from each Member State based on their own gross national income.

21.107 The Decision on Own Resources is renegotiated every seven years as part of a wider package of measures, 'the financial perspective', intended to allow longer-term planning of expenditure in line with the Union's revenue. Central to this is the Multiannual Financial Framework[88]—agreed unanimously by the Council with the consent of the European Parliament, which places annual ceilings on various general categories of expenditure over the seven-year period.[89] While this helps planning and facilitates agreement on the annual budgets it also means that the periodic negotiation of the financial perspective is one of the most significant exercises undertaken within the Union—for Member States and the institutions alike.

21.108 The negotiation of Member States' financial contributions can prove particularly contentious given not only divergent views about how much the Union should itself do (and thus spend) but the often important differences in the extent to which States contribute to and benefit from the EU budget. The United Kingdom's concerns about what it regarded as significant imbalances in its budget contributions and distortions in EU expenditure led to one of the most difficult negotiations within the EU with UK Prime Minister Margaret Thatcher finally securing a budget abatement (the 'rebate') in 1984. The British Permanent Representative during this episode concluded: 'You can only get your way in the Community by sustained will-power, careful planning and skilled negotiation; ... if you have these things and a good case, the Community has in the end to take account of it.'[90]

---

[87] For the Own Resources Decision in force from 2007 see Council Decision 2014/335/EC, Euratom published in the *Official Journal* at OJ L168/105, 07/06/2014.

[88] Art 312 TFEU. Prior to the Lisbon Treaty the practice was to adopt an interinstitutional agreement between the Council, Commission, and European Parliament. The Treaties now provide that an MFF Regulation must be adopted at least every five years—but current practice is to cover a seven-year period.

[89] The text of the Regulation setting out the MFF for 2014–20 is published in the *Official Journal* at L347/884, 20/12/13. This provides for €960 billion commitment appropriations and €908 billion payment appropriations over this period allocated under the main headings of Growth, Natural Resources (including agricultural resources), Security & Citizenship, Global Matters (including development aid and CFSP). and administration.

[90] M Butler, *Europe: More than a Continent* (London: Heinemann, 1988).

22

THE EUROPEAN UNION—II
EXTERNAL RELATIONS

Paul Berman

'Who do I call when I want to call Europe?', a much-quoted phrase often attrib- **22.1**
uted to the former US Secretary of State Henry Kissinger,[1] reflects the ambiguity of the European Union's position on the international stage. The Union's
extensive common policies and legislation, and its extensive relations with third
States and international organizations, can create the expectation that the
European Union can or should act at the international level in a manner akin to

---

[1] It would appear that Kissinger never actually made the remark. According to Kissinger himself,
'I'm not sure I actually said it, but it's a good phrase.' Quoted in the *Wall Street Journal*, 27 June 2012.

that of a single State. However the Union can only act within the limits of the powers conferred on it by its Member States under the EU Treaties and the complex division of responsibilities amongst the Union's own institutions means that dealing with the European Union at the international level can indeed be perplexing.

22.2 What is clear is that the European Union, and its predecessor the European Community, have acquired wider powers to conduct international relations than any other international organization. Most of this book describes the diplomatic practice of States in conducting their relations with other States either bilaterally or within a multilateral framework. However, within the limits of the powers conferred on them, international organizations can themselves carry out many of the functions exercised by States including concluding international agreements, participating in other international organizations, making formal statements and representations, and undertaking actions engaging their own international responsibility.

22.3 The significant extent to which the European Union has developed and exercised these functions, including in areas where it has replaced its constituent Member States, has made it a major diplomatic actor in its own right. It is party to an extensive range of agreements with third States and international organizations covering everything from trade to military matters, is a full member or observer in a number of international bodies, maintains a global network of delegations, is a major donor of development aid, and promotes common foreign policy objectives through a range of tools including declarations and démarches, sanctions, and civilian and military operations.

22.4 The term 'European Union' can sometimes be used in international relations to refer either to the Union itself or more loosely to include the Union's Member States. Of course the European Union is an important means by which its Member States collectively pursue their economic and foreign policy objectives—they play an important role in its internal decision-making, contribute their own assets to the delivery of its international objectives, and seek to coordinate their positions in international fora even when not acting formally through EU institutions. It is however in the former sense that the term is used here—to describe the action taken by the European Union in its relations with third States and organizations as an actor in its own right exercising the legal powers and institutional framework described in the preceding chapter. Understanding the unique characteristics of the Union in conducting its external relations, including its limitations and complex division of responsibilities, is key for a diplomatic practitioner in the twenty-first century and in knowing precisely whom to 'call'.

Historical Development of the Union's External Relations

Founding Treaties to Single European Union Act

From the outset[2] the treaties establishing the original three European Com-   **22.5**
munities in the 1950s—the European Coal and Steel Community (ECSC), the
European Economic Community (EEC), and the European Atomic Energy
Community (Euratom)—envisaged an external role for the organizations as
a corollary of their internal responsibilities. The 1951 Treaty of Paris did not
confer express treaty-making powers on the ECSC but did provide that 'in its
international relationships, the Community shall enjoy the juridical capacity
necessary to the exercise of its functions and the attainment of its ends'.[3] The
1957 Treaties establishing Euratom and the EEC both conferred legal personality on their respective organizations[4] and Euratom was given a general power
to conclude agreements with third parties within the limits of its power and
jurisdiction.

The EEC itself was given the express powers to conclude international agree-   **22.6**
ments in two areas: the common commercial policy and association agreements.
The common commercial policy was a necessary corollary of the establishment of a customs union among the Member States and the common external
customs tariff.[5] The European Commission negotiated international commercial agreements on behalf of the Community pursuant to negotiating
directives agreed by the Council of Ministers which also then approved and
concluded the agreements. Under these arrangements numerous agreements
were drawn up on trade matters, tariffs, quotas, and rules for exports, and
imports.

Association Agreements—'agreements establishing an association involving   **22.7**
reciprocal rights and obligations, common action and special procedures'—had
a much larger scope including financial and technical assistance and cooperation in a wide range of areas. While originally aimed at countries having historical ties with Member States, they were used more extensively and in particular
for arrangements with States aspiring to join the Community—including the

---

[2] On the history and development of the Union more generally see Chapter **21**, paragraphs **21.2**
et seq. On the historical development of the EU's external action see also n 29.

[3] Art 6. The ECSC was considered to have implied treaty-making powers.

[4] This was held to include international legal personality.

[5] If Member States had continued to conclude separate agreements with third countries on tariffs
and quotas that would have undermined the principle under which goods from those countries
entering the Community could then circulate freely within the common market.

first two such agreements with Greece (signed in 1961) and Turkey (the Ankara Agreement of 1963).[6]

22.8   Of particular importance were the successive Conventions with countries in Africa, the Caribbean, and the Pacific (the ACP) covering trade preferences and financial and technical assistance as well as matters such as competitive tendering, democracy, and human rights. The first such agreement, the Yaoundé Convention, was signed with eighteen African countries in 1963.[7] The Treaty of Rome had already provided in 1957 for the establishment of a European Development Fund including the provision of assistance to countries still under the colonial rule of EEC States[8] and Yaoundé, underlining the sovereignty of all participants, reflected the transition to the post-colonial era.

22.9   The EEC Treaty also provided for the Community to establish relations with the United Nations and its Specialized Agencies, with the Council of Europe, and with the Organisation for European Economic Cooperation (later the OECD) and the Community became an observer in all of these bodies as well as in other international organizations covering areas within its competence. In the United Nations General Assembly the Community was entitled to speak in debates but not to vote.[9]

22.10   The EEC was also given the power to establish appropriate relations with the organs of the 1947 General Agreement on Tariffs and Trade (GATT). While the GATT did not permit the Community to become a member, it came to be treated as if it were, with the Commission acting as negotiator for the Community as a whole under the authorization and mandate of the Council of Ministers. When the GATT was subsumed within the World Trade Organization in 1995, the Community became a full member alongside EC Member States.

22.11   The attitudes of third countries to the emerging role of the Community as an international actor were mixed. The United States was in principle a strong supporter of European integration. In his Independence Day speech in Philadelphia in 1962, President Kennedy lauded the 'great new edifice' and a 'united Europe [which] will be capable of playing a greater role'.[10] At the same time differences

---

[6] In practice such agreements also covered areas falling within the responsibility of Member States and were therefore concluded as 'mixed agreements'—see paragraph 22.79.

[7] This was succeeded by a second Yaoundé Convention (1969), the Lomé Convention (1974), and latterly the Cotonou Agreement signed with seventy-eight ACP countries in 2000, amended in 2005.

[8] Classified then as Overseas Countries and Territories.

[9] GA resolution 3208 (XXIX) of 11 October 1974.

[10] See D Basosi, 'New or Larger? JFK's Diverging Visions of Europe', in S Kosc, et al. (eds), *The Transatlantic Sixties* (Bielefeld: Transcript Verlag, 2013). More generally, see A de Porte, *Europe Between the Superpowers* (New Haven: Yale University Press, 1987).

over trade and other economic matters occasionally led to strains in international fora such as GATT. The Soviet Union for its part was openly hostile to European integration with Foreign Minister Gromyko issuing a memorandum in March 1957 condemning the establishment of the EEC and Euratom.[11]

Even countries sympathetic to the Community found it difficult to adapt to the notion of an international organization participating in negotiations in a manner akin to sovereign States. Acceptance of the Community as a member in international organizations—usually by the insertion of a provision in the constituent agreement allowing for the accession of 'regional economic integration organizations' (REIOs)—was slow. It was not until 1991 that the first UN agency, the Food and Agriculture Organization (FAO), accepted the Community as a member in its own right.   **22.12**

The Community's external powers were not just based on the EEC Treaty's express provisions but were also extensively developed by the Court of Justice's interpretations of that Treaty—most significantly the AETR judgment of March 1971.[12] This held that the Community's wider powers to adopt internal legislation implied a corresponding power to conclude international agreements on the same subject-matter. Moreover the Court held that only the Community, and not Member States, had the power to conclude international agreements which might affect the Community's internal rules—otherwise the effectiveness and coherence of these rules would be undermined: the principle of exclusive external competence. This 'AETR doctrine' has continued to be elaborated over subsequent decades. Given the increasing scope of the Community's internal powers it has represented a significant basis for the Community's external action and, in relation to areas subject to exclusive competence, an important constraint on Member States' own treaty-making powers.   **22.13**

The EEC was however accorded no general power in relation to the conduct of foreign policy. This remained the preserve of Member States who were reluctant to give the Community, and its supranational institutions, a role in the sensitive areas of foreign policy. In 1970 an intergovernmental arrangement known as European Political Cooperation (EPC) was established under which Member States' Foreign Ministers and diplomats consulted and might reach consensus on political matters of common concern such as the Arab–Israel conflict, notably   **22.14**

---

[11] See 'Historical Events in the European Integration Process', Centre Virtuel de la Connaissance sur l'Europe, Luxembourg (<http://www.cvce.eu/en/home>).
[12] Case 22/70, *Commission v Council* [1970] ECR 263. The judgment concerned the European Agreement Concerning the Work of Crews of Vehicles Engaged in International Road Transport (ERTA or AETR in French).

in the Venice Declaration of 1980,[13] or the negotiations with the Communist bloc in the Conference on Security and Cooperation in Europe (CSCE). This was 'conducted by diplomatists for diplomatists, employing informal and highly flexible procedures'.[14]

22.15 In 1986 EPC was given a basis in the EC Treaties by the Single European Act. It was however kept strictly separate from the legal arrangements applicable to the European Community. It was for the Member States to 'endeavour jointly to formulate and implement a European foreign policy'[15] on an intergovernmental basis. Using this framework, consultation and cooperation on foreign policy issues continued to intensify among Foreign Ministers, officials, and diplomats. Common positions were increasingly implemented in diplomatic démarches and coordinated action in international conferences and through initiatives such as the establishment in August 1991 of the Badinter Arbitration Commission relating to the former Yugoslavia, the adoption of Guidelines on the Recognition of New States in Eastern Europe and in the Soviet Union in December of the same year,[16] and the sending of observer missions to elections such as those in post-Soviet Russia in 1993 and South Africa in 1994.

From Maastricht to Lisbon

22.16 The most significant change in the treaty and institutional arrangements relating to the conduct of foreign policy came with the Treaty on European Union (TEU), the Maastricht Treaty, signed at Maastricht in February 1992 and entering into force in November 1993. As described in the preceding chapter,[17] this introduced the European Union as the term for a new overarching 'three-pillar structure' comprising the existing three Communities ('the first pillar') and two new intergovernmental pillars for Justice and Home Affairs and the Common Foreign and Security Policy.

22.17 The Common Foreign and Security Policy (CFSP—'the second pillar') placed foreign policy cooperation on a firm institutional and legal basis. Unlike EPC, decision-making was undertaken by the Council itself which was given powers to adopt legal instruments—notably common positions and joint actions[18]—binding

---

[13] Adopted by the Heads of State or Government and Foreign Ministers of the then nine Member States of the European Community.

[14] S J Nuttall, 'European Political Cooperation and the Single European Act', *Yearbook of European Law* (1985) 203.

[15] Art 30(2) Single European Act.

[16] See Chapter 4, paragraphs 4.12–4.13.

[17] See Chapter 21, paragraphs 21.19 and 21.37.

[18] Arts J.2 and J.3. Common positions dealt generally with establishing positions on matters of policy while joint actions related to more operational matters.

on Member States. The scope and objectives of CFSP were broadly defined including safeguarding the common values, fundamental interests, and independence of the Union, preserving peace and strengthening international security, promoting democracy and the rule of law, and respect for human rights.[19] In addition, obligations were placed on Member States to coordinate in international organizations and conferences and for their embassies and consulates, together with Commission delegations, to cooperate in implementing Union measures.[20]

CFSP was also to include all questions relating to the security of the Union— 'including the eventual framing of a common defence policy which might in time lead to a common defence'.[21] It was only following the St Malo Declaration[22] that the first steps were taken to implement this security dimension with the first EU military operation, Operation Concordia in the former Yugoslav Republic of Macedonia (FYROM), being launched in 2003.   **22.18**

The TEU marked a step change in the elaboration of a common foreign policy on the part of what was now termed the European Union. It saw the start of an adoption of a series of legal measures, as well as the continuing elaboration of political statements and declarations and coordination in international conferences, relating both to specific situations in third countries and horizontal foreign policy issues. While the European Union, unlike the European Community, was not expressly accorded legal personality it also became accepted in due course that it had the functional legal personality necessary to conclude international agreements with third countries and organizations in relation to CFSP matters.[23]   **22.19**

Reflecting Member States' ongoing concerns to maintain control over the sensitive area of foreign policy, CFSP remained strictly distinct from the continuing conduct of external relations by the European Community under the first pillar. The latter had continued to extend its powers at the international level both as the corollary of its increasing internal powers, such as the environment (placed on a treaty basis by the Single European Act), and in developing distinct areas of external action notably development cooperation (placed on a treaty basis by the Maastricht Treaty). While the European Community continued to conduct its external relations using the Community method, CFSP was subject   **22.20**

---

[19] Art J.1.
[20] See D McGoldrick, *International Relations Law of the European Union* (London: Longman, 1997) ch 8, 'From European political cooperation to a common foreign and security policy'.
[21] Art J.4
[22] See paragraph **22.122**.
[23] See Chapter **21**, paragraph **21.39**.

to essentially intergovernmental decision-making.[24] The role of the supranational institutions—the Commission, the European Parliament, and the Court of Justice—was limited or excluded and unanimity was the default voting rule in the Council.

22.21 The subsequent amending Treaties of Amsterdam (1997) and Nice (2001) refined and expanded, but did not fundamentally alter, these arrangements.[25] The Amsterdam Treaty extended the range of CFSP legal instruments, introduced express powers to conclude international agreements, and modified the voting rules (including introducing 'constructive abstention'[26]). It also provided for the appointment of special representatives with a mandate for a specific issue or country and paved the way for the establishment of the Political and Security Committee—a standing committee of ambassadors in the Council responsible for oversight of CFSP matters—subsequently confirmed by the Nice Treaty.

22.22 In particular the Amsterdam Treaty established the post of High Representative for the Common Foreign and Security Policy—to be held jointly with the post of the Secretary General of the Council. This was a high-profile CFSP role to assist the Council by contributing to the formulation, preparation, and implementation of policy decisions and conducting political dialogue with third parties.[27] Javier Solana, a former Spanish Foreign Minister and Secretary-General of NATO, held the post from 1999 until the entry into force of the Lisbon Treaty in 2009 bringing political weight and experience to his multiple roles.

22.23 The 'organized schizophrenia'[28] of the pillar structure created by the TEU was a continuing preoccupation particularly in relation to the Union's external relations. External action was starkly divided between the first-pillar Community supranational decision-making and institutional arrangements, covering areas such as trade, development, and the environment, and the second-pillar intergovernmental Common Foreign and Security Policy, covering the broader political areas of foreign and security policy. This created the challenge both of ensuring coherence between the EU's action under the different pillars and explaining these complex arrangements to Union's interlocutors. Equally third countries and international organizations were confronted with a range of

---

[24] See Chapter 21, paragraphs 21.34 *et seq*.
[25] See R A Wessel, *The European Union's Foreign and Security Policy: A Legal Institutional Perspective* (The Hague: Kluwer, 1999); and R Gosalbo Bono, 'Some Reflections of on the CFSP Legal Order' (2006) 43(2) *Common Market Law Review* 337–94.
[26] See paragraph 22.35.
[27] Art J.15 TEU as amended by the Amsterdam Treaty.
[28] See Chapter 21, paragraph 21.38.

different institutional actors, depending on the subject-matter, and even two different legal persons—the European Community and the European Union.

A key part of the discussions of the Convention on the Future of Europe estab- 22.24
lished in 2001 to review the operation of the Union therefore focused on international relations with working groups on legal personality, external action, and defence. While the resulting 2004 Constitutional Treaty was rejected in referendums many of the innovations relating to external action were taken up in the 2007 Lisbon Treaty which entered into force in 2009.

These innovations were principally focused on seeking to ensure greater coherence 22.25
in the Union's external relations. Importantly, the Lisbon Treaty did not abolish the distinction between CFSP and non-CFSP areas of external action. The former remained a separate, essentially intergovernmental area of decision-making with separate procedures and institutional arrangements. However the distinction between the European Community and the European Union was abolished and the previous structures and arrangements subsumed under a single legal person, the European Union. Moreover common external objectives were introduced covering both CFSP and non-CFSP policy areas with the European Council empowered to identify the strategic interests and powers of the Union in this field.

Perhaps most significantly, attempts were made to straddle the institutional 22.26
arrangements for CFSP and non-CFSP areas of external action by creating a so-called 'double-hatted' post of High Representative of the Union for Foreign Affairs and Security Policy who *ex officio* also held the post of Vice-President of the Commission responsible for external relations. This post replaced that previously held by Javier Solana and was intended to be a high-profile, political position; as well as conducting CFSP as mandated by the Council, the incumbent was also to be responsible for chairing the Foreign Affairs Council—a role previously undertaken by the rotating Presidency. In the Constitutional Treaty the post was originally entitled the 'Union Minister for Foreign Affairs' but this was rejected as being too suggestive of acting on behalf of a State.

To support the High Representative both in her CFSP role and that of Vice- 22.27
President of the Commission, a European External Action Service (EEAS) was established drawing its officials from Member States, the Commission, and the Council Secretariat and the existing global network of Commission delegations were re-designated as EU delegations—reflecting their broader responsibilities including CFSP matters—and placed under the authority of the High Representative. The first High Representative, the former British minister and EC Trade Commissioner, Catherine Ashton, was appointed in November 2009 and she was succeeded in November 2014 by the former Italian Foreign Minister, Federica Mogherini.

22.28　There was much debate as to whether these innovations would indeed inject greater coherence into the EU's overall external action and whether the incumbent in the post of High Representative and Vice-President of the Commission would be able to fulfil such a demanding role and respect the distinct powers and prerogatives of the institutions—Council and Commission—which they served. Moreover, within the Commission itself important external portfolios—trade, development, and enlargement—remained the responsibility of other Commissioners.

22.29　In the years following the entry into force of the Lisbon Treaty there have been achievements in implementing its provisions—notably in setting up the External Action Service—while the successive High Representatives have been personally associated with what have been widely regarded as diplomatic successes for the Union such as the normalization of Serbia–Kosovo relations in April 2013 and the agreement with Iran on its nuclear programme in January 2015. But institutional tensions have continued and delivering coherent and effective Union action at the international level, while respecting the powers and roles of the EU institutions and its Member States, remains as challenging as ever.

The Legal and Institutional Framework

22.30　External relations are of course but one dimension of the European Union's wider policy-making, legislative, and executive responsibilities and as such use the same legal powers and institutions—as described in Chapter 21—as apply to the Union as whole. There are however aspects of the Union's legal powers and institutional arrangements that are specific to the conduct of external relations involving as they do legal and political relationships with third States and organizations, distinct areas of specialist expertise and operational action, and institutional and decision-making arrangements reflecting the particular sensitivities of foreign policy.[29]

---

[29] On the EU's external action and foreign policy generally see K E Jorgensen, et al. (eds), *The SAGE Handbook of European Foreign Policy* (London: Sage, 2015); S Keukeleire and T Delreux, *The Foreign Policy of the European Union* (2nd edn, Basingstoke: Palgrave Macmillan, 2014); C Hill and M Smith (eds), *International Relations and the European Union* (2nd edn, Oxford: Oxford University Press, 2011); P Koutrakos (ed), *European Foreign Policy: Legal and Political Perspectives* (Cheltenham: Edward Elgar Publishing, 2011); F Cameron, *An Introduction to European Foreign Policy* (2nd edn, London: Routledge, 2012).

Legal Powers

Like other international organizations, the Union can only act within the limits   **22.31**
of the powers conferred on it by its constituent Member States. All the Union's
powers to conduct external relations are based on the EU Treaties, the Treaty
Establishing the European Union (TEU) and the Treaty on the Functioning of
the European Union (TFEU)[30]—either on the Treaties' express provisions or on
the legal principles which have been elaborated by the Court of Justice on the
basis of those Treaties.[31]

The aims of the Union laid down in Article 3 TEU include 'in its relations with   **22.32**
the wider world': promoting its values, interests, and protection of its citizens;
contributing to peace, security, and sustainable development; free and fair trade;
eradicating poverty; protecting human rights; and strict observance and development of international law. These are further elaborated in Article 21 TEU
which sets out overarching objectives for the Union's external action in relation
to both CFSP and non-CFSP policies.[32] These general aims and objectives are
given effect using the specific powers and procedures, and under the conditions,
set out in the Treaties—in particular Articles 23 to 46 of the Treaty on European
Union relating to CFSP and Part Five of the Treaty on the Functioning of the
European Union (Articles 205 to 222) setting out other provisions relating to
the Union's external action.

The scope of CFSP is broadly defined as 'covering all areas of foreign policy and   **22.33**
all questions relating to the Union's security'.[33] As noted earlier, following the
entry into force of the Lisbon Treaty, CFSP retained its distinct, essentially intergovernmental, character.[34] Article 24 TEU makes clear that it continues to be
'subject to specific rules and procedures' in which the jurisdiction of the Court
of Justice is largely excluded, the roles of the Commission and the European

---

[30] Other international agreements concluded by the EU Member States may also be relevant to
the conduct of external relations—notably the Accession Agreements concluded with new Member
States. This chapter does not deal with Euratom which as noted in Chapter 21 and at paragraph 22.5
has continued, after the Lisbon Treaty, as a separate organization outside the Union and has its own
legal personality and treaty-making powers.

[31] On the legal aspects of the EU's external action and foreign policy see P Koutrakos, *EU
International Relations Law* (2nd edn, Oxford: Bloomsbury Publishing, 2015); B Van Vooren and
R A Wessel, *EU External Relations Law: Text, Cases and Materials* (Cambridge: Cambridge University
Press, 2014); G De Baere. *Constitutional Principles of EU External Relations* (Oxford, Oxford
University Press, 2008); P Eeckhout, *EU External Relations Law* (2nd edn, Oxford: Oxford
University Press, 2011).

[32] Art 22 TEU also gives the European Council the possibility of adopting decisions identifying
strategic interests and objectives covering both CFSP and non-CFSP areas.

[33] Art 24(1) TEU.

[34] See paragraph 22.19 and Chapter 21, paragraph 21.37.

Parliament are limited and, in contrast to other areas of decision-making, unanimity remains the default rule.

22.34　Under the Lisbon Treaty the range of legal instruments used under CFSP has been simplified and is now largely limited to decisions adopted by the Council whether relating to operational action undertaken by the Union (previously covered by measures known as 'joint actions'), the definition of the Union's approach to a particular matter of a thematic or geographical nature (previously covered by 'common positions'), or the implementation of existing decisions.[35] Decisions of an operational character include those establishing civilian and military operations and appointing special representatives. Decisions defining the Union's approach include those imposing sanctions, setting out a policy position towards a particular country or regional conflict, or supporting a particular international initiative (such as the arms trade treaty or International Criminal Court).

22.35　Such decisions are binding on Member States but, unlike much EU law, they do not have direct effect—that is, they do not apply directly in Member States' legal systems. They may be proposed either by the High Representative (with or without the Commission's support) or by a Member State. While, as noted, unanimity remains the default rule, a Member State may abstain from a vote indicating that it does not intend to be bound by a decision ('constructive abstention');[36] equally in a limited number of cases qualified majority does apply, notably when implementing an existing decision or when appointing special representatives. In line with the specific character of CFSP, the adoption of legislative acts[37]—involving the European Parliament and subject to particular rules including on transparency—are expressly excluded.

22.36　Part Five of the TFEU, 'the Union's External Actions', sets out the provisions relating to the non-CFSP aspects of the EU's external relations—previously falling within the remit of the European Community and subject to the community method or supranational decision-making. It also covers the arrangements for concluding international agreements, and for relations with third countries and organizations, which apply to both CFSP and non-CFSP matters.[38]

---

[35] See Arts 25, 28, and 29 TEU. In addition, Art 25 TEU provides for the adoption of 'general guidelines' while Art 26 TEU provides for the European Council to adopt decisions on strategic interests, objectives, and general guidelines for CFSP.

[36] Art 31(1) TEU. Under constructive abstention, a Member State must refrain from any action likely to conflict with impeded Union action.

[37] See Chapter 21, paragraph 21.48.

[38] See paragraphs 22.75 *et seq*, 22.84 *et seq*, and 22.100 *et seq*.

The key external policy areas set out in Part V include the common commercial 22.37 policy, that is the EU's trade policy;[39] development cooperation, whose primary objective is defined as the eradication of poverty;[40] the provision of economic, financial, and technical cooperation to non-developing countries;[41] and the provision of humanitarian aid, a new article introduced by the Lisbon Treaty.[42] In all cases the provisions define the scope of the policy covered in each area and the measures which may be adopted to implement them whether by way of internal EU laws, arrangements with third countries and organizations, or other initiatives. Unlike CFSP, there is no limitation on, or exclusion of, the roles of the Commission, European Parliament, and Court of Justice in these policy areas and the full range of EU legal instruments, including legislative acts, may be involved.

As noted at paragraph 22.13, the Union's external powers are not limited to 22.38 those set out expressly in the Treaties. Since its 1971 AETR judgment, the Court of Justice has delivered a series of key rulings determining that the Union's power to act externally may be implied from its internal powers and, significantly, the circumstances in which only the Union, and not Member States, may act in relation to a certain matter—so-called exclusive, external competence.[43] Thus in addition to areas where express provision is made for the Union to act externally, the Union may also act externally notably by concluding international agreements—in pursuance of its internal policy objectives. The Union, and previously the Community, has concluded a large and significant range of agreements relating to matters such as transport, the environment, energy, and social policy. In some cases the Treaty provisions relating to these areas also make reference to the international dimension of the policy concerned.[44]

It is however the notion of *exclusive*, external competence which is the most 22.39 important aspect of the Union's external powers and arguably one of the Union's most significant characteristics. Its application means that there are large areas of external action—including in relation to the conclusion of international agreements and participation in international conferences and organizations— where Member States are no longer able to act in their own right at the international level. The impact of this can be significant. In its 'Open Skies' judgments

---

[39] Arts 206–7 TFEU.

[40] Arts 208–11 TFEU.

[41] Arts 212–13 TFEU.

[42] Art 214 TFEU.

[43] On Union competences generally see Chapter 21, paragraphs 21.31 and 21.32.

[44] Thus Art 191 TFEU defining the Union's policy objectives on the environment includes 'promoting measures at the international level to deal with regional or worldwide environment problems, and in particular climate change'.

of 2002,[45] the Court of Justice struck down a series of bilateral air services agreements concluded by the United Kingdom, Sweden, Finland, Belgium, Luxembourg, Austria, and Germany on grounds that elements of the agreements violated the Community's exclusive competence.

22.40 The Lisbon Treaty catalogued for the first time, in Articles 2 to 6 TFEU, the different types of competence exercised by the Union including, in Article 3, those which are exclusive. Thus the common commercial policy as a whole is regarded as an area of exclusive competence—since this is a corollary of the Union's common external tariff and customs union it would clearly not be compatible with this for Member States to conclude their own separate agreements with third States.

22.41 Article 3(2) TFEU attempted to codify the principles arising from the line of case law developed from the AETR judgment onwards. It provides that exclusive external competence for the conclusion of an international agreement would also arise 'where its conclusion is provided for in a legislative act of the Union, or is necessary to enable the Union to exercise its internal competence, or insofar as its conclusion may affect common rules or alter their scope'.[46] These principles—intended to ensure that individual agreements concluded by Member States cannot cut across the application of the Union's own common rules—are of general and potentially wide-ranging application and explain why the extent and nature of the competences exercised by the Union are such a sensitive, and often highly contested, matter for Member States.

22.42 Conversely development cooperation and humanitarian aid are areas of what is termed 'parallel competence' where both the Union and Member States are free to act since the provision of assistance by one does not in any way preclude the provision of assistance by the other. Equally CFSP is set out as a separate *sui generis* area of competence. While Member States must of course comply with any legal measures adopted in this area, the application of the CFSP provisions does not give rise to exclusive Union competence; provided they comply with their CFSP obligations, Member States remain free to act individually in relation to all areas of foreign policy.

22.43 The above paragraphs set out the Union's legal powers in the area of external relations as set out in, or based on, the EU Treaties. In addition the European

---

[45] Cases C-466/98, C-467/98, C-468/98, C-469/98, C-471/98, C-472/98, C-475/98, and C-476/98.

[46] The principles set out in the Court's case law have been continually refined since the AETR judgment and the extent to which these are adequately reflected in Art 3(2) has been the subject of debate.

Council and the Council, including the Foreign Affairs Council, frequently agree on policy positions in the form of Conclusions—indeed this is the usual outcome of their meetings and a common vehicle for setting out the Union's position on CFSP matters. Such Conclusions on policy are not legally binding measures and are not provided for in the Treaties—as such they are adopted by consensus.

Where a matter does not fall within an area of exclusive Union competence, Member States of course remain free to exercise their own inherent powers at the international level as sovereign States. They may equally decide to do so in a coordinated manner—for example, in adopting a political statement or negotiating an international instrument—and in such cases it is for all Member States to agree on the proposed approach. Such coordinated action may also be undertaken alongside the Union—where for example an agreement or international conference straddles matters falling within both the Union's and Member States' powers. Where such powers are inextricably interlinked then under the duty of sincere cooperation set out in Article 4(3) TEU it is incumbent on Member States and the Union to coordinate their positions so as to ensure a 'unity of representation'. **22.44**

The Institutional Framework

The European Council and Council

The European Council and Council[47] occupy a central decision-making role across all areas of the EU's external relations—both CFSP and non-CFSP—reflecting in part Member States' concern to maintain control over these sensitive areas of EU activity. **22.45**

As indicated above, the European Council has the power to adopt decisions on the Union's strategic interests across both CFSP and non-CFSP areas as well as to define guidelines and strategic interests specifically for CFSP. The Conclusions issued at the end of its regular meetings frequently deal with foreign policy and other external relations matters setting the political agenda for the Union as whole. Moreover the President of the European Council is responsible for representing the Union externally on CFSP matters 'at his level'.[48] **22.46**

The Council maintains a key decision-making role in the negotiation and conclusion of international agreements.[49] It must authorize the opening of all negotiations, issue negotiating directives, and agree to both signature and conclusion **22.47**

---

[47] See also Chapter 21, paragraphs 21.58 *et seq.*
[48] See paragraph 22.95.
[49] On the role of the European Parliament see paragraph 22.72.

of all agreements. In some areas of non-CFSP external action, such as the implementation of sanctions measures and the provision of urgent financial assistance to third countries, it remains the sole decision-maker. Crucially, it is also the sole decision-maker across all areas of CFSP. The Council also provides the forum within which Member States usually coordinate their action when exercising their own powers, either separately or alongside the Union, for example in the negotiation of mixed agreements.[50]

22.48 Most external relations matters—both CFSP and non-CFSP—are handled by the Foreign Affairs Council (FAC). As well as the principal meetings composed of Foreign Ministers this also meets in other formats—Trade, Development, and Defence—bringing together ministers with specific responsibilities. Since the Lisbon Treaty, all FAC meetings are chaired by the High Representative who is replaced by the rotating Presidency when not available; Trade and Development Councils are also in practice chaired by the rotating Presidency. Like other Councils, the FAC may also meet informally for policy discussions—these informal Foreign Affairs Councils are traditionally known as 'Gymnich' meetings.[51] External relations issues are not however solely confined to the FAC—the external aspects of internal EU policies, such as the conclusion of international agreements and participation in international bodies, frequently crop up in other Council formations while enlargement is handled by the General Affairs Council (GAC).

22.49 Like other Councils, the work of the FAC is prepared by the Committee of Permanent Representatives, Coreper—specifically Coreper II.[52] But in addition there is a Political and Security Committee (PSC) charged with monitoring and advising on the international situation in relation to matters covered by CFSP. Set up in its current form in 2001,[53] the PSC is composed of Brussels-based ambassadors more junior than those of Coreper II but with a specific foreign policy remit and expertise. While its responsibility is specifically for CFSP matters, and it does not therefore deal with issues such as trade and development, it maintains an overview of the Union's foreign relations. Matters passing from the PSC to the FAC are generally handled with a lighter touch in Coreper and the PSC also has specific decision-making responsibilities in relation to the conduct of CFSP operations.

22.50 As with other areas of the Council's work, much of the preparatory work on external relations matters is done by working groups staffed by officials from

---

[50] See paragraph 22.79.

[51] After the castle in Erfstadt, Germany where the first informal FAC meeting was held.

[52] See Chapter 21, paragraph 21.61.

[53] By Council Decision 2001/78/CFSP. A political committee for PSC was envisaged in the Amsterdam Treaty; its establishment in its current form was confirmed in subsequent treaties.

capitals and the Permanent Representations. There are about fifty such groups dealing specifically with external relations covering areas such as trade, certain international organizations, geographical regions, thematic issues (such as human rights or consular matters), and civilian and military operations. Following the entry into force of the Lisbon Treaty a number of these groups, and specifically those dealing with CFSP matters, are chaired by officials from the European External Action Service—as is the PSC—with the remainder continuing to be chaired by the rotating Presidency. While the General Secretariat of the Council continues to provide administrative support and legal advice to all these groups, policy support to the EEAS-chaired groups is now provided by the relevant teams in the External Action Service.

Particular arrangements apply to the groups dealing with military matters in **22.51** view of the specialist expertise, and distinct chains of command, applicable in this area. The body responsible for advising the PSC on military matters is the EU Military Committee (EUMC) also established in 2001[54] and composed in principle of the Chiefs of Defence Staff of each Member State but in practice by Military Representatives (of one to three-star rank) some of whom also serve as their country's Military Representative to NATO. The Chair of the EUMC, who also acts as military adviser to the High Representative, is, unusually, chosen by the Committee members. The Committee and the High Representative are supported by the EU Military Staff, a team of military personnel seconded from national armed forces and forming part of the External Action Service.

The Commission

For many diplomats and officials from third countries and international organ- **22.52** izations, their principal dealings with the European Community, and now the Union, have been with officials from the Commission.[55] On non-CFSP matters, the Commission is responsible for the external representation of the Union and in particular for the negotiation of international agreements. Until the Lisbon Treaty, it was the Commission which maintained a network of its own delegations around the world and was the most visible face of the Community in international conferences and organizations.

Within the Union, the Commission plays a powerful role in relation to the **22.53** development and implementation of the external policies of the Union outside the CFSP—covering key areas such as trade, development and the external aspects of environment, migration, agriculture, and transport. It is responsible

---

[54] Council Decision 2001/79/CFSP.
[55] See also Chapter 21, paragraphs 21.70 *et seq.*

for making all proposals and recommendations in these areas—both for legislation and the negotiation of agreements—and, once adopted, for their implementation.

22.54 Responsibility for external relations issues continues to be shared among a number of different Commissioners each supported by their own Directorate General. The person holding the post as High Representative and in parallel that of one of the Vice-Presidents of the Commission is charged, in that latter role, with the 'responsibilities incumbent on it in external relations and for coordinating other aspects of the Commission's action'. In that capacity, but only in that capacity, the post holder is fully bound by Commission procedures like any other Commissioner and has assumed the responsibilities held prior to entry into force of the Lisbon Treaty by the Commissioner for External Relations. She[56] is advised in relation to her Commission responsibilities by her staff in the External Action Staff and the posts in the former Commission Directorate General for External Relations have in practice been transferred to the EEAS.

22.55 Other Commissioners with roles specifically relating to external relations are those with responsibilities for trade, development and cooperation, neighbourhood policy and enlargement, and for humanitarian aid and crisis management each supported and advised by a Directorate-General covering these areas (DG TRADE, DG DEVCO, DG NEAR)—or the European Humanitarian Aid Civil and Protection Department (ECHO) in the case of humanitarian aid. It is officials from these departments who are responsible for drawing up proposals for policy, agreements, legislation, and operational initiatives in these non-CFSP areas and for their implementation. However as already noted external issues can also arise frequently within the areas of responsibility of other Commissioners and Directorates-General—thus for example the Directorate-General for Climate Action (DG CLIMA) takes the lead on international negotiations on climate change.

22.56 All this work is coordinated under the auspices of the Commission President, who himself represents the Commission at EU summits[57] and certain international meetings. The introduction of five 'project teams' to improve coordination across the Commission appointed in 2014 includes a team for 'Europe in the World' chaired by the Vice-President holding the post of High Representative and comprising the seven other Commissioners responsible for enlargement,

---

[56] As noted at paragraph 22.27, both the incumbents at the time of publication have been women and while the legal texts relating to the post use the masculine pronoun, the female pronoun is used in this chapter to refer to the post holder.

[57] See paragraph 22.96.

trade, climate change, transport, migration, development cooperation, and humanitarian aid—itself demonstrative of the cross-cutting scope of external relations in the Commission.

Conversely the role of the Commission itself in relation to CFSP is much more **22.57** curtailed. Responsibilities that it has in relation to non-CFSP matters, including negotiating international agreements, proposing legal measures and representing the Union externally, are, in the area of CFSP, the preserve of the High Representative in her CFSP role or of Member States or of the President of the European Council. The Commission and Council, assisted by the High Representative, are jointly charged with ensuring coherence between CFSP and non-CFSP activities, and as with other Council bodies, the Commission attends meetings of the Foreign Affairs Council, PSC, and working groups dealing with CFSP matters. But following the entry into force of the Lisbon Treaty, the Commission can no longer make its own CFSP proposals but only support those submitted by the High Representative.[58]

The EU budget[59] is however an area where the Commission plays an important **22.58** role including in relation to CFSP matters. As discussed in Chapter 21, the annual budget is agreed jointly by the Council and European Parliament within the parameters laid down by the Multiannual Financial Framework (MFF). The MFF for 2014–20 earmarked €58.7 billion[60] for Heading 4, 'Global Europe', covering expenditure on both CSFP and non-CFSP activities. This does not include funding provided outside the EU budget on an intergovernmental basis in the framework of the Cotonou Agreement[61] (the European Development Fund) and for CSFP operations having 'defence or military implications' (provided through the 'Athena' mechanism).

The Commission is responsible for the implementation of expenditure from the **22.59** EU budget[62] including for external action, in accordance with the requirements and limits laid down in EU law. All budgetary expenditure requires a legal basis and much of the Union's funding for external action is thus channelled through arrangements and programmes established under nine external financing instruments[63]—legislation covering the same period as the MFF.

---

[58] Art 30 TEU.

[59] On the MFF and EU budget see Chapter 21, paragraphs 21.104 *et seq*.

[60] Commitment appropriations out of a total of €960 billion for the MFF as a whole.

[61] See paragraph 22.9.

[62] Art 317 TFEU—'The Commission shall implement the budget in cooperation with Member States ...'.

[63] These include the Development Cooperation Instrument, the Instrument for pre-Accession Assistance, the European Neighbourhood Instrument, the Partnership Instrument (covering the external aspect of internal Union policies as well as responses to global challenges such as climate

22.60 Heading 4 also includes funding for CFSP and thus the responsibilities that both the Commission and European Parliament exercise for budgetary matters can become a means by which these institutions seek to exercise influence over an area in which their role is otherwise curtailed. This is particularly the cases in determining how much funding should be allocated to CFSP as opposed to non-CFSP aspects of external action—under the 2014–20 MFF, CFSP was allocated €2.334 billion. The Commission's Service for Foreign Policy Instruments is responsible for dealing with budgetary expenditure under CFSP, as well as under certain external funding instruments. It is co-located with the External Action Service reflecting both the importance of budgetary issues in this area and the complex interaction of the institutions' different responsibilities

The High Representative and European External Action Service

22.61 The Lisbon Treaty's creation of the role of the High Representative for Foreign Policy for Foreign Affairs and Security Policy—held successively by Catherine Ashton and Federica Mogherini[64]—supported by an European External Action Service (EEAS),[65] was the most important innovation in the conduct of the EU's external relation since the establishment of CFSP by the Maastricht Treaty some 25 years earlier.

22.62 The post of High Representative replaced that created by the Amsterdam Treaty and previously exercised concurrently with the role of Secretary-General of the Council. But while the earlier post owed much of its profile to the personal qualities of its occupant, Javier Solana, the new role was from the outset intentionally designed to be a high-profile, political role—reflected in the original, abandoned title proposed in the Constitutional Treaty of 'EU Foreign Minister'. Its most defining characteristic was that the occupant was to hold the post concurrently with that of Vice-President of the Commission responsible for external relations—a so-called 'double-hatting' which was intended to ensure coherence in the Union's external action in the CFSP and non-CFSP areas of policy and which places a significant range of responsibilities, and burden of work, on the shoulders of one individual.

---

change), the European Instrument for Democracy and Human Rights, and the Instrument contributing to Stability and Peace (largely covering pre- and post-conflict situations as well as natural disasters). For more information on the external funding instruments see the Commission website: <https://ec.europa.eu/europeaid/funding/funding-instruments-programming/funding-instruments_en>.

[64] See paragraph 22.26.

[65] See B Van Vooren, 'A Legal-Institutional Perspective on the European External Action Service' (2011) 48(2) *Common Market Law Review* 475–502.

Reflecting this dual responsibility, the incumbent is often referred to as the **22.63** 'HR/VP' (High Representative and Vice-President) as shorthand for what is in practice a complex arrangement. But formally the role and responsibilities of the two posts are distinct. As High Representative, she is responsible for conducting CFSP as mandated by the Council. She is thus responsible, amongst other things, for making proposals for CFSP policies and measures, implementing CFSP measures adopted by the European Council and Council, recommending and negotiating agreements relating exclusively or principally to CFSP, and representing the Union on CFSP matters in relation to third countries and organizations.[66]

In addition, the High Representative takes part in meetings of the European **22.64** Council and, as a reflection of the political significance of the post, she is responsible for chairing meetings of the Foreign Affairs Council—a previous undertaking by the rotating Presidency—which gives her an important role in overseeing the development of the Council's policy on CFSP matters. While this function is formally an aspect of her role as High Representative, it is sometimes referred to as a 'third hat'. Certainly the impartial responsibilities of chairing a Council—otherwise undertaken by the rotating Presidency—are different from the executive responsibilities of the High Representative and the FAC's remit is not itself limited to CFSP. When not available, the High Representative is replaced by the rotating Presidency who also in practice continues to chair the trade and development formations of the FAC.[67]

These functions are distinct from those of Vice-President of the Commission **22.65** described at paragraphs 22.54 *et seq*. This double-hatted role makes the procedure of appointment, and resignation, rather complicated. The High Representative is appointed by a qualified majority of the European Council with the agreement of the Commission President. But the appointment of the Commission as a whole, including the High Representative, is also subject to the consent of the European Parliament. If the Commission as a body is required to resign following a vote of censure from the Parliament, the High Representative must resign the duties she 'carries out in the Commission', i.e. as Vice-President.[68]

There has been much discussion as to whether the approach of 'double-hatting' **22.66** has in practice helped to improve the coherence between CFSP and non-CFSP

---

[66] See Arts 18 and 27 TEU.

[67] This also applies to the High Representative's responsibilities at the political level so that the rotating Presidency also replaces her when unavailable in answering European Parliament questions on CFSP. Equally, the High Representative's EEAS officials who chair Council working groups are, when unavailable, replaced by the rotating Presidency.

[68] See Arts 17 and 18 TFEU.

areas of decision-making notwithstanding that the institutional and decision-making procedures remain distinct. There was also much speculation as to whether this would lead to an encroachment of non-CFSP policies and institutional arrangements into areas of CFSP or the reverse.[69] Rather like kremlinologists, some observers have read much into the symbolism of where the High Representatives located their offices, their choice of officials, and their use of terminology. Certainly having a single person covering responsibilities for CFSP and non-CFSP matters has helped avoid narrow, technical debates when dealing with third parties or responding to international crises. But the political realities and legal requirements underlying the distinction between CFSP and non-CFSP remain and navigating these differences has been one aspect of a demanding and challenging role.

22.67   One of the main challenges for Catherine Ashton was the establishment from scratch of a European External Action Service (EEAS).[70] This Service was envisaged as a complement to the High Representative's own cross-cutting role. Comprising officials from the General Secretariat of the Council, the Commission, and seconded from national diplomatic services, the role of the Service is to assist the High Representative in fulfilling her mandate. Mandated to work 'in cooperation with the diplomatic services of the Member States', the EEAS is itself sometimes informally described as the European Union's 'diplomatic service'. Clearly the Union is not a State and as such does not exercise the full range of diplomatic functions and powers of a State but the term gives an indication of the range of functions—including representation and advice on policy—which the Service carries out across the range of EU external policy areas.

22.68   The Service's own powers and responsibilities are derived from their role in supporting the High Representative herself. It is not an institution in its own right. When supporting and advising the High Representative in her concurrent role as Vice-President of the Commission, the EEAS officials have the same functions as would any officials supporting or advising their Commissioner—and any responsibilities exercised on her behalf in this capacity are those of the Commission. Similarly it is the High Representative's own role and powers in relation to CFSP, as laid down in the Treaties, which determines EEAS officials' own role in this area. Thus any proposals for CFSP legal acts are made by the High Representative herself, not by the EEAS. Her role in chairing the FAC is similarly mirrored in the chairing by EEAS officials of the PSC and of Council working groups dealing with CFSP matters. Their role is to chair in an

---

[69] Art 40 TEU emphasizes that the implementation of CFSP shall not affect the procedures and powers relating to non-CFSP policies and vice versa.
[70] See Art 27(3) TEU.

impartial manner, in accordance with the rules and procedure of the Council, facilitating the work of the group rather than promoting a particular agenda or perspective.

The External Action Service was established by a 2001 Council Decision.[71] By **22.69** December 2014 the EEAS comprised some 4,000 staff[72] the core of whom, in accordance with the EU Treaties, were recruited on roughly equal basis from the diplomatic services of Member States, from the General Secretariat of the Council (in particular those units providing policy advice and support on CFSP under the pre-Lisbon Treaty arrangements) and from the Commission (in particular from what was previously DG Relex). Following a reorganization in 2015, the most senior officials are the Secretary-General[73] and three Deputy Secretaries-General covering respectively Economic and Global Issues, Political Affairs and CSFP, and crisis operations. Below them are a number of managing directors and directors overseeing a series of teams covering geographical and thematic areas which would be familiar in any larger ministry of foreign affairs. The establishment in Brussels also includes specific structures, such as the EU Intelligence and Situation Centre[74] (Intcen) and the EU Military Staff, while much of the EEAS's resources are focused on the global network of EU delegations, comprising some 60 per cent of its personnel, discussed at paragraphs 22.100 *et seq*.[75]

EU Agencies and EUSRs

As well as the EEAS, there are other actors with specific responsibilities for **22.70** external action. Many EU agencies'[76] activities necessarily involve external aspects—such as Frontex, the bodies dealing with European border management—while there are a number of agencies with specific responsibilities for CFSP issues: the European Institute for Security Studies, the European Satellite Centre, and the European Defence Agency (EDA). The EDA, whose head is the High Representative and which acts under the Council's authority, is charged

---

[71] Council Decision 2010/427/EU adopted on a proposal of the High Representative with the consent of the Commission.

[72] Policy and support staff including both permanent and temporary personnel. Source: EEAS Human Resources Report 2014, Brussels, May 2015.

[73] Helga Schmid, a senior EU official and former German diplomat and adviser to successive German Foreign Ministers, took office in September 2016. She was preceded by Alain Le Roy, a French diplomat and formerly UN Under-Secretary General for Peacekeeping, and Pierre Vimont, similarly a French diplomat and former French ambassador to Washington.

[74] Providing intelligence analysis to the EEAS and other EU bodies dealing with CFSP and counter-terrorism; formerly the Joint Situation Centre established under Javier Solana. On the Military Staff see paragraph 22.51.

[75] See paragraph 22.100.

[76] See Chapter 21, paragraph 21.57.

with improving defence capabilities and armaments cooperation within the Union.[77]

22.71 The Amsterdam Treaty also established arrangements—already trailed in the appointment in 1996 of Special Envoys dealing with the crisis in the African Great Lakes and with the Middle East Peace Process—for appointing EU Special Representatives (EUSRs). These are appointed by the Council by qualified majority voting to carry out a mandate in relation to particular policy issues under the authority of the High Representative.[78] As of the start of 2016 there were nine such EUSRs covering Central Asia, the Middle East Peace Process, Afghanistan, Bosnia and Herzegovina, Kosovo, the South Caucasus and the crisis in Georgia, Horn of Africa, Human Rights, and the Sahel.[79] Previous holders of these posts have included high-profile political figures such the former Spanish prime minister, Felipe González appointed to cover the former Yugoslavia from 1998 to 1999 and Lord (Paddy) Ashdown who held the post as EUSR for Bosnia and Herzegovina from 2002 to 2006 alongside that of High Representative for Bosnia and Herzegovina responsible for oversight of the implementation of the Dayton Agreement.

The European Parliament

22.72 Like the Commission, the European Parliament's[80] principal role is in relation to non-CFSP policies—the former Community first pillar. There are now a number of areas of external action which are co-decided by the Council with the European Parliament such as measures on development cooperation, humanitarian aid, assistance to third countries, and the framework on the implementation of the common commercial policy. The many areas covered by co-decided internal policies can also give rise to external competence while the European Parliament must consent to the conclusion of agreements in these and certain other areas as well as being kept 'immediately and fully informed' at all stages of the negotiation of international agreements.[81]

22.73 A number of EP Committees deal specifically with external issues—including not only the Foreign Affairs Committee (AFET), with its two subcommittees on Human Rights (DROI) and Security and Defence (SEDE), but also

---

[77] The EDA's membership includes all Member States except Denmark and is the only EU Agency whose governing body—the Steering Committee—meets at ministerial level.

[78] Art 33 TEU.

[79] As well as the African Great Lakes, former posts have included those covering the Sudan, the former Yugoslav Republic of Macedonia, Moldova, the African Union, the Southern Mediterranean, and South-East Europe.

[80] On the European Parliament generally see Chapter 21, paragraphs 21.80 *et seq.*

[81] See paragraph 22.82.

International Trade (INTA) and Development (DEVE)—while others will frequently deal with external issues as part of their wider responsibilities. MEPs, like their counterparts in national parliaments, undertake fact-finding and other missions to third countries, as well as maintaining relations with parliaments and parliamentary assemblies outside the Union through various delegations. In 2016 there were forty-one such delegations including bilateral Joint Parliamentary Committees and Parliamentary Cooperation Committees—established pursuant to EU Association and Cooperation Agreements—and delegations to multilateral parliamentary assemblies such as those with Africa, Caribbean and Pacific, Mediterranean, and Eastern European countries.

As well as its legislative responsibilities, the European Parliament frequently **22.74** adopts resolutions setting out its position on wider foreign policy issues, receives visits from third country Heads of State and Government, ministers, and other policy-makers,[82] and produces reports on the full range of EU external action. As noted earlier, the EP's formal role in relation to CFSP is strictly limited. But the High Representative is required[83] to 'regularly consult the European Parliament on the main aspects and basic choices' of CFSP and to inform it of how those policies evolve and on this basis issues annual reports to the Parliament.[84] In addition, as set out at paragraphs **22.58–22.60**, the EP has sought to exercise its influence through its responsibilities in relation to the EU budget.

International Agreements and Organizations

International Agreements

The conclusion of international agreements with third States and international **22.75** organizations has been the principal means by which the Community, and later the Union, has exercised its external, legal powers.[85] Thousands of such agreements have been concluded by the Community, and now the Union. They cover the full range of the EU's policies—including trade, development, environmental protection, fisheries, customs, immigration, social affairs, science and technology, transport, and CFSP operations—and may be either specific in scope, dealing with a particular subject, or wide-ranging covering cooperation

---

[82] From 1979 to 2013, Heads of State from about a third of the world's countries visited the European Parliament. Source: European Parliament news, 25 July 2013.

[83] Art 36 TEU.

[84] For copies of these reports see <http://eeas.europa.eu/topics/common-foreign-security-policy-cfsp/8427/cfsp-annual-reports_en>.

[85] References to agreements concluded by the Union here include agreements concluded by the European Community prior to the entry into force of the Lisbon Treaty at which point the Union replaced the Community assuming all its rights and responsibilities.

on a broad range of issues. Agreements may be concluded with a specific country or international organization, with a group of third countries (such as the Cotonou Agreement with the African, Caribbean, and Pacific States or the 2012 Association Agreement with Central American States) or on a multilateral basis (for example within the framework of the UN, WTO, or Council of Europe).[86] To give a flavour of the variety and range of agreements entered into the Union during any period, those signed in the last quarter of 2015 included a wide-ranging Partnership and Cooperation Agreement with Kazakhstan; fisheries agreements with Liberia, Mauritania, and Denmark (in respect of Greenland); visa-waiver agreements with Tonga, Palau, and Colombia; savings taxation agreements with Lichtenstein and San Marino; and an agreement with Bosnia and Herzegovina on the latter's contribution to CFSP operations.[87]

22.76　Among the most significant agreements for the Union, certainly in terms of its bilateral relations with third States, are association agreements. As already noted,[88] the conclusion of association agreements was one of the first external powers provided for in the EEC Treaty and is still enshrined in what is now Article 217 TFEU envisaging the establishment of 'associations involving reciprocal rights and obligations, common action and special procedure'. They represent the most extensive arrangements with third countries generally involving close and privileged political and economic cooperation and the establishment of a standing body of both parties—an association council—to oversee the implementation of the arrangement and with the power to adopt binding decisions.

22.77　The earliest association agreements were concluded with potential candidates for EU membership—Greece and Turkey—and all Member States acceding from 2004 onwards were previously parties to such agreements. A series of association agreements have been negotiated with other Mediterranean States and the Palestinian Authority—many termed Euro-Mediterranean Agreements—and with East European States in the framework of the European Neighbourhood Policy as well as with Western Balkan countries as part of the Union's Stabilisation and Association process in that region. But association agreements have also

---

[86] For a full list of the agreements concluded by the European Union, including analyses by category (subject-matter, Contracting Parties, bilateral/multilateral, in force etc), see the databases maintained by Eur-Lex (<http://eur-lex.europa.eu/browse/directories/inter-agree.html>), the Council Secretariat (<http://www.consilium.europa.eu/en/documents-publications/agreements-conventions>), and the European External Action Service (<http://ec.europa.eu/world/agreements/default.home.do>).

[87] The same period also saw the conclusion of high-profile negotiations, involving the European Union, on the Paris Agreement, within the framework of the United Nations Framework Convention on Climate Change, and the 10th WTO Ministerial Conference in Nairobi.

[88] Paragraph 22.7.

been concluded with countries in other regions—most notably the Cotonou Agreement with seventy-eight African, Caribbean, and Pacific countries.[89] The political significance of such agreements was demonstrated by the protests in Kiev in November 2013 after President Yanukovych stalled the signature of the EU–Ukraine association agreement, in favour of closer ties with Russia, leading to the overthrow of his government.

Other bilateral trade and cooperation agreements, while not association agree-   **22.78** ments as such, may also have great political and economic significance and the weight of the European Union as a leading global economic and trading power[90] makes it an important partner. A key objective of the common commercial policy is the progressive abolition of restrictions on international trade and many of these agreements are aimed at promoting free trade. The scope and ambition of the Union's bilateral agreements varies from country to country, depending on the degree of economic development in the country concerned and its political and economic relations with the EU, and is reflected in a variety of titles including Deep and Comprehensive Free Trade Agreements, Free Trade Agreements, and Partnership and Cooperation Agreements. As well as covering trade and investment matters, such agreements may also cover other areas such as economic cooperation, regulatory cooperation, environmental protection, sustainable development, political dialogue, and immigration. Negotiations for one of the EU's most ambitious, and debated, bilateral agreements between the world's two largest economies—the Transatlantic and Trade Investment Partnership with the United States (TTIP)—were launched in 2013.[91]

Many agreements concluded by the European Union, both bilateral and multi-   **22.79** lateral, are 'mixed'—that is, they are concluded by the EU Member States alongside the Union itself. Mixed agreements are used where the subject-matter straddles matters both within the competence (or legal powers) of the Union— whether exclusive competence where only the Union can act or shared competence where, as a matter of choice, it has been decided that the Union should act—and those of the Member States. This requires careful coordination between Member States and the Union particularly where their respective responsibilities are closely intertwined.[92] Rather than negotiate separately in relation to their own areas of responsibility, Member States usually designate the Commission

---

[89] See paragraph 22.7.

[90] In 2014 the European Union had both the world's largest share of both GDP (23.98 per cent) and world trade (16.6 per cent).

[91] This is estimated as capable of adding €120 billion and €95 billion respectively to the EU and US economies. See 'Transatlantic Trade and Partnership Investment Agreement—the Economic Analysis Explained', European Commission, September 2013.

[92] See paragraph 22.44.

or the rotating Presidency to negotiate on their behalf. As Member States are parties to such agreements in their own right they must be concluded in accordance with their respective constitutional requirements including where appropriate by their national parliaments. This can in turn lead to tensions with some pressing for 'EU only' agreements as being more efficient—taking an expansive view of the competences that the EU must, or should, exercise—and others defending the right of Member State to exercise their own powers and the involvement of national parliaments.[93]

22.80　The internal allocation of powers between the Union and its Member States, and their respective responsibilities for implementing the provisions of a mixed agreement, can understandably be confusing and opaque for the third countries or organizations with whom they are concluding such agreements. In some cases detailed 'declarations of competence' have been made at the time of concluding agreements indicating the areas for which the Union (or its predecessor the Community) or its Member States have responsibility.[94] In particular detailed declarations of competence were made when the Union acceded to the Constitution of the Food and Agriculture Organization in 1991, to the UN Convention on the Law of the Sea in 1993, and the UN Convention on the Rights of Persons with Disabilities in 2010. But in view of the complex, evolving, and often contested scope of Union competence such declarations can be difficult to negotiate between the Union and Member States and may only give a general and time-limited picture of the allocation of responsibilities. It is ultimately for the Union and Member States to ensure as between themselves that obligations under mixed agreements are fully implemented in relation to third parties which also means that such agreements must be concluded in a concerted fashion so that the Union and Member States enter into their responsibilities together.

22.81　The procedures for negotiating and concluding international agreements—for those covering both CFSP and non-CFSP matters—are now set out in Article 218 TFEU; more specific arrangements for trade agreements are set out in Article 207 TFEU. It is for the Commission (or the High Representative where an agreement relates primarily or exclusively to CFSP matters) to submit a recommendation to the Council which then authorizes the opening of negotiations,

---

[93] See e.g. Opinion 2/15 submitted to the Court of Justice by Commission on whether the proposed Free Trade Agreement with Singapore should be concluded as a mixed or EU only agreement. A particularly sensitive issue when, under new national arrangements, a Dutch referendum in April 2016 opposed ratification by the Netherlands of the Association Agreement with Ukraine.

[94] See the External Action Service database cited at n 79 for a list of agreements in relation to which declarations of competence have been made.

appoints a negotiator for the Union (normally the Commission or High Representative depending on the subject-matter), and provides the latter with negotiating instructions ('directives').

Those acting on behalf of the Commission or the High Representative then **22.82** conduct the negotiations with the third country or organization in regular consultation with a committee appointed by the Council—usually the relevant Council working group. At the end of the negotiations it is again for the Council to authorize signature and conclusion[95] of the agreement. The voting rule to be used throughout the procedure depends on the subject-matter of the agreement. The European Parliament must be kept informed at all stages of the negotiation and in certain cases—such as association agreements, agreements with budgetary implications, and those covering internal policies to which co-decision[96] applies—must give its consent to the approval of the agreement.

Once concluded international agreements are of course binding under international law on the European Union as an international legal person. Under the **22.83** EU Treaties,[97] they are binding upon the EU institutions and Member States and form part of the EU legal order. As such their provisions may be interpreted by the Court of Justice and, where an agreement's provisions are sufficiently precise and unconditional, they can be relied upon by individuals before the courts as having 'direct effect'.[98] The Court of Justice cannot annul an international agreement concluded under international law but it may rule on the legality of the internal Union decision authorizing the conclusion of the agreement. The Court can also issue an opinion on whether an *envisaged* agreement is compatible with the EU Treaties; this has led to a number of rulings in which the Court has held that an agreement would need to be modified before it entered into force because, for example, its provisions encroached on the Union's own judicial procedures.[99]

International Organizations

The Union's participation in international organizations is one of the most visible **22.84** forms of its role as an international actor. However the forms of its participation,

---

[95] The EU Treaties do not use the term ratification. The procedure on conclusion refers to the step which confirms the Union's consent to be bound including ratification.

[96] See Chapter 21, paragraph 21.86.

[97] Art 216(2) TFEU.

[98] Thus the provisions of association agreements, such as those providing for non-discrimination between nationals of EU Member States and those of the third country concerned, have frequently been relied upon by third country nationals; conversely, the Court of Justice held that the provisions of the GATT did not fulfil the conditions for having direct effect.

[99] See e.g. Opinion 2/13 on the proposed accession of the European Union to the European Convention on Human Rights.

whether as a full member or as an observer, vary from organization to organization depending upon both the membership rules of the organization concerned and the extent of the Union's competence in relation to the issues for which the organization has responsibility.

22.85 Article 220 TEU provides that the Union shall establish 'all appropriate forms of cooperation' with the organs of the United Nations and its Specialized Agencies, the Council of Europe, the OECD, and to maintain such forms of cooperation as appropriate with other international organizations. This provision, which now applies to both non-CFSP and CFSP areas of activity, does not envisage that the Union should become a member of these bodies[100] but rather provides for cooperation—in relation to matters within the EU's areas of responsibility—on an organization to organization basis such as exchange of information, administrative cooperation, and coordination of activities. An example of the matters covered by such cooperation is set out in the May 2007 Memorandum of Understanding between the Council of Europe and the European Union.[101]

22.86 Such relations also extend to the sending of delegations to such international organizations and, where the organizations allow, participating as observers in their meetings. Thus under United Nations General Assembly resolution 3208 (XXIX) of October 1974, the Community could speak in General Assembly meetings but not vote. Under General Assembly resolution GA/65/276 of May 2011, the UN granted additional participatory rights to the Union under which it can present EU agreed common positions, make interventions, present proposals, and circulate EU communications as official documents.

22.87 The EU presence at the United Nations also extends to the Security Council (UNSC). The UNSC includes two permanent members from the EU and other Member States are regularly elected as non-permanent members. Article 34 TEU provides that they should keep other Member States informed of developments in the UNSC and request that the High Representative be invited to present matters on which there is a defined Union position. As such the High Representative provides regular updates to formal meetings of the Council. In February 2014 the Security Council delivered its first Presidential statement[102] on cooperation between the UN and the Union commending the latter's work in the Western Balkans and on negotiations on Iran's nuclear programme, its

---

[100] On EU membership of international organizations see paragraphs **22.88** *et seq.*

[101] EU cooperation with international organizations may also extend to the conclusion of formal agreements such as the 2007 Agreement on cooperation and assistance with the International Criminal Court—adopted under CFSP powers, this was the first such agreement adopted between the ICC and a regional actor.

[102] S/PRST/2014/4.

crisis management operations in Africa, and its humanitarian assistance to Syria.[103]

EU membership of international organizations, participating as a full member with voting rights, is a material step beyond cooperation or attending as an observer.[104] It involves assuming the full obligations of membership and participating in the adoption of, and being subject to, new rules and commitments on matters within the sphere of responsibility of the international organization—matters for which the Union, and previously the Community, may have acquired competence in place of its constituent Member States.

22.88

As noted earlier,[105] in the early days of the EEC third countries found it difficult to adapt to the notion of the Community participating in international organizations on a basis akin to a sovereign State. The constituent treaties of most international organizations in any event limited membership to States. It was only when new organizations were established allowing for membership of what were termed regional economic integration organizations, or the constituent treaties of existing organizations were amended, that admission of the Community became possible. Even then, membership was initially largely confined to very specific, technical bodies, and in particular commodity organizations, such as the International Wheat Council which the Community joined in 1971, and fisheries organizations. The Food and Agriculture Organization was the first UN agency to admit the Community as a member in 1991 on the basis of a declaration of competence as described earlier[106] and it became a member of the World Trade Organization when the latter subsumed the GATT in 1995.[107]

22.89

Where the Union does accede to an international organization then it can clearly only do so in relation to matters for which it has competence under the EU Treaties and, as regards its instrument of accession, in accordance with the procedures in Article 218 TFEU as set out earlier. This article also sets out

22.90

---

[103] In 2015, the EU delivered more than 220 statements at the United Nations in New York, including thirty-one at the Security Council (source—the website of the EU Delegation to the United Nations: <http://eu-un.europa.eu>).

[104] For a survey of legal and policy issues relating to the Union membership of international organizations see J Wouters, J Odermatt, and T Ramopoulos, 'The EU in the World of International Organizations', Leuven Centre for Global Governance Studies, September 2013.

[105] Paragraph 22.12.

[106] Paragraph 22.80.

[107] See J Sack, 'The EC's Membership of International Organizations' (1995) *Common Market Law Review* 1227; and E Denza, 'The Community as a Member of International Organizations', in N Emiliou and D O'Keeffe, *The European Union and World Trade Law after the GATT Uruguay Round* (Chichester and Colorado Springs: Wiley, 1996).

the procedure for establishing the Union position on acts having legal effects to be adopted within an international organization. In many cases the Union is a member of an international organization alongside its Member States and in these cases careful coordination is needed to ensure that their respective powers are respected when speaking or voting. In the case of interventions this may be addressed by agreeing a joint statement of the Union and its Member States. In the case of voting, the terms under which the Union has adhered to the international organization are generally strict in ensuring that there can be no double-voting—only the Union (usually exercising a vote equivalent to those of the number of its Member States) or the Member States may vote but not both.[108]

22.91   There are of course a number of international organizations whose responsibilities include matters for which the Union has competence but of which the EU is not a member—usually due to a reluctance to change the membership rules to admit non-State members. Initiatives[109] have been proposed from time to time by the Commission to seek membership, or upgrade the status of, the Union in bodies such as the IMO, ICAO, and IAEA where the Union has particular interests but these have not been taken up. In these circumstances, where an international organization is dealing with matters within the competence of the Union, and not of Member States, the latter can only act jointly in the interests of the Union.[110] As regards interventions covering areas of Union competence, or straddling areas of Union and Member States' responsibility, this may again be addressed by adhering to a coordinated position which might, depending on the arrangements applicable in that organization, be delivered by the Union representative or the rotating Presidency.[111]

---

[108] See e.g. Art II(10) of the FAO Constitution: 'a Member Organization may exercise on matters within its competence, in any meeting of the Organization in which it is entitled to participate, a number of votes equal to the number of its Member States which are entitled to vote in such meeting. Whenever a Member Organization exercises its right to vote, its Member States shall not exercise theirs, and conversely.'

[109] See European Commission (2002) 'Recommendation from the Commission to the Council in order to authorise the Commission to open and conduct negotiations with the International Civil Aviation Organization (ICAO) on the conditions and arrangements for accession by the European Community', 9.4.2002, SEC/2002/0381 final; and European Commission (2012a) Communication to the Commission from the President in Agreement with Vice-President Ashton, 'Strategy for the progressive improvement of the EU status in international organisations in line with the objectives of the Treaty of Lisbon', Brussels, 20 December 2012, C(2012) 9420 final.

[110] See e.g. the ECJ judgment of October 2014 in C399/12 *Germany v Council* regarding the procedure for establishing the position to be taken by Member States on behalf of the Union in the Organization of Vine and Wine of which the EU is not a member.

[111] See also paragraph 22.99.

External Representation

Representation of the Union

The arrangements for representing the European Union in its relations at the international level—whether in a bilateral or multilateral framework—depend upon a variety of factors: the level at which the relations are conducted, the subject-area covered (and in particular whether it is CFSP or non-CFSP), the nature of the powers being exercised (including whether they also engage those of Member States), the forum in which negotiations or contacts are being conducted, and the particular actors available or empowered to represent the Union.   **22.92**

The basic framework laid down by the Treaties is that in relation to CFSP matters, the High Representative is responsible for representing the Union,[112] or 'at his level'—that is, at the level of Heads of State or Government—the President of the European Council. The Commission is responsible for representing the Union in relation to non-CFSP matters[113]—that is, those matters formerly covered by the European Community.[114] The Treaties also provide that Union delegations, under the authority of the High Representative, based in third countries and at international organizations shall represent the Union.[115] Their role, covering both CFSP and non-CFSP matters, is discussed at paragraph 22.100.   **22.93**

These arrangements reflect changes made to the Lisbon Treaty in relation to external representation on CFSP matters. Prior to the Lisbon Treaty, representation of the Union in this area was the responsibility of the Member State holding the rotating Presidency supported by the then High Representative. It was thus the local representative of the Presidency, whether in a bilateral mission or in an international organization or conference, who would present the coordinated Union position. Equally while the High Representative had a specific role in conducting political dialogue with third countries, representation at the political level was formally a matter for the Head of State or Government or Foreign Minister of the Presidency. This was exemplified in particular by the 'troika'[116] arrangement   **22.94**

---

[112] Art 27(2) TEU: 'The High Representative shall represent the Union for matters relating to the common foreign and security policy. He shall conduct dialogue with third parties on the Union's behalf and shall express the Union's position in international organisations and at the international level.'

[113] Art 17 TEU.

[114] As well as those areas of Justice and Home Affairs which prior to the entry into force of the Lisbon were part of the intergovernmental 'third pillar'; see Chapter 21, paragraph 21.41.

[115] Art 221 TFEU.

[116] The term 'troika' was originally introduced to describe team-working, particularly in the framework of European Political Cooperation, between the current, former, and future Presidencies.

introduced after the Treaty of Amsterdam in which the Union was represented at the political level by the Foreign Minister of the Presidency together with the High Representative and the Commissioner for External Relations.[117]

22.95   Representation of the Union on CFSP matters at the political level is thus now either a matter for the High Representative, who is responsible for most day-to-day political contacts, or the President of the European Council. The latter receives visiting Heads of State or Government, attends the G7 (former G8) and G20 meetings and other summit meetings where appropriate, and also represents the Union at bilateral 'EU summits' with third countries. At these EU summits with the Heads of State or Government of third countries, the Union is represented by the President of the European Commission (who also attends G7 and G20 meetings) and the President of the European Council reflecting the fact that their scope covers CFSP and non-CFSP issues. Less frequently there may also be summits at which all the Heads of State or Government of Member States are present, together with the Presidents of the European Commission and European Union, dealing with issues of particular significance and straddling areas of Member State and Union responsibility.[118]

22.96   Conversely, the Lisbon Treaty did not propose any changes to responsibilities for ensuring representation on non-CFSP matters, simply confirming that this continued to be the responsibility of the Commission. In practical terms however this can now often be done at the political level by the High Representative exercising her concurrent responsibilities as Vice-President of the Commission while at the local level EU delegations have taken over the responsibilities of what were previously Commission delegations. But other Commissioners, and at summit level the Commission President, continue to represent the Union at the political level and, as well as acting through the EU delegations, the Commission continues to send officials, for example, to represent the Union in international conferences and the negotiation of bilateral agreements.

22.97   Equally the Council continues to exercise its policy-making and coordinating responsibilities[119] in relation to both CFSP and non-CFSP areas of responsibility which may include meeting at official or ministerial level *sur place*[120] to

---

More recently it has been used informally to refer to the wholly distinct notion of the group of the Commission, ECB, and IMF dealing with the Eurozone crisis.

[117] Reflecting the previous Treaty provision under Art J.8 (4) that the Commission was to be 'fully associated' with representation of the Union.

[118] Such as the Valletta Summit of November 2015 with Heads of State or Government of African countries and dealing with migration.

[119] Art 16(1) TEU.

[120] The French term is frequently used in EU practice to describe the geographical location in which negotiations or other international conferences or meetings are being held.

determine the policy relating to an ongoing negotiation—thus the trade formation of the Foreign Affairs Council meets in the location of ministerial WTO negotiations. For its part, the rotating Presidency retains its role, where appropriate, for chairing such meetings, for representing the coordinated position of Member States as required at international conferences and negotiations on matters falling within their own areas of responsibility, and exceptionally for substituting for the High Representative or her officials on CFSP matters where they are not available or represented locally.

Despite the ambitions of the Lisbon Treaty to promote greater coherence in the **22.98** EU's external representation, it left—perhaps unavoidably—some issues unresolved, as well as raising new ones, and there have continued to be disagreements both about the extent of different EU actors' representational responsibilities as well as the allocation of responsibilities between the Union and its Member States. Attempts have been made to clarify some of these issues[121] but they can continue to take up much time and be a source of frustration both to those within the Union and to those engaging with it at the international level.

Particular areas of sensitivity have been the distinction between responsibilities **22.99** for representation and policy-making—such as on intervention in international legal proceedings[122] and responsibilities for chairing meetings *sur place*—and more generally the arrangements for coordination and representation on matters which straddle areas of Union and Member States' responsibility. As regards coordination and representation, practice can continue to vary from place to place, particularly in multilateral fora, depending on the nature and extent of the powers being exercised, the established practices of the local Member State missions and EU delegations, and the attitude of third parties. But with flexibility pragmatic solutions can be found which respect the powers and responsibilities of the respective institutions and Member States.

Diplomatic Relations and Consular Protection

EU Delegations

The Lisbon Treaty replaced the previous network of delegations established and **22.100** staffed by the Commission and dealing with matters, such as trade and development, within the Commission's area of responsibility. These Commission

---

[121] For example, through the establishment in October 2011 of General Arrangements on EU statements in multilateral organizations.

[122] See e.g. the ruling of the Court of Justice of October 2015 in *Council v Commission* concerning a written intervention on behalf of the Union in a case before the International Tribunal on the Law of the Sea.

delegations became EU delegations, staffed by the EEAS, and covering both CFSP and non-CFSP matters.[123] There are some 140 EU delegations around the world—accredited both to third States and to international organizations—comprising some 60 per cent of the personnel of the External Action Service. Decisions to open and close delegations are taken by the High Representative in agreement with the Council and Commission.[124] Like the EEAS generally the staff of delegations are drawn both from diplomats seconded from Member States and from the Commission and the General Secretariat of the Council in addition to locally engaged staff.

22.101   In view of their responsibility to represent the Union, their remit, as regards non-CFSP issues, is not limited to matters falling within the specific portfolio of the High Representative in her capacity as Vice-President of Commission, but also covers trade, development, climate change, and other areas. It therefore falls to such delegations to represent the Union on both CFSP and non-CFSP matters both bilaterally in third countries and in international organizations and the Commission may issue instructions to EU delegations under matters for which it is responsible.[125]

22.102   While the heads of EU delegations are accorded the courtesy title of ambassador, and their delegations referred to as diplomatic missions, they do not exercise the full functions of the diplomatic mission of a State. They can only act within the limit of the powers conferred on the Union. Nor are such delegations covered by the provisions of the Vienna Convention on Diplomatic Relations (VCDR) where participation is limited to States.[126] They are rather covered by a wide network of agreements concluded with the host States and generally conferring on the EU delegations privileges and immunities broadly similar to those conferred under the VCDR.[127] Letters of credence for heads of delegations to be presented to the host State are signed by both the President of the

---

[123] EU Delegations also replaced the handful of missions established by the Council Secretariat in New York and elsewhere.

[124] Art 5(1) of the Council Decision establishing the EEAS.

[125] See Art 5(3) of the Council Decision establishing the EEAS: 'In areas where the Commission exercises the powers conferred upon it by the Treaties, the Commission may, in accordance with Article 221(2) TFEU, also issue instructions to delegations, which shall be executed under the overall responsibility of the Head of Delegation.'

[126] On diplomatic privileges and immunities see Chapter 13.

[127] Under Art 5(6) of the 2011 Decision establishing the EEAS, 'The High Representative shall enter into the necessary arrangements with the host country, the international organisation, or the third country concerned. In particular, the High Representative shall take the necessary measures to ensure that host States grant the Union delegations, their staff and their property, privileges and immunities equivalent to those referred to in the Vienna Convention on Diplomatic Relations of 18 April 1961.'

European Council and the European Commission reflecting the scope of the role of delegations.

Member States' Diplomatic Missions

The EU Treaties provide that the EU delegations shall act in close cooperation **22.103** with Member States' diplomatic and consular missions.[128] Declarations accompanying the Lisbon Treaty emphasize that establishment of the EEAS did not in any way affect national diplomatic services or national representation in third countries or participation in international organizations.[129] EU delegations do not therefore replace national diplomatic missions but may, where the Union's powers so allow, assist them in certain of their responsibilities—notably consular protection.

The EU Treaties also stipulate that Member States' diplomatic missions and EU **22.104** delegations shall cooperate in ensuring the implementation of CFSP measures and more generally 'step up cooperation' by exchanging information and carrying out joint assessments.[130] Cooperation between heads of national diplomatic missions, and with EU delegations—including exchange of information and coordination of positions—is therefore frequent and substantial in both third country capitals and international organizations.[131]

While Article 6 of the Vienna Convention on Diplomatic Relations permits **22.105** two or more States to accredit a single ambassador to another State, this has not been used by EU Member States.[132] Conversely, the downgrading or (re-)establishment of diplomatic relations with a third State may be coordinated as reflected in the joint presentation of credentials by five Member States to the President of Somalia in February 2013.[133] In addition, increasing use has been made of the co-location of the embassies of EU Member States both amongst themselves and with EU delegations. By 2014, the EEAS had concluded some fifty memoranda of understanding providing for co-location with EU Member

---

[128] Art 221 TFEU.

[129] Declarations 13 and 14 concerning the Common Foreign & Security Policy. See also P Berman, 'The Lisbon Treaty: The End of the Foreign Office?', Chatham House, 12/01/10, <https://www.chathamhouse.org/sites/files/chathamhouse/public/Meetings/Meeting%20Transcripts/120110berman.pdf>.

[130] Art 35 TEU—the provision was introduced by the Maastricht Treaty.

[131] According to the website of the EU Delegation to the United Nations in New York, at n 103, the Delegation hosts more than 1,300 coordination meetings annually while in 2014 Member States voted together on 92 per cent of the resolutions adopted by the UN General Assembly.

[132] Moreover, for Member States such as France, a constitutional amendment would be needed for a national of another State to represent its diplomatic interests. See E Denza, *Diplomatic Law* (4th edn, Oxford: Oxford University Press, 2016) 47.

[133] Germany, France, Spain, Belgium, and Finland. Press release of EU Delegation in Kenya, 26 February 2013.

States' embassies with seventeen being signed in that year alone.[134] Most of these provided for national embassies to be located in the premises of EU delegations[135] but in some cases, for example the UK embassy in Iraq, the Member State mission has hosted the EU delegation. The most extensive exercise has been Europe House in Abuja, Nigeria, launched in 1994, providing shared facilities for the embassies of a number of EU Member States as well as the EU delegation.

Consular Protection

22.106 One of the most significant areas of cooperation between Member States' diplomatic and consular missions, and between those missions and EU delegations, is in relation to consular protection. Under Article 8 of the 1963 Vienna Convention on Consular Relations, a State may exercise consular functions on behalf of a third State unless the receiving State objects. The Maastricht Treaty introduced the concept of EU citizenship, to be held in addition to national citizenship, and with it the right to enjoy 'in the territory in which the Member State of which they are nationals is not represented, the protection of the diplomatic and consular authorities on the same conditions as the nationals of the State'.[136]

22.107 Arrangements for implementing this provision are now set out in Council Directive 2015/637 adopted in April 2015. This stipulates, for example, the type of consular protection and the categories of persons which are covered and the practical arrangements for coordination, information sharing, and reimbursement of financial costs.[137] It provides for local coordination meetings, chaired by a Member State representative, with particular responsibilities being conferred on a 'lead State'—a concept already established under guidelines established in 2008[138]—as well as the involvement of the EEAS and EU delegations in providing logistical support and facilitating the exchange of information. The emphasis however in both the Treaty provisions and the Directive is on the role of Member States underlining that the exercise of consular protection remains a matter for States.

22.108 The practical implications of these arrangements are potentially significant. According to the European Commission in 2015, '7 million EU citizens travel

---

[134] EEAS Activity Report 2014. For a detailed table of co-location missions, involving EU delegations and Member States, as at 2013, see the EEAS Activity Report 2013.

[135] Thus in 2012 the EEAS concluded memoranda of understanding with Luxembourg and Spain providing for the location of those States' embassies in the EU delegations in Ethiopia and Yemen respectively. EAS Press Release, Brussels, 10 December 2012, A 568/12.

[136] Now provided for in Art 9 TEU and Art 20 TFEU.

[137] Art 23 TFEU.

[138] OJ C317, 12.12.2008.

or live outside the EU in places where their own EU country does not have an embassy or consulate. The only four countries where all 28 EU countries are represented are the United States, China, India and Russia.'[139] A notable example of EU consular cooperation was in relation to the conflict in Lebanon in July 2006 during which tens of thousands of evacuees, including EU citizens, were transferred to Cyprus.[140]

Third States' Relations with the European Union

In view of the European Union's extensive external responsibilities, many non-Member States have, since the early days of the European Communities, established missions to the European Union to engage directly with the responsible institutions and decision-makers.[141] The heads of such missions previously presented their letters of credence, signed by their Head of State, to both the President of the European Commission and the rotating Presidency. Since the entry into force of the Lisbon Treaty, such letters are to be addressed to the Presidents of the European Council and European Commission[142] while, since 2014, credentials are in practice presented only to the President of the European Council.   **22.109**

Under Article 16 of the Protocol on Privileges and Immunities annexed to the EU Treaties, the Member State in which the Union has its seat shall 'accord the customary diplomatic immunities and privileges to missions of third countries accredited to the Union'. Belgium is thus responsible for according the full range of diplomatic immunities and privileges to such missions some of whose heads are also accredited as bilateral ambassadors to Belgium or to other States.   **22.110**

The process of *agrément* for accreditation to the EU involves consulting Member States as well as the Council, Commission, and EEAS. This is particularly pertinent as regards recognition of States which remains a matter for Member States. While EU Member States seek to coordinate as far as possible their positions on State recognition,[143] there have been occasions—such as in relation to   **22.111**

---

[139] European Commission Press Release, 30 April 2015.

[140] Joint (Presidency, Council, Commission) Press Release, July 2006. However, for some these and other international crises also highlighted the need to improve coordination mechanisms particularly for large scale emergencies—see J Melissan and A M Fernadez (eds), *Consular Affairs and Diplomacy* (Leiden: Martinus Nijhoff, 2011) 102.

[141] By April 2016 over 140 States were accredited to the European Union. For a list of accredited States see Commission website at: <http://ec.europa.eu/dgs/secretariat_general/corps>.

[142] See 'Vade-mecum for the use of the diplomatic corps accredited to the European Union and to the European Atomic Energy Community', on the Commission website cited at n 141.

[143] See the 1991 Guidelines on the Recognition of the New States in the Eastern Europe and the Soviet Union (see paragraph **22.15**).

Kosovo—where they disagree.[144] In such situations great care is taken in references to the entity concerned to avoid prejudicing the individual positions of Member States as well as in ensuring that there is consensus before the Union itself takes a position, for example in international negotiations or organizations, affecting recognition. This has however still been able to accommodate a pragmatic approach leading to, for example, the signature of a Stabilisation and Association Agreement with Kosovo in October 2015.

Common Foreign and Security Policy

22.112 The previous sections illustrate the wide-ranging scope of the EU's external policies across both non-CFSP and CFSP areas. However two areas of (principally) CFSP policy merit separate mention both because they provide a visible demonstration of the breadth of the EU's action at the international level and because they raise specific policy and institutional issues. While these areas—sanctions and the common security and defence policy—use the same CFSP legal powers[145] and institutional arrangements as previously outlined (and in the case of sanctions may also involve non-CFSP powers) they are also subject to particular arrangements and procedures.

Sanctions

22.113 The imposition of sanctions[146] on third countries, organizations, and individuals is perhaps CFSP's most important, and most used, foreign policy tool. As of 2016 there were some forty sanctions regimes[147] in force targeting, amongst others, terrorist organizations, those involved in committing violations of human rights or humanitarian law, those undermining democracy and the rule of law, and regimes and their supporters deemed to be a threat to international or regional peace and security or otherwise undermining the rights of their citizens or violating international law. As well as sanctions against terrorist organizations, their geographical scope extends to countries in four continents and includes those adopted in implementation of UN Security Council resolutions (UNSCRs) and those adopted independently by the European Union—'autonomous sanctions'—in pursuit of specific EU foreign policy goals.

---

[144] Twenty-three EU Member States have recognized Kosovo while Spain, Cyprus, Greece, Romania, and Slovakia have not done so.

[145] See paragraphs 22.33–22.35.

[146] See C Portela, *EU Sanctions and Foreign Policy: When and Why Do They Work* (London and New York: Routledge, 2010).

[147] For a complete list of sanctions measures currently in force see the EEAS website at: <http://eeas.europa.eu/cfsp/sanctions/docs/measures_en.pdf>.

The imposition of sanctions already arose, in the then Community context, in   **22.114**
relation to the implementation of United Nations sanctions against Rhodesia
between 1965 and 1968[148] while more systematic efforts to align Member
States' positions, within the framework of the EPC, date back to the 1980s.
Thus Foreign Ministers agreed to impose economic sanctions on Iran in
1980 in response to the detention of hostages in the US embassy in Tehran,
albeit hampered by differences in national implementation[149] and on the Soviet
Union in 1982 after the declaration of martial law in Poland. In the same year
they rapidly agreed to impose both an import ban and arms embargo on
Argentina in response to the latter's invasion of the Falklands Islands with
one Community official claiming 'we have done in a day what would normally
take a year to do'.[150]

These cases however demonstrated the tensions between the political decision   **22.115**
to impose sanctions on a third county, a foreign policy matter for Member
States, and the implementation of such sanctions through interrupting trade, a
competence of the Community. This was addressed by the Maastricht Treaty[151]
which introduced a provision enabling action to be taken under the Community
pillar to implement CFSP measures calling for the interruption of economic
relations with a third country. This provision was further refined by the Lisbon
Treaty but the basic approach in what is now Article 215 TFEU remains the
same—the imposition of sanctions is a matter to be decided under CFSP and,
where these impact on economic or financial relations with third countries,
then implemented by non-CFSP measures.

While the imposition of economic and financial restrictions—such as trade   **22.116**
embargoes, capital restrictions, and the freezing of individuals' assets—remain
an important part of Union sanctions they also extend to other elements such as
arms embargoes, diplomatic restrictions, and visa bans. The choice of measures
depends on the particular circumstances that the Union is seeking to address.
However, a significant development in sanctions practice over the past decades
has been the move against imposing sanctions on a country as a whole—with
consequent hardship for the entire population—and to target those individuals
whose conduct the measures are intended to address.

---

[148] See P Koutrakos, *Trade, Foreign Policy & Defence in EU Law* (Oxford: Hart Publishing, 2001).
[149] The UK House of Commons for example refused to apply such sanctions retroactively to the
date of the seizure of the Embassy.
[150] See L Martin, 'Institutions and Cooperation: Sanctions during the Falklands Conflict' (1992)
16(4) *International Security* 143. After a rapid initial response, disagreements subsequently emerged
on the renewal of sanctions.
[151] Art 301 TEC. Art 60 TEC was used to restrict capital movements and payments to third
countries.

22.117 Such targeted or 'smart' sanctions, while designed to avoid harm to the general population, have led to hundreds of legal challenges to EU sanctions decisions in the Court of Justice. Although such sanctions are not criminal penalties but are rather intended to deter illegal or harmful conduct—for example by depriving a terrorist of the means of carrying out future attacks—they have often been annulled, in particular on the grounds that the procedural rights of the individuals concerned have not been respected. Most significantly, and contentiously, the Court of Justice held that sanctions imposed on an individual in implementation of a mandatory Chapter VII resolution of the UN Security Council should be annulled[152] on human rights grounds. However, the procedures for listing have been continually refined, reducing the risk of legal challenge, and sanctions policy continues to be a major aspect of CFSP and the Union's overall external action.[153]

Security and Defence

22.118 The security and defence element of CFSP, now termed the Common Security and Defence Policy (CSDP), is conversely one of the most recent areas of CFSP, and EU external action, to be developed.[154] After attempts to establish a European Defence Community failed in 1954,[155] efforts on European integration were focused on economic matters with States being particularly concerned to keep the sensitive areas of security and defence away from supranational decision-making. Defence cooperation between Western European countries was rather expressed in intergovernmental, mutual defence arrangements—first the Western European Union[156] (WEU) established in 1948 but principally through NATO established a year later.

---

[152] Cases C-402/05 P and C-415/05, *P Kadi and Al Barakaat International Foundation v Council and Commission* [2008] ECR I–6351.

[153] An illustration of the use and range of such sanctions was the action taken by the Union in response to Russia's annexation of Crimea in March 2014 which included diplomatic sanctions (e.g. cancellation of EU and bilateral summits); the imposition of asset freezes and visa bans on those whose actions threatened to undermine the territorial integrity of Ukraine; asset freezes on those responsible for the misappropriation of Ukrainian assets; import, investment, and tourist services ban in relation to Crimea and Sevastopol; suspension of economic cooperation with Russia; and a ban on arms trade with Russia and targeting of other Russian economic sectors.

[154] See P Koutrakos, *The EU Common Security and Defence Policy* (Oxford: Oxford University Press, 2013).

[155] This proposal to establish a pan-European defence force, involving what were to become the six founding members of the EEC, was blocked by the French National Assembly. The events form a perhaps unlikely backdrop to the final novel in Nancy Mitford's 'Love in a Cold Climate' trilogy set in the British Embassy in Paris.

[156] Originally comprising France, the Netherlands, Belgium, Netherlands, Luxembourg, and the UK and then expanded first in 1954 to include Germany and Italy and then in the 1990s to include Spain, Portugal, and Greece. See also Chapter 23.

Once again the significant change came with the 1991 Maastricht Treaty   **22.119**
which specified that CFSP 'shall include all questions related to the security
of the Union including the eventual framing of a common defence policy,
which might in time lead to a common defence'. It also requested 'the WEU,
which is an integral part of the development of the Union, to elaborate and
implement decisions and actions of the Union which have defence implications'.[157]

From the end of the 1980s, the WEU had tentatively started to develop a post-   **22.120**
Cold War role in undertaking limited external operations such as minesweeping
in the Gulf and it was co-opted by the EU to provide the military capacity for
its new security policy. The range of tasks that the WEU was to undertake were
set out in the 1992 Petersberg Declaration.[158] These 'Petersberg tasks'—including humanitarian and rescue missions, disarmament, peacekeeping, military
advice and assistance, and post-conflict stabilization—set the agenda for the
development of the EU's own security operations and were subsequently incorporated into the EU Treaties.[159]

The development of a security, and in particular military, aspect to the EU's   **22.121**
activities nevertheless remained sensitive. As part of the arrangements under
which it ratified the Maastricht Treaty, Denmark opted out of all EU decisions
with defence implications. Some Member States had a tradition or policy of
neutrality and were, and are, not part of NATO.[160] Others were concerned not
to create a rival to NATO as the transatlantic basis for European defence. The
Maastricht Treaty made clear that the EU's own security policy would 'not prejudice the specific character of the security and defence policy of certain Member
States and shall respect the obligations of certain Member States under the
North Atlantic Treaty'.[161]

These sensitivities meant that it was only several years after the entry into force   **22.122**
of the Lisbon Treaty that the security dimension of CFSP began to be developed.[162] The catalyst was the commitment to developing the Union's military
capacity made in the 1998 St Malo Declaration by the leaders of the EU's two
main military powers—President Chirac of France and Prime Minister Blair of

---

[157] Art J.4 of the then Treaty on European Union.
[158] Named after the Hotel Petersberg in Bonn where the declaration was agreed.
[159] By the Lisbon Treaty. They are now set out in Art 43(1) TEU.
[160] As of 2016, six of the twenty-eight EU Member States were not NATO members: Austria,
Cyprus, Finland, Ireland, Malta, and Sweden.
[161] Similar language is now set out in Art 42(2) TEU.
[162] Although the EU did task WEU with certain operations such as demining operations in
Croatia from 1999–2001.

the United Kingdom.[163] Thereafter progress was rapid. The specific institutional structures required for operational planning and decision-making were established by 2001,[164] arrangements to allow the EU to use NATO assets—the 'Berlin Plus' agreement—were established in 2002, and a European Security Strategy defining the Union's main security challenges was drawn up in 2003.[165] The same year the first military mission directly under EU auspices, Operation Concordia in the former Yugoslav Republic of Macedonia was launched.[166]

22.123   From 2003 to 2016, the Union has launched thirty-two operations, known as 'crisis management operations', of which sixteen were ongoing in 2016. These have comprised twenty-one civilian operations—drawing on a range of civilian experts—and eleven military operations—drawing in each case on the armed forces of individual Member States. Their main focus has been on areas of particular foreign policy concern to the Union in neighbouring regions or in countries with historical ties to Member States—thus seventeen missions have been undertaken in Africa, nine in Europe, five in the Middle East, and only one further afield in Asia. They range in size from a few dozen members to major operations involving several thousand personnel and significant military assets and their objectives have included combating piracy and people smuggling, post-conflict stabilization and monitoring, military training and strengthening of security capacities, and police and border assistance.[167]

22.124   Whilst one of the most distinctive areas of EU external action, EU military operations are still far removed from the notion of a pan-European armed force. The Maastricht Treaty did introduce the possibility of moving to a 'common defence' when the European Union 'acting unanimously, so decides'[168] but the prospect of a proposal for a European army securing unanimous support has

---

[163] This stated that 'the Union must have the capacity for autonomous action, backed up by credible military forces, the means to decide to use them, and a readiness to do so, in order to respond to international crises'.

[164] See paragraphs 22.49–22.51.

[165] See <http://www.consilium.europa.eu/uedocs/cmsUpload/78367.pdf>. The five key threats were defined as terrorism, proliferation of weapons of mass destruction, regional conflicts, failed States, and organized crime. In June 2016, High Representative Mogherini presented to the European Council a new 'Global Strategy for the Common Foreign and Security Policy'—see <https://europa.eu/globalstrategy/en>.

[166] With the establishment of the EU's own military capacity, and mutual defence clause, the WEU was finally dissolved in June 2011. See also Chapter 23.

[167] Four of the largest missions are Eufor Althea which replaced NATO's SFOR mission in Bosnia in 2004, the Eulex mission supporting rule of law institutions in Kosovo (launched in 2008), Operation Eunav for Atalanta combating piracy off the Horn of Africa (2008), and another maritime operation Operation Eunavfor Sophia combating people smuggling in the Mediterranean (2015).

[168] Art 42(2) TEU.

been remote.[169] Conversely, the Lisbon Treaty introduced a mutual assistance clause obliging Member States to provide aid and support if one of their number were to be a victim of armed aggression on its territory.[170] This provision was invoked for the first time by France in November 2015 following major terrorist attacks in Paris. This was as much about sending a political message of mutual solidarity and resolve as about practical support—and involved providing support on a government to government basis rather than through EU bodies.

The wide range of external threats and challenges confronting the European Union in both its neighbouring regions and further afield—including confronting international terrorism, countering so-called 'hybrid threats',[171] addressing international migration, and dealing with conflicts and post-conflict situations in the Middle East, Africa, and Europe itself—continue to shape CSDP's development and priorities. But other factors—including the evolving relationship with NATO,[172] the prospect of the withdrawal of the United Kingdom as one of the Union's main military and diplomatic powers, and the readiness or otherwise of Member States to contribute to the development of the Union's operational capabilities—will also play an important role in the future development of CSDP. **22.125**

---

[169] In March 2015 Commission President Juncker revived the notion of a European army stating: 'you would not create a European army to use it immediately but a common European army would send a clear message to Russia that we are serious about defending the values of the European Union'. A UK government spokesman was quoted as responding: 'Our position is crystal clear that defence is a national—not an EU—responsibility and that there is no prospect of that position changing and no prospect of a European army.' *The Guardian*, 8 March 2015.

[170] Art 42(7) TEU.

[171] See Foreign Affairs Council Conclusions on 'Countering Hybrid Threats', April 2016, <http://www.consilium.europa.eu/en/press/press-releases/2016/04/19-fac-conclusions-hybrid-threats/>.

[172] At the NATO Summit in Warsaw in July 2016, the NATO Secretary-General and the Presidents of the European Council and Commission issued a Joint Declaration identifying areas for reinforcing cooperation 'as a strategic priority' between the EU and NATO.

23

OTHER INTERNATIONAL AND REGIONAL ORGANIZATIONS

Commonwealth, NATO, Council of Europe, OAS, AU, ASEAN, CIS, Francophonie, Arab League, Organization of Islamic Cooperation, Gulf Cooperation Council, OSCE

Ivor Roberts

The Commonwealth

Balfour Definition

The idea of the Commonwealth goes back to the nineteenth century when, **23.1** after Canada had become a self-governing Dominion, the future prime minister, Lord Rosebery, referred to the Empire as a Commonwealth of Nations. The first modern definition associated with Lord Balfour of the Commonwealth of Nations emerged from the Imperial Conference of 1926. The status of the group of self-governing communities composed of Britain and the Dominions was described as follows:

> They are autonomous communities within the British Empire, equal in status, in no way subordinate one to another in any aspect of their domestic or external affairs, though united by a common allegiance to the Crown and freely associated as members of the British Commonwealth of Nations.[1]

Statute of Westminster

Under the Statute of Westminster 1931, remaining restrictions on the powers of **23.2** Dominion parliaments were largely removed.

The turning point in the history of the Commonwealth came with the London **23.3** Declaration of April 1949, in which member countries accepted India's intention to adopt a republican constitution, at the same time continuing 'her full membership of the Commonwealth of Nations and her acceptance of The King as the symbol of the free association of its independent member nations and as such the Head of the Commonwealth'.[2]

It was also in 1949 that the title 'Commonwealth of Nations' was first used as an **23.4** alternative to the former title 'British Commonwealth of Nations', which in time it replaced completely. Nowadays it is simply referred to as the Commonwealth.

---

[1] The Imperial Conference 1926, Summary of Proceedings, Cmd 2768. At that time the self-governing Dominions were Canada, Australia, New Zealand, the Union of South Africa, and the Irish Free State. Newfoundland is also mentioned in the Statute of Westminster (it was also a dominion until 1934) but is omitted from the previous sentence as its constitutional development led away from independent international status.

[2] The Declaration regarding the future of the Commonwealth was incorporated in the communiqué issued at the end of the Commonwealth Prime Ministers Meeting in April 1949.

Thus, the concept of the Commonwealth has changed from a group of countries owing allegiance to a single crown, to an association of sovereign independent nations which includes alongside those members both republics and countries with their own monarchs.

23.5 Since 1950, some forty-six former dependent territories have become independent and full members of the Commonwealth. Member countries (2016) number fifty-three.[3] Today the Commonwealth is, after the UN and its Specialized Agencies, one of the world's largest intergovernmental organizations, with more than a quarter of the UN's membership, about a third of the world's population, and about a fifth of the world's trade.

Freedom of Decision

23.6 In 1947, on the occasion of the Burma Independence Bill, the then British prime minister, Clement Attlee, emphasized that '[t]he British Commonwealth of Nations is a free association of peoples, not a collection of subject nations'. Burma was thus free to become an independent State outside the Commonwealth and it so decided, as did Ireland under the Ireland Act of 1949. The Sudan took the same course in 1956 and between that date and 1967 British Somaliland and Protectorate,[4] Kuwait, Southern Cameroons, and the South Arabian Federation (including Aden)[5] ended their earlier, sometimes tenuous, imperial connections. By contrast Namibia and Cameroon joined the Commonwealth in 1990 and 1995 respectively and Mozambique and Rwanda, neither of which had had any imperial connection with Britain, joined in 1995 and 2009 respectively.[6]

23.7 Of the above countries only Ireland had enjoyed the status of member country of the Commonwealth at the time of decision. The Union of South Africa on its declaration of a republic in 1961 and Pakistan in 1972, following the recognition by Commonwealth governments of Bangladesh, the former east wing of Pakistan, as an independent State, also voluntarily ceased existing membership. There has been no case of any country being expelled, but suspension has occurred (see below). The withdrawal of South Africa in 1961 was, however, due to what was felt to be the pressure of the majority of Commonwealth governments on the South African government for an essential change in the system of racial *apartheid* to which the South Africans were not willing to agree. South Africa was readmitted to the Commonwealth in 1994 after the end of *apartheid*.

---

[3] A full list of current member countries is to be found at <http://www.thecommonwealth.org>.
[4] Now Somalia.
[5] Now Southern Yemen.
[6] L Lloyd, *Diplomacy with a Difference: The Commonwealth Office of High Commissioner, 1880–2006* (Leiden and Boston: Martinus Nijhoff, 2007) 278–9.

Pakistan rejoined in 1989. In recent times, several members have been suspended from the councils of the Commonwealth for failing to uphold democracy. The Fiji Islands, Nigeria, and Pakistan have all been suspended and readmitted. Fiji was re-suspended in 2006 and readmitted in 2014. Zimbabwe was suspended in 2002 and withdrew from the Commonwealth the following year when the Abuja Commonwealth Heads of Government Meeting (CHOGM) decided to maintain Zimbabwe's suspension. The Gambia left the Commonwealth in 2013.

From 1949 on, as numerous dependent territories assumed independent status, **23.8** a preponderance of countries opted for republican status either at the time of transition or shortly afterwards. On the other hand, some traditionally monarchical communities retained their own monarchies.

Head of the Commonwealth

Despite such wide constitutional divergences, one common factor remains: that **23.9** of the Queen as the symbolic head of the Commonwealth. No specific functions attach to this title as such, though the Queen issues a Commonwealth Day Message and has usually addressed the Opening Ceremony of CHOGM. Nor has it any constitutional significance. It is, however, seen as the outward and visible mark of the special Commonwealth relationship. Today the Queen is Head of State in sixteen of the fifty-three Commonwealth member countries, all of them fully independent. When the Queen dies or were she to abdicate, her heir will not automatically become head of the Commonwealth. It will be up to the Commonwealth Heads of Government to decide on a successor as head.

Governors-General

In those member countries apart from Britain where she is Head of State, the **23.10** Queen is represented by a Governor-General. He or she is charged with many, though not all, of the functions performed in Britain by the sovereign personally, such as the summoning, proroguing, and dissolution of Parliament, the giving of the Royal Assent to Bills, the appointment of cabinet ministers (on the advice of the prime minister) and judges, and the issuing of credentials.

The Governor-General has direct links with the Queen and is not the represen- **23.11** tative or agent of the British government or of any department of that government. He or she is appointed on the advice of ministers of the member country concerned and not, as formerly, of British ministers.

In Australia the sovereign is still also represented in each State by a Governor. **23.12** Their functions are generally similar to those of a Governor-General, except that since 1986 they are appointed formally on the advice of the state premier.

Previously a Governor was appointed on the advice of British ministers. Similarly, Canadian provinces have a Lieutenant-General.

Commonwealth Heads of Government Meetings (CHOGM)

23.13 While ministerial and functional conferences now take place throughout the Commonwealth on an increasing scale, ranging from gatherings, sometimes in a UN context, of ministers of foreign affairs, finance, justice, health, or trade to those of cabinet secretaries, officials, or technicians, the meetings of heads of government have become the most obvious symbol of continuing Commonwealth cooperation. When such meetings were resumed in 1944, they took on a more informal character than the pre-war Imperial Conferences. (They were known as Prime Ministers' Meetings until 1971 when they were renamed CHOGMs.) During the two following decades they were held almost without question in London under the chairmanship of the British prime minister of the day. Servicing of the meetings remained in the joint hands of the British Cabinet Office and of the Dominions (later Commonwealth Relations) Office. Even following the independence of India, Pakistan, and Ceylon in 1947–8, the gatherings remained small (not surprisingly given the smallness of the Commonwealth at that time) and retained something of a family atmosphere.

23.14 It was not until 1966, shortly after the unilateral declaration of independence by Rhodesia, that a further precedent was set. In that year not only were two heads of government meetings held, but for the first time one of them took place outside London—in Nigeria—and was devoted to the single subject of Rhodesia. While a further conference was convened in London in 1969, the concept of 'rotation' is now firmly established. Recent CHOGMs, now held biennially, have taken place in Abuja, Valletta, Kampala, Port of Spain, Perth, Colombo, and Malta (Valletta and Fort St Angelo, Birgu) in 2015. The Colombo meeting was dogged by controversy over the host government's human rights record and in particular alleged war crimes during the last stages of Sri Lanka's civil war. The prime ministers of Canada, India and Mauritius declined to attend the summit over this human rights issue. From the second CHOGM onwards, to preserve informality, the practice has developed for the leaders of each country's delegation to foregather in a retreat with no more than one and sometimes no adviser present.

The Commonwealth Secretariat

23.15 With the growing numbers of Commonwealth members by the mid 1960s, it was agreed that the time had come to set up a secretariat on a Commonwealth-wide basis. Accordingly in 1964 the heads of government decided to establish a Commonwealth Secretariat to be located at Marlborough House in London, a royal palace.

The early Secretaries-General Arnold Smith, a senior Canadian diplomat, and **23.16** his successor Sir Shridath Ramphal, a distinguished legal and political personality from Guyana, ensured that the Secretariat developed from being, as originally understood, a servicing organization into an initiator of programmes in the fields of development, technical cooperation, health, youth affairs, and education and, within the limits imposed by differences of alignment (political, defence, and regional) between individual members, a coordinator of Commonwealth policies and activities. Both interpreted their roles dynamically to establish the value of the Secretariat and played a prominent role in combating racism in southern Africa. The Secretariat also effectively took over the prerogative of organizing Commonwealth meetings at high political levels which had traditionally fallen to the British government.

From 2008–16, the Secretary-General was Mr Kamalesh Sharma, a former senior **23.17** ior Indian diplomat. The former Attorney General for England and Wales, Baroness (Patricia) Scotland, originally from Dominica, was elected at the Malta CHOGM of 2015 as the sixth Secretary-General, taking office in April 2016.

Organization within the British Government

Within the British government relations with what were to become Common- **23.18** wealth countries were originally handled by a separate Department of State called the Dominions Office established in 1925. In 1947, when India and Pakistan became independent, the name of the Office was changed to Commonwealth Relations Office.[7] With increasing numbers of colonies becoming independent in the next two decades, most of the territories which had been administered by the Colonial and the Dominion Offices became the responsibility of the Commonwealth Relations Office.

It was decided in 1966 that the remaining responsibilities in this field no longer **23.19** justified the maintenance of a separate Colonial Office, which was accordingly absorbed by the Commonwealth Relations Office, then renamed Commonwealth Office.[8] But only two years later, in October 1968 the Foreign Office and Commonwealth Office were merged to form the Foreign and Commonwealth Office (FCO).

Since that year the Secretary of State for Foreign and Commonwealth Affairs **23.20** has been responsible for the conduct of relations with other member countries

---

[7] The newly named department thus took over the work of the former India Office in so far as that remained appropriate to the changed conditions.

[8] *The Merger of the Foreign Office and the Commonwealth Office 1968* (1968). This publication gives a clear, brief account not only of this later merger but of its historical background.

of the Commonwealth and for the administration of the remaining British dependencies. Although the conduct of diplomatic business between Commonwealth governments is carried out in much the same way as that with foreign countries, Commonwealth high commissioners and their staffs in London traditionally deal direct with a wider range of government departments, and in general in a more informal manner, than do most of their foreign counterparts.[9]

Diplomatic Representation

23.21 All members of the Commonwealth have permanent representatives at the seat of the UN in New York. Between Commonwealth countries however, a head of mission is styled 'high commissioner' rather than 'ambassador', and the office 'high commission'.

High Commissioners

23.22 All high commissioners, to whatever Commonwealth country they may be accredited, have a status equivalent to that of ambassador. So far as Britain is concerned, its high commissioner will be either termed the representative of the British government or, in those Commonwealth countries whose Head of State is other than the Queen, Her Majesty's representative. The duties of high commissioners from any Commonwealth country will be similar to those of ambassadors, namely to advise their government on the politics of the country to which they are accredited, to interpret and project the policies of their own country, and to look after its interests.

Privileges and Immunities

23.23 Article 14 of the Vienna Convention of 1961 on Diplomatic Relations contains a special provision enabling high commissioners to be included in the first class of heads of mission. This class comprises 'ambassadors or nuncios accredited to Heads of State, and other heads of mission of equivalent rank'. High commissioners are technically not 'accredited' when the countries between which they are exchanged share the same Head of State.[10] Since high commissions have the status of diplomatic missions, all privileges and immunities under the Vienna Convention are accorded on that basis. The United Kingdom in one respect extends more favourable treatment to members of Commonwealth high commissions than is extended to members of other diplomatic missions. A member of a Commonwealth high commission who is a dual citizen (of the sending

---

[9] For direct contacts between diplomatic missions and government departments other than those regularly responsible for external affairs, see Chapter **12**, paragraphs **12.45–12.46**.
[10] See Chapter 7, paragraph 7.14.

country and also of the United Kingdom) is treated as though he were not a UK citizen in that he does not lose his privileges and immunities because he is a 'national of the receiving state'.

Agents-general

While the Commonwealth of Australia and Canada are represented in London as **23.24** sovereign States by high commissioners, the constituent states of Australia and the provinces of Canada are separately represented by agents-general. The agents-general are not diplomatic agents under the Vienna Convention, but under the Commonwealth Countries and Republic of Ireland (Immunities and Privileges) Order 1971 they, their families, their staffs, and their offices are accorded privileges and immunities on the scale set out in the Vienna Convention on Consular Relations 1963. They are not, however, entitled to any special precedence.

Consular Functions

In those Commonwealth countries (as previously in Pakistan), where the inter- **23.25** ests of Britain dictated the need for a presence outside the capital, for example in Canada, Australia, New Zealand, India, or Nigeria, British representatives were, with the agreement of the receiving member country, styled variously as 'Deputy High Commissioner' or 'Senior Trade Commissioner'. Such officers were treated as members detached for local service from the diplomatic staff of the British high commissioner in the capital concerned.

In 1970, however, given the continuing expansion in the independent member- **23.26** ship of the Commonwealth, it became an acceptable practice to make consular appointments within the Commonwealth and to adopt consular titles. Some functions which are consular in nature, such as trade, welfare, and immigration, are carried out by representatives whose titles are varied—trade commissioners, immigration officers, and assistant commissioners are among those used. In Britain these officers are also given privileges and immunities on the consular scale under the Commonwealth Countries and Republic of Ireland (Immunities and Privileges) Order 1971.

Links with the Judicial Committee of the Privy Council

In the days of Empire, appeals could be made from higher courts overseas to the **23.27** Judicial Committee of the Privy Council. Since 1949, however, with the increasing number of republics within the Commonwealth, the numbers of countries exercising the right of ultimate appeal to the Judicial Committee have diminished considerably. In the majority of countries, the right of appeal has terminated often following controversial cases, e.g. the imposition of death penalties in cases in the Caribbean. However, a number of member countries, namely the Commonwealth realms of Antigua and Barbuda, The Bahamas, Belize, Grenada, Jamaica, Saint Kitts and Nevis, Saint Lucia, Saint Vincent and the Grenadines and Tuvalu and the Commonwealth of Dominica, Mauritius, Trinidad and Tobago, and if the case involves constitutional rights, Kiribati, still maintain the right of appeal to the Judicial Committee. The Sultan of Brunei, where appeals have been made to him, refers the case to the Judicial Committee, which then reports back to him.

North Atlantic Treaty Organization (NATO)

23.28 At the end of the Second World War, Western Europe faced the need to repair the physical destruction and human deprivation, to ensure peace in Western Europe and its economic development, and to take necessary precautions against any danger from the Soviet Union and its allies. The first two were obvious for all to see. The last showed itself in numerous ways, one of the most conspicuous being the commitment of the Western Powers to a united Germany democratically governed, as opposed to the Soviet policy of keeping Germany divided with one zone in the east under a Communist régime. The Western governments accepted that there would need to be arrangements between them not only for mutual economic help but also for physical defence not simply against a possible revival of German power, but also against potential dangers from the East, both to military security and to human rights and individual and national freedoms as understood in the West.

23.29 A series of treaties of variable geometry was entered into by the major Western countries in the following decades, the earlier ones (Dunkirk, Brussels, Paris) being superseded by more comprehensive treaties signed later. The Brussels Treaty, for instance, signed in 1948 between the United Kingdom, France, Belgium, the Netherlands, and Luxembourg led to the establishment of a Permanent Defence Organization, which became the Western European Union (WEU), a body which saw in 2000 its capabilities and functions transferred to the EU under its developing European Security and Defence Policy (ESDP) now termed the Common Security and Defence Policy (CSDP).[11] In 2011 the WEU formally ceased to exist.

The North Atlantic Treaty

23.30 While the Brussels Treaty provided a framework for cooperation between the five Western European Allied Powers even at the time of its signature in 1948

---

[11] See Chapter 22, paragraphs 22.118–22.124.

there was a growing realization on both sides of the Atlantic, prompted by the USSR's progressive takeover of much of Eastern Europe, that a wider alliance, combining the strengths of Europe and North America, would be essential. That same year 'the idea of a single mutual defence system, including and superseding the Brussels Treaty, was publicly put forward by [the prime minister of Canada] in the Canadian House of Commons'.[12] No doubt assisted by the USSR's Berlin blockade of 1947/48, a bipartisan resolution in the US Senate, despite the predictable opposition of isolationists, embodying what would be for the US an unprecedented overseas commitment, was adopted on 11 June. Talks immediately began with the governments of the Brussels Treaty countries, and by the end of October, agreement had been reached on 'the principle of a defensive pact for the North Atlantic area'. The Brussels Treaty Powers and Canada and the United States invited Denmark, Iceland, Italy, Norway, and Portugal to accede to the proposed North Atlantic Treaty so that on 4 April 1949, the Treaty was signed in Washington on behalf of these twelve countries.[13] It came into force on 24 August 1949. Greece and Turkey were invited to join the Alliance in 1951 and acceded on 18 February 1952. The Federal Republic of Germany was invited to accede in October 1954, and formally became a member of NATO in May 1955.[14]

The Provisions of the North Atlantic Treaty (1949)

The preamble affirms the determination of the parties: **23.31**

> to safeguard the freedom, common heritage and civilisation of their peoples... to promote stability and well-being in the North Atlantic area... to unite their efforts for collective defence and for the preservation of peace and security.

Article 1 significantly relates the Atlantic Treaty and the future actions of the Alliance to the purposes and actions of the United Nations. Thus in Article 1:

> The Parties undertake, as set forth in the Charter of the United Nations, to settle any international dispute in which they may be involved by peaceful means in such

---

[12] These words are quoted directly from *NATO, Facts and Figures* (Brussels, 1976) because they represent a brief, authoritative definition of what was to happen.

[13] Cmd 7789.

[14] This occurred after an abortive attempt the previous year at creating a European Defence Community. While there had been general recognition that Germany should participate in her own defence and in that of Western Europe, there was also a natural reluctance in Europe, and particularly in France, to allow uncontrolled German rearmament. The French government thereupon proposed a compromise arrangement which came to be known as the 'Pleven Plan'; Germany should be rearmed within a European army in which national units would be welded together under a supranational command. Effect was given to this idea in the European Defence Community (EDC) Treaty signed in Paris on 27 May 1952, by France, the Federal Republic of Germany, Italy, Belgium, the Netherlands, and Luxembourg. In August 1954, however, the French National Assembly finally decided not to accept the EDC Treaty.

a manner that international peace and security and justice are not endangered, and to refrain in their international relations from the threat or use of force in any manner inconsistent with the purposes of the United Nations.

The signatories undertook to contribute towards the further development of peaceful and friendly international relations 'by strengthening their free institutions . . . and by promoting conditions of stability and well-being' and to seek 'to eliminate conflict in their international economic policies. . . .'[15] (Article 2). They undertake to 'maintain and develop their individual and collective capacity to resist armed attack' (Article 3) and to 'consult together whenever, in the opinion of any of them, the territorial integrity, political independence or security of any of the Parties is threatened' (Article 4). In Article 5, the parties crucially:

> agree that an armed attack against one or more of them in Europe or North America shall be considered an attack against them all; and consequently they agree that, if such an armed attack occurs, each of them, in exercise of the right of individual or collective self-defence recognised by Article 51 of the Charter of the United Nations, will assist the Party or Parties so attacked by taking forthwith, individually and in concert with the other Parties, such action as it deems necessary, including the use of armed force, to restore and maintain the security of the North Atlantic area.

Article 6 describes the circumstances in which Article 5 becomes operative. Since the accession of Turkey, Article 6 has read:

> For the purpose of Article 5, an armed attack on one or more of the Parties is deemed to include an armed attack:
>
> (i) on the territory of any of the Parties in Europe or North America, on the Algerian Departments of France, on the territory of Turkey or on the islands under the jurisdiction of any of the Parties in the North Atlantic area north of the Tropic of Cancer;
> (ii) on the forces, vessels or aircraft of any of the Parties, when in or over these territories or any other area in Europe in which occupation forces of any of the Parties were stationed on the date when the Treaty entered into force or the Mediterranean Sea or the North Atlantic area north of the Tropic of Cancer.[16]

Machinery

23.32 The Atlantic Treaty did not attempt to set up a constitution. It delegated this power to:

---

[15] It is characteristic of those who work in NATO to emphasize that the preamble and Art 2 are not routine sentiments but genuinely animate the work of the Organization.

[16] Protocol Regarding the Accession of Greece and Turkey to the North Atlantic Treaty of 4 April, 1949; signed in London on 17 October 1951 (Cmd 8407).

a Council, so organised as to be able to meet promptly at any time. The Council shall set up such subsidiary bodies as may be necessary; in particular it shall establish immediately a defence committee ...

The first meeting of the Council was held in Washington in September 1949 at foreign ministerial level.[17] They immediately created a Defence Committee, consisting of ministers of defence, and a Military Committee, consisting of national chiefs of staff.

But in 1950 the Alliance lacked two essentials. First, the edifice had no unified apex, a situation which would mean weakness and delay in an emergency. At its Brussels meeting in December 1950, the Council agreed to create an integrated European Defence Force and a Supreme Headquarters under the command of an American officer. General Dwight D Eisenhower became the first Supreme Allied Commander (SACEUR).[18]   **23.33**

On the civilian side, the Council decided in May 1950 to set up a civilian body to execute its directives, coordinate the work of the Alliance's civilian and military bodies, and act as a forum for regular political exchanges between member governments.[19] Later, to enable the new Council to act in the absence of some, or indeed all, of the ministers, it was agreed to appoint a permanent (resident) representative (PR), usually a senior ambassador. Nowadays, the North Atlantic Council meets weekly at PR level and only occasionally at ministerial or higher level, and very occasionally a visiting minister might sit in the national seat for the weekly meeting. It carries its full authority under the Treaty. The NAC is chaired by an international civil servant (invariably a distinguished former minister) who has been appointed as Secretary-General of NATO.[20]   **23.34**

Developments and Structural Adaptation

It is not possible in this book to follow, even in brief detail, the events and developments affecting so large and many-sided an organization as NATO. But a few landmarks stand out. In 1956, East/West tensions arose as a result of the   **23.35**

---

[17] The Council can meet at any level from Head of Government, or Head of State, to permanent (official) representative, subject to the agreement of member governments on the appropriateness of the subject to the level of the meeting.

[18] General Eisenhower applied for release in 1952 to enter political life.

[19] *Nato Facts and Figures*, 28.

[20] The current Secretary-General is Jens Stoltenberg, the former prime minister of Norway, whose predecessors have been: Anders Fogh Rasmussen (2009–14), Jaap de Hoop Scheffer (2004–9), Lord Robertson (1999–2003), Javier Solana (1995–9), Willy Claes (1994–5), Manfred Wörner (1988–94), Lord Carrington (1984–8), Joseph Luns (1971–84), Manlio Brosio (1964–71), Dirk U Stikker (1961–4), Paul Henri Spaak (1957–61), and Lord Ismay (1952–7).

year of the brutal suppression of the Hungarian uprising and of the failure of the Anglo-French enterprise in Suez.

23.36 On 10 March 1966 President Charles de Gaulle announced that France intended to withdraw French personnel from the NATO integrated military headquarters and to request the transfer from French territory of the NATO international headquarters and of Allied units and installations or bases not falling under the control of the French authorities. NATO duly made Brussels the Council's headquarters.

23.37 As has been evident from the foregoing, NATO has been engaged throughout close to six decades in a process of structural experiment and adaptation. The principal change had been the formation of a Defence Planning Committee which was in practice the Council, meeting under the Defence Planning title and with that function. When in 1966 France remained in the Alliance but ceased taking part in NATO military discussions, a possibly serious difficulty was circumvented through the discussion of these items by the Council, meeting as its own Defence Planning Committee.

23.38 Although the US involvement in the Vietnam War created some tensions within the Alliance, the continuing threat from the Soviet Union and its allies in the Warsaw Pact ensured unity of purpose. Strategic arms limitation agreements in the 1970s were not however sufficient to prevent a major build-up of Soviet arms in the late 1970s and early 1980s. NATO adopted a dual-track approach matching increased arms build-up of their own with a commitment to détente. The Soviet Union made strenuous efforts to divide the Alliance in the early to mid 1980s encouraging the mobilization of anti-nuclear weapons demonstrators in Alliance countries against the deployment in Western Europe of intermediate range nuclear weapons. But the Alliance stood firm and it was in the Warsaw Pact that cracks appeared as Communism collapsed throughout Eastern Europe in 1989 leading to the reunification of Germany in 1990 and the dissolution of the Warsaw Pact and the Soviet Union in 1991. This led to existential questions in some quarters about the continuing purpose of NATO but, as hot war returned to Europe, in the 1990s in former Yugoslavia, for the first time since 1945, the question was clearly resolved in favour of NATO's continuing existence, strengthened by the organization's capacity to adapt its goals.

23.39 In the early post-Cold War period, NATO moved to build up relations with the former Warsaw Pact countries. The North Atlantic Cooperation Council established in 1991 sought to provide a framework for this activity. (It was subsumed into the Euro-Atlantic Partnership Council (EAPC) in 1997, an enhanced forum for security consultation and cooperation, comprising all NATO member countries (currently twenty-eight) and twenty-two partners. In 1993, NATO decided to offer former members of the Warsaw Pact an association with NATO known as Partnership for Peace (PfP). Those countries so associated with NATO take part in a specific menu of activities focusing in particular on defence-related work, defence reform, but which touch on virtually every field of NATO activity. These include defence policy and planning, civil–military relations, education and training, air defence, communications and information systems, crisis management, civil emergency planning, joint exercises, peacekeeping operations, and information sharing. Members of PfP may apply for membership of NATO and be accepted, subject to meeting the criteria (to date, as of 2015, twelve former PfP members have become full members of NATO: Hungary, Poland, and the Czech Republic in 1999; Bulgaria, Estonia, Latvia, Lithuania, Romania, Slovenia, and Slovakia in 2004; and Albania and Croatia in 2009). A full list of PfP members can be found at <http://www.nato.int/cps/en/natolive/topics_82584.htm>. This process was facilitated by the decision of the NATO Summit meeting in Washington in April 1999 to create Membership Action Plans to assist individual countries aspiring and judged ready to open negotiations for membership. A full list of current members of NATO is to be found at <http://www.nato.int>. In May 2002, a NATO–Russia Summit in Rome agreed the establishment of a NATO-Russia Council which replaced the Permanent Joint Council. Progress in this body has been fitful, influenced by strategic relations.

In 1995, France returned to the Military Committee of NATO after a 30-year **23.40** absence. In the same year, NATO aircraft bombed Bosnian Serb positions to force the withdrawal of heavy artillery from around Sarajevo where the city had been effectively besieged for three years. This helped bring an end to the Bosnian war. The peace agreement concluded at Dayton, Ohio in November 1995 made provision for the deployment of NATO troops to enforce the peace agreement militarily. The implementation force of up to 54,000 troops in country (known as IFOR) was succeeded by a smaller stabilization force known as SFOR the following year. It concluded its mission in December 2004 handing over to a 7,000-strong EU force known as EUFOR, the first full military deployment by the European Union under the European Security and Defence Policy (ESDP).

In Autumn 1998 NATO issued an ultimatum to President Milošević of the then **23.41** Federal Republic of Yugoslavia (FRY) threatening the use of force unless attacks on the Albanian population in Kosovo stopped. There then followed negotiations in Rambouillet between representatives of the Federal Republic and the Kosovar Albanians, under the chairmanship of France and the United Kingdom, with the aim of agreeing substantial autonomy for Kosovo. A draft agreement was not accepted by the FRY. Accordingly, after a further warning without effect, on 24 March 1999, NATO began a campaign against the FRY in an effort to stop continued FRY action against the Kosovar Albanians, to encourage FRY acceptance of the international peace agreement, which had been rejected by Milošević's representatives at Rambouillet (and which would have granted extensive autonomy to Kosovo), and to force the withdrawal of FRY troops and security forces from there. This action was taken without explicit UN Security Council authorization. Each member of NATO satisfied itself that military action in the circumstances, including the need for humanitarian intervention, was legal. The arguments in favour included the need for a proportionate response to protect the Albanians, all other means having failed.

23.42   After 11 weeks of bombing which had extended to infrastructure targets in Serbia and as it began to look as though only the threat of an attack by ground forces would compel the FRY's surrender, the Yugoslav President, Slobodan Milošević agreed to NATO's demands after an intervention by two envoys on behalf of the international community, the former Finnish President Martti Ahtisaari and Viktor Chernomyrdin the former Russian prime minister. The terms were incorporated into a UN Security Council resolution, SCR 1244. Under the terms of the SCR, Yugoslav troops withdrew from Kosovo and were replaced by a NATO-led force (KFOR) under a United Nations mandate, and a UN mission assumed responsibility for the administration of Kosovo. The campaign demonstrated clearly the importance of maintaining Alliance cohesion during such a relatively extended campaign, both militarily and politically. The operation was particularly sensitive for Greece, which voted for it, but stood aside from the military activity. Targeting was the responsibility of the NATO Secretary-General and the Supreme Commander. This became a sensitive point as the French government insisted on generic approval of targets to the frustration of NATO military commanders and the irritation of the US government. This, NATO's largest military and first offensive operation, was remarkable in being conducted despite the fact that no member of NATO had been attacked. Russia denounced the attacks and broke off all diplomatic links with NATO. They were resumed in 2000. China was also incensed by the accidental bombing with fatalities of the Chinese embassy in Belgrade and NATO missions in Beijing were attacked by demonstrators.

23.43   In August–September 2001, the Alliance also mounted a mission to disarm ethnic Albanian militias in the Former Yugoslav Republic of Macedonia (FYROM) and, working with the European Union and the Organization for Security and Cooperation in Europe (OSCE), averted the risk of a civil war.

23.44   The 9/11 attacks on New York and Washington in 2001 prompted NATO to invoke Article 5 ('agree that an armed attack against one or more of them in Europe or North America shall be considered an attack against them all') of the

NATO Charter for the first time in its history. Despite this prompt demonstration of solidarity, the US chose not to involve NATO directly in its initial response against Al Qaeda and their Taleban protectors in Afghanistan. NATO did however take command of the International Security Assistance Force (ISAF) in Afghanistan in April 2003. The handover of control to NATO took place in August that year and marked the first time in NATO's history that it had taken charge of a mission outside the (North Atlantic) area. The troops, including those from eleven non-NATO countries, then numbered some 30,000.

At its summit in Bucharest in April 2008, NATO invited Croatia and Albania **23.45** to apply for membership (they became members on 1 April 2009), and asserted that Ukraine and Georgia would become members of NATO. After a 43-year break, in March 2009, President Sarkozy announced that France would rejoin NATO's integrated military command.

Doubts about the relevance of NATO have been assuaged, not least by the num- **23.46** ber of countries who have joined and those who aspire to membership. It retains its primary responsibility for collective defence, is a forum for transatlantic debate, provides the means for a key expeditionary role to combat threats and promote stability, while on the European continent, it has encouraged reform of the security sector, democratic accountability, and cooperation between States. In moving forward, it also has a cooperative arrangement (known as Berlin Plus) with the European Union's European Security and Defence Policy, ESDP, under which for some operations, NATO can provide military assets and command structures for EU operations.

In NATO's new Strategic Concept agreed in 2010, the Alliance committed itself **23.47** to dealing with 'all stages of a crisis—before, during and after'—a comprehensive principle that suggested a greater role for cooperative security. This has led NATO to develop security partnerships with countries throughout the Mediterranean, the Gulf, and even as far away as the Pacific area (e.g. Australia) and with other international organizations. One example was UN–NATO cooperation during the 2011 crisis in Libya, a crisis which led the Alliance to develop contacts with the Arab League, who had an important role in the crisis.[21]

The resurgence of Russian expansionism, notably with the annexation of the **23.48** Crimea in 2014, but also the conflict with Georgia over South Ossetia in 2008 and the continuing active Russian military support for secessionists in Eastern Ukraine, has disquieted those NATO countries with borders with or near Russia. This in turn has led to strong rhetorical support for Poland and the Baltic States

---

[21] <http://www.nato.int/history/nato-history.html>.

and the holding of NATO military exercises in these countries to deter any thought of Russian aggression and reaffirm the Article V NATO commitment to mutual defence.

23.49   Russia has in turn accused the West of breaking promises made at the time of the unification of Germany and subsequently not to enlarge NATO to Russia's borders. NATO's arguments that its policy is only to integrate Central and Eastern European States into an Atlantic security space, have failed to shake the persistent Russian belief that NATO has taken advantage of Russian weakness in the early 1990s and had acted to humiliate it. NATO has further argued that any undertakings made about the further expansion of NATO were made in the context of German reunification and could not in any event prevent independent countries, albeit formerly members of the Warsaw Pact, from freely seeking to join a different security alliance.

23.50   Nevertheless, NATO military intervention in Kosovo, in the face of strenuous Russian opposition and in the absence of a specific UN Security Council resolution, was used by Russia to support their own narrative. And Western recognition of Kosovo's independence from Serbia, despite the latter's opposition, was cited by President Putin as a precedent for Russia's annexation of the Crimea.

23.51   The NATO Wales Summit was held in 2014 and took decisions on desirable levels of defence spending by member countries, further reform of NATO, contemporary threats, and the Military Covenant. This took place against a challenging international environment and poor relations with Russia. In July 2016, the NATO Summit was held in Warsaw and decided to strengthen the Alliance's military presence in the east, with four battalions in Poland, Estonia, Latvia, and Lithuania on a rotational basis—to be in place starting 2017.

The Council of Europe

23.52   The Council of Europe is Europe's leading human rights organization, dedicated to the promotion and protection of human rights, democracy, and the rule of law.[22] Its Statute was signed in London in 1949. The original signatories were: Belgium, Denmark, France, Ireland, Italy, Luxembourg, Netherlands, Norway, Sweden, and the United Kingdom. The current membership, which greatly expanded after the fall of the Berlin Wall, stands at forty-seven member States, that is, nearly every European country, covering a combined population

---

[22] Winston Churchill, in his celebrated speech in Zurich in September 1946, called for 'a kind of United States of Europe' and added 'The first step is to form a Council of Europe.'

of 820 million. The Council of Europe also has five observer countries: Canada, the Holy See, Japan, Mexico, and the US. The Council of Europe should not be confused with the European Union (see Chapters **21** and **22**) or the European Council, the meeting of Heads of State or Government of the EU. However the EU shares unofficially the Council of Europe's flag and anthem. As the Council of Europe's focus is on human rights, democracy, legal standards and the rule of law, and the promotion and extension of democracy and cultural cooperation, it implements its aims largely through Conventions (i.e. public international law) to which member countries voluntarily adhere. Unlike the EU, the Council of Europe does not involve a commitment to supranational law, but its members are bound by those Conventions to which they have subscribed and to any relevant judgments of the European Court of Human Rights, which enforces the European Convention on Human Rights, to which all members of the Council belong. Membership of the Council of Europe is open to any European State 'which is deemed to be able and willing to fulfil' the Statute's provisions and which is invited to accede by the Committee of Ministers.

The organs of the Council are the Committee of Ministers, the Parliamentary   **23.53** Assembly of the Council of Europe (PACE), the Congress of Local and Regional Authorities of the Council of Europe, the European Court of Human Rights, a Commissioner for Human Rights who independently addresses and calls atten tion to human rights violations, a Conference of some 400 International Non-Governmental Organizations (INGOs) to bring the views of civil society to the attention of the Council, and the Secretary-General served by the Secretariat. The permanent seat of the Council is at Strasbourg.

The Committee of Ministers is the intergovernmental decision-making organ of the   **23.54** Council. Its members are the Foreign Ministers of member States or their permanent diplomatic representatives in Strasbourg. The Committee deals with recommendations made by the Parliamentary Assembly, any other matters of general concern which it decides to place on the agenda, and with administrative and financial questions affecting the Council. It is the only organ of the Council empowered to take decisions. Meetings of the Committee are held two to three times a year. The preliminary work is undertaken by ambassadors or permanent representatives of member States who meet between sessions to discuss current matters.

The Parliamentary Assembly[23] which is the 'deliberative organ' of the Council,   **23.55** is composed of 318 representatives (and 318 substitutes) elected by national

---

[23] In July 1974 the Standing Committee decided that the name Parliamentary Assembly should be used instead of Consultative Assembly since it reflects the role and composition of the Assembly more accurately.

parliaments or appointed in such manner as the parliaments may decide. The number of seats allotted to each member State in the Assembly is governed by the need to keep the size of the Assembly to reasonable proportions and at the same time to ensure that the smaller States are adequately represented.

23.56 The Assembly holds four ordinary sessions each year, and there is a provision for the calling of extraordinary sessions. It holds an annual meeting with the European Parliament on a subject of topical interest. The Assembly's views may be incorporated in resolutions or recommendations. The latter, which may propose specific action by member governments, come before the Committee of Ministers for consideration. Major decisions require a two-thirds majority. The Assembly also elects the Secretary-General, the Human Rights Commissioner, and the judges to the European Court of Human Rights.

23.57 The work of the Assembly between sessions is carried on by a group of committees of which the most important is the Standing Committee, consisting of the Bureau and the chairmen of the other committees. The Congress of Local and Regional Authorities of the Council established in 1994 includes 636 political representatives from local and regional authorities of the member States.

23.58 The first Convention to be drawn up by the Council of Europe was the European Convention on Human Rights (ECHR). Referring back to the Congress of Europe (held at The Hague in May 1948 to discuss the structure of the future Council of Europe), which had proclaimed that '[a]n independent European Court should be created to which any member of the Council could refer cases in which it appeared that the Declaration of Rights had been violated', the Council of Europe approved, after some extremely complex technical negotiations, the European Convention on Human Rights. This entered into force in September 1953. It provided for the creation of a European Court of Human Rights (ECtHR), established in 1959, which represented a far stronger instrument than had existed hitherto. (A Commissioner for Human Rights elected by the Parliamentary Assembly was created in 1999.)

23.59 The Court hears applications from individuals or groups of individuals (and even though rarely from one or more contracting States) alleging breaches of the human rights provisions set out in the ECHR by a contracting State. Its workload increased dramatically after the fall of the Berlin Wall and the consequent accession of new States. Such was the backlog (in 2009 there were more than 119,000 pending applications) that the Committee of Ministers adopted a Protocol to the ECHR aimed at reducing the ECtHR's workload, allowing it to filter applications and focus on cases raising important human rights issues. After much initial resistance from Russia, the Protocol entered into force in June 2010.

In the UK, and in other countries, the Court has been criticized as being too **23.60** judicially expansionist, beyond what the authors of the ECHR envisaged. While the clear majority view among the British judiciary is that UK courts are bound by the decisions of the ECtHR, a senior British judge in 2015 opined that UK judges were not bound by the decisions of the ECtHR and instead were only obliged to take that Court's rulings 'into consideration'.[24] The Conservative government elected in the same year committed itself to withdraw from the ECHR if the UK Parliament failed to secure the right to veto judgments from the Strasbourg Court.

Since the adoption of the EHCR, over two hundred further Conventions on **23.61** widely varied subjects (social, professional, economic, and cultural) have passed successfully through the Council of Europe including a Convention on the Prevention of Terrorism. Recent examples include Conventions on Action against Trafficking in Human Beings, the Protection of Children against Sexual Exploitation and Sexual Abuse, Preventing and Combating Violence against Women and Domestic Violence, and Trafficking in Human Organs.

The main activities and agreements on social policy are the European Social **23.62** Charter (signed 1964), the European Code of Social Security (signed 1968), and the European Convention on Social Security. The Charter seeks to improve social and economic rights of individuals generally, the Code to establish acceptable standards of social benefits, and the European Convention on Social Security to solve social security problems raised by the movement of employees, tourists, etc across national frontiers. On cultural policy, one of the main agreements is the European Charter for Regional or Minority Languages.

The Parliamentary Assembly raises, largely through its twelve committees of **23.63** members of parliaments, subjects of the greatest variety such as, to mention only very few, migrant workers, the European cultural heritage, the prevention of terrorism, and soil conservation. This kind of work will be found at all stages of development and can lead to anything from harmonization in purely practical terms to a formal Convention. The Committee of Ministers has, in its turn, rapporteur groups, working parties, and liaison committees to advise on propositions initiated by the Assembly.

The Council of Europe handles matters not covered by any other European **23.64** organization. Much of it, while not attracting immediate public attention, has long-term value. Its interests inevitably overlap in part with those of the

---

[24] Sir Brian Leveson, President of the Queen's Bench Division, speaking at the Hay Literary Festival, 23 May 2015.

European Union (e.g. human rights, protection of personal data, extradition, mutual assistance in criminal matters, and terrorism). Reference to the ECHR, for example, has been included within the preamble of an EU Treaty. The future technical and political relationships between each organization will continue to be important as was recognized in May 2007, when the Council of Europe and the European Union signed a Memorandum of Understanding which sets out the priorities and focal areas of cooperation between them. Further information on the Council of Europe can be found at <http://www.coe.int>.

The Organization of American States (OAS)

23.65   The Organization of American States was formed in 1948, but efforts to establish some system of inter-American organization are as old as the independence of the Latin American republics. A Congress of American States, the first attempt of its kind, was convened by Simón Bolívar[25] at Panama in 1826 with the aim of creating an association of States in the hemisphere but was unsuccessful in laying down any permanent structures. From 1889 to 1890, the First International Conference of American States was held in Washington DC and established the International Union of American Republics and its secretariat, the Commercial Bureau of the American Republics, the forerunner of the OAS. This organization became the Pan-American Union in 1910. When established, its seat was at Washington. It developed smoothly into the OAS when at its Ninth Conference in 1948 in Bogotá the twenty-one participants signed the OAS Charter and the American Declaration of the Rights and Duties of Man, the first international expression of human rights principles.

23.66   Fundamental to the Western hemisphere idea is the so-called Monroe Doctrine,[26] which laid down that the United States should 'consider any attempt [on the part of the European Powers] to extend their system to any portion of this

---

[25] Simón Bolívar, called El Libertador, born at Caracas in Venezuela in 1783. After travelling in Europe and the USA he joined the independence movement in Venezuela in 1809 and commanded insurgent forces with varying success until he defeated the Spaniards in 1821 and became the first President of Colombia, later helping to bring both Ecuador and Peru to independence. He died in 1830.

[26] President James Monroe embodied this doctrine, now universally known by his name, in a message (largely written by John Quincy Adams, Secretary of State and future President) to Congress on 2 December 1823. The so-called Roosevelt Corollary, enunciated by President Theodore Roosevelt in 1904, seemed to be an extension of the doctrine presaging claims by the USA to the right of intervention in the affairs of Latin American States. In 1923 Secretary of State Hughes formally stated that the US had no such intention, and in 1930 a memorandum, previously prepared by Under-Secretary J Reuben Clark, was published stating that the Corollary was not justified by the terms of the Monroe Doctrine.

hemisphere as dangerous to our peace and safety'. Latin Americans have, however, been less inclined to regard this declaration as a guarantee of their independence than as the implied assertion of United States' hegemony in the Western hemisphere. Thus their concern to defend Latin America from potential US encroachment goes a long way towards accounting for the slowness of some Latin American governments to oppose the challenge of the Axis Powers before and during the Second World War and that of the Communist powers after it.

The Charter

The OAS's purposes are: **23.67**

(a) To strengthen the peace and security of the continent;
(b) To promote and consolidate representative democracy, with due respect for the principle of non-intervention;
(c) To prevent possible causes of difficulties and to ensure the pacific settlement of disputes that may arise among the Member States;
(d) To provide for common action on the part of those States in the event of aggression;
(e) To seek the solution of political, juridical, and economic problems that may arise among them;
(f) To promote, by cooperative action, their economic, social, and cultural development;
(g) To eradicate extreme poverty, which constitutes an obstacle to the full democratic development of the peoples of the hemisphere; and
(h) To achieve an effective limitation of conventional weapons that will make it possible to devote the largest amount of resources to the economic and social development of the Member States.

The OAS uses a four-pronged approach effectively to implement these purposes, based on its main pillars: democracy, human rights, security, and development.

The OAS Charter sets out principles which include the effective exercise of **23.68** representative democracy; respect for the rights of the individual 'without distinction as to race, nationality, creed or sex'; and condemnation of aggression, adding that 'victory does not give rights'—a phrase on which the Argentine representative in its negotiation laid particular stress. The Charter also sets out the principle of non-intervention in unequivocal terms.

> No State or group of States has the right to intervene, directly or indirectly, for any reason whatever, in the internal or external affairs of any other State. The foregoing principle prohibits not only armed force but also any other form of interference or attempted threat against the personality of the State or against its political, economic and cultural elements.

and:

> The territory of a State is inviolable; it may not be the object, even temporarily, of military occupation or of other measures of force taken by another State, directly or indirectly, on any grounds whatever. No territorial acquisitions or special advantages obtained either by force or by other means of coercion shall be recognised.

23.69　Membership of the OAS in 2016 includes all thirty-five American States as follows: Argentina; Bolivia; Brazil; Chile; Colombia; Costa Rica; Cuba; Dominican Republic; Ecuador; El Salvador; Guatemala; Haiti; Honduras; Mexico; Nicaragua; Panama; Paraguay; Peru; Uruguay; Venezuela; United States; Trinidad and Tobago (1976); Barbados (1968); Jamaica (1969); Grenada (1975); Suriname (1977); Dominica (1979); Saint Lucia (1979); Antigua and Barbuda (1981); Saint Vincent and the Grenadines (1981); Bahamas (1982); Saint Kitts and Nevis (1984); Canada (1990); Belize (1991); Guyana (1991). Up–to-date membership details can be found at: <http://www.oas.org>.

23.70　The OAS has country offices in thirty-five American states. In addition to the United Nations sixty countries and the EU have Permanent Observer status at the OAS. The OAS Secretary-General (currently Luis Almagro) is entitled to attend the United Nations General Assembly as an Observer while the United Nations has Observer status at all OAS inter-American conferences and Meetings of Consultation (see paragraph **23.**71). Although there is no formal political cooperation between the OAS and the UN, organs of the OAS have adopted texts in support of UN actions (e.g. the Suez and Hungarian questions in 1956) and have from time to time reported to the UN Secretary-General (in accordance with Article 54 of the UN Charter) on OAS decisions and on developments within the region.

Structure and Work Programme of the OAS

23.71　The member countries set major policies and goals through the General Assembly, which gathers the hemisphere's ministers of foreign affairs once a year in regular session. A Permanent Council, made up of ambassadors appointed by the Member States deals with day-to-day work. A Meeting of Consultation of Ministers of Foreign Affairs is held in order to consider problems of an urgent nature and of common interest to the American States, and to serve as the Organ of Consultation. Any member State may request that the Meeting of Consultation be called. The request must be addressed to the Permanent Council of the organization, which decides by an absolute majority whether a meeting should be held.

23.72　As the Cold War came to an end and as democratic regimes increasingly became the norm in Latin America, the OAS adjusted its priorities and its work programme to reflect the new realities. Thus the organization has worked increasingly to support and strengthen democratic institutions, e.g. by adopting in

2001 the Inter-American Democratic Charter, which sets out key principles of democratic practice and guidelines for action when democracy is considered to be at risk in the region; and by sending a large number of observer missions to monitor free and fair elections in the member States and investigating irregularities. Special OAS missions have helped to resolve political crises in Bolivia, Ecuador, Haiti, Nicaragua, and Venezuela, and to support the demobilization of paramilitary groups in Colombia. The OAS has also played an important 'facilitator' role in the long-running border dispute between Belize and Guatemala. Both the Inter-American Human Rights Commission (set up in 1959) which has been increasingly active in reporting on the human rights situations in member States and in denouncing individual human rights violations, and the Inter-American Court of Human Rights (created in 1979) are well-established, active, and highly regarded. These bodies carry out serious scrutiny of national laws and illegal practices, such as the systematic elimination of political opponents through forced disappearances. The Inter-American Drug Abuse Control Commission was established in 1986 to coordinate efforts and facilitate cross-border cooperation.

US–Latin American Relations

In the early years of the OAS, the US was pushing an anti-Communist line **23.73** aimed initially at Guatemala. Neither the non-interference principles of the OAS nor its peacekeeping machinery prevented the overthrow of the Arbenz regime in Guatemala in 1954 or that of the Allende government in Chile in 1973, both CIA-sponsored coups against democratically elected Marxist governments. In 1961 six of the most important Latin American States refused to vote for a Meeting of Consultation to consider what should be done about the violations of human rights and the subversive activities against his neighbours of which President Fidel Castro of Cuba was accused. Nevertheless a meeting was eventually held in February 1962 at Punta del Este, where the Alliance for Progress[27] had been launched the previous year, at which sixteen delegations supported a ban on military supplies to Castro, and fourteen the exclusion (i.e. in practice the suspension) of the Cuban government from the OAS. There was, however, sharp disagreement regarding the juridical soundness of this exclusion as the terms of the Charter make no express provision for suspension. Again, when the Cuban missile crisis arose in October 1962, President Kennedy

---

[27] Established by the Charter of Punta del Este, under which $20 billion, largely from US governmental sources, would be made available over a period of 10 years for national development projects in Latin America.

appealed simultaneously to the Security Council and to the OAS. The latter adopted a resolution calling for the dismantling and withdrawal from Cuba of all missiles and sanctioning the use of armed force to ensure that the government of Cuba could not 'continue to receive from the Sino-Soviet powers military supplies and related material which may threaten the peace and security of the continent'. However, Mexico, Bolivia, and Brazil made it clear that they would not support armed invasion of Cuba to remove the missiles. Nor did the United States succeed in securing the removal of all Soviet forces from Cuba, still less the downfall of Fidel Castro. (He has now been succeeded as President by his brother Raúl.) Although ministers of foreign affairs of the Americas voted in 2009 to lift Cuba's suspension, the latter, while welcoming the vote, stated that it would not return to the OAS.

23.74   Since the advent of the populist President of Venezuela, Hugo Chávez, in 1999, US relations with that country have almost matched in antipathy those with Cuba. The US government claimed that Chávez and his policies were a threat to democracy in Latin America. US–Venezuela relations have not improved since Chavez' successor, Nicolás Maduro, took office in 2013; nor has the Venezuelan economy despite the country's oil assets (much diminished now by the collapse in oil prices). Bolivian President Evo Morales has very much taken Venezuela's side and has been openly critical of the US. Indeed a series of socialist victories in presidential elections in Latin America in the 2000s (the so-called 'pink tide') has led some countries to distance themselves from Washington and reject neo-liberal economic policies promoted by the US.

Summit of the Americas

23.75   The first Summit of the Americas took place in 1994 in Miami at President Clinton's initiative. Although it resolved to establish a hemispheric free trade area within 10 years, an ambitious goal that has not been achieved, the OAS has not recently been extensively active in the economic sphere. There have instead been partial solutions which have so far not proved complementary. Thus MERCOSUR (the Common Market of the South) currently groups only five countries: Brazil, Argentina, Paraguay, Uruguay, and Venezuela. Bolivia is in the process of accession (2016). MERCOSUR has made considerable progress in establishing a free trade in services but further progress in this area and on an Association Agreement with the European Union (under negotiation since 2000) has been hampered by the huge economic disparity between Brazil and the other members (Brazil has over 70 per cent of the GDP of MERCOSUR) and by the priority accorded by Brazil to the liberalization of agricultural trade given its relative efficiency. The Andean Community (previously Pact) is a customs union of Bolivia, Colombia, Ecuador, and Peru set up in 1969. The North American Free Trade Agreement (NAFTA) which came into force in 1994 comprises the US, Canada, and Mexico. The United States has bilateral free trade agreements with Chile, Colombia, Costa Rica, Dominican Republic, El Salvador, Guatemala, Honduras, Nicaragua, Panama, and Peru.

Since the Miami Summit, the Heads of State and Government of the Americas **23.76** have decided to meet on a regular basis and to institutionalize the summit meetings. This institutionalization had been lacking during the Cold War summits which were organized on an ad hoc basis. The most recent Summit of the Americas took place in Panama City in 2015 and was notable for the meeting and handshake between the Cuban and US Presidents which was followed by the reopening of diplomatic relations and consequently of the respective embassies after a gap of 54 years.

African Union (AU) formerly the Organization of African Unity (OAU)

The Organization of African Unity was established in 1963. By 1977, there were **23.77** forty-nine members of the OAU. Given the very recent experience of colonialism for many of the OAU members, it was no surprise that the OAU Charter dedicated the organization to eradicating all forms of colonialism from Africa. European colonialism in Africa was historically short-lived and although it survived two world wars in which some European countries had colonies in Africa who fought on opposite sides, and for another decade post-war, the pace of decolonization picked up quickly in the 1960s.

Some pressures for independence existed before the Second World War—his- **23.78** toric American disapproval of colonies, contact of African students in Europe and the United States with libertarian doctrines, teaching, and practice—but perhaps the most telling influence on African hopes was the success of the Indian sub-continent and Ceylon (Sri Lanka) in 1947 in gaining independence from Britain.

Ten years after the Second World War the first sub-Saharan African State, **23.79** Ghana (previously the Gold Coast), became independent.[28] The dynamic radicalism of the first president, first President, Dr Kwame Nkrumah, had two

---

[28] Apart, of course, from South Africa.

positive effects: it provided African radicals with a persuasive theoretician and it enabled him through his friendship with other African radicals like M. Sekou Touré of (French) Guinea to create a bridge between English-speaking and French-speaking Africa. This would be essential to any future organization claiming to represent Africa as a whole. On the other hand, his very radical line aroused suspicions in Muslim North Africa and other countries whose participation was essential to success.

23.80   A period of rival conferences and drafting of charters from 1958–61 which threatened to lead to separate Anglophone and Francophone regional groupings was followed by a meeting bringing together all the rival groupings at a preparatory conference in Addis Ababa at the beginning of May 1963 at which the Foreign Ministers of thirty African States met to discuss items of principle which would have to be covered by a Charter. Each region of Africa (except the Portuguese and Spanish colonies, which had not yet gained independence, and South Africa, Rhodesia, and Namibia) and each political trend were represented. The Heads of State met on 16 May and drew up a draft of a Charter for an Organization of African Unity which was signed on 26 May 1963 by the representatives of thirty-one States. The Charter represented a compromise between those who, like Ghana, favoured something as close as possible to federation, and those who insisted on as loose an association as was compatible with the word 'unity'. This tension was still evident 40 years later when, in July 2002, the African Union (AU) was formed as a successor to the OAU and the African Economic Community (AEC). A crucial early decision of the OAU was to recognize and confirm the boundaries which the independent States had inherited. The OAU had been criticized as both ineffectual and insouciant of human rights abuses by the continent's own leaders giving it the unfortunate epithet of 'the Dictators' Club'. The Libyan Head of State Muammar al-Qaddafi was a particularly strong advocate of the closer union approach from the mid-1990s. It was not unexpected then when the Heads of State and Government of the OAU issued the Sirte (in Libya) Declaration in September 1999, calling for the establishment of an African Union. At subsequent summits in Lomé in 2000 and Lusaka in 2001, detailed plans were elaborated for the creation of the AU, coinciding with the initiative for the establishment of the New Partnership for Africa's Development (NEPAD) which is the AU's strategic framework for pan-African socio-economic development.

23.81   The African Union was launched in Durban in July 2002, by its first President, the South African President Thabo Mbeki. In the following years, the debates within the OAU have been replicated within the AU with some countries (notably Libya) advocating a maximalist view leading to a common Union government with an AU army; and others (especially the southern African States) supporting rather a strengthening of the existing structures, with some reforms to deal with administrative and political challenges in making the AU Commission and other bodies truly effective.

While the OAU had a focus on support for liberation movements to remove the **23.82** last vestiges of colonialism and apartheid, the AU has a vision of 'an integrated, prosperous and peaceful Africa, driven by its own citizens and representing a dynamic force in the global arena'. Accordingly, the AU's objectives include the achievement of greater unity and solidarity between the African countries and the peoples of Africa, to defend the sovereignty, territorial integrity, and independence of its member States and to accelerate the political and socio-economic integration of the continent. It also aims to encourage international cooperation, taking due account of the Charter of the United Nations and the Universal Declaration of Human Rights; to promote peace, security, and stability on the continent; to promote democratic principles and institutions, popular participation, and good governance; and to promote and protect human and peoples' rights in accordance with the African Charter on Human and Peoples' Rights and other relevant human rights instruments.

The organs of the AU include an Assembly, composed of Heads of State and **23.83** Government or their duly accredited representatives, which is the supreme organ of the Union; an Executive Council composed of ministers or authorities designated by the governments of Member States; a Commission composed of the chairperson, the deputy chairperson, eight commissioners, and staff members, with each commissioner responsible for a portfolio; a Permanent Representatives' Committee charged with the responsibility of preparing the work of the Executive Council; a Peace and Security Council (PSC); and a Pan-African Parliament, to ensure the full participation of African peoples in governance, development, and economic integration of the continent. The Protocol relating to the composition, powers, functions, and organization of the Pan-African Parliament is in the process of ratification. The PSC is a significant body with substantial powers and claims responsibility for continental peace and security. It cooperates with the Security Council of the United Nations, and has coordinated the deployment of peacekeeping forces representing the AU. There are also plans to establish a Court of Justice. Lastly, the AU's financial institutions are the African Central Bank, the African Monetary Fund, and the African Investment Bank.

Membership of the AU

There are fifty-four member States: Algeria; Angola; Benin; Botswana; Burkina **23.84** Faso; Burundi; Cameroon; Cape Verde Islands; Central African Republic; Chad; Comoro Islands; Democratic Republic of the Congo; Congo; Djibouti; Egypt;

Equatorial Guinea; Eritrea; Ethiopia; Gabon; The Gambia; Ghana; Guinea; Guinea-Bissau; Ivory Coast; Kenya; Lesotho; Liberia; Libya; Madagascar; Malawi; Mali; Mauritania; Mauritius; Mozambique; Namibia; Niger; Nigeria; Rwanda; Western Sahara (SADR); São Tomé and Principe; Senegal; Seychelles; Sierra Leone; Somalia; South Africa; Sudan; South Sudan; Swaziland; Tanzania; Togo; Tunisia; Uganda; Zambia; and Zimbabwe. The only African State that is not a member of the African Union is Morocco. She left the AU's predecessor, the Organization of African Unity (OAU), in 1984, in protest at the support of many OAU member States for the Polisario Front's Sahrawi Arab Democratic Republic (SADR), a partially recognized state which controls about a quarter of the former Spanish colony of Western Sahara (incorporated into Morocco and Mauritania after its cession by Spain in 1976) and claims the rest, which is controlled by Morocco.

23.85 The African Union does have provision for suspension of members in case of unconstitutional change of regime and has applied the provision to the Central African Republic, Togo, and recently to Mauritania and Guinea. In 2008 there was further discussion of strong action against Zimbabwe, with a number of States supporting sanctions, and Kenya suggested suspension but received insufficient support. Instead the Council recommended that the two parties should negotiate to bridge their differences. Given its post-colonial history, it is perhaps unsurprising that within the AU there tends to be more emphasis on unconstitutional or undemocratic change than on intrusive monitoring of wider human rights performance. By contrast, in March 2009 the Tribunal of the Southern Africa Development Community delivered a judgment on the application by dispossessed land owners in Zimbabwe which declared that the seizures of land were 'arbitrary, discriminatory and contrary to the rule of law'. The Tribunal ordered protection for remaining land owners and compensation for those evicted, and further declared that the provision in the constitution of Zimbabwe denying access to the courts to those dispossessed by land reforms was contrary to the treaty of the Southern Africa Development Community. In Togo, after a military coup in 2005, the AU's protests led to elections to elect a President constitutionally. And in 2012, after a military coup in Mali which was reversed with the help of French troops, the AU intervened to support a caretaker government and the holding of fresh presidential elections.

Problems in Meeting the Objectives of the OAU and the AU

23.86 The OAU and the AU have faced hugely ambitious tasks of both policy and administration. The administrative problems were and are obvious—the sheer difficulty of adequate communication, interpretation, and consultation between over fifty nations inhabiting an enormous continent and its adjacent islands.

The policy task has been governed by two sets of tensions, those indigenous to Africa itself and those resulting from past and present encounters between Africa and the outside world. Some contained elements of both.

Confronted by these tensions, the OAU applied both conciliation and pressure. **23.87** An important first step in conciliation was the acceptance by the organization in 1964 of a Protocol under which member States would accept the boundaries set up in the colonial period. The acceptance proved far from complete in the days of the OAU. In Nigeria, a civil war broke out in 1967 over Biafra's attempt to secede. War broke out between Somalia and Ethiopia in 1977 over the Ogaden area; Libya had frontier claims against Chad and there have been inter-State or internal wars over the last 20 years in Angola, Burundi, Democratic Republic of the Congo, Rwanda, Darfur (part of Sudan), and Ethiopia resulting in the creation of the State of Eritrea, Somalia, Sierra Leone, Ivory Coast, Comoros, South Sudan, Mali, and Nigeria and many more instances of internal turmoil such as in Zimbabwe which has increasingly failed to deliver minimum standards of stability, health care, adequate food and water, or human rights. Several boundary disputes in Africa have gone to the ICJ (Chapter 25). It has been estimated that over a quarter of the countries of the AU are engaged in war or are suffering post-war conflict. The AU's Peace and Security Council has since its first meeting in 2004 been active in relation to current crises and has sent over 64,000 AU peacekeeping forces to missions on the continent which have included deployments in Burundi, Darfur, the Democratic Republic of the Congo, Mali, Somalia, and Sudan, some of which have had an offensive character, as well as two multinational task forces to fight against the Lord's Resistance Army and Boko Haram in Nigeria and surrounding countries. It is also involved in the creation of an African Stand-by Force to operate as a permanent peacekeeping reserve body of some 20,000 peacekeepers.

The AU and the Outside World

To these crises of conflict should be added the huge challenges posed by migra- **23.88** tionary pressures towards Europe (not all refugees from areas of conflict), disease, notably HIV/AIDS (which is at least as much a security as a health issue) and malaria, climate change and desertification, and the aggravating pressures these are exerting on poverty in the world's poorest continent. The AU's ability to provide a contribution to the solution of these problems in collaboration with external actors such as the UN, the EU, and the G7 will be the touchstone of its success not the institutional discussions over the creation of a Union government.

With fifty-four member States, all members of the United Nations, the AU **23.89** constitutes 28 per cent of the total United Nations membership. Apart from the mathematical effect on voting in the UN General Assembly, a voting bloc of this magnitude cannot fail to affect the general atmosphere there and the votes in Committee meetings in which African members may take a particular interest. These are changes which cannot be ignored despite the limitations on the Assembly's power.

23.90 As a result of the lessons of the last 50 years, the concept of unity among the peoples of Africa has grown at great speed, measured against the scale of world history. How rapidly this unity can be translated into yet further practice by so large a number of relatively young States will depend partly on active understanding of Africa's problems by the international community and partly on the skill shown in resolving outstanding differences, in particular those which, if they persist or recur, could inhibit urgently needed economic growth. More positively, commonality of interest and cooperation between African States need to develop, in particular to encourage trade, economic, transport, and a myriad of other practical links between them. For further information on the African Union see <http://www.au.int>.

23.91 In addition there are a number of regional organizations in Africa bringing together groupings of States. These include the Arab Maghreb Union (AMU), East African Community (EAC), Southern Africa Development Community (SADC), Economic Community of Central African States (ECCAS), and the Economic Community of West African States (ECOWAS). They espouse practical cooperation, and have different levels of ambition and indeed effectiveness.

Association of South-East Asian Nations (ASEAN)

23.92 The reasons for the formation of ASEAN in 1967 were a complete contrast to those which lay behind the founding of the Organization of African Unity. Whereas in Africa there was a clear political objective to bring independence to all African countries that had not yet achieved it, and to remove racial discrimination from the African continent, the position in Asia in the mid 1960s was much more complex. First there were a number of States either at war or at least in sharp conflict with each other—notably the two Vietnams and the two Koreas—or with internal conflicts. There was also the confrontation between Malaysia, supported by the United Kingdom, and Indonesia. In addition, the activities of Communist dissidents were a continuing problem for countries such as Thailand and the Philippines, and even to some extent Malaysia: these countries therefore sought the reassurance of continued links with the West. Thailand and the Philippines were members of SEATO (designed to be a South East Asian version of NATO and dissolved in 1977): Malaysia and Singapore had defence ties with Britain. At the same time, they were concerned that too much reliance on the West would only serve to attract increased hostility from the Communist world, with particular concerns about China's intentions. They therefore felt the need to group together in what was seen as the middle ground between the Communist and non-Communist worlds.

Moves towards the formation of an organized 'middle' group in South-East Asia, **23.93** were accelerated by two developments. During 1965, fears grew in Indonesia, particularly among military leaders, that President Sukarno might press his policies of friendliness to the Communist Party at home and to Communist States abroad to the point that Indonesia would become wholly committed to the 'Communist Camp'. On 30 September of that year an attempted coup by left-wing groups, including the leaders of the Communist Party, was thwarted by the Army. President Sukarno, whose attitude to the coup had been equivocal, subsequently fell from power and was succeeded by a military regime under the leadership of General Suharto. The new government was anti-Communist, sought improvement of relations with non-Communist countries, and the end of confrontation with Malaysia and Britain. Indonesia thus became one of the 'middle' countries of the area whose location, size, population, and resources made its membership essential if any effective South-East Asian Organization independent of outside alliances were to be formed. Secondly, the failure in the 1960s to find a solution to hostilities in Indo-China left a feeling among the non-Communist countries that closer cooperation would benefit their interests.

After various abortive attempts at forming a regional grouping, on 8 August **23.94** 1967 a meeting of political representatives of Indonesia, Malaysia, the Philippines, Singapore,[29] and Thailand issued in Bangkok an announcement under the title 'ASEAN [often known as the Bangkok] Declaration'. The Declaration states that the aims and purposes of the Association are:

1. To accelerate the economic growth, social progress and cultural development in the region through joint endeavours in the spirit of equality and partnership in order to strengthen the foundation for a prosperous and peaceful community of Southeast Asian Nations;
2. To promote regional peace and stability through abiding respect for justice and the rule of law in the relationship among countries of the region and adherence to the principles of the United Nations Charter;
3. To promote active collaboration and mutual assistance on matters of common interest in the economic, social, cultural, technical, scientific and administrative fields;

---

[29] The amalgamation in 1963 of Malaya, Sarawak, and Sabah (former North Borneo) and Singapore as an independent Malaysia had not worked satisfactorily, and Singapore left to become an independent State in August 1965. The name Malaysia was, however, retained as a better designation for the State.

4. To provide assistance to each other in the form of training and research facilities in the educational, professional, technical and administrative spheres;

5. To collaborate more effectively for the greater utilisation of their agriculture and industries, the expansion of their trade, including the study of the problems of international commodity trade, the improvement of their transportation and communications facilities and the raising of the living standards of their peoples;

6. To promote Southeast Asian studies; and

7. To maintain close and beneficial cooperation with existing international and regional organisations with similar aims and purposes, and explore all avenues for even closer cooperation among themselves.

23.95 As part of the Declaration, the ministers agreed upon an annual meeting of Foreign Ministers and a standing committee of the accredited ambassadors of the other member countries, to carry on the work of the Association in between meetings of Foreign Ministers.

23.96 In 1973 the ASEAN Ministerial Meeting decided that there should be a permanent centralized secretariat located in Jakarta. In 1976, at a summit meeting in Indonesia, held at Den Pasar in Bali, ministers took steps to formalize the corporate status and purposes of the Association and signed three important agreements:

(a) a Treaty of Amity and Cooperation in South-East Asia;

(b) a Declaration of ASEAN Concord;

(c) an agreement on the establishment of an ASEAN secretariat.

In the preamble of the Declaration, the signatories: '[u]ndertake to consolidate the achievement of ASEAN and expand ASEAN cooperation in the economic, social, cultural and political fields'. The last item mentioned was new and significant as seen in the Declaration itself, where the members define the first item of their principles as the pursuit of political stability:

> The stability of each member state and of the ASEAN region is an essential contribution to international peace and security. Each member state resolves to eliminate threats posed by subversion to its stability, thus strengthening national and ASEAN resilience.

Another important political point was the call for the establishment of a Zone of Peace, Freedom and Neutrality (ZOPFAN) in South-East Asia, to keep the region 'free from any form or manner of interference by outside powers'. At this Conference the ministers also appointed the first ASEAN Secretary-General, a special adviser on Indo-Chinese affairs to the Foreign Minister of Indonesia.

23.97 The ASEAN Vision 2020, adopted by the ASEAN Leaders on the thirtieth anniversary of ASEAN in 1997, agreed on a shared vision of ASEAN as a concert of South-East Asian nations, living in peace, stability and prosperity, cooperating in economic development and in fostering a community of inclusive societies. In 2003, the ASEAN Leaders resolved that an ASEAN Community should be established comprising three pillars, namely, an ASEAN Security Community, an Economic Community, and a Socio-Cultural Community.

In recognition of security interdependence in the Asia-Pacific region, ASEAN had already established regional dialogue through the ASEAN Regional Forum (ARF) in 1994. The ARF's agenda is a three-stage one, namely the promotion of confidence-building, development of preventive diplomacy, and elaboration of approaches to conflicts. The present participants in the ARF include: Australia, Bangladesh, Brunei Darussalam, Cambodia, Canada, China, European Union, India, Indonesia, Japan, Democratic People's Republic of Korea, Republic of Korea (ROK), Lao PDR, Malaysia, Mongolia, Burma (Myanmar), New Zealand, Pakistan, Papua New Guinea, the Philippines, the Russian Federation, Singapore, Thailand, Timor-Leste, the United States, and Vietnam. The ARF discusses major regional security issues in the region, including the relationship amongst the major powers, non-proliferation, counter-terrorism, transnational crime, South China Sea, and the Korean Peninsula, among others. **23.98**

The ASEAN Economic Community has as its end-goal economic integration measures to create a stable, prosperous, and highly competitive ASEAN economic region with a free flow of goods, services, investment, skilled labour and a freer flow of capital, equitable economic development, and reduced poverty and socio-economic disparities to be established by 2015. In aiming at this ambitious target the Economic Community is building on the ASEAN Free Trade Area (AFTA) launched in 1992. This aimed to promote the region's competitive advantage as a single production unit. The elimination of tariff and non-tariff barriers among member countries is being progressively introduced to promote greater economic efficiency, productivity, and competitiveness. **23.99**

ASEAN holds bi-annual summits during which meetings may be held with, regularly, China, Japan and South Korea (the ASEAN Plus Three grouping), and less regularly with Australia (a Commemorative Summit to mark the fortieth anniversary of ASEAN-Australia relations was held in Burma (Myanmar) in 2014) among others. Joint meetings with both Australia and New Zealand (ASEAN-CER) were held most recently at ministerial level in 2014. ASEAN is also a prime mover in ASEM, an Asia–Europe meeting of fifty-three members. The first ASEAN–Russia Summit took place in 2005 in Kuala Lumpur. An ASEAN–EU Summit was held in 2007. **23.100**

At their summit in November 2007, ASEAN endorsed the ASEAN Charter. The Charter gives ASEAN legal personality, and will develop the concept of the three core 'ASEAN Communities'. The aim of the Charter is to move ASEAN further towards integration and to strengthen ASEAN so that it can remain the **23.101** driving force in the South-East Asian region. The ASEAN Charter provides for the establishment of a human rights body, which will 'operate in accordance with the terms of reference to be determined by the ASEAN Foreign Ministers'. In 2009, this was given concrete expression by the establishment of an ASEAN Intergovernmental Commission on Human Rights (AICHR). The Charter was ratified, by all ten members, in December 2008 and entered into force, at which point ASEAN became an international governmental organization with full legal personality.

23.102   While its favourite modus operandi is the so-called 'ASEAN way' of quiet diplomacy, compromise, and consensus-building, ASEAN has not shrunk from speaking out on occasions even against fellow members and other regional powers. ASEAN was robust in criticizing Vietnam after its invasion of Cambodia in 1978 and more recently in 2007, when the regime in Burma (Myanmar) crushed the protests against it led by monks and pro-democracy groups, ASEAN issued a strongly critical statement expressing its 'revulsion' at the use of such force. The following year after Cyclone Nargis had devastated Burma (Myanmar) leaving more than a hundred thousand dead and missing and many times that number homeless, ASEAN asked the regime what ASEAN meant to it when the Burmese authorities initially refused to allow any foreign humanitarian relief workers to enter the country. Nevertheless, it is also true that the ASEAN human rights body, AICHR, has tended under its terms of reference to focus more on declarations and promoting human rights awareness than on rigorous enforcement.[30] The Singaporean Foreign Minister in 2008 commented on the body that 'while lacking in teeth, [it] will at least have a tongue, and a tongue will have its uses'.[31] ASEAN States have in general eschewed public criticism of each other.

Membership

23.103   Membership has expanded from the original five (Indonesia, Philippines, Malaysia, Singapore, and Thailand) to ten with the addition of Brunei in 1984, Vietnam in 1995, Laos and Burma (Myanmar) in 1997, and Cambodia in 1999. Enlargement of ASEAN's membership to include all South-East Asian nations in the late 1990s was a major advance for ASEAN. As well as fulfilling ASEAN's mandate geographically (except for Timor Leste-East Timor, which has applied for membership and hopes to join as soon as it has fulfilled the necessary obligations), the accession of the Indochinese countries marked the substantial end of South-East Asia's ideological division (significant, given ASEAN's founding

---

[30] See D McGoldrick and D Seah, 'I. The ASEAN Charter' (2009) 58 *ICLQ*,197–212 doi:10.1017/S0020589308000882.

[31] Singapore Parliamentary Reports, Vol 84 (23 February 2008).

rationale as an anti-Communist grouping) as economic and trading interests dominated. However, enlargement has also brought new challenges for ASEAN. Economically, ASEAN is more sharply divided between developed and developing countries, which complicates integration and block trade negotiations. As already noted, politically, Myanmar (Burma) has been an albatross around ASEAN's neck for much of the time since it was admitted to membership, though the reforms enacted in that country since 2011, the release from house arrest of the opposition leader Aung San Suu Kyi, and the return to an at least notional civilian government have brought Myanmar far more into the ASEAN mainstream. This trend accelerated following the elections of November 2015 which brought Aung San Suu Kyi's party, the National League for Democracy, to power. Further details on ASEAN can be found at <http://www.asean.org>.

Commonwealth of Independent States (CIS)

In December 1991—after the collapse of the Soviet Union—Russia, Belarus, and Ukraine founded a Commonwealth of Independent States. They were joined later the same month by eight other former Soviet republics: Armenia, Azerbaijan, Kazakhstan, Kyrgyzstan, Moldova, Turkmenistan, Tajikistan, and Uzbekistan. One more former Soviet republic, Georgia, joined two years later while the three Baltic States declined to join making clear that their priority was to become members of the EU. (They joined it in 2004.) Ukraine, Georgia, and Moldova harbour ambitions in that direction. After the armed conflict between Russia and Georgia over South Ossetia in August 2008, Georgia announced its intention to withdraw from the CIS. This took effect in August 2009. Turkmenistan became an associate member in 2005. The long or even the medium-term viability of the CIS is in doubt as many of its members have publicly expressed their doubts about its efficacy and two of its members (one now ex), Georgia and Russia, have actually been in armed conflict. Its headquarters are in the Belarus capital while its chairman, the Executive Secretary, has been either from Russia or Belarus since its inception. Ukraine has never ratified the CIS Treaty and is not therefore formally a member. While it became an associate member in 1993, in the light of the Russian annexation of Crimea and its military intervention in Eastern Ukraine, legislation has been introduced in the Ukrainian parliament to denounce the 1991 agreement establishing the CIS. For similar reasons, including Russian support of breakaway regions of Moldova, the latter's parliament has debated legislation to denounce the CIS's founding agreement.

23.104

Among the CIS's more concrete achievements have been the creation of a free trade zone (set up in 2005) and participation *qua* CIS in UN peacekeeping. Its

23.105

participation in election monitoring in each other's member States has often been highly controversial, favouring as it has pro-Russian parties. While the CIS has established a Human Rights Commission, its members are often distinguished by their poor human rights record. Further information can be obtained at <http://www.cisstat.com>.

Francophonie

23.106 The International Organization of La Francophonie was created in 1970. It claims as its mission the embodiment of the active solidarity between its eighty member States and governments (fifty-seven members and twenty-three observers, which together represent over one-third of the United Nations' member States and account for a population of over 890 million people, including 220 million French speakers) and the sharing not merely of the French language and its culture but also the humanist values promoted by the French language. A full list of members and observers can be found at <http://www.francophonie.org>.

23.107 Many of the members are former French colonies but the criterion of membership is a significant presence of the French language and culture in the make-up of the member State. The organization's headquarters are in Paris. It has a Parliamentary Assembly and four permanent representatives to major regional organizations in Addis Ababa, Brussels, New York, and Geneva. Summits are held every two years, the most recent, the 15th, in Dakar in 2014 and the 16th in Antananarivo (Madagascar) in 2016. While the main aim of the organization is self-evidently promotion of the French language, the organization's stated aims include promoting peace, democracy, and human rights; support for education and research; and sustainable development and interdependence.

Arab League

23.108 An important organization which can be termed regional, but is not wholly parallel with regional associations analysed in this chapter, is the Arab League. The idea of such a league came in 1942 from the British who saw it as a means to unite the Arab countries against Germany and Italy in the Second World War. It was eventually founded in 1945 at a time when its focus was on decolonization of Arab countries and the prevention of the creation of a State of Israel. It is currently an association of twenty-two Arab States. One of these as recognized by the League is the State of Palestine. Syria's seat is currently occupied by an opposition body, the Syrian National Coalition, given the government's repressive actions during the civil war. The League, whose member countries currently have a population of around 410 million, has a Council, Specialized Committees and Agencies and a secretariat administered by a Secretary-General resident in Cairo. Between 1979 and 2006 the secretariat moved to Tunis in response to Egypt's signature of a peace treaty with Israel. The current Secretary-General (since 2016) is a former Egyptian diplomat, Ahmed Aboul Gheit.

While the Arab League is an intergovernmental organization, the emphasis of **23.109** its work differs from that of other regional associations in that it consists less in the day-to-day handling of intergovernmental business than in the organizing of conferences, largely on economic and social questions, cultural exchanges and investment protection, and particularly in the handling of the Palestinian issue, through speeches, publications, and personal contacts. Part of the reason for this lies in the divisions which have long been present in the organization initially between those countries more aligned with the Soviet Union and its allies and those more oriented towards the West. More recently the divisions have been between the traditional monarchies and the more radical republics which in turn are mirrored in their degree of hostility to Israel. This has been illustrated in the reactions to the war in Iraq where some of the traditional Arab League States provided logistic and other support for the US-led invasion while others were fiercely hostile. Currently its States are grappling with the consequences of the so-called Arab Spring, the democratic uprising which began in Tunisia in December 2010 and quickly spread. The League's most striking success as an organization was its successful economic boycott of Israel between the creation of that State in 1948 and 1993. The League has a resident observer at the United Nations. Representatives with ambassadorial status are posted at a number of capitals. The League also concerns itself with the maintenance of the Islamic faith (but see the OIC below).

Organization of Islamic Cooperation (OIC) formerly the Organization of the Islamic Conference

The Organization of Islamic Cooperation (Arabic منظمة التعاون الإسلامي) (formerly **23.110** the Organization of the Islamic Conference) is second only to the UN in numbers of members. There are currently fifty-seven in four continents representing some 1.5 billion Muslims. A full list of members can be found at <http://www.oic-oci.org>.

The OIC was founded with thirty members in 1969 as a reaction to the arson **23.111** attack on the Al Aqsa mosque in Jerusalem. In 1970 the first ever meeting of the

Islamic Conference of Foreign Ministers (ICFM) was held in Jeddah which decided to establish a permanent secretariat there headed by the organization's Secretary-General. It describes itself as the collective voice of the Muslim world aiming to safeguard and protect the interests of that world. The Islamic Summit, composed of kings and Heads of State and Government of member States, is the supreme authority of the organization. It convenes once every three years to deliberate, take policy decisions, and provide guidance on all issues relating to the realization of its objectives and consider other issues of concern to the member States and the Muslim world, the *ummah*.

23.112   The Council of Foreign Ministers, which meets once a year, considers the means for the implementation of the general policy of the organization by, inter alia:

(a)   adopting decisions and resolutions on matters of common interest in the implementation of the objectives and the general policy of the organization;

(b)   reviewing progress of the implementation of the decisions and resolutions adopted at the previous summits and Councils of Foreign Ministers.

On 23 June 2011 during the 38th Council of Foreign Ministers meeting in Astana, Kazakhstan, the organization changed its name from Organization of the Islamic Conference (Arabic: منظمة المؤتمر الإسلامي) to its current name.

23.113   The General Secretariat is the executive organ of the organization, entrusted with the implementation of the decisions of the two preceding bodies. The Secretary-General is Mr Iyad Ameen Madani of Saudi Arabia. So far thirteen Islamic Summit Conferences and forty-three Councils of Foreign Ministers (CFM) have been held. The Twelfth Islamic Summit Conference was held in Cairo in 2013. The thirteenth was held in 2016 in Istanbul, Turkey.

23.114   The OIC has been criticized for its passivity and its failure to react promptly and forcibly to events of concern to the *ummah*. On the other hand, it has been criticized vigorously by non-Muslim States with Muslim minorities (e.g. Thailand and India) for what have been perceived as unwarranted interference and failure to take a balanced view between Muslims and non-Muslims.

Gulf Cooperation Council (GCC)

(Arabic: مجلس التعاون لدول الخليج العربية)

23.115   The GCC is a political and economic alliance of six Gulf States—Saudi Arabia, Bahrain, Kuwait, Oman, the United Arab Emirates, and Qatar—set up in Riyadh, Saudi Arabia, in May 1981 against the backdrop of the Islamic revolution in Iran and the Iraq–Iran war. All share similar political systems—a form of monarchy, with limited democratic participation—and a culture rooted in Islam.

The GCC aims to develop economic cooperation between members (collect-   **23.116**
ively they possess some 40 per cent of the world's proven oil reserves) and,
through collective security, to guard against any threat to any of their members
from neighbouring States and from Islamic extremism. The highest decision-
making entity of the GCC is the Supreme Council, which meets on an annual
basis and consists of GCC Heads of State. Its Presidency rotates annually.
Decisions of the Supreme Council are adopted by unanimous approval and
each State has one vote.

In 1984, the GCC created a joint military venture—the Saudi-based Peninsula   **23.117**
Shield. While it made no attempt to counter the Iraqi invasion of Kuwait in
1991, it was controversially deployed to Bahrain in March 2011 to strengthen
security during anti-government protests which were part of the Arab Spring.

GCC members signed an intelligence-sharing pact in 2004, aimed at counter-   **23.118**
ing Islamic extremism and terrorism and in 2003 declared a customs union
which came into existence as a common market in 2008. Progress since has
been slow and incremental. Agreement was reached in 2009 on the goal of a
single regional currency similar to the euro but so far progress has been limited
to the use of a basket of the national currencies by business.

Organization for Security and Co-operation in Europe (OSCE)

With fifty-seven States from Europe, Central Asia and North America, the   **23.119**
Organization for Security and Co-operation in Europe (OSCE) is the largest
regional security organization in the world. A list of current members can be
found at <http://www.osce.org>.

Its origins go back to the period of détente in the Cold War in the early 1970s,   **23.120**
when the Conference on Security and Co-operation in Europe (CSCE) was established as a forum for dialogue and negotiation between East and West. After two
years of negotiations in Helsinki and Geneva, the CSCE reached agreement on
the Helsinki Final Act, which was signed on 1 August 1975. This document contained a number of key political commitments on politico-military, economic,
and human rights issues that became central to the so-called 'Helsinki process'. It
also established ten fundamental principles (the 'Decalogue') governing the
behaviour of States towards their citizens, as well as towards each other. This
document was an important contributor to the developments which led to the
fall of the Berlin Wall and the new democracies of central and Eastern Europe.

23.121   Until 1990, the CSCE organized itself principally around a programme of meetings and conferences which developed and monitored the commitments which the member States had assumed. However, with the end of the Cold War, the Paris Summit of November 1990 marked a step change in the CSCE's activities. The Summit issued a Charter of Paris for a New Europe in which the CSCE was given a key role to play in effecting the change in Europe and responding to the new challenges of the post-Cold War period. This involved, inter alia, the establishment of permanent institutions with a secretariat in Vienna and real operational capabilities. This process led at the Budapest Summit of Heads of State or Government in December 1994 to the 'Conference' name being changed to 'Organization' hence the OSCE.

23.122   The OSCE provides an early warning system for potential crises, and is actively involved in conflict prevention, crisis management, and post-conflict rehabilitation in its area. It has sixteen missions or field operations in South-Eastern Europe, Eastern Europe, the South Caucasus, and Central Asia enabling the OSCE to tackle crises as they arise and to play a critical post-conflict role. They also underpin the capacity of host countries through specific projects including initiatives to support law enforcement, minority rights, legislative reform, the rule of law, and press freedom.

23.123   There is a Parliamentary Assembly of 323 full members from fifty-six member States. The Holy See which has no national parliament sends two representatives to the Assembly meetings as guests of honour. It has international partners in the CIS, European Parliament, Inter-Parliamentary Union, the NATO Parliamentary Assembly, and the Parliamentary Assembly of the Council of Europe. The most recent summit took place in the Kazakh capital Astana in December 2010.

23.124   Like its predecessor, the organization deals with three areas of security—the politico-military, the economic and environmental, and human rights. It therefore concerns itself with a wide range of activities, including arms control, confidence-building measures, human rights, minorities questions, policing and counter-terrorism, promotion of democracy (specifically election monitoring, including monitoring of elections in all member States) through its Office for Democratic Institutions and Human Rights (ODIHR), and the security aspects of economic and environmental activities. As all fifty-seven participating States have equal status, decisions are taken by consensus. The OSCE retains relations with a number of partner States in the Mediterranean and Asia.

Book V

INTERNATIONAL DISPUTES AND COURTS

24

PREVENTION AND MANAGEMENT OF CONFLICT AND SETTLEMENT OF DISPUTES

Emyr Jones Parry

The Nature of Conflict

Conflict-related issues[1] occupy a spectrum, ranging from its absence, peace; **24.1**
through emerging conflict; actual conflict or war; ending hostilities; to the
challenge of building stable, peaceful societies and States. Inter-State war has
diminished since 1945, partly because of the system of international peace

---

[1] For further reading, see J G Merills, *International Dispute Settlement* (5th edn, Cambridge: Cambridge University Press, 2011); Ian Brownlie. *Peaceful Settlement of International Disputes* (Oxford: Oxford University Press, 2009); United Nations Handbook on Peaceful Settlement of Disputes (1992).

preservation put in place, primarily through the United Nations, and perhaps because such conflict is less likely with more democratically elected governments of States participating in the international trade and financial system. But conflict within States remains potent with armed non-State actors a frequent characteristic.

Identifying and Promoting Conflict Resolution

24.2   The old proverb is so relevant. Prevention is better than cure. Successful conflict prevention is in effect dispute resolution before escalation into actual conflict. The benefits are obvious. The costs of prevention are dwarfed by the human and financial consequences of conflict and the subsequent investment needed to create successful peaceful States. Identification of potential conflict or dispute is key. Causes can include grievances and traditional hatreds, weak States and poor governance, ideological or belief-motivated pressures, resource exploitation, ethnicities and poverty, the ability to finance and support rebellion, and more. Early warning of disputes and nascent conflict is essential. The UN system, governments, diplomats, international and non-governmental organizations often have access to information indicating a looming problem, the more so given the spread of internet and cell phone networks. But knowledge is not enough. There then needs to be action, preferably coordinated, and those in dispute have to accept help if the problems are to be tackled. Possible techniques to promote dispute resolution are discussed later. Additionally, external players can provide targeted financial, development assistance to support peace initiatives. Pressure can also be applied on the parties directly by governments and international organizations and through sanctions, for example to confiscate assets or deny access to travel or financial markets; arms embargoes; and the preventative deployment of international troops.

Negotiating Solutions to Conflict

24.3   Better than conflict is that the parties to a dispute should negotiate a diplomatic solution to resolve the dispute. This depends on getting the parties or their representatives to the table. This can depend on whether the timing is ripe, particularly if conflict has already broken out. It is also invariably more difficult in an intra-State dispute, partly because the degree of commitment to a cause can be great, as in identity or recognition of minorities, and partly because of the difficulty in identifying and gaining acceptance of which parties are entitled to participate in the negotiations. Those excluded can often be spoilers to deny a successful outcome. It is important to emphasize the role of women in negotiations. United Nations Security Council resolution 1325 adopted in 2000 insists that women should participate in decisions, including mechanisms for prevention of conflict and peace negotiations. This resolution has been followed by others developing its themes and the subject is debated annually in the Security Council. It is for States to comply with the spirit of the resolutions which the United Nations family also seeks to implement.

Negotiating an end to conflict requires a comprehensive approach starting with **24.4** a cessation of hostilities and some form of agreement between the belligerent parties, which in an intra-State conflict will require accepting peaceful coexistence within agreed State structures. Agreements need to provide for demobilization, disarmament and reintegration of fighting forces, and frequently a system of validation. The challenge then is to stop any re-emergence of fighting and ensure security, through both military and police presence, with perhaps an international element; provide economic prospects; and move to establish political and social structures, the rule of law, respect for human rights, and justice for victims. A 'winner takes all' approach is rarely successful. Usually each party will expect to derive some benefit from the arrangements.

Peacebuilding

Peacebuilding after conflict is difficult, but achieved successfully can resolve **24.5** conflict for the long term. Successful peacebuilding in countries emerging from conflict requires stability, a secure environment without conflict, a prospect of economic progress, and institutions which ensure the rule of law and deliver a sense of justice acceptable to combatants and victims. It entails a sustained effort over many years, and the risk of recidivism into conflict is always present, and indeed is the case with many conflicts. The challenge of preventing re-emergence of conflict diminishes only as the parameters listed above are successfully established. In 2005 the Security Council and the General Assembly each adopted resolutions setting up a Peacebuilding Commission, which is an intergovernmental advisory body available to support peace efforts in countries emerging from conflict. It has three aims: to bring together all the relevant actors, including international donors, the International Financial Institutions, and national governments; to marshal resources and advise on and propose integrated strategies for post-conflict recovery and development; and to improve the coordination of support. It is the State itself which decides its policies for recovery drawing on the advice, encouragement, and resources provided.

Role of the Security Council

24.6 When conflict has emerged or appears likely, the situation can be brought to the United Nations Security Council if its members agree that there is a threat to international peace and security. The range of options available to the Council include the deployment of UN Peacekeepers. Although not mentioned in the Charter, such deployments, which began in 1948, are now a frequent measure to prevent the re-emergence of conflict. Each deployment is approved by the Security Council in a resolution which mandates the purpose and conditions for the deployment of 'blue helmets', a common term for a United Nation Peacekeeping mission. The basic principles for deployment are that there should be a peace agreement between the warring parties who have consented to the presence of international troops, that the mission is impartial, and that generally the use of force is only sanctioned in self-defence, and in defence of the mandate and of civilians. The budget for this peacekeeping is separate from the general United Nations budget. The African Union has also approved its own peacekeeping deployments; in 2007 a hybrid operation with the United Nations in Darfur, the United Nations African Union Mission in Darfur, and alone in Somalia, also in 2007, the African Union Mission in Somalia, which drew its troops from many African States.

Threats to States

24.7 Intra-State conflict poses more of a threat in general than that between States. But today's States can face a myriad of external threats which include weapons of mass destruction, international terrorism, espionage, climate change, and increasingly cyber threats. This last category can affect individuals, organizations, companies, and governments. Hackers have many motives. These may include greed or criminal purpose. It may be to steal intellectual property or gain an advantage. It may be capricious or seriously intended to maim, damage, or do physical or economic harm. All of us to some extent have to protect against this threat. For governments the primary aim of ensuring the protection of citizens and ensuring their economic well-being is paramount. It also potentially affects the way in which business is transacted within and between governments as measures have to be put in place to maximize security and minimize risk.

Inter-State Disputes

There is little new in disputes between States—in some ways, they are as inevi-   **24.8**
table as disputes between individuals. Here we will concentrate on disputes
between States while recognizing that many 'international' disputes may not
involve States as parties.[2] Disputes have varied subject-matter and need not
concern political matters; they may, for example, be commercial in nature. A
dispute can be defined as a specific disagreement relating to rights or interests
where a party considers that it has a claim against another which that other rejects.
The *Mavrommatis* case[3] defined a dispute as 'a disagreement over a point of law
or fact, a conflict of legal views or interests between two persons'.

Among early efforts to settle disputes, prominent was the 1899 Hague Conven-   **24.9**
tion for the Pacific Settlement of International Disputes, followed by further
efforts in 1907 to provide for a number of mechanisms which might be deployed.[4]
The options available permitted parties to agree on the process which they considered most likely to produce a satisfactory outcome. Any reference to any form
of judicial and binding process required the prior agreement of the parties.

Resolution of disputes became a central tenet of the Charter of the United   **24.10**
Nations. Article 1.1 sets out a primary purpose: 'to bring about by peaceful
means, and in conformity with the principles of justice and international law,
adjustment or settlement of international disputes or situations which might
lead to a breach of the peace'. Article 2.3 requires that '[all] members shall settle
their international disputes by peaceful means in such a manner that international peace and security, and justice, are not endangered'. In Chapter VI on
Pacific Settlement of Disputes, Article 33 sets out a possible menu through
which the parties to a threat which may endanger the maintenance of international peace and security shall first of all seek a solution 'by negotiation, enquiry,
mediation, conciliation, arbitration, judicial settlement, resort to regional agencies
or arrangements, or other peaceful means of their own choice'.

The United Nations has devoted much, if not always efficient, consideration   **24.11**
to this issue. The General Assembly on 15 November 1982 approved the Manila

---

[2] For example, international investment disputes between States on the one hand and individuals
or companies on the other may, since the entry into force in 1966 of the Convention on the
Settlement of Investment Disputes between States and Nationals of Other States, be submitted to
independent conciliation commissions and arbitral tribunals constituted in each case under the
framework laid down by the Convention.
[3] PCIJ, Series A, No 2 (1924) 11.
[4] 1907 Hague Convention for the Pacific Settlement of International Disputes.

Declaration on the Peaceful Settlement of International Disputes.[5] It underlined the principles of peaceful settlement of international disputes and the non-use of force in international relations. The Declaration drew on the Charter provisions to underline the need for the UN to increase its effectiveness in this area. All States were enjoined to settle disputes exclusively by peaceful means on the basis of sovereign equality of States and on the basis of free choice as to means; the resolution elaborated the different ways of settling disputes. States Parties to regional arrangements were asked to make every effort to find a solution through those arrangements. Continuing effort is the order of the day, with the prospect of a reference to the Security Council if a threat to international peace and security emerges. In practice, such references have been few, partly because of sovereignty concerns, partly resentment of the Council by those who hanker for a General Assembly role, and partly because successive Secretaries-General of the United Nations have been reluctant to use their prerogative under the Charter to make such reference. Despite the demand and potential powers available to it, the United Nations has not responded sufficiently well to the challenge, particularly where disputes have their origin within a member State. The principle of non-interference in matters essentially within the domestic affairs of a sovereign State in Article 2.7 is widely invoked to inhibit involvement in intra-State disputes, although this is countered by the Responsibility to Protect doctrine (see Chapter 2, paragraph 2.24) which is not a Charter provision. Nor in general have the resources and mediation support capacities been adequate to the demand, or has enough been done to work with regional organizations and civil society.

24.12 The methods and techniques available to help resolve international disputes are similar, within and without the United Nations context. The principle of free choice of means should apply to decisions made by States. We will now summarize them in turn.

Direct Negotiation and Consultation between the Parties

24.13 This is the most common means of settlement and involves the conduct of direct talks between the parties to a dispute, aimed at resolving the dispute; negotiations are used at some stage of almost every dispute. They are often conducted through 'diplomatic channels'; that is, through foreign offices or diplomatic representatives, the delegations often including or comprising

---

[5] General Assembly resolution 37/10 of 15 November 1982.

representatives from different departments of government. If settlement of the dispute through these means fails, the negotiations may be raised to the level of Heads of State or Government. A precondition for success is that the parties should have the political will to work for agreement, and that customarily where relevant, politics and public opinion in the States concerned permit the negotiations to proceed. This process is entirely in the hands of the parties and does not involve a third party. Negotiations are bilateral or multilateral depending on the number of parties involved. Such negotiations are sometimes conducted in secret, this being the only basis for the parties agreeing to a process. The Norwegian government successfully facilitated in secret the Oslo Accord on Palestine in 1993. Another example would be Henry Kissinger's negotiations with the North Vietnamese from 1969–73.

If the subject-matter of the dispute means that substantive settlement is very **24.14** difficult, different techniques may be used to assist with the process. Agreement may be possible on procedures, rather than substance; for example the result of the negotiations may be agreement to submit the dispute to a third party, either for advice or for a resolution which the parties agree in advance will be binding. Or a 'without prejudice' clause may be agreed which allows the parties to discuss certain matters while leaving the most contentious alone; for example, the sovereignty 'umbrella' under which the United Kingdom and Argentina negotiated on Falkland Islands matters without raising the question of sovereignty.[6] This followed the precedent of the Antarctic Treaty 1959 which creates the basis for continuing cooperation between the parties while 'freezing' the sovereignty claims of some of the parties and their non-recognition by others.

Some treaties impose an obligation on parties to consult together before taking **24.15** any other action, as in Article 283 of the UN Convention on the Law of the Sea; refusal by one party to take part in such consultations does not prevent the other party from resorting to another process. But there is no general duty to attempt settlement by negotiation and negotiations do not have to be exhausted before resort is made to another option. The means of settlement set out in Article 33 of the Charter are alternatives. However, at least some exchanges between governments will be necessary before a difference of view can be called a dispute and it is only if there is a 'dispute' that the matter can be taken to the International Court of Justice (ICJ). Sometimes, bilateral treaties can include a formalized negotiating process to settle disputes. An example is the permanent commission established as part of the Canada–US International Joint Commission.

---

[6] See 1989 Joint Statement in 29 *ILM* 1291.

Negotiation Facilitated by Third Parties

24.16 Negotiations between disagreeing parties may be encouraged by other governments or organizations. The parties to the dispute, at least initially, may not be prepared to meet face to face. The third party tries to establish a basis of trust with the protagonists, seeks to understand their concerns and interests, and then attempts to narrow the differences. This can involve shuttle diplomacy between the parties and many contacts over a period of time. This then constitutes what might be termed a peace process. President Carter's efforts in 1978 produced two Accords: a Framework for a Peace Treaty between Israel and Egypt and a Framework for wider Middle East peace. The countries constituting the Friends of Guatemala supported the peace process which ended the 1990–6 civil war.

Inquiry and Fact-finding

24.17 The aim, in terms used in the 1907 Hague Convention,[7] is 'to facilitate a solution of...disputes by elucidating the facts by means of an impartial and conscientious investigation'. Fact-finding is a process performed by all tribunals, but it can also be a means of settlement of disputes separate from other mechanisms. While it should not involve the application of rules of law if the dispute has its basis in fact, it may also contribute to a solution if the dispute has legal content. The resulting acceptance by both parties of established facts should help find solutions, and can contribute to a successful outcome by a range of methods. The General Assembly in 1991 defined fact-finding as 'any activity designed to obtain detailed knowledge of the relevant facts of any dispute or situation which the competent United Nations organs need in order to exercise effectively their functions in relation to the maintenance of international peace and security'.[8] Prior approval by the States concerned is usually required.

24.18 A commission of inquiry was established by the British and Danish governments following the Red Crusader incident in 1961. A British trawler of that name had been arrested by a Danish fisheries protection vessel by having two Danish officers put on board; the trawler had in turn incapacitated these officers and

---

[7] This followed from an earlier version of arrangements for inquiry commissions in the 1899 Hague Convention.

[8] Declaration on Fact-finding by the United Nations in the Field of the Maintenance of International Peace and Security A/RES/46/59 of 9 December 1991.

changed course. The Danish vessel fired on the fleeing trawler. The commission of inquiry found the facts which facilitated the settlement of the dispute. Although it took nearly a year after the commission's report, the governments agreed mutually to waive their claims. The commission did in practice approach the role of an arbitration in that it made some legal rulings as well as finding the facts. A further example was the investigation by the UN Secretary-General in 1984 of the use of chemical weapons in the war between Iran and Iraq.

The UN Compensation Commission was established by the Security Council **24.19** in 1991 to consider claims against Iraq arising from its invasion of Kuwait.[9] It was described by the Secretary-General as having a fact-finding role in the settlement of claims by governments, companies, and organizations.[10] Claims for compensation have been assessed by expert panels and several billion dollars of compensation paid. The role is not judicial or arbitral but administrative, since the issue of overall liability was settled by Security Council resolution 687 (1991).

Mediation and Good Offices

If relations between the parties are not conducive to successful negotiations or **24.20** if negotiations have not succeeded, intervention by a third party may help. This third party must be acceptable to all the parties to the dispute. Good offices provide an additional channel of communication for the parties. Mediation involves the intervention of a third State or States, a disinterested party, or UN organ with the disputing States in an effort to advance proposals aimed at a compromise solution. As Article 4 of the 1899 Hague Convention put it: 'The part of the mediator consists in reconciling the opposing claims and appeasing the feeling of resentment which may have arisen between the States at variance.' Usually action is by a third party of particular standing or reputation who seeks to bring about, initiate, or secure the continuation of negotiations, without necessarily himself participating in the negotiations. To succeed, this method requires the agreement and cooperation of the parties. Any proposals are non-binding on the parties. The settlement is likely to require compromise on both sides, because the aim of the mediator will be to suggest proposals which both parties can willingly accept. Both the Security Council and the General Assembly are competent to recommend the use of good offices or mediation by a member State, agency, or organ of the UN. The terms are broadly interchangeable,

---

[9] Established by Security Council resolution 687 (1991).
[10] Report of the UN Secretary-General, 2 May 1991 (S/22559) para 20.

However, a mediator in seeking to reconcile different claims is likely to advance proposals aimed at an acceptable compromise solution.

24.21 Five examples demonstrate the diversity of interventions. The UN Secretary-General, Perez de Cuellar, mediated between France and New Zealand over the *Rainbow Warrior* affair in 1986.[11] Although the process was termed 'mediation', the parties agreed in advance that the result would be binding, and they entered into an agreement to implement its terms.[12] The Beagle Channel dispute between Chile and Argentina arose in 1978 as a result of failure by Argentina to accept or implement an award by an arbitral tribunal. A mediation by envoys of the Pope produced a settlement in 1984 which did not depend on the terms of the legal award. The Catholic Community of Sant'Egido mediated in the Mozambique civil war which concluded in 1992. Civil war in Macedonia was averted in 2000 through the coordinated and active mediation by the Secretaries-General of the Organization for Security and Cooperation in Europe (OSCE) and NATO, and the High Representative of the European Union (EU). In 2006 UN Secretary-General Kofi Annan successfully mediated in a territorial dispute between Nigeria and Cameroon over ownership of the Bakassi peninsula.

24.22 In September 2008, the Security Council considered a paper on mediation tabled by the President of the Council, Burkina Faso, encouraged by its success in March 2007 in brokering an agreement between the Ivorian government forces and the former rebel Forces Nouvelles. The resulting Presidential Statement[13] issued by the Council focused on the role of mediation in settling disputes. It emphasized the importance of mediation and the role of the Secretary-General and his special representatives and envoys, exhorted the Secretariat to build up its mediation capabilities, welcomed regional efforts, and encouraged participation by women in the settlement of disputes.

Conciliation

24.23 This technique combines the characteristics of inquiry and mediation. Again, a person enjoying the confidence of the parties or a conciliation panel is

---

[11] In 1985, the *Rainbow Warrior*, a ship owned by the environmental organization Greenpeace, was in Auckland harbour about to go on a protest voyage to Moruroa Atoll, a French nuclear test site, when it was sunk by agents of DGSE, the French foreign intelligence service. A photographer was drowned on the sinking ship.

[12] The agreement was later broken by France, and an arbitration was necessary before that further dispute was finally resolved.

[13] Presidential statement of 23 September 2008 (S/PRST/2008/36).

tasked to establish the facts and put forward non-binding proposals for consideration by the parties within an informal third party machinery for negotiation. Some treaties provide for resort to conciliation if there is a dispute under the terms of the treaty concerned; while this is not now common with bilateral treaties it is more frequent in multilateral treaties. Detailed conciliation procedures are provided, for example, in the Vienna Convention on the Law of Treaties and the Convention on the Law of the Sea. In spite of the existence of these treaties, conciliation is now rarely used. The model rules for conciliation set out in General Assembly resolution 50/50[14] are unlikely to serve much practical use. One reason for its unpopularity may be that the time and expense of setting up and appearing before a conciliation panel may come close to the resources needed for an arbitration tribunal, but the parties are left without a binding result.

Arbitration

This is the determination of an outcome by a legally binding decision of one or more arbitrators or a tribunal, chosen by the parties or by a method agreed by the parties. Arbitration may be agreed between the parties on an entirely ad hoc basis or be built into particular treaty arrangements. The judges are called arbitrators and their judgment is known as an award. For the parties, recourse to the procedure implies submission, in good faith, to the award. Arbitration has a long history. But the Permanent Court of Arbitration, established under the 1899 Hague Convention, has a misleading name; it provides not an arbitral court but a mechanism for facilitating arbitrations. **24.24**

Compulsory settlement of disputes, such as is provided by arbitration, was a move away from a power-based system to a more principled approach. Arbitration is not dissimilar to a judicial settlement by the International Court of Justice in that the result is binding on the parties. But usually the tribunal is created for a specific purpose. Unlike resort to the ICJ, the parties have to bear the costs of the tribunal, and these can be very heavy; this will be a consideration in deciding whether to put a dispute to the Court or to arbitration. Since the tribunal's award will be final, the parties need to be quite clear about the detail to which they are signing up before entering into the proposed arbitration, and consider the likely outcomes given the assumption that they will submit in good faith to the outcome. **24.25**

---

[14] United Nations Model Rules for the Conciliation of Disputes between States; GA resolution 50/50 adopted on 29 January 1996.

24.26 Arbitration can only settle a dispute, of course, if the parties accept the result. An example where they did not do so is the award of the Boundary Commission established to settle the boundary dispute between Ethiopia and Eritrea.[15] The arbitration used the facilities of the Permanent Court of Arbitration. Although the two States agreed to accept the award as final and binding, Ethiopia found it impossible to do so. It can be argued that arbitrators, in interpreting the facts and the law, need also to take into account the probable reaction of the parties to possible decisions. A successful example was the Kishenganga Arbitration which resolved the dispute between India and Pakistan over a vital water resource.

Judicial Settlement

24.27 Judicial settlements and arbitration are the two compulsory means of settlement of disputes. However, in contrast to arbitration, judicial settlement is established by international agreement between States transferring jurisdiction over specified disputes to an international court or tribunal, or to the national courts of States. The composition of such courts or tribunals may not be within the control of the parties, and their decisions not always appealable. Recourse is often to the International Court of Justice, but Article 95 of the UN Charter makes clear that States may use other tribunals of choice.

Compromis (Special Agreement)

24.28 This term denotes an agreement to refer a dispute to arbitration or to judicial settlement, the matters in dispute being defined more clearly in the agreement itself. The normal English equivalent of the term is 'special agreement' (though 'Arbitration Agreement' is frequently used in the case of an arbitration); and in French or Spanish the single word '*compromis*' or '*compromiso*' is used. Article 40.1 of the Statute of the International Court of Justice provides that:

> [c]ases are brought before the Court, as the case may be, either by the notification of the special agreement (*compromis*) or by a written application addressed to the Registrar. In either case the subject of the dispute and the parties shall be indicated.

24.29 An example is the Special Agreement for Submission to the International Court of Justice of the Dispute between Malaysia and Singapore concerning Sovereignty over Pedra Branca/Pulau Batu Puteh, Middle Rocks and South Ledge, which

---

[15] Established under the Comprehensive Peace Agreement, signed in Algiers in December 2000.

was jointly notified to the Court on 24 July 2003.[16] The special agreement comprised six short Articles including the submission of the dispute to the Court, the subject of the litigation, the applicable law (in those proceedings the principles and rules of international law recognized in Article 38(1) of the Statute of the Court), and the agreement of the parties to accept the judgment of the Court as final and binding upon them.[17]

The content of a special agreement *(compromis)* referring a dispute to the International Court of Justice can be relatively simple since the composition of the Court and the procedure to be followed are already determined by the Statute of the Court and the Rules of Court. More complex arrangements are necessary when the parties wish to refer a dispute to an ad hoc court of arbitration. **24.30**

In 1958 the International Law Commission drew up a set of Model Rules on Arbitral Procedure which the General Assembly brought to the attention of Member States 'for their consideration and use, in such cases and to such extent as they consider appropriate, in drawing up treaties of arbitration or *compromis*'.[18] **24.31**

The Permanent Court of Arbitration (PCA) is a body established under The Hague Conventions of 1899 and 1907 with the aim of facilitating the settlement of international disputes by recourse to arbitration. Its headquarters are in the Peace Palace at The Hague, alongside the International Court of Justice. As now organized, the PCA offers hearing facilities and ancillary administrative services to arbitral tribunals operating ad hoc or under the auspices of another institution, and as part of these services has drawn up a list of model clauses for the submission of disputes to arbitration. It has also in recent years revised, or drawn up afresh, a series of Rules of Procedure suitable for the conduct of arbitrations between States, arbitrations involving international organizations, and other combinations of disputing parties, most notably the Permanent Court of Arbitration Optional Rules for Arbitrating Disputes between Two States, adopted in 1992.[19] **24.32**

A recent example of a *compromis* for reference of a dispute to ad hoc arbitration, making use of the facilities of the PCA, is provided by the Arbitration Agreement **24.33**

---

[16] See <http://www.icj-cij.org/docket/files/130/1785.pdf>.

[17] For the judgment of the Court in the case, given on 23 May 2008, see <http://www.icj-cij.org/docket/files/130/14492.pdf>.

[18] <http://legal.un.org/ilc/texts/instruments/english/commentaries/10_1_1958.pdf>; General Assembly resolution 1262 (XIII) of 14 November 1958.

[19] Text at <http://www.pca-cpa.org/upload/files/2STATENG.pdf>. See too the UN Handbook on the Peaceful Settlement of Disputes between States, paras 168–95, 1992: <http://www.un.org/law/books/HandbookOnPSD.pdf>.

of July 2003 between the Belgian and Netherlands governments.[20] This concerned the reactivation of the so-called 'Iron Rhine' railway line, and how the associated costs are to be borne. The two governments agreed that the Tribunal should operate under the PCA's Optional Rules as modified by agreement between them.

Regional and Other Special Arrangements

24.34   Article 33 of the Charter of the United Nations mentions 'resort to regional agencies or arrangements' among peaceful means to find a solution to a dispute. This is further developed in Chapter VIII, and specifically in Article 52. Regional organizations often have their own provisions for addressing disputes and technical means to do so. Indeed, there is often an obligation that parties belonging to such organizations will, if in dispute with each other, follow the resolution procedures established by or within that organization.[21] Thus the Council of Europe and its Regional Court of Human Rights, established by the European Court of Human Rights by the European Convention for Human Rights 1952 exercises jurisdiction over member States in respect of member States' observance of human rights.

24.35   The three founding treaties of the European Union, as amended by successive treaty amendments, established the European Court of Justice with compulsory jurisdiction over certain matters within the Treaties; basing itself on the body of European law, it gives binding judgments on actions brought by the European Commission or a Member State against a particular State or States. The Court also has other forms of jurisdiction in relation to companies and individuals, it rules on challenges to the legality of acts of the Community, and national courts refer issues of EU law to it for its decision. The OSCE has a large number of mechanisms for the avoidance and settlement of disputes, emphasizing dispute prevention and management, as much as settlement.[22]

24.36   The African Union (AU), established to replace the Organization of African Unity, has a Peace and Security Council with functions that include the use of good offices, mediation, conciliation, and enquiry. Members of the Commission

---

[20] Full text, with English translation, available at <http://www.pca-cpa.org/upload/files/BE-NL%20Arbitration%20Agreement.pdf>. For other such agreements see <http://www.pca-cpa.org/showpage.asp?pag_id=1029>.

[21] See also the coverage of regional organizations and their dispute settlement procedures in Chapter 23.

[22] A useful summary is at <http://www.osce.org/documents/sg/2004/06/4056_en.pdf>. However, the so-called 'Valetta mechanism' for the peaceful settlement of disputes was never used.

(the Secretariat) of the AU have been active in political interventions to resolve disputes both between and within States. Similarly, at a regional level in Africa, groupings have become increasingly active in resolving disputes. In 2004 and 2005, office-holders of the Economic Community of West African States were instrumental in coping with the consequences of a coup in Guinea Bissau and the possible inauguration of an unelected President in Togo. In 2008, the Southern African Development Community attempted to secure the implementation of the power-sharing agreement in Zimbabwe.

There are many conventions, or organizations set up under their auspices, which **24.37** have their own dispute settlement provisions, some of them of great complexity. The United Nations Convention on the Law of the Sea is one of these. Part XV of the Convention is entirely devoted to the settlement of disputes between parties concerning the interpretation or application of the Convention. If no solution has been reached by other means, Article 286 of the Convention stipulates that the dispute be submitted at the request of any party to the dispute to a court or tribunal having jurisdiction. Article 287 of the Convention defines these as: the International Tribunal for Law of the Sea, set up by the Convention (with its seat in Hamburg); the International Court of Justice; an arbitral tribunal constituted in accordance with Annex VII of the Convention; or a special arbitral tribunal constituted in accordance with Annex VIII. States may declare, when they become party to the Convention, which means of settlement they choose. There are particular settlement provisions for particular kinds of disputes.

The World Trade Organization (WTO), established in 1994 to replace the **24.38** General Agreement on Tariffs and Trade (GATT), has a binding dispute settlement system which has generally proved effective. Understanding on Rules and Procedures Governing the Settlement of Disputes provides the basis for resolving disputes relating to the application of WTO rules. The Dispute Settlement Body includes panels established where necessary and an appellate body to consider and make recommendations on specific complaints, which are then referred to the Dispute Settlement Body. The Understanding also makes reference to good offices, conciliation, mediation, or arbitration, undertaken with the consent of the parties.

Procedures Envisaged in the Charter of the United Nations

For completeness we should underline the role of the Security Council and **24.39** the General Assembly. The Council, having the primary responsibility for the maintenance of international peace and security, may under Chapter VI of the Charter, inter alia, investigate any dispute or any situation which might lead to international friction or give rise to dispute. It may then recommend appropriate procedures or methods of adjustment, and can decide to use its powers to act to preserve international peace and security. For its part, the General Assembly is empowered under Chapter IV of the Charter to discuss any question within the scope of the Charter and to make recommendations to the Council.

International Administration of Territory

24.40 The principle of non-intervention in the domestic jurisdiction of a State is set out in Article 2.7 of the United Nations Charter. Yet the involvement of international organizations in territorial administration goes back at least to the League of Nations. Namibia, a former German colony, was mandated to South Africa by the League in 1920. In 1973 the United Nations recognized the South West African People's Organization as the official representative of the Namibian people, although the territory remained under South African administration until it became independent in 1980. The practice has been surprisingly common. The United Nations High Commissioner for Refugees administers camps housing refugees and internally displaced persons, and international organizations are responsible for the administration of assistance programmes in various territories. These are usually implemented with the consent of the State. Wider administration of territory or even all the territory of a State can arise from a dispute as to who is entitled to exercise control or if there is a grave problem with the governance of a territory. In each case there needs to be a legitimate process for deciding who should take on the administration and why this should occur. This is wholly different from administration by an occupying power, and is usually confirmed by the United Nations. Three examples illustrate the practice. Security Council resolution 1244 in 1999 established the United Nations Interim Administration in Kosovo, and in the same year resolution 1246 set up the Transitional Administration in East Timor. The United Nations Security Council welcomed the Dayton Accords of 1996 which created the role of High Representative of the International Community in Bosnia Herzegovina, bestowing defined governmental responsibilities on the post.

25

THE INTERNATIONAL COURT OF JUSTICE

Elizabeth Wilmshurst

General

Located in the Peace Palace at The Hague, the International Court of Justice was **25.1** established by the United Nations Charter as a forum for settling international disputes. It is a principal organ of the UN, replacing the Permanent Court of International Justice which had functioned since 1922. It is now one of a number of international courts,[1] but it remains 'the principal judicial organ of the United Nations'.[2] Most of the detailed provisions relating to its functions and powers are to be found in the Statute of the Court which is annexed to the UN Charter and forms an integral part of it.[3] While few diplomats in the course of their careers are likely to appear before the Court as representatives of their governments, the use of the Court to settle disputes, and the impact of the Court's decisions more generally, are significant features of the conduct of international affairs.

---

[1] For other international courts, see Chapter 24, paragraphs 24.34–24.35.

[2] Arts 7.1 and 92 of the Charter.

[3] Art 92. Other provisions regarding the Court are to be found in Chapter XIV of the Charter (Arts 92–6). The website of the Court gives useful information: <http://www.icj-cij.org/>. Further discussion of the Court and its procedures may be found in J G Merrills, *International Dispute Settlement* (5th edn, Cambridge: Cambridge University Press, 2011) chs 6 and 7.

Jurisdiction of the Court

25.2 The Court's role is to decide, in accordance with international law, disputes which are submitted to it by States and to give advisory opinions on questions referred to it by certain United Nations organs and specialized agencies. The first of these two kinds of cases are referred to as contentious cases, the second as advisory proceedings.

Contentious Cases

25.3 Only States may be parties to contentious cases before the Court. Individuals, corporations, and organizations cannot. Although the Court is sometimes referred to as the 'World Court', it is not a supreme court which national courts or individuals can use as a last resort. Nor is it an appeal court for any other international tribunal. The United Nations cannot itself bring a case against a State in its own judicial organ; however, a United Nations organ may initiate advisory proceedings if it has a right to do so.[4]

25.4 A State may be a party to a contentious case only if it is a member of the United Nations, or has become a party to the Statute of the Court, or has accepted its jurisdiction under certain conditions. All members of the United Nations are parties to the Statute by virtue of their UN membership. A State which is not a UN member may become a party to the Statute on conditions determined by the General Assembly upon the recommendation of the Security Council. Before they became UN members, Japan, Liechtenstein, San Marino, Nauru, and Switzerland were all parties to the Statute of the Court, in accordance with conditions (the same in each case) set by General Assembly resolution.[5] At present, however, all parties to the Statute of the Court are members of the United Nations.[6]

25.5 The fact that a State is a party to the Court's Statute does not mean that the Court has jurisdiction to hear any case against it. The Court may hear a case only if the States concerned have *agreed* to accept its jurisdiction. There is no prescribed form in which the consent of a State to the Court's jurisdiction must be expressed, and consent may be given either after a particular dispute has

---

[4] See paragraphs 25.15–25.18.

[5] These conditions were set for the first time in relation to Switzerland in resolution 91(I) (1946) of 11 December 1946.

[6] States which are not even parties to the Statute may appear before the Court upon certain conditions laid down by the Security Council (Art 35.2 of the Statute; and see Security Council resolution 9 (1946)). While there is normally no difficulty in establishing whether a State is a UN member and, accordingly, a party to the Statute, the question had to be decided in cases brought by or against Serbia and Montenegro in relation to the period when the legal position of the former Republic of Yugoslavia vis-à-vis the UN was uncertain; see in particular *Case concerning the Legality of Use of Force (Serbia and Montenegro v Belgium)* Preliminary Objections [2004] ICJ Reports 1307, paras 46–91.

arisen or in advance. The Court has jurisdiction over cases brought to it in one or more of three ways: (i) if the parties have agreed to refer the particular case to the Court, (ii) if the parties have previously agreed in a treaty to refer such disputes to the Court, or (iii) if each party has made a declaration accepting the jurisdiction of the Court as compulsory in the event of a dispute with another State which has made a similar declaration (Article 36.1 and 36.2 of the Statute).

Thus, the first way in which a case may be brought before the Court is by the **25.6** consent of the parties to refer that case. Usually, but not invariably, this consent is given in the form of a written agreement or treaty, known as a 'special agreement' or *compromis*.[7] No particular form of agreement has to be used, so long as the consent is unequivocally given.[8] Consent may be deduced from acts of a State. A State may file an application in the Court and invite another State to consent to the Court's jurisdiction. For example, Djibouti made an application to the Court in 2006 against France alleging that France was in violation of a treaty of mutual cooperation for not assisting with a Djibouti investigation of the murder of a French judge in Djibouti; France, rather surprisingly, sent in a letter of acceptance agreeing to the Court's jurisdiction, and the Court was therefore able to hear the case.[9]

The second way to bring a case before the Court is under a treaty providing for **25.7** the submission of a certain class of disputes to the Court when one of the parties so decides; usually these will be disputes relating to the interpretation or application of that treaty. In each case the jurisdiction of the Court depends upon whether the dispute referred to the Court is or is not within the category covered by the treaty. So, for example, in the case brought by the government of Iran against the US in 1992 seeking reparations for attacks by US naval vessels against three Iranian oil platforms, the US argued that the Iranian claims fell outside the obligations in the 1955 Treaty of Amity, Economic Relations and Consular Rights between the US and Iran, which contained a compromissory clause giving jurisdiction to the Court. The dispute as to jurisdiction was settled, as in all such cases, by the decision of the Court, the Court here finding that the dispute between the two States did concern the interpretation and application of the Treaty and that the Court therefore had jurisdiction under the compromissory clause.[10]

---

[7] See Chapter 24, paragraphs 24.28–24.33. In the *North Sea Continental Shelf* cases, jurisdiction was based on two agreements between Denmark and the FRG and between the Netherlands and the FRG ([1969] ICJ Reports 5–7).

[8] *Corfu Channel case (UK v Albania)* Preliminary Objection [1948] ICJ Reports 27.

[9] *Case concerning certain questions of Mutual Assistance in Criminal Matters (Djibouti v France)* [2008] ICJ Reports 177.

[10] *Oil Platforms (Islamic Republic of Iran v United States of America)*, Preliminary Objection, Judgment [1996] ICJ Reports 803.

25.8 The third way to bring a case before the Court is by use of declarations made under Article 36.2 of the Statute (usually known as the 'Optional Clause'). Under this provision a State may declare that it recognizes as compulsory, without special agreement, the jurisdiction of the Court in a legal dispute. As between two States, both of which have made a declaration, one of them is entitled to institute proceedings before the Court against the other, and the Court will have jurisdiction so long as the subject-matter of the dispute is covered by the declarations and is not excluded by any reservation. For this purpose, the respondent State is entitled to rely upon any reservation made by the applicant State: the Court's jurisdiction depends on reciprocity. Thus in the case of *Whaling in the Antarctic (Australia v Japan)* Japan challenged the jurisdiction of the Court by seeking to rely on the wording of Australia's reservation regarding the exploitation of certain maritime areas. The case had been brought by Australia against Japan and concerned the interpretation of the International Convention for the Regulation of Whaling. The Court found that the substance of the case fell outside Australia's reservation and the ICJ therefore had jurisdiction. (Japan failed also on the merits of the case.)[11]

25.9 The United Kingdom is the only permanent member of the Security Council to have a current declaration under the Optional Clause. Its most recent declaration, made on 30 December 2014, provides an example of some of the kinds of reservations that States make. It reads as follows:

1. The Government of the United Kingdom of Great Britain and Northern Ireland accept as compulsory ipso facto and without special convention, on condition of reciprocity, the jurisdiction of the International Court of Justice, in conformity with paragraph 2 of Article 36 of the Statute of the Court, until such time as notice may be given to terminate the acceptance, over all disputes arising after 1 January 1984, with regard to situations or facts subsequent to the same date, other than:
   (i) any dispute which the United Kingdom has agreed with the other Party or Parties thereto to settle by some other method of peaceful settlement;
   (ii) any dispute with the government of any other country which is or has been a Member of the Commonwealth;
   (iii) any dispute in respect of which any other Party to the dispute has accepted the compulsory jurisdiction of the International Court of Justice only in relation to or for the purpose of the dispute; or where the acceptance of the Court's compulsory jurisdiction on behalf of any other Party to the dispute was deposited or ratified less than twelve months prior to the filing of the application bringing the dispute before the Court;
   (iv) any dispute which is substantially the same as a dispute previously submitted to the Court by the same or another Party.
2. The Government of the United Kingdom also reserve the right at any time, by means of a notification addressed to the Secretary-General of the United

---

[11] *Whaling in the Antarctic (Australia v Japan: New Zealand intervening)*, Judgment [2014] ICJ Reports 226.

Nations, and with effect as from the moment of such notification, either to add to, amend or withdraw any of the foregoing reservations, or any that may hereafter be added.

In the *Aerial Incident* case, Pakistan claimed that India was in breach of inter- **25.10** national law for the shooting down on 10 August 1999 of an unarmed aircraft of the Pakistani navy, resulting in the death of all sixteen on board, who allegedly were on a routine training mission over Pakistani territory. As one of the grounds for the Court's jurisdiction, Pakistan relied on the declarations made by the two States accepting the Court's compulsory jurisdiction under the Optional Clause; India however countered that its declaration excluded disputes with any State 'which is or has been a Member of the Commonwealth of Nations'. Pakistan argued that this reservation lay outside the range of reservations permitted by the Court's Statute and was obsolete. The Court decided that the limitation on India's consent to accept the Court's jurisdiction must prevail, and since Pakistan and India were both members of the Commonwealth, the Optional Clause provided no basis of jurisdiction in this case.[12]

The Court's jurisdiction in contentious cases covers only 'disputes' between **25.11** States. What is a 'dispute' for this purpose? As indicated in Chapter 24, the Court has adopted the definition of the Permanent Court of International Justice: 'A dispute is a disagreement over a point of law or fact, a conflict of legal views or interests between two persons.'[13]

Under Article 94 of the Charter, States are required to comply with the decision **25.12** of the Court in any case to which they are parties. This will usually involve action by only the government of the State concerned, but if the decision in a case requires action to be taken within a country, the State must ensure that its domestic law will allow it to comply with the judgment. An example where a State was not able to comply with a judgment of the Court, despite its government's wish to do so, can be found in the proceedings following the *Avena* case.[14] The Court had determined that the US should review and reconsider the convictions and sentences of some Mexican nationals as a result of US violation of their obligations to allow consular access to prisoners under the

---

[12] *Aerial Incident of 10 August 1999 (Pakistan v India), Jurisdiction of the Court,* Judgment [2000] ICJ Reports 12. Pakistan put forward other bases of jurisdiction for the Court but these were also ruled invalid by the Court, and the case did not proceed to the merits.

[13] The *Mavrommatis* case PCIJ, Series A, No 2 (1924) 11; cited by the ICJ in, for example, *Questions of Interpretation and Application of the 1971 Montreal Convention arising from the Aerial Incident at Lockerbie (Libyan Arab Jamahiriya v United Kingdom), Preliminary Objections,* Judgment [1998] ICJ Reports 9, para 22.

[14] *Avena and Other Mexican Nationals (Mexico v United States of America),* Judgment [2004] ICJ Reports 12.

terms of the Vienna Convention on Consular Relations. Although the US administration sought to comply with this decision, the US Supreme Court concluded that the decisions of the International Court of Justice were not directly enforceable in United States courts and that, in effect, the President's actions to try to give effect to *Avena* were ineffective under United States constitutional law.[15]

25.13　If a party to a case fails to comply with a judgment of the Court, the other party may resort to the Security Council, which may make recommendations or decide upon measures to be taken to give effect to the judgment. Under this provision Nicaragua asked for an emergency meeting of the Council in October 1986 to consider the non-compliance by the US with the judgment of the Court in the *Case of the Military and Paramilitary Activities in and against Nicaragua.* This case concerned the involvement of the US in the activities of the Contras and other actions against Nicaragua. The United States twice vetoed draft Council resolutions which called for 'full and immediate compliance' with the Court's judgment.

25.14　The existence of the International Court of Justice does not of course limit the right of members of the United Nations to settle their disputes by other means. Indeed, Article 33.1 of the Charter lays down the general principle that:

> [t]he parties to any dispute, the continuance of which is likely to endanger the maintenance of international peace and security, shall, first of all, seek a solution by negotiation, enquiry, mediation, conciliation, arbitration, judicial settlement, resort to regional agencies or arrangements, or other peaceful means of their own choice.

Advisory Opinions

25.15　The General Assembly or the Security Council may request the Court to give an advisory opinion on any legal question (Article 96 of the Charter). Other organs of the United Nations and, if they are authorized to do so by the General Assembly, its specialized agencies may also request advisory opinions on legal questions within the scope of their activities. No other body, and no State on its own, can ask for an advisory opinion.

25.16　What is a legal question within the meaning of Article 96? The Court has stated that 'the contingency that there may be factual issues underlying the question posed does not alter its character as a legal question'.[16] Further, the fact that an

---

[15] The story can be found in the judgment of 19 January 2009 in the *Request for Interpretation of the Judgment of 31 March 2004 in the Case concerning Avena and other Mexican Nationals (Mexico v United States of America).*

[16] *Legal Consequences of the Continued Presence of South Africa in Namibia* [1971] ICJ Reports 27.

advisory opinion has been requested on a political issue does not make the question a political rather than a legal one. Indeed, issues surrounding the request and giving of advisory opinions can be intensely political, as can be seen from three recent opinions: *Nuclear Weapons, the Wall in the Occupied Palestinian Territory,* and *Kosovo.*[17]

While the Court is not *obliged* to give an advisory opinion when requested, it **25.17** has never refused to respond if it has jurisdiction. If there is jurisdiction, the Court will decline to meet a request only for compelling reasons[18] and in order to remain faithful to the requirements of its judicial character.[19] In the *Wall* opinion the Court was asked, by resolution of the General Assembly, 'What are the legal consequences arising from the construction of the wall being built by Israel, the occupying Power, in the Occupied Palestinian Territory, including in and around East Jerusalem?' Some participants in the Court's proceedings asked the Court to exercise its discretion and refuse to give an opinion for the following reasons: because the request concerned a contentious matter between Israel and Palestine, in respect of which Israel had not consented to the exercise of that jurisdiction; because it could impede a political, negotiated solution to the Israeli–Palestinian conflict; because the Court could not give an opinion on issues which raised questions of fact that could not be elucidated without hearing all parties to the conflict; because an opinion would lack any useful purpose; and because Palestine, given its responsibility for acts of violence against Israel and its population which the wall is aimed at addressing, could not seek from the Court a remedy for a situation resulting from its own wrongdoing. The Court decided that none of these was a ground for it to decline to issue an advisory opinion and it went on to do so.[20] It should be noted that the opinion had little effect as regards the continuing actions of the government whom it primarily concerned.

As the term makes clear, advisory opinions are only advisory and have no binding force. But they are 'authoritative in the sense that their legal correctness cannot **25.18** be officially or formally questioned, by the organ to which they are rendered, acting in its corporate capacity'.[21] If the Court were to indicate that a certain

---

[17] *Legality of the Threat or Use of Nuclear Weapons*, Advisory Opinion [1996] ICJ Reports 226 (hereafter the *Nuclear Weapons* opinion); *Legal Consequences of the Construction of a Wall in the Occupied Palestinian Territory*, Advisory Opinion [2004] ICJ Reports 136 (hereafter the *Wall* opinion); *Accordance with International Law of The Unilateral Declaration of Independence in Respect of Kosovo* [2010] ICJ Reports 403.

[18] *Judgments of the Administrative Tribunal of the ILO* [1956] ICJ Reports 86.

[19] *Western Sahara*, Advisory Opinion [1975] ICJ Reports 21.

[20] See para 65.

[21] Sir Gerald Fitzmaurice in (1952) 29 *BYIL* 54.

course of action would be definitely illegal or that, of various courses of action proposed only one would be legal, it would be difficult in practice for the organ requesting the opinion not to follow the course advocated by the Court. It is a different matter for States, which are not formally addressed by the opinion. But, since the opinions are given by the principal judicial organ of the United Nations, 'whatever be their formal authority, their persuasive character and substantive authority must be great'.[22] Finally, there is nothing to prevent advisory opinions being given binding force by agreement.[23]

The Judges of the Court

25.19   The Court has fifteen judges, no two of whom may be nationals of the same State. The judges are elected by the General Assembly and the Security Council, voting simultaneously but independently of each other. In order to be elected, a candidate must receive an absolute majority of the votes in both bodies. For voting in the Security Council, the permanent members do not have a veto.

25.20   The judges are elected from candidates in a list of persons nominated by 'the national groups in the Permanent Court of Arbitration' (Article 4 of the Statute). This means that governments of States do not have the right to propose candidates; that is the role of the four jurists in each State who can be called upon to serve as members of an arbitral tribunal under the Hague Conventions of 1899 and 1907.[24] Each group may nominate up to four candidates, not more than two of whom may be of their own nationality.

25.21   The judges must be 'persons of high moral character, who possess the qualifications required in their respective countries for appointment to the highest judicial offices or are jurisconsults of recognized competence in international law' (Article 2 of the Statute). It is the intention that in the Court as a whole there should be representation of the main forms of civilization and of the

---

[22] Ibid, 55.

[23] Thus, section 30 of the General Convention on the Privileges and Immunities of the United Nations 1946 provides as follows: 'If a difference arises between the United Nations on the one hand and a Member on the other hand, a request shall be made for an advisory opinion on any legal question involved in accordance with Article 96 of the Charter and Article 65 of the Statute of the Court. The opinion given by the Court shall be accepted as decisive by the parties.'

[24] For States not represented on the Permanent Court of Arbitration, candidates are nominated by national groups appointed by their governments for this purpose and under the same conditions.

principal legal systems of the world, and as a result, the judges are in practice chosen from the different regional groups of the United Nations as follows: three from Africa, three from Asia, two from Latin America and the Caribbean, five from Western Europe and other States, and two from Eastern Europe. Of these, judges of the nationality of the permanent members of the Security Council have always been included in the Court. Judges are elected for nine-year terms and may be re-elected.[25]

Before taking up their duties, the judges make a solemn declaration that they will exercise their powers impartially and conscientiously. A judge cannot be dismissed unless, in the unanimous opinion of the other judges, he or she can no longer fulfil the required conditions. This has never happened. The judges may not exercise any political or administrative function or engage in any other occupation of a professional nature, nor act as agent, counsel, or advocate in any case, nor participate in cases in which, before their election, they have taken part in any capacity. The judges enjoy diplomatic privileges and immunities when engaged on the business of the Court.[26]   **25.22**

The Court usually sits as a full court, but it can be formed into chambers. Article 26.1 of the Statute allows the Court to create a chamber to deal with certain categories of cases; under this provision the Court set up a Chamber for Environmental Matters in 1993. It was never used, however, since no State ever asked that a case be dealt with by it, and in 2006 the Court decided not to continue holding elections for the chamber. Under Article 26.2 of the Statute, an ad hoc chamber can be formed to deal with a particular case and this has been done in six cases so far, at the request of the parties. The informal practice is to allow the parties to choose the judges who will sit in the chamber. Each of the chambers has so far comprised five members; in three of the cases the chamber was composed of three ICJ judges and two ad hoc judges chosen by the parties.[27]   **25.23**

---

[25] The manner of selection of candidates for the ICJ and for other international courts have been the subject of proposals for reform to improve transparency and the quality of the process; see e.g. R Mackenzie et al., *Selecting International Judges* (Oxford: Oxford University Press, 2010).

[26] In an exchange of letters between the President of the Court and the Dutch Minister of Foreign Affairs on 26 June 1946, it was arranged that members of the Court would, in a general way, enjoy the same privileges, immunities, facilities, and prerogatives as heads of diplomatic missions in The Hague (<http://www.icj-cij.org/documents/?p1=4&p2=5&p3=3>). In The Hague the President of the Court takes precedence over the dean of the Diplomatic Corps.

[27] The six cases were: the *Delimitation of the Maritime Boundary in the Gulf of Maine Area* between Canada and the United States, the case concerning the *Frontier Dispute* between Burkina Faso and the Republic of Mali, the case concerning *Elettronica Sicula SpA (ELSI)* between the United States of America and Italy, the case concerning the *Land, Island and Maritime Frontier Dispute* between El Salvador and Honduras, the *Frontier Dispute (Benin/Niger)* case, and the *Application for Revision of*

Applicable Law

25.24 Article 38, which is one of the most important articles in the whole Statute, states:

> 1. The Court, whose function it is to decide in accordance with international law such disputes as are submitted to it, shall apply:
>   (a) international conventions, whether general or particular, establishing rules expressly recognized by the contesting States;
>   (b) international custom as evidence of a general practice accepted as law;
>   (c) the general principles of law recognized by civilized nations;
>   (d) subject to the provisions of Article 59, judicial decisions and the teachings of the most highly qualified publicists of the various nations, as subsidiary means for the determination of rules of law.
> 2. This shall not prejudice the power of the Court to decide a case ex aequo et bono, if the parties agree thereto.

25.25 The sources of law mentioned in subparagraphs (a), (b), and (c) of paragraph 1 above are now generally regarded as the sources of international law which *any* international tribunal should apply in the absence of an express direction to the contrary. The Court may also decide a case *ex aequo et bono* (thus without limiting itself to existing rules of international law) if the parties agree; it has not done so yet.

25.26 Since a decision of the Court has no binding force except between the parties and in respect of that particular case, the Court is, in strict law, not bound even by its own precedents, let alone by the decisions of other international tribunals. In practice, however, the Court attaches great weight to previous decisions, not only its own and those of the Permanent Court of International Justice, but also on occasions those of arbitral tribunals of high standing.

Procedure before the Court

25.27 Contentious cases are begun by filing with the Court either an application, or the *compromis* or special agreement, where one exists. The application is signed by the agent or some other duly authorized person. As agent it is usual to appoint a legal adviser to the foreign ministry or a diplomatic representative in The Hague. The agent, who acts as the link between the Court and the applicant State, is responsible generally and at all stages for the handling of the case. In

---

the Judgment of 11 September 1992 in the *Case concerning the Land, Island and Maritime Frontier Dispute (El Salvador/Honduras: Nicaragua intervening) (El Salvador v Honduras)*. The last three comprised three members of the Court and two judges ad hoc chosen by the parties.

drawing up pleadings and presenting argument orally the agent is generally assisted by Counsel, including in some cases law officers, and international law academics. An application must identify the parties, the basis of the Court's jurisdiction, the nature of the dispute, and the precise nature of the claim. It must summarize the main facts and grounds on which the claim is based. These are developed in detail in the Memorial, to which documentary evidence is attached.[28]

The official languages of the Court are French and English, although there is nothing to prevent a party using another language provided it arranges for a translation to be made into one or other of the official languages. The procedure consists of two parts: written and oral, and the oral proceedings may include the hearing of the evidence of witnesses. The hearing is public, unless the Court decides otherwise, or unless the parties demand that the public are not admitted. **25.28**

Sometimes a State has chosen not to appear before the Court. Nevertheless, the Court will decide on its jurisdiction and on the merits of the case. For example, Iran did not appear in a case brought to the Court by the US after some of its embassy staff had been taken hostage and its diplomatic premises taken over.[29] The Court proceeded to decide the case, establishing the facts by reference to material provided by the US and from public sources. **25.29**

If a case is brought before the Court by the application of one party alone, the other party may object to the jurisdiction of the Court or to the admissibility of the case, provided that is done before the expiry of the time-limit fixed for the delivery of the first pleading. This will cause the proceedings on the merits to be suspended while the Court hears the objection. It is for the Court itself to judge whether the objection is valid. Three possibilities are open to the Court: to uphold the objection, to overrule it, or to join it to the merits of the case to be heard at the same time.[30] **25.30**

Objections to jurisdiction have already been discussed. Admissibility is a concept separate from that of jurisdiction and goes to the nature of a case. If, for example, the applicant's claim is found to concern a dispute which has disappeared or if a case is found to be moot, academic, or devoid of object and purpose, then the Court will declare the case inadmissible and decline to **25.31**

---

[28] Rule 35 of the Rules of Court.

[29] *Case concerning United States Diplomatic and Consular Staff in Tehran*, Judgment [1980] ICJ Reports 3; see Chapter 13, paragraph 13.16 for further details of the case.

[30] The rules governing preliminary objections which are usually, though not necessarily, objections to the jurisdiction are contained in Article 67 of the Rules of Court.

adjudicate upon its merits.[31] The reason is to safeguard the judicial function of the Court. A case can become moot after the filing of the application, for example as a result of a change of practice or the giving of undertakings on the part of the respondent.[32]

25.32 The deliberations of the Court take place in private and remain secret. All questions are to be decided by a majority of the judges present, and in the event of an equality of votes, the President or the judge who acts in his place has a casting vote. The judgment states the reasons on which it is based and any judge may deliver a separate opinion, which may be either a 'dissenting opinion', or an 'individual opinion' agreeing with the conclusions of the judgment, though not necessarily with the reasons on which it is based. The judgment is final and without appeal. The Court may, however, be asked to interpret it if a dispute arises as to its meaning or scope[33] or even to revise it in the event of a new decisive fact being discovered.

25.33 A State which considers that it has an interest of a legal nature which may be affected by the decision in the case may ask the Court to be permitted to intervene. Such requests are rare. However, third parties have an automatic right to intervene whenever the Court has to decide on the interpretation of a treaty to which they are party. If they exercise this right, they are bound by the judgment. Usually each party has to bear its own costs; having regard to the fees charged by counsel and the expenses necessary in obtaining evidence, those costs can be substantial. For States to whom the cost of taking a dispute to the Court would be prohibitive, a trust fund has been created to provide financial assistance in certain circumstances. Funds are provided only in cases where the jurisdiction of the Court is not in doubt.[34] The costs of the Court itself are met not by the parties (as is the case with arbitrations) but from the UN budget.

25.34 If the Court already includes judges of the nationality of both the parties, these judges retain their right to sit in the case. If the Court includes a judge of the nationality of one of the parties only, the other party has the right to choose a judge for that particular case, who will usually, but not always, be of that party's nationality. If the Court does not include a judge of the nationality of either of the parties, both parties have the right to choose a judge for the case.

---

[31] *Northern Cameroons* case [1963] ICJ Reports 15.

[32] *Nuclear Tests* cases *(Australia v France)* and *(New Zealand v France)* [1974] ICJ Reports 253 and 457.

[33] As in the *Request for Interpretation of the Judgment of 31 March 2004 in the Case concerning Avena and other Mexican Nationals (Mexico v United States of America)* [2009] ICJ Reports 3.

[34] Information about the trust fund may be found on <http://www.un.org/law/trustfund/trust-fund.htm>.

The procedure for applications for advisory opinions is a little different. The **25**.35
Court may hold written and oral proceedings. States and international organizations will be asked to give information on the question before the Court,
in particular the States Members of the organization which has requested
the opinion. Those States are not in the same position as parties to contentious
proceedings. Any State not consulted by the Court may ask to take part.
Participants may submit written statements, and States are then usually invited
to present oral statements at public hearings. Palestine was invited to (and did)
participate in the proceedings relating to the *Wall* opinion and the 'Provisional
Institutions of Self-Government of Kosovo' were invited to (and did) participate
in the proceedings for the advisory opinion which concerned the declaration of
independence.[35]

Provisional Measures

The Court may order provisional or interim measures 'which ought to be taken **25**.36
to preserve the respective rights of either party' (Article 41 of the Statute).[36] In
some cases, the Court has ordered both parties to refrain from taking any action
'which might aggravate or extend the dispute...or prejudice   rights...in respect
of the carrying out of whatever decision the Court may render in the case'.[37] If
the rights are such that any breach of them eventually found could be repaired
(for example, by the payment of compensation), or if the parties have already
accepted obligations to refrain from actions which would aggravate the dispute
(for example, through the Security Council), the Court will not order provisional
measures.[38]

---

[35] *Accordance with International Law of the Unilateral Declaration of Independence by the Provisional
Institutions of Self-Government of Kosovo*, Advisory Opinion [2010] ICJ Reports 403. On 22 July
2010 the ICJ, having held unanimously that it had jurisdiction, decided by 9 votes to 5 that it would
comply with the request to give an opinion. It concluded that it was not required by the request to
take a position on whether international law conferred a positive entitlement on Kosovo unilaterally
to declare its independence; accordingly, by 10 votes to 4 the Court confined its advisory opinion to
stating that the declaration of independence made by such institutions did not constitute a breach
of international law.

[36] Further information about provisional measures can be found in S Rosenne, *Provisional
Measures in International Law: The International Court of Justice and the International Tribunal for the
Law of the Sea* (Oxford: Oxford University Press, 2005).

[37] *Nuclear Tests* cases [1973] ICJ Reports 93 and 135, at 106 and 142 respectively). Similar orders
are frequently made.

[38] *Aegean Sea Continental Shelf* case (*Greece v Turkey*) Interim Protection, Order, [1976] ICJ
Reports 3. Nor will interim measures be ordered in cases where the need for such measures is not
urgent: *Interhandel* case (*Switzerland v US*) [1957] ICJ Reports 105 and 112; and *Pakistani Prisoners
of War* case (*Pakistan v India*) [1973] ICJ Reports 330.

25.37   Under Article 66 of the Rules of Court, requests for such measures will be treated as a matter of urgency; if the Court is not sitting, the judges will be convened by the President forthwith. The Court has power to indicate provisional measures where it *prima facie* has jurisdiction; where there is no basis on which jurisdiction can be founded, it will not issue such measures, as in the *Case concerning Legality of Use of Force (Yugoslavia v Belgium)*, one of the cases brought by the Federal Republic of Yugoslavia against NATO States in relation to the bombing of the FRY in 1999.[39] The Court is entitled to indicate measures other than those proposed in the request and even to indicate measures *proprio motu* (i.e. without any request having been made).

25.38   It was once a controversial question whether the measures indicated by the Court are legally binding or not. The words 'indicate' and 'suggested' in Article 41 may give the impression that the measures are not intended to be binding, but the Court has decided that provisional measures do have a binding effect. In a case brought by Germany against the US in relation to the rights under the Vienna Convention on Consular Relations of two German brothers sentenced to death in US courts, the Court ordered that the US should take 'all measures at its disposal' to ensure that the remaining brother was not executed prior to the Court's judgment in the case. The US government transmitted the order to the Governor of Arizona, who did not give effect to it and the German national was executed. The Court found that the US had failed to take the measures at its disposal to prevent the execution before the Court had disposed of the case and the US was accordingly in breach of its obligation under the order for provisional measures.[40]

---

[39] *Legality of Use of Force (Yugoslavia v Belgium)*, Provisional Measures, Order of 2 June 1999 [1999] ICJ Reports 124.

[40] *LaGrand (Germany v United States of America)*, Judgment [2001] ICJ Reports 466, paras 98–109; the Court's reasoning drew on the French text of the Statute and its object and purpose.

26

PROSECUTIONS

The International Criminal Court and other Tribunals

Elizabeth Wilmshurst

When the Nuremberg trial ended, it was thought that it might be a precedent **26.1** for international trials in other contexts. Judge Robert Jackson, one of the Nuremberg prosecutors, said in his opening speech for the prosecution that 'while this law is first applied against German aggressors, the law includes, and if it is to serve a useful purpose it must condemn, aggression by any other nations, including those which sit here now in judgment'.[1] Cold War divisions and other factors combined to make international agreement on an early successor to Nuremberg impossible. No new international criminal courts were established

---

[1] *Trial of Major War Criminals, Nuremberg* (London, 1946).

until the 1990s, when the Security Council set up the ad hoc Tribunals for the former Yugoslavia and for Rwanda. The relative success of the creation of these two bodies contributed to the impetus for the establishment of the International Criminal Court (ICC), a permanent institution, in 1998. Other courts with international elements have since been created. All these courts and tribunals share the characteristic that they have jurisdiction over individuals, not States, and their purpose is to investigate and prosecute for various international crimes.

26.2 Of these courts and tribunals, the ICC is the only one with a substantial continuing caseload and the only permanent international criminal court; the work of the two ad hoc Tribunals is coming to an end. This chapter therefore begins with discussion of the ICC, although it is not first in time, and then addresses more briefly the residual mechanism set up to deal with the remaining work of the two ad hoc Tribunals and finally, even more briefly, other courts with international elements.

26.3 The diplomat cannot leave these institutions to the lawyers. The impact of the courts and tribunals and of the body of international criminal law which they apply is felt in many areas. Negotiations for resolving a conflict can no longer ignore questions of responsibility for atrocities committed in the course of the conflict. Proposals for post-conflict reconstruction will need to deal with such questions as whether alleged criminals should be tried within their own countries or by an international court. If the choice is for national trials, the national judicial systems may need to be supported by the international community. The tension between peace and justice may have to be addressed: with the new international institutions has come a widespread acceptance that victims of atrocities demand retribution, but at the same time the possibility of international trials for leaders may make peace negotiations with them more difficult.

26.4 Government officials will also need to be aware of the obligations their governments must respect when they are faced with requests and orders from the international courts for assistance and cooperation. These requests may ask for the provision of evidence, assistance with investigations, and the transfer of suspects to the court concerned. These matters are dealt with at paragraphs 26.35 to 26.38.

26.5 Finally, for all persons who are engaged in a conflict themselves, in whatever capacity, the existence of the ICC, with its wide jurisdiction, must be taken into account. The creation of the Court emphasizes the importance of complying with international law on matters such as the conduct of hostilities and the treatment of civilians. If war crimes are committed, those responsible for participating in or ordering them may be vulnerable to international prosecution if their national courts cannot or will not undertake proceedings themselves.

The International Criminal Court (ICC)

The idea of a permanent international criminal court[2] had been current long **26.6** before the Nuremberg trial,[3] but nothing came of it until the government of Trinidad and Tobago provided the impetus in 1989. Wanting to secure international prosecutions for drugs offences which were proving difficult to deal with on a national basis, the government of Trinidad and Tobago proposed that the creation of a permanent international criminal court be put back on the agenda of the United Nations. The government succeeded in their objective of establishing a new court—but the Court that was finally agreed upon does not have any jurisdiction over drugs offences.

The negotiations for the treaty which was to set up the new permanent court **26.7** began at the United Nations in New York, and culminated in a five-week conference in Rome; the Statute for the International Criminal Court was adopted there on 17 July 1998. At the time of writing, there are 124 States Parties to the Statute. Whether or not a State is a party is relevant as to whether that State will have the obligation to cooperate with the Court, and as to the extent of the Court's jurisdiction, as will be seen later.

Jurisdiction

The ICC has jurisdiction over genocide, crimes against humanity, war crimes, **26.8** and aggression—but the crime of aggression cannot be tried until the amendments to the Statute agreed at the Review Conference in June 2010 have entered into force under the prescribed conditions.[4] The ICC Statute spells out in some detail the 'elements' of the crimes which it can try; these follow by and large the definitions of the crimes under existing international law, with some changes. In brief, genocide is defined, as in the Genocide Convention 1948, as:

any of the following acts committed with intent to destroy, in whole or in part, a national, ethnical, racial or religious group, as such:

---

[2] For further reading see W Schabas, *An Introduction to the International Criminal Court* (4th edn, Cambridge: Cambridge University Press, 2011).

[3] The first formal proposal for such a court was probably that of Gustav Moynier, one of the founders of the International Committee of the Red Cross; see C K Hall, 'The First Proposal for a Permanent International Criminal Court' (1998) 322 *International Review of the Red Cross* 57.

[4] The amendments, including the conditions for entry into force, are to be found at <https://treaties.un.org/doc/Publication/CN/2010/CN.651.2010-Eng.pdf>.

    (a) killing members of the group;

    (b) causing serious bodily or mental harm to members of the group;

    (c) deliberately inflicting on the group conditions of life calculated to bring about its physical destruction in whole or in part;

    (d) imposing measures intended to prevent births within the group;

    (e) forcibly transferring children of the group to another group.[5]

'Crimes against humanity' are defined as a list of acts such as murder, deportation, torture, rape, persecution of a group, and enforced disappearance, 'when committed as part of a widespread or systematic attack directed against any civilian population, with knowledge of the attack'.[6] There is a long list of war crimes, loosely drawn from the Geneva Conventions and the two Protocols, divided into crimes committed in international conflict and those committed in non-international conflict.[7] Aggression is committed by 'the planning, preparation, initiation or execution, by a person in a position effectively to exercise control over or to direct the political or military action of a State, of an act of aggression which, by its character, gravity and scale, constitutes a manifest violation of the Charter of the United Nations'.

26.9   The Court cannot try a crime unless it has jurisdiction over the suspects. It may try genocide, crimes against humanity and war crimes only (i) if the State on whose territory the crime was committed, or the State of which the suspect is a national, is a party to the Statute or has formally accepted the jurisdiction of the Court in relation to the particular crime; *or* (ii) where a situation has been referred to the Court by the Security Council under Chapter VII of the UN Charter.[8] For example, Sudan was not a party to the ICC Statute when the Security Council referred the situation in Darfur to the Court in 2005;[9] the Court now has jurisdiction over Sudanese nationals and any others who have

---

    [5] Art 6 of the ICC Statute.

    [6] Art 7 of the Statute. The full list of acts is '(a) murder; (b) extermination; (c) enslavement; (d) deportation or forcible transfer of population; (e) imprisonment or other severe deprivation of physical liberty in violation of fundamental rules of international law; (f) torture; (g) rape, sexual slavery, enforced prostitution, forced pregnancy, enforced sterilization, or any other form of sexual violence of comparable gravity; (h) persecution against any identifiable group or collectivity on political, racial, national, ethnic, cultural, religious, gender as defined in paragraph 3, or other grounds that are universally recognized as impermissible under international law, in connection with any act referred to in this paragraph or any crime within the jurisdiction of the Court; (i) enforced disappearance of persons; (j) the crime of apartheid; (k) other inhumane acts of a similar character intentionally causing great suffering, or serious injury to body or to mental or physical health.'

    [7] Art 8 of the Statute, amended to insert an additional two crimes in non-international armed conflict at the Review Conference in 2010.

    [8] Arts 12 and 13 of the Statute.

    [9] By resolution 1593 (2005).

committed crimes in Darfur, but this would not have been so if the Council had not referred the situation to the Court. The conditions for jurisdiction over the crime of aggression are slightly different and depend in part on whether a State concerned has accepted the 2010 amendments.[10]

The ICC may try only crimes committed after 1 July 2002, the date on which   **26.10**
the Statute entered into force (or after 27 June 2017 for aggression). There is no jurisdiction for crimes a long way back in history. If a State becomes party to the Statute later than that date, the relevant date for the Court's jurisdiction will be the date of entry into force of the Statute for that State, but a State may also voluntarily accept the jurisdiction of the Court for periods before that date (but after 1 July 2002). (Again the rules for aggression differ.)

Complementarity

It is not enough that the ICC has jurisdiction over a crime and over the suspect.   **26.11**
It will not be able to try the case (because the case will be 'inadmissible') if national authorities are investigating or prosecuting, or have done so—unless national authorities have shown themselves unable or unwilling 'genuinely' to investigate or try the case. Inability and unwillingness have been defined in the ICC Statute as follows:

Article 17:
2. In order to determine unwillingness in a particular case, the Court shall consider, having regard to the principles of due process recognized by international law, whether one or more of the following exist, as applicable:
   (a) The proceedings were or are being undertaken or the national decision was made for the purpose of shielding the person concerned from criminal responsibility for crimes within the jurisdiction of the Court...;
   (b) There has been an unjustified delay in the proceedings which in the circumstances is inconsistent with an intent to bring the person concerned to justice;
   (c) The proceedings were not or are not being conducted independently or impartially, and they were or are being conducted in a manner which, in the circumstances, is inconsistent with an intent to bring the person concerned to justice.
3. In order to determine inability in a particular case, the Court shall consider whether, due to a total or substantial collapse or unavailability of its national judicial system, the State is unable to obtain the accused or the necessary evidence and testimony or otherwise unable to carry out its proceedings.

---

[10] For the conditions as to jurisdiction, see the wording of the amendments at <https://www.icc-cpi.int/iccdocs/asp_docs/RC2010/AMENDMENTS/CN.651.2010-ENG-CoA.pdf>.

26.12　The relationship of the ICC with national authorities is termed 'complementarity' and is a major feature of the Court. It means that the ICC does not have primacy over national jurisdictions; rather the reverse. It is a court of last resort. States themselves have the responsibility to prosecute offenders if they are able properly to do so. Indeed, the former Prosecutor in an oft-quoted statement said:

> The effectiveness of the International Criminal Court should not be measured by the number of cases that reach the Court. On the contrary, the absence of trials by the ICC, as a consequence of the effective functioning of national systems, would be a major success.[11]

While this is an exaggeration, it makes the point nicely.

Initiating and Suspending Proceedings

26.13　Unlike national criminal systems which allow the launching of a prosecution after an investigation by police or prosecutors, the ICC has special provisions regarding the institution of its proceedings. A 'situation' may be referred to the Court by a State Party to the Statute, or by the Security Council. The Prosecutor then decides whether to open an investigation of the situation and to apply to the Pre-Trial Chamber for arrest warrants. Alternatively, the Prosecutor may begin an investigation of a situation without a referral, if the Pre-Trial Chamber authorizes it.

26.14　Two examples of referrals of situations to the Court by States are those in Uganda and the Democratic Republic of Congo (DRC). The Lord's Resistance Army (LRA) had been engaged in murder, the brutalization of children, rape, and slavery for almost two decades when the government of Uganda referred the situation to the ICC. The Court issued arrest warrants for Joseph Kony and his fellow leaders for crimes against humanity and war crimes. Then the government of the DRC, where millions of civilians had been killed during the years of civil war and internationally sponsored conflicts, referred that situation to the Court. From the DRC referral came the first case to be tried by the Court— that of Thomas Lubanga Dyilo, charged with the war crime of enlisting child soldiers. The Security Council has referred two situations to the Court—that in Darfur, leading to arrest warrants being issued against persons including the President of Sudan, and that in Libya. The Prosecutor has exercised the initiative of opening an investigation without referral by a State or the Security Council in cases arising from the post-election violence in Kenya of 2007–8, in Côte

---

[11] 'Paper on some policy issues before the Office of the Prosecutor', September 2003, on the website of the ICC: <https://www.icc-cpi.int/nr/rdonlyres/1fa7c4c6-de5f-42b7-8b25-60aa962ed8b6/143594/030905_policy_paper.pdf>.

d'Ivoire in the context of post-electoral violence between 2010 and 2011, and in Georgia in the context of the armed conflict of August 2008. In each case authorization for the investigation was required from the Pre-Trial Chamber.

The Security Council has another role. The ICC must suspend any proceedings **26.15** for a year if the Council decides under Chapter VII of the Charter to request it to do so; the Council may renew its request year by year. This unusual provision is to be found in Article 16, which was intended to ensure that ICC proceedings would not prejudice the interests of international peace and security.

The Court and its Procedures

Of the various chambers among which the judges are divided (Pre-Trial, Trial, **26.16** and Appeals Chambers) the Pre-Trials Division is a compromise between the common law prosecutorial system and the French system of *juges d'instruction*. The judges of the Court must have competence either in criminal law or in relevant areas of international law. States, in electing the judges, must take into account the need for representation of the principal legal systems of the world, equitable geographical representation and, for the first time in criteria for elections to an international tribunal, the need for a fair representation of female and male judges. Complex voting rules have been adopted with these criteria in mind (except for the representation of the world's legal systems—an exclusion justified on the basis that this criterion should largely be met if geographical representation is equitable). Unfortunately, the ICC suffers from the standard international practice for elections, whereby votes are sometimes 'traded' among States for reasons other than the personal and professional qualities and attributes of the judges and this means that the composition of the Court has not always been constituted entirely of the best judges available.

The ICC has innovative procedures allowing victims to participate in its **26.17** proceedings at various stages. The judges give directions as to the timing and manner of participation which is generally by means of legal representatives. The Court may make orders for reparations to be paid to victims. The Trust Fund for Victims has been established to implement awards for reparations against a convicted person and to use other resources from voluntary contributions—to provide victims under Court jurisdiction with physical rehabilitation, psychological rehabilitation, and material support.

Challenges to the ICC

There is not universal support for the Court. Some of the States that are not **26.18** parties to the Court's Statute have expressed concerns that their nationals may be tried by the Court without their consent. The United States at one time worked actively to undermine the Court,[12] but in 2005 supported the Court's proceedings with regard to Darfur, abstaining rather than exercising a veto on the resolution referring the situation to the Court, and has since given practical assistance to the Court. Other governmental opposition has come from among the members of the African Union; resolutions from the African Union have encouraged their member States not to cooperate with the Court.[13] Their concern is not so much about jurisdiction being taken over their nationals generally but about jurisdiction over their Heads of State and other government leaders. Concern has also been expressed that almost all the situations being investigated by the ICC are in Africa.[14] The response is that many of the situations in question were referred by the governments themselves, and that for victims it is not a cause of concern but of thankfulness that the crimes for which they suffered are being investigated.

26.19 The ICC faces unique problems. The crimes subject to its jurisdiction will in most cases be ones committed in situations of ongoing conflict where investigations on the ground are risky or impossible. Effective witness protection schemes are necessary if evidence is to be collected. The initiation of ICC investigations with the threat of arrest warrants to follow should have a deterrent effect on the commission of further crimes but it is not always apparent that there is such an effect. There may also be allegations, as with northern Uganda and the LRA, that peace negotiations will be prejudiced by the claims of retributive justice. These allegations may not be justified, but they complicate the task of the Court. The warrants against the President of Sudan and against Kenyan leaders led to (unmet) demands from the African Union that the

---

[12] In 2002, the US vetoed the renewal by the Security Council of a peacekeeping operation in Bosnia and Herzegovina and insisted that US nationals who were engaged in the operation be exempted from ICC jurisdiction, leading to the adoption of resolution 1422 (2002), which requested the ICC, in accordance with Article 16 of its Statute, to defer any exercise of its jurisdiction for 12 months 'if a case arises involving current or former officials or personnel from a contributing State not a party to the Rome Statute over acts or omissions relating to a United Nations established or authorised operation'. The resolution was renewed for 12 months the next year in a similarly worded resolution, 1487 (2003). The resolutions have had no impact in practice, since no ICC proceedings were envisaged in the relevant periods. Two later Council resolutions had provisions giving States not parties to the ICC Statute sole jurisdiction over their personnel in relation to forces in Liberia and in Darfur, thus excluding the jurisdiction of the Court (resolutions 1497 (2003) para 7 and 1593 (2005) para 6). The US also entered into bilateral agreements with a number of States, to bar US personnel from ever being transferred to the Court. Acceptance of these agreements was forced upon some States by threats to remove US military and other aid, threats that were backed by US legislation, the American Service-members' Protection Act.

[13] AU Assembly decision of October 2013, 'Decision on Africa's Relationship with the International Criminal Court (ICC)', Ext/Assembly/AU/Dec.1) is one of many.

[14] At the time of writing, nine of the ten situations (two in Central African Republic) under investigation and/or trial are from Africa.

Security Council request the suspension of Court proceedings under Article 16 of the Statute. Because it does not have the enforcement mechanisms enjoyed by any national judicial system, the Court has to rely on the cooperation of States to enforce its orders and to cooperate with investigations and the arrest and surrender of suspects. This cooperation is not always available,[15] particularly where the State concerned does not support the proceedings of the Court, and some of the persons charged by the Court are still at liberty.

The International Residual Mechanism for Criminal Tribunals (MICT)

This strangely worded name is in fact that of a court, set up to complete the **26**.20 remaining work of the International Criminal Tribunal for the former Yugoslavia and the International Criminal Tribunal for Rwanda, the two ad hoc Tribunals which were established by the Security Council in 1993 and 1994 respectively.

International Criminal Tribunal for the Former Yugoslavia

The armed conflicts which led to the dissolution of Yugoslavia were accompanied **26**.21 by large-scale atrocities. The UN Secretary-General consulted member States about the creation of a tribunal to try the crimes concerned and the result was a recommendation from the Secretary-General that the Security Council create a tribunal by Council resolution, the alternative course of establishing a tribunal by intergovernmental treaty having been rejected as taking too much time. The 'International Tribunal for the Prosecution of Persons Responsible for Serious Violations of International Humanitarian Law Committed in the Territory of the Former Yugoslavia since 1991' was established by Council resolution 827 (1993); the Tribunal is more briefly known as the International Criminal Tribunal for the Former Yugoslavia, or more briefly still as ICTY.

Based in The Hague, the powers, composition, and jurisdiction of the Tribunal **26**.22 were set out in a Statute prepared by the UN Secretariat.[16] It was given jurisdiction over certain war crimes, crimes against humanity, and genocide, committed after 1 January 1991 in those countries which are within the territory of the former Yugoslavia. Its jurisdiction was not given an end limit in time, so that

---

[15] Particularly egregious examples of non-cooperation with the Court include the action of the South African government in June 2015 allowing President Bashir of Sudan, under warrant of arrest from the ICC, to leave South Africa although the South African courts had ordered that he be prevented from leaving the country until the issue had been adjudicated by the (South African) courts.

[16] The Statute of ICTY may be found on the Tribunal's website: <http://www.un.org/icty/>.

the later conflicts in Macedonia and the NATO military intervention in 1999 relating to Kosovo were also included. As regards the latter, the Prosecutor considered opening an investigation into crimes alleged to have been committed by NATO States, but she decided after inquiry that no formal investigation was justified, thus coming under criticism from different quarters for both decisions—to order an inquiry at all and not to open an investigation.

26.23 ICTY was given primacy over national courts. Cases arising from some of the worst incidents in the different conflicts resulting from the dissolution of the former Yugoslavia, and the conflict in Kosovo, have been brought before the Tribunal. For example, the Srebrenica massacre of some 8,000 Muslim men and boys gave rise to ICTY indictments and trials for genocide. The most high-profile trial of the Tribunal was that of Milošević, formerly President of Serbia and later of the rump Yugoslavia, the FRY, which lasted for four years and one month and was far from complete when it ended in his death in detention. The trial of Radovan Karadžić, formerly President of the Republika Srpska and one of the last to be tried by the Tribunal, ended with convictions for the genocide in Srebrenica and crimes against humanity.

26.24 The Tribunal was not set up as a permanent body and at the time of writing its proceedings are being drawn to a close. A few proceedings are ongoing. It has been responsible for the substantial development of international criminal law and the creation of a large body of case law which is used by other international courts and tribunals.

The International Criminal Tribunal for Rwanda

26.25 The genocide which took place in Rwanda in 1994, causing the deaths of some 800,000 Tutsis and moderate Hutus, produced waves of horror and also of guilt for the international failure to prevent the commission of the atrocities. It was felt that if a tribunal was appropriate in Europe, the same model should be used for Africa. The Security Council accordingly set up first a fact-finding Commission and later the International Criminal Tribunal for Rwanda. Like ICTY, the Rwanda Tribunal (or ICTR) was established by a resolution adopted under Chapter VII of the UN Charter,[17] thus giving binding legal force to its orders.

26.26 The Tribunal was based in Arusha, Tanzania but shared the Appeals Chamber of ICTY, which remained in The Hague. It had jurisdiction over genocide, war crimes, and crimes against humanity, like ICTY, though the definitions of the

---

[17] Resolution 955 (1994).

last two crimes had differed slightly from those in the ICTY Statute. The Tribunal affirmed that genocide had indeed been committed in Rwanda. The first conviction for genocide was of Mayor Jean-Paul Akayesu, followed two days later by the conviction, after a guilty plea, of Jean Kambanda, the former prime minister of Rwanda. These trials were historic, marking the first convictions for genocide by an international court.

The Tribunal closed its doors in December 2015 after 21 years of judicial work. **26.27** It had convicted and sentenced sixty-one persons and referred ten to national courts for trial. The main contribution of the Tribunal to international criminal law has been in its case law on genocide. The crime is notoriously difficult to prosecute due to the narrow definition in the 1948 Genocide Convention. It was the first international tribunal to recognize rape as a means of perpetrating genocide.

The MICT

The Residual Mechanism[18] was established to continue the jurisdiction, rights **26.28** and obligations, and essential functions of the ICTY and the ICTR after the completion of their respective mandates.[19] As well as tracking and trying the three persons indicted by ICTR who have evaded capture (ICTY has no outstanding fugitives), and completing appeals from convicted persons, it has continuing functions to oversee the enforcement of sentences, to monitor the protection of victims and witnesses, and to preserve the archives of the two Tribunals.

The Mechanism has two branches: one in Arusha and one in The Hague. It is **26.29** intended to be a lean and efficient court: it has a roster of judges to undertake work as necessary at the request of the President, and a full-time President, Prosecutor, and Registrar, common to both its branches.

Other Courts with International Elements

The focus on justice for the victims of conflict-driven crimes has given rise to **26.30** different kinds of international assistance in the provision of courts with international elements. There is not a single model for such courts.[20]

---

[18] For further information, see the website: <http://www.unmict.org/>.
[19] It was established by UN Security Council resolution 1966 (2010) of 22 December 2010.
[20] For a fuller overview see chapter 9 of R Cryer et al., *An Introduction to International Criminal Law and Procedure* (3rd edn, Cambridge: Cambridge University Press, 2011).

The Special Court for Sierra Leone

26.31   The Special Court for Sierra Leone was created in 2002 by treaty between the UN and Sierra Leone, following years of violent civil war. The UN Secretary-General appointed the international judges to the Court; they were in the majority, while the minority are appointed by the government of Sierra Leone. The Court had jurisdiction to prosecute persons 'who bear the greatest responsibility' for crimes against humanity, certain war crimes, and specified breaches of domestic law, committed in the territory of the country since 30 November 1996. The most high-profile accused was Charles Taylor, the former President of Liberia, who was convicted, sentenced to 50 years' imprisonment, and sent to the UK to serve his sentence. The Court has now ended its work and is replaced by the Residual Special Court, established pursuant to another agreement between the UN and Sierra Leone,[21] with the mandate of overseeing witness protection, supervising prison sentences, and managing the Court's archives. Like other courts with international elements, the Special Court had financial difficulties, having to rely on voluntary funding. This is a factor which should give pause to the creation of other such courts in the future.

Extraordinary Chambers in the Courts of Cambodia

26.32   The slaughter of hundreds of thousands of victims during the period of the Khmer Rouge regime in Cambodia led eventually to the creation of the so-called 'extraordinary chambers' of Cambodia, though more than two decades after the event. Although supported by a treaty between the UN and the government, the chambers form part of the domestic system. National judges are in the majority. Crimes which can be tried by the chambers include genocide as defined in the 1948 Genocide Convention, crimes against humanity, and some war crimes. The jurisdiction of the chambers is limited to the relevant period: 17 April 1975 to 6 January 1979. The death of Pol Pot means that the one person who was almost certainly most responsible for the crimes will not be brought to justice.

Special Tribunal for Lebanon

26.33   Another treaty-based court is the Special Tribunal for Lebanon, set up to try those responsible for the assassination of Rafik Hariri, the former prime minister of Lebanon, and for other connected terrorist incidents. When a political impasse

---

[21] Dated 11 August 2010. For this and the other documents of the Residual Court and the former court see <http://www.rscsl.org/>.

led to the impossibility of bringing the treaty into force under Lebanese constitutional procedures, the Security Council adopted a resolution (1757(2007)) under Chapter VII of the Charter to bring it into force. The Tribunal has its seat outside Lebanon and the international judges are in the majority. Although the Tribunal was set up by an international process, it is to apply only domestic law and its jurisdiction is over terrorist acts and other crimes under Lebanese law. No other State but Lebanon is under an obligation to cooperate with the Tribunal. The Tribunal has charged five men, who are being tried in their absence for the assassination of Hariri and has also issued charges for contempt and obstruction of justice against journalists, stemming from the publishing of information on the identities of confidential tribunal witnesses.

Other Courts with International Elements

Other courts with international elements and with jurisdiction over international crimes have included the 'Regulation 64 Panels' in Kosovo set up by the United Nations mission in Kosovo, now replaced; the 'Serious Crimes Panels' set up by the UN Transitional Administration in East Timor, but now disbanded; and the War Crimes Chamber in Bosnia and Herzegovina. Two courts which are entirely national but were given international support in their establishment are the Iraqi Higher Tribunal and the War Crimes Chamber of the Belgrade District Court in Serbia. **26.34**

Impact on National Law

States Parties to the Statute of the International Criminal Court have an obligation to cooperate with the Court. Where the Security Council refers a case to the ICC under Chapter VII of the UN Charter, this obligation can be extended to all member States of the UN—though that has not been the case with the two situations, Darfur and Libya, so far referred to the Court. The Security Council also imposed an obligation on all States to cooperate with the Tribunals for the former Yugoslavia and for Rwanda. **26.35**

The extent to which States are obliged to cooperate with other courts with international elements depends on what is said in the agreement or other instrument establishing the court concerned. States must, if necessary, change their national law to allow them to cooperate with the ICC or the other tribunals, complying with requests to identify and locate suspects, to take evidence, to search premises, and to require the production of documents and other materials, as well as to freeze assets and, crucially, to surrender a person to a court or tribunal where it has issued a warrant of arrest. For the two Tribunals, **26.36** there is no bar under national or international law to the prosecution of Heads of State, Foreign Ministers, diplomats, and others, and all States must hand over any such person if sought by one of the Tribunals. The same goes for the ICC, so far as the Heads of State and other representatives of States Parties are concerned. The Security Council has the power by resolution to require cooperation from States not parties, thus effectively removing immunity from Heads of State and others.

26.37　It is a matter for the national law of each State to designate the appropriate authorities for the handling of requests for cooperation from the Court and Tribunals, and the diplomat, whether in a posting or at home, must turn to the legal advisers of his or her own country for guidance in the event of a request.

26.38　The primacy of national jurisdictions over the ICC—the principle of complementarity—has been mentioned at paragraph 26.11. The ICC is a court of last resort. This creates an incentive for States to make punishable under their national law the offences under the Statute, and to ensure that the jurisdiction of their courts is at least as wide as that required under the Statute. How this is to be done is left to the individual States Parties. For example, in the United Kingdom's International Criminal Court Act 2001 the offences listed in the Statute are made offences in British law, without further definitions and without listing already existing offences corresponding to them. Provided that a State is acting genuinely in pursuing an alleged offender, the case can be dealt with by its own courts and the ICC is shut out.

Book VI

ALTERNATIVE (INCLUDING TRACK 2) DIPLOMACY

27

PUBLIC DIPLOMACY AND ITS OFFSHOOTS

Tom Fletcher

Public diplomacy has, at one level, probably been around nearly as long as **27.1** diplomacy itself. After the Conference of Sparta in 432 BC where the Spartans were deciding whether or not go to war with Athens, it is not too fanciful to think that the Athenian delegation in Sparta (who happened to be in Sparta on other unspecified business), having failed to persuade the gerontocracy of the Conference against war and exasperated by 'the secrecy of their government',[1] may have taken their arguments to the Spartan agora (the word gives us the verb ἀγορεύω, *agoreúō*, 'I speak in public').[2]

The actual phrase, public diplomacy, was, if not coined by, certainly given **27.2** institutional currency in 1965 by a former US diplomat Edmund Gullion and in an increasing number of diplomatic services, modern diplomats are progressively expected to project their government's message. While they should not become main actors in their host country's affairs, they have no reason to maintain a low profile. The means of delivering their message shift constantly as

---

[1] Thucydides, *The Landmark Thucydides: A Comprehensive Guide to the Peloponnesian War*, ed Strassler (New York: Simon & Schuster, 1998) 5.68.2.
[2] See Chapter 1, paragraph 1.6.

new information technology is developed (see paragraphs **27**.13 *et seq*) but projecting the diplomat's government's message publicly in an attempt to influence mass public opinion is for some scholars of diplomatic studies little more than a form of propaganda (the term was originally used in a sixteenth-century religious context to propagate the faith). 'In the hard world of governments, "public diplomacy" is simply propaganda rebranded.'[3] Nevertheless, while public diplomacy can on occasions be guilty of selectivity about the facts, it is now an accepted and established part of the practice of diplomacy not just in Western capitals but globally. From African capitals to the Far East, from the Middle East to Latin America foreign ministries throughout the world have migrated online. As such, all these ministries are now struggling to institutionalize the use of social media and digital tools by training diplomats, authoring guidelines, and developing best practices. Public diplomacy is now a major weapon in a diplomat's armoury. To ignore its potential, risks diplomacy losing opportunities both to understand and encourage political developments.

27.3 Diplomats now have an increasingly public role to play in projecting their government's message locally, not just by media appearances and newspaper articles, but by regular use of social media, blogging, Twitter, and evolving techniques. This is not to minimize what has often been the powerful use the media by diplomats to put their case to the host country's people. Sir Nicholas Henderson, when ambassador in Washington during the Falklands War carried out an invaluable media campaign (frequent TV appearances (with his trademark eye-catching dishevelled shirt collar) at a time when the US administration was deeply split between those who saw support for the UK as being disastrous for US relations with the whole of Latin America and those who believed in the 'special [UK–US] relationship'). Sir Nicholas's efforts were a real tour de force of public diplomacy. But he might have found his task easier in the digital age where an important statement by a minister can be re-tweeted at the touch of a smartphone and a local debate can ensue on Google, Facebook, or Twitter which will determine how that policy is perceived, accepted, or rejected. Today's social media unlike previous forms of communication used to deliver public diplomacy (e.g. radio and television) has the advantage of being interactive. Twitter is based on immediate and continuous dialogue between its subscribers. Thus, an ambassador's tweet is immediately commented on by a (sometimes knowledgeable and regularly opinionated) online public. While this is not without pitfalls for diplomats, it also offers many opportunities. Digital diplomacy may now be used to converse with online publics, to stimulate debate on important

---

[3] G R Berridge, *Diplomacy: Theory and Practice* (5th edn, Basingstoke and New York: Palgrave, 2015) 200.

issues, to foster relations with foreign publics, and gauge public opinion in host countries. Thus, Twitter is more than a powerful megaphone—it is a key to the city street or square, and helps avoid the risk of capital/establishment reporting which can present a distorted picture of events, as was the case when the Shah of Iran was deposed.

Lord Palmerston, on receiving his first telegram in the 1840s, is famously said to   **27.4** have exclaimed 'By God, this is the end of diplomacy!' The modern diplomat must continue to demonstrate the fallacy: as a digital interventionist fully engaging with social media because it can amplify the message far more widely and swiftly than can be achieved through traditional means. A digital démarche carried out with many followers can be far more effective than a traditional démarche through the usual elite channels: the diplomat can mobilize public opinion to change another country's policies. (This can, of course, be a high-risk venture particularly when operating in an authoritarian country or even in a democratic former colony, where attempts to influence public opinion by the former colonial power can be perceived as a form of neo-colonialism or subversion and strongly resented by the government.)

It is through embracing new methods of creating and sharing information,   **27.5** delivering services, and networking that the modern diplomat will keep the profession influential and relevant in a crowded market place. It will involve far less co-creation of reports in stark contrast to traditional practice where an initial draft might be seen and commented on by several (usually senior) colleagues; it will use big data not only to determine the overall tone of media and popular debate but also to check the number of the embassy's citizens in country, registered through an embassy app and their location; and to engage with activists or to counter the efforts of radical groups.

Social media complicates policy-making. Of course, in the wake of Wikileaks   **27.6** and Snowden, governments need to convince their publics that they will use the data collected responsibly. Sensible use of digital space will allow the diplomats to take their services to people, not vice versa, so the businessman or tourist arriving in a country will receive on their smartphone information on how to do business, get help if needed, and advice on where to go and not to go. And an invitation to get in touch. But the speed at which information is publicly available creates expectations that governments react as quickly, despite having incomplete and undigested information. At another level the confidentiality of negotiations can be difficult to sustain when participants are tweeting the proceedings live. Procedures are required to ensure that wrongful disclosure does not inhibit progress.

In the event of a terrorist incident, or other crisis, humanitarian or otherwise,   **27.7** given globalization and the speed of modern communications, the diplomat cannot hope to compete with 24/7 news services but it will often fall to the resident diplomat to respond to media pressure, sometimes quite unreasonable, not only by addressing the problem in terms of aid supplies or other support but to be seen with a physical presence to be doing so.

27.8 The digital revolution has changed the world faster than any previous technology. It is 70 years since mainframes arrived in academic and military institutions. Fifty years since the arrival of the microprocessor. Twenty years since personal computing started a mass migration of human effort and attention towards digital. Today, more than 3 billion people are connected to the internet, nearly half the world's population. There are more mobile phones in Brazil than people. Thirty-six million British people use the internet every day, double the figure in 2006.

27.9 The patterns show us—data, computer chip advancement, global temperatures, portable telephone size—that change is now speeding up at a bewildering rate. Sociologist Ian Morris has asserted[4] that in just a century we will go through the equivalent in technological transformation of the shift from cave paintings to nuclear weapons.

27.10 These trends will have a significant impact on established States, ideas, and professions. The new hyper-connectivity reduces trust in traditional political and media elites, and empowers citizen commentators. The transformation of how we meet our needs for security, dignity, and community will change the political equilibrium, and shift power away from governments towards citizens. The internet accelerates that process in as important a way as the printing press did.

Implications for Diplomacy

27.11 In an age therefore when knowledge (and therefore power) is again diffusing, diplomacy is again having to reconnect to new sources of power. Writing in 1961,[5] against a backdrop of social change and the spectre of nuclear war, Harold Nicolson saw that the fundamentals on which the diplomacy and indeed the politics that he knew had been built were shaky. The rules of the game—an elite talking to fellow elites in Europe—were changing. 'The old diplomacy was based on the creation of confidence, the acquisition of credit...the old currency has been withdrawn...we are now dealing in a new coinage.'

---

[4] I Morris, *Why The West Rules For Now* (London: Profile Books, 2010).
[5] H Nicolson, 'Diplomacy Then and Now' (1961) 40(1) *Foreign Affairs* 39.

That coinage is increasingly digital. This presents three major issues for diplomacy **27.12** as a profession. It is going to be disrupted at a time when it lacks resource, will, and energy. What it represents—States, hierarchies, the status quo—is becoming weaker. And the challenges it needs to confront are becoming greater. There will be many times when digital media feel to professional diplomats an obstacle to traditional diplomacy. New digital media will create different and sometimes uncomfortable oversight of what diplomats do. They will further empower rival sources of influence and power and may make the government's task more difficult in gaining and retaining public support for their policies.

Digital Diplomacy

Yet diplomats are putting new digital tools to increasingly creative use. Both the **27.13** US and UK had virtual embassies—allowing them online engagement without the physical risks of locating diplomats—in Iran. Since its independence in 2008, Kosovo has been recognized by only half the world. So its deputy Foreign Minister, Petrit Selimi, persuaded Facebook to allow users to place their location in Kosovo, and not in neighbouring Serbia. The success of this effort means that Kosovo's existence is more widely recognized online than offline.

The first email between Heads of Government was sent in 1994, from Swedish **27.14** Prime Minister Carl Bildt to US President Bill Clinton. He congratulated Clinton on the lifting of the Vietnam embargo, and added that 'it is only appropriate that we [Sweden] should be among the first to use the internet for political contacts and communications around the globe'.[6] Clinton replied the following day, in hindsight perhaps with less panache than the moment required: 'I appreciate your enthusiasm for the potential of emerging technologies. This demonstration of electronic communication is an important step toward building the global information highway.' Leaders now text, email, or tweet each other direct. During negotiations, the text messages between them (and between their advisers) are often more important than the conversation at the table. It may become less necessary for them to meet as often, yet they will get to know each other better.

Neither Bildt nor Clinton could have anticipated the speed at which the 'global **27.15** information highway' was being built around them. In terms of diplomacy, it is Twitter and Facebook that have built it. The first tweet was sent in 2006. Within three years, a billion tweets had been sent. Facebook has well over a billion users

---

[6] Both texts in the William J Clinton Library.

at present. and this figure has grown by a third a year. Most of these users are now on mobile devices. Diplomats are among them. Bildt was the first Foreign Minister to make it compulsory for ambassadors to have social media accounts. It is now virtually mandatory for world leaders from the US President to the Pope to do the same.

27.16   Digital media are also increasingly important resources for those responding to humanitarian crises. Humanitarian agencies now aim to get social media channels and devices to those hit by disasters, and use Google Earth to locate survivors. For those diplomats using these new digital tools to connect in new and innovative ways, there are some helpful guidelines.

27.17   Firstly, as offline, diplomats using these tools need to understand those with whom they are engaging. Are the majority in other countries or in their home country? Are they hostile, curious, or supportive? Diplomats need to reach out, but not fall into the trap of courting popularity.

27.18   Secondly, as in offline communication, online engagement still demands consistency and quality. And just as diplomats fail when their telegram report matters more to them than the action they are reporting the best digital diplomacy is action not reportage-based, purpose not platitudes. In this new environment, diplomats must also understand and manage the risks, especially where the personal blurs with the political. They should judge the local context for their messages, especially when they are on more controversial terrain. A British ambassador to Lebanon (not the author of this chapter) had her blog taken down by the Foreign Office in 2010 when it praised the spiritual leader of Hizbollah, Ayatollah Fadlallah, describing his death as sad news, calling the religious leader a decent man and saying 'the world needs more men like him'.[7]

27.19   Finally, modern diplomats should not forget their mission. Transnational debates can be fascinating, and alliances will become more issue-based, more fluid. But diplomats should not lose sight of the core aim of foreign policy: contributing to creating and maintaining a secure and prosperous international environment, because through that national prosperity and security are best advanced.

The Challenge to Secrecy, Authority, and Trust

27.20   The modern reality is that the boundaries between secrecy and privacy are being rapidly eroded. In the digital age, no comment can pass as off the record. For

---

[7] *The Guardian*, 9 July 2010.

diplomats, that is a problem—most of their work has tended to be confidential, protected by codes and laws, hidden from public sight.

The two biggest recent challenges to confidentiality in statecraft and espionage have come from Julian Assange and Edward Snowden. Assange and his Wikileaks insurgents tracked down and released masses of mainly US government confidential information. They did this without discrimination, believing that everything should be exposed for examination. Meanwhile, whistle-blowing US intelligence analyst Snowden exposed systematic efforts by Western governments to monitor the communications of other governments, and even their own populations. These revelations have accelerated a debate about surveillance and the internet. Security agencies argue that they have to mine an ocean of data to identify the new threats from legitimate intelligence targets. Some involved in diplomacy argue that some of the greatest threats to security come from increased transparency. In condemning Wikileaks, US Secretary of State Hillary Clinton suggested: 'It puts people's lives in danger, threatens our national security and undermines our efforts to work with other countries to solve shared problems...disclosures like these tear at the fabric of the proper function of responsible government.'   **27.21**

More widely, the ability of diplomats and governments to protect confidential information and exchanges is under threat. Public and media expectations of oversight of policy-making are increasing and inquiries, an essential component of accountability, are an increasingly familiar aspect of the diplomatic landscape. As an example, policy-makers and their advisers have given evidence to the various Iraq inquiries, which have been a constant feature of the last decade. There is quite rightly an intense interest in what advice goes to leaders, especially on issues relating to war and peace. Recent inquiries have shown that few emerge with much credit when their real-time communications are put under an intense spotlight. Advice also becomes less candid, and more cautious.   **27.22**

Everyone in diplomacy knows that detailed records are kept by most of their interlocutors. For those involved, the more honest, colourful, and bold that these reports are, the more useful. So there is a danger that fear of disclosure makes them more cautious. After Wikileaks, diplomats are writing less down with the consequence that future historians will have less to work with. The way in which advice is given to leaders will change, and so future generations analysing decisions will have different data sets.   **27.23**

The public rightly demands greater insight into the workings of government. Meanwhile, security agencies argue that they must sift through information from those who are not targets. As GCHQ's last Director Iain Lobban has put   **27.24** it, 'we're looking for the needle, not at the hay'.[8] Robert Hannigan, his successor, argues[9] that US technology giants are becoming more reluctant—following Edward Snowden's whistle-blowing revelations—to cooperate with the FBI, NSA, and GCHQ. Yet privacy can never be absolute and US tech giants are 'the command-and-control networks of choice for terrorists and criminals'.[10] So while ISIS/ISIL and other organized terror groups are using digital media in a more targeted and intelligent way than their predecessors (including Al Qaeda) monitoring them is getting harder.

27.25　However, the need for secrecy should not be allowed to become a barrier from scrutiny, or used to conceal mistakes. A system is needed that allows diplomats to do their jobs, while reassuring the public. Foreign policy should never be wholly secret but negotiations must be confidential.

The Next Wave of Innovation in Diplomacy

27.26　Social media will transform the way that governments engage with citizens. But while the internet defies boundaries, most governments find it hard to escape the confines of national responses. Data is not sufficiently shared and regulation struggles to keep pace. Governments have not yet tackled the big questions on the balance between privacy and transparency, or found the right formula to nurture innovation. Set-piece events are being replaced by more fluid, open interaction with the people whose interests diplomats are there to represent.

27.27　Future diplomatic innovation will be driven by big data which will reshape how diplomats find and use information; how they deliver a service; and how they network and influence. Digital technology should also make government better at discovering and delivering what people want from it. Modern diplomats will have to accept that everything they do will have to pass the test of whether it can be done by new tools. Can, for instance, Google Translate replace language training; can a computer write a better press summary than a diplomat, or issue a visa faster and more fairly?

The Politics of Digital Change

27.28　Even without the pressures of massive technological change, there is a strong case to be made for greater openness and transparency. The US, more than any

---

[8] BBC, 7 November 2013.
[9] *Financial Times*, 3 November 2014.
[10] Ibid.

other nation, has sought to use these new public diplomacy instruments to promote democratic values in other countries, whether through presidential YouTube messages to the Iranian people or energetic defence of the rights of the free speech of bloggers facing greater restrictions. And even where there is limited free speech, digitally monitored uprisings of the Arab Spring fed off each other and spread protest. Activists could for the first time watch the simultaneous successes and failures of their counterparts in other parts of the region. Individuals could now document what was happening around them in real time; share it more easily; and organize themselves more effectively. Anyone can now be a broadcaster or commentator. Political action is becoming a franchise rather than a controlled party operation. Global protest politics—from Wikileaks to Anonymous—is breaking down old power monopolies. Social media will continue to play a part in breaking down barriers everywhere where people are connected to the internet. Digital media alone did not create the Arab Spring. But it made it less predictable, and more widespread. It is no longer possible to imagine an uprising or revolution that does not deploy social media.

But there are, beyond terrorist and violent non-State actors, negative forces at **27.29** work. Of the estimated 5 billion people who will become connected in the next decade, most will be in more repressive societies. Some States, such as Turkey, have already taken on Twitter directly. In Russia, oligarchs have forced more independent operators out of control of large sections of the internet. This repression is increasingly sophisticated and well resourced. The challenge will be to find new ways of communicating with those fighting censorship or living in otherwise repressive societies. Digital technology will also allow those opposed to basic liberties a platform to suppress them, promote their atrocities, and recruit their foot soldiers. Shrewd authoritarian regimes will crack down on digital freedom, and turn it against activists. Social media campaigns will also be used to fuel extremism and polarize debate—the modern equivalent of the use of hate radio during the Rwanda genocide. ISIS/ISIL sent 40,000 tweets in one day as they took Mosul in June 2014.

Conclusion

Technological change is, as it always was, here to stay. The last time it went **27.30** backwards was in the Dark Ages after the fall of the (Western) Roman Empire. The overall effect of this technological revolution is positive. It is better ultimately to have too much information than too little. But it is not painless. Diplomats will be part of the debate on our digital rights, tackling the toughest issues around trust and transparency, and helping to find the balance between freedom of expression and the rights of others. Governments will continue to lose their monopoly on information and influence. Secrets will become harder to justify and harder to keep. The answers to the tough questions on the balance between digital freedoms and oversight predate the digital era. We still need to understand where authority begins and ends; what issues fall under the rule of law; and how to balance the rights of individuals and communities.

27.31   The role of diplomats is being transformed faster than at any point in history. But diplomacy existed before States, and will exist even were there to be a genuine post-modern geo-political world. We need diplomats more than ever because the implications of diplomatic failure are potentially catastrophic. In the digital age the need is not for something to replace diplomacy, but for better deployed diplomacy.

28

NON-GOVERNMENTAL ORGANIZATIONS (NGOS) AND VIOLENT NON-STATE ACTORS (VNSAs)

Ivor Roberts

Non-Governmental Organizations		Violent Non-State Actors	
(NGOs)	28.1	(VNSAs)	28.12
ICRC	28.8		

Non-Governmental Organizations (NGOs)

Civil society, that offshoot of the enlightenment, has developed in the early **28.1** twenty-first century into a benchmark of a fully functioning democracy. One of its key manifestations is the flourishing of organizations outside the state sector. India for example is estimated to have over 1 million non-governmental organizations (NGOs). In 1997, the then UN Secretary-General discussed the increasing influence of civil society within the United Nations and pointed out that civil society actors were 'now perceived not only as disseminators of information or providers of services but also as shapers of policy, be it in peace and security matters, in development or in humanitarian affairs'.[1] Non-governmental organizations come in many shapes and sizes. Many have a charitable base and some will have humanitarian or human rights objectives; others focus on sustainable development and aid. Often their concern will be a single issue, e.g. climate change. Their objectives will be focused and invariably single-minded,

---

[1] Renewing the United Nations: A Programme for Reform, Report of the Secretary-General A/51/950, para 212.

less able or willing to take into account other aspects. As a result, their relationship with governments, although sometimes harmonious, may be one of tension and occasionally confrontation. Whereas an NGO will usually have a bias in favour of bringing matters into the open, a government needs a comprehensive policy which balances out all the interests involved. Moreover, governments are generally predisposed to favour confidentiality and discretion in formulating their policies so as to maximize political advantage, and avoid embarrassment or damage to relations with other governments. Increasingly NGOs scrutinize and criticize the performance of government, and indeed NGOs are active in the diplomatic field, sometimes duplicating, often monitoring, the performance of governments and international or national organizations. NGOs such as Amnesty International traditionally saw their role as one of challenge to States which they considered to be failing to meet their human rights obligations. While they were often seriously disadvantaged compared to States in terms of resources and access to information, their activities increasingly enjoy support, including from, usually, Western governments, in pushing human rights issues.

28.2   Why have NGOs been able to move into a field which was for centuries the monopoly of a politico-diplomatic class? One of the consequences of globalization, with its speed of communication and easy access to information for all, has been to weaken States' monopoly on diplomacy. Availability of information puts pressure on governments for early responses and action. Campaigning by NGOs has become an important political driver. This has also led to a parallel growth in so-called track two diplomacy,[2] carried out either by private individuals or NGOs, a form of diplomacy which 'has increased rapidly over recent decades'.[3] NGOs and other international bodies have 'revived the medieval right of non-sovereign entities to send and receive envoys, conduct negotiations and conclude agreements'.[4] The rise in importance of such bodies is partly a function of the way foreign policy, particularly among Western governments, is now less vertical and more horizontal in its interests. Global issues are vital

---

[2] As opposed to track one diplomacy by governmental or international organizations. See also Chapter 1, paragraph 1.24. 'Formerly known as "citizen diplomacy", mediation in an inter- or intra-State conflict conducted by any agency other than a state or an intergovernmental organization, typically by an NGO. The term was coined in 1981 by Joseph Montville, then a US diplomat. Track two diplomacy may be pursued on its own or in partnership with track one diplomacy, in which case it will form part of an instance of twin-track diplomacy.' G R Berridge and L Lloyd, *The Palgrave Macmillan Dictionary of Diplomacy* (3rd edn, London: Palgrave Macmillan, 2012) 368.

[3] G R Berridge, *Diplomacy: Theory and Practice* (5th edn, Basingstoke and New York: Palgrave Macmillan, 2015) 257.

[4] R Cohen, 'Reflections on the New Global Diplomacy', in J Melissen (ed), *Innovation in Diplomatic Practice* (London: Macmillan, 1999).

challenges for governments and for international relations. Governments are having to pay increasing attention to issues like human rights and climate change, terrorism and nuclear non-proliferation as well as to the purely territorial or geographical issues which were the more traditional stuff of diplomacy. The influence of NGOs has grown, partly as a result of the spread of literacy, the generation gap and 'counter culture' of the 1960s, and the popularity of pressure group politics. NGOs in countries with non-democratic or authoritarian regimes, often with the support of international NGOs, seek to influence government policies to reflect human rights and the people's needs, rather than what they regard as merely the wishes of the ruling elite, and this is relevant to foreign as well as domestic policies where we have seen the rise of pressure groups in domestic affairs mobilized against the State, or those perceived as acting as arms of the State, in defence of the environment or whatever.

Communications, television in particular, have brought humanitarian crises **28.3** direct to the homes of the public, thus mobilizing rapid support for action by government and by public subscription. The famine in Ethiopia in the late 1980s was brought vividly to the TV screen, picked up, and amplified by pop stars. The result was a mobilization of effort to bring relief. Similarly, in that decade, skilful manipulation of communication and films of the clubbing of seal pups, accompanied by targeted NGO pressure on EU governments, led to an EU ban on the import of seal skins from Canada. More and more, NGOs will be on the front line in areas of conflict, not just providing much needed aid and medical assistance but bringing abuses and violations of human rights to world attention. Traditionally, NGOs working in such theatres were universally respected and enjoyed de facto protection. Increasingly this is no longer the case, and NGO workers are often attacked. This brings into sharp focus their relationship with any peacekeepers or troops present, as NGOs have always wanted to maintain their neutrality and impartiality. However, combatants, and particularly extreme jihadist groups like Al Qaeda and ISIS/so-called Islamic State, are less and less likely to respect this role, often claiming that aid workers are Western spies. Attacks (including many instances of kidnapping) on aid workers (and on journalists) have increased significantly in recent years with 2012 being the worst so far, with 167 incidents of major violence on aid workers.[5] Some incidents are accidental. In one attack in 2015, six staff including doctors of Médecins sans Frontières (MSF) were killed in a US military air strike in Kunduz, Afghanistan.

The relationship between NGOs and governments is a complex and often sym-**28.4** biotic one which can to some degree compromise the former's independence.

---

[5] <https://aidworkersecurity.org/sites/default/files/AidWorkerSecurityReport_2013_web.pdf>.

As has been said, '[I]f civil society becomes state-sponsored, it ceases to be civil, and NGOs become quangos.'[6] But increasingly governments see the advantage of working with NGOs, particularly where their objectives match those of governments. The work of Amnesty International and Human Rights Watch in the human rights field is a case in point.

28.5 By contrast with the often ambivalent attitude of governments, the UN has since its inception sought to involve NGOs in its work.[7] International, regional, sub-regional, and national NGOs can claim consultative status where their programmes are of direct relevance to the aims of the UN. For instance, at present, more than 3,000 NGOs enjoy consultative status with ECOSOC (the UN Economic and Social Council, see Chapter 19) in accordance with Article 71 of the UN Charter.[8] Similarly the right to participation of NGOs in the regular and special sessions of the Human Rights Council (paragraph 19.21) was enshrined in the UN General Assembly resolution setting up the Council in 2006 and is a prerogative of NGOs enjoying consultative status with ECOSOC. NGOs play an important role in the work of UN human rights 'treaty bodies' such as the committees which monitor the implementation of the two Human Rights Covenants and the Committee against Torture (which monitors the Conventions against Torture). They supply the treaty bodies with information about human rights abuses and developments which enable the committees to verify or question the versions presented in governmental reports. While NGOs have different arrangements with different multilateral or international organizations, increasingly the latter involve and accommodate the former in their work (e.g. the Council of Europe and the African Union) with progressively closer relationships. For example, while ECOSOC and the ILO continue to use the term 'consultation' to describe their relationship with NGOs, the term 'participation' is becoming more common elsewhere.

28.6 It is now common for NGOs to be involved in preparations for international conferences.[9] The UN and its agencies are increasingly open to some form of participation by NGOs in conferences under their aegis. Issues as to rights of

---

[6] E Mortimer, 'At arm's length: Non-profit groups should not be beholden to governments', *Financial Times*, 22 March 1995.

[7] The Report of the Panel of Eminent Persons on Civil Society and UN Relationships recommends a still stronger relationship (11 June 2004, A/58/817).

[8] General Assembly resolution 1996/31 lays down the arrangements for consultative status, and the principles to be applied in the establishment of consultative relations. Consultative status is granted by decision of ECOSOC on the recommendation of the standing Committee on Non-Governmental Organizations; decisions can be politically sensitive and are often adopted by vote.

[9] See Chapter 30, paragraph 30.25. For further reading on NGO participation in international conferences, see chapter 8 of A-K Lindblom, *Non-Governmental Organisations in International Law* (Cambridge: Cambridge University Press, 2005).

access, rights to receive information, and rights to speak or make proposals are often a major part of negotiations on a conference's Rules of Procedure. The best recent example is the 2015 Conference of the Parties to the UN Framework Convention on Climate Change which adopted the Paris agreement on the reduction of carbon dioxide emissions where there were substantial numbers of observers as well as non-governmental organizations (NGOs).[10] The 1998 Conference on the establishment of the International Criminal Court (Chapter 26) provided another example of a high level of NGO participation (though not on the Paris scale) in a conference held under UN auspices. An interesting feature of such conferences was the secondment of NGO experts (particularly international law academics) to government delegations, especially delegations from small developing States.[11] The inclusion of NGO experts in government delegations provides expertise, responds to political pressures, and may be particularly helpful to assist smaller governments which lack adequate resources. The rationale of other governments which include NGO representatives as part of their delegations may have both domestic and foreign policy roots. It may be at least in part to mute domestic criticism of a particular policy and perhaps 'to attract the support of a younger generation concerned with internationalist issues'.[12] It is also the case that mutual needs do not necessarily imply cooperative relationships.[13] Thus, while NGOs will feel that their voice is being heard in the formulation of policy and their inclusion in delegations, with a consequently higher profile, their expectations to see their aims delivered will also increase. They may also feel the need to retain distance and consequently their independence.

The role of most NGOs is not of course confined to the conference hall. They **28.7** are more often in the front line in conflict areas (e.g. the work of Médecins sans Frontières in places like Darfur, Gaza, and Afghanistan) and in development. Oxfam, to give another example, has a world reputation for supplying clean water and sanitation. Moreover, some of the larger NGOs are far more than collectors and disbursers of money. Amnesty International campaigns, inter alia, on behalf of political prisoners, in favour of free speech and human rights, and against torture and the death penalty. Oxfam has a sizeable policy unit which

---

[10] See Chapter **30**, paragraph **30**.24 n 28.

[11] For example, the NGO 'Peace without Justice' implemented its Judicial Assistance Programme in this way, both at the ICC conference and at the preceding negotiations in the Preparatory Commission.

[12] D MacShane, 'The Left-wing Wizards of Oz', *The Guardian*, 4 September 1995 quoted by Brian Hocking in 'Catalytic Diplomacy'.

[13] B Hocking, 'Catalytic Diplomacy: Beyond "Newness" and "Decline"', in J Melissen (ed), *Innovation in Diplomatic Practice* (London: Macmillan, 1999).

covers areas as diverse as the implications of climate change and women's rights in Africa. NGOs regularly report on situations and lobby for improvements. Some NGOs, particularly those operating in the development field, will see themselves as essentially development diplomats, though NGOs will from time to time lack the capabilities for full economic rigour and therefore be criticized by those who, for example, point out that without investment in a secure environment we would be naive to believe that 'Oxfam can right all the world's ills—admirable as it and other NGOs may be'.[14] But the NGOs of course lack both the legitimacy which comes with official representation of a government or international organization like the UN and, more specifically, democratic legitimacy. In some cases, they can be said to represent only narrow interest groups. Yet they fulfil an important role in what they do on the ground and for the causes which they champion, and are usually uninhibited in holding governments, both donors and recipients, to account.

ICRC

28.8 A notable exception to these general comments about NGOs is the International Committee of the Red Cross (ICRC). Established in 1863 with its headquarters in Geneva, the ICRC is an association under Swiss law overseen by a committee of Swiss nationals. However, it has many of the characteristics of an intergovernmental organization.[15] It has observer status in the UN General Assembly (the other two anomalous organizations with humanitarian roles which also have this status are the International Federation of the Red Cross and Red Crescent, and the Sovereign Military Order of Malta). The ICRC is largely funded by voluntary donations by national governments and is treated by many States as having international legal personality: it has special privileges and legal immunities in many countries (it is represented in over eighty). While the committee itself remains exclusively Swiss, the ICRC's delegates are now drawn from countries around the world. The ICRC is accorded specific responsibilities under the Geneva Conventions and has played a key role in the development of these and other International Humanitarian Law instruments.[16] The ICRC has an exclusively humanitarian mission to protect and assist the victims of war and

---

[14] C Patten, *What Next?: Surviving the Twenty-first Century* (London: Allen Lane, 2008) 210 and 265.

[15] <http://www.icrc.org/Web/Eng/siteeng0.nsf/html/5W9FJY>.

[16] Conventions governing the conduct of war and the treatment of prisoners and other non-combatants; the first was drawn up and signed in Geneva under the aegis of the Swiss government in 1864.

internal violence (including prisoners of war and civilians and its policy of strict neutrality and independence often allows it access (for example visiting detainees) not available to other actors.

It is worth noting that the UN and its agencies such as UNICEF and UNHCR **28.9** have taken to appointing as 'good will ambassadors', stars from the world of entertainment and other celebrities, to focus world attention on problems as diverse as land mines, refugees, the use of rape as a weapon in war, and reproductive health. The use of the traditional nomenclature of diplomacy is significant and the authority conferred by the UN Secretary-General's blessing and in particular the name recognition of the individual is usually a powerful element in promoting a particular cause and creating acceptance by governments.

What is the lesson for conventional ambassadors or other diplomats? Not that **28.10** they have lost their role but that they no longer enjoy a monopoly as actors in the field of international relations. There are many advantages to working constructively with NGOs and other representatives of civil society. NGOs make excellent allies where governments are keen for their diplomats to promote wider respect for human rights and democracy.[17] Working with the grain of NGOs can result in good information; moreover, failure to engage with them on matters of common interest can invite public and parliamentary criticism for non-cooperation.

As we have already noted (with more examples to come in the next chapter), the **28.11** field of diplomatic activity is an increasingly crowded one. Yet the diplomats' aim remains the same: to advance and protect their government's interests, making use of all the tools under their control, and as necessary bartering information and intelligence with other actors such as NGOs. It is futile jealously to guard one's turf but a diplomat will as always want to be cautious about sharing sensitive information with others. It would not for instance be sensible for diplomats to share with an NGO information, even at a good exchange rate, which could be damaging or embarrassing to their government if it emerged into the public domain. An NGO has no obligation to protect the information it acquires. When NGOs act in the diplomatic field and are assisting governments, they are doing so as auxiliaries to diplomats, that is to say as paradiplomats.[18] On other

---

[17] See Chapters 17 and 36.

[18] Keith Hamilton and Richard Langhorne in *The Practice of Diplomacy* (2nd edn, London: Routledge, 2011) 151–2 refer to paradiplomacy in the use by Woodrow Wilson of his friend, Colonel Edward House, and of the intelligence officer, Sir William Wiseman, by the British for 'diplomatic' purposes during the First World War: 'Paradiplomacy on this scale was frustrating for an ambassador of Spring Rice's calibre and temperament.' Spring Rice was the British ambassador at Washington until January 1918. More recently, Tony Blair's use of Lord Levy in the Middle East during his

occasions they are acting as representatives of interest groups of civil society and thus, at their best, helping to remedy what may be a democratic deficit if negotiations are conducted at a purely governmental level.

Violent Non-State Actors (VNSAs)

28.12   The intersection of terrorism and diplomacy has been covered in Chapter 11 but there are other categories of non-State actors whose activities are at the opposite pole to those whose benign activity has been described earlier and where States have lost their monopoly. Generically described as violent non-State actors (VNSAs) their categories number warlords, militias, insurgencies, and criminal organizations, including pirates and people traffickers. Such actors flourish in ungoverned spaces, failed states, or in territories where the governance is weak and/or oppressive. Although there is considerable scope for overlap between these groups and terrorists (they share for instance the challenge to the nation state's monopoly of violence) their aim can be to provide alternative state structures in the absence of the traditional Westphalian model or more often to profit from the absence of governance to further illicit, purely criminal, ends. The re-emergence of piracy and the rapid increase in people trafficking within refugee flows are recent examples of the latter. The weaknesses of society can lead to a reversion to family or tribal-based loyalties. Globalization has assisted and often amplified the effects of VNSAs, facilitating arms flows and illegal sources of funding. The modern diplomat may be required to negotiate with other governments measures to curb the activities of these groups. We have seen for instance the use of Chinese naval vessels to combat piracy in the Indian Ocean and Western governments have had to swallow hard and collaborate with some fairly unpalatable bedfellows in the common cause of extirpating ISIS/so-called Islamic State. The requirement may extend to negotiating with

---

premiership in a paradiplomatic role caused similar frustrations for the British ambassadors in the region.

A full definition is to be found in Berridge and Lloyd, *The Palgrave Macmillan Dictionary of Diplomacy*, 3rd edn, 276:

paradiplomacy. (1) Generally, activity analogous to diplomacy conducted by anyone without diplomatic status, in particular a member of a non-governmental organization or private individual acting independently. (2) Specifically, international activity (typically lobbying) by regional governments such as the Canadian province of Quebec and stateless nations such as that of the Kurds. Paradiplomacy of this kind is sometimes prefixed with one or other of the following adjectives: sub-national, sub-state, or regional.

By analogy with 'paramedics', 'paramilitaries', and so on, practitioners of both kinds of paradiplomacy are sometimes called paradiplomats, although the term is rare.

these VNSAs humanitarian access for international development agencies or the evacuation of civilian populations from conflict zones.

It is no exaggeration to state that 'VNSAs play a prominent, often destabilizing **28**.13 role in nearly every humanitarian and political crisis faced by the international community'[19] and 'have become a pervasive challenge to nation-states'[20] in our time.

---

[19] T Thomas, S Kiser, and W Casebeer, *Warlords Rising: Confronting Violent Non-State Actors* (Lanham, MD: Lexington Books, 2005).
[20] P Williams, 'Violent Non-State Actors' (PDF), International Relations and Security Network, Center for Security Studies (CSS) (Swiss Federal Institute of Technology, Zurich, 2008) 4.

29

SECRET OR BACK-CHANNEL DIPLOMACY, SECRET INTELLIGENCE, RELIGIOUS AND OTHER UNCONVENTIONAL DIPLOMATIC ACTORS

Ivor Roberts

Secret or Back-Channel Diplomacy

29.1 A single definition of secret or back-channel diplomacy is hard to construct. Berridge describes back-channel diplomacy thus: 'A line of diplomatic communication which bypasses the normal diplomatic channels. The reason for this is to maximize secrecy and avoid opposition to a new line of policy. This does not necessarily entail sidelining all professional diplomats, just most of them.'[1] Those undertaking secret diplomacy may want to conceal the fact that negotiations are taking place and/or their content and will usually want to control the timing of any announcement of a successful outcome. With failure, the fact of such a negotiation having taken place may never be revealed.

---

[1] G R Berridge and L Lloyd, *The Palgrave Macmillan Dictionary of Diplomacy* (3rd edn, London: Palgrave Macmillan, 2012) 27.

A corollary of this is often the secrecy of the identity of the person or persons **29.2** involved in the negotiation. Successful instances of secret or back-channel diplomacy include the negotiations to bring the Vietnam War to an end conducted by Henry Kissinger and Le Duc Tho in 1972 and 1973. By 1972, both sides in the Vietnam War were ready to compromise. The US was no longer insisting on the withdrawal of North Vietnamese forces from the South and the North Vietnamese were not demanding the replacement of the South Vietnamese leader Thieu with a coalition government. In this new situation, Kissinger and the North Vietnamese envoy Le Duc Tho negotiated in secret a peace agreement in October 1972. The Thieu government, however, denounced the agreement and Kissinger after President Nixon's re-election attempted to renegotiate it. This led the North Vietnamese to reject the proposed changes and to advance their own. Nixon decided to coerce the North by the so-called Christmas bombing campaign, the most intense campaign of the war. After eight days, the North Vietnamese agreed to sign an agreement much the same as that agreed upon in October. After a combination of carrot and stick, President Thieu also consented. On 27 January 1973, the Agreement on Ending the War and Restoring Peace in Viet-Nam was signed by the US, North Vietnam, South Vietnam, and representatives of the South Vietnamese Communist forces.

Another example was the secret negotiation over the Oslo Accords in 1993. In **29.3** 1992, after a Middle East peace conference in Madrid had made limited progress, the Israeli Vice-Minister of Foreign Affairs Yossi Beilin and Norwegian researcher Terje Rød-Larsen arranged a meeting in secret between the PLO representative Ahmed Qurei and an Israeli professor, Yair Hirschfeld, who met in a series of meetings in Oslo which was then taken over by senior officials sent by the then Israeli Minister of Foreign Affairs Shimon Peres. The two delegations usually shared accommodation and meals while the Norwegian government dealt with the logistics and kept the meetings confidential, even providing a cover through the Norwegian Fafo Institute for Applied International Studies. An agreement was reached in August 1993. In both cases conventional diplomacy was in some respects acting as a front for the real negotiations. The Vietnam Peace Conference in Paris continued its weekly meetings while the real activity was going on elsewhere. The same was true of the Madrid peace negotiations and the Oslo Accords.

Secrecy has the advantage of speed very often over conventional procedure and **29.4** is sometimes essential where disclosure of ongoing negotiations—particularly towards the final stages—could have an impact on financial markets. Active but discreet negotiations took place over 10 years to settle the 60-year-old dispute between the United Kingdom and the Soviet Union over claims for bonds and private property taken during the Russian Revolution and counter-claims for the British part in the intervention aimed at defeating the Revolution. They ended with the signature in 1986 by Sir Geoffrey Howe as UK Foreign Secretary and Eduard Shevardnadze, then Soviet Foreign Minister, of an Agreement[2] which in the words of *The Times* on the following day 'took the financial markets by surprise'.[3] On the day the Agreement was to be signed at noon, dealings in pre-1939 Russian bonds were suspended at the start of business on the London Stock Exchange. Although the bonds held by private claimants had not been honoured for 60 years many were in the hands of speculators and collectors as well as heirs to the original holders, and those who claimed eventually received a dividend of over 50 per cent from Soviet assets—mostly the so-called 'Baring balances'—which passed to the United Kingdom under the Agreement.

29.5 Back-channel diplomacy, another phrase for secret diplomacy, was used in helping to bring the 'troubles' in Northern Ireland to an end. Since 1973, a Northern Irish businessman with strong links to the IRA, and Michael Oatley, his SIS (MI6) case officer, had maintained a channel of communication between the IRA leadership and 10 Downing Street, as Jonathan Powell, Tony Blair's Chief of Staff, revealed. 'It is very hard for democratic governments to admit to talking to terrorist groups while those groups are still killing innocent people. Luckily for this process, the British government's back channel to the Provisional IRA had been in existence whenever required from 1973 onwards.'[4] In other words, one of the advantages of back-channel diplomacy is its deniability, particularly appropriate when the other party is neither another government nor even an NGO, while another is the ability to talk to those with whom it is official policy not to engage in negotiation. The secret link was only used on three major occasions: to negotiate an IRA cease-fire in the mid-1970s; during the first IRA hunger strike in 1980; and in the early stages of the peace process in the 1990s. There are of course disadvantages: certain key points in the negotiation may be missed but principally there is irritation caused to those who are the visible face of the diplomatic process. These are often the same (demoralized) people who have to implement any agreement reached via the back channel. Much to his annoyance, the US Secretary of State, William Rogers, was kept in the dark by Henry Kissinger, President Nixon's National Security Adviser, over his negotiations with the Chinese on reopening relations for the

---

[2] Agreement between the Government of the United Kingdom of Great Britain and Northern Ireland and the Government of the Union of Soviet Socialist Republics concerning the Settlement of Mutual Financial and Property Claims arising before 1939, UKTS No 65 (1986).

[3] *The Times*, 16 July 1986.

[4] J Powell, *The Guardian*, 18 March 2008.

first time since the Communist takeover.[5] Ministers and others have to be prepared to deny the existence of a process when questioned in a legislature or by the press.

Secret Intelligence

Secret or back-channel diplomacy needs to be distinguished from secret intelligence gathering. *Pace* the example quoted earlier of an MI6 officer conducting 'back-channel' diplomacy with the IRA, the former tends to be conducted by diplomats and/or ultimately ministers (e.g. Kissinger). **29.6**

By contrast, secret intelligence gathering is in modern times the virtual domain of intelligence officers. In Britain, external intelligence is the responsibility of the Secret Intelligence Service (SIS), colloquially referred to as MI6, their Second World War cover name. Their equivalents in the US are the CIA; in Russia the FSB (formerly the KGB in the days of the Soviet Union); in France the DGSE and so on. In the British case, the SIS are responsible to the Foreign Secretary whose officials and ultimately the minister authorize all important operations. The CIA is by contrast a free-standing agency whose Director answers to the US President. **29.7**

It was not always thus. Until the late nineteenth and early twentieth centuries, an ambassador might well and often did regard his role as information and intelligence gathering rolled into one and by whatever means, including bribery. With the beginning of the arrival of service (military and naval) attachés into embassies and consulates, the professional diplomat could divorce his activity from those of *sub rosa* intelligence gatherers. Later, and particularly from the Second World War onwards, the service attachés' work in intelligence gathering was complemented by civilian foreign intelligence or espionage officers. This is now widely established practice. Where spies are based in embassies or consulates (attachés invariably are) they operate under diplomatic cover which affords them a base with security of communications and immunity from arrest or prosecution if their activities are uncovered by the host government. This immunity does not of course prevent them from being declared *persona non grata* and expelled, an outcome to be avoided by spies as their expulsion tends to become public and their consequent usefulness in the secret world abroad much diminished. Such expulsions are normally justified by stating that the diplomats have been carrying **29.8**

---

[5] Margaret MacMillan, *Seize the Hour: When Nixon met Mao* (London: John Murray, 2007) 178–86.

out activity incompatible with their diplomatic status.[6] Another practice is where the intelligence officer is declared to the host government and where the officer works cooperatively with representatives of that government to tackle common problems such as terrorism or drug trafficking.

29.9 Spies do not always work with diplomatic cover but those who do not, known as 'illegals', need not concern us here as they do not have much or any interaction with genuine diplomats. Those who do work within embassies may therefore do so either as 'declared' intelligence officers, working with the local intelligence agencies in areas of mutual interest, or as 'undeclared', often working against the interests of the host government in acquiring information which might be used against that government in a future negotiation. In some embassies, colleagues will not know the role of the intelligence officer who will 'work' his or her cover. In other words, if they are described as a press officer, a commercial, or consular officer, they will devote part of each day to their cover task. In other cases, they will spend 100 per cent of their time on espionage activities. Naturally, where they are seen to be lending a helping hand with conventional embassy tasks, their relations with their own diplomatic colleagues are likely to be warmer.

29.10 To complement this human intelligence (humint) work, some embassies have sophisticated communication interception equipment installed in and/or on top of the embassy building. Although in many cases, the host government will be alive to this risk, there are other occasions where, perhaps relying on the friendly relations between the countries concerned, the hosts will assume that their own internal communications will not be targeted.

29.11 A particularly embarrassing example of how this confidence was misplaced arose in 2013 when press reports, *not* denied by the US government and therefore assumed to be accurate, indicated that the US government had been intercepting the phone calls of Angela Merkel, the German Chancellor. It was presumed that this was being carried out through the signals intelligence (sigint) gathering activity of the US embassy in Berlin. The US ambassador was summoned to explain himself and it was reported that there was a lengthy and difficult conversation between Mrs Merkel and President Obama.[7]

---

[6] These are covered in Arts 3.1(d), 41.1, and 41.3 of the Vienna Convention on Diplomatic Relations.

[7] '[O]ther information, most of which comes from the archive of former NSA contractor Edward Snowden, led to the conclusion that the US diplomatic mission in the German capital has not merely been promoting German-American friendship. On the contrary, it is a nest of espionage. From the roof of the embassy, a special unit of the CIA and NSA can apparently monitor a large part of cell phone communication in the government quarter. And there is evidence that agents based at

Disaffected intelligence officers, like the US military intelligence analyst, Private 29.12
Manning and Edward Snowden of the US National Security Agency (NSA),
have caused serious damage to diplomatic relations. The release by Wikileaks in
2010 of diplomatic exchanges made two years earlier between the Saudi King
Abdullah and the US ambassador Ryan Crocker over Iran with the former
urging the US 'to cut off the head of the [Iranian] snake' were acutely embarrassing and damaging to all concerned, not least to Saudi Arabia whose relations
with Iran were already severely strained.[8] And of course, the King's willingness
to share confidences with a friendly ambassador whose government could not
be trusted to protect such sensitive information must have compromised relations, at least in the short term.

Religious Diplomacy

At the other end of the spectrum of unconventional diplomacy comes religious 29.13
diplomacy. Given their spiritual and humanitarian concerns it is not surprising
that religious bodies have been active in international relations for many years,
even for centuries. The Quakers, with their strong pacifist roots, are a classic
case in point. More recently, the Community of Sant'Egidio, which began in
1968 as a Roman Catholic lay organization focused on the poor of Rome, has
since spread to be represented in seventy countries and has been active in bringing an end to the civil war in Mozambique and in mediation and conflict resolution in Lebanon, Algeria, Albania, Guatemala, and Kosovo.

Between 1979 and 1984, the Vatican mediated in the Beagle Channel dispute 29.14
between Argentina and Chile which included navigation rights, delimitation of
the Straits of Magellan, and maritime boundaries stretching to Cape Horn and

---

Pariser Platz recently targeted the cell phone that Merkel uses the most.... Last Wednesday Merkel
placed a strongly worded phone call to US President Barack Obama.... In a gesture of displeasure
usually reserved for rogue states, German Foreign Minister Guido Westerwelle summoned the new
US ambassador, John Emerson, for a meeting at the Foreign Ministry.' *Der Spiegel,* Issue 44/2013,
28 October 2013.

[8] 'The Need to Resist Iran

... 10. (S) [i.e. classified Secret] The King, Foreign Minister, Prince Muqrin, and Prince Nayif all agreed that
the Kingdom needs to cooperate with the US on resisting and rolling back Iranian influence and subversion
in Iraq. The King was particularly adamant on this point, and it was echoed by the senior princes as well.
*Al-Jubeir [Saudi Ambassador to the US] recalled the King's frequent exhortations to the US to attack Iran and so
put an end to its nuclear weapons program. "He told you to cut off the head of the snake," he recalled to the [US]
Chargé, adding that working with the US to roll back Iranian influence in Iraq is a strategic priority for the King
and his government.'*

Extract (paragraph 10) from a telegram/cable classified 'Secret' from the US Embassy in Riyadh to
Washington on Sunday, 20 April 2008, published by *The Guardian* on 28 November 2010.

beyond. Pope John Paul II sent a personal envoy to lead the mediation. The process took six years to resolve and culminated in 1984 with the signature of a Treaty of Peace and Friendship brokered by the Vatican.

29.15 Perhaps drawing on this precedent, the Argentine President Cristina Fernandez Kirchner approached (the Argentine) Pope Francis within days of his assuming the Pontificate in 2013 asking him to intervene in the Falklands dispute between her country and the UK and to promote dialogue between the two sides, a poisoned chalice which the Pope wisely decided not to accept. More recently, however, the Pope's intervention, even if only through using his good offices, has been demonstrated to have considerable efficacy in bringing about the renewal of diplomatic ties between Cuba and the US in 2015.[9]

Security Consultancies

29.16 Another manifestation of track two diplomacy has been the emergence of specialist consultancies on security matters that not only offer their business-orientated political analysis to companies and on occasion governments but will also mediate in areas where governments fear to tread. Control Risks is an example of a specialist risk consultancy that has engaged in activities such as negotiating ransoms for kidnapped businessmen, which have gone against the policies of most Western governments which refuse, at least in public, to pay ransoms and in some cases make doing so illegal.

Multinational Corporations

29.17 Global or multinational corporations must now be added to the list of diplomatic actors. Many follow the UN Code of Conduct for Transnational Companies and the range of similar provisions adopted by the OECD and individual governments. Leading companies are conscious of their corporate responsibilities, increasingly requiring to report to their shareholders on issues such as employment practices and environmental impact. As a result, like NGOs, their numbers involved in diplomatic activity have grown significantly in recent years. They may need to engage with governments, international institutions

---

[9] 'Within hours of the rapprochement being announced last December, it emerged that the first Latin American Pope in history had hosted secret talks at the Vatican between US and Cuban officials…. The Holy See confirmed in a statement that it had provided "its good offices to facilitate a constructive dialogue on delicate matters, resulting in solutions acceptable to both parties.'" *The Telegraph*, 18 September 2015.

including development banks, their shareholders, and NGOs on a variety of issues. Their aim understandably is to further and protect their company's interests which may bring them into collision, particularly with NGOs whose agendas on, for example, environmental and social matters may be severely at odds with those of the corporation. Again like governments and NGOs, multinational corporations will increasingly want to project their message and cast themselves in the most favourable light, an activity which is redolent of a government's public diplomacy. They will often need to open their own 'embassies' or offices to allow them to engage face-to-face with governmental or international institutions' representatives or indeed with a particularly active local NGO.

It is perhaps no surprise that major transnational firms should behave in this **29.18** way. Historically many such firms enjoyed governmental support in their trading activities. Examples include the Hudson's Bay Company and the respective East India companies of the British and Dutch governments. Indeed, such was their power that they effectively arrogated to themselves or were granted quasi-governmental powers. For instance, the Hudson's Bay Company, at one time the largest landowner in the world, was incorporated by royal charter of 1670 as *The Governor and Company of Adventurers of England trading into Hudson's Bay*, after which it was no surprise that it functioned as the de facto government of large tracts of North America. Its modern successors often find themselves in collision with government over competition law, monopolistic practices, and use and abuse of tax regimes. They will normally have specifically designated employees who are tasked with government or external relations. However, not all transnational corporations' activities are exclusively focused on profit-making. Some of the largest are among the world's major philanthropists— as they can afford to be.

Book VII

TREATIES AND TREATY-MAKING

30

INTERNATIONAL CONFERENCES

Frank Berman and David Bentley

Introductory

International meetings[1] in all formats and at all levels are now a ubiquitous **30.1** feature of international life. The tensions—likewise the pleasures, professional and personal—of modern conference diplomacy are hard to describe succinctly, but are reflected at many places in earlier chapters, and can often best be appreciated by reading personal memoirs and biographies.[2]

The present chapter is confined to international conferences in the more formal **30.2** sense of high-level meetings of state representatives for the discussion or settlement

---

[1] Permanent organizations having their own standing arrangements and rules of procedure, such as the United Nations and the Specialized Agencies, are treated as a separate subject in Book IV. Cross-references to that Book have therefore been kept to a minimum.

[2] The aficionado of contemporary international conferences can always, if the subject is of general interest, remain glued to an astonishingly wide selection of conference blogs and Twitter feeds.

of questions of international concern. The term 'congress' was used in the past to refer to formal assemblies of Plenipotentiaries for the conclusion of peace and the redistribution of territory,[3] but is now entirely out of use, even for these purposes:[4] cf, e.g. the Peace Conferences of 1919 and 1946–7 at the end of the two World Wars, and, more recently, the Conference on Security and Cooperation in Europe (CSCE),[5] which met for some three years in the early 1970s.[6] The term 'conference' is now universally used to describe all international meetings of this kind, whatever the subject-matter, whether convened with a view to arriving at particular agreements, including those not designed to be legally binding, or simply with a view to ventilating matters of concern or importance, or making recommendations to governments for action.

30.3 Many of the functions served by international conferences are nowadays equally capable of being performed either by a separate conference convened for a specific purpose or alternatively through the medium of a plenary gathering of the principal organ of an international organization. An intermediate solution, which is nowadays the most usual, is for a conference to be convened by decision of an international organization, but to take place separately from the meetings of the organization itself.[7] One increasingly common modern format is for multilateral treaty arrangements to provide for periodic 'Conferences of the Parties'. These may be simply for reviewing the operation of the treaty, or they may have specific functions conferred on them by the parent treaty for the modification, amendment, or supplementation of the treaty arrangements themselves.[8]

---

[3] As, for example, the Congresses of Vienna (1814–15) after the Napoleonic Wars, Paris (1856) after the Crimean War, and Berlin (1884–5) for the settlement of colonial claims in Africa.

[4] Although the Universal Postal Convention continues to be revised periodically at 'Congresses' of the Universal Postal Union.

[5] See Cmnd 6932 (1977) for the Final Act and other main documents, as well as a report on the Conference's outcome. The Final Act is also available at <http://www.osce.org/mc/39501>.

[6] And retained a semi-permanent character thereafter. On 1 January 1995 its name was changed from 'Conference' to 'Organization': see <http://www.osce.org/mc/39554>.

[7] Under Article 62.4 of the United Nations Charter, the Economic and Social Council (ECOSOC) is given an express power to call international conferences on matters falling within its competence, which it has made use of to convene important conferences on the environment and development (1972), hunger and world food (1974), population growth (1974), the role of women (1975), employment (1976), human settlements (1978), and science and technology (1979). A recent example is the series of conferences on financing for sustainable development, the latest of which took place in Addis Ababa in 2015 (<http://www.un.org/esa/ffd/ffd3/conference.html>).

[8] Striking recent examples of the latter are the 2010 Review Conference of the Statute of the International Criminal Court which adopted the amendment covering the crime of aggression, and the 2015 Conference of the Parties to the UN Framework Convention on Climate Change which adopted the Paris agreement on the reduction of carbon dioxide emissions.

Venue

In earlier times conferences of these kinds might be held at a neutral venue, or **30.4**
at some place expressly neutralized for the purpose of the meeting. There were
often mediators who presided over the discussions, whether carried on orally or
in writing. In the nineteenth century congresses and conferences were mostly
held at the capital of one of the Powers concerned, and then the Chancellor or
Minister for Foreign Affairs of that Power usually presided. Besides the Plenipotentiaries specially deputed for the occasion, the local diplomatic representatives
of the Powers were also appointed as delegates.

Nowadays, although traces of the earlier practices remain, the usual pattern, **30.5**
where a conference is convened by an international organization, is for the decision on the seat of the conference, as well as other necessary details about its
date, duration, participation in the conference, and the organizational arrangements, to be incorporated in the formal decision or resolution convening the
conference and setting out its purpose or terms of reference. This does not,
however, exclude the possibility of a conference's being convened at the invitation of a particular government or group of governments. In that event, the
modalities mentioned above will have been established by agreement on the
diplomatic plane in advance, and then Incorporated in the invitation issued
by the convening government, perhaps with some of them left to be worked
out by the conference itself in its initial stages.

The place of meeting of an international conference will be determined **30.6**
according to the pattern employed for convening it. An international organization convening a conference will often do so at its own permanent headquarters, but will sometimes be dependent on an offer from a member State to act
as host and to provide premises for the conference, and meet at least part of the
organizational and financial burden. In that event, the myriad details that arise
to be regulated will be covered in a host country agreement concluded between
the host government and the international organization, often following a
standard model. Moreover, even where the idea behind the conference had been
initiated by the international organization, it would be normal for a host government to assume for practical purposes the responsibilities of sponsor and
convener. Quite apart from any political considerations, the problems of
finance, location, and accommodation, and notably nowadays those of security,
may prove unexpectedly formidable, and the detailed advance planning may
occupy many months. Where the conference is convened at the invitation of a
State, its site will usually be the capital of that State. Sometimes, on the other
hand, the site is chosen on the basis of its convenience as a location for all parties. On other occasions, the choice may be expressly designed to enable discus-

sions to be carried on in a neutral atmosphere, or in seclusion away from the glare of publicity, or protected from security threats or public demonstrations, in which case the place chosen may well not be a capital city.[9] For periodic meetings, such as review conferences of a multilateral treaty or conferences of the parties as mentioned earlier, the place may be determined by a provision in the treaty itself, or by an understanding reached at the previous conference.

Invitations to a Conference

30.7 Before formal invitations to a conference are issued, there will invariably have been an exchange of views between the governments concerned, or at any rate those chiefly affected, and may in many modern cases also include international bodies as well as non-governmental organizations (NGOs) and other entities whose participation may be essential for the conference to achieve its purpose. In that event, and notably for example where the purpose of the conference is to deal with an internal, or mixed internal and external, armed conflict, or to resolve disputed claims to territory or statehood, the terms on which entities not yet recognized as States or governments are admitted to participate in the conference may be as delicate to settle as they are crucial to the prospects of the conference succeeding. Questions of this nature aside, it is always desirable, and may be essential, for the scope of the conference to be determined in advance, so as to reduce the risk of the conference coming to grief when differences on this central issue prove insurmountable. In many cases the conference will have been preceded by intensive prior negotiation over the shape of the substantive outcome, even though the political will to reach general agreement may only become possible under the enhanced pressure of the conference itself.

30.8 It is usual for the invitations to a conference to be accompanied by a draft of the proposed rules of procedure, specifying among other things the type of credentials required; the arrangements for observers; the main committee structure; the keeping of records; interpretation and translation; open and closed meetings; the working languages; and the system of voting to be used.[10] Where the conference is convened by an international organization, the draft rules of

---

[9] The face-to-face meetings between representatives of Israel and the Palestine Liberation Organization, which led to the Oslo Accords of 1993, were held under cover of a Norwegian research institute (Fafo); the Norwegian government covered the expenses, provided security, and were able to keep the meetings away from the public eye. The negotiation of a subsequent important appendage took place in a Paris hotel in the full glare of publicity, and the resulting agreement was signed in Washington. See also Chapter 29, paragraph 29.3.

[10] A useful comparative model is the standing Rules of Procedure for the UN General Assembly, which can be found at <http://www.un.org/en/ga/about/ropga/>.

procedure will have been produced and discussed within the framework of the organization, and then transmitted for formal adoption by the conference itself when it convenes. Similarly, the conference agenda may need to have been pre-negotiated in advance. All this presupposes the appointment of a secretariat on which the administrative work of the conference is to fall. If the conference is not convened by an international organization, the host government will have to make itself responsible for the provision of a secretariat.[11]

Delegates

Normally, in the case of conferences of a non-political or technical character, **30.9** diplomats are appointed as chief delegates and their delegations will include whatever specialized knowledge or expertise the subject requires. The names of the members of each delegation will have been communicated in advance to the convening international organization or host government. The most senior representative of each participant will be designated the head of delegation, and will sometimes, for important conferences, be a minister or high official who might in turn attend only the opening and closing stages, leaving the detailed work under the charge of a deputy. The importance of the occasion, as well as the resources available to the individual participating governments, will dictate the size of their delegations, which often include legal or technical experts, secretaries, interpreters and translators, press spokesmen, etc. If the agenda ranges over a wide or complex field, delegations may be of a considerable size, not only on the part of the host State. At the Third United Nations Conference on the Law of the Sea, which met for an extended period in the 1970s and 80s, the delegation of the United States had two joint heads and fifteen alternate representatives, assisted by fifteen Congressional advisers and their staff and a senator from Micronesia; thirty-eight advisers representing the Departments of State, Commerce, Defense, Interior, Transportation, the Treasury, and numerous federal agencies, as well as experts on geography, cartography, navigation, international law, and international relations; and twenty-six technical experts in the fields of fisheries, petroleum, hard minerals, the marine environment, marine science, and maritime industries: a total of 112 delegates in all (excluding secretarial, administrative, and service staff).

Full Powers and Credentials

Many international conferences are convened for the purpose of negotiating **30.10** and concluding treaties. A conference of this kind may be designated as a

---

[11] See further paragraphs **30.26–30.27**.

Conference of Plenipotentiaries; in that case, as the name implies, the expectation would be that the heads of delegation or their representatives had been furnished with Full Powers,[12] empowering them not only to take part in the negotiations, but to conclude, subject if necessary to ratification, any treaty instrument which may result. Where a State appoints more than one Plenipotentiary, Full Powers may be issued to each, or their names may be included in a single document which authorizes them to act jointly or severally.

30.11 Whether or not they hold Full Powers, all delegates will require credentials, without which they will not be entitled to gain admission or to take part in the work of the conference. Credentials usually take the form of a letter from the responsible minister of the sending government, giving the delegates' names, titles, and functions, and specifying their capacity within the delegation, depending on the requirements of the rules of procedure. A single letter of credentials covers all members of the delegation. A credentials committee of limited size will invariably be established at the outset of the proceedings to examine the letters of credentials and recommend their approval by the plenary body. This will normally be a pure formality, but severe difficulties can on occasion arise, for example when two authorities claim to represent a participant. The resulting gap is frequently bridged by a provision in the rules to the effect that, pending approval of their credentials, delegations may be seated provisionally, and that can on occasion be manipulated to allow all delegations to be seated 'provisionally' while postponing the intractable credentials issue until the closing sessions.[13]

Languages at Conferences

30.12 Before the First World War, the language employed at an international conference was usually French, but since then practice on this question has undergone substantial changes. At the Paris Peace Conference of 1919, and at League of Nations conferences, French and English were used. For conferences convened under the auspices of an international organization, it is now invariably the case that all of the official languages of the organization will be official languages of the conference, but that does not necessarily mean that they will all have the same status as working languages. The applicable rules on the question will form part of the rules of procedure, and will regulate, for example, the languages into

---

[12] See also Chapter 31, paragraphs 31.11–31.12, and, more generally, Chapter 7, paragraphs 7.54–7.57.

[13] An equivalent rule can be found in Rule 29 of the standing Rules of Procedure for the UN General Assembly (see n 10).

which conference documents will be translated and the languages into and out of which interpretation will be provided. In the case of the United Nations and other organizations within the UN system there are six official languages: Arabic, Chinese, English, French, Russian, and Spanish. Within the European Union, on the other hand, the national languages of all Member States have equal status, a total of twenty-four in all.[14] Although English is now the language most commonly used at international conferences of all kinds, this is a matter of empirical practice only.

The development of modern equipment allowing for simultaneous interpret- **30.13** ation of speeches has made the use of two or more languages much easier, but success depends on the quality of the interpretation.[15] The standard of simultaneous interpretation, which has always had a few exponents of legendary skill, is nowadays generally high, and the International Association of Conference Interpreters (AIIC), with headquarters in Geneva, has helped to bring this about.[16] An international organization may have at its disposal its own staff of interpreters or translators,[17] though it is commonplace for the interpreters at least to be hired from outside for the occasion or provided by the host government. The choice of equipment for interpretation and its proper functioning requires constant technical supervision, and its lay-out may impose limitations of its own on the premises suitable for conference use.[18]

The President of a Conference

An international conference is usually, but not always, presided over by the **30.14** principal representative of the country in which it is held, if that country is a participant. Often this is the Minister for Foreign Affairs or some other member of the government. There may on occasion however, depending on the way in which the conference was initiated, or on the political sensitivities affecting the

---

[14] Internally within the European Union, the language régime for the community institutions is determined by the Council (Art 342 of the consolidated version of the Treaty on the Functioning of the European Union).

[15] See also Chapters 31 and 35 for treaties in more than one language.

[16] The AIIC administers an accreditation process, and its members are bound by codes of ethics and professional standards. There is a similar organization for conference translators, also with its headquarters in Switzerland. For a fuller description of the part played by interpreters, see R Roland, *Interpreters as Diplomats: A Diplomatic History of the Role of Interpreters in World Politics* (Ottawa: University of Ottawa Press, 1999).

[17] With the benefit of modern methods of communication, it may sometimes be simpler and more effective for documents to be sent back for translation to the organization's headquarters.

[18] And so may the security implications.

particular subject-matter, be a joint presidency held by more than one country, or a series of vice-presidents. The choice of president (and vice-presidents), as well as the main committee chairmanships and other offices, will in practice have been settled informally in advance, so that the election of the president will be a purely formal motion which the conference will be expected to accept by acclamation.

30.15   The functions of the president of an international conference are to open the proceedings; to secure formal endorsement of the rules of procedure, of the committee structure and chairmanships, and of other questions of procedure previously agreed to informally; to direct the course of the discussions throughout the formal proceedings of the conference proper; to control the final voting (if any); and ultimately to declare the conference closed. Frequently, however, the most important function of the presidency will be to bring its prestige to bear behind the scenes to cajole or persuade delegations to come to agreement on the most difficult points. Adroit conduct of the presidential function is often the key to a successful conference outcome.

Ceremonial and Precedence

30.16   In the past, a great deal of the work of a congress or conference might relate to the nice adjustment of matters of ceremonial and precedence. It is recorded that on the signature of the treaty of peace between France and Spain at the Congress of Nijmegen (1676–9), the French and Spanish copies of the treaty had been prepared, and laid on the table at which the English mediators sat. The three French Plenipotentiaries then entered by one door at the same moment as the three Spanish Plenipotentiaries entered at the other, they sat down simultaneously in exactly similar armchairs, and signed both copies at the same instant.

30.17   Older rules about precedence among Plenipotentiaries have now been supplanted by the principle of equality between all delegations. Seating is normally arranged in alphabetical order in a conference hall, starting from the right of the president.[19] Which delegation occupies the first place on the right of the president

---

[19] The entry of the two halves of the divided Germany into UN membership in 1973 necessitated some delicate diplomacy over titles; by informal arrangement, while East Germany was seated under its official name (German Democratic Republic), West Germany carried the title 'Germany, Federal Republic of', with the consequence that the two delegations were seated next to one another. In the case of the new Macedonian State that emerged from the break-up of the former Yugoslavia, it was eventually, after difficult negotiation (including over whether 'f' should appear as upper- or lower-

may be determined by arrangement or by drawing lots. At a peace conference or its equivalent the representatives of the belligerent States may be seated in two opposite groups; often, however, the device of a 'round table conference' or some other special seating arrangement is deliberately chosen to sidestep awkward questions of this kind.[20]

Procedure

Plenary Organ; Committees and Sub-committees

It will frequently be the case that the main organ of the conference will adjourn **30.18** after disposing of the formal opening business and conducting a general debate; the substantive proceedings will then be remitted to a committee of the whole, under the control of which further committees may be set up to discuss particular agenda items or sections of the draft final instrument. Sub-committees may be formed to deal with specific points and these in turn report back to the committee which appointed them. Apart from these, it is nearly always necessary to have a drafting committee of limited size to prepare the text of the treaty, concluding document, or other instrument resulting from the work of the conference, though it is also possible that informal drafting processes will be used, especially when the expectation is that the final outcome will be approved by consensus.

Each of these committees will have its own chairman, and will often appoint a **30.19** 'rapporteur' to prepare the report to be furnished to the parent body, who may or may not also be the chairman of the committee; the functions of the rapporteur are to summarize the conclusions arrived at by the committee and the discussions that led to them. The report is first submitted to the members of the committee, and the rapporteur is then the mouthpiece of the committee in placing its report before the parent body.

Plenary Meetings and Recording of Proceedings

As the work of the conference proceeds, plenary meetings of the main organ **30.20** take place from time to time, either for further policy debate or to receive and consider the reports of the committees. In a typical case, where the outcome of the work is embodied in a treaty, the plenary organ will be asked to adopt the

---

case), seated under the letter 't' as 'the former Yugoslav Republic of Macedonia'; see M Wood, *Max Planck Yearbook of United Nations Law*, Vol 1 (1997) 231.

[20] See Appendix II for some examples.

text, article by article, if necessary by vote,[21] after which the resulting text will be submitted for adoption as a whole by the conference; it will then be incorporated in or appended to the Final Act of the conference, which will be signed at the concluding session by the heads of all delegations.[22] A Final Act of this kind is particularly common when the results of the conference are embodied in treaty instruments together with decisions or recommendations which do not themselves form part of the treaty texts adopted.[23]

30.21 Careful record keeping is an important function of all significant conferences. It used to be the practice for minutes (*procès-verbaux*) to be prepared by the secretary or secretaries covering each sitting in minute detail, which would then be signed by all the Plenipotentiaries, and the originals preserved by the government of the host State, which would supply copies to the others. In recent years, practice has become both less regular and far less formal. There is generally a verbatim record, either stenographic or recorded on tape or disc, from which the secretariat will be responsible for producing, often under the supervision of a rapporteur, a summary record for circulation to delegations. Participants may be given an opportunity of altering wording in the summary, but not the sense. Adoption of records by the conference and their signature by the president are unusual, although they are normally submitted to the delegations before being drawn up in final form. Drafts, declarations, etc are often circulated as conference documents and are not always appended to the daily record of proceedings.

30.22 In modern practice, the signatures both on the Final Act and on a treaty adopted by a conference appear in the alphabetical order of the States represented.[24] Earlier special practices have fallen away.

---

[21] The Vienna Convention on the Law of Treaties (see Chapter 31) now lays down a rule that the adoption of a treaty at an international conference takes place by the vote of two-thirds of the States present and voting, which is widely accepted as an accurate statement of international practice. The rule is however expressly qualified by an exception for the case where the application of a different voting rule is decided 'by the same majority'. In actual practice, however, there has been a marked contemporary move towards the use of a 'consensus' rule, where possible, for international conferences in general, although the term 'consensus' has no formal definition and can be applied in a variety of forms.

[22] See also Chapter 33, paragraphs 33.25–33.27.

[23] The Vienna Conference on the Law of Treaties, for example, adopted a Declaration on the prohibition of military, political, or economic coercion in the conclusion of treaties, a Declaration on universal participation in the Vienna Convention on the Law of Treaties, a Resolution relating to Article 1 of the Convention, a Resolution relating to the Declaration on the prohibition of military, political, or economic coercion in the conclusion of treaties, and a Resolution relating to Article 66 of the Convention, all of which were annexed to the Final Act of the Conference.

[24] Within the EU, the alphabetical order follows the name of each Member State in its own language.

Codification of Procedures

Both the League of Nations and the United Nations have tried, without success, **30.23**
to codify in standard form the procedures to be followed at international conferences. It was one of the topics remitted to the League of Nations Committee
of Experts for the Progressive Codification of International Law in the 1920s,
but the work was deferred *sine die* in 1928. The subject was likewise looked at
intermittently by the UN General Assembly in the 1980s but the work was
again deferred without outcome.[25] The General Assembly did however draw up
in 1979 a set of standard rules for Pledging Conferences, which would seem to
have been beneficial in avoiding wasteful duplication.[26]

Participation in International Conferences

The question of who is to participate in a conference can vary from the straight- **30.24**
forward to the intensely problematic. Even at a Conference of the Parties or
review conference,[27] where the primary criterion for attendance is a given, questions may still arise as to the admission of States entitled to become party to the
treaty in question even though they have not yet done so, or have not yet completed the processes for accession. Similar questions may arise for conferences
convened by an international organization. During the Cold War, when the
continued existence of divided States prevented the admission of either part to
the United Nations and other organizations, a formula had to be found for
general conferences which permitted sufficiently wide attendance but avoided
unacceptable conclusions being drawn over recognition. That particular problem is now largely a thing of the past, but problems of a not dissimilar kind
may have to be solved ad hoc—for example at a conference to settle an internal
conflict—in order to avoid untoward implications as to the varying statuses of
the participants. Similar problems arise in respect of the admission of 'observers', which are dealt with in the next paragraph.[28]

---

[25] See R Sabel, *Procedure at International Conferences* (2nd edn, Cambridge: Cambridge University Press, 2006) 13–17.
[26] Ibid, 18.
[27] See paragraph **30.3**.
[28] For a particularly complex contemporary example, see the Paris Conference (see n 8 and Appendix II), where the parties were divided (though for substantive reasons) into three categories, and there was a massive presence of observer organizations as well as NGOs (details can be found at <http://unfccc.int/parties_and_observers/items/2704.ph>).

Observers

30.25 The creation of a category of 'observers' is a device frequently resorted to as a way to side-step awkward questions of status, recognition, or participation.[29] Typically, observers will have the right to attend a conference and to be present at most, if not all, of its meetings, but not to play a formal part in its work, e.g. by voting on proposals and decisions. So the status of observer may be opened to: States not members of an international organization; other international organizations; state-like entities not generally recognized;[30] other bodies with a special international status;[31] or (quite frequently nowadays in the context of particular international conferences) NGOs.[32]

The Secretariat

30.26 The principal secretary at a conference—often called its Executive Secretary—is usually an official of the country in which it is held, if that country is the convener of the conference, and the members of the secretariat are also often furnished by it, perhaps supplemented by others drawn from the permanent secretariat of an international organization. The secretariat comes under the control and authority of the president of the conference. For conferences convened by international organizations, it is invariably the case that a senior member of the organization's permanent staff will be designated as Executive Secretary of the conference. In such cases, the necessary services are normally provided by the secretariat of the organization concerned, supplemented possibly by the host State.

30.27 One of the major functions of the Secretariat will be relations with the media, print, television, and online, ranging from the provision of facilities, and arrangements for media accreditation, to the regular feeding of information. There will

---

[29] On the detail, see Sabel, *Procedure*.

[30] The Palestine Liberation Organization, for example, was granted in 1974 the status of a permanent observer in the UN General Assembly by GA resolution 3237 (XXIX) (later under the title of 'Palestine' following GA resolution 43/177 of 1988), and was subsequently granted the 'additional rights and privileges' set out in the Annex to GA resolution 52/250 of 1998, which applied as well to conferences convened under UN auspices. Finally, under GA resolution 67/19 of 2012, Palestine was granted 'non-member observer State status' in the United Nations. Similar arrangements had been in effect for the Holy See which became a 'Permanent Observer State' in 1964, and were further enhanced in 2004; see the Annex to GA resolution 58/314.

[31] Notably the International Committee of the Red Cross 'in consideration of the special role and mandates conferred upon it by the Geneva Conventions of 12 August 1949' (GA resolution 45/6 of 1990).

[32] See, in general, <http://www.un.org/esa/coordination/ngo/>. The significance of NGOs in general is dealt with at length in Chapter 28.

seldom be a conference spokesman as such; the media function is likely to be divided between the conference presidency and the executive secretary and senior officials.

Note. Lists of the more important congresses and conferences from the middle of the seventeenth century onwards were given in the second edition of this work; and in his further treatise, *International Congresses,* the late Sir Ernest Satow dealt more fully with those held since the beginning of the last century. None of this material is included in the present edition. But in view of certain peculiarities with regard to the way in which the respective Peace Treaties were negotiated and drawn up by the Paris Peace Conference of 1946, the Japanese Peace Conference of 1951, and the Geneva Conference of 1954, the notes on them which appeared in the fourth edition have been retained and are reprinted in an edited form in Appendix II of this book, supplemented by a section on the International Conference on the Former Yugoslavia of 1992–5.

31

TREATIES AND OTHER INTERNATIONAL INSTRUMENTS—I GENERAL DEFINITION, TREATY FORMALITIES

Frank Berman and David Bentley

General Definition

31.1 The most frequently cited definition of a treaty is that contained in the Vienna Convention on the Law of Treaties.[1, 2] It defines the term 'treaty' as 'an international agreement concluded between States in written form and governed by international law, whether embodied in a single instrument or in two or more

---

[1] Much useful material is nowadays to be found on the Foreign & Commonwealth Office's treaty pages, at <https://www.gov.uk/guidance/uk-treaties> (hereinafter 'FCO Guidance'). The United Nations Office of Legal Affairs also publishes a Treaty Handbook containing similar material; it can be found at <https://treaties.un.org/doc/source/publications/THB/English.pdf>.

[2] Opened for signature on 25 May 1969; entered into force on 27 January 1980; 1155 UNTS 331. There are now 114 States Parties.

related instruments and whatever its particular designation'.[3] This definition is however expressly for the purposes of the Convention only. It consciously excludes, for example, international agreements concluded between States and international organizations or between international organizations themselves, and equally excludes international agreements not in written form, while providing at the same time that the omission of these cases is without prejudice to their legal force or to the application to them of the rules of international law.[4] Amongst the leading authorities, McNair uses the term 'treaty' to denote 'a written agreement by which two or more States or international organizations create or intend to create a relation between themselves operating within the sphere of international law';[5] while Reuter, at a higher level of generality, speaks of: 'une manifestation de volontés concordantes imputables à deux ou à plusieurs sujets de droit international et destinée à produire des effets de droit selon les règles de droit international'.[6]

Particular Aspects of a General Definition

Agreements Involving International Organizations and Oral Agreements

It is thus apparent that there is no single, all-embracing definition of the term 'treaty', and that the Vienna Convention, for all its great authority in the field, does not set out to provide one. The Convention is however now supplemented by a second Vienna Convention, of 1986, equally adopted on the basis of thorough and lengthy preparation by the International Law Commission, and designed to regulate the treaties of international organizations, both those concluded between themselves and by them with States.[7] With the sole exception of the references to international organizations, the terms used in the 1986 Convention to define 'treaty' for its own purposes are substantially identical to those used in the 1969 Convention. It is thus possible to extract the following

31.2

---

[3] Art 2.1(a). In formal terms, the Convention has no retroactive effect (Art 4); but for a brief analysis of how far the Convention represents a codification of existing customary international law: see I M Sinclair, *The Vienna Convention on the Law of Treaties* (2nd edn, Manchester: Manchester University Press, 1984) ch I. The International Court of Justice has on repeated occasions recognized this effect for provisions of the Convention.

[4] Art 3. While it is now widely accepted that a State may be bound by a unilateral or purely oral statement where the intention to create a binding obligation under international law should be inferred, engagements of this kind are not covered by most of the formal, and even substantial, rules and practices dealt with in this and following chapters. They may nevertheless be governed *mutatis mutandis* by some aspects at least of the law of treaties, as the Vienna Convention implies.

[5] Lord McNair, *Law of Treaties* (Oxford: Clarendon Press, 1961) 4.

[6] *Introduction au droit des traités* (3rd rev edn, Paris: PUF, 1995).

[7] But not yet in force, failing ratification by more than thirty of the requisite thirty-five States; twelve international organizations have however become parties to it. See <https://treaties.un.org/Pages/showDetails.aspx?objid=080000028004bfbd>.

elements as central to a modern general definition of the term 'treaty': an *agreement*, of a suitably *formal character*, designed to give rise to *legal rights and obligations*, operating *within the sphere of international law*, and concluded between two or more parties possessing *legal personality under international law*. This should be read together with the fact that, whereas States are automatically endowed with treaty-making capacity, as an aspect of their sovereignty,[8] the extent to which a particular international organization will be competent to conclude treaties will be a function of its constituent instruments and other rules of the organization, based on the fulfilment of the organization's functions and purposes.[9]

31.3 It is also established that, although the overwhelming majority of transactions meeting these criteria will be recorded in writing,[10] there is no reason in law or practice why this must be the case.[11] The position is now beyond doubt, following the judgments of the Permanent Court of International Justice in the *Legal Status of Eastern Greenland* case in 1933, and of the International Court of Justice in the *Nuclear Tests* cases (*Australia v France, New Zealand v France*) in 1974. In the first of these, the Court had to consider the legal significance of an oral declaration made by the Norwegian Minister for Foreign Affairs to the Danish diplomatic representative, and concluded:

> that a reply of this nature given by the Minister for Foreign Affairs on behalf of his Government in response to a request by the diplomatic representative of a foreign Power, in regard to a question falling within his province, is binding upon the country to which the Minister belongs.[12]

In the second, the Court attributed special weight to a series of statements by the President of the French Republic, and by the French ministers of defence and foreign affairs, made subsequent to the oral proceedings in the case, which the Court said had to be held to constitute an engagement of the State having legal effect, whatever the form in which they were expressed, in writing or not.[13] The International Law Commission has recently had the subject under study and adopted a set of Guiding Principles, for what it termed 'formal declarations formulated by a State with the intent to produce obligations under international

---

[8] Vienna Convention, Art 6.

[9] Arts 1 and 6 and the Preamble to the 1986 Convention (see n 7).

[10] Though by no means necessarily in one single document.

[11] McNair, *Law of Treaties*, 7.

[12] PCIJ, Series A/B, No 53, 71.

[13] [1974] ICJ Reports 267: 'With regard to the question of form, it should be observed that this is not a domain in which international law imposes any special or strict requirements. Whether a statement is made orally or in writing makes no essential difference, for such statements made in particular circumstances may create commitments in international law, which does not require that they should be couched in written form.'

law'. The Guiding Principles indicate that to determine the legal effects of such declarations, it is necessary to take account of their content, of all the factual circumstances in which they were made, 'and of the reactions to which they gave rise'.[14]

It should finally be noted that, so long as it evidences a clear indication of con- **31.4** sent by the parties to be bound, it is not necessary for a treaty, even one in writing, to take the form of an instrument signed, and as the case may be rati- fied, by each of them. The Algiers Accords, which settled a series of questions in dispute between the United States and Iran following the revolution that deposed the Shah of Iran, takes the form of declarations made by the government of Algeria in which it records, as intermediary, 'the ... interdependent commitments ... made by the two governments', and annexes the terms of an escrow agreement between the United States government and certain banks.[15] In the case between Qatar and Bahrain on *Maritime Delimitation and Territorial Questions*,[16] the International Court of Justice found that separate exchanges of letters between the King of Saudi Arabia and the Amirs of Qatar and Bahrain, together with a document headed 'Minutes' and signed by the Foreign Ministers of the three States, were international agreements creating rights and obliga- tions for the parties sufficient to establish the jurisdiction of the Court.

For practical purposes, therefore, neither agreements not in written form, nor **31.5** treaties concluded by international organizations, nor treaties cast in a non- conventional shape, need be regarded as a special case when it comes to the application to them of the law of treaties. But several of the central elements set out earlier warrant further analysis.

Requirement that Agreement Should be Governed by International Law

First there is the requirement that the agreement should be 'governed by inter- **31.6** national law'.[17] This serves to distinguish a treaty from other agreements which, although concluded between States or other subjects of international law, are regulated not by international law but by the national law of one of the parties (or by some other legal system chosen by the parties). An example would be a State contract concluded between the competent State authorities of two countries,

---

[14] The full text of the Guiding Principles is at <http://legal.un.org/ilc/texts/instruments/english/commentaries/9_9_2006.pdf>.

[15] Texts available at <http://www.iusct.org/index-english.html>. A main purpose of the Accords was to establish a Claims Tribunal, which has since its foundation in 1981 presided over one of the largest claims settlement processes in history.

[16] [1995] ICJ Reports 6.

[17] Operate 'within the sphere of international law' (McNair); or be intended to produce legal effects 'selon les règles de droit international' (Reuter).

under which one agreed to supply the energy needs of the other through a gas pipeline on the basis of a standard form of contract used in the energy trade. Other transactions of a private law nature, such as leases of land and buildings and loan agreements, may also be entered into between governments; in such cases, it may be difficult to determine whether the parties intended the transaction to be governed by international law, or by general principles of law, or by a particular system of national law.[18] Conversely, it is perfectly possible for transactions between non-State parties, or between a State and a foreign private party, to be governed, by agreement, by international law, either on its own or as a supplement to the application of national law; this is very frequently the case for investment contracts, notably those concluded under the cover of bilateral treaties for the protection and promotion of investments.[19] A treaty of 1965, concluded under the auspices of the World Bank, established a Centre, based in Washington, for the settlement of investment disputes by arbitration,[20] and provides that, in the absence of agreement, the tribunal shall apply the national law of the State Party 'and such rules of international law as may be applicable'.[21]

Instruments not Intended to Give Rise to Legal Relations

31.7 The requirement also serves moreover to distinguish a further category of international transactions which, although cast in writing and representing the result of an agreement between governments, are nevertheless not intended to give rise to legal relations, i.e. to a set of binding rights and obligations. Lacking this essential element, these instruments, however important they may be, cannot properly be classed as treaties.

31.8 An example is the Final Act of the Conference on Security and Cooperation in Europe.[22] It is plain on the internal evidence[23] that the Final Act was not considered to amount to a treaty. Another example is the Universal Declaration of Human Rights adopted by the General Assembly of the United Nations on 10 December 1948,[24] which required subsequent lengthy discussion and

---

[18] See F A Mann, *Studies in International Law* (Oxford: Clarendon Press, 1973) 140–255.

[19] See <http://investmentpolicyhub.unctad.org/IIA>.

[20] Or, though far less frequently, by conciliation.

[21] The Washington Convention of 1965 on the Settlement of Investment Disputes between States and Nationals of Other States, Art 42(1); <https://icsid.worldbank.org/apps/ICSIDWEB/icsiddocs/Pages/ICSID-Convention.aspx>.

[22] See Chapter **30**, paragraph **30.2** and related footnotes; the text of the Final Act is at <http://www.osce.org/mc/39501>.

[23] Including that it was specifically stated not to be 'eligible for registration under Article 102 of the Charter of the United Nations' (see further paragraphs **31.18–31.19**).

[24] General Assembly resolution 217 (III).

negotiation to turn its contents into legally binding form in the two International Covenants of 1966 on Civil and Political Rights, and on Economic, Social and Cultural Rights.[25]

Questions of Form and Terminology

'Terminology' refers here to the title given by the parties to their treaty, and **31.9** 'form' to its formal structure. Although the question of terminology was once the source of much confusion, it is now well established that the title given to a treaty instrument is entirely a matter of the free choice of the parties, and has no bearing on the legal quality of the instrument or on the application to it of the law of treaties. The Vienna Convention definition cited earlier[26] makes this explicit by providing in terms that it applies to all such agreements, whatever their particular designation. Conversely, the title given to an instrument, although it may be an indicator, and sometimes even a strong indicator, of the intentions of the parties, is not in itself conclusive of the status of the instrument, which would have to fulfil in substance the criteria listed[27] in order to rank as a treaty. Although Article 102 of the United Nations Charter, when laying down the obligation of registration,[28] uses the dual terminology '[e]very treaty and every international agreement', the term 'treaty' may be taken as having the broadest generic scope. It may also, depending upon the intention of the parties, cover agreed minutes and (subject to paragraphs 33.20–33.24) memoranda of understanding.

A rationalization of the terminology employed in international practice to **31.10** describe treaty instruments is difficult to attempt, and hardly seems profitable. So far as trends are discernible at all in modern practice, it might be said that 'treaty' and 'convention' tend to be invested with the most solemnity, the former being frequently (but by no means exclusively) employed for bilateral engagements and the latter (but again by no means exclusively) for general multilateral engagements; whereas 'statute' is most commonly reserved for the constitutive instruments of international organizations. But any statement of this kind is subject to so many exceptions as to let it serve as no more than the most general guidance, and then of a purely descriptive character. It would nevertheless appear that the most frequently utilized designations for treaty instruments are

---

[25] For an account of the process, see A Cassese, in P Alston, *The United Nations and Human Rights* (Oxford: Oxford University Press, 1992) 25–54. A similar pattern was followed for Outer Space (GA resolution 1962 (XVIII)), and for the Deep Sea Bed (GA resolution 2749 (XXV)).

[26] Paragraph **31.1**.

[27] Paragraph **31.2**.

[28] See paragraphs **31.18–31.19**.

treaty, convention, agreement, exchange of Notes, protocol, and declaration. These particular usages will be discussed in Chapters 32–33.

Formalities in the Drawing up of Treaties

Initialling and Signature

31.11 The 'single-instrument' type of treaty (whether designated as treaty, convention, agreement, protocol, or declaration) is normally concluded, and the authenticity of its text established, by means of the signatures of the negotiators, who will, as a general rule, have to produce Full Powers for the purpose.[29] It will depend on the circumstances, but primarily on the intention of the parties as signified in the treaty, whether signature alone is sufficient to bring the treaty into force or whether some further step, such as ratification, is necessary.[30]

31.12 Sometimes, however, and particularly when there may be a significant interval between the conclusion of the negotiations and the signature of a treaty (for example, in order to enable the governments concerned to satisfy themselves as to the acceptability or otherwise of the agreement as a whole), the negotiators initial the treaty in its final version as a guarantee of the authenticity of the text. Even when a treaty is opened for signature immediately upon the conclusion of the negotiations, the separate pages of the text are sometimes initialled prior to its reproduction in a form suitable for signature (this practice applies to bilateral rather than multilateral treaties). The act of initialling a treaty can of itself constitute a signature of the treaty when it is established that the negotiating States have so agreed.[31] The International Law Commission point out that in practice initialling, especially by a Head of State, Prime Minister, or Foreign Minister, is not infrequently intended as the equivalent of full signature.[32] But initialling by lesser dignitaries may equally have the effect of full signature if this is the clear intention of the parties.[33]

---

[29] Vienna Convention, Art 7. Heads of State, Heads of Government, and ministers for foreign affairs are however, in virtue of their functions and without having to produce Full Powers, considered as representing their State for the purposes of performing all acts relating to the conclusion of a treaty. Credentials notifying the composition of a delegation to an international conference at which a treaty may be negotiated and signed do not constitute Full Powers for the purposes of signature.

[30] See Chapter 34, paragraphs 34.13–34.18.

[31] Vienna Convention on the Law of Treaties (Art 12.2).

[32] [1966] ILC Reports 29.

[33] A 'Memorandum of Understanding' of 5 October 1954, between the Governments of the United Kingdom, the United States of America, Italy and Yugoslavia about the Free Territory of Trieste provides that certain things were to be done 'as soon as this Memorandum of Understanding has been initialled' or within a specified period from the date of initialling.

Preparation of Signature Texts

The preparation for signature of a bilateral single-instrument treaty is under- **31.13**
taken by the country in whose capital the treaty is to be signed. The style and
presentation used will follow the practices of that country. Bilateral treaties
are prepared for signature in duplicate, so allowing each party to retain a signed
original version. Each of the two countries is entitled to precedence in the
original retained by it, that is to say, its language will (where the treaty text is
printed on facing pages or in parallel columns) appear in the first or left-hand
page or column; its title (or the title of its representative) will be named first
in the preamble; and the signature of its representative will appear above, or
to the left of, the signature of the representative of the other party. For multilateral treaties, these formalities will usually fall to the secretariat of the conference
at which the treaty is negotiated and concluded (see Chapter **30**) together,
where necessary, with the host government, but there will be one signature
text only.

If a treaty covers more than a single sheet of paper, the sheets will be united by **31.14**
ribbon or fancy cord and the ends of the ribbon will be sealed. A cover will
normally be supplied by the host government.

Personal seals (i.e. a hand-seal or signet-ring showing crest, emblem, or other **31.15**
device, or the initial letters of the owner's names) are used only when the treaty
is drawn up in Heads of State form and when the *testimonium* requires that the
Plenipotentiaries should affix their seals to the treaty. Where a negotiator has no
personal seal—as is nowadays usually the case—an official wax seal or wafer seal
is used.[34]

Languages

A bilateral treaty between two countries which share the same language will be **31.16**
drawn up in that language. If, as is more common, each country has its own
language, the standard rule is that the treaty is drawn up in equally authentic
versions in each language, but all the language versions will be bound together
as a single signature text.

Sometimes, however, a treaty may be drawn up in a language or languages **31.17**
which are not those of the Contracting Parties. The Treaty of Peace between
Japan and Russia of 1905[35] was drawn up in English and French. Again a treaty

---

[34] In United Kingdom practice, the seal bears the Royal Arms and the name of the diplomatic
mission or the Foreign and Commonwealth Office as the case may be.
[35] *BFSP*, Vol 98, 75.

may be drawn up not only in the languages of the Contracting Parties, but also in a third language, which prevails in the event of any divergence of interpretation.[36] Although this practice had fallen out of favour, it has now re-emerged in bilateral treaties for the promotion and protection of investments, which in several recent instances make an English-language version prevail even though it is not the language of either treaty party—presumably on the basis that English is regarded as the language of modern commerce and finance.[37]

Registration and Publication

31.18 Article 102 of the UN Charter lays down that:

1. Every treaty and every international agreement entered into by any Member of the United Nations after the present Charter comes into force shall as soon as possible be registered with the Secretariat and published by it.
2. No party to any such treaty or international agreement which has not been registered in accordance with the provisions of paragraph 1 of this Article may invoke that treaty or agreement before any organ of the United Nations.

31.19 In 1946 the General Assembly adopted a set of Regulations to give effect to Article 102, subsequently amended; their current contents are more fully explained in Section 5 of the UN Treaty Handbook.[38] Under Article 10 of the Regulations, the Secretariat accepts for 'filing and recording' treaties or international agreements voluntarily submitted to it which are not subject to registration under Article 102 or under the Regulations. The direct obligation falling on the Secretariat under Article 102 to publish treaties registered with it was met by the creation of the United Nations Treaty Series, the most comprehensive collection of treaty texts and related information in publication, now running to over 2,500 volumes containing more than 200,000 entries.[39]

31.20 Many States have similar national requirements for the official publication of the texts of treaties entered into by the State, together with related information about their status and entry into force. This is particularly necessary when treaties automatically become part of the local law and are applied directly by the

---

[36] Examples are the Treaty of Peace between Indonesia and Japan of 20 January 1958 (UNTS, Vol 324, 241) which is drawn up in the Japanese, Indonesian, and English languages, the English text to prevail in case of any divergence of interpretation; and the Treaty of Friendship between Japan and Ethiopia of 19 December 1957 (UNTS, Vol 325, 99) drawn up in the Japanese, Amharic, and French languages, the French text to be authentic in case of any divergence of interpretation.

[37] Further detail about the interpretation of treaties in more than one language can be found in Chapter 35.

[38] See n 1.

[39] See further <https://treaties.un.org/pages/Publications.aspx?pathpub=Publication/UNTS/Page1_en.xml> which offers a direct link to the UN Treaty Series itself.

Court, but is not limited to those situations, and numerous governments maintain published treaty series simply for the purpose of general information. Among the best known national treaty series are those of the UK,[40] the USA,[41] and France.[42]

---

[40] UK Treaty Series (UKTS), accessible via <https://data.gov.uk/dataset/treaties-database>.

[41] Treaties and other International Acts (TIAS); see <http://www.state.gov/s/l/treaty/tias/pubtias/>, or <http://www.state.gov/s/l/treaty/tif/> for an annual list of treaties in force.

[42] Accessible via <http://basedoc.diplomatie.gouv.fr/Traites/Accords_Traites.php>.

32

TREATIES AND OTHER INTERNATIONAL INSTRUMENTS—II TREATY, CONVENTION, AGREEMENT, PROTOCOL

Frank Berman and David Bentley

Introduction

32.1 This chapter will discuss the most common forms of treaty instrument, namely those entitled 'treaty', 'convention', 'agreement', and 'protocol'. It should however always be borne in mind that, as the Vienna Convention definition shows, the title used is of no significance in and of itself for a treaty's legal status.[1] Chapter **33** will look at various other types of treaty or treaty-related instrument. The type of instrument known as a Memorandum of Understanding will also be dealt with in Chapter **33**, although its most common use is to record terms that are not intended to be legally binding.

Treaty

32.2 Of those international instruments which are clearly intended to have an obligatory or binding character, many of the most significant bear the title

---

[1] For a fuller list of treaty titles that have been employed, see A Aust, *Modern Treaty Law and Practice* (3rd edn, Cambridge: Cambridge University Press, 2013) 22–4.

'treaty'. The word 'treaty' is derived from the French word *traiter*, which means to negotiate, and is used in both a general and a restricted sense. The definition of the term 'treaty' in the Vienna Convention is of course based on the general sense and covers all formal instruments of agreement by which two or more States establish or seek to establish a relation under international law between themselves. But the restricted sense of the term 'treaty' which is considered here refers simply to instruments of that kind which bear the title of 'treaty'.

Generally speaking, the designation 'treaty' has been reserved for international **32.3** agreements of a particularly significant character, for example treaties of peace or alliance. The designation 'treaty' may also be employed to mark the political importance of the particular international agreement—as for example the North Atlantic Treaty of 4 April 1949,[2] and all of the treaties establishing, first, the European Communities and then the European Union,[3] as well as the treaties providing for the accession of new member States to them.[4] It was once the case that treaties of this kind were always concluded between Heads of State; but modern practice demonstrates that important and significant treaties can be concluded, alternatively, in Head of State form, in inter-State form, or in intergovernmental form. The choice of form may depend partly on the political importance of the treaty and partly on the constitutional requirements of the Contracting Parties; otherwise it is not possible to discern any general principle governing the choice between these forms, as the following illustrations from practice illustrate.

Treaties between Heads of State, though rare, are still concluded. The European **32.4** Community and European Union Treaties are cast in this form, as are the accession arrangements for new Member States.[5] The Head of State form has virtually died out, however, for bilateral treaties; the last example in British practice dates from 1986.[6]

---

[2] 34 UNTS 244.

[3] Texts available at <http://eur-lex.europa.eu/collection/eu-law/treaties.html>; subsequent modifications of these constitutional instruments have, however, not always been entitled 'Treaty', e.g. the Single European Act of 1986.

[4] The accession instruments typically include an 'Act of Accession', which sets out the detailed provisions, but it forms an annex to the Accession Treaty; texts available at <http://eur-lex.europa. eu/collection/eu-law/treaties.html>.

[5] See further Chapter 33, paragraph 33.5.

[6] Treaty between the United Kingdom of Great Britain and Northern Ireland and the French Republic concerning the Construction and Operation by Private Concessionaires of a Channel Fixed Link, with an Exchange of Letters, done at Canterbury on 12 February 1986 (Treaty Series No 15 (1992) Cm 1827).

32.5 The inter-State form, by contrast, is now in far more frequent use. The North Atlantic Treaty of 4 April 1949, and the Treaties of Peace with Italy (1947),[7] and Japan (1951),[8] were all concluded between States rather than between Heads of State. The Treaty on the Non-Proliferation of Nuclear Weapons of 1968[9] is another example of an important multilateral treaty concluded in inter-State form.

32.6 Treaties between States are rather less formal in their terminology than treaties between Heads of State.[10] In place of the term 'High Contracting Parties', the expression 'Contracting Parties' or 'Contracting States' (or sometimes simply 'the Parties' or 'the States Parties')[11] is used. It is, however, customary, as in the case of a Heads of States treaty, to include a formal preamble setting out the object of the treaty.

32.7 Treaties between governments are also less formal. The parties normally refer to themselves as the 'Contracting Governments' or the 'Contracting Parties', although occasionally one may come across the use of such terms as 'Signatory Governments' or 'Participating Governments'. Again, however, the preamble will usually contain a statement of the reason for the treaty and the purposes it is intended to achieve.

Convention

32.8 The designation 'convention' tends to be utilized for multilateral treaties of a law-making type. The tendency goes back to the various Hague Conventions emanating from the First and Second Hague Peace Conferences (of 1899 and 1907 respectively) and the practice followed by the League of Nations, as, for example, with the Barcelona Conventions of 1921 and the Slavery Convention of 1926. It can be seen perpetuated in the various conventions concluded since the Second World War as part of the progressive development and codification of international law within the framework of Article 13 of the UN Charter.

---

[7] 49 UNTS 126.

[8] 136 UNTS 49.

[9] 729 UNTS 169.

[10] Occasionally, one may come across a treaty which is in 'mixed' form. Thus, the Treaty of Versailles of 28 June 1919 is expressed to be concluded between the 'Principal Allied and Associated Powers' and Germany, but the High Contracting Parties (on the Allied side) are the various Heads of State 'represented' by certain ministers and ambassadors. This formula was probably chosen for the purpose of enabling the British Self-governing Dominions and India to participate separately in the Peace Treaty without raising what would have been regarded at that time as difficult questions of their treaty-making capacity: see McNair, *Law of Treaties*, 16.

[11] Some casual modern usage tends to refer to 'State Parties' (with State in the singular) but this is incorrect, and should be avoided as it can raise a misleading inference that there exist other categories of parties.

Examples are the Vienna Convention on Diplomatic Relations of 1961;[12] the Vienna Convention on the Law of Treaties of 1969;[13] the Convention on the Prevention and Punishment of Crimes against Internationally Protected Persons, including Diplomatic Agents, of 1973;[14] the Third United Nations Convention on the Law of the Sea of 1982;[15] the Convention against Torture and Other Cruel, Inhuman or Degrading Treatment or Punishment, of 1984; the Vienna Convention on the Depletion of the Ozone Layer of 1985; and the United Nations Framework Convention on Climate Change of 1992.[16] Law-making or regulatory treaties concluded under the auspices of one or other of the Specialized Agencies of the United Nations will also normally take the form of conventions: examples are the Hague Convention for the Suppression of Unlawful Seizure of Aircraft of 1970,[17] the Montreal Convention for the Suppression of Unlawful Acts against the Safety of Civil Aviation of 1971[18] (both negotiated within the framework of the International Civil Aviation Organization (ICAO)), and the Framework Convention on Tobacco Control of 2003 (WHO). Following recent practice, some of these treaties are called 'Framework Conventions', being expressly designed not as a final regulation but to create a framework for coordinated efforts to tackle a longer-term problem. Treaties which establish international bodies of a technical character may also take the form of conventions—for example, the Universal Postal Convention, the International Telecommunications Convention, and the various conventions for the protection of intellectual property.

The Council of Europe maintains a carefully ordered practice in this regard, **32.9** namely:

> Once a 'Convention' or an 'Agreement' is concluded, they have the same legal effect. The only distinguishing feature is the form in which a State may express its wish to be bound by one or the other. While a European Convention is usually the object of the deposit of an instrument of ratification, acceptance or approval, a European Agreement may be signed with or without reservation as to ratification, acceptance or approval. Moreover, the model final clauses adopted by the Committee of Ministers in 1963 and revised in 1980 contain clauses regarding the procedure whereby non-member States of the Council of Europe may become Parties to European Conventions or Agreements; in principle, these clauses enable them only to accede.[19]

---

[12] 500 UNTS 95.

[13] Misc. No 19 (1971), Cmnd 4818.

[14] 1035 UNTS 167.

[15] 1833 UNTS 3 (likewise the four earlier conventions on the law of the sea of 29 April 1958).

[16] 1465 UNTS 85.

[17] 860 UNTS 106; <http://www.icao.int/icao/en/leb/Hague.pdf>.

[18] 974 UNTS 178; <http://www.icao.int/icao/en/leb/mtl71.pdf>.

[19] See <http://www.coe.int/web/conventions/about-treaties>.

32.10 It should not however be thought that the designation 'convention' is used only for multilateral treaties of a law-making or normative type. The title is also in common use for a range of bilateral treaties, in the fields, for example, of extradition, double taxation, and judicial cooperation.

Agreement

32.11 Purely numerically, 'agreement' is currently the most commonly used title for treaties. The term 'agreement', like the term 'treaty' itself, is used in both a generic and a restricted sense. In a generic sense, it covers any meeting of minds—in this case, the minds of two or more international persons. But, as has already been said, a distinction must be drawn between agreements intended to have an obligatory character and agreements not intended to be legally binding. In its restricted sense, the term 'agreement' means an agreement intended to be binding, but usually of a less formal or significant nature than a treaty or convention. Like treaties and conventions, agreements in this restricted sense may be concluded between Heads of State, or between States, or between governments.

32.12 The treaty instrument in the form of an 'agreement' is, as it were, the workhorse of the treaty-maker. Agreements take a wide variety of forms, and the title is used for a wide variety of subject-matters. While it can be used for multilateral treaties—for example, the Agreement regarding the Status of Forces of Parties to the North Atlantic Treaty of 1951[20]—it is more commonly used for bilateral treaties of a fairly routine nature. It may be noted that bilateral treaties concluded between the United Kingdom and other Commonwealth countries usually take the form of 'agreements' expressed to be concluded as between governments rather than as between Heads of State or as between States.[21]

32.13 It should finally be noted that instruments called 'agreements' are sometimes concluded between a government department in one country and a government department in another. It depends on the circumstances (see earlier) whether or not such interdepartmental agreements amount to treaties binding under international law.[22]

---

[20] 199 UNTS 68.

[21] For the particular historical and constitutional background, see F Berman, 'Treaty-Making within the British Commonwealth' (2015) 38 *Melbourne University Law Review* 897.

[22] See Chapter 31, paragraph 31.6.

Protocol

The term 'protocol' derives from the Low-Latin *protocollum*, itself deriving from **32.14** a word in the original Greek meaning the 'first glued-in' to a book—that is to say, a summary or digest of the contents. In diplomacy, it gradually came to mean the register in which the minutes of a conference were held. It is, of course, also employed in diplomacy to signify the forms to be observed in the official correspondence of the Minister for Foreign Affairs and in the drafting of diplomatic documents such as treaties, Full Powers, letters of credence and recall, etc. Finally, it has come also to embrace the concept of something which is added to a treaty in order to perfect or complete the treaty. The word 'protocol' may accordingly, depending upon the context in which it is used, signify 'an addition to a treaty, a summary of official proceedings or a technique of the proper method of doing things, including official etiquette'.[23] In this last very broad sense, the word will, of course, cover such matters as protecting sensitive national dignities on major occasions and the practical arrangement of even informal occasions where there might well be difficulties if no rules existed.[24]

When used in the sense of a treaty instrument, the designation 'protocol' usually **32.15** refers to a single instrument which amends or supplements an earlier international agreement. The designation 'protocol' may also be given to a treaty instrument which is ancillary to a treaty or convention, although concluded simultaneously. Thus nine such protocols are annexed to the treaties providing for the accession of the Czech Republic, Estonia, Cyprus, Latvia, Lithuania, Hungary, Malta, Poland, Slovenia, and Slovakia to the EU in 2003.

Compulsory dispute settlement provisions are frequently put into a separate **32.16** protocol, so that their acceptance can be made optional. Thus there are Optional Protocols on the Compulsory Settlement of Disputes to the Vienna Conventions on Diplomatic Relations and Consular Relations and the Convention on Special Missions.[25] The right of petition to the European Court of Human Rights was originally optional, and governed by a separate protocol, but has since 1998 been an integral part of the Convention on Human Rights and Fundamental Freedoms, following its amendment by Protocol No 11.[26]

---

[23] Denys P Myers, 'The Names and Scope of Treaties' (1957) 51 *AJIL* 575, 586.

[24] See especially Chapters 7, **12**, **13**, and **36**.

[25] The Optional Protocol to the Consular Relations Convention has recently provided the jurisdictional base for a series of important judgments of the International Court of Justice in cases brought against the USA by Paraguay, by Germany, and by Mexico.

[26] See <http://conventions.coe.int/Treaty/en/Summaries/Html/005.htm>.

32.17 The term 'protocol' may also be given to a treaty instrument which prolongs the duration of a treaty or convention that is about to expire. Examples are the Protocol for the Continuation in Force of the International Coffee Agreement, 1968, as extended,[27] and the Protocol of 1967,[28] for the extension of the period of validity of the Convention on the Declaration of Death of Missing Persons.

32.18 In its secondary sense of a summary of official proceedings, the term 'protocol' has much the same meaning as the minutes of a conference, and has been used as the vehicle to record, on the conclusion of a multilateral treaty or convention, observations, declarations, and ancillary agreements relating to the text or to its interpretation.[29]

32.19 Treaties dealing with some particular topic are sometimes entitled 'protocols', though not differing other than in the title from other treaties or agreements. The form has been used to conclude an armistice (Protocol between the United States and Spain of 1898;[30] and between Poland and Lithuania of 1920);[31] to provide for the delimitation of a boundary (Protocol concerning the delimitation and marking of the Argentine–Uruguayan Boundary Line in the River Uruguay of 1968);[32] to re-establish diplomatic relations (Protocol between the Netherlands and Venezuela of 1894);[33] to regulate the status of international military headquarters (Protocol of 1952, between the Parties to the North Atlantic Treaty);[34] and to regulate the exercise of criminal jurisdiction over UN armed forces (Protocol of 1953, between Japan, the United States, Australia, Canada, and the United Kingdom).[35] There is a Protocol on Arbitration Clauses, signed at Geneva in 1923, concerning the recognition and enforcement of certain arbitration agreements and arbitral awards.[36] Finally, mention should be made of the important Geneva Protocol of 1925 for the Prohibition of the Use of Asphyxiating, Poisonous or Other Gases, and of Bacteriological Methods of Warfare.[37]

---

[27] 982 UNTS 332.

[28] 588 UNTS 290.

[29] Nowadays however items of that kind would be recorded in the Final Act of the Conference (see Chapter 33, paragraphs 33.25–33.27) or in the records of an international organization when it formally adopts the treaty text and opens it for signature (cf GA resolution 59/38, adopting the United Nations Convention on Jurisdictional Immunities of States and Their Property, which formally took into account a statement by the Chairman of the relevant Committee recording certain working understandings relating to the text, which were then annexed to the Convention).

[30] *British and Foreign State Papers (BFSP)*, Vol 90, 1049.

[31] Ibid, Vol 114, 875.

[32] 671 UNTS 57.

[33] *BFSP*, Vol 86, 543.

[34] 200 UNTS 340.

[35] 207 UNTS 237.

[36] 27 UNTS 157.

[37] Available at <http://www.icrc.org/ihl.nsf/FULL/280?OpenDocument>.

It is, however, correct to say that the protocol is now used principally as an instrument subsidiary to a treaty or convention, usually (but not necessarily) drawn up by the same negotiators, and dealing with ancillary or incidental matters such as the interpretation of particular articles of the main treaty or any supplementary provision of a minor character. Ratification of the treaty or convention[38] will normally *ipso facto* involve ratification of any supplementary or additional protocol of this nature. In 1993 the English Divisional Court held, with reference to the Maastricht Treaty, that ratification of the Treaty 'will automatically involve' ratification of the Protocols to it.[39] Where the protocol is concluded independently at a later date (as, for example, an amending protocol), it will of course be subject to independent ratification.   **32**.20

Alternatively, the protocol form may be used as the means for subsequently adding to or expanding, sometimes in a significant way, the terms or scope of an earlier treaty, as in the case of the three Additional Protocols to the Geneva Conventions of 1949 on the protection of victims of armed conflict (Red Cross Conventions).[40]   **32**.21

An interesting special case is the Convention on Prohibitions or Restrictions on the Use of Certain Conventional Weapons which may be Deemed to be Excessively Injurious or to have Indiscriminate Effects of 1980,[41] which is drawn up as a framework convention for the separate regulation of particular weapons through individual protocols. Three such protocols are annexed to the Convention itself, and two have been adopted since, one on blinding laser weapons,[42] and one on explosive remnants of war.[43]   **32**.22

---

[38] See Chapter 34, paragraph 34.3.

[39] Citing in support the fifth edition of the present work; *R v Secretary of State for Foreign & Commonwealth Affairs, ex parte Rees-Mogg* [1994] QB 552 at 564G.

[40] The Protocols deal, respectively, with the amendment of the rules relating to international armed conflict, with the adoption of new rules relating to non-international armed conflict, and with the adoption of a further distinctive emblem alongside the Red Cross and Red Crescent; texts of the Conventions and Protocols available at <https://www.icrc.org/applic/ihl/ihl.nsf/vwTreatiesByTopics.xsp>.

[41] 1342 UNTS 137.

[42] Vienna, 13 October 1995; <http://www.icrc.org/ihl.nsf/FULL/570?OpenDocument>.

[43] Geneva, 28 November 2003; <http://www.icrc.org/ihl.nsf/FULL/610?OpenDocument>.

33

TREATIES AND OTHER INTERNATIONAL INSTRUMENTS—III PACT, ACT, *MODUS VIVENDI*, DECLARATION, EXCHANGE OF NOTES, MEMORANDUM OF UNDERSTANDING

Frank Berman and David Bentley

Introduction

33.1   This chapter continues the typology of treaties begun in Chapter **32**; it should be read subject to the caveat in paragraph 1 of that chapter.

Pact

33.2   The term 'pact' derives from the Latin word *pactum* (plural *pacta*) meaning 'agreement'. It has a long and respectable colloquial usage to signify an agreement of any kind,[1] and in an international context to refer to a formal agreement between States, as in 'a non-aggression pact'. One of the most basic rules of international

---

[1] As in the phrase, 'I'll make a pact with you.'

law, which underlies the entire law of treaties, is that '[e]very treaty in force is binding upon the parties to it and must be performed by them in good faith', and appears in Article 26 of the Vienna Convention on the Law of Treaties and in the preamble to the Convention under the Latin heading *pacta sunt servanda*.

The term has been used to denote an especially solemn international agreement, **33.3** though it is sometimes loosely used as shorthand for a treaty which bears another title. The General Treaty for Renunciation of War as an Instrument of National Policy, signed at Paris in 1928,[2] is accordingly commonly referred to as the 'Kellogg–Briand Pact' or the 'Pact of Paris' (and was cited as the latter in various resolutions of the League of Nations).[3] The former Mutual Assistance Treaty between the States of the Communist bloc was universally known as the 'Warsaw Pact'.

More recently, the formal designation 'Pact' was given to several treaties which **33.4** the negotiating parties regarded as being of a particularly solemn nature, such as the Pact of the League of Arab States signed in Cairo in 1945,[4] but the term is now largely out of fashion; so the Arab League, for example, refers to its Pact as 'Charter' in its official usage.

Act

The term 'Act' (as distinguished from 'General Act' or 'Final Act') is an old form **33.5** of treaty nomenclature, sometimes used to designate an international instrument which, in and of itself, may lack some of the formal characteristics of a treaty, but which nevertheless forms part of a complex of treaty instruments. In this sense, an 'Act' will constitute a piece of international law-making and may indeed embody the decisive terms of the treaty complex. A recent example of this kind of usage is the 'Act' annexed to the Treaty of 2012 concerning the Accession of the Republic of Croatia to the European Union[5] setting out the conditions of admission and the adjustments to the EU Treaties entailed by such admission, and which, under Article 1(3) of the Treaty, forms an integral part of it. The Act of Accession consists of fifty-two substantive articles, together with nine annexes and a Protocol.

---

[2] LNTS No. 2137.
[3] So also, the American Treaty on Pacific Settlement 1948 (30 UNTS 55) was deliberately given the name Pact of Bogotá by its Art LX.
[4] 70 UNTS 248.
[5] <http://eur-lex.europa.eu/legal-content/EN/TXT/PDF/?uri=CELEX:12012J/TXT&from=EN>.

Modus Vivendi

33.6 This title is used for a temporary or provisional agreement, usually intended to be replaced later on, if circumstances permit, by one of a more permanent and detailed character. The term is not, however, always employed; more often than not, what is in substance a *modus vivendi* may be more straightforwardly designated a 'temporary agreement' or an 'interim agreement'.

33.7 An example of a treaty which is in fact formally called a *modus vivendi* is the Modus Vivendi between the Belgo-Luxembourg Economic Union and Turkey of 1947,[6] providing for most-favoured-nation treatment over navigation and customs duties, formalities, and charges, pending the entry into force of a treaty of commerce and navigation between the parties. An earlier Commercial Agreement of 1930 between the Governments of the United Kingdom and the USSR records that, pending the conclusion as soon as possible of a Treaty of Commerce and Navigation, the two governments 'have meanwhile agreed upon the following temporary Agreement to serve as a modus vivendi pending the conclusion of such a Treaty'.[7]

33.8 A more recent example is an Exchange of Notes of 13 November 1973, between the United Kingdom and Iceland, concluded after the United Kingdom had already instituted proceedings against Iceland before the International Court of Justice in relation to the underlying fisheries dispute,[8] which recites that:

> the following arrangements have been worked out for an interim agreement relating to fisheries in the disputed area, pending a settlement of the dispute and without prejudice to the legal position or rights of either Government in relation thereto…

In its judgment on the merits of the Fisheries Jurisdiction case, the International Court says:

> The interim agreement of 1973, unlike the 1961 Exchange of Notes, does not describe itself as a 'settlement' of the dispute and, apart from being of limited duration, clearly possesses the character of a provisional arrangement adopted without prejudice to the rights of the Parties, nor does it provide for the waiver of claims by either Party in respect of the matters in dispute.[9]

The Court accordingly concluded that there still existed an actual controversy involving a conflict of legal interests between the parties which could properly be adjudicated.

---

[6] 37 UNTS 223.
[7] Treaty Series No 19 (1930) Cmd 3552.
[8] Treaty Series No 122 (1973) Cmnd 5484.
[9] [1974] ICJ Reports 18.

Declaration

Oppenheim's *International Law* places declarations, whether made by a single **33.9** State or several States, under a general heading of 'unilateral acts', since any legal significance they may possess is not dependent on the response of an addressee. Sometimes however a declaration, 'perhaps for reasons of dignity', as Oppenheim puts it, is just a treaty or convention by another name.[10] A particularly good contemporary example is furnished by the Joint Declaration of China and the United Kingdom on the Question of Hong Kong of 1984, where it seems likely that the studiously neutral title was chosen in order to bridge the fundamental gap between the legal views of the two parties as to British authority over Hong Kong. Although its terms were largely written into the Basic Law of the Hong Kong Special Administrative Region on the territory's restoration to China,[11] the Joint Declaration undoubtedly establishes between the two States legal rights and obligations sounding in international law, and was registered as such with the UN Secretariat on 12 June 1985. Similar considerations may however apply to multilateral instruments as well, like the Declaration of Paris of 1856,[12] which aimed at defining the rules of international law relating to blockade and contraband. Other law-making (or law-declaring) declarations are the Declaration of St Petersburg of 1868 (explosive bullets),[13] the (unratified) Declaration of London of 1909 (blockade and contraband),[14] and the Barcelona Declaration of 1921 recognizing the Right to a Flag of States having no Sea-Coast.[15] But declarations are not confined to law-making treaties; the Declaration on the Neutrality of Laos signed at Geneva in 1962[16] contains a number of specific undertakings by the signatory governments and, in accordance with its terms, is to be 'regarded as constituting an international agreement'.

It may sometimes be difficult to determine whether an instrument which is **33.10** styled a declaration amounts to a treaty rather than a pronouncement of policy expressive of a shared or common purpose. The Declaration by United Nations of 1 January 1942[17] should almost certainly be regarded as a treaty, since acceptance of the Declaration was a condition of original membership of the United Nations. On the other hand, the type of instrument which became increasingly

---

[10] *The Law of Peace* (9th edn, Longman, 1992) ss 576–7.
[11] See Chapter **34**, paragraph **34**.42.
[12] *BFSP*, Vol 46, 63.
[13] <http://www.icrc.org/ihl.nsf/FULL/130?OpenDocument>.
[14] <http://www.icrc.org/ihl.nsf/FULL/255?OpenDocument>.
[15] 7 LNTS 73.
[16] Treaty Series No 27 (1963) Cmnd 2025.
[17] *Yearbook of the United Nations* (1946–7) 1.

common during the Second World War (and has persisted to this day), namely, a declaration published after a meeting between Heads of State or Government,[18] presents rather special features. The contents of a declaration of this kind may be partly agreements to do or not to do something, and partly statements of common policy; accordingly, it is unsafe to generalize on how far declarations of this somewhat unorthodox nature may constitute treaty instruments.[19] An instructive recent example is the Council of Europe's Declaration on Jurisdictional Immunities of State Owned Cultural Property of 4 December 2015 for which, despite its treaty-like similarities in point of form, the title 'declaration' was chosen in order to demonstrate that it 'had been elaborated as a legally non-binding document expressing a common understanding on *opinio juris* on the basic rule that certain kind of State property (cultural property on exhibition) enjoyed jurisdictional immunity'.[20]

33.11 Secondly, under the general heading of unilateral acts, unilateral declarations are undoubtedly capable of creating rights and duties for other States.[21] One would previously have listed among these: declarations of war, declarations on the part of belligerents concerning the goods they will condemn as contraband, and declarations at the outbreak of war on the part of third States that they will remain neutral. Present-day practice is less amenable to a listing of this kind. The International Law Commission had the subject under study from 1996 to 2006 and reported in terms of general 'Conclusions', to the effect that 'formal declarations formulated by a State with the intent to produce obligations under international law', and publicly made, may have the effect of creating legal obligations, the binding character of which is based on good faith. The Commission went on to say that a unilateral declaration entails obligations for the formulating State only if it is expressed in clear and specific terms, and that, in the case of doubt as to the scope of the obligations resulting from such a declaration, such obligations must be interpreted 'in a restrictive manner'.[22]

33.12 Thirdly, the term 'declaration' is used to describe the action taken when States communicate to other States, or to the world at large, an explanation and justification of their policy or conduct, or an explanation of their views and intentions.[23]

---

[18] Such as the conferences which took place at Yalta and Potsdam in 1945.

[19] A McNair, *The Law of Treaties* (Oxford: Clarendon Press, 1961) 23, n 2.

[20] Text and explanatory note available at <http://www.coe.int/en/web/cahdi/cahdi/-/asset_publisher/ym6zfUP2IxDn/content/declaration-on-jurisdictional-immunities-of-state-owned-cultural-property?redirect=%2Fen%2Fweb%2Fcahdi%2F&inheritRedirect=true>. The Declaration remains open for signature and has to date been signed by thirteen Foreign Ministers.

[21] See the examples cited at paragraph 33.9.

[22] UN Doc A/61/10 (2006) at para 176.

[23] A recent example of this type is the Joint Declaration of January 2016 by the Višegrad States on immigration and terrorism (text available at <http://www.visegradgroup.eu/calendar/2016/joint-declaration-of>).

Declarations of these second or third types, whether they give rise to legal obliga-   **33.13**
tions or not, do not constitute treaties as such.

In the *Ambatielos* case[24] the International Court of Justice held that a Declaration   **33.14**
annexed to the Treaty of Commerce and Navigation between Great Britain and
Greece of 1926, and separately signed by the parties, was a 'provision' of the
Treaty to which it was annexed, within the meaning of Article 29 of the Treaty,
and consequently founded the jurisdiction of the Court to determine a dispute
relating to the interpretation of the Declaration. In reaching this conclusion,
the Court drew on the wording of the instruments of ratification of the Treaty,
the fact that the Plenipotentiaries had included the Treaty and the Declaration
in a single document, as had the United Kingdom government in publishing
them in the Treaty Series, and that both countries had registered them with the
League of Nations under a single number.[25]

The name 'declaration' is also very occasionally given to agreements between gov-   **33.15**
ernments regarding some relatively minor matter. An example is the Declaration
on the Construction of Main International Traffic Arteries of 1950.[26]

Exchange of Notes

The treaty concluded in the form of an Exchange of Notes or letters is, in mod-   **33.16**
ern times, the most frequently used device for formally recording the agreement
of two governments on all kinds of transactions.[27] It takes the form not of a
single instrument but of an ordinary exchange of correspondence between the
ambassador of one State and the Minister for Foreign Affairs of the State to which
he is accredited. The content of the agreement to be recorded by the Exchange of
Notes will of course have been agreed in advance between the two governments.
The initiating Note sets out the provisions of the proposed agreement and goes
on to suggest that if the proposals are acceptable to the other government the
initiating Note and the other government's reply to that effect should constitute
an agreement in the matter. The exchange is then concluded by way of a Note in
reply accepting the proposal in the initiating Note.

---

[24] [1952] ICJ Reports 28: the case arose out of a claim by a Greek ship owner who alleged that he
had suffered considerable loss in consequence of a contract which he concluded in 1919 with the
British government.

[25] No 1425. Treaty of Commerce and Navigation between the United Kingdom and Greece and
accompanying Declaration signed at London, 16 July 1926.

[26] 96 UNTS 91.

[27] Anthony Aust, *Modern Treaty Law and Practice* (3rd edn, Cambridge: Cambridge University
Press, 2013) has, at 425–8, examples of Exchanges of Notes respectively constituting a treaty and
recording an understanding (MOU).

33.17   It is not customary to present Full Powers[28] for an Exchange of Notes. Nor are Exchanges of Notes normally subject to ratification, although in some cases they may be. The International Law Commission in their commentary to what is now Article 14 of the Vienna Convention on the Law of Treaties, summarizes the position as follows:

> Meanwhile, however, the expansion of intercourse between States, especially in economic and technical fields, led to an ever-increasing use of less formal types of international agreements, amongst which were exchanges of Notes, and these agreements are usually intended by the parties to become binding by signature alone. On the other hand, an exchange of notes or other informal agreement, though employed for its ease of convenience, has sometimes expressly been made subject to ratification because of constitutional requirements in one or other of the contracting States.[29]

The fact that Exchanges of Notes do not normally require ratification, and accordingly enter into force as soon as the exchange has been effected, makes them a very convenient and flexible instrument for treaty-makers. Although the form is used for recording agreement between two governments on a wide variety of routine matters, it has also been used to regulate transactions of considerable political importance. Thus, Exchanges of Notes have dealt with such matters as the transfer and lease of military bases, the maintenance of armed forces and military missions on foreign soil, settlement of war claims, settlement of boundary disputes, delimitation of territorial waters, and jurisdiction over foreign armed forces for criminal offences.[30]

33.18   Normally the Notes exchanged recording the agreement bear the same date, in which case, unless they provide otherwise, the agreement has effect from that date. If they bear different dates, that of the last Note, or at any rate the date of its receipt, is the governing date (unless otherwise provided), since it is the acceptance of the initiating proposal that constitutes the agreement on both sides. It is also now commonplace for the coming into force of an Exchange of Notes to be postponed until the necessary internal requirements (less formal than ratification) have been completed on both sides. In that case the Exchange of Notes will provide for each side to notify the other formally when its internal requirements have been met.

33.19   Agreements embodied in Exchanges of Notes are, as a general rule, bilateral. Exceptionally, there may be more than two States concerned in an Exchange of

---

[28] See Chapter **30**, paragraph **30**.10.

[29] [1966] ILC Reports 30.

[30] These and other examples are given by J L Weinstein, 'Exchanges of Notes' (1952) 29 *BYIL* 205–26. See also paragraph **33**.8 for the Exchange of Notes used to record the interim agreement between the United Kingdom and Iceland in connection with the fisheries dispute.

Notes or letters. The agreement between the Bank for International Settlements, on the one hand, and the United Kingdom, United States, and French governments, on the other hand, for the return to those governments of gold looted by Germany was constituted by a letter addressed to representatives of the three governments by the chairman of the Bank and by a letter in reply signed by the representatives of the three governments.[31] A somewhat unorthodox example of a 'multilateral' exchange is afforded by the exchange of letters on monetary questions annexed to the Treaty concerning the Accession of Denmark, Ireland, Norway, and the United Kingdom to the EEC and EURATOM of 1972. The initiating letter was addressed by Mr Geoffrey Rippon (the minister in charge of the United Kingdom delegation for the entry negotiations) to M. Thorn (Minister for Foreign Affairs of Luxembourg) in his capacity as President of the EEC Council of Ministers, and sought confirmation from 'the Governments of the Member States of the Community and of the Governments of the Kingdom of Denmark, Ireland and the Kingdom of Norway' that they agreed to a declaration made by Mr Rippon in the course of the negotiations. The letter in reply was signed by M. Thorn and countersigned by the eight other Foreign Ministers.[32]

Memorandum of Understanding

Modern practice is replete with cases in which governments reach agreement which **33.20** they record in writing, but deliberately choose not to make legally binding.[33] Such instruments are very often entitled 'Memorandum of Understanding' (MOU), or are referred to as such, as a specific indicator of their non-binding character. The FCO Guidance[34] summarizes the essential character of an MOU as follows: 'An MOU records international "commitments" but in a form and with wording which expresses an intention that it is not to be legally binding.' Whether the practice of recording commitments in MOUs is desirable or undesirable is a matter of debate, but various reasons may enter into the choice of the non-binding form over

---

[31] Treaty Series No 38 (1948) Cmd 7456. So also, an Exchange of Notes between the United Kingdom and Italian governments for the allocation to Italy of a share in the proceeds of sale by the International Refugee Organization of certain valuables, currencies, and securities, presumed looted by the German forces and taken from them in Italy by the forces of the Allies, was linked to a parallel Exchange of Notes between the United States and Italian governments; see Treaty Series No 52 (1951) Cmd 8294.

[32] Treaty Series No 1 (1973)–Part I, Cmnd 5179–1, 272–4.

[33] See Aust, *Modern Treaty Law*, 28 *et seq*. For a more general treatment of this subject see H Hillgenberg, 'A Fresh Look at Soft Law' (1999) 10 *EJIL* 499.

[34] <https://www.gov.uk/government/publications/treaties-and-mous-guidance-on-practice-and -procedures>.

the treaty form. One might be the wish to avoid the publicity resulting from inclusion in a national treaty series or registration with the United Nations,[35] if for example the agreement deals with sensitive or secret matters, like nuclear technology, weapons production, intelligence cooperation, or joint action against terrorism. Another might be the wish to avoid having to submit the agreement to a process of formal internal approval before the national parliament. Yet another might be the simple preference for a commitment depending for its fulfilment more on political harmony and good faith than on the possibility of bringing formal claims in the event of a future breach.[36] Valid as these reasons may be—and indeed are—in particular cases, they can as easily be called into play to shore up less noble motives in other cases.

33.21 British practice in the drawing up of MOUs follows, as far as possible, a set terminology in order to distinguish MOUs from treaties. Standard terminology for use in MOUs can be found in the FCO Guidance: for instance, use 'governments' or 'participants', not 'parties', 'provisions' not 'terms', and 'will' not 'shall'. MOUs are expressed to 'come into operation' or 'effect', while treaties 'come into force'. An MOU, and any Exchange of Notes confirming it, should record the 'understanding' of the governments concerned in the matter, not their 'agreement'. If this terminology is followed, it will generally be plain that the intention is not to create legally binding rights and obligations.[37]

33.22 Many other States are similarly consistent in the use of particular terminology. Confusion has however been caused by the fact that the practice of the United States, in particular, has been less consistent, with the result that the US has regarded some instruments as treaties which other States would regard as MOUs.[38] It is of course possible to provide expressly to the effect that the instrument is not legally

---

[35] See Chapter 31, paragraphs 31.18–31.19.

[36] As explained in the FCO Guidance (n 34) '[An] MOU is used where it is considered preferable to avoid the formalities of a treaty—for example, where there are detailed provisions which change frequently or the matters dealt with are essentially of a technical or administrative character; in matters of defence or technology where there is a need for such documents to be classified; or where a treaty requires subsidiary documents to fill out the details.'

[37] At the Vienna Conference on the Law of Treaties, the UK representative maintained that 'many agreed minutes and memoranda of understanding were not international agreements subject to the law of treaties, because the parties had not intended to create legal rights or obligations, or a legal relationship, between themselves'. He also pointed out that 'international practice had consistently upheld the distinction between international agreements properly so-called, where the parties intended to create rights and obligations, and declarations and other similar instruments simply setting out policy objectives or agreed views'. *Official Records. Second Session* (1969) 228.

[38] There is a discussion of this question in the Tribunal's Award in the *Heathrow User Charges Arbitration (US v UK)*, 102 ILR 215, at 351 *et seq*.

binding, but this is not commonly done, and the absence of such a provision would not on its own be conclusive.[39]

The fact that an MOU is not legally binding does not however mean that enter- **33.23** ing into one entails no commitment; as indicated earlier, the commitment is one of a policy rather than a legal kind, and issues of good faith and reputation are just as much at stake in the one case as in the other. For instance, by the Budapest Memorandum of 1994, a non-treaty instrument, the United Kingdom, the United States, and Russia[40] confirmed their commitment to respect the independence and sovereignty and the existing borders of Ukraine in return for the commitment of Ukraine to eliminate all nuclear weapons from its territory; when Russia subsequently annexed Crimea, in breach of that commitment, it met with the strongest condemnation. While the MOU form can thus in practice be used, not simply for mundane exchanges on technical subjects, but as the vehicle for commitments of considerable consequences beyond the merely political, for example projects for the joint development or procurement of sophisticated weapons systems involving substantial investment, its limitations have to borne in mind. For instance, MOUs have also been concluded in recent years between the United Kingdom and countries in the Middle East and North Africa intended to facilitate the deportation or extradition of terrorist suspects by providing assurances about their treatment on return to their home country sufficient to meet the United Kingdom's human rights obligations. Whether the vehicle is in fact sturdy enough to carry this weight of freight has been cast into doubt in national courts. A national court, faced with a question (arising for example out of legislation on human rights) as to whether another State can be relied upon to uphold its commitments, might well take an adverse view of the fact that the State was not willing to give those commitments legal form. How far this kind of assurance may be relied upon, given conditions in the receiving countries, has been the frequent subject of challenge in British courts,

---

[39] For elaborate denials of legal commitment, see the US–Israel Declaration on Trade in Services 1985 (24 ILM 679), or the US–Israel Memorandum of Mutual Understanding on Homeland Security 2007: 'This Memorandum does not impose any legal commitments on the Participants. It does not create, nor is it intended to create any enforceable legal rights or private rights of action, nor does it affect the Participants' rights and obligations under any other international treaties, agreements, or arrangements, nor under each Participant's national laws, regulations and practices. This Memorandum is not intended to displace or supersede any existing channels of communication or cooperative endeavors between the Participants.' (<http://www.jewishvirtuallibrary.org/jsource/US-Israel/homelandmou.html>).

[40] UN Document S/1994/1399, 5 December 1994.

with varying results, and the possibility of further recourse to the European Court of Human Rights.[41]

33.24　Nor does the absence of legal obligation mean that an MOU is devoid of legal consequences. The principle that States must conduct their dealings with each other in good faith may have the effect that a State is legally precluded from going back on commitments made in an MOU where the other State has acted in reliance on them; this is, however, a still developing area of international law.

Final Act

33.25　The term 'Final Act' is normally used to designate a document recording the formal summary of the proceedings and outcome of an international conference, including, as the case may be, the treaties or other instruments drawn up, together with any resolutions adopted by the conference. But it may also be similarly used to record the outcome of a complex negotiation taking place by different means.[42] As such, it is signed by the heads of all delegations taking part, but this signature goes only to approving the content of the Final Act, and does not in itself entail any expression of consent to be bound by the treaties or other instruments listed in it. An example of this type of Final Act is provided by that of the Vienna Conference on the Law of Treaties.[43] It is self-evident that an instrument of this nature does not in itself constitute a treaty, since it is simply a summary of the proceedings of the Conference which drew up the Vienna Convention.

33.26　Most modern international conferences convened to draw up international conventions, including those convened under the auspices of international organizations, conclude by adopting a Final Act of this nature. A recent example is the Final Act of the United Nations Diplomatic Conference of Plenipotentiaries on the Establishment of an International Criminal Court done at Rome on 17 July 1998.[44]

---

[41] So the ECtHR found inadequate a flimsy arrangement between Italy and Tunisia (*Saadi v Italy*, 28 February 2008). In *RB and Anor (Algeria) v Home Sec*, and *OO (Jordan) v Home Secretary* [2009] UKHL 10, paras 106–26, Lord Phillips set out the approach to be taken where assurances given by a foreign State are challenged; despite assurances in that instance at the highest level, the difficulties were only overcome when the necessary guarantees were eventually incorporated in a treaty between the United Kingdom and Jordan in 2013 (<https://www.gov.uk/government/publications/treaty-on-mutual-legal-assistance-between-the-uk-and-jordan>).

[42] As in the EU example cited in n 5.

[43] See the fuller description in Chapter 30, n 23.

[44] UN Doc A/Conf.183/10; <http://legal.un.org/icc/statute/finalfra.htm>.

It is possible for a Final Act to constitute a treaty in its own right, but this would **33.27** be highly exceptional.[45] The Final Act of the Wheat Conference done at London on 25 August 1933 appears to be an example of an international agreement drawn up in the form of a Final Act.[46]

---

[45] See H W Briggs, 'The Final Act of the London Conference on Germany' (1955) 49 *AJIL* 148–65, especially at 149–52.
[46] Treaty Series No 38 (1933) Cmd 4449.

34

TREATIES AND OTHER INTERNATIONAL INSTRUMENTS—IV RATIFICATION, ACCESSION, ACCEPTANCE AND APPROVAL, TREATY SUCCESSION

Frank Berman and David Bentley

Introduction

34.1 A treaty becomes binding through the expression by the parties of their consent to be bound. This consent may be expressed by various means, notably signature, exchange of instruments constituting a treaty, ratification, acceptance, approval, or accession, or by any other means if so agreed.[1] The treaty itself may provide that it is to enter into force upon signature, in which case the act of signature definitively expresses the consent of the signatory States to be bound by the treaty. In exceptional cases, the initialling of a text may also express the consent of the States concerned to be bound by it, when it is established that the negotiating States have so agreed.[2] It sometimes happens that a representative of a State is unable to receive definite instructions from his government by the time of signature; or it may be that the treaty is to enter into force on signature but the government concerned wants the opportunity to study the agreed text in greater detail before

---

[1] Art 11 of the Vienna Convention on the Law of Treaties.
[2] See Chapter 31, paragraph 31.12.

taking the final decision. In such circumstances, the representative may sign the treaty *ad referendum*, which, if subsequently confirmed, will constitute a valid expression of consent to be bound, effective retroactively as from the date of the signature *ad referendum*.[3] Alternatively, the formal signature of the treaty may simply be postponed until the States concerned are all in a position to commit themselves.

The very great majority of multilateral treaties, and a significant proportion of bilateral treaties are, however, nowadays concluded subject to ratification or some other process of subsequent confirmation, and it is these processes which are considered in what follows. **34**.2

Ratification

Ratification is a solemn act on the part of a sovereign or other Head of State declaring that a treaty, convention, or other international instrument has been submitted to the Head of State and that after examination it has been given formal approval, with a promise of its complete and faithful observance. The instrument of ratification is signed by the Head of State, and sealed with the seal of State, though practice varies as to whether the complete text of the treaty and related instruments should be reproduced in it. Where the treaty is not in Head of State form, but in inter-State or intergovernmental form, the form of the instrument of ratification is adjusted accordingly.[4] **34**.3

In the case of a bilateral treaty, instruments of ratification are exchanged, in other words each party delivers to the other its instrument of ratification and receives the corresponding one from the other party in return. The fact of exchange is recorded in a certificate of exchange, which is ordinarily drawn up in the respective languages of the two parties, and signed in duplicate, each party retaining an original in which it is given precedence. As a rule, the exchange is effected by the head of the department concerned with treaty formalities in the ministry of foreign affairs of the one country and a diplomatic representative of the other. The issue of Full Powers for such a purpose is unnecessary, unless, as occasionally happens, one of the parties should insist on this additional formality; normally, however, the production of the instruments of ratification by the **34**.4

---

[3] Art 12.2(b) of the Vienna Convention on the Law of Treaties.
[4] Standard forms for instruments of ratification are reproduced in the UN Treaty Handbook (see Chapter **31** n 1) and in A Aust, *Modern Treaty Law and Practice* (3rd edn, Cambridge: Cambridge University Press, 2013).

officials undertaking the exchange is regarded as sufficient evidence that they are authorized to proceed to the exchange.

34.5 For bilateral treaties, it is now far more common in practice for the ceremonial exchange of ratifications to be replaced by the mutual notification of the completion of the internal procedures necessary to enable the treaty to be brought into force.

34.6 When there are more than two Contracting Parties to a treaty, it is customary to have only one original text of the treaty (in all language versions), which is signed by the negotiators and deposited either in the archives of the State where it was signed, or in the archives of the international organization under whose auspices it was concluded, each of the other parties being furnished with a certified copy.[5] The instruments of ratification are then as a rule deposited with whichever government or international organ has been designated as the 'depositary'.[6] Amongst the duties of the depositary will be to deliver a formal acknowledgement of each deposit to the State concerned, and to notify the other States Parties or States entitled to become parties. The procedure to be followed in these cases is normally laid down in the treaty itself.

34.7 In the United Kingdom, the treaty-making power is vested in the Sovereign and the ratification of a treaty concluded in Heads of State form is effected by means of an instrument of ratification signed by the Sovereign and sealed with the Great Seal.[7] Constitutionally the Sovereign acts on the advice of the responsible ministers and, in certain circumstances, notably where the execution of a treaty involves financial commitments or a cession of territory, the approval of Parliament will first be sought. Furthermore, if legislation is required to carry out the provisions of the treaty, it is a firm rule that the United Kingdom instrument of ratification will not be exchanged or deposited until Parliament has enacted the necessary implementing legislation. Even where specific implementing legislation is not required, however, the standing practice is to lay before Parliament the texts of all treaty instruments requiring ratification, accompanied in recent years by an

---

[5] Though there are occasional exceptions to this rule. For some multilateral agreements the 'triple depositary' technique was devised during the period of divided States as a special exception to the general rule, so as to allow each of the component parts of a divided State to sign the treaty or deposit an instrument of ratification or accession with a depositary power that recognized it as a State and thus as entitled to ratify or accede. Examples are: the Treaty on Principles Governing the Activities of States in the Exploration and Use of Outer Space, including The Moon and Other Celestial Bodies 1967; the Treaty on the Non-Proliferation of Nuclear Weapons 1968; and the Hague Convention for the Suppression of Unlawful Seizure of Aircraft 1972.

[6] For the functions of a treaty depositary, see Art 77 of the Vienna Convention on the Law of Treaties.

[7] Practice, of course, varies widely as regards the form and wording of an instrument of ratification. The UN Treaty Handbook (see Chapter **31** n 1) contains model texts in the Annexes.

explanatory memorandum, and not to proceed to ratification until a period of 21 sitting days has elapsed.[8]

Most, if not all, States will have corresponding constitutional procedures of their **34.8** own. If, for a given State, the constitutional position is that treaties duly concluded by the State become part of national law, or in some cases rank higher than ordinary legislation, the procedures for treaty approval are likely to reflect that fact. But the procedures are too varied from one country to another, as are their legal effects, to make it possible to offer any kind of summary.[9]

It should be noted that there is often confusion over what the term 'ratification' **34.9** precisely connotes. In common parlance it can be used, variously, to refer to:

(a) the act of the appropriate organ of the State (sovereign, president, federal council, etc) which signifies the consent of the State to be bound by the treaty;
(b) the internationally agreed procedure whereby a treaty formally enters into force, that is to say, the formal exchange or deposit of instruments of ratification;
(c) the actual document or instrument whereby a State expresses its consent to be bound by the treaty; and
(d) more loosely, the approval of the legislature or other state organ whose approval may be constitutionally necessary as a condition precedent to ratification in the sense of (a) above.

As ratification is a technical term of international law, the usage under (d) above, which is sometimes popularly translated into 'parliamentary ratification' is inaccurate. In the United Kingdom, for example, it is the Crown which ratifies, not Parliament, though Parliament may, as a condition precedent to ratification, be invited to approve and, if necessary, to legislate. Thus, (a) is the correct technical sense of the term, and corresponds to the definition of ratification in the Vienna Convention on the Law of Treaties as 'the *international* act so named whereby a State establishes on the international plane its consent to be bound by a treaty'.[10] Where (b) is intended, reference should be made to the exchange or deposit of instruments of ratification; and, strictly speaking, where (c) is

---

[8] This is popularly known as the 'Ponsonby rule'; see the FCO Guidance (see Chapter 31 n 1), in particular the descriptive note on the operation of the rule. The Ponsonby Rule is now enacted into law with some changes by ss 20–25 of the Constitutional Reform and Governance Act 2010.

[9] A wide selection of national systems is described in D Hollis, M Blakeslee, and B Ederington (eds), *National Treaty Law and Practice* (Leiden, Boston: Martinus Nijhoff, for the American Society of International Law, 2005).

[10] Art 2(b) (emphasis supplied). In the analogous situation of the withdrawal of a reservation, the International Court has drawn a firm distinction between the adoption of internal legislation authorizing withdrawal and the formal notification of withdrawal on the international plane: *Case concerning Armed Activities on the Territory of the Congo* [2006] ICJ Reports 6, 23–7 (for Reservations, see Chapter 35).

intended, reference should be made to the instrument of ratification rather than to ratification *tout court*.

34.10 A further point relates to the purpose which ratification (or indeed any other form of subsequent confirmation) is designed to serve. McNair explains the position succinctly:

> Ratification is not (or, at any rate, since the days of absolute monarchs it has not been) a mere formality, like the use of a seal, or parchment, or tape. Ratification has a value which should not be minimized. The interval between the signature and the ratification of a treaty gives the appropriate departments of the Governments that have negotiated the treaty an opportunity of studying the advantages and disadvantages involved in the proposed treaty as a whole, and of doing so in a manner more detached, more leisurely, and more comprehensive than is usually open to their representatives while negotiating the treaty. However careful may have been the preparation of their instructions, it rarely happens that the representatives of both parties can succeed in producing a draft which embodies the whole of their respective instructions; some concession on one side and some element of compromise are present in practically every negotiation. It is therefore useful that in the case of important treaties Governments should have the opportunity of reflection afforded by the requirement of ratification. Moreover, the more careful the preparation of the treaty and the more deliberate the decision to accept it, the more likely is the treaty to be founded upon the interests of the parties and to be observed by them.[11]

34.11 It should also be noted that ratification must, on principle, be unconditional. Unless the treaty itself specifically so provides, the operative effect of ratifying cannot be made conditional on ratifications by other States. The need for a degree of reciprocity will be met in the treaty itself, either by providing for a minimum number of ratifications before its entry into force,[12] or by providing that the ratification of all the signatories is required for entry into force.[13]

34.12 A final point is that ratification, being in part a confirmation of a signature already given, must relate to what the signature relates to, i.e. to the treaty as a whole, and not merely to a part of it, unless the treaty itself provides that States may elect to become bound by a certain part or parts only.[14]

34.13 Older controversies over which treaties required ratification and which did not, or over whether or not there is any duty to ratify, are now a thing of the past, to a large extent as a result of the Vienna Convention on the Law of Treaties.

---

[11] Arnold McNair, *The Law of Treaties* (Oxford: Clarendon Press, 1961) 133–4.

[12] For multilateral conventions concluded under the auspices of the UN, thirty-five is often the chosen number, but there may be further qualifications as well: the UN Charter required the ratification of all five States designated as permanent members of the Security Council, and the same rule applies to all amendments to the Charter.

[13] As, for example, with all of the constitutional treaties of the European Union.

[14] For the possibility of making ratification subject to reservations, see Chapter 35.

The traditional view had been that, in principle, all treaties required ratification **34.14** in order to become valid and binding. The International Law Commission explained the reasons for this view:

> The modern institution of ratification in international law developed in the course of the nineteenth century. Earlier, ratification had been an essentially formal and limited act by which, after a treaty had been drawn up, a sovereign confirmed, or finally verified, the full powers previously issued to his representative to negotiate the treaty. It was then not an approval of the treaty itself, but a confirmation that the representative had been invested with authority to negotiate it and, that being so, there was an obligation upon the sovereign to ratify his representative's full powers, if these had been in order. Ratification came, however, to be used in the majority of cases as the means of submitting the treaty-making power of the executive to parliamentary control, and ultimately the doctrine of ratification underwent a fundamental change.
>
> It was established that the treaty itself was subject to subsequent ratification by the State before it became binding. Furthermore, this development took place at a time when the great majority of international agreements were formal treaties. Not unnaturally, therefore, it came to be the opinion that the general rule is that ratification is necessary to render a treaty binding.[15]

As late as 1929, the Permanent Court of International Justice referred, in the **34.15** *Territorial Jurisdiction of the International Commission of the River Oder* case, to the rule that 'conventions, save in certain exceptional cases, are binding only by virtue of their ratification'.[16] But the generally accepted view is now the one expressed in Article 14 of the Vienna Convention on the Law of Treaties that whether a treaty requires ratification or not depends essentially on the intention of the parties to the particular treaty.

Fortunately, the dispute as to the nature of the underlying rule is more theoreti- **34.16** cal than real; for it is now the invariable practice for the treaty itself to contain either an express clause or some other clear indication as to whether ratification is required. Where the parties do not regard ratification as necessary, the treaty usually states that it will come into force upon signature, or on a certain date, or upon the happening of a certain event.

At the Vienna Conference on the Law of Treaties, there was extended, but incon- **34.17** clusive, discussion on whether there should be incorporated in the Law of Treaties Convention a residual presumption in favour of signature or of ratification when a treaty was silent as to how consent to be bound should be expressed. The Convention as adopted makes no attempt to resolve the argument, and simply

---

[15] [1966] ILC Reports 30; see also J Mervyn Jones, *Full Powers and Ratification* (Cambridge: Cambridge University Press, 1946) 12–20 and 74–90.

[16] PCIJ, Series A, No 23, 20.

enumerates the circumstances in which consent to be bound is expressed by signature, and the circumstances in which consent to be bound is expressed by ratification, acceptance, approval, or accession.[17]

34.18 Although ratification is a matter of discretion, it is not generally the practice of a democratic government to sign a treaty unless it means to make an effort in good faith to ratify it in due course. Successive British governments have held to that principle as a rule of policy. But, as is well known, governments may meet with insuperable political difficulties which prevent ratification.[18] No time limit is normally set for ratification and, subject to the terms of the treaty, there is no rule of law as to the date within which, if at all, it must take place. Frequently several years elapse between signature and ratification.[19] Article 18 of the Vienna Convention on the Law of Treaties lays down a rule that, pending ratification, a signatory State is under an obligation 'to refrain from acts which would defeat the object and purpose of a treaty', until it had made clear its intention not to become party to the treaty; but it has been doubted whether this represents a rule of customary international law.[20]

Accession

34.19 Accession is the process under which a State may become a party to a treaty of which it is not a signatory.[21]

34.20 Accession is normally a secondary process, but it can exceptionally constitute the primary (or even the exclusive) process for a State to express its consent to be

---

[17] Arts 12, 14, and 15; see also Ian Sinclair, *The Vienna Convention on the Law of Treaties* (2nd edn, Manchester: Manchester University Press, 1984) 40–1.

[18] For example, the then French government failed to obtain in 1954 the necessary parliamentary approval required to enable France to ratify the European Defence Community Treaty. More recently, the difficulties are well known that have faced the Treaty establishing a Constitution for Europe of 29 October 2004, and the subsequent Treaty of Lisbon of 13 December 2007, following their failure to be approved by referendum in certain EU Member States. US accession to the Third UN Convention on the Law of the Sea has been pending in the Senate for more than 20 years.

[19] Though it is rare that the gap between signature and ratification is as long as 63 years, as for the United Kingdom ratification (in 1970) of the 1907 Hague Convention for the Pacific Settlement of International Disputes. A more modern example is the Additional Protocols to the Geneva Conventions of 1949, signed by the United Kingdom in 1977, but not ratified until 1998.

[20] In 2002 the USA, which had signed on 31 December 2000 the Statute of the International Criminal Court, gave formal written notice to the Government of Italy, as depositary of the treaty, of its intention not to proceed to ratification; this has vulgarly, but not entirely accurately, been written about as an attempt to 'un-sign' the treaty as a result of the unhappy use in the US notification of the phrase 'suspend' in respect of the US signature.

[21] The process is sometimes called 'adherence' or 'adhesion' (in French 'adhésion'), but the Vienna Convention on the Law of Treaties uses the term 'accession'.

bound by a treaty. The 1928 General Act for the Pacific Settlement of International Disputes was drafted by a Commission set up by the Assembly of the League of Nations, subsequently discussed and modified, and eventually adopted by the Assembly itself, and then left open for accession. There was no provision for signature and ratification, so that accession was the only means of becoming a party to it.[22] The Revised General Act adopted by the United Nations General Assembly in 1949 follows the same pattern.[23]

A similar process is laid down in the Convention on the Privileges and Immunities **34.21** of the United Nations.[24] The relevant provisions are:

> *Section 31*—This Convention is submitted to every Member of the United Nations for accession.
> *Section 32*—Accession shall be effected by deposit of an instrument with the Secretary-General of the United Nations and the Convention shall come into force as regards each Member on the date of deposit of each instrument of accession.

Similar, but slightly more complex, provisions are contained in the Convention of 1947 on the Privileges and Immunities of the Specialized Agencies of the United Nations.[25]

It should be stressed, however, that these cases are exceptional. Multilateral trea- **34.22** ties will normally make provision for the treaty to be open for signature until a stipulated date and thereafter to be open for accession, often indefinitely, an example being the Vienna Convention on the Law of Treaties itself.[26]

It used to be thought that it was legally impossible to accede to a treaty which **34.23** was not yet formally in force. The rationale of the view was that accession amounted in essence to acceptance of a contract already entered into, thereby implying an operative instrument to accede to. Modern practice is however in the contrary sense, as the International Law Commission pointed out in 1966.[27] It is therefore open to the States negotiating a treaty to provide that it should be open to accession at once (or after the expiry of a set period), even before the

---

[22] Art 43 simply provides that 'the present General Act shall be open to accession by all the Heads of State or other competent authorities of the Members of the League of Nations and the non-Member States to which the Council of the League of Nations has communicated a copy for this purpose'; 93 LNTS 343.

[23] 71 UNTS 101.

[24] Approved by the UN General Assembly on 13 February 1946: 1 UNTS 15 and 90 UNTS 327.

[25] 33 UNTS 261.

[26] Under Art 81 the Convention was opened for signature until 30 November 1969, at the Federal Ministry for Foreign Affairs of the Republic of Austria, and subsequently, until 30 April 1970, at United Nations Headquarters in New York; and under Art 83 it is to remain 'open for accession' thereafter.

[27] [1966] ILC Reports 32.

treaty has formally entered into force; and likewise to provide that accessions rank equally with ratifications in making up the number of consents to be bound required to bring the treaty into force.[28]

34.24 Accession as a secondary process can take place as of right (where the treaty expressly provides that certain States or categories of States may accede to it) or by invitation (where the treaty expressly provides that non-signatory States may accede only upon the invitation of the Contracting Parties or of some representative body). There are many examples of treaties, accession to which is by invitation only. Thus, Article 10 of the North Atlantic Treaty of 1949[29] provides that:

> [t]he Parties may, by unanimous agreement, invite any other European State in a position to further the principles of this Treaty and to contribute to the security of the North Atlantic area to accede to this Treaty. Any State so invited may become a party to the Treaty by depositing its instrument of accession with the Government of the United States of America.

Later members have all joined the alliance pursuant to Protocols to the North Atlantic Treaty by which the parties give their unanimous consent to the issue of an invitation to accede to the Treaty.

34.25 The nature of a treaty may be such that the Contracting Parties may wish to make an invitation to accede subject to conditions to be agreed between them and the State so invited. The best-known example of this kind is the European Union, the admission of a new member to which will of necessity require enormously detailed negotiation between the existing Member States and the applicant State. Article 49 of the Treaty on European Union (Consolidated Version)[30] provides that:

> [a]ny European State which respects the values referred to in Article 2 and is committed to promoting them may apply to become a member of the Union. The European Parliament and national Parliaments shall be notified of this application. The applicant State shall address its application to the Council, which shall act unanimously after consulting the Commission and after receiving the consent of the European Parliament, which shall act by a majority of its component members. The conditions of eligibility agreed upon by the European Council shall be taken into account.

> The conditions of admission and the adjustments to the Treaties on which the Union is founded, which such admission entails, shall be the subject of an agreement

---

[28] For example, under Art 84 of the Vienna Convention on the Law of Treaties itself, the Convention 'shall enter into force on the thirtieth day following the date of deposit of the thirty-fifth instrument of ratification or accession'.

[29] Treaty Series No 56 (1949) Cmd 7789.

[30] Text available at <http://eru-lex.europa.eu/resource.html?uri=cellar:2bf140bf-a3f8-4ab2-b506-fd71826e6da6.0023.02/DOC_1&format=PDF >.

between the Member States and the applicant State. This agreement shall be submitted for ratification by all the contracting States in accordance with their respective constitutional requirements.

Where a treaty is the constitutive instrument of an international organization, the admission of a new Member State (on such terms and conditions as the constitutive instrument may lay down) may be regarded as equivalent to accession. The Charter of the United Nations stipulates (Article 4) that: **34.26**

1. Membership in the United Nations is open to all other peace-loving States which accept the obligations contained in the present Charter and, in the judgement of the Organization, are able and willing to carry out these obligations.

2. The admission of any such State to membership in the United Nations will be effected by a decision of the General Assembly upon the recommendation of the Security Council.

The applicant State is required to embody in its formal written application a declaration that it accepts the obligations contained in the Charter; and, if the application is approved, membership becomes effective on the date on which the General Assembly takes its decision on the application.[31]

In cases such as these, where the constitutive treaties have their own inbuilt dynamic, accession (or admission) may be rendered possible on terms which put the new Member State in a different position from the other Contracting Parties, at least for a transitional period. Normally speaking, however, any State exercising the right of accession given to it in a treaty enjoys the same rights and becomes subject to the same obligations as the other Contracting Parties, without regard to whether they are original signatories or have subsequently acceded. **34.27**

The question was discussed in the Assembly of the League of Nations in 1927 whether a State might properly express a purported instrument of accession as 'subject to ratification'. Present-day practice discourages this. In his role as depositary of multilateral treaties, the Secretary-General of the United Nations has long considered an instrument of accession declared to be subject to ratification 'simply as a notification of the government's intention to become a party'; he has drawn the attention of the government concerned to the fact that the instrument does not entitle it to become a party and underlines that 'it is only when an instrument containing no reference to subsequent ratification is deposited that the State **34.28**

---

[31] Previously, once a favourable decision was taken by the General Assembly, membership became effective on the date on which the applicant State presented to the Secretary-General an instrument of adherence. The first six new members (Afghanistan, Iceland, Pakistan, Sweden, Thailand, and Yemen) were admitted to membership of the United Nations in this way.

will be included among the parties to the agreement and the other governments concerned notified to that effect'.

34.29 Which States may accede to a treaty? It would seem beyond dispute that no State, uninvited, has a right to make itself a party to a treaty by accession; accession can accordingly only take place when the original parties to the treaty consent, either generally by means of a provision in the treaty, or ad hoc, and only upon whatever conditions they may have laid down for accession. It was at one time suggested that a principle of universality required that all States should be entitled to participate in general multilateral treaties, defined for this purpose as treaties which concern general norms of international law or which deal with matters of general interest to States as a whole. A proposal to that effect advanced at the Vienna Conference on the Law of Treaties was, however, rejected by the Conference mainly on the ground that it ran contrary to the principle that States are, and should be, free to choose their treaty partners.[32]

34.30 International law prescribes no particular form for an instrument of accession, though the treaty itself may do so. An instrument of accession is a formal instrument, and it seems inconceivable that an oral communication would suffice. Accession is carried out in accordance with the procedure prescribed by the particular treaty, either by the deposit of a formal instrument of accession with, or by a written notification addressed to, the depositary.[33] The instrument or notification emanates from the executive authority of the State. It will enter into force on the date of deposit or notification, unless the treaty otherwise provides. Where the deposit or notification takes place before the date of entry into force of the treaty, the accession will not take effect unless and until the treaty itself enters into force.

Acceptance and Approval

34.31 Acceptance and approval are alternative methods of participation in a multilateral treaty, which have relatively recently become established in international practice as a new procedure for becoming party to treaties. They are, as the International Law Commission pointed out, 'an innovation which is more one of terminology than of method'.[34]

---

[32] Sinclair, *The Vienna Convention*, 230–1; but see S Nahlik, 'La Conférence de Vienne sur le droit des traités. Une vue d'ensemble' (1969) 15(1) *Annuaire Français de Droit International* 48–9.

[33] The UN Handbook (at para 3.3.4) indicates that '[t]he Secretary-General, as depositary, has tended to treat instruments of ratification that have not been preceded by signature as instruments of accession, and the States concerned have been advised accordingly'.

[34] [1966] ILC Reports 31.

Where a treaty is made open to 'acceptance' without prior signature, the process is akin to accession. Thus, Article 14 of the Statute of the Hague Conference on Private International Law of 1951 provides that it 'shall be submitted for the acceptance of the Governments of the States which participated in one or more sessions of the Conference. It shall enter into force from the date that it is accepted by the majority of the States represented at the Seventh Session.'[35]   **34.32**

Reference to 'acceptance' as a method of participation in a treaty may also be found in the so-called 'triple option' clause to be found in many international conventions. An example is the Convention on the Intergovernmental Maritime Consultative Organization of 1948,[36] Article 57 of which provides that: **34.33**

> the present Convention shall remain open for signature or acceptance and States may become parties to the Convention by:
>
> (a) Signature without reservation as to acceptance;
> (b) Signature subject to acceptance followed by acceptance; or
> (c) Acceptance.

Acceptance shall be effected by the deposit of an instrument with the Secretary-General of the United Nations.[37]

The advantage of a provision for acceptance in a treaty is that it may enable the treaty to enter into force earlier than if the treaty had provided for 'ratification' as such. The constitutional procedures of some States require the assent of the legislature before a treaty can be formally ratified, and it may be possible to accomplish the process of 'acceptance' by executive action alone.[38]   **34.34**

What has just been said about 'acceptance' applies *mutatis mutandis* to 'approval'. 'Approval' appears more often in the form of 'signature subject to approval', where, according to Liang,[39] approval is apparently used 'to indicate the approbation, by the process of municipal law, of the terms of a treaty, as distinguished from "acceptance" which is used to indicate the formal act evidencing the actual acceptance of the treaty by the State'. The opening of a treaty to 'approval' without signature is rare.[40]   **34.35**

---

[35] Treaty Series No 65 (1955) Cmd 9582.
[36] Now the Intergovernmental Maritime Organization (IMO); the consolidated text of the Convention as revised is available at <http://www.imo.org/>.
[37] Similar provisions can be found in other IMO Conventions.
[38] See Liang in (1950) 44 *AJIL* 342–9.
[39] Ibid.
[40] [1966] ILC Reports 31.

Treaty Succession

34.36 Finally, a word needs to be said about treaty succession, a subject which has gained in importance in recent decades. Whenever a change takes place in the international status of a particular territory (or, to put the matter more precisely, when one State is replaced by another in the responsibility for the international relations of a particular territory), questions are bound to arise in regard to the effect of this change on the status of treaties that formerly applied to the territory, or at least its effect in regard to legal relations under such treaties. The subject is known as treaty succession, and is merely one aspect of the more general question of State succession.[41] The situations that may give rise to succession are classified in a United Nations Convention of 1978 on Succession of States in respect of Treaties, as: the transfer of territory from one State to another, the case where two or more States unite into one successor State, and the case when 'a part or parts of the territory of a State separate to form one or more States, whether or not the predecessor State continues to exist'.[42] The Convention (which did not enter into force until 1996; see further below) also devotes considerable attention to what it refers to as 'newly independent States', i.e. territories that had previously been colonial dependencies, a situation that attracted much international attention at the time, but is now of far less practical interest.

34.37 Unlike the Vienna Convention on the Law of Treaties itself, the 1978 Succession Convention cannot be regarded as an expression of the generally accepted law and practice in this area. It has only twenty-two parties, of whom eight are accounted for by the six States emerging from the break-up of the former Yugoslavia, together with the Czech Republic and Slovakia, and none of the leading States has shown interest in becoming party to it. Whereas the Convention sought to diminish the role either of agreements reached between predecessor and successor States for the assumption of treaty obligations in anticipation of the succession, or of general declarations made by the successor State to the same effect after the event, international practice has shown itself to be characterized by a far greater degree of pragmatic flexibility. The Convention favoured, in essence a 'clean slate' for newly independent States (see paragraph **34**.36), by contrast with substantial continuity in the cases of the uniting and separating of

---

[41] Questions of an equivalent kind arise in respect of the property of the State in all its forms, the liabilities of the State (including its debts), and the ownership of and access to historical, archival, and cultural materials.

[42] 1946 UNTS 3.

States.[43] The particular case of decolonization aside, the needs of international life have shown the great desirability of mechanisms by which successor States can express a position in respect of their treaty relations, to which other treaty parties can then react, whether by way of express acceptance, tacit acquiescence, or (where the case demands) formal refusal, and the treaty depositary may have an important administrative role to play in this process, especially when the depositary function is carried out by an international organization.[44] In some practical respects, the attainment of clarity may be as important as establishing whether treaty relations do continue to subsist. In summary, rather than a rigid reliance on abstract rules, practice has favoured empirically derived outcomes case by case, in which subsequent consent or acquiescence by the States concerned has played a substantial role. This is as one would have expected, given that agreement represents the fundamental basis for treaty relations in general.

It is generally accepted, however, that a succession of States has no effect on boundary regimes or other territorial regimes, and this rule is reflected in Articles 11 and 12 of the Succession Convention.[45]   **34.38**

Conversely, highly personal and highly political treaties are liable to expire rather than to be continued. A special rule also applies to membership of international organizations, where in principle membership cannot be inherited, even though it has as its formal origin the member State's becoming party to the treaty which forms the constitutive instrument of the organization. Therefore, where two States unite, both of whom had been members of an international organization, their membership can be merged into the membership of the new State, but the process does not operate in reverse; on a separation of States, it would normally be expected that the new State (or States) would apply for membership in its (or their) own name.   **34.39**

---

[43] Though the continuity was qualified, for uniting States, by the proviso that the application of inherited treaties would remain limited to the territory to which they originally applied, in other words not to the entire territory of the new State, a limitation that was found particularly difficult to accept in the case of Germany; see further at paragraph **34.41**.

[44] Though this may in turn require a more active role than the purely neutral and mechanical one that many depositaries had come to accustom themselves to playing.

[45] It has also been suggested, notably by monitoring bodies under these instruments, that human rights treaties have a special character, in that their purpose and effect is to guarantee fundamental rights for the benefit of individuals, and that 'once the people are accorded the protection of the rights under the Covenant, such protection devolves with territory and continues to belong to them, notwithstanding changes in government of the State Party, including dismemberment in more than one State or State succession or any subsequent action of the State Party designed to divest them of the rights guaranteed by the Covenant': General Comment No 26 of 8 December 1997 by the Committee under the International Covenant on Civil and Political Rights (Document CCPR/C/21/Rev.1/Add.8/Rev.1, available at <http://www.unhchr.ch/tbs/doc.nsf/(Symbol)/06b6d70077 b4df2c8025655400387939?Opendocument>.

34.40 There is however an important qualification to the above, which has come into focus latterly with the disintegration of composite States, notably the former Socialist Federal Republic of Yugoslavia and the former Union of Soviet Socialist Republics, but also in a more limited way the former Republic of Czechoslovakia. In such cases, it may be possible to discern (though this is not always so) that there is a single central sovereignty that has been maintained, initially through the accretion of additional units of territory, and later through their loss. In a case of this kind, it is possible to speak of a 'continuing State' (sometimes referred to as 'continuator State') which will have a different status for succession purposes than the other territorial entities, whose treaty relations will be determined as 'successor States'.[46] The distinction can be of fundamental importance. It explains, for example, why the Russian Federation was able, by simple notification, not merely to continue the membership of the Soviet Union in the United Nations, but to assume the special prerogatives of a permanent member of the Security Council. It explains also how the Russian Federation retained the special status of nuclear-weapon State under the Treaty on the Non-Proliferation of Nuclear Weapons, while the other component parts of the former Soviet Union either succeeded or acceded to the Treaty as non-nuclear-weapon States. Contrast the outcome of the dissolution of the former Yugoslavia, where in a series of cases, the International Court of Justice has noted (without pronouncing definitively on them) the doubts remaining over membership in the United Nations of the rump State entitled 'Federal Republic of Yugoslavia (FRY)' until the eventual admission of the State of Serbia and Montenegro as a new member on 1 November 2000. The Court nevertheless decided, on the one hand, that it could proceed with cases brought before that date by or against the FRY; conversely that, after the separation of Montenegro, a case pending against Serbia and Montenegro should proceed against Serbia alone.[47]

34.41 Two other cases of special interest should be noted. One is the eventual reunification of Germany in 1990, after close on half a century during which the eastern part of Germany had gradually acquired recognition of separate statehood as the 'German Democratic Republic' (GDR). Although the GDR ultimately acceded to the Federal Republic of Germany under the latter's Constitution, this was

---

[46] The same distinction is made in the Analyses published by the British government in advance of the referendum on Scottish independence in 2014; see Cm 8554 of February 2013 and Cm 8765 of January 2014, especially the legal expert opinion annexed to the latter.

[47] *Legality of Use of Force (Yugoslavia v United Kingdom)* [1999] ICJ Reports 826, later *sub nom. Serbia and Montenegro v United Kingdom* [2004] ICJ Reports 1307; *Case concerning Application of the Convention on the Prevention and Punishment of the Crime of Genocide (Bosnia and Herzegovina v Yugoslavia)* [1996] ICJ Reports 595, [2003] ICJ Reports 7, later *sub nom. Bosnia and Herzegovina v Serbia and Montenegro* [2003] ICJ Reports 43.

done on the basis of a treaty between the two States, which in turn made specific provision for treaty succession: the Federal Republic's treaties would in principle continue, and be extended to the entire territory (subject where necessary to consultations with the other treaty parties), whereas all the GDR's treaties were to be subject to discussion with the other parties 'with a view to regulating or confirming their continued application, adjustment or expiry'. It would seem that discussions took place with 135 treaty partners, and that the outcome was to discard or disapply the overwhelming proportion of the GDR's very substantial corpus of treaties.[48]

The second case of special interest is that of Hong Kong. The Sino-British Joint **34.42** Declaration of 19 December 1984, which laid the ground for the return of Hong Kong to Chinese sovereignty in 1997, stipulated that Hong Kong would be enabled to conduct within limits its own external relations, including the power to conclude international agreements, using the name 'Hong Kong, China'. As spelled out more fully in Annex 1 to the Joint Declaration and in the Basic Law (enacted by China—though in agreed terms—to serve as the constitutional instrument for the Hong Kong Special Administrative Region), this international capacity was to include both the continued application to Hong Kong of international agreements concluded before the handover and also Hong Kong's continued participation, in an appropriate form, in international organizations. These arrangements were seen by both parties as an important element in the preservation of Hong Kong's own way of life, including the maintenance of the capitalist economic system. In exercise thereof, an extensive campaign of 'localizing' Hong Kong's treaty relations (for example, in the fields of trade and air services) was pursued in the period preceding the handover.[49]

---

[48] For a full account see D Papenfuss, 'The Fate of the International Treaties of the GDR within the Framework of German Unification' (1998) 92 *AJIL* 469, who points out that the GDR had pursued a hyper-active policy of treaty making as a device for seeking recognition.

[49] Now see the Treaties and International Agreements website of the Hong Kong Department of Justice: <http://www.legislation.gov.hk/choice.htm>.

35

TREATIES AND OTHER INTERNATIONAL INSTRUMENTS—V INTERPRETATION, RESERVATIONS, TERMINATION, THE EFFECT OF WAR, *IUS COGENS*

Frank Berman and David Bentley

35.1 This chapter is devoted to certain miscellaneous aspects of the law of treaties, which are important all the same, and in some cases controversial. Treaty interpretation, for example, is the daily meat and drink of much international activity. It is also of considerable importance at the national level. On other topics dealt with here, the treatment is inevitably somewhat technical, and non-lawyers may prefer to note the existence of difficulties without feeling obliged to explore the issues fully—much less to take a firm position where uncertainty exists. But it is important to grasp for instance what reservations are (and what they are not), and what effect they might have, these being difficult and delicate questions that arise both when a treaty is under negotiation and after its conclusion. Similarly, claims by States to be freed from, or to bring an end to, their treaty obligations are a frequent source of international friction. The same goes for claims that a treaty, or part of it, should be regarded as void, because it conflicts with a fundamental rule of international law (*ius cogens*). Finally, the effect, temporary or permanent, of armed conflict on treaty rights and obligations cannot be ignored by diplomats, for whom indeed it may have immediate consequences.

Interpretation

Treaty compliance, and the effective implementation of treaty commitments, are **35.2** critically dependent on being able to ascertain reliably what the treaty means in its application to particular sets of circumstances. Treaty interpretation is therefore the one aspect of treaty law and practice that is most likely to be of practical importance to a wide range of interested parties, not limited to governments and their advisers, but extending to national courts, practising lawyers, non-governmental bodies, the media, and even the private citizen. It is also the one area, more than most others, in which the work of the International Law Commission, now embodied in the Vienna Convention, has swept aside old controversies in favour of a set of logical and accessible principles, which are now universally accepted as authoritative.[1]

The 'Golden Rule'

Article 31.1 of the Vienna Convention states what might be regarded as the **35.3** 'golden rule' of treaty interpretation:

> A treaty shall be interpreted in good faith in accordance with the ordinary meaning to be given to the terms of the treaty in their context and in the light of its object and purpose.

That is amplified, in paragraph (2), by a definition of 'context' which is deliberately broad; paragraph (3) then lists extraneous materials which are to be taken into account together with the context, and paragraph (4) provides for the case where the Parties intended a term to have a special meaning.

---

[1] There is a complete and up to the minute treatment of the entire subject in R K Gardiner, *Treaty Interpretation* (2nd edn, Oxford: Oxford University Press, 2015).

35.4 It should be emphasized that the International Law Commission saw all of these, not as separate or disaggregated elements, but as parts of a single composite rule, as underlined by the heading, which describes Article 31 as the '*General rule*' of interpretation. It should also be noted that the opening reference to 'good faith' is not mere window dressing, but informs the entire process of interpretation, so as to rule out of consideration, for example, suggested interpretations of a treaty that are plainly one-sided and self-serving.[2] An important aspect of good faith in interpretation is to seek to give meaning to treaty terms, not to deprive them of meaning.

Context, 'Object and Purpose', Negotiating History

35.5 It will be apparent that what the Vienna Convention envisages as the key to establishing the proper meaning of a treaty is the shared common intention of the Parties, but—and this is crucial—that it sees as the safest guide to identifying that shared common intention the terms on which the treaty parties had reached formal agreement. The plain good sense of this is obvious; it becomes even more manifest when the proposition is applied, not to the simplest case of a single-subject bilateral treaty, but instead to a major multilateral treaty, which may involve multiple linked subjects and close on 200 negotiating parties. But the Convention is equally clear that to arrive at the meaning of a treaty, or part of it, individual treaty terms cannot be taken on their own but must be looked at in the context of the text as a whole, and that regard has to be paid as well to the circumstances surrounding the conclusion of the treaty.

35.6 As already indicated, the definition of 'context' is broad; it includes, besides the treaty preamble and any annexes, extraneous material such as agreements between the treaty parties relating to the treaty's interpretation, and even unilateral instruments made by individual parties if they are accepted by the others as instruments relating to the treaty. The guiding principle is that, if the negotiating process that led to ultimate agreement on the treaty text also generated collateral understandings about how it should be interpreted, these understandings constitute a valid part of the interpretative process.

35.7 Of special interest, however, are the extraneous materials specified in paragraph (3): any subsequent agreement between the parties regarding the interpretation of the treaty or the application of its provisions, and any subsequent practice in the application of the treaty which establishes the agreement of the parties

---

[2] The term was considered at length in connection with the Convention on the Status of Refugees by the House of Lords in *R v Immigration Officer at Prague Airport, ex parte European Roma Rights Centre* [2004] UKHL 55, but this seems on closer examination to be less a question of treaty interpretation and more one of implementation in good faith under Art 26 of the Vienna Convention.

regarding its interpretation. These go beyond what is normally admissible for interpretation in national legal systems. The guiding principle here is that treaties are living instruments 'owned' by their parties, whose understanding of what the treaty properly entails may be shaped over time. Subsequent practice in putting the treaty into effect may be particularly instructive of what the parties understand their treaty rights and obligations to be. Finally, paragraph (3) also brings into play 'any relevant rules of international law applicable in the relations between the parties'. The guiding principle here is that all or part of the purpose of a treaty may have been to adapt, or even to disapply, the rules of customary international law that would otherwise have regulated the relations between the parties, and the latter can therefore usefully illuminate what they had in mind in concluding the treaty in that particular form.

The 'golden rule' lays down that the terms of the treaty are to be interpreted not just in context but also in the light of the treaty's 'object and purpose' which is discussed further in paragraphs 35.11–35.12 in connection with 'teleological interpretation'. **35.8**

Last of all, Article 32 of the Convention allows (though it does not require) recourse to 'supplementary means of interpretation' in either of two circumstances: to *confirm* the meaning, or to *determine the meaning* when the application of Article 31 either still leaves it ambiguous or obscure, or leads to a result which is 'manifestly absurd or unreasonable'. The most commonly encountered supplementary means is the negotiating history of the treaty, but this has to be treated with caution as it is often incomplete,[3] or can lack objectivity. International tribunals will almost invariably look at the negotiating history for what it is worth, but will hardly ever be inclined to give it decisive effect on its own. **35.9**

Multilateral and Bilateral Treaties

There is no difference in principle or in legal status between bilateral and multilateral treaties. But the application of the legal rules can sometimes vary in a practical sense according to the number of parties and the purpose of the treaty. This can become evident in the area of treaty interpretation, where, for example, a direct investigation into the intentions of each party may be practicable and sensible for a carefully negotiated bilateral treaty, but unthinkable in any workable sense for a major multilateral treaty, so that the text of the treaty on its own will acquire greater significance than any extraneous material, including the negotiating history. This may be particularly so where the disputed question **35.10**

---

[3] See Chapter **30**, paragraph **30.21** for the records of international conferences. Sad to say, for reasons of economy, full records are no longer published of all significant treaty-making conferences.

of interpretation involves a State that was not part of the original negotiation but subsequently acceded to the treaty.[4] Similar considerations can have particular importance in the case of treaties setting up international organizations or arrangements of unlimited duration, as will be discussed in the next section.

'Teleological' Interpretation

35.11 The term (also sometimes used in the form 'purposive') is a convenient shorthand for an approach to interpretation which sets as its aim to achieve the treaty's purpose by enhancing its effectiveness. It is characterized by the way it looks for the underlying objective rather than taking a strictly textual approach. The tendency is particularly marked in the case of treaties establishing close, long-term relations, notably those containing an institutional element, and where the same treaty provision comes up for repeated application to changing sets of circumstances.

35.12 The teleological technique is not inherently incompatible with the Vienna Convention's 'golden rule'. It is, however, entirely dependent not only on the ascertainment of what Article 31.1 refers to as the treaty's 'object and purpose', but in addition on deciding what action is appropriate to that end, from one situation to another.[5] The first is a question of law, and the second one of policy, though the tendency is to run the two together as if they were one. When that is done by the parties themselves, or by discussion in a competent policy organ, it raises less difficulty than when the treaty arrangement is endowed with a standing judicial organ, which proceeds to carry out the task, so to speak on the parties' behalf. The problem is exacerbated by the fact that international law (including specifically the Vienna Convention) offers no clear guide on how to extract a treaty's object and purpose, or at least to do so convincingly at a level which is not so general and abstract as to be of little genuine assistance in the interpretative process.[6] It is further exacerbated by the tendency in these circumstances to overlook that what the Vienna Convention has in view is the object and purpose of the treaty as a whole, and instead to purport to isolate the 'object and purpose' of particular treaty provisions.

35.13 There is thus inevitably a systemic tension between the teleological and the textual approach towards the interpretation of international treaties that have a more or less constitutional character,[7] and it is this that underlies in part the

---

[4] For accession, see Chapter 34, paragraphs 34.19 *et seq.*

[5] See paragraphs 35.37 *et seq* for the use of the same concept in the context of reservations.

[6] The first port of call is normally the treaty's preamble, but all too often the preamble is either a short collection of lapidary pronouncements, or else an extended recital of assorted desiderata, some designed to appeal to one part of the constituency, others to others. Neither case offers much to help the diligent interpreter, but both offer temptations (seldom resisted) to cherry-pick. The same problem poses itself in respect of reservations.

[7] The phenomenon is entirely analogous to processes at the national level, such as the perpetual tension between the liberal and conservative wings of the US Supreme Court.

current backlash against the rules of the European Union, or against the human rights régimes, especially those with standing judicial organs of compulsory jurisdiction. Yet without the availability of purposive approaches towards the application of their provisions to changed circumstances, and sometimes dramatically changed social attitudes, many treaty régimes would founder, so that it has to be assumed that the negotiators intended at the outset that the treaty should be capable of adaptation over time.

Treaties in More than One Language

Where a treaty is drawn up in two or more languages, great care has to be taken to ensure the closest correspondence possible between the texts. But this may sometimes be difficult, more especially when the languages differ widely in character. The faith of negotiators that they have achieved concordance between differing language texts of a treaty may sometimes be sadly misplaced. In the important instance of the Four-Power Agreement on Berlin of 1971–2, significant nuances of difference between the English and French texts, on the one hand, and the Russian text, on the other, emerged at a very late stage immediately before signature and were never resolved.[8] And the 2007 Arbitration between the British and French governments and their respective concessionaires over the Concession Agreement for the Channel Tunnel revealed, in the words of the Tribunal, 'many discrepancies between its two equal and authoritative texts', which the Tribunal resolved by reference to the parent Treaty between the United Kingdom and France.[9]   **35.14**

Desirable as it may be in theory to pre-empt problems of this kind by specifying in the treaty that one language text is to be regarded as authoritative, national sensitivities and the circumstances of negotiation will nowadays normally make this wholly unrealistic.[10]   **35.15**

The number of language texts in a multilateral treaty may vary from one to as many as six (Arabic, Chinese, English, French, Russian, and Spanish) for treaties concluded under the auspices of the UN, or twenty-three for the treaties providing for the accession of Romania and Bulgaria to the European Union in   **35.16**

---

[8] An attempt to mediate the practical consequences of this through the production of an agreed German version between the East and West German authorities who would have to implement its terms was equally unsuccessful, but the problem ultimately disappeared with the unification of Germany in 1990.

[9] <http://www.pca-cpa.org/upload/files/ET_PAen.pdf>.

[10] Provisions to this effect nevertheless continue in older treaties, such as, for example, the Warsaw Convention of 1929, which governs liability in respect of the carriage of passenger luggage by air; thus the French text was applied by the House of Lords in *Fothergill v Monarch Airlines* [1981] AC 251, as the implementing Act of Parliament required. And the 1982 version of the International Telecommunication Convention retains the provision for the French text to prevail in case of dispute. See also Chapter 31 paragraphs 31.16–31.17.

2005, all being equally authentic.[11] But a multilateral treaty may be drawn up in two or three widely spoken language texts only (for example, in English, French, and Spanish), with provision for 'agreed translations (or official texts) of the treaty to be established in other languages also').[12]

35.17 It is sometimes argued that the language (or languages) in which a multilateral treaty was negotiated should be given more weight in its interpretation than the other language texts. In the case of the United Nations Charter, for example, the working languages of the San Francisco Conference of 1945 were English and French, and the text of the Charter finally approved by the Coordination Committee—and from which the translations into other languages were made—was in English. There is however no evidence of international tribunals approaching questions of interpretation in this way, even though in practice it is likely that more judges and arbitrators work in English or French (or Spanish) than in other languages, and it is also true that the official and working languages of the International Court of Justice are English and French only.

35.18 The rule laid down in Article 33 of the Vienna Convention on the Law of Treaties is that 'the terms of the treaty are presumed to have the same meaning in each authentic text'. It then goes on to deal with the case where a comparison of the authentic texts discloses a difference of meaning which the application of accepted rules of treaty interpretation does not remove, and lays down that, leaving aside the case where the treaty has provided or the parties have agreed that a particular text shall prevail, the meaning is to be adopted 'which best reconciles the texts, having regard to the object and purpose of the treaty'.[13]

35.19 In the *LaGrand* case[14] the International Court, finding itself 'faced with two texts [of its own Statute] which are not in total harmony', resolved the issue, in application of the rule in Article 33 of the Vienna Convention, by reference to the object and purpose of the Statute, together with the context of the provision in question.[15] Some years previously, the tribunal in the *Young Loan Arbitration*[16]

---

[11] See <http://eur-lex.europa.eu/en/treaties/index.htm#accession>.

[12] An example is the Universal Copyright Convention of 1952; 943 UNTS 194.

[13] For a full and up-to-date account of the history of this provision and its application in practice, see Gardiner, *Interpretation*, ch 9.

[14] [2001] ICJ Reports 466.

[15] See also the decision of a Chamber of the Court in the *Elettronica Sicula (ELSI)* case [1989] ICJ Reports 15; and the express refusal of an arbitration tribunal to follow an inconvenient earlier ruling on the interpretation of a bilingual text of a bilateral investment treaty: *Sehil v Turkmenistan* (ICSID Case No ARB/12/6) Decision on Respondent's Objection to Jurisdiction, 13 February 2015; *Kılıç v Turkmenistan* (ICSID Case No ARB/10/1) Decision on Article VII.2 of Turkey-Turkmenistan BIT, 7 May 2012.

[16] 59 ILR 494.

had expressly rejected a submission that it should give special weight to the English text, as the language of negotiation, and had similarly applied the Vienna Convention rules by referring to other articles in the treaty, to its object and purpose, and to the negotiating history. In the Taba Arbitration of 1988, on the other hand, the Tribunal applied an English-language translation (out of an Arabic translation) of a treaty in the Turkish language, on the basis that it was this translation the parties had relied upon in practice.[17]

Reservations

Reservations are a peculiar, and somewhat anomalous, institution of the law of **35.20** treaties, an institution which has given rise to as much difficulty in its practical implementation as controversy at the doctrinal level. The origins of the institution lie in the difficulty frequently encountered of securing the complete agreement of each negotiating party to every detail of a complex treaty text. When that happens, the choices may lie between watering down the final terms of the treaty to something below a worthwhile level of agreement; facing the possibility that one or more negotiating States may decline to (or be unable to) become party to the treaty; or trying to find a special accommodation to meet the demands of the dissenter or dissenters. If an accommodation of that kind can be found, and is incorporated in the treaty text, the problem falls away, as will be indicated in what follows. If not, the tension will remain unresolved between the conflicting demands of the integrity of the treaty bargain, on the one hand, and the wish for widespread participation on the other. The institution of reservations is the attempt to mediate that tension.

The treatment of the institution of reservations that follows is unavoidably long. **35.21** Those interested simply in the current position may skip to paragraphs 35.41 and following. But much of what appears in those paragraphs can only be fully understood in the light of the account of the development of law and practice that precedes them.

The Vienna Convention on the Law of Treaties contains the following defin- **35.22** ition of a reservation:

> a unilateral statement, however phrased or named, made by a State when signing, ratifying, accepting, approving or acceding to a treaty, whereby it purports to exclude or modify the legal effect of certain provisions of the treaty in their application to that State.[18]

---

[17] 80 ILR 226.
[18] Art 2.1(d).

It should be noted at once that the crux is the effect intended by the statement, not how it is described; and, secondly, that (as indicated by the deliberate choice of the word 'purports') it is not for the reserving State on its own to determine the ultimate effect of its reservation.

35.23 Ideally, the treaty will specify whether reservations can be made, and if so which ones, and it may also provide expressly for their legal consequences and for the procedure to be followed. To the extent that the treaty does so, the terms of the treaty will prevail. The practice of the Council of Europe affords a good illustration of the variety of reservations clauses that may be found in multilateral conventions, on the basis of agreement reached within the framework of the negotiations and then incorporated in the final treaty text.

35.24 Thus a reservations clause may be expressed in fairly general terms, but related closely to the contents of the particular treaty, for example the European Convention on the Peaceful Settlement of Disputes, 1957,[19] under Article 35 of which:

1. The High Contracting Parties may only make reservations which exclude from the application of this Convention disputes concerning particular cases or clearly specified subject matters, such as territorial status, or disputes falling within clearly defined categories. If one of the High Contracting Parties has made a reservation, the other Parties may enforce the same reservation in regard to that Party.

2. Any reservation made shall, unless otherwise expressly stated, be deemed not to apply to the procedure of conciliation.

35.25 The best-known reservations clause of this type is however Article 57 of the European Convention on Human Rights:

1. Any State may, when signing this Convention or when depositing its instrument of ratification, make a reservation in respect of any particular provision of the Convention to the extent that any law then in force in its territory is not in conformity with the provision. Reservations of a general character shall not be permitted under this article.

2. Any reservation made under this article shall contain a brief statement of the law concerned.[20]

35.26 Other reservations clauses may be expressed in more particular terms and even specify the precise reservations which are permissible. So, for example, under the European Convention on Compulsory Insurance against Civil Liability in respect of Motor Vehicles, 1959,[21] the Contracting Parties are allowed to avail themselves

---

[19] <http://conventions.coe.int/Treaty/en/Treaties/Html/023.htm>.
[20] For the interpretation and application of these provisions by the European Court of Human Rights in the specific context of the Convention, see n 32.
[21] <http://conventions.coe.int/Treaty/en/Treaties/Html/029.htm>.

of one or more of the reservations provided for in an Annex to the Convention, which then lists sixteen precisely formulated reservations (for example, 'to exempt from compulsory insurance damages for pain and suffering').[22]

In other cases, the particular convention may prohibit reservations altogether. **35.27** Thus, Article 39 of the European Convention on State Immunity, 1972, provides that '[n]o reservation is permitted to the present Convention'.[23]

A similar provision prohibiting reservations altogether is now regularly to be **35.28** found in major international treaties, as an expression of the fact that the integrity of the treaty bargain as a whole was regarded as a primary value by the negotiating States. This approach may be applied even to treaty texts of very great complexity, such as the Third United Nations Convention on the Law of the Sea, 1982,[24] or more recently the Statute of the International Criminal Court, 1998.[25] Here the thought is that the complex régime established by the treaty constitutes an intricate balance of concessions and compromises on all sides, so that to allow any one State to qualify the extent of its commitment on becoming party to it might well lead to others following suit, with the risk of unravelling the entire bargain between them.

However, in cases where the treaty does contain a clause of this kind expressly **35.29** prohibiting the making of reservations, States may seek instead to attach 'interpretative declarations' to their expression of consent. Whether this amounts to an attempt to circumvent the prohibition on reservations depends, as has been seen, on the intention and effect of the statement, not on its description.[26] It is well established in international practice that States may, when signing or expressing consent to be bound, make formal written statements relating to the interpretation of the treaty or particular provisions in it, which the depositary is asked to circulate to all other signatory States.[27] As the Special Rapporteur of

---

[22] A similar example is the European Convention providing for a Uniform Law on Arbitration, 1966 (<http://conventions.coe.int/Treaty/en/Treaties/Html/056.htm>), with fifteen precise reservations. In certain cases, the right to reserve may be limited to particular States, as in the European Convention on the Place of Payment of Money Liabilities, 1972 (<http://conventions.coe.int/Treaty/en/Treaties/Html/075.htm>); here Art 7 and Annex II open a specific reservation to Italy and the Netherlands by name.

[23] <http://conventions.coe.int/Treaty/en/Treaties/Html/074.htm>.

[24] 1833 UNTS 3.

[25] 2187 UNTS 3.

[26] Paragraph 35.22.

[27] It may also be that the terms of such declarations will have been discussed and even accepted at the conference which drew up the treaty; so, for example, the Treaty of Nice of the European Union has annexed to its official publication twenty-four common Declarations adopted by the Conference, and three national Declarations 'of which the Conference took note'; see <http://eur-lex.europa.eu/legal-content/EN/TXT/?qid=1451931039383&uri=CELEX:12001C>.

the International Law Commission put it, with reference to the definition of a reservation contained in the Vienna Convention on the Law of Treaties:

> The…Commission had taken cognizance of the existence of declarations as to interpretation and had accordingly drafted [the definition] in its present form. Some such declarations were of a general nature and represented an objective interpretation of what was understood to be the meaning of a treaty. The purpose of others was to clarify the meaning of doubtful clauses or of clauses which were controversial for certain States. Others again dealt with the application of a treaty in certain circumstances peculiar to a State. The Commission had considered that reservations should be understood to mean declarations which purported to exclude or vary the legal effect of certain provisions in their application to a particular State. That question called for thorough examination, but the Conference should be very cautious about the application of the term 'reservations' to declarations as to interpretation in general.[28]

35.30   That notwithstanding, it may sometimes be difficult, when a State makes an interpretative statement or declaration of this kind on expressing its consent to be bound by a treaty, to distinguish it from a reservation;[29] and while, in principle, interpretative statements or declarations are not subject to the legal régime applicable to reservations as such, the International Law Commission found it necessary to devote a section of its later study of the subject to them.[30] While noting (correctly) that the distinction between an interpretative declaration and a reservation lies in the legal effect that its author purports to produce, the Commission contemplates the application to interpretative declarations of a régime which would in certain respects apply to them rules analogous to those applying to reservations, but without amalgamating the one with the other. A particular example is what the Commission calls 'conditional interpretative declarations', by which a State conditions its acceptance of the treaty on its being interpreted in a specified way; a declaration of this kind can be indistinguishable from a reservation.[31]

35.31   Where the particular treaty contains its own reservations clause, questions concerning the legal effect of reservations made to that treaty will in the first instance be governed by the terms of that clause, taken in its context in the treaty as a whole; and it is only when the terms of the treaty are ambiguous or unclear, or

---

[28] Sir Humphrey Waldock, United Nations Conference on the Law of Treaties, *Official Records, First Session*, 34.

[29] See the analysis by Nelson (2001) *ICLQ* 767, of 'disguised reservations' to the UN Convention on the Law of the Sea, which does not permit reservations; for the texts of formal objections taken by other States to declarations of this kind, see <https://treaties.un.org/Pages/Treaties.aspx?id=21&subid=A&lang=en>, Ch XI.

[30] See paragraphs 35.44 *et seq*. See also the description of EU practice by E Denza, in C Stefanou and H Xanthaki (eds), *Legislative Drafting: A Modern Approach* (Aldershot: Ashgate, 2008) 238.

[31] 13th Report of the ILC's Special Rapporteur, 2008, UN Doc A/CN.4/600.

when the reservations clause is not comprehensive, that reference may have to be made to the rules of general international law about the formulation of reservations and their legal effect. These rules have however been the subject of great controversy for more than 50 years, and the controversy shows no signs of abating. It is now clear that the areas of current controversy go far wider than the case of those multilateral conventions which contain no reservations clause, and extend also to the role and effect of the objection (or lack of objection) by other parties to a reservation formulated by a would-be party; to the legal effect of reservations once validly established; and even to whether different rules apply, or should apply, to reservations to treaties of different types.

It may be said at the outset, however, that the question of reservations does not **35.32** in principle arise in the case of *bilateral* treaties, since it is generally accepted that an attempt by one of the two negotiating States unilaterally to vary the terms of the agreed text after the conclusion of the negotiations will simply mean that negotiations will have to be resumed until agreement can be reached on the text.

That said, the tendency in recent years for the United States Senate to attach, **35.33** even in the case of bilateral treaties, what it terms 'reservations' as the condition for giving its constitutional 'advice and consent' to ratification has given rise to particular problems, the solution to which is not always straightforward. In the case of the Supplementary Extradition Treaty with the United Kingdom of 1985,[32] Aust describes what happened as follows:

> The US Senate approved [the Treaty] on condition that certain amendments were made. The US Government having informed the UK Government of this, it was decided to amend the treaty by an exchange of notes. The US note recorded the Senate's condition and attached the articles of the Treaty as they would read if so amended. The note explained that the US President could not execute the instrument of ratification unless the amendments were made, and asked if they would be acceptable to the UK Government. The UK note confirmed that the amendments were acceptable and instruments of ratification were finally exchanged in December 1986.[33]

The Traditional View

Traditionally, the generally accepted view was that a State which sought subse- **35.34** quently to attach a reservation to a multilateral convention the text of which had been finally agreed could only do so with the assent of the other parties or

---

[32] 1556 UNTS 369.
[33] A Aust, *Modern Treaty Law and Practice* (3rd edn, Cambridge: Cambridge University Press, 2011) 132.

potential parties to the convention. This view was based, inter alia, on the practice of the League of Nations.[34]

35.35 There was however an inner link between the unanimity rule for the adoption of the *text* of a multilateral convention and the unanimity rule for the admissibility of reservations to that text. So long as it was accepted that the text of a multilateral convention could be established only by the unanimous agreement of the participating States, so long was it understood that subsequent reservations to that text required, in order to be accepted as valid, the unanimous consent of the parties to the convention. However, with the weakening of the unanimity rule, including at international treaty-making conferences,[35] later accelerated under the practical impact of the enormous increase in the size of the international community of States from the 1960s onwards, it was inevitable that the foundations for the unanimity rule for reservations would be called into question.

The *Genocide Convention* Case

35.36 The traditional unanimity rule governing the admissibility of reservations to multilateral conventions had been applied in the depositary practice of the League of Nations Secretariat and was taken over by the Secretariat of the United Nations.[36] The traditional rule was not, however, universally accepted. A small number of States, notably the Soviet Union and its allies, laid claim to a principle that every State has a sovereign right to make reservations at will and unilaterally, and to become a party to treaties subject to such reservations, even against the objection of other Contracting States. A larger group of Latin-American States applied a more flexible system based upon a resolution of 1932 by the Governing Board of the Pan-American Union, which would allow a treaty to come into force between a reserving State and other parties which accepted the reservation, but not between it and parties which did not accept the reservation.[37]

35.37 Matters came to a head in 1950 over the Convention on the Prevention and Punishment of the Crime of Genocide (the 'Genocide Convention'), which contains no provision governing reservations and had attracted a certain number of reservations to which other States had objected on the grounds that the reser-

---

[34] See the Report of June 1927 by the Committee of Experts for the Progressive Codification of International Law, League of Nations Document C.212: 1927 V: the full text is published in A McNair, *The Law of Treaties* (Oxford: Clarendon Press, 1961) 173–7.

[35] The Vienna Convention lays down, in Art 9.2, a general two-thirds majority rule for the adoption of the text of a treaty at an international conference (see Chapter 30).

[36] See the Secretary-General's Report to the General Assembly of 20 September 1950 on Reservations to Multilateral Conventions, UN Doc A/1372.

[37] See the historical summary in *ILC Yearbook* 1962, Vol 2, 73–80.

vations were impermissible.[38] The United Nations Secretary-General, as depositary for the Convention, was in a quandary as to whether to count the ratifications subject to these reservations towards the number required for the Convention to enter into force, and the General Assembly decided to seek an advisory opinion from the International Court of Justice on various questions, including whether a reserving State could be regarded as being a party to the Convention if its reservation is objected to by some parties to the Convention but not by others; and, if so, what the effect of the reservation would be as between the reserving State and objecting parties, on the one hand, and accepting parties, on the other. The Court in due course pronounced, by a narrow majority, in the following Delphic terms:[39]

> that a state which has made and maintained a reservation which has been objected to by one or more of the parties to the Convention but not by others, can be regarded as being a party to the Convention if the reservation is compatible with the object and purpose of the Convention; otherwise, that state cannot be regarded as being a party to the Convention;

> that if a party to the Convention objects to a reservation which it considers to be incompatible with the object and purpose of the Convention, it can in fact consider that the reserving state is not a party to the Convention...if, on the other hand, a party accepts the reservation as being compatible with the object and purpose of the Convention, it can in fact consider that the reserving state is a party to the Convention.

Developments Subsequent to the *Genocide Convention* Case

Simultaneously with seeking the advisory opinion, the General Assembly had **35.38** invited the International Law Commission to study the question of reservations to multilateral conventions urgently. In its first report, in 1951, the Commission took the view that the 'compatibility' criterion, as formulated by the International Court, was too subjective and not suitable for application to multilateral conventions in general.[40] In addition, so long as the application of the criterion of compatibility remained a matter of subjective discretion, if some parties were willing to accept a reservation and others not, the status of a reserving State in relation to the Convention would remain uncertain; and this could throw doubt on the status of the Convention itself.[41]

---

[38] It is of some historical interest to note that the reservations were to the provision (Art IX) conferring jurisdiction over disputes on the International Court of Justice, and that, after the fall of communism in the 1990s the majority of the reservations in question were withdrawn.

[39] [1951] ICJ Reports 15.

[40] [1951] ILC Reports 5.

[41] Precisely the point that had led to the request for an advisory opinion in relation to the Genocide Convention; see paragraph 35.37.

35.39 The Commission's recommendation to retain the unanimity rule met with a mixed reception in the United Nations General Assembly, and, in the context of its continuing work on the draft of the Vienna Convention, the Commission ultimately reached the conclusion that 'the very number of potential participants in multilateral treaties now seems to make the unanimity principle less appropriate and less practicable', and aligned itself with the view that, where the treaty is silent in regard to reservations, the International Court's principle of 'compatibility with the object and purpose of the treaty' was suitable for adoption as a general criterion of the legitimacy of reservations to multilateral treaties.[42] The difficulty lay rather, the Commission thought, in the process by which that principle was to be applied, especially where there is no tribunal or other organ vested with standing competence to interpret the treaty.[43]

35.40 After considering various possible solutions, including a 'collegiate' system under which the reserving State would only become a party to the treaty if the reservation were accepted by a given proportion of the other States concerned, the Commission came down in favour of 'a flexible system, under which it is for each State individually to decide whether to accept a reservation and to regard the reserving State as a party to the treaty for the purpose of the relations between the two States'.[44] This is the system which, with minor modifications, is now embodied in the Vienna Convention on the Law of Treaties.

Reservations in the Vienna Convention on the Law of Treaties

35.41 The régime on reservations is set out in Articles 19–23 of the Vienna Convention. Articles 19–21 are the most significant and warrant being set out in full:

> Article 19
>
> *Formulation of reservations*
> A State may, when signing, ratifying, accepting, approving or acceding to a treaty, formulate a reservation unless:
>
> (a) the reservation is prohibited by the treaty;
> (b) the treaty provides that only specified reservations, which do not include the reservation in question, may be made, or
> (c) in cases not falling under sub-paragraphs (a) and (b) the reservation is incompatible with the object and purpose of the treaty.
>
> Article 20
>
> *Acceptance of and objection to reservations*
> 1. A reservation expressly authorized by a treaty does not require any subsequent acceptance by the other contracting States unless the treaty so provides.

---

[42] [1966] ILC Reports 37.
[43] *ILC Yearbook* 1962, Vol 2, 178–9.
[44] *ILC Yearbook* 1962, Vol 2, 180.

2. When it appears from the limited number of the negotiating States and the object and purpose of a treaty that the application of the treaty in its entirety between all the parties is an essential condition of the consent of each one to be bound by the treaty, a reservation requires acceptance by all the parties.

3. When a treaty is a constituent instrument of an international organization and unless it otherwise provides, a reservation requires the acceptance of the competent organ of that organization.

4. In cases not falling under the preceding paragraphs and unless the treaty otherwise provides:

   (a) acceptance by another contracting State of a reservation constitutes the reserving State a party to the treaty in relation to that other State if or when the treaty is in force for those States;

   (b) an objection by another contracting State to a reservation does not preclude the entry into force of the treaty as between the objecting and reserving States unless a contrary intention is definitely expressed by the objecting State;

   (c) an act expressing a State's consent to be bound by the treaty and containing a reservation is effective as soon as at least one other contracting State has accepted the reservation.

5. For the purposes of paragraphs 2 and 4 and unless the treaty otherwise provides, a reservation is considered to have been accepted by a State if it shall have raised no objection to the reservation by the end of a period of twelve months after it was notified of the reservation or by the date on which it expressed its consent to be bound by the treaty, whichever is later.

Article 21

Legal effects of reservations and of objections to reservations

1. A reservation established with regard to another party in accordance with Articles 19, 20 and 23:

   (a) modifies for the reserving State in its relations with that other party the provisions of the treaty to which the reservation relates to the extent of the reservation; and

   (b) modifies those provisions to the same extent for that other party in its relations with the reserving State.

2. The reservation does not modify the provisions of the treaty for the other parties to the treaty *inter se.*

3. When a State objecting to a reservation has not opposed the entry into force of the treaty between itself and the reserving State, the provisions to which the reservation relates do not apply as between the two States to the extent of the reservation.

Broadly speaking, this corresponds to the 'flexible' system proposed by the **35**.42 Commission in 1962. The most significant departure from the Commission's proposals is the reversal of the rule concerning the legal effect of an objection to a reservation (Article 20.4(b)). The Commission had proposed that an objection to a reservation should preclude the entry into force of a treaty as between the objecting and reserving States unless a contrary intention was expressed by the objecting State, whereas the Conference[45] put the onus on the objecting State to declare positively that its objection had the effect of precluding the entry into force of the treaty between the two States.[46]

Comment

35.43 Since the entry into force of the Vienna Convention in 1980, and despite the widespread effect of its provisions on shaping the development of the general law of treaties, the controversy surrounding the making of reservations, and the rules regulating them, has continued. State practice has not settled down into a uniform pattern, and some of the bodies created to exercise a monitoring or adjudicatory role under certain conventions on human rights have adopted decisions that are not entirely consistent with one another, and which in addition have been criticized by States Parties to those conventions.[47]

35.44 In 1993, the UN General Assembly took note of these continuing difficulties and misunderstandings and endorsed the proposal that the International Law Commission should be tasked with reporting once more on the law and practice relating to reservations. The Commission noted at the outset that the Vienna Conventions of 1969 and 1986 set out some principles concerning reservations to treaties, but

> did so in terms that were too general to act as a guide for State practice and left a number of important matters in the dark. These conventions provide ambiguous answers to the questions of differentiating between reservations and declarations of interpretation, the scope of declarations of interpretation, the validity of reservations (the conditions for the lawfulness of reservations and their applicability to another State) and the regime of objections to reservations (in particular, the admissibility and scope of objections to a reservation which is neither prohibited by the treaty nor contrary to its object and purpose). These conventions are also silent on the effect of reservations on the entry into force of treaties, problems pertaining to the particular object of some treaties (in particular the constituent instruments of international organizations and human rights treaties), reservations to codification treaties and problems resulting from particular treaty techniques.[48]

---

[45] On the basis of a proposal by the Soviet Union, the main proponent of a unilateral right to make reservations; see paragraph 35.36.

[46] I Sinclair, *The Vienna Convention on the Law of Treaties* (2nd edn, Manchester: University of Manchester, 1984) 62–3.

[47] See in particular the Judgments of the European Court of Human Rights in the *Belilos* ((1988) 10 EHRR 466) and *Louizidou* ((1995) 20 EHRR 99) cases, drawing on the special character of the European human rights régime. On the wider canvas, see General Comment No 24, adopted in 1994 by the Committee under the International Covenant on Civil and Political Rights (<http://www2.ohchr.org/english/bodies/hrc/comments.htm>), and the strong reactions it called forth from France, the United States, and the United Kingdom, as well as the comments thereon of the ILC's Special Rapporteur in his second Report (1996), Doc A/CN.4/477/Add.1.

[48] See 1993 ILC Report, at paras 428 *et seq* (Doc A/48/10).

After very lengthy consideration, the Commission eventually brought its study to **35.45** an end in a 'Guide to Practice'[49] consisting of nearly 200 guidelines, together with elaborate commentary, which are too complex to be summarized.[50] Of particular interest will however be the Commission's sustained effort to grapple with the central problem of invalid reservations and the status of the author of a reservation of that kind in relation to the treaty (see paragraph **35**.23). The Commission's proposals are contained in Guidelines 4.5.2 and 4.5.3, which read as follows:

4.5.2 Reactions to a reservation considered invalid

1. The nullity of an invalid reservation does not depend on the objection or the acceptance by a contracting State or a contracting organization.
2. Nevertheless, a State or an international organization which considers that a reservation is invalid should formulate a reasoned objection as soon as possible.

4.5.3 Status of the author of an invalid reservation in relation to the treaty

1. The status of the author of an invalid reservation in relation to a treaty depends on the intention expressed by the reserving State or international organization on whether it intends to be bound by the treaty without the benefit of the reservation or whether it considers that it is not bound by the treaty.
2. Unless the author of the invalid reservation has expressed a contrary intention or such an intention is otherwise established, it is considered a contracting State or a contracting organization without the benefit of the reservation.
3. Notwithstanding paragraphs 1 and 2, the author of the invalid reservation may express at any time its intention not to be bound by the treaty without the benefit of the reservation.
4. If a treaty monitoring body expresses the view that a reservation is invalid and the reserving State or international organization intends not to be bound by the treaty without the benefit of the reservation, it should express its intention to that effect within a period of twelve months from the date at which the treaty monitoring body made its assessment.

This represents a sustained attempt to find a régime that, from the starting point of the nullity of the reservation, would allow reasonable effect to be given to the subjective intentions of the reserving State, while recognizing the additional dimension introduced in particular by those human rights treaties endowed with treaty monitoring mechanisms. Its prospects of general acceptance remain for the time being unclear, but it will undoubtedly act as the focus for future development in this difficult area.

A further element of the International Law Commission's work deserving atten- **35.46** tion is the annex to the Guide to Practice on the so-called 'reservations dialogue', which has the great merit of recalling to international attention that the

---

[49] Available at <http://legal.un.org/ilc/guide/1_8.shtml>.
[50] And may also, by that token, be of less practical use to governments than had been hoped.

formulation of a reservation and its possible rejection by other States does not bring the story to a final end, but that scope remains (and should be encouraged) for further discussion and clarification, which might in some cases lead to a reservation being withdrawn, or reformulated in more acceptable terms, to the benefit of all the States concerned and that of the treaty régime itself.

Termination

35.47　A treaty continues to have operative effect for any party to it so long as it remains in force generally or for the party concerned. A treaty remains in force generally so long as it has not come to an end, either automatically by virtue of a provision in the treaty concerning expiry or lapse, or at any time by consent of all the parties. Many treaties provide that they are to remain in force for a specified period of years or until a particular date or event. All these are examples of treaties which come to an end by operation of their own terms; they are perhaps more accurately characterized as examples of *expiry* clauses than of *termination* clauses.

35.48　As to termination proper (that is, action by one or more of the Contracting Parties to bring to an end a treaty still in force), there are, as so often, two cases: termination through the application of a treaty's own provisions, and termination in circumstances not specifically provided for. A further important distinction is between termination of the treaty as a whole, and termination only of a given party's participation in the treaty.

Termination of a Treaty through the Application of its Own Provisions

35.49　The majority of modern treaties contain clauses which provide for a right to denounce[51] or withdraw from the treaty upon the giving of a specified period of notice. Sometimes it is a case of an open right to give notice of withdrawal at will, in others the right is conditioned by the presence of particular circumstances (see further paragraphs 35.51–35.52). In all these cases however the termination of the treaty or the termination of the participation of a Contracting Party in the treaty is brought about by operation of the treaty itself, and when this may happen is essentially a question of interpreting and applying the treaty. As the International Law Commission pointed out:

---

[51] A terminology which is open to misunderstanding on the part of the lay audience; 'denunciation' is simply a lawyer's term of art meaning withdrawal, and does not carry any necessary connotation of condemnation.

The treaty clauses are very varied. Many treaties provide that they are to remain in force for a specified period of years or until a particular date or event; others provide for the termination of the treaty through the operation of a resolutory condition…More common in modern practice are treaties which fix a comparatively short initial period for their duration, such as five or ten years, but at the same time provide for their continuance in force after the expiry of the period subject to a right of denunciation or withdrawal. These provisions normally take the form either of an indefinite continuance in force of the treaty subject to a right of denunciation or withdrawal on six or twelve months' notice, or of a renewal of the treaty for successive periods of years subject to a right of denunciation or withdrawal on giving notice to that effect six months before the expiry of each period. Some treaties fix no period for their duration and simply provide for a right to denounce or withdraw from the treaty, either with or without a period of notice. Occasionally, a treaty which fixes a single specific period, such as five or ten years, for its duration allows a right of denunciation or withdrawal even during the currency of the period.[52]

It will accordingly be seen that withdrawal or denunciation clauses may vary **35.50** widely in their form and effect. Examples of the types of clauses which may be found in modern treaties can be found in Aust.[53] These illustrate the more usual forms of withdrawal or denunciation clause currently in use. An interesting, but unusual, example of a specific clause of this type, which is the subject of much debate at the time this volume goes to press, is Article 50 of the Lisbon Treaty, under which an existing EU Member State, if it decides to withdraw from the European Union, is required to 'notify the European Council of its intention', following which the Union is to negotiate and conclude an agreement with the Member State setting out the arrangements for its withdrawal in the light of its future relationship with the Union, and the withdrawal will take effect either on the entry into force of the withdrawal agreement or, failing that, on the expiry of a specified period.

In particular cases (and this depends essentially upon the nature of the treaty in **35.51** question), a party wishing to exercise a right of withdrawal or denunciation may have to show special cause. Thus, a series of important treaties in the field of arms control contain similar clauses covering the right of withdrawal for special cause, e.g. Article X.1 of the Non-Proliferation Treaty:

Each Party shall in exercising its national sovereignty have the right to withdraw from the Treaty if it decides that extraordinary events, related to the subject matter of this Treaty, have jeopardized the supreme interests of its country. It shall give notice of such withdrawal to all other Parties to the Treaty and to the United Nations Security Council three months in advance. Such notice shall include

---

[52] [1966] ILC Reports 78.
[53] Aust, *Modern Treaty Law*, 278 *et seq.*

a statement of the extraordinary events it regards as having jeopardized its supreme interests.[54]

35.52 Practice under these special clauses is sparse. However, in 1993 North Korea (the Democratic People's Republic of Korea) did give notice of withdrawal from the Non-Proliferation Treaty under this provision, citing as justification certain activities of the United States of America on the one hand and the International Atomic Energy Agency (IAEA) on the other.[55] Following a statement issued jointly by the United Kingdom, the United States, and the Russian Federation, as the depositaries of the Treaty, which called this justification into doubt, the United Nations Security Council adopted a resolution calling on North Korea to reconsider its announcement 'and thus to reaffirm its commitment to the Treaty'.[56] The resolution also urged all Member States to encourage North Korea to respond positively. In due course, an announcement was made of North Korea's decision 'to suspend...the effectuation of its withdrawal', but 10 years later North Korea claimed to reactivate its withdrawal forthwith in response to a resolution adopted by the Board of Governors of the IAEA. North Korea is currently subject to economic sanctions imposed by the Security Council in this connection.

Termination of a Treaty Containing no Termination Clause

35.53 Even if a treaty contains no express provisions governing its expiry or conferring a party right of withdrawal, it can still be terminated at any time by consent of all the parties.[57]

35.54 More controversial is the question whether, and if so in what circumstances and subject to what conditions, a State has the right unilaterally to terminate its participation in a treaty which contains no provision for withdrawal or denunciation.

35.55 McNair talks in terms of a presumption against unilateral termination:

> the normal basis of approach adopted in the United Kingdom and, it is believed, in most States, towards a treaty is that it is intended to be of perpetual duration and incapable of unilateral termination, unless, expressly or by implication, it contains a right of unilateral termination or some other provision for its coming to an end. There is nothing juridically impossible in the existence of a treaty creating obligations which are incapable of termination except by the agreement of all parties.[58]

---

[54] 729 UNTS 169.
[55] The account which follows is based on the rather fuller treatment in Aust, *Modern Treaty Law*, 282.
[56] SC resolution 825 (1993) of 11 May 1993.
[57] Art 54(b) of the Vienna Convention on the Law of Treaties.
[58] McNair, *Law of Treaties*, 493–4.

If such a presumption exists, it is not an absolute one, since there may be evidence that the treaty parties intended to admit a right of withdrawal on notice; or the nature of the treaty itself may be such as to imply the existence of such a right. Article 56.1 of the Vienna Convention accordingly provides that:

[a] treaty which contains no provision regarding its termination and which does not provide for denunciation or withdrawal is not subject to denunciation or withdrawal unless:

(a) it is established that the parties intended to admit the possibility of denunciation or withdrawal; or

(b) a right of denunciation or withdrawal may be implied by the nature of the treaty.

While these principles are generally accepted, it is more difficult to specify which treaties are of such a nature as to imply the existence of a right of unilateral denunciation.[59] One example frequently cited is treaties of alliance, on the basis that they can be presumed not to have been intended for all eternity. Another is commercial or trade treaties. Yet it is easier to suggest general categories in this way than it is to tie them firmly to state practice, in view of the fact that some alliances (for example, the North Atlantic Alliance (NATO)) are clearly intended to be of long duration, as indeed are some treaty relationships in the trade and economic fields (for example, the European Union). Moreover, it is nowadays a virtually universal practice to include in treaties a duration or termination clause.[60] **35.56**

An interesting example of the handling of matters of this kind is provided by Indonesia's purported withdrawal from the United Nations in 1965, in protest against the election of Malaysia to a non-permanent seat on the Security Council. The Charter of the United Nations does not contain any express provision regulating the question of withdrawal from the organization. It is nevertheless clear from the records of the San Francisco Conference that the founding members intended to concede the right to withdraw in exceptional circumstances.[61] **35.57**

Against this background, the Secretary-General sent a carefully considered reply to the Indonesian letter which referred to the absence of express provision in the **35.58**

---

[59] See K Widdows, 'The Unilateral Denunciation of Treaties Containing no Denunciation Clause' (1982) 53(1) *BYIL* 83.

[60] Although EU Treaties tend to be concluded 'for an unlimited period'; e.g. Art 3 of the Treaty of Lisbon of 13 December 2007 (<http://eur-lex.europa.eu/en/treaties/dat/12007L/htm/12007L.html>).

[61] As appears from the commentary of the competent Committee at the San Francisco Conference; see 7 UNCIO 267. For differing views as to the status and legal effect of this commentary on withdrawal, see H Kelsen, *The Law of the United Nations* (London: Stevens, 1951) 127; H Rolin, *Annuaire de l'Institut de Droit International* (1961), Vol 1, 237; and L M Goodrich, A P Simons, and E Hambro, *Charter of the United Nations* (New York: Columbia University Press, 1969) 75.

Charter and to the declaration of the San Francisco Conference, and concluded by expressing, in carefully chosen words:

> both the profound regret which is widely felt in the United Nations that Indonesia has found it necessary to adopt the course of action outlined in your letter and the earnest hope that in due time it will resume full co-operation with the United Nations.[62]

35.59 On 19 September 1966, the Indonesian ambassador to the United States addressed a telegram to the Secretary-General in which, with reference to the Indonesian letter and the Secretary-General's reply, he indicated that the Indonesian government 'has decided to resume full co-operation with the United Nations and to resume participation in its activities starting with the Twenty-first session of the General Assembly',[63] and on 28 September, the president of the General Assembly reported to the Assembly, following discussions with the Indonesian Foreign Minister and the Secretary-General:

> It would therefore appear that the Government of Indonesia considers that its recent absence from the Organization was based not upon a withdrawal from the Organization but upon a cessation of cooperation. The action so far taken by the United Nations on this matter would not appear to preclude this view. If this is also the general view of the membership, the Secretary-General would give instructions for the necessary administrative actions to be taken for Indonesia to participate again in the proceedings of the Organization. It may be assumed that, from the time that Indonesia resumes participation, it will meet in full its budgetary obligations. If it is the general view that the bond of membership has continued throughout the period of non-participation, it would be the intention of the Secretary-General to negotiate an appropriate payment with the representatives of Indonesia for that period and to report the outcome of his negotiations to the Fifth Committee for its consideration.[64]

No objection having been raised to the president's statement, the representatives of Indonesia were invited to take their seats in the General Assembly, and the Secretary-General took action on the lines suggested.[65]

35.60 But if controversy surrounds the asserted right of unilateral withdrawal from or denunciation of a treaty which contains no provision on withdrawal or denunciation, controversy equally surrounds the questions of what other grounds a party may invoke for terminating or withdrawing from a treaty. The Vienna Convention on the Law of Treaties lists three possible grounds of this nature,

---

[62] UN Doc A/5899; S/6202 of 26 February 1965.
[63] UN Doc A/6419; S/6498 of 19 September 1966.
[64] UN Doc A/PV. 1420 of 28 September 1966.
[65] See generally, F Livingstone, 'Withdrawal from the United Nations—Indonesia' (1965) 14 *ICLQ* 637.

namely, breach, impossibility of performance, and fundamental change of circumstances.[66]

A material breach of a bilateral treaty by one of the parties entitles the other to **35.61** invoke the breach as a ground for terminating the treaty or suspending its operation in whole or in part.[67] As regards multilateral treaties, a material breach by one of the parties entitles the other parties by unanimous agreement to suspend the operation of the treaty in whole or in part or to terminate it either in the relations between themselves and the defaulting State, or as between all the parties. Irrespective of whether that happens or not, a party which is specially affected by the breach may invoke it as a ground for suspending the operation of the treaty in whole or in part in the relations between itself and the defaulting State. In addition, if the treaty is of such a character that a material breach of its provisions by one party 'radically changes the position of every party with respect to the further performance of its obligations under the treaty', any party other than the defaulting State will have the right to invoke the breach as a ground for suspending the operation of the treaty with respect to itself.[68]

In its Advisory Opinion in the *Namibia* (South West Africa) case,[69] the Court **35.62** approved these rules as constituting in many respects a codification of customary law, to the effect that only a material breach of a treaty justifies termination, such breach being defined as: 'a repudiation of the treaty not sanctioned by the Vienna Convention; or the violation of a provision essential to the accomplishment of the object or purpose of the treaty'. The Court went on to hold that the General Assembly had determined, by resolution 2145(XXI), that both forms of material breach had occurred in this case, and concluded that: '[t]he resolution in question is therefore to be viewed as the exercise of the right to determine a relationship in case of a deliberate and persistent violation of obligations which destroys the very object and purpose of that relationship'.[70]

Impossibility of Performance

Article 61.1 of the Vienna Convention on the Law of Treaties stipulates that: **35.63**

A party may invoke the impossibility of performing a treaty as a ground for terminating or withdrawing from it if the impossibility results from the permanent

---

[66] A treaty may also be considered as terminated by operation of law if all the parties to it conclude a later treaty relating to the same subject-matter which is so far incompatible with the earlier one that they must be considered to have intended to abrogate it (Art 59 of the Vienna Convention).

[67] Vienna Convention, Art 60.1.

[68] Vienna Convention, Art 60.2.

[69] [1971] ICJ Reports 16.

[70] [1971] ICJ Reports 47. See also H W Briggs, 'Unilateral Denunciation of Treaties: The Vienna Convention and the International Court of Justice' (1974) 68 *AJIL* 51–68.

disappearance or destruction of an object indispensable for the execution of the treaty. If the impossibility is temporary, it may be invoked only as a ground for suspending the operation of the treaty.

The usual examples given of the rare cases of supervening impossibility of performance are 'the submergence of an island, the drying up of a river or the destruction of a dam or hydroelectric installation indispensable for the execution of a treaty'.[71]

35.64 Naturally, impossibility of performance may not be invoked by a party if the impossibility is the result of a breach by that party of an obligation under the treaty or any other international obligation owed to any other party to the treaty.[72]

Fundamental Change of Circumstances

35.65 Linked with the concept of supervening impossibility of performance, but much more controversial in its formulation and application, is the doctrine that political (as opposed to physical) changes of circumstances may be invoked as a ground for terminating a treaty. This is the so-called doctrine of *rebus sic stantibus*. It is spelt out, in suitably restrictive terms, in Article 62.1 of the Vienna Convention:

> A fundamental change of circumstances which has occurred with regard to those existing at the time of the conclusion of a treaty, and which was not foreseen by the parties, may not be invoked as a ground for terminating or withdrawing from a treaty unless:
> (a) the existence of those circumstances constituted an essential basis of the consent of the parties to be bound by the treaty; and
> (b) the effect of the change is radically to transform the extent of obligations still to be performed under the treaty.

The remaining paragraphs of the Article then go on to make plain that the doctrine may not be invoked in respect of a treaty which establishes a boundary or if the change of circumstances results from a breach by the party invoking it either of the treaty or of any other international obligation.

35.66 There have been relatively few cases in which the doctrine of *rebus sic stantibus* has been invoked before an international tribunal and in no case has the right to terminate a treaty on the ground of fundamental change of circumstances been upheld. When the International Court of Justice was confronted with an Icelandic contention that, owing to changed circumstances resulting from the ever-increasing exploitation of the fishery resources in the seas surrounding

---

[71] [1966] ILC Reports 84.
[72] Art 61.2.

Iceland a 1961 Exchange of Notes was no longer applicable, the Court acknowledged the validity of the principle, but declined to accept that the change of circumstances invoked by Iceland had resulted in a radical transformation of the extent of obligations still to be performed, pointing out that:

> [t]he present dispute is exactly of the character anticipated in the compromissory clauses of the Exchange of Notes. Not only has the jurisdictional obligation not been radically transformed in its extent; it has remained precisely what it was in 1961.[73]

Finally, the Court held that a change of circumstances can never extinguish **35.67** a treaty automatically or allow an unchallengeable unilateral denunciation by one party; it only operates 'to submit the dispute to some organ or body competent to determine whether the conditions for the operation of the doctrine are present'.[74]

Procedure for Termination

A notice of termination, withdrawal, or denunciation ('notice') is a formal noti- **35.68** fication from the competent authority of the State concerned and communicated through the diplomatic channel to the other party or parties to the treaty or to such depositary government or authority as the treaty may specify. Any notice given under a treaty must comply with the conditions specified in the treaty. It is not sufficient to announce termination or withdrawal or to publish a notice of it in the press.

Notices take effect only with their formal communication as above, and any **35.69** period to which the notice is subject runs from then. Unless the treaty provides otherwise, notices must be unconditional, and will apply automatically to all annexes, protocols, Notes, letters, and declarations attached to the treaty and forming an integral part of it.

Unless the treaty provides otherwise, a notice may be withdrawn or revoked at **35.70** any time before it takes effect provided that the withdrawal or revocation is consented to by any other party which, in consequence of the original notice, has itself given notice of termination or has otherwise changed its position.

Where notice is given in accordance with the terms of the treaty itself, the notice **35.71** may or may not be accompanied by a statement of the reasons.[75]

---

[73] *Fisheries Jurisdiction* case (*United Kingdom v Iceland*) [1973] ICJ Reports 3, para 43.
[74] At para 44.
[75] But see paragraphs 35.51–35.52.

The Effect of War on Treaties

35.72　Treaties, depending as they do for their efficacy on the twin principles of agreement and good faith, are inherently subject to the possibility of disturbance if a situation of armed conflict should subsist for any sustained period of time between the treaty parties, or between two or more of the parties in the case of a multilateral treaty.[76] The Vienna Convention does not purport to deal with the subject, but merely sets it aside as a matter not prejudged by the terms of the Convention. The subject has, however, recently been under discussion by the International Law Commission, in the light of experience in recent conflicts, leading to the adoption of a set of draft articles, which were in turn commended by the UN General Assembly to the attention of governments;[77] it is not clear whether further action is likely to follow towards turning the draft articles into a formal legal instrument of any kind.

35.73　It can however be said with some confidence that not all treaties will automatically be brought to an end, or temporarily suspended in their operation, even by the existence of extended hostilities. Mere local skirmishes, for example, are not likely to put at issue the general relations between the contending States. Similarly, some treaties may expressly contemplate their operation during armed conflict, or include explicit provision as to what is to happen in the event of armed conflict: an example of the former is the 1949 Geneva Conventions on the Protection of the Victims of Armed Conflict (Red Cross Conventions) and their Additional Protocols; an example of the latter is a human rights convention containing provision for derogation in time of armed conflict or other national emergency. If the treaty does contain explicit provision for the situation, that provision will govern. Likewise, it is generally accepted that certain categories of treaty are not in principle set aside by armed conflict. In addition to those just mentioned, these categories would include, amongst others, boundary treaties and treaties regulating territorial status; treaties regulating international trade and transport; treaties governing international watercourses, or the protection of the environment; treaties governing the status of diplomats or consular representatives; treaties for the settlement of international disputes; and treaties which represent the constitutive instruments of international organizations.[78] Many of these treaties, however,

---

[76] It should be emphasized that this section deals with the effect of war on the treaty as such, i.e. as an instrument creating rights and obligations under international law. The effects of war on private rights, under domestic legal systems, are a different matter altogether, but are outside the scope of this book.

[77] GA resolution 66/99 of 9 December 2011.

[78] Cf the Annex to the ILC draft articles (n 77).

even if they continue in being, will nevertheless find their operation inevitably affected, at least to some extent, by wartime conditions, such as treaties on the environment, on transit, or those providing for freedom of trade or transport. In cases of that kind, it may well be that the treaty parties find themselves obliged to settle on agreed measures to adjust aspects of the treaty régime to the exigencies of the wartime situation. Nothing stands in the way, legally speaking, of States making agreed adjustments of this kind in the general interest, perhaps under the aegis of a competent international body; the existence of armed conflict does not of itself affect their treaty-making capacity, as witness the fact that a cease-fire or armistice, or the definitive ending of the conflict, may in due course have to be brought about by the conclusion of new treaty instruments of some kind between the conflicting States. An especially difficult challenge may be posed by disarmament treaties—as opposed, that is, to treaties definitively banning the possession or use of particular weapons or methods of warfare.

In cases other than those already mentioned, the survival or fate of the treaty **35.74** will be dependent on the particular circumstances, including the nature of the treaty, the number of the parties to it, and the characteristics of the armed conflict itself, e.g. its intensity and territorial extent. In all cases, however, suspension, termination, or withdrawal by a State Party will have to be preceded by due formal notification of its intentions.

It should finally be noted that, in the case of a multilateral treaty, the fact that **35.75** armed conflict may affect the treaty relations between the hostile parties, or between them and other States Parties, does not necessarily mean that mutual relations under the treaty are also affected as between the other States Parties, not themselves involved in the conflict.

Ius Cogens

The chapter concludes with a brief mention of the difficult topic of *ius cogens* **35.76** despite its problematical and highly controversial character. This is because the Vienna Convention on the Law of Treaties is one of the few leading instruments to deal with the subject explicitly and because, notwithstanding the broad mention in Chapter **31** of the inherent treaty-making capacity of States, it would now be generally recognized that the impact of *ius cogens* sets at least a theoretical limit on that capacity. There is moreover an increasing tendency to draw the concept of *ius cogens* into international advocacy, despite the many subsisting problems in the way of a generally accepted understanding of the scope of the doctrine or of its legal consequences.

The fact that the doctrine is often referred to by its Latin name is a signal of its **35.77** out-of-the-ordinary nature, but is partly also the result of the lack of a suitable

English-language equivalent. The Vienna Convention resorts to the periphrasis 'peremptory norm of general international law',[79] which it defines as 'a norm accepted and recognized by the international community of States as a whole as a norm from which no derogation is permitted and which can be modified only by a subsequent norm of general international law having the same character', though this formula is in reality too circular to serve as an adequate definition. The Vienna Convention goes on to provide (in its Article 53) that a treaty which, at the time of its conclusion, was in conflict with a norm of this character is void; by 'void' is meant that the treaty never came into legal existence, i.e. that its provisions have no legal force. The Vienna Convention similarly provides (in its Article 64) that, if a new 'peremptory norm' emerges, any existing treaty in conflict with that norm becomes void, and terminates, but without attempting to make adequate provision for the element of retroactivity that would entail.[80]

35.78   It will be evident that any attempt to apply this apparently simple régime will throw up a series of tricky, and perhaps intractable questions, including: what are the norms that potentially qualify as rules of *ius cogens*?[81] How does one of them actually become established as such? How is it to be determined *when* that happened? Who decides? For reasons of that kind, and in view of the great potential of the doctrine to undermine the stability of treaty relations, its adoption at the Vienna Conference and incorporation into the Vienna Convention remained highly controversial to the last. It was eventually accepted at the very final stage of the negotiation, but only in return for the inclusion of a special provision (Article 66(a)) under which disputes over the invocation of *ius cogens* to invalidate a treaty were made subject to the compulsory jurisdiction of the International Court of Justice.[82] Article 66(a) would however only be effective to confer jurisdiction on the International Court[83] if the treaty is itself one directly covered, as a matter of treaty law, by the Vienna Convention,[84] and the provision has never been called into play to date. The International Court has,

---

[79] 'norme impérative du droit international générale' in the French text.

[80] See Art 71.2, on which Reuter has commented, '[l]es incertitudes qui touchent aux effets du *ius cogens* sont atteintes d'une incertitude aussi grave que la notion elle-même'.

[81] The records show that the International Law Commission deliberately refrained from offering any list of illustrative examples of possible *ius cogens* rules, for fear of the misunderstanding which that might lead to; the most commonly cited examples today are the rules prohibiting aggression, genocide, the slave trade, and torture, though not all would meet with the same degree of agreement, and further problems of definition would in any case ensue.

[82] A detailed account can be found in Sinclair, *Vienna Convention*, 228 *et seq*.

[83] See Chapter 24 on the settlement of disputes.

[84] i.e. a treaty 'concluded by States after the entry into force of the present Convention with regard to such States' (Art 4 of the Vienna Convention).

however, shown itself very cautious over the endorsement of the alleged *ius cogens* status of a rule of general international law where a claim of that kind has featured in a case brought before it by other means. Nor has the Court shown any inclination to go beyond the limited and circumscribed effect of *ius cogens* rules as described above, e.g. by accepting arguments that a rule of *ius cogens* possesses a sort of 'trump card' status that would displace the operation of other accepted rules of international law.[85]

---

[85] So in the *Case between the Democratic Republic of the Congo and Rwanda* [2006] ICJ Reports 6, the Court declined to contemplate that different rules would apply to reservations to a multilateral treaty if the reservations related to treaty provisions reflecting rules of general international law said to have a *ius cogens* character. A similar reluctance can be seen (outside the treaty field) in the Court's refusal to find any contradiction between *ius cogens* and the principles of state immunity; *Jurisdictional Immunities of the State (Germany v Italy: Greece intervening)* [2012] ICJ Reports 99. Similar reticence has been displayed by the International Criminal Tribunal for the former Yugoslavia and the European Court of Human Rights.

Book VIII

ENVOI

36

ADVICE TO DIPLOMATS

Ivor Roberts and Emyr Jones Parry

François de Callières's (1645–1717) classic work *De la manière de négocier avec les* **36.1**
souverains,[1] including his observations on the qualities necessary for the profession of a diplomat, though made exactly 300 years ago, still has a good deal to commend it. A brief summary of the main points is given here. In modern days, methods of diplomacy are certainly less subtle and tortuous than were those of the past; while the rapidity of communication now enables a negotiator to remain in constant touch with his government throughout. But national character and human nature have not changed to any appreciable extent. Callières's advice is summarized as hints that should prove useful to younger diplomats and as a suitable introduction to the present chapter:

> A good negotiator should have enough self-control not to speak without having asked himself what he has to say. He shouldn't fall into the error of a famous ambassador of our times who was so intemperate in debate that he revealed secrets in order to support his arguments.
>
> He shouldn't err in the other direction by making a secret out of nothing and by being incapable of distinguishing between matters of importance and trifles.
>
> One calls an ambassador an honourable spy as he tries to discover the secrets of the Court where he is accredited and he should spend what is necessary to pay those who can tell him.

---

[1] H M A Keens-Soper and Karl W Schweizer (eds) (New York: University Press of America, 1993).

A good negotiator should never base a successful negotiation on false promises or bad faith. Craftiness is an illustration of smallness of mind and an indication that the person hasn't enough intellectual breadth to achieve his aims by fair and reasonable means.

A man who displays self-possession and calmness under pressure has a great advantage in negotiation over a man who is lively and fiery. To succeed in this profession, you need to speak much less than to listen: you need phlegm, reserve, plenty of discretion and patience.

A wise and capable negotiator needs to adjust himself to the habits and customs of the country where he lives without showing repugnance or contempt for them. He shouldn't publicly criticize the form of government he finds [Ed. unless that is a clear instruction from his own government]; indeed he should praise what is good about the country's form of government as no country's governance has a monopoly of good points.

He should know or learn the history of the country where he is resident and so recount the great deeds of the ancestors of the country's leaders or indeed their own deeds which will incline them to look kindly on the negotiator.

It's more of an advantage for a negotiator to carry out his business orally. This way he has more opportunity to discover the feelings and aims of his interlocutors and to put over his own arguments more forcefully.

One of the greatest secrets of negotiating is knowing how to distil drop by drop into the mind of interlocutors the matter of which one wants to persuade them [Ed. so that the interlocutor himself comes to a different view].

There is hardly anyone who wants to admit to being wrong or having made a mistake or who will give up his opinions in favour of yours if all you ever do is contradict him, however good your reasons. There are however many who will give up some of their opinions where you can find arguments which flatter their amour propre and advance their own interests thus justifying their change of view...one should avoid bitter and obstinate discussions with Princes and their ministers but reason with them without passion and without always wanting to have the last word.

36.2   A century later the first Earl of Malmesbury[2] wrote to Lord Camden, at the latter's request, on his nephew, Mr James, being destined for the foreign service:

Park Place, April 11, 1813.

MY DEAR LORD,

It is not an easy matter in times like these, to write anything on the subject of a Foreign Minister's conduct that might not be rendered inapplicable to the purpose by daily events.[3] Mr. James' best school will be the advantage he will derive from the abilities of his Principal, and from his own observations.

The first and best advice I can give a young man on entering this career, is *to listen, not to talk*—at least, not more than is necessary to induce others to talk. I have in

---

[2] James Harris, first Earl of Malmesbury, British ambassador at St Petersburg, 1777–82.
[3] At the beginning of the nineteenth century reference to a Foreign Minister was usually to a diplomat not a political figure.

the course of my life, by endeavouring to follow this method, drawn from my opponents much information, and concealed from them my own views, much more than by the employment of spies or money.

To be very cautious in *any* country, or at *any* court, of such as, on your first arrival, appear the most eager to make your acquaintance and communicate their ideas to you. I have ever found their professions insincere, and their intelligence false. They have been the first I have wished to shake off, whenever I have been so imprudent as to give them credit for sincerity. They are either persons who are not considered or respected in their own country, or are put about you to entrap and circumvent you as newly arrived.

We should be most particularly on their guard against such men, for we have none such on our side of the water, and are ourselves so little *coming* towards foreigners, that we are astonished and gratified when we find a different treatment from that which strangers experience here; but our reserve and *ill manners* are infinitely less dangerous to the stranger than these premature and hollow civilities.

To avoid what is termed abroad an *attachement.* If the other party concerned should happen to be sincere, it absorbs too much time, occupies too much your thoughts; if insincere, it leaves you at the mercy of a profligate and probably interested character.

Never to attempt to export our own habits and manners, but to conform as far as possible to those of the country where you reside—to do this even in the most trivial things—to learn to speak their language, and never to sneer at what may strike you as singular and absurd. Nothing goes to conciliate so much, or to amalgamate you more cordially with its inhabitants, as this very easy sacrifice of *your* national prejudices to *theirs.*

To keep your cypher and all your official papers under a very secure lock and key; but not to *boast* of your precautions, as Mr Drake did to Mehée de la Touche.

Not to allow any opponent to carry away any official document, under the pretext that he wishes 'to study it more carefully;' let him read it as often as he wishes, and, if it is necessary, allow him to take minutes of it, but *both in your presence.*

Not to be carried away by any real or supposed distinctions from the sovereign at whose Court you reside, or to imagine, because he may say a few more common-place sentences to you than to your colleagues, that he entertains a special personal predilection for you, or is more disposed to favour the views and interests of your Court than if he did not notice you at all. This is a species of royal stage-trick, often practised, and for which it is right to be prepared.

Whenever you receive *discretionary* instructions (this is, when authority is given you) in order to obtain any very desirable end, to decrease your demands or increase your concessions according as you find the temper and disposition of the Court where you are employed and to be extremely careful not to let it be supposed that you have any such authority; to make a firm, resolute stand on the first offer you are instructed to make, and, if you find *'this nail will not drive,'* to bring forward your others *most gradually,* and not, either from an apprehension of not succeeding at all, or from an over-eagerness to succeed too rapidly, injure essentially the interests of your Court.

It is scarcely necessary to say that no occasion, no provocation, no anxiety to rebut an unjust accusation, no idea, however tempting, of promoting the object you have in view, can *need,* much less justify, a *falsehood.* Success obtained by one is a precarious and baseless success. Detection would ruin, not only your own reputation for ever, but deeply wound the honour of your Court. If, as frequently happens, an indiscreet question, which seems to require a distinct answer, is put to you abruptly by an artful minister, parry it either by treating it as an indiscreet question, or get rid of it by a grave and serious look: but on no account contradict the assertion flatly if it be true, or admit it as true, if false and of a dangerous tendency.

In ministerial conferences, to exert every effort of *memory* to carry away faithfully and correctly what *you hear* (what *you say* in them yourself you will not forget); and, in drawing your report, to be most careful it should be faithful and correct. I dwell the more on this (seemingly a useless hint) because it is a most seducing temptation, and one to which we often give way almost unconsciously, in order to give a better turn to a phrase, or to enhance our skill in negotiation; but we must remember we mislead and deceive our Government by it.

I am, etc.[4]

36.3 These antique examples clearly need adapting to modern times and supplementing.[5] Diplomats need to know their own country; it is that country which diplomats represent and whose interests they are sent abroad to advance. Diplomats do not represent NGOs however laudable a particular NGO's aims might seem. As diplomats abroad representing their country, it is assumed that the views they express are those of their government. Care should be taken to avoid personal views which can be wrongly interpreted as official views.

36.4 A diplomat must be on guard against the notion that his or her own post is the centre of international politics, and against an exaggerated estimate of the part assigned to that post and its staff. Diplomats should aim to understand how their work contributes to national objectives in the general scheme of things. (In this respect it is invaluable to have experience of working in one's own ministry even in a different area.) While ministers and senior officials at home have the responsibility to decide what should be the main direction of foreign policy, and to gauge the relative value of political friendships and alliances, they should appreciate well-argued and proportionate advice. Conciseness and an ability to simplify knowledge will always be appreciated. It is of overriding importance to retain the confidence of one's own capital while being willing to 'speak truth to power'.[6]

36.5 Diplomats need to be conscious of the responsibility of representing their country. They should never give in to the temptation of a negative comment about

---

[4] *Diaries and Correspondence*, Vol 4, 420.

[5] A modern, comprehensive, and often entertaining account of what diplomats do and shouldn't do is to be found in Brian Barder, *What Diplomats Do: The Life and Work of Diplomats* (Lanham: Rowman and Littlefield, 2014).

[6] Variously attributed either to the African-American civil rights leader, Bayard Rustin (1912–87) or to a 1955 Quaker pamphlet of that name by Milton Mayer.

their own government. Diplomats are there to represent it and their country's values and to provide an accurate picture of their government's views to the government to which the diplomat is accredited (the host government). The diplomat's government will, however, even when there are sharp differences between governments, want to see them retain productive working relationships with the host government. If that breaks down, the diplomat's value is much diminished.

Good diplomats will know how to target the right people. There is little use in **36.6** cultivating someone on the way out or expected to be moved in a reshuffle. It is important instead to anticipate the more promising in the upcoming generation and cultivate them. While diplomatic colleagues from other missions should always be treated with courtesy and respect, it is often too easy to fall into the trap of reporting diplomatic corps tittle-tattle as though it were gospel. Direct local contacts will usually prove a much better source of information. And it is important to keep one's network of contacts broad. Too much reliance on the institutional elites and insufficient attention to the views on the street and in the souk can blind even an experienced diplomat to political trends and even to impending major changes of régime.[7]

As the lesson of the Iranian revolution demonstrates, while it is a constant and **36.7** invigorating challenge for any diplomat to analyse the country to which they are posted, the traps are numerous. In particular, it is essential to differentiate between the desirable from the diplomat's government's perspective and what is objectively likely. Hence the importance of getting outside the capital, listening to the concerns and interests of those outside of the establishment elites, and approaching official news sources with appropriate scepticism. In a relatively closed society, the diplomat may be engaged in an updated form of Kremlinology, scanning the papers for who is standing next to whom at national events. In other countries the challenge may instead be one more of selection: cutting through the noise to decide which economic measures, civil society leaders, or social media users are most insightful and influential. And if the diplomat has a resident spouse or partner with an individual life, and quite possibly employment outside the embassy, there might be few readier sources for out-of-the-ordinary local contacts.

---

[7] Sir Nick Browne's influential report commissioned by the British Foreign Secretary on why Britain had failed to predict the fall of the Shah pulled no punches. 'The conclusion that the embassy drew from their analysis [of the Shah's position] consistently proved to be too optimistic.' It had 'overstated the personal popularity of the Shah . . . knew too little about the activities of Khomeini's followers . . . saw no need to report on the financial activities of leading Iranians . . . [and] failed to foresee that the pace of events would become so fast.' He went on to criticize Sir Anthony Parsons, the British ambassador to Iran from 1974 to 1979, as inadequately informed and had not sufficiently pursued contacts with the opposition to the Shah and in particular, supporters of Khomeini. As a result, he had 'underestimated the attractions of [Khomeini's] simple and consistent message that the Shah must be overthrown'.

36.8 Spotting potential political upheavals is famously difficult. No capital likes an embassy that constantly cries wolf. But nor does any embassy want to miss a revolution in the offing. Particular care should be taken to recognize a deteriorating security situation. Foreign ministries will, or perhaps should, be focused on the security of their staff at post. And an embassy that is perceived to gloss over security concerns may be considered a boiling frog—that, is an observer unaware about how hot the water around it is becoming until it is too late. The surest and best way to understand a country is to get to know its language and in so doing to understand the feelings of the people; getting to know a country's economy and energy relationships and dependence on its neighbours, its geographic diversity, even the background and context of the national anthem can all be a valuable part of pre-posting preparation. Once in post, it should be a priority to maintain a lively interest in the topics which are likely to be uppermost in the minds of one's contacts; they are likely to enjoy conversation with a well-informed diplomat far more and be more confident in sharing information.

36.9 In negotiating with the host government, diplomats should always try to put themselves in the position of the person with whom they are negotiating, to understand their interlocutors' psychology, objectives, and needs, and try to imagine what they would wish, do, and say, under those circumstances and consider their own assets in making a case: convening power and particularly soft power. Simple lobbying may well be appropriate but in terms of influencing public opinion, the modern diplomat may well choose to make use of social media to engage the local media and the civil society (see Chapter 27). Being aware of major themes trending in social media, like opinion polls, can be a help to understand local politics.

36.10 A diplomat should always take care to protect the dignity of the State which he or she represents. However, it is not always easy to avoid making mistakes in precedence and protocol in a foreign country and it's generally unwise, if the victim of such a mistake, to attempt to make a fuss. Such mistakes are seldom made maliciously or deliberately. A sense of humour is often the best solution. (See also paragraphs **36.27–36.31**.)

36.11 Diplomats should not hold commercial real estate, engage in trade or hold directorships, or speculate on the stock exchange in the territory of the host State. Such activity may well have a significant effect on privileges and immunities to the detriment of the mission. There is, moreover, the risk of judgement as to the financial stability of the State or of local commercial undertakings being clouded by personal interest (see Chapter 13, paragraphs **13.4** and **13.6**). Diplomatic service regulations of some States (e.g. the US) prohibit investment by their own diplomats in companies or enterprises in countries where they are posted.

In earlier times ambassadors enjoyed a wide discretion in the interpretation of **36.12**
their instructions, in case it became necessary to take a sudden decision, but in
these days, when communication is virtually instantaneous, if heads of mission
think that their instructions are not best expressed to secure the government's
objectives, they can easily ask for them to be modified. In doing this it will be
important to explain the reasoning and suggest alternative wording.

Occasionally, a diplomat may wish to pass a copy of the instructions received to **36.13**
his or her host government. This requires considerable trust, and in doing so,
great care should be taken to ensure that there is nothing in the instructions
which is best left uncommunicated in writing or indeed orally. On the other
hand, there will be occasions when it is advisable to leave a written copy of
instructions so that no ambiguity can remain. The interview of the US ambassador with Saddam Hussein shortly before the Iraqi invasion of Kuwait in 1990
is a case in point. According to one school, Saddam Hussein would have inferred
from his exchange with the ambassador that an invasion of Kuwait by Iraq
would be regarded as undesirable by the US but would certainly not be regarded
as a *casus belli* by that government.[8] This was later contradicted by Tariq Aziz,
who was present at the meeting as the Foreign Minister, and who claimed that
there were no mixed messages and that the ambassador was there to receive a
message from Saddam Hussein, not deliver one.[9] Whatever the truth of the
matter, misunderstandings can prove fatal. In critical circumstances it is not the
job of the diplomat to make his message more palatable to the recipient. Any
message, even if tactfully worded and tailored to the recipient, must always
retain clarity so that it is unambiguously understood.

The negotiation of agreements with the host State requires particular care. In very **36.14**
many cases a delegation will be sent out from the home State to do the negotiating

---

[8] According to an Iraqi transcript reprinted in the *New York Times* on 23 September 1990,
Ambassador Glaspie said 'we have no opinion on the Arab-Arab conflicts, like your border disagreement with Kuwait. I was in the American Embassy in Kuwait during the late 60's. The instruction
we had during this period was that we should express no opinion on this issue and that the issue is
not associated with America. James Baker has directed our official spokesmen to emphasize this
instruction. We hope you can solve this problem using any suitable methods via Klibi or via President
Mubarak. All that we hope is that these issues are solved quickly.'

[9] *Frontline*, January 2000, Interview with Tariq Aziz. 'There were no mixed signals. We should not
forget that the whole period before August 2 witnessed a negative American policy towards Iraq. So
it would be quite foolish to think that, if we go to Kuwait, then America would like that... So how
could we imagine that such a step was going to be appreciated by the Americans? About the meeting
with April Glaspie—it was a routine meeting. There was nothing extraordinary in it. She did not ask
for an audience with the president. She was summoned by the president. He telephoned me and
said, "Bring the American ambassador. I want to see her." ... So, what she said were routine, classical
comments on what the president was asking her to convey to President Bush. He wanted her to carry
a message to George Bush——not to receive a message through her from Washington.'

with the support of the local mission. But where the negotiation is left to the mission on the spot, the diplomat should take time to study not only the substance, but also the form and the drafting. If the proposal comes from the host State, the substance will obviously need careful checking to ensure that it meets policy instructions, but the diplomat will also be expected to try to avoid ambiguity or lack of clarity in the terms used, especially when the agreement is to be in the local language as well as that of the home State. And particular care may also be needed over the form if the intention is *not* to conclude a binding treaty. Other than in the most exceptional circumstances, the final text of any written agreement should always be vetted by the legal adviser to the mission, if there is one, before being sent back for formal clearance by one's own capital and authority for signature. Further particulars about treaty form and substance can be found in Chapters 31–32.

36.15   Reporting to the ministry at home is a key requirement. This covers the range of activities, negotiations, opinions on developments and political/economic prospects and much more. Brevity, clarity, and an indication of the importance of the report are necessary elements. Accounts should be accurate and avoid self-praise, while bringing out truthfully the role of the writer. If asked to advocate a particular policy, the account should summarize the positive points made, set out the reaction, and if opposed or criticized, bring out the arguments which the advocate used so as to make clear that instructions were robustly followed. This can be very helpful in the home capital. Senior staff in embassies should aim to encourage junior colleagues, help those learning the basics of the profession, and try to mentor by example. That should include pointing out pitfalls which may await a young diplomat. However, responsibility for more formal training invariably lies with the ministry's central administration who will generally organize courses in such skills as drafting, negotiating with professional trainers, languages, consular practice, and international law.

36.16   The duties of the head of a mission and consuls in particular include also the giving of advice to their own country's citizens when in difficulties, attending the scene of any major incident or disaster and, for example, intervention on their behalf when they are arrested and detained in custody, where they are the subject of rape and sexual assault, when there is a death overseas, forced marriage, child abduction, mental health cases, etc. Because diplomatic and consular staff cannot interfere in another country's processes, the guidance to British diplomats and consuls is that they should not interfere in the legal processes that may be brought against their nationals. Representations could be made where proper legal procedures have not been followed or where the sentence imposed on them is excessive by international norms (e.g. death sentence, floggings) or there are concerns about prisoner welfare or medical provisions.

It used to be the rule that without specific authorization from their government   **36.17**
in high-profile cases (e.g. those of Nelson Mandela and Aung San Suu Kyi),
diplomats did not occupy themselves with the interests of individual citizens of
their host country.[10] Now, however, interest in the human rights of the citizens
of a country, and the behaviour of a government towards its citizens, is increasingly important for the diplomat and many Western embassies encourage their
staff to engage with and support local human rights activists and defenders. An
important adage, however, is to do no harm. Where prominent public engagement with a human rights group is likely to prove damaging to that group, it
will be essential to ensure that no action is taken against their wishes. Heads of
mission will be best placed to offer their staff advice on how public their support for NGOs and human rights defenders should be. Diplomats whose active
and public support for NGOs and other human rights activists is deemed too
provocative by the host government may find themselves expelled, declared *persona non grata*, which is neither to their mission's advantage nor usually to the
human rights group concerned.

The reader will by now appreciate that the art of negotiation is not new and that   **36.18**
wisdom from the past is every bit as valid today as it was in the times of Callières
and Malmesbury. The twenty-first-century psychologist may analyse what the
skilled practitioner has always known instinctively. Negotiation is a dialogue
made up of give and take, and diplomats will be poor performers if they are so
full of their own ideas that they can only think about getting themselves lis-
tened to, and can barely bring themselves to listen in their turn. It is worth
noting that this insistence on the virtue of listening is common to both Callières
and Malmesbury. Perhaps the advice of the latter to a young man 'to listen, not
to talk'—at least not more than is necessary to induce others to talk—is a touch
cynical, or at least too sweeping. Sometimes there is a long or complex message
to deliver which may need clarifying. Sometimes, maybe, the other interlocutor
has a legitimate wish to listen. Everyone knows the colleague who asks everything and gives nothing; and Callières warned against this too. Malmesbury
has a good point for beginners; but Callières, aware of the strength of suggestion, recommends learning the secret of distilling 'drop by drop' into the mind
of the listener the substance of which one wishes to persuade him.[11] And it may
happen that the advice to listen becomes more rather than less important with
experience; the more one has to say, the greater the temptation to say it, whether
appropriate or not.

---

[10] See Chapter 17, paragraph 17.100.
[11] Paragraph 36.2.

The Nicolson Definition

36.19 There is one more classic statement on what a diplomat ought to be, say, and do, 'the Nicolson test':

> These, then, are the qualities of my ideal diplomatist. Truth, accuracy, calm, patience, good temper, modesty, loyalty. They are also the qualities of an ideal diplomacy.
>
> 'But,' the reader may object, 'you have forgotten intelligence, knowledge, discernment, prudence, hospitality, charm, industry, courage and even tact.' I have not forgotten them. I have taken them for granted.[12]

36.20 It's worth reflecting on 'truth'. When a Soviet Foreign Minister told the president of the United States in 1962 that there were no Soviet missile launchers in Cuba, President Kennedy happened to have in his desk drawer a photograph of just such weapons. What could be his view of the Foreign Minister? Perhaps that of Aristotle who when asked what a person could gain by telling a lie, replied, 'Not to be believed when he speaks the truth'. The incident did not change the power position in the world. It merely undermined one politician's trust in the word of another.

36.21 The same comment could be applied to relations with the former Iraqi leader Saddam Hussein whose lies and deception both over his plans to invade Kuwait and his weapons programme meant that when he claimed in 2002 that he had no weapons of mass destruction (WMD), there was widespread scepticism. This scepticism led directly to the invasion of Iraq in 2003. Similarly, Bismarck earned a dubious reputation when it became known that, by sending in 1870 the famous Ems telegram,[13] a message deliberately economical with the truth,

---

[12] H Nicolson, *Diplomacy* (Oxford, 1939) 126.

[13] 'The Ems telegram was a report of an encounter between King William I of Prussia and the French ambassador; the telegram was sent from Ems (Bad Ems) in the Prussian Rhineland on July 13, 1870, to the Prussian chancellor, Otto von Bismarck. Its publication in a version edited by Bismarck so as to purposely offend the French government precipitated the Franco-German War. Early in July, the candidacy of Prince Leopold of Hohenzollern-Sigmaringen, a relative of the Prussian king, for the Spanish throne had alarmed the French, who feared that the extension of Prussian influence into Spain would threaten France. Leopold's candidacy was withdrawn on July 12; the following day, the French ambassador to Prussia, Count Vincent Benedetti, approached King William at Ems to request an assurance that no member of his family would again be a candidate for the Spanish throne. The king politely refused Benedetti's demand, and their discussion ended. A telegram describing the incident was sent to Bismarck. Bismarck's edited version, which he published the next day, omitted the courtesies in the two men's exchange and instead made it seem that each man had insulted the other. This touched off an intensified demand for war in Paris and Berlin, and France declared war on July 19. The incident provided the excuse for a trial of strength that was sought by both France and Prussia, but because of Bismarck's dishonest editing of the Ems telegram, it was France that was the first to declare war. This circumstance helped enlist the southern German states to Prussia's side in the ensuing war, which resulted in the unification of all the German states (except Austria) into modern Germany.' *Encyclopaedia Britannica* Online Edition.

he had made sure that war between Prussia and France, a war he sought as the means to unify Germany, could not be prevented. As Bismarck himself put it, 'The Ems Telegram should have the desired effect of waving a red cape in front of the face of the Gallic Bull.'[14]

Multilateral Diplomacy

For the practitioner of multilateral diplomacy, particular skills are involved. **36.22** Unlike the classic bilateral diplomat, the individual representing his or her country in a multilateral organization will spend much of the time with diplomats from other States. Essential background is to know the rules, provisions of a charter or treaty which govern the organization, as well as much of the *acquis* of previous decisions. Familiarity with the rules of procedure which determine the conduct of meetings is also invaluable. Getting to know colleagues and where possible establishing a relationship of trust is also important. Obviously some key members are priorities, but it is best to have the widest range of relationships. No one likes being acknowledged only when a favour is being sought. These links are vital when it comes to identifying the bases for eventual agreement and securing coalitions to get the necessary votes. Understanding the position, interests, and aims of others is essential. In most negotiations, each of the participants will usually expect to derive some benefit from the final outcome. It is also wise to seek the advice of permanent officials of the organization, especially on matters of procedure. A simpatico member of a secretariat can be of considerable help as a source of knowledge and advice. While it is wise to be on good terms with the secretariat, diplomats, dealing with members of the secretariat of their own nationality, need to respect their independence and their responsibilities to the organization (see Chapter 16, paragraph 16.4).

In meetings, individuals represent their State and are assumed to be setting out **36.23** formally the position of that State on the issue or proposal under discussion. It is therefore important to have clear instructions from the capital and agreement on how much flexibility the representative is to enjoy. As necessary, communication with the capital on developments in negotiations permits instructions to be updated or revised. Instructions can, of course, be interpreted in different ways. Positive constructive approaches always encourage a good atmosphere and help foster agreements. Perversely positive instructions deliberately presented in a negative manner can have the opposite effect.

---

[14] A J P Taylor: *Bismarck: The Man and the Statesman* (New York: Vintage Books. 1967) 121.

36.24 On the basis of instructions, knowledge of the issue, and appreciation of the views of others, the representative will set out a position. This should be done clearly, without polemics and remembering that jokes seldom travel well. It is useful to indicate in the introduction the points to be made, then to set out those points in some detail, and in conclusion summarize succinctly the arguments made. In this way note-takers will catch the points. It is often a tactical decision when to speak in a debate, and if there are interpreters involved, they appreciate having a written text where it exists, or a speed of oral delivery which permits a good interpretation. The role of the chair is important, as are relations with the chair. Understanding in advance what the chair expects to achieve and the intended conduct of business is vital to deciding how and when to intervene in discussion. If a written text is being discussed it is always an advantage to have influenced the content of the draft. In discussion, as necessary, clear amendments, often discussed in advance with colleagues, are tabled to help secure outcomes compatible with instructions. It is best to avoid ambiguous language, particularly in legally binding texts—the only exception perhaps being when limited constructive ambiguity may be the price of securing an agreement.[15]

36.25 Negotiations can take place in a quiet formal way or at the other extreme in a heated emotional atmosphere. At all times, the negotiator will do well to remember his or her instructions and the objectives which have been set. It does not pay to get carried away by the search for agreement and by the satisfaction of producing acceptable texts to overcome objections, if the result does not achieve what is required by the instructions. It is also salutary to remember that when the chair asks if there is agreement, that is the moment of maximum attention and the occasion to object if the representative believes the text to be in some way unacceptable to his or her government. It is too late to say no after the chair has pronounced agreement without any objection. If there is any doubt that the chair's proposal is acceptable, given the instructions, then the best course is to make a reservation before the chair concludes. It is much easier at the next meeting to lift a reservation than it is to renege on agreement unwisely given previously. After agreement, or indeed lack of agreement, there is often press interest. It is always a good idea to have two or three points ready to brief the press, whatever the outcome, after the meeting.

Problems of Protocol and Precedence

36.26 A sure way of making oneself look foolish is to 'make a scene' about matters of precedence and protocol. In 1508 Dr de Puebla, the Spanish ambassador in London

---

[15] See E Denza, 'Compromise and Clarity in International Drafting', in C Stefanou and H Xanthaki (eds), *Legislative Drafting: A Modern Approach* (Aldershot: Ashgate, 2008).

(and incidentally the first resident ambassador there) informed his successor that 'it was his custom to attend court ceremonies when he was invited and to sit or stand wherever he was placed, since his business was to maintain friendship between his master and the King of England and he thought it would be ill served by making a fuss over trifles'.[16]

One should never forget that protocol is a means to an end and not an end in itself. As Sir William Temple, British ambassador to the Viceregal Court at Brussels, put it, 'ceremonies were made to facilitate business, not to hinder it'.[17] If protocol goes beyond this, then the proper sense of proportion has been lost, and that frequent phrase, 'It's not for me, it's for my country' has lost its integrity.   **36.27**

In the more informal diplomatic society of the twenty-first century, younger diplomats may feel an impatience with protocol and ask whether it is really necessary. Put generally, if no rules governed diplomatic and other official occasions, the problem of seating would be solved by a free-for-all with unfair results. In this respect diplomats would behave neither better nor worse than other human beings. Obviously in public life some people are more powerful or more interesting than others, and a seat next to one (or two) of them is both a privilege and an advantage. If there were no rules there would be pushing and shoving, and unscrupulous characters would, with whatever pretence of politeness, position themselves more effectively than other more courteous and less pushy souls. This would inevitably lead to much bad blood and the host government would rightly be criticized for letting it happen. At least, if the rules are followed, there is no argument. No one has been able to improve on the wisdom of the Congress of Vienna in assigning precedence according to date of arrival in post.   **36.28**

When host at some diplomatic occasion if in any doubt about precedence or *placement*, rather than trusting to instinct or to an ostensibly knowledgeable colleague's advice, it is safer to consult the host government's protocol department. It is their job to know and to advise.   **36.29**

Protocol in the shape of *placement* should not, however, be rigid. Suppose that, as can quite possibly happen, the balance of acceptances and refusals for a sit-down luncheon leaves the host in a situation where all the diplomatic guests outrank all the guests from the host country. To seat them accordingly would probably defeat the whole purpose of the party. In which case, adjust the *placement* to suit common sense, by mixing diplomatic and host country guests. It is   **36.30**

---

[16] G Mattingly, *Renaissance Diplomacy* (London: Jonathan Cape, 1955) ch 25.

[17] Sir William Temple (1628–99), distinguished British diplomat and writer much involved in the succession of William III and Mary to the British throne in 1689. In 1669 he applied the principle quoted above in the brilliantly swift negotiation of an alliance to protect the Netherlands and Flanders against French pressure.

now regarded as perfectly acceptable to vary protocol requirements to ensure that all guests are seated next to one person at least they can speak to in a language with which they are comfortable. The welcome and good humour of the host, together with explanations in advance as to what is intended, can help prevent any misunderstandings. It is also essential to take account of gender balance and be sensitive to the position of partners accompanying diplomatic officers, many of whom are pursuing their own careers and interests.

36.31   Sir Mark Young, when the Governor of Hong Kong in 1946 was faced with a guest who was aggrieved to find herself on Sir Mark's left instead of his right. In response to her acid remark: 'I suppose it is really very difficult...always to put your guests in their right places?' Sir Mark blandly replied 'Not at all, for those who matter don't mind, and those who mind don't matter.'[18]

Public Occasions

36.32   The real difficulty occurs when on a public occasion, or an occasion which will be known about publicly, a mistake is made by the host government or by, say, a diplomatic colleague, which could legitimately be thought to cause embarrassment or give rise to misunderstanding. The situation is particularly difficult to handle when the person whose position is adversely affected has only a few seconds in which either to object at once or to let the matter pass. At the funeral of Pope John Paul II in 2005, Prince Charles was put in an embarrassing position by being seated, by the Holy See, one place away from President Mugabe of Zimbabwe and being surprised into shaking hands with him when relations between the United Kingdom and the Mugabe régime had reached rock bottom. It is best to avoid public fuss and the drawing of attention to the problem but the press aspects are important; better not to be photographed in an embarrassing handshake.

36.33   Strange events such as these are the oddities affecting modern diplomacy. In authoritarian régimes, it is worth remembering that, as on public occasions in such countries every detail of speech and conduct may be planned and watched with an eye to its potential use in propaganda, a diplomat should refrain from applauding an official speech unless it is understood, even though applause might be intended merely as a courtesy to the host government. The elementary principle recurs that the diplomat arriving at a new post must try to develop a feel for the way in which the host country manages its external policy.

---

[18] *Empire Digest*, February 1946.

Diplomats who serve in the United States, will be conscious of the important 36.34
and active role played by the Congress, and particularly by the Senate Foreign
Relations Committee, in the supervision of policy and the confirmation of US
ambassadors. This perspective is reflected in those Latin American countries
which maintain democratic government on the United States model.

In countries with political organizations of the French type, diplomats will find 36.35
that they have to learn to understand and work with the so-called *cabinet* system.[19]
The minister, as in all governments, derives information and support from his or
her department. But there is also a personal supporting team, consisting partly
of officials and partly of people from political, academic, and professional life
who, while familiar with foreign policy issues, are the minister's personal eyes
and ears as to what the rest of the government is thinking and doing. Contact
with such officials can be particularly helpful for the diplomat.

Since the institutions of the European Union are based very largely on a Latin 36.36
rather than an Anglo-Saxon tradition, it is natural that a *cabinet* system should
prevail there; and the diplomat in Brussels, whether representing a Member
State or a non-member, will need to develop relations with the *cabinet* as well as
the department of any Commissioners with whom the post is in contact.

Internal Differences

Diplomacy, like any other worldwide activity, enjoys and suffers its own peculiar 36.37
rewards and deprivations: against absorbing interest must be set the disadvantages of family separation and/or the negative impact on a spouse's or partner's
career; against exciting variety, periods of unexpected monotony. Despite the
many challenges and pitfalls, the young diplomat should try to enjoy the experience and privilege of representing one's country and appreciate the opportunity
to study and understand the host country. It is more often, with hindsight, the
failure to take opportunities which is the cause of subsequent regret. On the
positive side, some of the contacts made, provided of course that they are kept
up, will prove some of one's best lifelong friends.

There are, of course, aspects of personal relationships which can, at least over short 36.38
periods, make or mar the good functioning of the diplomatic machine One of
these, while common enough in other walks of life, has particular dangers in diplomacy. It has been called the Us and Them complex; and it can still arise even in
an age when instant communication links the post abroad with the ministry at

---

[19] In this context, the word '*cabinet*' is always used with the French pronunciation.

home. Honest differences of view between different diplomatic missions serving the same government, or between a mission and the home department, are unavoidable and indeed essential to proper analysis of future policy. But there is a dangerous by-product if such disagreement proves corrosive. It is only too easy to build up in an embassy abroad a picture of Us as hardworking, conscientious, and prompt, battling with a disobliging foreign government and a disagreeable climate, while They are living comfortably at home, taking their bureaucratic time over correspondence and callous about Our physical afflictions. Or, in reverse. We are commuting uncomfortably, cramped bureaucratically, and (to Our way of thinking) financially disadvantaged; why is this not obvious to Them?

36.39 None of this is unreasonable; its only fault is that, if it is allowed to grow, it is fatal, first to personal relationships between post and ministry, and later to the conduct of the diplomatic machine. The main responsibility for avoiding this development of the Us and Them disease lies with the head of the post or the head of the department. But no one should be unaware of the possible danger, or too lazy, or too timid, to do something about it when its symptoms appear. The search for the right way is one of the challenges to diplomats and to a diplomatic service. Neither total complacency nor total officiousness is helpful, and tattle is apt to be worse still.[20] Disagreement on policy and tactics at the formative stage is helpful to identifying the best course of action, but once there is agreement or Head Office has decided, all should support that policy.

36.40 Most advice to diplomats falls under the heading 'organized common sense'. But among the traps that can be difficult to detect without advice is the following. An abnormally heavy responsibility may suddenly be imposed on a young diplomat when an unexpected crisis occurs in the absence of the head of mission or leader of delegation. The young diplomat performs brilliantly, possibly in a way that attracts public attention. But while it is clearly right that the more senior colleagues should recognize and reward good performance, it is wise for the young diplomat to acknowledge that experience is the best ally of true talent.

36.41 But that is enough precept. Shakespeare should have the last word. No one is quite sure whether Polonius's advice to Laertes is to be taken as parody, irony, or high seriousness. But to say to a diplomat:

> … to thine own self be true,
> And it must follow, as the night the day,
> Thou canst not then be false to any man[21]

---

[20] For some comment on certain concrete cases, see P Gore-Booth, *With Great Truth and Respect* (London: Constable, 1974) 80–1.

[21] *Hamlet,* Act I, Scene 3, l. 78.

is to get as near to the kernel of truth as this guide can travel. And if the diplomat, aspiring or experienced, who has read so far should feel overloaded with instructions and exhortations, some consolation can be found in Warwick's exclamation:

Alas! How should you govern any kingdom

That know not how to use ambassadors?[22]

---

[22] *King Henry VI, Part III,* Act IV, Scene 3, l. 35.

APPENDIX I

The Language of Diplomacy

The following selective explanations of certain terms and expressions are meant to be illustrative (and interesting) rather than exhaustive:

Acta jure imperii, acta jure gestionis. Terms used particularly in connection with the exercise of jurisdiction by a national court over a foreign State or its officials to distinguish acts in the exercise of sovereign or governmental authority and acts performed of a commercial or private law nature.

Ad referendum. In these days of instant communication between capitals even the most distant from each other, prudent diplomats will not commit their governments by a provisional acceptance of proposals advanced by the receiving State unless it is supported by their previous instructions. Instead they will receive the proposal *ad referendum.* This term is in regular use for provisional acceptance by negotiators on the understanding that they propose immediately to seek specific instructions.

Ask for/Demand one's passports. For an ambassador to ask for his passports was usually a strong expression of disapproval or displeasure with the receiving State's actions, tantamount to a breaking of diplomatic relations. If accompanied by an ultimatum (see later), it could be the prelude to a declaration of war. An ambassador would deposit diplomatic passports designating him as ambassador with the foreign ministry on arrival in a post. This practice, which may, inter alia, have served the purpose historically of ensuring that an envoy had paid his debts before departure, has long been discontinued. And as formal declarations of war are now virtually unknown, the term is of historic interest only. Thus Sir Edward Goschen, British ambassador in Berlin, reported on his conversations with German Foreign Minister, Gottlieb von Jagow, and later with Arthur Zimmermann, German Under Secretary of State, on 4 August 1914 as follows:

> I said [to von Jagow] that in that case [Germany refusing to refrain from further violating Belgian neutrality] I should have to demand my passports. . . . After expressing his deep regret that the very friendly official and personal relations between us were about to cease, [Zimmermann] asked me casually whether a demand for passports was equivalent to a declaration of war. I said that such an authority on international law as he was known to be must know as well or better than I what was usual in such cases. I added that there were many cases where diplomatic relations had been broken off, and, nevertheless, war had not ensued; but that in this case he would have seen from my instructions, of which I had given Herr von Jagow a written summary, that His Majesty's Government expected an answer to a definite question by 12 o'clock that night and that in default of a satisfactory answer they would be forced to take such steps as their engagements required. Herr Zimmermann said that that was, in fact, a declaration of war, as the Imperial Government could not possibly give the assurance required either that night or any other night.

See also: *Ultimatum*

Casus belli and *Casus foederis* (literally *case of war* and *case of treaty* respectively). These terms appear to be sometimes confused. The former signifies an act or proceeding of a provocative nature on the part of one Power which, in the opinion of the offended Power, justifies it in making or declaring war. Palmerston defined it in 1853 as 'a case which would justify war'.[1] The latter is an offensive act or offensive behaviour of one State towards another, or any occurrence which gives the latter a reason to invoke a treaty with an ally and to require the ally to fulfil the undertakings of the alliance existing between them. With the demise, however, of the formal declaration of war and state of war under the legal regime of the UN Charter, both terms have fallen out of use.

Customs union. An agreement made by two or more countries to impose a common tariff on goods imported by them from non-member countries.

Démarche. Any diplomatic representations or protests usually delivered in person and supported by written material in the shape of an aide-mémoire, a letter, or a 'non-paper' which provides a written version of the verbal presentation or 'talking points'. (See also Chapter **6**, paragraph **6**.19.)

Détente. A relaxation of tension in the relations between countries, not necessarily implying *rapprochement* on matters of political or ideological conviction, or a reduction in the means of defence. (See also Chapter **1**, paragraph **1**.20 and n 39.)

Domino theory. The contention that in specific circumstances the collapse of a government or State will cause the collapse of a neighbouring government or State, which in turn will produce a series of similar collapses, on the analogy of falling dominoes.

Donner la main (in English give the hand, German *Oberhand*) means to give the seat of honour, i.e. on the right hand of the host or diplomatic agent receiving a visit from a person of lower rank. The Elector Max Joseph of Bavaria was reported in 1765 to have bestowed this mark of deference on the Imperial Ambassador 'which certainly no crowned head in Europe would do'.[2] In the instructions to Lord Gower, on his appointment as ambassador to Paris in 1790, he is directed to act in accordance with the Order in Council of 26 August 1668, and 'to take the hand of envoys' in his own house, i.e. to place them on his left hand.[3]

En clair. Used of a message sent uncoded: literally in plain language.

Executive agreement. An international agreement made by executive officers of the State without reference to the legislature (e.g. in the United States an agreement not requiring the assent of the Senate).

Explanation of Vote (EOV). After a vote in the UN General Assembly or Security Council, it is common that certain members will want to make a short speech explaining why their government has voted in a particular way. The same practice operates in other international bodies and at international conferences.

Flag of convenience. The flag of a State whose laws are less onerous on shipowners than those of other States. They are for this reason controversial. Vessels registered in such a State fly its flag and their crews are subject to its laws.

---

[1] E Ollivier, *L'Empire libéral* (1895) Vol 2, 363.
[2] O Browning, *The Despatches of Earl Gower* (1885) 2.
[3] See also *Annual Digest, etc.* (1927–8), Case No 24.

Force majeure. Compulsion or coercion by circumstances which one cannot control.

Free trade area. Two or more countries agreeing to the abolition of tariffs on goods imported from each other, but not necessarily to the imposition of a common tariff on imports from outside the area.

Placement. The placing round a table of guests at a formal meal, or of officials at a meeting, by reference usually to rank and seniority. (See Chapter **10**, paragraph **10**.2 and Chapter **36** paragraphs **36**.29–**36**.31 and n 18.)

Prendre Acte. Donner Acte. The legal definition of *acte* is 'a declaration made before a court, whether spontaneously or in consequence of an order of a court, and which has been certified to have been made'. In diplomacy it is applied to any document recording an international agreement by which an obligation is undertaken; such as, for instance, the convention for the suspension of hostilities of 23 April 1814, signed between France and the four allied Great Powers.[4] 'Instrument' is the proper English equivalent, though we sometimes find it rendered by 'Act'.

Prendre acte. This is to declare that one will avail oneself, should the necessity arise, of a declaration or admission made by the other party, without conceding that one is in any way bound by that declaration. 'To take note of' is perhaps the English equivalent. Yet it may sometimes conveniently be rendered by 'recognize' or 'acknowledge'.

> Mais les sagesses tardives ne suffisent point; et même quand elles veulent être prudentes, l'esprit politique manque aux nations qui ne sont pas exercées à faire elles-mêmes leurs affaires et leur destinée. Dans le déplorable état où l'entreprise d'un égoïsme héroïque et chimérique avait jeté la France, il n'y avait évidemment qu'une conduite à tenir; reconnaître Louis XVIII, prendre acte de ses dispositions libérales et se concerter avec lui pour traiter avec les étrangers.[5]

Donner acte. This is to give recognition to another party that he has performed a certain necessary act.

Raison d'état or Realpolitik. The interest of the State taking precedence over normally accepted morality.

Sine qua non denotes a condition that must be accepted, if an agreement is desired by the party to whom it is proposed.

Special Representative. In United States' usage someone appointed or assigned by the President to a particular function or task (usually on a non-residential basis) without confirmation by the Senate. Also used increasingly by the UN Secretary-General (where it can often be residential) and by other governments and regional organizations. The EU Special Representative for Bosnia and Herzegovina is also High Representative for the same country, a pro-consular position created after the Dayton Peace Agreement in 1995 and based in Sarajevo.

Ultimatum. This term signifies a Note or memorandum in which a government or its diplomatic representative sets forth the conditions on which the State in whose name the declaration is made will insist. It should contain an express demand for a prompt, clear, and categorical reply, and it may also require the answer to be given within a fixed limit of time. This is as much as to say that an *ultimatum* embodies the final condition or concession, 'the

---

[4] F Guizot, *Mémoires pour servir à l'histoire de mon temps* (1858) Vol 1, 95.
[5] H W V Temperley, *Frederick the Great and Kaiser Joseph: An Episode of War and Diplomacy in the Eighteenth Century* (London, 1915, reprinted 1968) 67.

last word', so to speak, of the person negotiating.[6] It ordinarily, but not always, implies a threat to use force, if the demand is not complied with.

Article I of The Hague Convention No 3 of 1907 declares that:

Les Puissances contractantes reconnaissent que les hostilités entre elles ne doivent pas commencer sans un avertissement préalable et non équivoque, qui aura, soit la forme d'une déclaration de guerre motivée, soit celle d'un ultimatum avec déclaration de guerre conditionnelle.

Some of the most graphic instances of *ultimata* are to be found in the period leading to the outbreaks of the two world wars. Four weeks after the assassination of Archduke Franz Ferdinand in Sarajevo, Austria-Hungary presented an *ultimatum* to Serbia. This took the form of a Note, dated 23 July 1914, to the Serbian government, containing various demands, and requiring an answer by six o'clock in the evening of the 25th. The reply of the Serbian government not being regarded as satisfactory, the Austro-Hungarian minister demanded his passports, left Belgrade, and war was declared against Serbia on the 28th.

The German *ultimatum* to Belgium of 2 August 1914, demanded permission to march through Belgian territory and threatened to regard Belgium as an enemy 'should Belgium react with hostility to German troops, should she, in particular, create difficulties to their advance through resistance at the fortresses at the Meuse or through the destruction of railways, roads, tunnels or other technical constructions'. The note of the German minister presenting this demand did not mention any length of time for an answer, but it appears he had verbally required an answer within 12 hours.

On 4 August the British government protested against a violation of the treaty by which Belgium was constituted a neutralized State, and requested an assurance that her neutrality would be respected by Germany. Later in the day a telegram was sent to Berlin, instructing the ambassador to ask for the same assurance to respect the neutrality of Belgium as had been given by France, and for a satisfactory reply to be received in London by midnight. These requests, especially the last, amounted in substance to an *ultimatum*.

On 3 September 1939 the British government instructed their ambassador in Berlin to deliver an *ultimatum* to the German Foreign Minister demanding confirmation that Germany had suspended all aggressive action against Poland and were prepared promptly to withdraw their forces from Polish territory, and that, failing receipt of such confirmation by 1100 British Summer Time, a state of war would exist between the two countries. (See Chapter **6**, paragraph **6**.10.)

The Nazi government in the Second World War more than once waited to present its *ultimata* until German troops had actually crossed the frontiers of the victim countries. Such action contrary to all the norms of diplomatic practice was, of course, a cynical if transparent ploy ostensibly to comply with diplomatic practice while in reality making a mockery of it.

More recent examples of what were effectively *ultimata* came in the form of the UN Security Council resolution 678 (1990) which authorized the use of force ('to use all necessary means' in the language of the UN) to secure the withdrawal of Iraq after its invasion of Kuwait in August of that year. The relevant paragraphs with the *ultimatum* language italicized are as follows:

---

[6] Cussy, Ferdinand de Cornot baron de, *Dictionnaire du Diplomate et du Consul* (F A Brockhaus, 1846) s.v.; Oppenheim, Vol 1, s 95.

1. Demands that Iraq comply fully with resolution 660 (1990) and all subsequent relevant resolutions, and decides, while maintaining all its decisions, *to allow Iraq one final opportunity, as a pause of goodwill,* to do so;

2. Authorizes Member States cooperating with the government of Kuwait, *unless Iraq on or before 15 January 1991 fully implements,* as set forth in paragraph 1 above, the above-mentioned resolutions, to use all necessary means to uphold and implement resolution 660 (1990) and all subsequent relevant resolutions and to restore international peace and security in the area...

And NATO repeatedly threatened Yugoslavia with air strikes in early 1999 to compel compliance with Western demands viz withdrawal of its military and security forces from the province of Kosovo and signature of a peace agreement negotiated at a conference in Rambouillet in February and March of that year. After the failure of the Rambouillet conference, US Assistant Secretary of State, Richard Holbrooke, travelled to Belgrade to deliver a final ultimatum to President Milošević on 22 March 1999 but without success. The bombing of Yugoslavia began two days later.

The meaning of *ultimatum* is not restricted to the sense which it bears in the above examples. During the course of a negotiation it may imply the *maximum* amount of concession which will be made in order to arrive at an agreement, where no resort to compulsion is contemplated in case of refusal. Cases have occurred in which it has been used as denoting an irreducible minimum which would be accepted, a plan or scheme of arrangement which it was sought to impose, a maximum of what would be conceded, and the like.

Uti possidetis and *status quo.* These two phrases often amount to the same thing, and are used to denote actual possession by right of conquest, occupation, or otherwise, at some particular moment, which has to be defined with as much exactness as possible in the proposals for a treaty of peace, or in the treaty itself.[7] But while *uti possidetis* relates to the possession of territory, the *status quo* may be the previously existing situation in regard to other matters, e.g. to privileges enjoyed by one of the parties at the expense of the other, such as the French privilege of taking and drying fish on a portion of the coast of Newfoundland. *Uti possidetis juris* is now recognized as a principle beyond the purely colonial context which secures respect for existing territorial boundaries at the time when independence is achieved unless the States concerned agree otherwise.

---

[7] J W Foster, *A Century of American Diplomacy* (Boston, 1900) 246, defines *uti possidetis* by the belligerents as the territory occupied by their armies at the end of the war, but this seems too absolute. Cf Oppenheim, Vol 1, s 263.

APPENDIX II

Conferences

(See Chapter 34.)

Paris Peace Conference, 1946

PEACE TREATIES WITH ITALY, ROMANIA, BULGARIA, HUNGARY, AND FINLAND

1. In the conditions that obtained after the cessation of hostilities in Europe, it became evident that the conclusion of any Peace Treaty by the ordinary process of calling a full-scale Peace Conference, to be attended by all the Allied countries, with such representation of the enemy countries as might be decided on, was likely to prove unduly difficult and long drawn out, and that it would be necessary to adopt some procedure directed to 'predigesting' the material to go into the proposed Peace Treaty before this actually got to a Peace Conference. It was accordingly decided to make use of the machinery of the Council of Foreign Ministers established by the Potsdam Conference in 1945 (the Council consisting for this purpose of the Foreign Ministers of France, the Soviet Union, the United Kingdom, and the United States). The Council of Foreign Ministers, so composed, accordingly met in Paris at the Palais du Luxembourg in April 1946. Each Foreign Minister was attended by a deputy, and the process was for the deputies to meet in the mornings and the Foreign Ministers in the afternoons. There were various Committees of Experts: military, economic and legal, etc. There was a double process by which questions were considered in these Committees and then passed up through the deputies to the Foreign Ministers; or, alternatively, by which questions were first considered by the Foreign Ministers or the deputies and then passed down, to come up again later. The deputies acted as the central clearing house of the process. Anything which they were able to agree upon normally stood agreed: what they could not agree upon would either be reserved for consideration by the Foreign Ministers or else sent back to the appropriate Committee.

2. The first meeting of the Council lasted for about a month, and was followed by a second meeting—in June and part of July. Opportunity was afforded to the enemy countries to express their views, and in some cases their representatives were heard at the Council table. In this way, the complete drafts of Peace Treaties with each of the five countries were drawn up. The remaining Allied Powers were then invited to a full-scale conference, also at the Luxembourg, which started early in August and went on until late in October. However, this conference was not empowered to take any final decisions: according to the Rules of Procedure which it adopted as its opening act, it could only proceed on the basis of the texts already drawn up by the Council of Foreign Ministers, though of course it was open to any delegation to propose amendments, which would then be carried or rejected by a majority vote. But even where carried, these amendments did not of themselves cause the text as drawn up by the Council of Foreign Ministers to be altered. Their status was simply that of *proposals* for

amendment made by the conference to the Council. The upshot was that at the end of the Peace Conference in October, a considerable part of the original texts as drawn up by the Council stood approved by the Conference, while in respect of the rest, the Conference had adopted a series of proposed amendments which the Council would now have to consider.

3. The Peace Conference then came to an end and never reconvened, and the remainder of the work was done by the Council of Foreign Ministers, meeting for this purpose in New York from early November until January, the Foreign Ministers themselves leaving about half-way through December. The meetings took place in one of the Tower Rooms of the Waldorf Astoria Hotel. At these meetings, the Foreign Ministers examined one by one the proposals for amendment to the original text adopted by the Peace Conference and either approved the amendment or rejected it, or possibly adopted some amendment of their own, using the same apparatus of deputies and Committees, etc. By the time the Foreign Ministers themselves left, complete and final texts had been drawn up, subject to a comparison of the texts in the different languages (French, English, and Russian), in the course of which some further purely drafting alterations were made.

4. These final texts were then opened for signature in Paris. A short signature ceremony took place on 10 February 1947, and the texts were signed by all the Allied Powers that had actually been at war with the five countries concerned.

Japanese Peace Conference, 1951

THE JAPANESE PEACE TREATY

5. The procedure adopted for the conclusion of this Treaty was of an even more unorthodox kind than in the case just considered. Some of the preparatory work was done by a body sitting in Washington, consisting of representatives of the principal countries that had been at war with Japan, and called the Far Eastern Commission. However, the actual *raison d'être* of this body was not the conclusion of a Peace Treaty, but the political supervision of the administration of Japan during the occupation period. The first actual drafts of a Peace Treaty were got out by diplomatic correspondence between the United States and United Kingdom governments during the latter part of 1950 and the early part of 1951. There then followed a series of meetings between officials and ministers of these two countries, some of which took place in Washington and some in London, between April and August 1951, at which progressive agreement was reached on the text of the Peace Treaty. Contact with other prospective signatories was maintained, partly by diplomatic correspondence conducted mainly through the State Department in Washington; partly by meetings between the State Department and the embassies of such countries in Washington; and partly by means of similar meetings between these embassies and the British embassy in Washington. In this way, the views of the different countries on the proposed text were ascertained, and progressive alterations were made in the texts to take account of these views. However, at no stage of the proceedings was there any general negotiating conference at which views could be exchanged across the table between all concerned.

6. Eventually, in August, final texts of a Treaty and various ancillary instruments were circulated to all the prospective signatories, and they were invited to attend a meeting at San Francisco which, it was emphasized, would be for the purpose of signing the Peace Treaty and other instruments and of hearing any accompanying declarations or speeches, but which was

not intended to be a forum for any negotiations or for proposing alterations in the existing texts.

7. The San Francisco meeting was duly held in the first part of September 1951, in the same buildings that had been utilized for the drafting of the United Nations Charter. Objections to the procedure adopted were voiced by certain countries which did not sign the Treaty. Apart from that, the Treaty and ancillary instruments, as presented, were found to be acceptable, and were signed on 8 September by twenty-six Allied Powers that had been at war with Japan, and by Japan.

8. This affords a unique example of a Peace Treaty concluded entirely by correspondence, by informal contacts, and by meetings between representatives of one or more interested countries without any general conference other than a meeting for the purpose of signature.

Geneva Conference, 1954

9. This Conference originated in a communiqué[1] of 18 February 1954, issued at the conclusion of a meeting in Berlin of the Foreign Ministers of the United States (John Foster Dulles), France (Georges Bidault), the United Kingdom (Anthony Eden), and the Soviet Union (Vyacheslav Molotov). The relevant part of the communiqué read as follows:

Considering that the establishment, by peaceful means, of a united and independent Korea would be an important factor in reducing international tension and in restoring peace in other parts of Asia,

Propose that a conference of representatives of the United States, France, the United Kingdom, the Union of Soviet Socialist Republics, the Chinese People's Republic, the Republic of Korea, the People's Democratic Republic of Korea and the other countries the armed forces of which participated in the hostilities in Korea, and which desire to attend, shall meet in Geneva on April 26th for the purpose of reaching a peaceful settlement of the Korean question.

Agree that the problem of restoring peace in Indo-China will also be discussed at the conference, to which representatives of the United States, France, the United Kingdom, the Union of Soviet Socialist Republics, the Chinese People's Republic and other interested States will be invited.

It is understood that neither the invitation to, nor the holding of, the above-mentioned Conference shall be deemed to imply diplomatic recognition in any case where it has not already been accorded.

10. The Conference was held in the Palais des Nations from 26 April to 21 July 1954.[2] It virtually became two conferences—one for the Korean question and one for the problem of restoring peace in Indo-China. This division was natural because, apart from the concern of the Four Powers and the People's Republic of China in both problems, they were entirely separate and distinct.

---

[1] Documents relating to the meeting of Foreign Ministers, Berlin, 25 January–18 February 1954, Cmd 9080, 180.

[2] See generally Documents relating to the discussion of Korea and Indo-China at the Geneva Conference, Cmd 9186.

11. On the conclusion of hostilities in 1945, Korea had been temporarily divided along the 38th parallel. In the following years, vain attempts were made by the United Nations to bring about the unification of Korea by democratic means, but on 25 June 1950, North Korean troops attacked South Korea. They were opposed by United Nations forces, and in spite of the support of very large numbers of Chinese Communist troops were in the end able to bring about no significant change in the division of Korea at the 38th parallel. Hostilities were ended by the Korean Armistice Agreement signed at Panmunjom on 27 July 1953. The result was a deadlock which neither the United Nations General Assembly nor, in the event, the Geneva Conference was able to break.[3]

12. The Indo-China phase of the Conference opened on 8 May 1954, a short time after the French garrison at Dien Bien Phu fell to the onslaught of the Viet Minh forces. The battle was the culmination of a nationalist and Communist struggle to wrest the Associate States of Vietnam, Laos, and Cambodia from the status of protection which France had tried to re-establish after the Second World War. At the time of the Conference, France had, in principle, recognized the independence of the Associate States and the primary task of the Conference was to put an end to hostilities so as to make possible a stable political settlement. The result was the signature of three Agreements on the cessation of hostilities in Cambodia, Laos, and Vietnam, respectively signed in each case by the appropriate military authorities. The conference contented itself with a declaration which, inter alia, took note of the three Agreements. Separate declarations were also made by the representatives of the United States, Cambodia, Laos, and France.[4]

13. The relations between the various governments and the non-recognition of some by others made the seating at the Conference both difficult and interesting. Ostensibly, the seating for the Korean phase followed the English alphabetical order and for the Indo-China phase the French alphabetical order.[5]

14. There was no Secretariat for the Conference as a whole, but the sixteen nations who had contributed military forces to the United Nations Command in Korea formed their own Secretariat for the Korean phase of the Conference. A Secretariat on a reduced scale was also maintained, on behalf of the Western Powers and their Indo-Chinese associates, by France and the United Kingdom during the Indo-Chinese phase of the Conference. In both cases, almost all the staff were provided by the United Nations Organization and their services were used to some extent by other delegations as well.

15. The procedure for both phases of the Conference was very informal. There was no voting. The most significant features of the procedure were the provisions relating to languages and the rotation of the chairmanship. For the Korean phase Prince Wan, M Molotov, and Sir Anthony Eden were the chairmen. For the Indo-China Phase Sir Anthony Eden and

---

[3] In the years since then, many developments have taken place, leading to the admission of both North Korea and South Korea as members of the United Nations (under the names of Democratic People's Republic of Korea and Republic of Korea, respectively), and both States are now widely recognized by other States and entertain relations with one another.

[4] For the text of the Agreements and declarations see Further Documents relating to the discussion of Indo-China at the Geneva Conference, 16 June–21 July 1954, Cmd 9239.

[5] During the later meetings on Indo-China, tables were arranged to form a continuous hollow square, but the retention of the same order of seating enabled any embarrassing proximities to be avoided.

M Molotov were the chairmen, although at some meetings their places were taken by their deputies.

16. The pattern of the Geneva Conference was reminiscent of many conferences of the eighteenth and nineteenth centuries. It had a character and dignity of its own, which, except during the final week, were unruffled by the pressure of drafting treaty texts and voting on numerous clauses and amendments which is typical of conferences in recent times. It aimed at a political settlement not by the production of a single treaty to which all participants might adhere, but by the formal statement of policies and views, the pronouncement of declarations, and the encouragement of agreement between the parties most directly concerned.

International Conference on the Former Yugoslavia, 1992

17. This offers an interesting example of a modern peace-making Conference, with a very special structure and organization designed to meet the complexity of the issues requiring to be settled in the aftermath of the bitter military hostilities that followed the collapse of the former Socialist Federal Republic of Yugoslavia, and to accommodate as well the unusual mixture of States, State-like and other entities, and international bodies who had or assumed an interest in the resolution of these issues.

18. The Conference was set up in August 1992 'to remain in being until a final settlement of the problems of the former Yugoslavia is reached'. It continued in being until the signature of the General Framework Agreement for Peace in Bosnia and Herzegovina, also known as the Dayton Agreement, in November 1995.[6]

19. The Conference had as its permanent co-chairmen the Secretary-General of the United Nations and the Head of State or Head of Government of the country holding for the time being the Presidency of the European Union (EU). Its main work was controlled by its Steering Committee, again under the co-chairmanship of the representatives of the permanent Co-Chairmen of the Conference, Cyrus Vance representing the UN and Lord (David) Owen representing the EU, together with representatives of: the States which composed the so-called 'troika' of the EU and that of the CSCE;[7] the five Permanent Members of the UN Security Council; the Organization of the Islamic Conference, and neighbouring States. A collateral agreement was subsequently reached under which one of the neighbouring State representations would rotate between Italy and Greece, and the other would be drawn from the non-EU Member States rotating in English alphabetical order beginning with Romania.

20. The Steering Committee was to be in continuous session at the Office of the United Nations in Geneva, as were its six Working Groups,[8] and was to be assisted by an Arbitration Commission. They would be serviced by a small secretariat provided jointly by the UN and

---

[6] Numerous documents of the Conference are published in *The International Conference on the Former Yugoslavia: Official Papers* (ed. Ramcharan) (The Hague, 1997).

[7] i.e. the current, former, and next following presidencies of those bodies; the term is of course borrowed from the Russian for a sleigh or other vehicle drawn by three horses abreast.

[8] Dealing respectively with: Bosnia and Herzegovina (cessation of hostilities and a constitutional settlement); humanitarian relief, including refugees; ethnic minorities; economic issues; and confidence- and security-building.

the EU, and the costs would be shared amongst the participants on a scale approved half-yearly by the Steering Committee.

21. The final phase of the negotiation over Bosnia and Herzegovina took place, under conditions of strict security (and total exclusion of the news media), at the Wright-Patterson Base of the US Air Force near Dayton, Ohio in 1995.

Paris Conference on Climate Change, December 2015

22. The purpose of the Paris Conference on Climate Change was 'to enhance the implementation' of the 1992 UN Framework Convention on Climate Change (UNFCC), itself one of a line of international agreements going back to the 1970s dealing with aspects of climate change, which had established a Conference of the Parties as its 'supreme body' to review and take forward the Convention's objectives at its annual sessions.[9] Three categories of participants were established for the purposes of meetings and conferences in the UNFCCC process: Parties to the Convention and Observer States, observer organizations, and the press and media. This reflected the acknowledgement 'that change in the Earth's climate and its adverse effects are a common concern of humankind', but that for that very reason measures to deal with it must take account of the widely differing circumstances of the countries of the world. The observer organizations were further categorized into three types: the United Nations System and its Specialized Agencies, and in addition other intergovernmental organizations (IGOs) and non-governmental organizations (NGOs), which became entitled to accredit delegates once they had been admitted as observer organizations by the Conference of the Parties. As of the date of the Paris conference, 100 IGOs and over 1,900 NGOs had been admitted as observers, the latter representing a broad spectrum of interests including business and industry, environmental groups, farming and agriculture, indigenous populations, local governments and municipal authorities, research and academic institutes, and trade unions, amongst others.

23. The structure of the Paris Conference followed a similar pattern, but in addition adopted the special device of dividing the negotiating States into three main categories for the purpose of negotiating and agreeing their different sets of commitments under the Agreement:

- Annex I Parties including the industrialized countries that were members of the OECD in 1992, plus countries with economies in transition (the EIT Parties), including the Russian Federation, the Baltic States, and several Central and Eastern European States.
- Annex II Parties consisting of the OECD members of Annex I, but not the EIT Parties, who are required to provide financial resources to enable developing countries to undertake emissions reduction activities under the Convention and to help them adapt to adverse effects of climate change.
- The Non-Annex I Parties are mostly developing countries, including certain groups of developing countries recognized as being especially vulnerable to the adverse impacts of climate change, such as those with low-lying coastal areas or prone to desertification and drought.

---

[9] See Chapter **30**, paragraph **30**.3, noting this 'increasingly common modern format'. An important intermediate step achieved via this mechanism was the 1997 Kyoto Protocol, which had set internationally binding emissions targets, while recognizing that parties would 'meet their targets primarily through national measures', which included market-based mechanisms, such as international emissions trading.

- Finally, the forty-nine parties classified as least developed countries (LDCs) by the United Nations are given special consideration on account of their limited capacity to respond to climate change and adapt to its adverse effects.[10]

At the time of writing, the Paris Agreement incorporating the above differentiated rights and responsibilities, although signed by 175 States and the EU, has been ratified by only fifteen parties; entry into force requires ratification by at least fifty-five parties accounting in total for at least an estimated 55 per cent of the total global greenhouse gas emissions.

---

[10] Fuller details are available on the UNFCC website at <http://unfccc.int/parties_and_observers/items/2704.php>.

BIBLIOGRAPHY

Acheson, D. *Present at the Creation* (New York: WW Norton, 1987).

Adair, E R. *The Extraterritoriality of Ambassadors in the 16th and 17th Centuries* (London: Longman, 1929).

Annales Rerum Anglicarum et Hibernicarum, regnante Elizabetha, translated by R N Gent (3rd edn, London, 1635).

Arnull, A. *The European Union and Its Court of Justice* (2nd edn, Oxford: Oxford University Press, 2006).

Arnull, A, and Chalmers, D. *The Oxford Handbook of European Law* (Oxford: Oxford University Press, 2015).

Ashman, C R and Trescott, P. *Outrage* (London: W H Allen, 1986).

Auchincloss, L. *Richelieu* (New York: Viking Press, 1972).

Aust, A. *Handbook of International Law* (2nd edn, Cambridge: Cambridge University Press, 2010).

Aust, A. *Modern Treaty Law and Practice* (3rd edn, Cambridge: Cambridge University Press, 2011).

Baere, G de. *Constitutional Principles of EU External Relations* (Oxford: Oxford University Press, 2008).

Bailey, S D. *The General Assembly of the United Nations* (rev edn, New York, 1964).

Bailey, S D. *Voting in the Security Council* (Bloomington: Indiana University Press, 1969).

Bailey, S D. *The Procedure of the Security Council* (Oxford: Clarendon Press, 1975).

Barder, B. *What Diplomats Do: The Life and Work of Diplomats* (Lanham: Rowman and Littlefield, 2014).

Barker, J C. *The Protection of Diplomatic Personnel* (Aldershot, England: Ashgate, 2006).

Barros, J (ed). *The United Nations, Past, Present and Future* (New York and London: The Free Press, 1972).

Bartels, L. 'The EU's Human Rights Obligations in Relation to Policies with Extraterritorial Effects' (2014) 25(4) *EJIL* 1071.

Basosi, D. 'New or Larger? JFK's Diverging Visions of Europe', in Kosc, S, Juncker, C, Monteith, S, and Waldschmidt-Nelso, B (eds), *The Transatlantic Sixties* (Bielefeld: Transcript Verlag, 2013).

Baumann, C E. *The Diplomatic Kidnappings* (The Hague: Martinus Nijhoff, 1973).

Bayley, Paul and Williams, Geoffrey (eds). *European Identity: What the Media Say* (Oxford: Oxford University Press, 2012).

Beck, G. *The Legal Reasoning of the Court of Justice of the EU* (Oxford: Hart Publishing, 2013).

Beckett, W E. 'Consular Immunities' (1944) *BYIL* 34.

Berman, F. 'Treaty-Making within the British Commonwealth' (2015) 38 *Melbourne University Law Review* 897.

Berman, P. 'From Laeken to Lisbon—The Origins and Negotiation of the Lisbon Treaty', in Biondi, A, Eeckhout, P, and Ripley, S (eds), *EU Law After Lisbon* (Oxford: Oxford University Press, 2012).

Berridge, G R. *Diplomacy: Theory and Practice* (5th edn, London: Palgrave Macmillan, 2015).

Berridge, G R and James, A. *A Dictionary of Diplomacy* (Basingstoke: Palgrave Macmillan, 2001).

Berridge, G R and Lloyd, L. *The Palgrave Macmillan Dictionary of Diplomacy* (3rd edn, 2012).

Berridge, G R, Keens-Soper, H M A, and Otte, T G. *Diplomatic Theory from Machiavelli to Kissinger* (Basingstoke: Palgrave Macmillan, 2001).

Blondel, J-F. *Entente Cordiale* (London: Caduceus Press, 1971).

Boeck, C de. 'L'Expulsion et les difficultés internationales qu'en soulève la pratique' (1927) *RdC* 502.

Boissieu, P de, et al. *National Leaders and the Making of Europe—Key Episodes in the Life of the European Council* (London: John Harper Publishing, 2015).

Briggs, H W. 'The Final Act of the London Conference on Germany' (1955) 49 *AJIL* 148–65.

Briggs, H W. 'Unilateral Denunciation of Treaties: The Vienna Convention and the International Court of Justice' (1974) 68 *AJIL* 51–68.

Browning, O. *The Despatches of Earl Gower* (1885).

Brownlie, I. *Peaceful Settlement of International Disputes* (Oxford: Oxford University Press, 2009).

Buchan, D. *Europe—The Strange Superpower* (Vermont: Dartmouth, 1993).

Bundy, W. *A Tangled Web: The Making of Foreign Policy in the Nixon Presidency* (London and New York: I B Tauris, 1998).

Butler, M. *Europe: More than a Continent* (London: Heinemann, 1988).

Callières, F de. *De la manière de négocier avec les souverains* (Paris and Amsterdam, 1746); ed Keens-Soper, H M A and Schweizer, Karl W (University of America Press, 1993).

Calvo, C. *International Law* (4th edn, Paris, 1896).

Cameron, F. *An Introduction to European Foreign Policy* (2nd edn, London: Routledge, 2012).

Caporaso, J A. *Multilateral Organization* (Massachusetts, 1992).

Cardinale H E. *The Holy See and the International Order* (Gerrards Cross: Smythe, 1976).

Cassese, A. In P Alston, *The United Nations and Human Rights* (Oxford: Oxford University Press, 1992).

Cassese, A. *Self Determination of Peoples: A Legal Reappraisal* (Cambridge: Cambridge University Press, 1995).

Chaplais, P. *English Diplomatic Practice in the Middle Ages* (London and New York, 2003).

Chatterjee, H. *International Law and Inter-State Relations in Ancient India* (London and Calcutta, 1958).

Churchill, Sir Winson. *The Second World War* (London: Cassell, 1950).

Cini, M and Pérez-Solórzano Borragán, N (eds). *European Union Politics* (4th edn, Oxford: Oxford University Press, 2013).

Clapham, A. *Brierly's Law of Nations* (7th edn, Oxford: Oxford University Press, 2012).

Cohen, R. 'Reflections on the New Global Diplomacy', in Melissen, J (ed), *Innovation in Diplomatic Practice* (Basingstoke: Macmillan, 1999).

Cooper, A, Heine, J, and Thakur, R (eds). *The Oxford Handbook of Modern Diplomacy* (Oxford: Oxford University Press, 2013).

Corbett, R, Jacobs, F, and Shackleton, M (eds). *The European Parliament* (8th edn, London: John Harper, 2011).

Craig, P. 'The Fall and Renewal of the Commission: Accountability, Contract and Administrative Organisation' (2000) 6 *ELJ* 6.

Craig, P and de Búrca, G. *EU Law: Text, Cases and Materials* (6th edn, Oxford: Oxford University Press, 2015).

Craven, M. 'Statehood, Self-determination and Recognition', in Evans, Malcolm D (ed), *International Law* (4th edn, Oxford: Oxford University Press, 2014).

Crawford, J. *The Creation of States in International Law* (2nd edn, Oxford: Oxford University Press, 2008).

Crawford, J. *Brownlie's Principles of Public International Law* (8th edn, Oxford: Oxford University Press, 2012).

Cryer, R, Friman, H, Robinson, D, and Wilmshurst, E. *An Introduction to International Criminal Law and Procedure* (3rd edn, Cambridge: Cambridge University Press, 2011).

Cussy, Ferdinand de Cornot, Baron de, *Dictionnaire du Diplomate et du Consul* (F A Brockhaus, 1846).

Dashwood, A, et al. *European Union Law* (6th edn, London: Sweet & Maxwell, 2011).

Denza, E 'The Community as a Member of International Organizations', in Emiliou, N and O'Keeffe, D (eds), *The European Union and World Trade Law* (Chichester and Colorado Springs: John Wiley, 1996).

Denza, E. *The Intergovernmental Pillars of the European Union* (Oxford: Oxford University Press, 2002).

Denza, E. 'Diplomatic Privileges and Immunities', in Grant, J P and Barker, J C (eds), *Harvard Research in International Law: Contemporary Analysis and Appraisal* (Buffalo: WS Hein, 2007).

Denza, E. 'Compromise and Clarity in International Drafting', in Stefanou, C and Xanthaki, H (eds), *Legislative Drafting: A Modern Approach* (Aldershot: Ashgate, 2008).

Denza, E. *The 1951 Convention Relating to the Status of Refugees and its 1967 Protocol*, ed A Zimmermann (Oxford: Oxford Univesity Press, 2011).

Denza, E. 'European Practice on the Recognition of States' (2011) 36 *ELR* 321.

Denza, E. *Diplomatic Law: Commentary on the Vienna Convention on Diplomatic Relations* (4th edn, Oxford: Oxford University Press, 2016).

Devuyst, Y. *The European Union Transformed: Community Method and Institutional Evolution from the Schuman Plan to the Constitution for Europe* (rev edn, Brussels: PIE-Peter Lang, 2006).

Dickie, J. *Inside the Foreign Office* (London: Chapmans, 1992).

Dickie, J. *The New Mandarins-How British Foreign Policy Works* (London and New York: I B Tauris, 2004).

Dinan, D. *Europe Recast: A History of the European Union* (2nd edn, London: Palgrave Macmillan, 2014).

Dumont, J C. *Corps universel diplomatique du droit des gens* (Paris, 1725–31).

Dunn, D H. *Diplomacy at the Highest Level: The Evolution of International Summitry* (Basingstoke: Macmillan, 1996).

Eeckhout, P. *EU External Relations Law* (2nd edn, Oxford: Oxford University Press, 2011).

Evans, Malcolm D, *International Law* (4th edn, Oxford: Oxford University Press, 2014).

Ewart-Biggs, J. *Pay, Pack and Follow* (London: Weidenfeld and Nicolson, 1984).

Fabry, M. *Recognizing States: International Society and the Establishment of New States since 1776* (Oxford: Oxford University Press, 2010).

Flassan, G de R de. *Histoire générale et raisonnée de la diplomatie française*, 7 vols, (2nd edn, Paris 1811).

Fletcher, T. *Naked Diplomacy: Power and Statecraft in the Digital Century* (London: Harper Collins, 2016).

Foakes, J. *The Position of Heads of State and Senior Officials in International Law* (Oxford: Oxford University Press, 2014).

Foster, J W. *A Century of American Diplomacy* (Boston, 1900).

Foster, J W. *The Practice of Diplomacy as Illustrated in the Foreign Relations of the United States* (Boston, 1906).

Fox, H and Webb, P. *The Law of State Immunity* (3rd edn, Oxford: Oxford University Press, 2015).

Freedman, L and Karsh, E. *The Gulf Conflict 1990–1991: Diplomacy and War in the New World Order* (London: Faber & Faber, 1993).

Frigo, D (ed). *Politics and Diplomacy in Early Modern Italy* (Cambridge: Cambridge University Press, 2000).

Gardiner, R K. *Treaty Interpretation* (2nd edn, Oxford: Oxford University Press, 2015).

Garner, R. 'State and Diplomatic Immunity and Employment Rights: Europe to the Rescue?' (2015) 64 *ICLQ* 783.

Garthoff, R L. *La Doctrine militaire soviétique* (Paris: Plon, 1956).

Genet, R. *Traité de diplomatie et de droit diplomatique*, Vol I (Paris: Pédone, 1931).

Gentilis, A. *De Legationibus Libri Tres* (1585).

Glanville, L. *Sovereignty and the Responsibility to Protect: A New History* (University of Chicago Press, 2013).

Glendon, M A. *A World Made New: Eleanor Roosevelt and the Universal Declaration of Human Rights* (New York: Random House, 2002).

Glendon, M A. *The Forum and the Tower: How Scholars and Politicians Have Imagined the World, from Plato to Eleanor Roosevelt* (New York, Oxford University Press, 2011).

Goodrich, L M, Simons, A P, and Hambro, E. *Charter of the United Nations* (New York: Columbia University Press, 1969).

Gore-Booth, P. *With Great Truth and Respect* (London: Constable, 1974).

Gosalbo Bono, R. 'Some Reflections on the CFSP Legal Order' (2006) 43(2) *CMLR* 337–94.

Green L C. 'Trends in the Law Concerning Diplomats' (1981) 132 *CYIL* 144–7.

Grotius, H. *De Jure Belli ac Pacis* (Paris, 1625).

Guizot, F. *Mémoires pour servir à l'histoire de mon temps*, Vol 1 (1858).

Hall, C K. 'The First Proposal for a Permanent International Criminal Court' (1998) 322 *International Review of the Red Cross* 57.

Hall, H D. *Mandates and Dependencies and Trusteeships* (London: Stevens, 1948).

Hall, W E. *A Treatise on International Law* (Oxford: Clarendon Press, 1924).

Hamilton, K and Langhorne, R. *The Practice of Diplomacy: Its Evolution, Theory and Administration* (2nd edn, London: Routledge, 2011).

Hannay, Lord (David). *New World Disorder* (London: I B Tauris, 2008).

Harris, D and Sivakumaran, S. *Cases and Materials on International Law* (8th edn, London: Sweet & Maxwell, 2015).

Hayes-Renshaw, F and H Wallace. *The Council of Ministers* (2nd edn, Basingstoke: Palgrave Macmillan, 2005).

Henkin, L. *How Nations Behave* (2nd edn, Columbia University Press, 1979).

Hickman, K. *Daughters of Britannia: The Lives and Times of Diplomatic Wives* (London: Flamingo, 2000).

Hill, C. *Foreign Policy in the 21st Century* (2nd edn, London: Palgrave, 2016).

Hill, C and Smith, M (eds). *International Relations and the European Union* (2nd edn, Oxford: Oxford University Press, 2011).

Hillgenberg, H. 'A Fresh Look at Soft Law' (1999) 10 *EJIL* 499.

Hocking, B. 'Catalytic Diplomacy: Beyond "Newness" and "Decline"', in Melissen, J (ed), *Innovation in Diplomatic Practice* (Basingstoke: Macmillan, 1999).

Hollis, D. *The Oxford Guide to Treaties* (Oxford: Oxford University Press, 2012).

Hollis, D, Blakeslee, M, and Ederington, B (eds). *National Treaty Law and Practice* (Leiden, Boston: Martinus Nijhoff, for the American Society of International Law, 2005).

Hurst, Sir C. 'Les Immunités diplomatiques' (1926) 2 *HR* 123.

Ingham, K (ed). *Foreign Relations of African States* (London: Butterworths, 1974).

Jackson, R. *Trial of Major War Criminals, Nuremberg* (London, 1946).

Jackson, Sir G. *People's Prison* (London; Faber & Faber, 1973).

Jones, J M. *Full Powers and Ratification* (Cambridge: Cambridge University Press, 1946).

Jorgensen, K E, Aarstad, K A, Drieskens, E, Laatikainen, K, and Tonra, B (eds). *The SAGE Handbook of European Foreign Policy* (London: Sage, 2015).

Judge, D and Earnshaw, D. *The European Parliament* (2nd edn, Basingstoke: Palgrave Macmillan, 2008).

Judt, T. *Postwar: A History of Europe since 1945* (London: William Heinemann, 2005).

Kassim, H, et al. *The European Commission of the 21st Century* (Oxford: Oxford University Press, 2013).

Keens-Soper, H M A and Schweizer, Karl W (eds). *The Art of Diplomacy* (Lanham: University Press of America, 1994).

Kelsen, H. *The Law of the United Nations* (London: Stevens, 1951).

Kennan, G F. 'The Sources of Soviet Conduct' (1947) 25 *Foreign Affairs* 581.

Keukeleire, S and Delreux, T. *The Foreign Policy of the European Union* (2nd edn, Basingstoke: Palgrave Macmillan, 2014).

Kissinger, H. *The White House Years* (Boston and London, 1979).

Kissinger, H. *Diplomacy* (London: Simon and Schuster, 1995).

Kissinger, H. *World Order* (New York: Penguin, 2014).

Kohler, M. *Multilateral Organization* (Massachusetts: Massachusetts Institute of Technology, 1992).

Koutrakos, P. Trade, *Foreign Policy & Defence in EU Law* (Oxford: Hart Publishing, 2001).

Koutrakos, P (ed). *European Foreign Policy: Legal and Political Perspectives* (Cheltenham: Edward Elgar Publishing, 2011).

Koutrakos, P. *The EU Common Security and Defence Policy* (Oxford: Oxford University Press, 2013).

Koutrakos, P. *EU International Relations Law* (2nd edn, Oxford: Bloomsbury, 2015).

Laatkainen, K V. 'Multilateral Leadership at the UN after the Lisbon Treaty' (2010) 15 *European Foreign Affairs Review* 475.

Lane Fox, R. *The Classical World: An Epic History from Homer to Hadrian* (London: Allen Lane, 2005) 327.

Lee, L T and Quigley, J B. *Consular Law and Practice* (3rd edn, Oxford: Oxford University Press, 2008).

Liang, Y-L. Notes on Legal Questions Concerning the United Nations including 'Use of the Term "Acceptance" in United Nations Treaty Practice' (1950) *AJIL* 333–49.

Lindblom, A-K. *Non-Governmental Organisations in International Law* (Cambridge: Cambridge University Press, 2005).

Linna, D K. *Sovereignty and Legitimacy in the Rule of Law Equation*, 'Sovereignty and the New Executive Authority Conference', CERL U Penn Law School, 19–20 April 2013, p. 15.

Livingstone, F. 'Withdrawal from the United Nations—Indonesia' (1965) 14 *ICLQ* 637.

Lloyd, E. 'The Development of the Law of Diplomatic Relations' (1964) 40 *BYIL* 149.

Lloyd, L. *Diplomacy with a Difference: The Commonwealth Office of High Commissioner, 1880–2006* (Leiden and Boston: Martinus Nijhoff, 2007).

Lockhart, R H B. *Memoirs of a British Agent* (London: Putnam, 1932).

Lowe, V. 'Diplomatic Law: Protecting Powers' (1990) 39 *ICLQ* 471–4.

Lowe, V. *International Law* (Oxford: Oxford University Press, 2007).

Lowe, V, with Roberts, A, Welsh, J, and Zaum, D (eds). *The United Nations Security Council and War...since 1945* (Oxford: Oxford University Press, 2008).

McGoldrick, D. *International Relations Law of the European Union* (London: Longman, 1997).

McGoldrick, D and Seah, D. 'I. The ASEAN Charter' (2009) 58 *ICLQ* 197–212.

Mackenzie, R, et al. *Selecting International Judges* (Oxford: Oxford University Press, 2010).

MacMillan, M. *Peacemakers: The Paris Conference of 1919 and its Attempt to End War* (London: John Murray, 2001).

MacMillan, M. *Seize the Hour: When Nixon met Mao* (London: John Murray, 2007).

McNair, Lord (Arnold). *International Law Opinions* (Cambridge: Cambridge University Press, 1956).

McNair, Lord (Arnold). *The Law of Treaties* (Oxford: Clarendon Press, 1961).

Malmesbury, J H. *Diaries and Correspondence* (London, 1844).

Mann, F A. *Studies in International Law* (Oxford: Clarendon Press, 1973).

Martens, Baron Charles de. *Causes Célèbres du Droit des Gens* (Leipzig, 1827).

Martin, L. 'Institutions and Cooperation: Sanctions during the Falklands Conflict' (1992) 16(4) *International Security* 143.

Mattingly, G. *Renaissance Diplomacy* (London: Jonathan Cape, 1955).

Melissan, J, and Fernadez, A M (eds). *Consular Affairs and Diplomacy* (Leiden: Martinus Nijhoff, 2011).

Merrills, J G. *International Dispute Settlement* (5th edn, Cambridge: Cambridge University Press, 2011).

Michalowski, P. *Letters from Early Mesopotamia*, ed E Reiner (Atlanta GA: Scholars Press, 1993).

Mills G. 'Trade and Investment Promotion', *The Oxford Handbook of Modern Diplomacy* (Oxford: Oxford University Press, 2013).

Montesquieu, Charles Louis de Secondat de. *De l'Esprit des Lois* (Geneva, 1748).

Moore, J B. *Digest of International Law*, Vol 4 (Washington, 1906).

Morris, I. *Why The West Rules for Now* (London: Profile Books, 2010).

Munn-Rankin, J M. 'Diplomacy in Western Asia in the Early Second Millenium BC' (Spring 1956) XVII(1) *Iraq* 87.

Myers, D P. 'The Names and Scope of Treaties' (1957) 51 *AJIL* 575.

Nahlik, S. 'La Conférence de Vienne sur le droit des traités. Une vue d'ensemble' (1969) 15(1) *Annuaire Français de Droit International* 24–53.

Neill, P. *European Court of Justice: A Case Study in Judicial Activism* (London: European Policy Forum, 1995).

Nicolson, H. *The Congress of Vienna* (London: Constable, 1946).

Nicolson, H. *The Evolution of Diplomatic Method* (London: Cassell, 1954).

Nicolson, H. 'Diplomacy Then and Now' (1961) 40(1) *Foreign Affairs* 39.

Nicolson, H. *Diplomacy* (3rd edn, London: Oxford University Press, 1963).

Noonan Jr, J-C. *The Church Visible: The Ceremonial Life and Protocol of the Roman Catholic Church* (New York: Viking, 1996).

Nuttall, S J. 'European Political Cooperation and the Single European Act' *Yearbook of European Law* (1985) 203.

O'Connell, D P. 'A Cause Célèbre in the History of Treaty-making: The Refusal to Ratify the Peace Treaty of Regensburg in 1630' (1968) *BYIL* 71.

Ollivier, E. *L'Empire libéral* (1895).

Oppenheim's *International Law*, Vol 1, *Peace*, ed Sir Robert Jennings and Sir Arthur Watts (9th edn, Oxford: Oxford University Press, 2008).

Ott, A. 'EU Regulatory Agencies in EU External Relations: Trapped in a Legal Minefield between European and International Law' (2008) *European Foreign Affairs Review* 515.

Otte, T G. 'Kissinger', in Berridge, G R, Keens-Soper, M, and Otte, T G. *Diplomatic Theory from Machiavelli to Kissinger* (Basingstoke: Palgrave, 2001).

Papenfuss, D. 'The Fate of the International Treaties of the GDR within the Framework of German Unification' (1998) 92 *AJIL* 469.

Parris, M. *Parting Shots* (London: Viking, 2011).

Patten, C. *What Next?: Surviving the Twenty-first Century* (London: Allen Lane, 2008).

Perrenoud, G. 'Les Restrictions à la liberté de déplacement des diplomates' (1953) 57 *RGDIP* 444.

Peterson, J and Shackleton, M (eds). *The Institutions of the European Union* (3rd edn, Oxford: Oxford University Press 2012).

Phillipson, C. 'The International Law and Custom of Ancient Greece and Rome' (1911) II *RDC* 552.

Piris, J-C. *The Lisbon Treaty: A Legal and Political Analysis* (Cambridge: Cambridge University Press, 2010).

Piris, J-C. *The Future of Europe: Towards a Two-Speed EU?* (Cambridge: Cambridge University Press, 2012).

Plöger, K. *England and the Avignon Popes: The Practice of Diplomacy in Late Medieval Europe* (London: Legenda, 2005).

Porte, A de. *Europe Between the Superpowers* (New Haven: Yale University Press, 1987).

Portela, C. *EU Sanctions and Foreign Policy: When and Why Do They Work* (London and New York: Routledge, 2010).

Pradier-Fodéré, P. *Cours de Droit Diplomatique*, Vol 2 (Paris, 1899).

Puetter, U. *The European Council and the Council* (Oxford: Oxford University Press, 2014).

Rasmussen, H. *On Law and Policy in the European Court of Justice* (Dordrecht: Martinus Nijhoff, 1986).

Reuter, P. *Introduction au droit des Traités* (3rd edn, Geneva: PUF, 1995).

Reynold, D. *Summits: Six Meetings that Shaped the Twentieth Century* (London: Allen Lane, 2007).

Richardson, L. *What Terrorists Want: Understanding the Terrorist Threat* (London: John Murray, 2006).

Rivier, A. *Principes du Droit des Gens*, Vol I (Paris, 1896).

Roland, R. *Interpreters as Diplomats: A Diplomatic History of the Role of Interpreters in World Politics* (Ottowa: University of Ottawa Press, 1999).

Rolin, H. *Annuaire de l'Institut de Droit International* (Salzburg, 1961), Vol 1.

Rosenne, S. *Provisional Measures in International Law: The International Court of Justice and the International Tribunal for the Law of the Sea* (Oxford: Oxford University Press, 2005).

Sabel, R. *Procedure at International Conferences* (2nd edn, Cambridge: Cambridge University Press, 2006).

Sack, J. 'The EC's Membership of International Organizations' (1995) *CMLR* 1227.

Salmon, J. *Manuel de droit diplomatique* (Bruxelles: Bruylant, 1994).

Sands, P and Klein, P. *Bowett's Law of International Institutions* (6th edn, London: Sweet and Maxwell, 2009).

Sands, P and Peel, J. *Principles of International Environmental Law* (3rd edn, Cambridge: Cambridge University Press, 2012).

Schabas, W. *An Introduction to the International Criminal Court* (4th edn, Cambridge: Cambridge University Press, 2011).

Scott, J B. *The Hague Conventions and Declarations of 1899 and 1907* (New York, 1915).

Sedley, S. 'Human Rights: A Twenty-first Century Agenda' (1995) *Public Law* 393.

Sfez, L. 'La Rupture des relations diplomatiques' (1966) *RGDIP* 359.

Shaw, M N. *International Law* (6th edn, Cambridge: Cambridge University Press, 2009).

Simma, B (ed). *The Charter of the United Nations: Commentary*, Vol I (2nd edn, Oxford: Oxford University Press, 2002).

Sinclair, I M. *The Vienna Convention on the Law of Treaties* (2nd edn, Manchester: Manchester University Press, 1984).

Slaughter, A-M. 'America's Edge' (January/February 2009) 88(1) *Foreign Affairs* 94–113.

Stirk, P and D Weigall (eds). *The Origins and Development of European Integration: A Reader and Commentary* (Pinter: London, 1999).

Sykes, P M. *The Right Honourable Sir Mortimer Durand: A Biography* (London: Cassell, 1926).

Taylor, A J P. *Bismarck: The Man and the Statesman* (New York: Vintage Books. 1967).

Temperley, H W V. *Frederick the Great and Kaiser Joseph: An Episode of War and Diplomacy in the Eighteenth Century* (London, 1915, reprinted 1968).

Ténékidès, G. 'Droit international et communautés fédérales dans la Grèce des cités' (1956) *HR* 552.

Thakur, R and Weiss, T G. 'R2P: From Idea to Norm-and Action?' (2009) 1(1) *Global Responsibility to Protect* 22–53.

Thody, P M W. *Europe Since 1945* (New York: Routledge, 2000).

Thomas, T, Kiser, S, and Casebeer, W. *Warlords Rising: Confronting Violent Non-State Actors* (Lanham: Lexington Books, 2005).

Thucydides. *The Landmark Thucydides: A Comprehensive Guide to the Peloponnesian War*, ed Strassler (New York: Simon & Schuster, 1998).

Touchard, J. *Le Gaullisme 1940–1969* (Paris: Seuil, Collection Points, 1978).

Trevelyan, H. *Diplomatic Channels* (Boston: Gambit, 1973).

Tridimas, T. 'The Court of Justice and Judicial Activism' (1996) 21 *ELR* 199.

UNOHCHR. *The Core International Human Rights Treaties* (United Nations Publications, 2006).

Vattel, E de. *Le Droit des Gens* (London, 1758).

Vattel, E de. *The Law of Nations*, Vol 3, 1758. Translated by C G Fenwick (Washington: Carnegie Institute, 1916).

Vel, G de. *The Committee of Ministers of the Council of Europe* (Council of Europe Press, 1995).

Vooren, B van. 'A Legal-Institutional Perspective on the European External Action Service' (2011) 48(2) *CMLR* 475–502.

Vooren, P B van and Wessel, R A. *EU External Relations Law: Text, Cases and Materials* (Cambridge: Cambridge University Press, 2014).

Wallace, H, Pollack, M, and Young, A (eds). *Policy-making in the European Union* (7th edn, Oxford: Oxford University Press, 2014).

Wallace, W. *The Foreign Policy Process in Britain* (London: RIIA, 1975).

Warbrick, C. 'British Policy and the National Transitional Council of Libya' (2012) 61 *ICLQ* 247.

Watson, A. *Diplomacy: The Dialogue between States* (London: Methuen, 1982).

Watts, A. 'The Legal Position in International Law of Heads of States, Heads of Governments and Foreign Ministers' (1995) 247 *HR* (994-III) 64.

Weiler, J. 'The Court of Justice on Trial' (1987) 24 *CMLR* 555.

Wessel, R A. *The European Union's Foreign and Security Policy: A Legal Institutional Perspective* (The Hague: Kluwer, 1999).

Widdows, K. 'The Unilateral Denunciation of Treaties Containing no Denunciation Clause' (1982) 53(1) *BYIL* 83–114.

Wood, M. 'The Convention on the Prevention and Punishment of Crimes against Internationally Protected Persons, including Diplomatic Agents' (1974) 23 *ICLQ* 791–817.

Wood, M. 'The European Convention on the Suppression of Terrorism' (1981) *Yearbook of European Law* 307.

Wood, M. 'The Immunity of Official Visitors' *Max Planck Yearbook of International Law*, in A von Bogdandy and R Wolfrum (eds) (February 2012) Vol 16, Issue 1, pp 35–98.

Xydis S C. In *The United Nations, Past, Present and Future*, ed Barros, J (New York and London: The Free Press, 1972).

Young, J W. *Twentieth-Century Diplomacy: A Case Study of British Practice: 1963–1976* (Cambridge: Cambridge University Press, 2008).

Zamoyski, A. *Rites of Peace: The Fall of Napoleon and the Congress of Vienna* (London: Harper Press, 2008).

Zaum, D. 'The Security Council, the General Assembly, and War: The Uniting for Peace Resolution', in Lowe, V, et al. (eds), *The United Nations Security Council and War* (Oxford: Oxford University Press, 2008).

INDEX

(The references are to **chapters** and paragraphs, or appendices, for example **21.29–21.30** refers to chapter 21 paragraphs 29–30)

Cases in international and national courts are in the Table of Cases.